UNEXPLORED CRETE

Written and Researched by
STEPHANOS PSIMENOS

Translated by
LENA HADJIIOANNOU
and
MICHALIS MONTESANTOS

YANNIS TEGOPOULOS
Publisher

Yannis was born in Athens in 1964 with a slight breathing problem: he breathes normally only above 70 km/h! Motorcycling is his cure of which he needs powerful doses. When he says "I've had enough, I need a breath," he means to pop by his village which is 360 kilometres away from Athens! His motorcycle is parked only when it's at the service shop, something that happens about two or three times a month. When he picks it up, he immediately makes an appointment for the next service!

In the army, Yannis served as a tank commander. It is then that he came to love the big BMW motorcycles and got the habit of moving on determinedly, disregarding even the hardest obstacles in his way.

Since 1985, Yannis has been working for ELEFTHEROTIPIA (ΕΛΕΥΘΕΡΟΤΥΠΙΑ), one of the largest daily Greek papers, where he is in charge of the press. When the pressure becomes unbearable... you know, he goes "for a breath of fresh air."

STEPHANOS PSIMENOS
Author

Stephanos was born in Athens in 1963. He has been travelling by bike since the age of... minus three months, since his pregnant mother and crazy father did not hesitate to ride a Vespa from Larissa to Athens (some 400 km on rough country roads!)

His first bike was - what a coincidence(!) - a 50cc Vespa that his incorrigible parents got for him, so he could attend some private lessons. Stephanos, of course, put it to good use, touring Greece from end to end... While in his second year as a Political Sciences and International Studies major at the Athens Panteion University, Stephanos bought his first motorcycle, which he used to tour Europe. At the same time, he wrote travel articles that were published in several motorcycle magazines.

In 1993, after eight years of work as a copywriter in several multinational advertising agencies (and a great many awards for his successful promotion of ice creams, gum and white elephants), he accepted Yannis's proposal to advertise something that is really worth it: travelling in Greece on a motorcycle.

AUTHOR'S NOTE

"Ποταμοίσι τοίσιν αυτοίσιν εμβαίνουσιν,
έτερα και έτερα ύδατα επιρρεί".

(No one can walk into the same river twice).
Heraclitos

There are as many worlds as there are people. Nothing that you see is identical to what I see. Even that very river that I see now is not the same river that I saw yesterday nor is it the river I shall see tomorrow. Because yesterday was rainy and the river was swollen with muddy water; today there is sunshine and the water is flowing quietly with crystal clearness.

The definition of **"Unexplored"** is fixed and self-evident in every country.You may be holding detailed maps of Greece and study carefully the existing literature. You may look at photographs and hear enchanting stories from your friends who have been to the places you are planning to visit. All these things may be the materials which you use for the preparation of your journey, but the journey begins once you have loaded your motorcycle and start off. It is in fact unique and irreproducible. What you are about to see has appeared in no book whatsoever in the way that you are going to see it. Greece unfolds and reveals itself before your eyes at the very moment you are travelling there. The landscape and the people, the roads, the houses, the colours and the smells are all changing continuously. However many times you travel in Greece, you will meet a different country each time, even if you ride along the same roads, stay in the same places and meet the same people. Every journey is a unique experience, **a work of art** with the traveller himself improvising as both leading actor and creator.

No one else has seen the Greece you are going to see. The people you meet in the street, laughters, shouts, the smell of food cooking in the narrow village streets, the wild flowers on the mountain slopes and the faint light of the oil lamps in small country churches, the shining pebbles on the seashore and the chorus of birds in the woods, the distant sound of a bell, the noise and bustle of the taverna and the quiet of the mountain; all these will make up a unique composition which is continually changing, like the clouds in the sky. You alone will be witness to it, even if you are travelling with your friends, on the pillion seat or on an another motorcycle. Different things will stimulate your senses and will attract your attention, and you will give different interpretations to the same stimuli, since you have different life experiences, different cultures and different characters. A painting is being created continually on an internal canvas with materials that you yourself choose during your journey. However much you describe it in the stories you tell, in your writings or in the photographs you have taken, there is no way that anyone can fully and clearly see the picture of the world you have inside you.

This book, like the rest of the series **"Unexplored Greece"**, is nothing but raw material, like the tube of paint a painter buys in order to start creating a work of art. It is really only a drop in an ocean of beauty, just enough to give you a taste and to whet your appetite for a dive into the endless beauty of Greece.

I am not an archaeologist, nor a writer of folklore, nor a historian. During the two years of my journey around Greece and the many more years which it took me to study the sources, I picked out those things that most impressed me personally and I have tried to present them by emphasising the elements which fascinated me. Neither have I hesitated to present those things that disappointed me and to express openly my indignation. The system I have followed in presenting my material is the one followed by most travellers on their journeys: using some town as a starting-point, I rush off in all directions and describe whatever impresses me on the way. If something important is missing or if a rather insignificant detail gets too much attention, this is but an inevitable shortcoming in an amateur's work. In three areas, however, I laid down strict professional rules.

Firstly, all historical accounts and descriptions of archaeological sites, if somewhat "Hollywood" in style so as to be more readable, are nevertheless based on the most reliable sources.

Secondly, I have seen and experienced in person whatever is described and recommended in the book. The routes, the beaches, the monasteries, the museums, the hotels, the bars, the tavernas - every paragraph in the tourist guides in the "Unexplored Greece" series is written from personal experience.

Thirdly, I did my research as an ordinary traveller and not as the writer of travel guides. Thus, the food I was served, the room I was given, the information I was told and the service I was offered are those that would be offered to any traveller, and as such they are presented in the guides. My subjective judgement was exercised within the bounds of accepted journalistic practice and precision.

I have also avoided artistic photographs which give an embellished picture of a place. In any case, I am an amateur photographer with amateur (although technologically advanced) photographic equipment. The images which you will see during your journey and which will be imprinted on the exceptionally sensitive "film" of your brain could not compare for beauty with even the most artistic photographs taken by a professional photographer. I am therefore letting the visual enjoyment be a living part of your journey and I limit myself to "informational" photographs that give a general picture of a place and of its atmosphere.

Finally, for the making of the maps included in this book, the so-called Road books, I had to rely on detailed forest maps, the tripmeter of my motorcycle, a good compass and a mountaineering altimeter. This may not be an example of cartographic accuracy but you will certainly not get lost in the wilds!

I hope that you will thoroughly enjoy your journey without any problems, and use every drop of your "fuel" to feed your senses with the endless beauties of Greece.

Stephanos Psimenos, Author

ROAD BOOK LEGEND

═══	Proposed main route	⎔	E4 sign (small diamond-shaped yellow sign with an E4 at the centre, marking the European Walk Path)
═══	Asphalt-paved road	■	Building (shepherd's hut, farmhouse etc.)
═══	Dirtroad	⛺	Spot suitable for rough camping
═══→	The road continues and is mapped out	⛨	Chapel
═══:::	The road continues in an unknown direction (a good chance for further exploration; send us details!)	⛪	Monastery
·······	Footpath	⛫	Archaeological site
══/══	Fenced pastureland	▒▒	Beach
♀ 800 ♀	Distance in metres	▭	Inhabited area
⛿	Sign (in the frame next to this symbol you see what exactly is on the sign)		

CITY MAP LEGEND

▭	Main traffic artery	▮	Hotels
▭	Pedestrian zone	✳	Restaurants
▥	Street with steps	▪	Entertainment
▭	Park	▲	Motorcycle dealers
✚	Hospital	▲	Repair shops, spare parts, motorcycle accessories
●	Sights and services of interest to the traveller		

The numbers next to the symbols on the city maps correspond to one of two things: the explanation in the table accompanying the maps or the explanations given in the travel guide where the cities are described.

TRAVEL GUIDE SYMBOLS

At the left margin of the travel guide and next to the route descriptions you will see certain symbols that are meant to facilitate you in going directly to the items of interest (and skipping those you don't care about). These symbols are the following:

 Main route - asphalt

 Panoramic view

 Main route - dirtroad

 Inhabited area

 Alternative route

 Hotel, Rooms to Let

 Historical information

 Camping ground (with facilities)

 Archaeological site

 Spot suitable for rough camping

 Fortress

 Tavern, restaurant

 Monastery

 Bar, disco

 Old church or chapel

 Danger

 Landscape of great beauty

 Parking

 Beach

 Sea transportation

 Cave

 Traditional recipe, local specialty

 Flora

 Traditional drink

 Fauna

ROAD CATEGORIES

The roads included in the maps and travel guides of ROAD EDITIONS have been classified into **8** categories depending on their quality. Asphalt-paved roads are described in the text as **A1, A2, A3 or A4** and dirtroads are described as **D1, D2, D3 or D4**. The symbols designate the following:

A1: National Road of European specifications - yes, there are such roads too in Greece! - with two or three lanes for each traffic direction and a parapet in the middle.

A2: Main road, wide, having one or two lanes per direction, protective bars at the side wherever needed, and helpful signs.

A3: The typical Greek country road with its... cute little potholes, its peculiarities, and its shining, smooth asphalt.

A4: Lousy road! Very narrow, full of potholes, worn at the edges, left without maintenance.

Signs are designated with one of three symbols: **E** for those written in English, **Gr** for those written in Greek and **Gr/E** for those written in both languages.

D1: Very good dirtroad. All vehicles can pass without a problem, including buses and Harleys!

D2: Good dirtroad with minor problems. All vehicles can pass and it is relatively easy.

D3: The typical Greek dirtroad. It requires careful driving. Jeeps and off-road motorcycles will have no trouble passing. All other vehicles must struggle a bit (or a lot) but they can make it.

D4: Lousy dirtroad! It features huge ditches (that are more like... ravines), gulf-like potholes, landslides, mud, fallen trees, rubble and steep inclinations. Only light off-road bikes and powerful jeeps with experienced drivers should attempt to pass.

CONTENTS

Editor's Note 10
Author's Introduction 12
Roadbook Legend, City Map Legend, Travel Guide Symbols 14

GENERAL INFORMATION ON CRETE
Cretan Geology 22
Cretan Mythology 24
History of Crete 30
Cretan Social Geography 48
Cretan Music and Dance 57
Cretan Cuisine 62
Cretan Landscape 66
Underwater World 70
Exploring Caves 74
Public Relations 76
Safety Matters 80
What to take along 87
When to come 98
On what motorcycle 104
Accommodations 106
Boats to Crete 112

THE ROUTES
Routes starting from Hania
Hania 118
1. Hania - Akrotiri 140
2. Hania - Paleochora 148
3. Hania - Samaria 164
4. Hania - Sphakia 176
5. Hania - Kasteli 194

Routes starting from Kasteli
Kasteli 202
6. Kasteli - Gramvoussa 206
7. Kasteli - Elafonissos 212
8. Kasteli - Paleochora (through the Topolian Gorge) 220
9. Kasteli - Paleochora (through Episkopi) 226
10. Kasteli - Sirikari 236

Routes starting from Sphakia
11. Sphakia - Rethimno (travelling inland) 242
12. Sphakia - Rethimno (following the coast) 250

Routes starting from Rethimno
Rethimno 260
13. Rethimno - Ierapetra (following the south coast) 276
14. Rethimno - Ierapetra (travelling inland) 316

Routes starting from Ierapetra
Ierapetra 350
15. Ierapetra - Zakros (coastal road) 356
16. Ierapetra - Zakros (inland route) 368

Routes starting from Iraklio
Iraklio 376
17. Iraklio - Rethimno (coastal road) 398
18. Iraklio - Rethimno (travelling inland) 406
19. Iraklio - Aghios Nikolaos (coastal road) 426
20. Iraklio - Aghios Nikolaos (travelling inland) 438

Routes starting from Aghios Nikolaos
Aghios Nikolaos 476
21. Aghios Nikolaos - Zakros 486

PRACTICAL INFORMATION
Useful information on the Greek law 510
In case of an accident 512
Gas stations 514
Postal services 514
Making phone calls 515
Banks 515
Drugstores 516
Traffic signs 516
Getting help on the road 516
Learn some Greek 518
Police 530
Port authorities 531
First Aid 532
Information for the motorcyclist 534
Area codes in Greece 540
Area codes abroad 542
A few words about ROAD EDITIONS 544
The people who worked for this book 546
Questionnaire 549
People you met on the trip 553
Travel calendar 556
Index 570

A NOTE ON THE TRANSLATION
The translation of this book was shared by two people.
Lena Hadjiioannou translated pages:
3-9, 14-19, 76-97, 106-355, 398-425 and 508-561
Michalis Montesantos translated pages:
10-13, 20-75, 98-105, 356-397 and 426-507

General information on Crete

CRETAN GEOLOGY
Crete has not always been as we know it today

As you lie on the sandy beach lulled by the waves, or as you rest in the armchair of your living room, it is hard to imagine that in reality you are surfing. Yes, indeed, you are surfing! To be precise you are "surfing geologically". You are on top of a gigantic "geologic swell" that moves slowly, very slowly, **tremendously slowly**, but it moves. With it it carries life since it first appeared.

Geologists have estimated that this swell (namely the Earth) started out some **4.5 billion years** ago, that is, long before life appeared on the planet. Then it was a fierce fiery swell covered by thick clouds of nitrogen and helium. Gradually it cooled off, forming lands here and seas there, but until it cooled off for good, there was mayhem. On the very spot of the planet that you are now (or will be soon) sunbathing, there was a deep sea at the time of creation. **25 million years** ago at the beginning of the Miocene epoch, an incredibly powerful tectonic upheaval lifted the bottom of the sea to the surface and, thus, was born - literally from the waves - Aegeis Land, although no human was then available to call it by that name. What was then available included huge elephants, deer, hippopotami, cave dwelling bears and various other beasts roaming undisturbed wherever they pleased. **This Aegeis Land** was not flat but full of jagged ranges and high peaks. The mountains of Crete were so formed (albeit not in the present shape) 25 million years ago.

Not very deep under the surface of the Earth, the unstable rocks (known as tectonic plates) were in motion causing tremendous uplift and subsidence on the fragile crust. During such a geologic upheaval **12 million years** ago, a large part of Aegeis Land sunk and the sea covered everything but the highest peaks. At that very distant era only four mountainous masses must have stuck out of the waters as separate islands, in the area where later Crete managed to float.

The natural see-saw continued for a long time until about 10000 BC. In the course of these hundreds of slow millennia, called Pleistocene epoch by geologists, severe climatic fluctuations created five Ice Ages. Ice, of course, in the form of glaciers, is nothing more than frozen water and it was formed by immense amounts of water borrowed from the sea. Consequently, in each Ice Age, the level of the sea would retreat by 100 to 200 metres! As a result, the four peaks-islands of Crete were joined together and in turn they joined the coast of Peloponnese. Next the ice would melt and everything would be flooded again. After the last ice age (just 12,000 years ago) and the successive ups and downs of sea waters, Crete found peace at last; woods covered the earth, cool water sources sprang out everywhere, a mini paradise was created ready to welcome the first humans.

It seems that humans were not late in coming to the island. Unfortunately, the science of palaeontology is not particularly advanced in Greece and, so, we know very little about the Palaeolithic inhabitants of Crete. Their oldest confirmed traces date from 10000 BC approxi-

CRETAN GEOLOGY

mately. After that, circa 2600 BC, an Indo-European people came from the east and mixed with the natives to form in tandem the famous Minoan civilisation. Afterwards, circa 1400 BC, Greek tribes came to settle here such as the Achaeans, to be followed shortly by the Dorians. Then, for short or long periods came here and settled Byzantines, Arabs, Genoans, Venetians, Turks, Germans, every man Jack. And now you, lying on the beach, are travelling carefree on top of the swell. Bon voyage, and be careful!

CRYPTOZOIC ERA (Precambrian)
total duration 4-5 billion years

PALAEOZOIC ERA
total duration 370 million years

MESOZOIC ERA *total duration 167 million years*			
Period	Epoch	Age*	Recipe
Triassic		230	Crete lies at the botton of the pot called Mediterranean and simmers
Jurassic		180	
Cretaceous		135	

CENOZOIC ERA *total duration 63 million years*			
Period	Epoch	Age*	Recipe
Tertiary	Palaeocene	63	
	Eocene	58	
	Oligocene	36	
	Miocene	25	Aegeis Land surfaces
	Pliocene	13	Large part of Aegeis Land sinks -4 islands float in the area of Crete.
Quaternary	Pleistocene	1	Ice Age. Successive phases of high and low temperatures. Crete is cooking.
	Holocene	0.1	Crete is server ready for habitation.

*Earth's age in millions of years

CRETAN MYTHOLOGY

What must primitive man have felt when, cocooned in the protection of his cave, he looked out and saw lightning flashing in the middle of a storm? Or just as he was unconcernedly hacking out his stone tools, the earth started to shake at its foundations and the uncanny rumbling of an earthquake covered everything? At such moments his heart, like that of all animals, will certainly have been seized by **fear.** But it was in his brain only, of all the species in the animal kingdom, that perplexity and doubt were born. Already, in that far - off time, there was a big "Why?" in the human brain. When he saw the death or the birth of his neighbour, natural phenomena, the grandeur of the natural world, early man wondered. But he also realised with despair how weak and fragile he was within this wonderful world.

His need to interpret the world in which he lived and his desire to overcome his weaknesses activated his creative imagination. In an era when logic was still in its infancy, the creations of his imagination acquired, with the passage of time, the validity of the most important truth. Using as raw materials his daily experiences and the forms that were familiar to him, i.e. the forms of animals and of humans, he interpreted everything that was incomprehensible to him and he created creatures which embodied his yearning to explain the marvellous phenomena of nature, to seek solace, to find the strength and courage to fight against endless difficulties and, of course, to dominate this world. Thus, **mythology** was born and was chiselled ever slowly over the centuries.

Mythology as an attempt to explain the world comes into the same area as religion and for this reason it is formed around the nucleus of the religions beliefs of a people. The religious nucleus of Cretan mythology is the worship of the Sun, the Moon and the Stars, which was brought from the East by the first colonisers of Crete. Indeed the names of many mythical Cretan heroes bear witness to this, for example **Asterionas,** the king of Crete, who took as his wife **Europa** (she with the big face). Europa's mother **Telephassa** (she which shines from afar); Minos' wife **Pasiphae** (she who shines on everyone), the daughters of Minos and Pasiphae **Phaidra** and **Ariadne** (the sparkling, the shining ones)

On the other hand, mythology as the expression of the human desire to dominate always has a historical nucleus of heroic deeds. The pride of the people who did them and the impression made on the neighbouring peoples who observed them were the reasons why these events were surrounded with the splendour of myth. With the passing of the centuries, the mythological "ivy" put out rich shoots and essentially concealed the historical "trunk", around which it was entwined. The historical nucleus of Cretan mythology is the power which Crete gained during the era of the Minoan Kings, her sea-empire and her expansion (by means of colonies and trading stations) throughout the Mediterranean. The leading mythical hero was King **Minos** of whom all the other Cretan heroes were either descendants or relations.

Mythology of course is not an artistic creation - this would give it an aesthetic dimension. Greek mythology, however, (to which Cretan mythology belongs) happens to have a unique beauty, an aesthetic wealth which has made it well-loved throughout the world. The ancient

CRETAN MYTHOLOGY

Babylonians or the Amazon Indians had a god of thunder, but only the Zeus of the ancient Greeks is widely known. The ancient Mongols Celts must have had a young hero who could easily kill wild beasts and monsters, but everybody knows only the invincible **Hercules** of the ancient Greeks for this reason. Greek mythology is not only the subject of study by specialists but is also an exciting world which appeals to everyone.

Cretan mythology is a part of the place that you are now preparing to explore. It is the deepest roots of the archaeological treasures that you will have the chance to admire at many museums and at archaeological sites in every corner of the island. For this reason, we chose to present Cretan mythology to you in sections, in the description of the areas connected with it, and here simply to mention briefly the main heroes, and to give a chart showing the relationship between them.

The abduction of Europa by Zeus-Bull

Amalthia

The nymph of Idaion Andron who brought up Zeus. She fed him on the milk of a goat called Aix (=goat) and on wild honey. One day, when Zeus was playing with this goat, he broke off one of her horns and gave it to Amalthia, telling her that all the fruits she could ever want would spring from out of the horn (the famous Horn of Amalthia, or Horn of Plenty).

Androgeos

One of the sons of Minos and Pasiphae who was a champion athlete in all athletic events. One day he went to Athens and took part in some local games, where he walked off with all the prizes. The Athenian athletes, green with envy, ambushed him just outside the city and killed him. When his father heard, he organised a military campaign against Athens, captured it and punished the Athenians by making them send seven young men and seven young women to Crete every year to be thrown to the Minotaur in the Labyrinth.

Ariadne

Daughter of Minos and Pasiphae. She fell in love with the Athenian hero, Theseus, when he came to Knossos to kill the Minotaur. Although she helped him greatly to succeed in his quest, with the famous skein of thread that she gave him, the ungrateful Theseus left her in Naxos where his ship put in on the way back to Athens. The god Dionyssos found her there, married her and took her up to mount Olympus.

Daedalus

An Athenian craftsman and the greatest inventor of ancient times. He was sent into exile for a crime he had committed in Athens. In this way, he found himself at the court of King Minos who employed him as an architect and sculptor at the Palace of Knossos. The king was very pleased with the variety of work done by Daedalos and most of all with the Labyrinth where the Minotaur was imprisoned. But when he found out that Daedalos had made the wooden cow in which his wife Pasiphae had had intercourse with a bull, and that Daedalos had advised his daughter Ariandne to give the skein of thread to Theseus, he became very angry with him and gave orders for him to be put to death. Daedalos, however, forestalled him and escaped by air, having made wings for himself and his son Ikaros. Ikaros was killed during the flight, but Daedalos landed and took refuge in the city of Camico in Sicily. After a long search, Minos found him there, but the inventive Daedalos managed to kill his pursuer by means of a trick.

Zeus

The son of Cronos and Rea, he belongs to the second generation of gods, i.e. to the gods of Olympus. Cronos had been told by an oracle that one of his children would usurp his power and so he did not allow any of them to live but swallowed them as soon as they were born. Rea became very angry, and when it was time for her to give birth to Zeus, she gave Cronos a rock to eat which was wrapped in swaddling-clothes and she went off and gave birth to Zeus in Diktaio Andro, a lonely cave on top of mount Dikti in Crete. Shortly after this, little Zeus was moved for reasons of safety to another Cretan cave, Idaion Andro on mount Idi, where a Nymph of the cave, Amalthia, undertook to bring him up (in another version of the story, she was a goat that brought Zeus up on her milk). When Zeus grew up, he put up a terrible fight and managed to topple the king from his throne and so he became king of the Gods. The other gods of Olympus were either his brothers and sisters or his children. His wife was Hera, although he had countless love affairs with other goddesses, but mainly with mortal women. One of these was Europa, whom he fell in love with in Tyre, Syria, and whom he brought to Crete to enjoy her love.

Europe

Daughter of the king of Tyre, Aginor and of Telephassa. One day, Zeus saw her playing with her friends on the beach and he fell in love with her. He appeared before her in the form of a likeable bull, the unsuspecting girl sat on his back and the Zeus-bull rushed into the water, carrying his darling on his back, and took her to Crete. They made their love-rest in an idyllic riverside place at the spot where Gortyna was later built. When he grew tired of her, he gave her to the king of Crete, Asterionas, who married her and adopted the three children she had had with Zeus (Minos, Sarpidonas and Radamanthys). When she died, the Cretans paid tribute to her with divine honours an gave her name to one of the earth's continents.

CRETAN MYTHOLOGY

Theseus
Son of the king of Athens, Aegeus, and the greatest mythical Athenian hero who did innumerable heroic good deeds. He became a volunteer for the team of fourteen young people who were sent as food for the Minotaur. Theseus managed to kill the Minotaur and got out of the Labyrinth by using a ball of thread (the famous skein of thread) which Ariadne had given him. When she left for Athens he took Ariadne with him as he had promised her, but after a few days he left her on Naxos and returned to Athens alone. He forgot however to change the black sails on his ship to white, which was the agreed signal to his father that the mission had been successful, and so his father, Aegeus, the king of Athens, threw himself into the sea and was drowned; the sea has since been called the Aegean.

Kourites
Seven good-tempered giant gods who came from Evoia. They roamed the Greek world, offering their good services where necessary. They happened to be in Crete when Zeus was born. Zeus' mother, Rea, asked them to stay outside the Idaio Andro and to dance and beat loudly on their copper shields so that Zeus' father, Cronos, would not hear his son crying. So Zeus managed to grow to manhood and later to become king of the Gods. Many years later, Zeus wife, Hera, asked them to get rid of Epaphos, a child that Zeus had had with a mortal woman. The Kourites carried out the goddess's wish but Zeus became very angry with them, forgot about the protection they had once given him, and killed them with a thunderbolt.

Minos
The most powerful and famous king of Crete, he was the son of Zeus and Europa and the heir of his stepfather Asterionas to the Cretan throne. He had the favour and protection of Zeus throughout his reign. Every nine years he went up to Idaio Andro and received directly from Zeus the laws with which he was to govern the Cretans. Under his rule, Crete enjoyed its greatest period of prosperity and expanded its power throughout the Aegean. His wife was Pasiphae with whom he had four daughters and four sons, but he also had many children by his many mistresses. He was killed in the city of Camico in Sicily in a campaign which he organised to hunt down Daedalus. After his death he became the judge of Souls in the Underworld with his brother Radamanthys and Aeakos, another son of Zeus!

The Minotaur
A monster with the body of a man and the head of a bull which was born from the Union of Pasiphae and the sacred bull of Poseidon. Minos closed him up inside the **Labyrinth,** a dark underground maze of passages which was designed and built under the Palace of Knossos by the Athenian craftsman Daedalus especially for this purpose. It was fed on human flesh and especially on the seven young men and seven young women which the Athenians had to send every year after their defeat in the war with Minos. It was killed by Theseus.

Pasiphae

A nobleman's daughter from an infamous generation. Her sister was the sorceress, **Circe,** who turned Odysseus's companions into pigs, and her brother was the blood-thirsty king of Kolchis, **Aeitis,** the father of the sorceress Medea who killed her children. Pasiphae was the wife of Minos and the mother of his eight legitimate children. She too had magic powers which she used to stop her husband from being unfaithful, but without satisfactory results. She was troubled not only by Minos' unfaithfulness but also by his perjury to Poseidon. The vexed god, in order to take revenge on Minos who had not sacrificed to him the bull he had promised him, instilled in Pasiphae an uncontrollable sexual desire for the animal. With the help of Daedalus, Pasiphae had sexual intercourse with the bull and that is how the Minotaur was born.

Radamanthys

Son of Zeus and Europa and the younger brother of Minos. He had such fair judgement that he was known as the fairest man on earth. When Minos succeeded Asterionas to the Cretan throne, he sent his brother into exile, afraid that he would over-shadow him. Radamanthys roamed around the Aegean islands and the coast of Asia Minor, where all the peoples respected his fair judgement and entrusted him with resolving their disputes. When he died, Zeus appointed him judge of human souls in the underworld, with his brother Minos

Sarpidonas

Son of Zeus and of Europa, brother of Minos. He also (together with his brother Radamanthys) took the road into exile when Minos ascended the throne of Crete. He ended up in Militos in Asia Minor, where he ruled until his death.

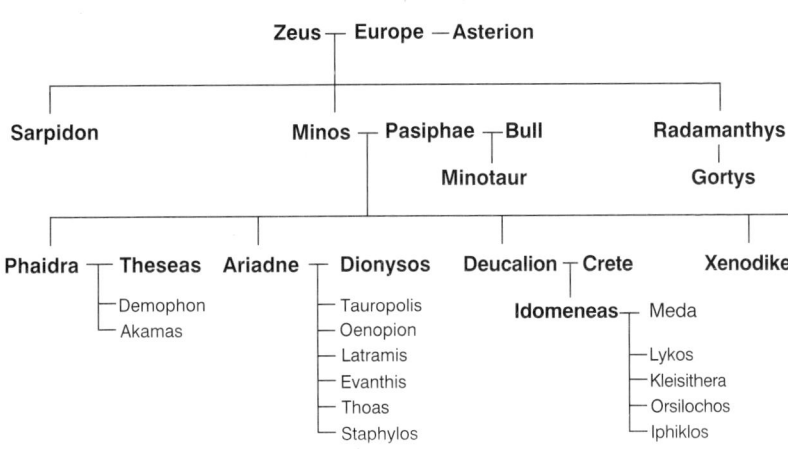

CRETAN MYTHOLOGY

Talos

The first robot to be born of the human imagination! Talos was a copper giant, the work of Hephaistus and the gods' gift to Minos. His job was to go round the whole of Crete (he could circle the island three times a day) and to protect it from invasion. His favourite weapons were enormous rocks which he catapulted on the enemy ships approaching the coast. If by any chance anyone managed to disembark, he had a warm welcome in store for them: he jumped in fire, made himself red-hot and then picked up the unfortunate invaders and crushed them in his arms, turning them into grilled steaks. However, he too had his "Achilles heel": a small vein in the back of his leg which he plugged with a metal stopper. When the Argonauts came to Crete, the sorceress Medea managed to pull out the stopper and the copper giant fell to pieces.

Phaedra

The daughter of Minos and Pasiphae and sister of Ariadne. Phaedra married Theseus when he became king of Athens despite his disgraceful behaviour some years earlier to her sister (he had left her high and dry on Naxos while she was asleep), and had two children by him -Demophon and Adamas. Phaedra was not only bolder but also more lively than her sister. She eventually became bored with Theseus and fell in love with Hippolytus, a son of Theseus by a previous wife (the Amazon, Antiopi). Hippolytus however did not reciprocate, and so Phaedra, afraid of being found out, lied about Hippolytus to Theseus saying that he had tried to rape her. Theseus believed her and soon after Hippolytus was dead. After this, Phaedra fell into deep despair and hanged herself in remorse.

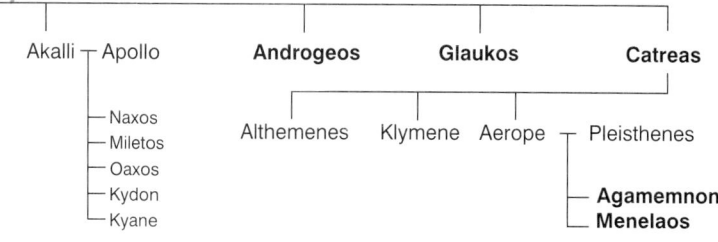

HISTORY OF CRETE

Okay, we know that this chapter is always the most boring in all travel guides, and nobody wants to fill his head with dates and historical facts, especially when he is on holiday. That at least is how most people feel at the outset. As you travel, however, and you hear stories, see monuments, archaeological sites, small country churches, even street names in the towns which excite your curiosity, you may very likely want to take a "stroll" through the history of the place. To help you as much as possible on this "stroll", we thought it best to give you a "map" (in the form of a chart) of Cretan history, so that, depending on the stimulus, you can go straight to the "area" that interests you. You can go from the end to the beginning, from the beginning to the end or jump from one part to another in whatever order you like, as if you were joining up the pieces of a big jigsaw puzzle. The more pieces of this puzzle that you join, combining them with your own impressions of the journey, the more complete will be your picture of Crete.

Late Palaeolithic Period (33000 - 8000 BC)

In the final period of the Ice Age, when the level of the sea was 100-200 metres lower than it is today and Crete was joined to the Pelopponese, some palaeolithic people came to Crete in search of mammals. Deer bones have been found in the Rethimnon area which bear clear signs of having been worked by human hand - these date back to approximately 10000 BC

Mesolithic Period (8000 - 7000 BC)

On a mountainside between Asfendos and Kallikratis (Rethimno prefecture), a group of palaeolithic hunters decorated the cave in which they lived, with rock-wall paintings (representations of deer, weapons, etc).

Early Neolithic Period (7000 - 5000 BC)

Groups of neolithic people, who came from the coast of Asia Minor, settled in caves in every corner of Crete. Some of these, however, were bold enough to venture out from their dark caves and to build their settlements outside, in the sunlight. The largest of these settlements (and one of the largest in the whole of the Eastern Mediterranean) was found in Knossos at exactly the same point as that where the magnificent Minoan palace was later built. Their houses were built of stakes. Their pots were very clumsy, with thick sides and decorated with white spots and linear patterns. Their weapons and their tools were simple but well-made of bone and stone. They cultivated small fields, raised small herds and knew how to weave.

Middle Neolithic Period (5000 - 4000 BC)

As they realised that they would not be eaten by lions, more and more groups of neolithic people settled outside caves. Their houses were no longer built hugging each other, but had small yards

HISTORY OF CRETE

Byzantine general Nikiforos Fokas victoriously entering Chandaka

and many small windows. Their pots were much more beautiful with thin sides and new, elegant designs. They were brownish-black in colour and had smooth surfaces and striped decorations. Their tools and weapons continued to be made of bone or stone.

Late Neolithic Period (4000 - 3000 BC)

Neolithic settlements were especially spread out in Knossos, Phaestos and Iraklio. The foundations of a house were found in Knossos which can be regarded as the forerunner of Minoan architecture, with a spacious central room equipped with a hearth and many small rooms around it. The remains of a small circular hut were found in Phaestos, and this seems to be the forerunner of the vaulted Minoan graves. The potters of this period showed a special love of **colour,** and they experimented with many new shapes. They engraved decorative motifs with lines or spots onto the smooth brown, black or red surfaces of their pots, or they drew ribbons in a bright red or white colour. Their weapons and tools were still of stone or bone, but the first **copper weapons** appeared, probably imported and not made in Crete.

Prepalatial Period (3000 - 2000 BC)

A new people from the East came via the coast of Asia Minor and the islands of the east Aegean to Crete. They intermarried with the local population and they brought new technical knowledge, such as working in copper. A new cultural thrust was created, a preliminary period for the fantastic Minoan civilisation which will soon flourish. Seafaring and trade were developed and social classes were formed whereby rich merchants dominated and achieved political power. Their pots were much more elegant and many of these were made on a primitive potter's wheel. Talented craftsmen made wonderful gold jewellery, seals, stone ceremonial vessels **(rhytons)** and works of art in ivory.

Paleopalatial Period (2000 - 1700 BC)

The first palaces were built in Knossos, Phaestos, Mallia and Zakros. These were luxurious multi-storied palaces with light, spacious rooms and many corridors, situated around a large central courtyard which had many storehouses, workrooms and places of worship. Around the palaces, towns were built which had no fortifications, a fact indicating that there were no internal conflicts in Crete. Industrial production (ceramics, seal-making, small sculptures) was concentrated in the palace centres and was under the direct control of the nobles. The industrial and agricultural products were exported to the main Mediterranean markets (Egypt, Cyprus, the Middle East, mainland Greece and its islands), from which the Minoans imported raw materials and merchandise (copper from Cyprus, pots and seals from Egypt, etc). In order to record their productive and commercial business, the Minoans used **hieroglyphic script** which remains completely indecipherable.

Neopalatial Period (1700 - 1450 BC)

Circa 1700 BC. A powerful earthquake shook Crete and destroyed the palaces. The Minoans found the courage to rebuild their towns and palaces from the beginning, bigger and more magnificent than the old ones and decorated with exceptional frescoes. The palace of Knossos covers an area of 22,000 square metres, of Phaestos and of Mallia 9.000 sq.m. and of Zakros 8,000 sq.m.

Circa 1600 BC. Linear A script was established. The palace secretaries kept notes on clay tablets, that no one has yet been able to decipher.

Circa 1600 BC. A powerful earthquake, which must have been related to the violent eruption of the volcano on Santorini that took place at that time, caused great destruction at the palace centres and throughout the Cretan countryside.

1600 - 1500 BC The Golden Age of Minoan Civilisation. Weaving, ceramics, stone-craft, goldwork, seal-making and small sculpture were at their height. The products of Cretan workshops and agricultural produce were loaded onto the spacious, seaworthy ships of the Minoan merchants and were sold throughout the Mediterranean. The wealth which accumulated gave thrust to all crafts and significantly raised the standard of living. The Minoan cities (at Gournia, Malia, Zakros and many other places) were exceptionally well-built, based on town planning, with paved roads and squares. As well as the palaces, luxury villas were built in many parts of Crete, where local noblemen and wealthy landowners lived, as were isolated farmhouses with many rooms (storerooms and workshops). The presence of the Minoans was dominant over the whole Mediterranean. They founded trading stations and colonies on the islands and in mainland Greece

Postpalatial Period (1450 - 1100 BC)

1450 BC. Destruction of the second palaces by an unexplained cause (a natural disaster of great intensity or an attack by invaders).

HISTORY OF CRETE

The Minoan civilisation took a great blow from which it was never to recover.

Circa 1400 BC Achaean colonisers from the Peloponnese became sovereign throughout Crete. The palace of Knossos was rebuilt, as was the palace of Archanes where the Achaean (Mycenaean) lords settled. Mycenaean style mansions were built in many part of Crete.

Circa 1400 BC the Linear A script was replaced by a more developed linguistic system, the **Linear B** script, which is an archaic form of the Greek language. This script was deciphered in 1952, but there are still quite a lot of obscure or uncertain points.

1380 BC Final destruction of the palace of Knossos by a powerful earthquake or by an attack by a second wave of invaders. The wonderful Minoan civilisation is wiped out completely

Circa 1200 BC As Homer tells us, the Cretans took part in the Trojan war on the side of the other Greeks, with 80 ships and king Idomeneas as leader. This is an indication that Crete, despite the destruction of the Minoan civilisation, maintained its nautical power and had a strong presence in Mediterranean waters.

Protogeometric Period (1100 - 900 BC)

Circa 1100 BC The first **Dorian** colonists arrived in Crete. They were armed with swords and javelins made from a new material, **iron,** which was much harder than copper. The weakened locals resisted as much as they could, but without success. The Dorians became masters of the island and settled in the towns of the previous inhabitants whom they enslaved and forced to work for them. Some small groups of locals (the so-called **Eteokrites,** i.e. genuine Cretans) took refuge in inaccessible mountain areas in Eastern Crete and continued to live under the traditions of their Minoan ancestors.

Circa 970 BC Protogeometric A order in ceramics. The decorators of the vases began to use **compasses** in order to draw straighter lines.

Geometric and Orientalising Period (900 - 650 BC)

900-800 BC Many Doric city-states were founded such as Axos, Lato, Driros, Rizinia and Lyttos. It is estimated that the total number of cities in Crete in this period exceeds 100, but only half of these have been located. The Dorians organised their social life in accordance with the strict Doric model.

840-810 BC Protogeometric B order in ceramics was developed in the Knossos workshops with obvious Eastern influence. The vases were decorated with bold curvilinear combinations and straight linear subjects, drawn freely by hand.

Archaic Period (650 - 500 BC)

650-600 BC The **Daedalic order**, whose first traces appeared at the end of the geometric period, now reached its peak. The decorative relief works and the statues took on movement and life. **This was a period of cultural flowering and prosperity in Doric Crete.**

600-500 BC Invasions from Greece and Asia created terrible disorder in Crete. Bloody battles and plundering ruined the local population, crafts and trade were neglected, and the best craftsmen (like the sculptors Dipoinos and Skyllis, and the architects Chersiphron and Metagenis) left Crete and went elsewhere to look for work. **The whole of the 6th century was a nightmare for Crete.**

Classical Period (500-330 BC).

490-480 BC During the period when the rest of the Greeks were frantically fighting against the Persian invaders, the Cretans chickened out! They put forward as the official excuse for their non-participation, the prophecy which Pythia had given them at the oracle at Delphi. When they asked her if they should participate in the war, the priestess of Apollo (who from the outset had taken the side of the Persians for financial reasons) answered plainly and clearly, without her well-known ambiguity: "don't be childish!".

431-404 BC During the period when the rest of the Greeks were fighting even more frantically against each other (the well-known Peloponnesian War), Crete was again totally absent because at that time it was busy fighting its own civil war: Knossos against Lyttos, Phaestos against Gortyna, Itanos against Ierapytna, Kydonia against Apollonia, Olous against Lato, a complete mess! In the end, Knossos and Gortyna predominated and the remaining cities attached themselves to these, forming two camps.

Hellenistic Period (330-67 BC)

circa 300 BC . Six mountain cities in south west Crete (Elyros, Lissos, Irtakina, Tarra, Poikilassos and Syia) joined forces an formed the **Koino ton Oreion** (Mountainous Commonwealth) with the aim of better protecting themselves against the many enemies who threatened them.

circa 250 BC On the initiative of Gortyna, the **Koino ton Kritaion** (Cretan Commonwealth) was founded, in which the following cities allied themselves: Gortyna, Knossos, Phaestos, Lyttos, Rafkos, Ierapytna, Eleftherna, Aptera, Polyrrinia, Syvrita, Lappa, Axos, Priansos, Allaria, Arkades, Keraia, Praesos, Lato, Viannos, Malla, Eronos, Chersonisos, Apollonia, Irtakina, Elyros, Eltynaia, Aradin, Anopolis, Istron and Tarra. It was the loosest kind of federation that created no type of obligation or bond on its members, while its general assemblies were limited to expressing good wishes!

220 BC Peace does not come about by good wishes alone. Old disputes never caome to an end and so Knossos made a sudden attack on Lytto and destroyed it, with the help of 1.000 Phokaian mercenary soldiers.

216-217 BC The Cretan cities elected the king of Macedonia, Philip V, as protector of the island. Macedonia, however, was a long way away and it seems that its protection never arrived. Civil conflict continued unabated.

210 BC War between Knossos and Gortyna.

172 BC War between Gortyna and Kydonia.

174 BC 29 Cretan cities formed an alliance with the kind of Pergamos **Eumenis II**.

155 BC War between Crete and Rhodes.

74 BC The Cretans finally realised the meaning of the phrase "strength in unity". For the first time in their history, they all joined together to confront an external threat, and they achieved the incredible: in a sea-battle just off the small island of Dia (opposite Iraklio), they beat the all-powerful Roman fleet of Mark Anthony. All prisoners taken were hanged without a second thought.....

69-67 BC If the Cretans had known what would happen next, they would never have hanged those unfortunate prisoners. The Romans were enraged and sent powerful forces against Crete, led by the Roman Consul Cuidus Cecilius **Metellus.** After a grueling three-year war, they occupied the entire island and destroyed any Cretan cities which offered resistance. Fortunately things calmed down quickly and not only did they stop the destruction, but they also rebuilt many cities and made them more beautiful than they had been previously.

Roman Period (67 BC - 330 AD)

67 BC Crete became an independent Roman prefecture, whose capital was **Gortyna,** where a Roman administrator with the title of Pro-Consul was installed. Gortyna was enriched with magnificent public buildings and a long period of prosperity began.

27 BC Crete ceased to be an independent Roman prefecture and was united administratively with the Cyrenean (the Roman prefecture of North Africa, in the region of today's Libya).

58 AD St. Paul himself ordained his disciple **Tito** as first Bishop of Crete, with the seat of his bishopric in Gortyna.

249-251 During the reign of Emperor Decius, the first serious persecutions of Christians in Crete took place. In Gortyna, ten young Christian died a martyr's death - the so-called **Holy Ten.**

Circa 295 The Emperor Diocletian made an administrative reorganisation of the Roman empire. The prefecture of Crete was taken out of the Cyrenian and included in the Administration of Mysia (a Roman prefecture in the Balkans).

300-330 The cartographers of this period must have gone crazy with scribing and rubbing out, as the borders of the dominions of the Roman Empire changed almost every month due to the continuous clashes between those claiming power (in one particular year, there were seven emperors simultaneously, each one claiming his own vital space!). The final triumph out of all this confusion belonged to the Emperor **Constantine the Great,** who abandoned Rome and built the new capital of his state, the splendid **Constantinople,** on the site of an old Megaran colony, Byzantium (after which it was- wrongly- named the Byzantine Empire). As for Crete, it followed developments without participating.

First Byzantine Period (330-824)

337 After the death of Constantine the Great, his three sons divided the Roman Empire into three. The youngest of the three brothers, the then underage **Constantas,** got **Crete** together with the Administration of Illyrium (which included the whole of mainland Greece), Italy and North Africa. The eldest brother, Constantinos II, got the West (i.e. the Administrations of Spain, France and Britain). The middle brother, Constantios II, got the East (i.e. Thrace, Asia, the Pontus and Egypt).

340 The eldest brother, Constantinos II, thought that it would not be difficult to push out his younger brother, Constantas, and take his state from him. But the young man tricked him, killed him and took his state from him instead (as we say, "the bites bit"!). So, on the map at that time remain the East Roman Empire and the West Roman Empire (to which Crete belonged)

395 The Emperor **Theodosius I** annexed East Illyrium to the east Roman State and so Crete joined its fortune to what later became the Byzantium Empire.

Circa 670 The Arab pirate Bavias conquered and plundered many Cretan towns, giving a foretaste of the harshness of his race which would soon ruin the island.

823 The Arabs who had conquered Spain were being increasingly driven into a corner by the Spanish and realised that they must soon look for new land to absorb. After extensive research, an Arab patrol of 20 ships, led by the cruel Abu Omar Haps, swallowed up the neglected and weakened Crete.

Arab Conquest (824-961)

824 A year after the first landing, the rest of the Arabs arrived with 40 ships. They made a sweeping attack on the interior of the island, leaving in their wake thousands of dead Cretans, ruins and burnt land. The land where the refined Minoan civilisation had once flowered, sank into the deepest darkness in its history, conquered by the ruthless Arabs. They made their capital at **Chandaka** (today's Iraklio), an insignificant settlement in the centre of the north coast which was once the port of Knossos and which now became the biggest base for pirate attacks and the centre of the **slave trade** in all the Mediterranean.

825 Alarmed, Constantinople immediately made the first attempt to free Crete on the orders of Emperor Michael II and his generals, Foteinos and Damianos, but without success.

826 The Byzantines made a second, more serious attempt with 70 ships and 23,000 men and managed to take Chandaka. The

HISTORY OF CRETE

Arabs retreated to the interior of the island and reformed themselves while the stupid Byzantine soldiers were celebrating with all-right drunken orgies. One evening, the Arabs suddenly attacked the unguarded city and murdered any Byzantines who did not have time to run away. Constantinople took many decades to get over this shock...

902 The Emperor Leon VI the Wise, wisely judged that the time had come to relieve the Mediterranean from the Arab pirates. He organised an expeditionary force of 180 ships and entrusted the leadership to Admiral Imerios who, however, proved to be deeply ignorant on matters of strategy: the Arabs went to meet him at Limnos, sank his fleet and killed most of his soldiers.

949 The Emperor Constantine VII made the fourth attempt to free Crete, but his general, Constantinos Gogylios, failed miserably.

960-961 The Emperor Romanos II made the freeing of Crete a priority matter and entrusted the organisation and leadership of the new campaign to his best general, **Nikiforos Fokas.** Fokas made careful preparations, determined to crush the Arabs; he armed **3,300 ships,** 2,000 of which had special launchers for the new super-weapon of the time, **liquid fire** (a mixture of petrol and other ingredients-a Byzantine invention). He landed outside Chandaka and fought the first decisive battle with the Arabs who had lined up outside the city walls. When the dust of battle settled, the ground was littered with 40,000 dead Arabs, while those who could, took refuge inside the walls. The Byzantines immediately began the siege, punishing the previous barbarity of the Arabs with the revenge they thought they deserved - they beheaded the dead and the prisoners of war and stuck the heads on stakes around the walls. They shot the left-over heads from their catapults over the walls, into the city. After they had shot over several thousand heads, the morale of the besieged men was shattered and the Byzantines entered Chandaka. They added another 160,000 to the mountain of chopped-off Arab heads and after that, the Arabs literally did not again raise their heads...

Second Byzantine Period (961-1204)

962-968 Nikiforos Fokas tried to move the capital of Crete to a safer place in the interior, and began to build a fortress which he called **Temenos.** After he was recalled to Constantinople, the inhabitants returned to the ruined Chandaka and rebuilt it.

1082 The Emperor Alexios II (Komninos) "inoculated" Crete with 12 Byzantine noble families, among whom was his son, Isaakios. This was the seed from which sprang the local **Cretan aristocracy** that quickly took ownership of large areas of fertile land, accumulated great economic and political power and played a leading part in the social and political life of Crete, even under Venetian rule.

1203 The Byzantine prince, Alexios, in his attempt to reinstate on the throne his deposed father, Isaakios II Angelos, **gave Crete** away to the Venetian leader of the Crusaders, Boniface Monferatico, in order to secure his support.

Venetian Rule (1204-1669)

1204 Boniface did not know what to do with Crete and he **sold** it to the Doge of Venice, Enrico Dandolo, for 5,000 gold ducats, i.e. for a pittance!

1206 Before the Venetians had time to settle themselves in Crete, their vindictive enemies the **Genoans,** led by the archpirate Enrico Pescatore, conquered a large part of the island and had time to build 14 fortresses to secure the conquered land. But their effort was in vain.

1206-1217 Venetian-Genoan war on foreign soil (in Crete). The Venetians won and threw the Genoans out of the island. The kingdom of Crete was founded **(Regnio di Candia)** with Chandaka as the capital, where the administrator of the island, who had the title of Duke, was installed. The island was divided into six areas (sestieri) that were given to Venetian feudal lords to exploit. The pre-existing Cretan aristocracy developed alongside the Venetian aristocracy.

1211 The Aghiostephanites Revolution, the first revolution by the Cretan nobles (specifically by the Aghiostephanites family with the support of the people, of course) against the Venetians. The Duke of Crete, Jacomo Tiepolo, could not suppress it and asked for the help of his colleague, Marco Sanoudo, the Duke of Naxos, promising him a handsome reward. Sanoudo, after much trouble and sacrifice, managed to put down the revolution, but Tiepolo refused to give him the agreed reward. So Sanoudo got angry, fought with the Cretans and captured Chandaka, Tiepolo had time to escape, disguised as a woman. The Venetian motherland then intervened, made a reconciliation between them, and Sanoudo returned to Naxos. It is not known whether Tiepolo continued to wear women's clothes.

1212 First large-scale colonisation of Crete by the Venetians. Venetian nobles settled on the island with their families. They selected the most fertile pieces of land and shared them out between themselves. The now landless locals worked without wages as serfs for the Venetian lords on the land which had previously been theirs.

1217-1219 The Skordilides and Melissinos Revolution. These Cretan Lords had great support from the people and managed to dominate the whole of West Crete. The Duke of Crete, Domenico Delfino, was forced to give them land and privileges.

1222 The second batch of Venetian colonisers arrived in Crete and grabbed even more land. The noble Melissinos family considered that they had suffered damage and rose in revolution for the second time (not on its own, of course, but with the support of the people!).

The Duke of Crete, Paolo Corino, came to a compromise with them and granted them new privileges.

1228-1236 The more you have, the more you want, and the greedy Melissinos again incited the Skordilides family and two other noble Cretan families (the Dracontopoulos and Arkoleos families) to revolution. The Venetian Duke was again unable to face them and, without much delay, he granted new privileges and feudal lands to the Cretan nobles in an attempt to avoid total defeat. So the Skordilidos and Melissinos families (who didn't care about freeing Crete and were interested only in lining their own pockets) betrayed the cause, whilst the Drakondopoulos family, who were patriots, continued on their own, but they were decimated and left the island.

1252 There was room for even more. The third batch of Venetian colonists came to Crete and grabbed whatever was left. More than **10.000** Venetian colonists in total (from the capture of the island to that date) had left their cramped, damp houses in Venice to settle in sunny, spacious Crete, mixed up with around **150.000** Cretans.

1261 After the recapturing of Constantinople, the Byzantine Emperor, Michael VIII, tried to pick up the pieces of the Byzantine empire, starting with Crete. He incited the Cretan Lords (the Chortatsides, Psaromiligos and Melissinos families) to revolution, but they confused the national and their personal interests and made a mess of it. The Venetians exploited their differences, immediately satisfied their personal demands (with grants of land and privileges) and things ended there.

1272-1278 The **Chortatsides Revolution,** with a genuine rational character this time. The rebels routed the Venetians and they laid siege to them at Chandaka. The man who saved the Venetians from certain defeat was a miserable traitor, the Cretan Lord Alexios Kallergis, who acted simply and solely for reasons of personal opposition to the other Cretan Lords. As soon as they recovered from the shock, the Venetians carried out horrible acts of revenge to set an example.

1282-1299 The **Kallergis Revolution.** It seems that the exchange made by the Venetians to Alexios Kallergis for his services did not satisfy him, so he made an unprecedented revolution! Indeed, it ended up in defeat for the Venetians and in the "Kallergis Treaty", which granted very large areas of land and the title of Venetian Noble to the all powerful Cretan Lord, Alexios Kallergis!

1319 Revolution at Sfakia, which was put down by the Venetians with the help of their friend Alexios Kallergis.

1330 Revolution by the Magarites family, which was also suppressed by the Venetians, with the help of George Kallergis, the son of Alexios.

1341-1347 Revolution by Leon Kallergis (almost the only Kallergis not to side with the Venetians), who stirred up other noble families such as the Psaromilirgos, Skordilides, Sevastos and Melissinos families. The Venetians put down this revolution too and took revenge on all the instigators and those under suspicion, with the most horrible tortures and the most barbaric executions. Alexios Kallergis, the grandson of the previous Alexios Kallergis, was an important helper and ally of the Venetians. As you can see, betrayal was a traditional sport in the wealthy Kallergis family.

1363-1366 The **Saint Titos Revolution.** For the first (and last) time, Venetian and Cretan nobles joined forces to rebel against the Venetian motherland with the aim of making Crete an autonomous Republic and for them to pocket the enormous tax revenues instead of sending them to Venice. The instigators of the revolution, which succeeded temporarily in its aim, were the Venetian nobles **Gradenigo** and **Venieri,** and the noble Cretan **Kallergis** family. This was too serious and enraged Venice, which immediately sent huge forces, suppressed the revolution and beheaded the instigators.

1415 One of the first travellers to visit Crete, the Italian **Cristoforo Buondelmonti,** wrote his impressions in a travel book which became the Bible of later travellers to Crete.

1508 A terrible earthquake almost completely destroyed Chandaka and killed thousands of its inhabitants.

1527 The **Revolution of George Kandanoleos,** or Lyssogiorgis, which the Venetians had little difficulty in suppressing. The instigators were beheaded, while the whole of the noble Kontos family (around 1,100 people), who were thought to be on friendly terms with the Kandanoleos family, were exiled.

1538 Cherentin Barbarosa, the most fearful pirate who ever operated in Mediterranean waters and arch-admiral of the Turkish fleet, attacked Crete. He was unable however to capture Chania, Rethimno and Chandaka, and he plundered the isolated Sitia and the whole of Lasithi.

1570 The **Turks,** the new power starting to dominate the Aegean, conquered Cyprus (as you can see, the Cypriots have old accounts to settle with the Turks). Their next target was Crete, which the Venetians were no longer in a position to protect effectively.

1577-1614 The Cretan painter, Dominicos Theotokopoulos known as **El Greco,** lived and worked in Toledo, Spain.

1550-1650 Period of peak intellectual achievement in Crete. Both, scholars and ordinary Cretans wrote pastoral poems, tragedies, and comedies, and this art reached its zenith with the narrative love poems **Erofili** by Chortatzis and **Erotokritos** by Vicenzo Kornaros, written in the language of the common people.

1644 A Turkish ship carrying pilgrims on their way to Mecca was arrested in the open sea off the coast of Crete, and the Turks used this as the official excuse they were looking for the invade Crete. The Turks accused the Venetians of harbouring Cretan pirates

HISTORY OF CRETE

and they prepared for one of the bigger military operations in their history.

1645 The Turks attacked Crete with 400 ships and 50.000 soldiers. They landed near Kasteli Kissamou and laid siege to Chania. After a siege of two months, they captured the city. The leader of the Turks was Yousouf Pasha and the defender of Chania was the Venetian general Kornaro.

1646 Rethimno fell into the hands of the Turks after a siege of 45 days

1648 The whole of Crete had now been captured by the Turks, except for the well-fortified Chandaka. The Turks gathered all their forces and began the siege of the capital. The Venetians together with the Greeks proved themselves to be hard nuts to crack and defended themselves effectively for **21 years,** the longest and hardest siege of a castle in history.

1669 Chandaka fell into the hands of the Turks, who had paid the heavy toll of 108,000 dead for their conquest. But the besieged too were in mourning for their approximately 30,000 victims. Those who were left had a time-limit of 12 days to abandon Chandaka, in accordance with the terms of surrender. The Turkish military commander during the final years of the siege was the Vizier Ahmed Kioprouli, and the leader of the defenders of Chandaka was the Venetian Fransisco Morozini.

The Turkish Rule (1669-1898)

1671 The Turks took a census of the population in order to impose their well-known poll-taxes and levies. At this time, it was found that around 60.000 Christians and 30.000 Moslems inhabited Crete.

1691 The Turks captured the fortress of Gramvousa which until then the Venetians had maintained control of.

1692 The Venetians sent their admiral, Domenico Motsenigo to Crete, stirred up the Cretans and attacked the Turks at Chania. The Turks defended themselves effectively and afterwards inflicted exemplary reprisals at the expense of the locals, naturally, and not of the Venetians, who got into their ships and sailed away.

1714 The Turks captured the fortress of Souda which was held by the Venetians.

1715 The Turks captured the fortress of Spinaloga, the last bastion of the Venetians in Crete, and they were at last absolute rulers of Crete.

1770 - 1771 The Daskaloyianni Revolution. The Russians, who had a dispute with the Turks, persuaded the Sfakians to rebel against the Turks, promising that they would help them. The help, however, never came and the 2,000 rebelling Sfakians, led by the legendary Yiannis Vlachos, or **Daskaloyiannis,** found themselves face to face with 15,000 better equipped Turks. After a few temporary successes on the part of the Sfakians, the Turks fought back and cornered them at Sfakia. They set fire to the villages and the property of the rebels, killed and captured many in the battles and, finally,

Daskaloyiannis surrendered. The Turks again demonstrated their cruelty - they **skinned Daskaloyiannis alive** in the central square of Iraklio...

1821 The great Greek revolution which broke out in Mainland Greece spread to Crete, the nucleus again being the inaccessible Sfakia. The Turks responded with plunder and mass slaughter (like the slaughter of 800 Christians at Iraklio) but the Cretan rebels managed to strike some powerful blows on the occupying forces in all corners of the island - in the battles of Therisos, Lakkon, Rethimno and elsewhere, the Turkish army suffered great losses. The Cretan chieftains, however, did not manage to avoid internal disputes and so they asked mainland Greece to send someone to undertake the general command. The leader of the Greek revolution Dimitrios Ypsilantis, sent **Michael Afentoulief** to Crete who did what he could to coordinate and organise the revolution in Crete. But the Cretans were stubborn and couldn't conquer their egotism. If they had had a little more accord, they would have thrown the Turks into the sea much earlier.

1822 The Sultan saw that he could not manage things on his own and he asked Mehmet Ali of Egypt for help. He landed at Crete with a very big Egyptian army and the scales turned again on the side of the Moslems who, after every victory, plundered, burned and ravaged everything before them. The morale of the Cretans was gradually lowered as they saw their country turning to ashes and ruins

1823 Afentoulief was deposed and **Emmanuel Tombazis** became leader. In a decisive battle on the plain of Mesara, the Turko-Egyptian army beat the Cretans. A few months later, Tombazis left Crete and the revolution was effectively over.

1825 A band of Cretan rebels came from the Peloponnese and captured the fortress of Gramvousa. The revolution rekindled.

1825-1828 The Gramvousa Revolution. With the fortress of Gramvousa as the centre of operations and under the direction of the "Council of Crete", whose chairman was the Warrior **Vassilis Chalis**, the revolution spread in west Crete.

1828 The Battle of Frangokastelo. The brave warrior from Epirus, Hatzimichalis Dalianis tried but could not beat the more numerous army of Mustafa Pasha. Dalianis himself was killed in battle, with the greater part of his army. But Mustafa also sustained a sudden attack by the Sfakian rebels during his return to Iraklio, and he suffered great losses.

1828 The first Governor of Greece, **Ioannis Kapodistrias,** realised that Crete was a lost cause and ordered the Cretans to stop fighting. The Cretans felt betrayed but they did not abandon their attempt to free themselves from the Turks and to be included in the newly formed Greek state.

1830 Despite the hard struggle the Cretans had put up all these years and the rivers of blood that had been shed, the London Protocol,

HISTORY OF CRETE

which was the first official international recognition of the Greek state, left Crete out of the Greek borders....

1830 -1840 Egyptian Occupation of Crete. The Sultan Mahmut IV ceded the whole of Crete to the Egyptian viceroy, **Mohammed Ali** in recompense for Egypt's help in putting down the Cretan revolution. In the beginning, the Egyptians showed themselves to be better masters than the Turks; they granted a general amnesty, asked the people to return to work, opened the schools and carried out many infrastructure works (roads, bridges, harbours, etc.), although at the expense of the people of course.

1833 The Mournies Revolution. Around 7.000 unarmed Cretans gathered at the village of Mournies to protest against the very heavy taxation, and in parallel sent a written protest to the Great Powers (England, France and Russia). The Egyptians showed their true face: they arrested the instigators and hanged them from the village trees, while they terrorised the inhabitants with similar acts throughout Crete.

1834 The English traveller **Robert Pashley** travelled for seven months through the whole of Crete and managed to locate and identify more positions of ancient Cretan cities than any previous investigator. His two-volume work "Travels in Crete", published in 1837, is one of the most important travel books ever written about Crete.

1840 The Egyptian Governor of Crete, Mohammed Ali, made a mess of his war operations in Syria. The Great Powers intervened and in the Treaty of London, Crete was taken away from the Egyptians and given back to the Sultan.

1841 The Chereti and Vasilogiorgi Revolution, which took its name from its two chieftains. Mustafa Pasha quickly crushed it and a new wave of violence broke out against the Christians.

1856 The Sultan realised that he could not continue being so tyrannical over his subjects and issued a firman (writ), the famous **Hati Houmayioun,** whereby he granted them important rights such as religious freedom, personal freedom, protection of property, etc.

1858 The firman mentioned above never arrived in Crete, so the **Mavroyeni Movement** arose. Around 5.000 unarmed Cretans gathered in Chania to protest and to send a written report to the Sultan and to the Great Powers. The Turks took a conciliatory stance, obviously fearing an international outcry, and promised to grant the Cretans the rights laid down in the Sultan's writ.

1865 The English admiral **T.A.B. Spratt,** who came to map the Cretan coast, took the opportunity to make an extended tour in the interior as well, and to write a very interesting travel book.

1866-1869 The Great Cretan Revolution. The Turks continued, as was expected, to violate the Christians' statutory rights, imposing new taxes. The Cretans rose up under the leadership of Yiannis Zymvrakakis in West Crete, Panayiotis Koroneos in central Crete and Michael Korakas in East Crete. The central slogan of the revolution was **"Union or Death"**. The Sultan, faced with this dilemma, obviously chose the second-death to the Cretans. To this effect, he sent to Crete his best (i.e. most brutal) general, Mustafa Giritli Pasha, who organised an army of 55.000 fanatical Turks. Terrible battles broke out throughout Crete with great losses on both sides. The Cretans had no help from the Great Powers, which in this case maintained a clearly pro-Turkish stance. The only ones who strengthened their struggle as much as they could, were fellow Greeks from free Greece.

1866 The peak moment of the revolution was the **Holocaust of Arkadi** in November 1866, when the 900 Christian defenders of the monastery, realising that they had no hope of being saved, blew up its powder magazine, bringing death to more than 1.500 Turks. This shocking event fired important Philhellenistic demonstrations throughout Europe, but the governments of the Great Powers remained unmoved and, on top of this, they obliged Greece to cut off the aid to Crete.

1869 The revolution was extinguished with the Treaty of Paris and the Turks consolidated their domination over the island, although they were obliged to grant significant privileges to the Cretans, with the so-called **Organic Law.**

1878 With the opportunity given by the Russo-Turkish war, a new revolution broke out in Crete with the demand that Crete be declared an autonomous state paying taxes to the Sultan, but with a Christian governor. The Turks naturally rejected the demand and the revolution took on enormous dimensions, with spectacular successes for the Cretans. The revolution ended with the **Agreement of Chalepa,** which granted significant political and economic rights to the Christians. Among other things, Greek was sanctioned as the official language of Crete, the publication of newspapers was allowed, and Crete acquired a General Assembly to which 49 Christians and 31 Moslem members of Parliament were elected. Turkish oppression was steadily losing ground and the time was approaching when it would be completely thrown off.

1878 Amid the general chaos, a sensitive, educated Cretan, **Minos Kalokerinos,** from Iraklio, did the first excavations at the ruins of Knossos. His findings (mainly earthen jars) were donated to foreign museums and to the Friends of Education Society of Iraklio.

1886 The German archaeologist, **Heinrich Schliemann,** already famous for his excavations in Troy, showed interest in excavating at Knossos and tried to buy a large piece of land in the area. But the money the owner of the field was asking seemed a lot to him and he left, angry!

1889 As if is wasn't enough for them to be ill-fated and barefoot under a powerful occupier, the Cretans argued amongst themselves! Such a civil political clash between the Cretan members of Parliament led to yet another revolution against the Turks, which the conquerors crushed immediately and which they used as a pretext to repeal the Agreement of Chalepa and to steep all of Crete in blood with indescribable acts of brutality. Europe continued to be unmoved.

1894 The English archaeologist, **Arthur Evans,** came to Crete for the first time and discovered that it was an unexplored archaeological paradise!

1895 A new revolution of the indomitable Cretans, which was also crushed by the indestructible Turks. Unbelievable new atrocities by the Moslems finally moved the Great Powers, who intervened and obliged the Sultan to ensure the Christians' political rights by way of a sketchy Constitution, the so-called **Memorandum.**

1897 Not only did the Turks never put into practice the Memorandum which the Great Powers had dictated to them, but they also began to act with undisguised cruelty towards the Christians. An unrestrained mob of Turks in Iraklio began to kill Christians and to burn down churches, as in the bad old days. But those days had finally gone into the past. The Greek government intervened strongly, ignoring the pro-Turkish stance of the Great Powers. It sent warships and 1.500 soldiers to Crete to reinforce the new revolution that had spread right throughout Crete. The Great Powers sent their own fleets, which blockaded the Cretan coast in order to obstruct the dispatch of Greek reinforcements, set a 6 kilometre zone around Chania which they forbade the Greek forces to approach, and proposed the declaration of Crete as an Autonomous State. The rebels rejected the proposal and continued their struggle, demanding unification with Greece.

1898 The Great Powers decided to impose their own choice and they captured Crete - The English took Iraklio, the Russians Rethimno, the Italians Chania, the Germans Souda, the French Sitia and the Austrians Kasteli Kissamou! Greece was then forced to withdraw its forces. The Cretan rebels were forced to accept the plan of the Europeans, who appointed Prince George of Greece as governor of the Autonomous Cretan State and placed it under their protection.

1898 Whilst the English were establishing the new administration in Iraklio, an enraged Turkish mob poured into the city, slaughtered hundreds of Christians, set fire to houses and churches and proceeded to all kinds of barbarous acts. While the river of Cretan blood spilled over so many years left the Europeans unmoved, the blood of the 17 English soldiers, killed in this final outbreak of Turkish barbarity, was the straw that broke the camel's back. The Europeans now realised what Turkish barbarity really meant, and they reacted strongly. They arrested and hanged the Turkish instigators and ordered the Turkish army to leave Crete immediately. On 2nd November, the last Turkish soldier left Crete. So, after 230 years, the period of Turkish occupation finally came to an end - it was one of the most nightmarish periods in Cretan history.

Autonomous Cretan State (1898-1913)

1899 Prince George, the Supreme High Commissioner (something like king, that is) of Crete appointed a 16 member committee that prepared a draft constitution and proclaimed elections, which took place in an absolutely orderly fashion and which set up the first Cretan government, where a powerful political personality stood out - **Eleftherios Venizelos.**

1900 The English archaeologist, Arthur Evans, came to Crete again, bought a large piece of land in the Knossos area and, by systematic excavations which lasted for 31 years, brought to light the ruins of **the Palace of Knossos.**

1901 Prince George believed that Crete should continue as an Autonomous State, while the Cretan people as a whole, with Venizelos as their chief spokesman, sought unification of Crete with Greece. As was to be expected, they came into collision. Prince George sacked Venizelos from the government (as he was empowered under the Cretan Constitution) and things started to get hot again. They were difficult times for princes....

1905 The Revolution of Therisso. With Venizelos as leader, around whom the most capable politicians in Crete and all the Cretan people were allied, the "Provisional Government of Crete" was formed in the village of Theriso.

1906 Prince George was forced to resign and his place was taken by **Alexandros Zaimis,** a person trusted by Greece, by Venizelos and by the Great Powers.

1907 The Cretan Civilian Guard was formed, which undertook to keep order and to protect the regime. The armies of the Great Powers were withdrawn from Crete.

1908-1909 As Austria had managed to annex (the diplomatic word for "grab") Bosnia-Herzegovina, and Bulgaria East Romylia, with no international reaction, why should Greece not annex Crete with which, when it came down to it, it had the closest national and religious bonds? The Cretan members of Parliament, headed by Venizelos, proclaimed unification with Greece and introduced the Greek Constitution to Crete. The High Commissioner, Zaimis, who at that time was away from Crete, received an order not to return to the island, where a temporary coalition government was being formed. Greece, so as not to provoke international reactions, did not officially accept the unification. In fact, the Great Powers did not intervene, despite Turkey's strong protests. When, however, the Greek flag was raised on the fortress of Firka in Chania, a detachment from the European fleet landed and took it down.

1910 Venizelos was elected Prime Minister of Greece. A brilliant politician and diplomat, he worked carefully in the direction of unification of Crete with Greece, and also of regaining Greek territory in Thessaly, Epirus, Macedonia, Thrace and the Dodecanese. He reinforced tacitly and very effectively Greece's military strength and when he finally felt ready, he declared war on Turkey.

1912-1913 First Balkan War. Greece allied with Bulgaria and Serbia. The allies attacked the Ottoman Empire, put down all resistance and freed significant parts of their territories. By the Treaty of London, which ratified the new borders of these countries, Crete was at last unified with Greece. **On 1st December 1913, the Greek flag was officially raised on the fortress of Firka in Chania.**

Province of Greece (1913-until today)

1923 Following the **Asia Minor Catastrophe** (the brave but unsuccessful attempt by Greece to free the very ancient Greek territories in Asia Minor from Turkish occupation), a large wave of Greek refugees came to settle on the hospitable land of Crete. By the Treaty of Lausanne, which regulated the question of population exchanges, all the Turkish minority in Crete (around 32.000 people) were forced to leave the island.

1941 The Battle of Crete. The German Staff, and specifically staff officers Gohring (chief of Luftwaffe) and Student (deputy chief of Luftwaffe) drew up the "Mercur" Plan for the capture of Crete. All day on 20th May, a cloud of 1.100 airplanes rained down German parachutists of the crack 7th Division. On the ground, they were "welcomed" by approximately 32.000 allies (English, Australian and New Zealanders) with 10.000 Greek soldiers (very badly armed) and the **whole** of the Cretan people who saw a foreign invader and ran amuck! Despite their terrible losses (4.000 dead parachutists and 170 crashed airplanes), the Germans captured Crete within ten days.

1941-1945 German occupation of Crete. The Cretan Resistance managed to strike some important blows on the occupier, the biggest event being the kidnapping of the German general Kreipe and his handing over to the Allies. German reprisals were cruel - they carried out mass indiscriminate executions of men, women and children, they burned villages or razed them to the ground, as in the case of Kantanos.

CRETAN SOCIAL GEOGRAPHY

With an area of 8,331 square kilometres, Crete is the **biggest island in Greece** and the fifth biggest in the Mediterranean (after Sicily, Sardinia, Cyprus and Corsica). Administratively it is divided into four countries and, according to the latest population census (1991), it has **540,000** inhabitants (see the table below). Of these, 200,000 live in the island's five biggest urban centres (Chania, Rethimno, Iraklio, Aghios Nikolaos and Ierapetra) and the remainder live in the 2,090 boroughs, communities and settlements which are scattered over every corner of the island.

Every summer, however, another **2,500,000** visitors from all over the world are added to the island's permanent inhabitants, i.e. five times more than the permanent inhabitants! As you can see, this is the main factor affecting Crete's social geography. The locals say characteristically that every summer, the island "sinks" under its many visitors!

Prefecture	Area in Km2	Population	Inhab./.Km2
Chania	2.376	134.000	56
Rethimno	1.396	70.000	47
Iraklio	2.641	265.000	100
Lasithi	1.818	71.000	39

Because of the need to service all these tourists, **40%** of the working population of Crete works directly or indirectly in the tourist sector, a sector which has an annual turnover of **1.5 billion dollars!** The average annual increase in tourist activity is estimated at 6%, which means that around the year 2005, Crete will reach saturation point, i.e. 5 million tourists, and a proportionate increase in turnover.

These lucrative prospects have of course changed completely the economic picture of the island. Many Cretans have sold their herds and have replaced them with herds of rented cars and motorcycles, while most of those who have land near the sea and tourist areas have ceased sowing wheat and barley and have planted hotels, rented rooms and restaurants instead. The pity is that the Greek State has not set strict specifications for tourist businesses, nor has it been in a position to car-

Tourist business has corrupted the authentic image of Crete

CRETAN SOCIAL GEOGRAPHY

ry out even some imperfect control to prevent arbitrary building and bad taste. Thus, architectural tradition and the natural landscape have been irrevocably damaged in many areas. Now, of course, the Cretans have realised that the tourists have demands and sensitivities

Cretan oranges are famous for top quality

and they are trying as much as they can to improve the tourist services which they supply.

Agriculture, although it has lost quite a lot of land, retains first position in the Cretan economy. Approximately 3.5 million stremmata (3,500 km2) is agricultural land, which grow potatoes (70.000 str), wheat (48.000 str), barley (46.000 str), Oats (39.000 str), tomatoes (25.000 str), water-melons (15.000 str), broad beans (13.000 str), onions (7.000 str), melons (5.500 str) and many other cereals, horticultural produce and vegetables, which sell well in Greece and throughout Europe because they are of high quality. The high temperatures that prevail all year round in Crete also favour the cultivation of exotic fruit, e.g. bananas and avocados, although their size is visibly smaller than fruit grown in tropical countries.

Viniculture has an important position (160.000 str) and produces exceptional table grapes and grapes for wine making, while the Cretan sultana, of world-wide reputation, is produced from a special variety of grapevines (280.000 str). Four vine-growing zones have been defined in Crete where they produce Appellation Origin Highest Quality wine. In **Archanes, Peza** and **Daphnes** (all three are in central Crete, south of Iraklio), they grow the Mantilaria and Kotsifali varieties, which give an exceptional dry red wine. In **Sitia** (on the eastern tip of Crete) they grow the Liatiko variety, which gives a light-coloured dry red wine. In Peza, they also grow the Vilana variety, which gives an aromatic dry white wine.

Tree-culture is however the absolute leader in Cretan agriculture. There are approximately **25 million olive trees,** which have literally covered the whole island from end to end, from which the famous Cretan olive oil, one of the best in Europe, is produced. There are also approximately 2.6 million orange trees, 1.6 million almond trees, 1 million peartrees and many fig-trees, mandarin-orange trees, lemon-trees, apple-trees, apricot-trees, peach-trees and cherry-trees.

Stock-breeding is not as developed as agriculture and continues to be carried out using traditional methods. There are approximately 900.000 sheep and 400.000 goats, which graze in both large and small herds on upland or mountain pastures. There are only a few cows (around 20.000) but around **1 million rabbits** are bred (almost half of those bred in the whole of Greece!) because they are a traditional Cretan food for which both locals and foreigners show a special preference.

There are also around 130.000 pigs many of which are domestic (you will see many families in the villages who are rearing their own pig, for their own consumption) and very many chickens (it is difficult to count them but they are estimated at around 2 million!) most of which are free range and you will often see them flying in front of your wheels in each village you pass.

Fishing also belongs to the traditional professions of the Cretans (it is certain that this has been practised since the Minoan years) but it has never seen any particular growth even though Cretan waters are very rich in fish. Unfortunately, many Cretans insist on fishing by the destructive and illegal dynamite method.

Industry is not particularly developed (as in the rest of Greece) but during recent years it has shown an upward trend. There are around 8.000 industrial and craftmaking units concerned with processing of agricultural products, mainly olive-presses, wine manufacturers, flour-mills, fruit juice production units and mineral water bottling plants, etc.

The Cretans did not always live off tourism

With so many hotels, restaurants, bars and all the kinds of tourist businesses you will see in almost every corner of Crete, you could easily get the impression that this place has been occupied with tourism since the old days. The tourist development of the island, however, basically began only twenty years ago. Until that time, the Cretans were occupied in other professions.

In the **neolithic period** (7000-3000 BC) the people who lived on this island (we cannot call them Cretans) lived mainly in caves and also in small settlements built on low hills. Their professional horizons were very limited - they were **hunters, small stock-breeders, small farmers and fishermen.** Neolithic man produced on his own all that he needed in order to live, but there must have been some talented people who specialised in the manufacture of stone tools and weapons, in the manufacture of clay vessels and in the building of huts. Certain others must have left their small fields to become the original **seamen** who went in their primitive boats to Milos, Nissyros and other places to bring back raw materials (obsidian) for making their tools with.

In the **Prepalatial Period** (3000-2000 BC), rapid developments took place, obviously under the influence of new colonists that came from the southwest shores of Asia Minor, who prepared the appearance of the Minoan civilisation. In this period, people gradually left their caves and built comfortable, square huts with stone foundations, brick walls and flat wooden roofs. The inhabitants continued to work in agriculture and stock-breeding, but ceramics and stonecraft developed a lot and new crafts emerged, such as **jewellery-making** and **weaving.** They loaded the surplus produce onto their ships (which had improved a lot in the meantime) and they sold it in the markets of the Aegean and of Egypt. Thus, alongside the farmers and the breeders, the first professional **merchants** slowly appeared.

In the **period of the Minoan Palaces** (2000-1450 BC), i.e. the peak period of the wonderful Minoan Civilisation, for some untraceable reason, authority was concentrated in the hands of the kings. Magnificent palace centres were founded and important changes took place in social and economic organisation. Populations gathered around the palaces and big cities, like Knossos, developed where new professions emerged and old ones saw great advances. Specialist Craftsmen, like **metalworkers, seal makers, sculptors, perfume makers and pharmacists** set up craft shops inside the palaces. Agricultural production was amplified by new irrigation techniques and by new tools that look much like the pick-axes and hoes of today. Home industry also saw a big development, mostly in **weaving** which employed women.

This long and very creative period came to an end, however, around 1450 BC, due to some unexplained violent cause. The palaces fell down in ruins, the cities became deserted, the fields were abandoned and went to waste and many people lost their lives. Immediately afterwards, Achaean colonisers appeared on the island, but they did not leave any special traces, nor do they appear to have clashed with the remaining distressed inhabitants.

Golden jewels from Malia. Paleopalatial Period (2000-1700 BC)

When, however, the war-happy, headstrong **Dorians** appeared (1100 BC), chaos ensued! After having captured the island relatively easily, they threw the previous inhabitants out of their houses and settled there themselves; they fortified their cities and organised their lives on the Spartan model. As for the locals, fate had five things in store for them. Those who had not resisted the invaders became **neighbours** and were allowed to make their homes near to the cities and to continue to cultivate their fields, although they paid a significant tax to the conquerors. Those who had resisted half-heartedly became **serfs;** they lost all their land and were forced to work on public projects (construction-sites, road-making, fortification works, etc). Those who dared to resist more seriously not only did they lose all their property and dignity, they also became **slaves** who did the haviest, dirtiest and most hazardous jobs. Those who resisted vigorously became **dead people!** Finally, there was a small group of Minoans who had realised in time that resistance was in vain and who had packed their bags and gone and climbed up to the most precipitous and inaccessible mountain-tops in the east part of the island, far out of the javelin range of the Dorians. The Dorians called these people **Eteocretans** (genuine Cretans). In the places they had climbed up to, they had very little cultivatable land and grazing pastures and it is certain that they were hard put to survive. Their last traces disappeared around the 3rd Century BC.

During ancient times and until the Roman Occupation (1100-69 BC) life in Crete was **a continuous clash** between the Cretan cities with long or short intervals of peace, of alliances and of reconciliations. There were around 150 large and small cities and an infinite combination of clashes and alliances between them, according to the interests of the moment. Generation upon generation of Cretans (as Homer refers to them for the first time) learned to use the spear much better than the ploughshare, and a new profession flowered during the whole of this period in Crete - **mercenary soldiers.** From out of this professional class, during periods of unemployment (i.e. during periods of peace) emerged another professional class - **the pirates!** The first pirates quickly and with little effort became very rich and thus became shining examples to younger people. Towards the end of the Hellenistic Period (the last pre-Christian centuries), the Cretan pirates joined together with the blood-thirsty Kilikian pirates and became the most daring and dangerous robbers in the Mediterranean. They did not hesitate to attack even Roman ships in the harbours.

When the situation became intolerable, the Romans took a trip and conquered Crete. The **Roman Conquest** lasted for 400 years (69 BC - 300 AD) and during this period the Cretans were forced, to their regret, to abandon piracy, robbery and mercenary soldiering and to return to their fields. The most fertile land had of course been taken by the Roman landowners, who set destitute locals to cultivate them under the terms and conditions of slaves. The Romans, however, did many good things - they built roads and harbours throughout the island thanks to which trade developed especially. Many craft activities also flourished, such as **copper-working** and **ceramics,** which now found new markets for their products on the shores of Phoenicia and Egypt, but stock-breeding and farming also developed gradually. In general, the Romans lived harmoniously beside the locals, maybe because they admired Greek civilisation and because there were not deep religious differences to divide them.

After the separation of the Roman Empire into west and east, Crete came under the jurisdiction of the east Roman Empire which later developed into the Byzantine Empire. The rearrangements and the conflicts were especially spread out throughout Europe but not much changed in the social and economic life of Crete. During the whole of the **first Byzantine Period** (330-824), Crete continued to be an important commercial junction in the heart of the Mediterranean while its stock-breeding and farm production flourished greatly. Despite its commercial and strategic importance, however, the Byzantines left it basically unfortified. Thus, in 824, the Saracen Arabs, who had been thrown out of Spain, found new land to plunder.

The period of the **Arab Occupation** (824-961) was the most catastrophic period the island had even known. The Arabs slaughtered as many Cretans as they could, plundered, pulled down and burned all the cities and villages that were in their path and they destroyed everything. Those Cretans who had time left the island, while those who stayed behind were converted to the Islamic religion to save their lives and enlisted in the Arab army. The fields were abandoned and became barren, the herds were exterminated and all the countryside was laid waste. Chandaka (the Iraklio of today) became the centre of

CRETAN SOCIAL GEOGRAPHY

During the Roman period, development of agriculture and brilliant public works brought new glamour to Crete. Here, Roman column in Gotryna.

Crete and this developed into the biggest centre of piracy and of the slave trade in the Mediterranean.

When the Byzantines finally managed to throw the Arabs out of Crete (to be accurate, they did not throw them out but killed them all, some 200.000 of them, either in battle or in executions), Crete was a destroyed and ruined place. In the 250 years that the **second Byzantine Period** (961-1204) lasted, Crete managed to heal its wounds gradually and to regain the old rhythms of its social and economic life. The Byzantines invited back the exiled Cretans, brought over new colonists from Constantinople for reinforcement, rebuilt the cities and the villages and got rid of all trace of the Arab nightmare. Commerce regained its old glory. The Greek population increased greatly and the island came to life again. A powerful class of big landowners was gradually created, in accordance with the models of Byzantine society, while small landowners were increasingly weakened. The landless villagers became labourers in the fields of the large landowners who amassed in their hands great economic and political power.

When the Byzantine empire began to decline, during a critical period of internal disputes, the Venetians managed to buy Crete from the Byzantines for a very low price! Thus began the long, painful period of the **Venetian occupation** (1204-1669) during which the Venetian rulers did not respect the political rights nor the religious conscience of the locals. The Regno di Candia (Kingdom of Crete) as they called it, was organised on the European feudal mode. The ruling class were the Venetian nobles who shared out the Cretan land between themselves and acquired tremendous economic and political power. A vigorous **urban class** developed in the cities (merchants, doctors, lawyers, civil servants), the members of which were mainly Greek orthodox people. In the countryside however the overwhelming majority of the Cretan people suffered greatly. Most of them had no land or property and they worked as slaves in the fields which the Venetians had grabbed. These grim feudal lords sold them or hired them to others and generally treated them as their inanimate property. The worst thing of all, however, was that they forced them to work on public projects, mainly fortification works (countless Cretan workers lost their lives due to beating and the miserable working conditions at the Venetian castles you see and admire today in Crete), and to serve as oarsmen in the Venetian galleys. This last was equivalent to a death sentence. Piracy, rough seas, hunger, sickness and exhausting rowing killed most of them. Despite their miserable condition, the Cretans resisted as much as they could. During the Venetian occupation, 27 large and small revolutions took place, but none had the desired result except for horrible revenge reprisals on the part of the Venetians who burned, killed and plundered without limit.

Authentic Cretans you will meet only in remote mountain villages

This terrible period eventually came to an end, but another even more terrible began. The Venetians were not able to prevent attack by the Turks and so in 1669 the period of the **Turkish occupation** (1669-1898) began. The new conquerors competed in barbarity with the old ones - tens of cities and villages were laid waste and their Christian inhabitants slaughtered, sent into exile or violently converted to Islam. The small urban Greek class was destroyed and all the urban professions devolved into Turkish hands. Commerce stagnated. But it was farming and stock-breeding which took the biggest blow - the taxes imposed by the Turks were so heavy that many Christians preferred to leave their fields and herds and to become guerrillas in the mountains (the legendary **chainides**). There were no more than 60.000 Greeks in Crete at the beginning of the Turkish conquest. They found a safe refuge however on top of the inaccessible mountains and isolated plateaux, where they managed not only to survive but also to increase: at the end of the 18th century it is estimated that they exceeded 200.000. They organised dynamic rebellions in which they mourned many victims, but they caused great damage to the conqueror. After many sacrifices an struggles, Crete at last was freed from the Turks (1898) and after a short transition period, was finally united with Greece (1913).

The adventures of the Cretan people through all these centuries left indelible marks on the Cretan mental make-up. One characteristic leftover is the special love of the Cretans for **guns.** Many Cretans of 14 years of age and over not only have their own gun but also carry it with them wherever they go, stuck into the belt of their trousers below their shirt. Some have two, three or four guns, usually automatic pistols or the latest type of revolvers, while there are some who maintain a whole arsenal of military rifles, hand-grenades, etc.! They spend a fortune To acquire them and to procure of ammunition, as everything is sold illegally on the black market. The gun is a part of a Cretan's body and no law can take it away from him despite sporadic attempts to do so. But what do they do with all these guns?

Firstly, they use them to shoot the famous **balothies,** i.e. shooting into the air at parties and festivals. If you happen to go to a Cretan celebration (a wedding, christening, or festival) you will think that war has broken out! Very often, when they are alone in the mounts, they do target practice or organise rough and ready shooting matches, firing at whatever they see, usually signs (with special preference for those reading "no hunting"). So if you are standing somewhere or when you pitch your tent in the wilds, make sure you're well away from signs!

More rarely, they use guns to solve their differences. Of course, they don't use them for small matters, nor in serious conflicts and clashes. But they use them without hesitating to punish anybody who dares to cause them the biggest possible damage - on insult against the honour of their family (e.g. raping their mother of their sister, or even making insulting insinuations against them). The first victim usually provokes the beginning of a chain reaction of killings - the so-called vendetta.

The sign advertises hunting equipment and school supplies! Naturally the gun becomes an appendix for many Cretans.

The close relatives of the murdered person do not rest until they have killed the murderer. Then the close relatives of the dead murdered do not rest until they have killed the murderer or murderers of the murderer. The remaining relatives of the dead murderers of the murderer of their relative do not rest until they have killed the murderers of the murderers - and so it goes on until everyone has been finally annihilated, or until the police manage to intervene effectively and to send the antagonists to prison. Even here however the dispute is not resolved but is simply covered up. When the murderer comes out of prison, even if this is after many years, the opposing relatives are lying in wait with their finger on the trigger, and the game starts all over again. So be careful how you talk and gesture to the beautiful Cretan girls, because their brothers don't mess around!

There are other penal crimes, however, which the Cretans not only are not ashamed of but which they also consider as an honour. **Sheep rustling,** for example, has a very great tradition in Crete and is almost an institution and a necessary stage in the coming of age process of Cretan shepherds. This tradition has its roots in the era of the Venetian occupation, if not even further back, when the people in the countryside were hungry and had to steal from the rich in order to live. Today, the Cretan shepherds steal neither to live nor to enlarge their herds (which are already quite big). They steal for **kapetania** as they say, because it is macho. But sometimes they overdo it and instead of stealing a symbolic five or six lambs, they steal whole herds. In this case, of course, tempers flare an often the pistols "speak".

But even the symbolic thefts of five or six sheep are capable of exterminating even a big herd very quickly when there are a lot of rustlers in the area. The only effective way a shepherd can protect his herd from rustlers is **Koumbaries.** This means that he takes care to make as many shepherds in the area as he can godfathers at his children's christenings. And if there are more shepherds in the area than his (usually many) children, then he asks two or three or sometimes even more people to be godfathers to each child! In this way, most Cretans have become related as **Koumbari** or **Syntekni** (ex officio brothers) as they call themselves and of course they avoid stealing from each other. Even if you are not a potential rustler, if you stay more than three or four months in Crete, you will almost certainly not leave without becoming a Koumbaros!

CRETAN MUSIC AND DANCE

By: **Hellenic Folklore Centre**
Vassilis Economou,
Mirella Konstantelou
Special Contributor: **Ioannis G. Panayiotakis**

From the most distant to modern times, the Cretans associate every moment of their social life with music and dance. At the harvest, when relaxing, at religious ceremonies and feasts, at weddings, births and deaths and in lamentations - at every opportunity, the Cretans sing and dance their joys, sorrows, bad luck, love, bravery, etc...

The songs and dances of Crete are many and differ from province to province, from area to area and even between villages. The same thing happens with the musical instruments which prevail in each area, depending on the historical and social conditions.

Musical instruments are used according to the occasion. At big celebrations, festivals and weddings, the *lyre* or the *violin* is played and is accompanied by the lute or the guitar. In East Crete, the *daoulaki* (small drum) and the *yerakokoudouna* (small bells fixed onto the bow of the lyre) are used as accompanying instruments.

The main musical instrument in Crete is the lyre, which made its first appearance in Crete during the 17th Century or the beginning of the 18th Century, and which has three shapes: the pear-shaped *lyraki* (small lyre) with a small shallow body and a sharp note; the also pear-shaped *vrontolyra* with a big, deep body and a loud deep note; and the *viololyra*, which is seldom played today.

The lyre that has predominated and is played today in Crete, was designed and first manufactured around 1940 by Manoli Stagaki in his instrument workshop which still exists today in Rethymnon.

Lyres are made of black mulberry, walnut or maple wood. The bow is made of loquat wood and hairs from a horse's tail. Once upon a time, lyre players made their own lyres. Today there are professional lyre manufacturers who sell them not only in Crete and the rest of Greece but also abroad. Antonis Stephanakis, in Zaro, Iraklio, is one of the best-known lyre manufacturers today.

For smaller groups of friends or for private family parties, apart from the lyre, the violin, the lute or the daoulaki, the **mandolin** or the **mandola** may be played. With these instruments, people sing the famous **mantinades**, improvised couplets which are mainly erotic, satirical, teasing, etc. The lyre-players are the best lyric-writers, but all Cretans are distinguished for the ease with which they compose mantinades at the drop of a hat.

The most common musical instrument in Crete from the time of Erotokritos to this day - with certain variations - must be the **lute**. Erotokritos himself:

"took his lute and walked quietly
and played it sweetly outside the palace
his hand was sugar and he had a voice like a nightingale
every heart that heard him cried and wept."

A very ancient pastoral instrument which, despite its long historical development in Cretan musical life is today tending to disappear, is the **askomantoura** (the ancient bag pipe). The same thing is happening to the **thambolia** or **sphyrochambiola** (pastoral flutes). The pilgrim to the monastery of St. Phanourios at Valsamonero, Iraklio, can see St. Phanourios playing the askomantoura on an icon of the 15th Century A.D.

It is very easy to organise a party in Crete. Good mezedes (bits and pieces to eat), plenty of wine and tsikoudia (a strong spirit), eager instrumentalist, the mandinada players with their improvised lyrics and the party has gelled. Until morning they exchange mandinades which touch on thousands of original topics. Most of them are about love, both requited and unrequited, and about the progress of the guests at work, at the hunt, with guns, etc.

In Crete we can distinguish two kinds of music. There is the dance music which we meet throughout the island, and the **rizitika** songs which are something like the slow kleftiko songs of the tavlas of mainland Greece. They are called rizitika because they sprang from, developed and are sung in the villages which are situated on the riza, i.e. on the slopes of the White Mountains in Chania prefecture.

Rizitika are divided into songs of the **tavla** and of the **strata**. There are more tavla songs. According to their verses they can be divided into akritika (featuring mainly Digenis Akritas), into songs about love, marriage, joy, into historical songs, into heroic and allegorical songs. The strata songs are mainly wedding songs, which they sing when they take the bridegroom or the bride to the church, or christening songs and others.

They still sing rizitika in **Anopoli**, as they do throughout Sfakia. The most important local narrative song, however, which has an epic character and great historical value is the song of Daskaloyiannis, the hero of Anopolis who was the leader of the first rebellion of the Sfakians against the Turks in 1770. The song, which has 1034 verses, was composed and dictated to someone who could write by the shepherd Uncle Pantzelio of Anopoli, seventeen years after the events it describes, namely in 1787.

In East Crete, the position of the tavla songs is taken by the **kondylies**, a series of repeated revised motifs on top of which they sing mandinades.

After a certain point, song cannot express the spiritual intensity of a festivity and here the code changes. Dance takes over. The most skillful join in a circle in various ways and create **tsambakia**, depending on the dance and the mood. They dance the Kondylies in a slow dance and then request **ortses**, the fast **pentozali**. They calm down with the wonderful **syrto** and finish up in a burst with the Kastrino, Sitiano or Roumathiano **pidichto** or with the Anogean ortses. If there are women in the group, they dance the **soustes** in pairs, where unconfessed desires erupt.

From the time of the Cretan rebellions and the repeated visits of allied fleets to Crete, a new dance appeared, the **polka**, which is still danced today.

Anogia is a big town in Mylopotamos county of Rethimnon prefecture. Weddings in Anogia still take place today with all the forms of the old customs. The women busy themselves with weaving. The Anogean woolen woven materials, with their wonderful folk motifs and their variety of colours and patterns, are very well known. Today, Anogia has acquired a great reputation for its good musicians and its excellent dancers. The Anogean pidichto is danced only here in Anogia, and there are only a few who still dance it.

The inhabitants of the village **Armeni**, in Sitia county of Lasithi prefecture, are well known for their festivities and they organise dances at every opportunity.

Kria Vrisi is a village in Aghios Vassilios county on the south-east side of Rethimno prefecture. The inhabitants are olive producers and stock-breeders As it is a mountain village, it has only a few orchards and vineyards. So to protect them in the springtime from hedgehogs and badgers that come out at night and destroy them by disturbing the freshly-turned soil, they invented the **moungrinara**. This is an instrument that sends off the pests with its loud note.

If you are genuinely interested in getting to know the wealth and depth of the Cretan soul, you must come to Crete during the off-peak periods and stay for some weeks in a non-tourist place. Only with the devotion of a pilgrim and the passion of a collector of treasures will you be able to discover the unknown life and the centuries-old traditions of the villages of Crete.

RELIGIOUS FESTIVALS IN CRETE
(Names of village/s are followed by the corresponding prefecture in brackets)

11/1 St. Antonios : Kasteli Pediados (Iraklio)
18/1 St. Kyrillos : Kalogeri (Rethimnon)
2/2 Candlemas Day : Skouvroula (Iraklio)
10/2 St. Charalambos : Xida (Iraklio)
11/2 St. Vlasis : Machairi (Hania)
25/3 The Annunciation : Paleochora (Hania), Tzermiado (Lasithi), Prasas (Iraklio)
23/4 St. Georgios : Selinari Mirambellou (Lasithi), Asi Gonia (Hania)
8/5 St. Ioannis Theologos (John the Baptist) : Stilos (Hania), Marmaketo (Lasithi)
12/5 St. Photeini : Avdou (Iraklio)
21/5 St. Constantine & St. Helen : Arkadi Monastery, Arkalochori (Iraklio)
30/5 St. Meletios : Chora Sphakion (Hania)
Holy Sririt : Moroni Kenourgio, Kalo Chorio (Iraklio)
24/6 St. John : Rethimno
30/6 Holy Apostles : Apostoli (Rethimno)
15/7 St. Kyrikos : Lambiotes (Rethimno)
17/7 St. Marina : Kato Chorio (Lasithi), Aghia Marina (Hania), Aghia Marina , Voni, Tsalikaki (Iraklio)
20/7 Prophet Elias : Kato Chorio (Lasithi), Gergeri (Iraklio), Kasteli Kissamou (Hania)
15/7 St. Anna : Kato Chorio (Lasithi), Geraki, Kato Asites (Iraklio)
26/7 St, Paraskevi : Kalives (Hania), Melambes, Sisarha (Rethimno), Skotino Pediados (Iraklio)
27/7 St. Panteleimon : Omalos (Hania), Kounavi, Harakas (Iraklio)
30/7 St. Syllas : Kalo Chorio Mirabello (Lasithi)
6/8 Transfiguration of Christ : Voukolies (Hania), Males Ierapetra, Voulismeni Mirabello, Zakros Sitia (Lasithi), Arkalochori (Iraklio), Ano Meros Imario
8/8 St. Myron : Aghios Mironas (Iraklio)
12/8 St. Mathew : Agh. Fotis, Kasteli (Hania)
15/8 Assumption of Virgin Mary : Neapoli, Piskokefalo, Orino (Lasithi), Agh. Vasilios, Archanes,

.................Aitania, Metaxochori, Mohos, Choudetsi (Iraklio),
......................Anogia, Axos, Eleftherna, Thronos, Kolivos,
.... Sisarcha (Rethimno), Kolimbari, Kalives (Hania)
24/8 St. Kosmas Aetolos : ....Kritsa Mirabello (Lasithi)
24/8 St. Eftychios : ....Kambanos (Hania)
25/8 St. Titos : ....Timbaki (Iraklio)
27/8 St. Phanourios : ....Vorizia (Iraklio), Agh. Pandes (Hania)
29/8 Decapitation of St. John : Tzermiado, Ziros, Agh. Georgios (Lasithi),
31/8 Holy Girdle : ....Psichro (Lasithi), Asfendou (Hania)
2/9 St. Mamas : ....Kiriakoselia (Hania)
14/9 Holy Cross : ....Tzermiado, Kalamafka, Savros (Lasithi)
15/9 St. Nikitas : ....Frangokastelo (Hania)
24/9 Birthday of Virgin Mary : ....Praesos Sitia (Lasithi)
8/10 St. Pelaghia : ....Aghia Pelaghia, Aghia Varvara, Vori (Iraklio)
26/10 St. Dimitrios : ....Ramni (Hania) Diavaide (Iraklio)
8/11 Archangels Michael & Gabriel : ....Potamies (Iraklio)
11/11 St. Minas : ....Iraklio, Archanes, Episkopi (Iraklio)
13/11 St. John Chrysostom : ....Stalida (Iraklio)
25/11 St. Catherine : ....Kalives (Hania)
5/12 St. Savvas : ....Kentri Sitia (Lasithi)
6/12 St. Nikolaos : ....Armeni (Hania)

CRETAN CUISINE

By: **Ilias Mamalakis**

(Lover of food, lover of good food and never a selfish eater!)

-*"Have some olives koumbare!"*
-*"The cheese is good too! " answers the witty, gourmand Cretan koumbaros, who instantly sums up the cheese as a better meal than the olives.*

Certainly for many centuries, Crete has offered a gastronomic education and a series of dishes which have travelled through time to arrive, almost unchanged, to the present day. Although the island has been a melting pot for almost all the peoples in the Mediterranean, it seems that Cretan cuisine, despite its international past, has remained strictly Cretan and minimally influenced by the conquerors - in any case, any intermingling between the peoples happened violently and not peacefully.

The Cretan people depended for their food almost exclusively on the products of their earth. They have their own sauces, dairy products, specialties, sweet dishes, pulses. This is a very egoistic opinion you will tell me. Well, come with me and let us see.

Have you heard anywhere else of eating **papoules, stamnagathi, rodiki, korfokoukia,** daisy shoots or mosses? Well, here are the specialty salads, always raw and always cooling, and with plenty of oil, vinegar and coarse salt, with a few wrinkled olives. So, if you find yourself in Crete during spring or autumn, don't forget to ask for some of these.

As far as cereals are concerned, barley has been cultivated more than wheat. The famous barley rusk has come down to us today - it is softened in water, soaked in oil and tomato, and it constitutes our national dish, the famous *"tako"* which is very tasty and very good for the digestion.

Crete has been grazed from the very old days until the present time almost exclusively by goats and sheep, which constitute the main body of Cretan stockbreeding. Their meat is tasty and is cooked with all types

| *The Cretan rusk (takos)*

of vegetables. It is not so long since, in every village, the butcher (meat seller) slaughtered a sheep or a goat having first orally ensured the sale, because if he was left with it, it would either have gone off (as there were no refrigerators of course) or he would have to eat it himself.

So we have ewe, which have given birth once or twice, lamb or goat or kid cooked with fennel, with delectable local artichokes, with wild mountain greens, with tomato or egg and lemon sauce, or simply boiled with rice drowned in staka.

Oh! that **staka**. A source of cholesterol and other unhealthy ingredients but extremely tasty, fatty, aromatic, it is none other than **cream of butter** (or "tsipa" as they call it in Crete), which is collected from the shepherd with great care, salted a little and kept in a cool place until needed at weddings and celebrations to prepare the proud *"gamopi-*

CRETAN CUISINE

lafo" (the rice used at weddings). It is difficult to find it these days if you do not have access as a friend to a Cretan family which in turn has a shepherd as a friend or relation.

But dairy products are not confined only to staka - we also have the fantastic, sweet-smelling **myzithres**, **anthotyro**, home-made **tyrozoulia** and the fantastic full-fat sheep's milk **graviera**, designated internationally as a cheese with appelation of origin. Light yellow in colour, salted, a little peppery (depending on its maturity) with all its fat, spicy with a totally characteristic taste, it is the queen of Greek **gravieras** and has already made its debut in the European and international markets which it will certainly capture with its fine qualities.

Returning to meat for a moment, we must mention the lovely **rabbit** which saved Crete from the famine caused every so often by the various conquerors, the Nazis being the most recent ones. Easy to reproduce (they breed like rabbits) and easy to rear because of the flora of the area, they existed and still exist in the garden of every village house. It is easy to cook and can be served in **stiphado** (stew with onions), fried or roasted in the oven with potatoes and it is always tasty and healthy. The Cretans owe it a lot and they show this by their preference for it. Just to give you an idea, I can tell you that half the number of rabbits in Greece are to be found in Crete.

Another native of Crete has contributed a lot to the everyday meal - we are of course talking about **snails**. They can be cooked in many ways: scalded in salt water for a meze in raki (a rare dish these days), with onions and fresh tomato sauce and, of course, the best recipe of all, the renowned **chochlii bourbouristi** (fried and simmered in vinegar and seasoned with rosemary) - something else!

Talking of vinegar, this is an important ingredient in the island's cooking. It is used everywhere, even in the preparation of sausages, to which it gives a very characteristic taste.

As far as pulses are concerned, broad beans make a classic speciality, one that was very popular in the old days - **broad beans *(koukia matsarista)***. This is very good and tasty and is basically broad beans with potatoes that have been crushed in a pestle and mortar with oil and vinegar. It is heavy, feeding and full of protein, a necessary food for the labourious life of the country people.

Don't let's forget that Crete is an island and a big island at that, and the Cretans have always valued and still value the produce of the sea which is getting rarer these days. Sargus, **rofos**, mullet, skorpidi, octopus, limpets and many more - these are all delicacies mainly of the seaside villages. I must make special mention however, of the prince of Cretan waters - the **skaros**. It's not necessary to say much - those who know, (mainly the fishermen and the village gourmets) classify it as the height of enjoyment. White compact meat, crispy skin and aromatic innards. Don't be surprised, skaros is eaten whole! yes, yes, whole! It must of course be caught early in the morning, before it feeds, so that its stomach is empty, so that when you eat it, the sand will not annoy you. The expert eater grills it in one piece. The only thing he takes out is the bitter liquid from the gall bladder (an operation of a few seconds done with a match), and then he grills it and enjoys his meze. What do you say now to a fish soup, the famous **kakavia** (bouillabaisse)? I remember they used to make it for us in my village in the old days with scorpion-fish, potatoes, a lot of lemon and oil and probably an onion or two - it was really terrific and nothing like the various bad versions of mediocre culinary imagination. If you know of a good fish taverna and you happen to go on the day they've made kakavia, you can order two bowls without thinking twice! Ask too if they have **achinosalata** (sea-urchin salad), a wonderful (and probably expensive) meze which is certainly worth trying.

Now that we've eaten well, even through descriptions, let's have a dessert - a **kalitsounaki** in the shape of a lamp, Crete's star sweet, although unfortunately available only during certain seasons of the year, mainly when sheep's milk is fat and plentiful. It is a tiny pie filled with fresh myzithra cheese, eggs, with or without aniseed and sesame seeds but with a little cinnamon. It is very pleasant to eat and can be kept for many days in a cool place. More often you will find crunchy **kserotigana**, fried doughy strips, wound in coils, steeped in heavy syrup and sprinkled with lots of grated walnut - you'll want to lick your fingers.

Freshly cut tomatoes, crisp cucumber, frangrant olive oil and the unique mizithra make an exquisite choriatiki salad (seek it in villages only).

While we are on the subject of traditional Cretan food, here are three restaurants where you will find some of the tastiest and best-cooked dishes in Crete.

Eutychia's taverna - outside Kolymbari still makes the rare dish called 'tourta', i.e. a pie filled with lamb and various local cheeses.

Kombos' taverna outside Rethimno on the road to Atsipopoulo makes a tasty splinogardouba (spleen) - and you'll be lucky if they have staka.

In Iraklio, in the suburb of Phoenikia, in **Zervos' taverna**, apart from the very tasty food, iced raki is served in a real ritual. For dessert, there are savoury and sweet mezedakia, like fried myzithra cheese with honey, water melon syrup preserve, green almonds and many more...

Dear travellers, whatever good things you have to eat, they lose some of their value if you don't wash them down with a good drink. Crete has two spirits to show off - **raki** or **tsikoudia**, and the traditional Cretan wine. Tsikoudia is an excellent drink for any occasion. Tsikoudia to whet your appetite, tsikoudia to help you digest, tsikoudia (warm, mixed half and half with honey and a little pepper) to warm you up, tsikoudia (iced) to cool you down, tsikoudia when you're tired, tsikoudia to help you relax. Tsikoudia for the body to ward off the evil eye, all your life swimming in tsikoudia and no complaints. Tsikoudia is a superb distillation of the skins of pressed grapes (tsikouda) which is done in old distillers (called **"kazania"** or boilers in Crete). Sometimes they flavour it with citron and other aromatic fruits and so we have **kitroraki** (with citron) **mournoraki** (with mulberries) and others. Tsikoudia is a

CRETAN CUISINE

genuinely alcoholic drink with the delicate aroma of ripe grapes and citrus fruits, and clear as crystal. It can be drunk through the whole range of temperatures, from hot straight from the distillery to iced from a shot glass, but you must be careful because it goes to your head if you are not used to it.

As far as wine is concerned, this has improved greatly in recent years thanks to the attempts made by many zealous vinegrowers and wine manufacturers. So it is of high quality which does justice to the produce, and its excellent quality never varies.

Home-made wine has all the characteristics of Cretan men. It is heavy, quick-tempered and serious, and it thunders and is sweetish at the same time. Finally, it breaks into a measured smile. It is loved by its producer, by Cretans in general and by specially educated palates. It has an earthy, deep red colour and has the fruity aroma of the grape.

We've eaten and drunk well so now let's have an after-dinner **digestif**. And what a digestif - the best! Cretan **diktamo** tea (ditary) known to the inhabitants of the island from the most distant past. The Cretans call it **eronda**, maybe because you must have a real love for it to go and look for the herb on the rough inaccessible slopes of Mt. Psiloreiti, where it grows. Nowadays it is cultivated regularly and it has lost some of its wildness, but cultivated **diktamo** is better than none.

Wherever you stop in the rough Cretan countryside, you will always find good company and a tasty treat with a little tsikoudia to calm you down - a treat expressing the traditional Cretan hospitality. If someone behaves coldly or professionally towards you forgive him, he certainly is not a local Cretan but from somewhere else and has come to Crete on business.

THE CRETAN LANDSCAPE

If you come to Hania by ship in the spring or early in the summer, you can make out, very far off, the snow-capped peaks of the **Lefka Ori** (the White Mountains). They owe their name not only to the fact that they are covered in snow for most months of the year, but also to the characteristic light grey/white colour of their limestone rock. This imposing mountain range rises smoothly from the northern shores of Crete, ends in 57 peaks above 2.000 metres (the higher peak being Pachnes at **2.452 m**) and falls steeply to the southern shores, forming imposing gorges. On the smooth northern slopes of the Lefka Ori are built dozens of interesting villages, both large and small, like the historic Theriso, the picturesque Thymia, Tsakistra, Madero and Melidoni. There are a few accessible dirt roads which climb to the heart of the mountain, the most impressive being the one that ascends from Theriso and reaches the foot of the Kaloros peak.

In the main massif of the Lefka Ori, there are only paths used by shepherds and mountaineers. There are also four very nice mountain refuges, those at Kalergi, Katsiveli, Volika and Tavris. They all belong to the E.O.S. of Hania (the Greek Mountaineering Association of Hania) with which you must get in touch if you want to use the refuges (tel. 0821-44647). The most impressive gorges in Crete are to be found on the southern precipitous slopes, such as the famous gorge of Samaria (or the **Farangas**, as the locals call it) and others which are less well-known but equally beautiful, like the Gorge of Tripiti (a part of which you can cross by motorcycle!), and the gorges of Eligia, of Aghia Irini (St Irene) and of Klados.

CRETAN LANDSCAPE

The famous **Omalos plateau** is situated at an altitude of 1.000 m in the western corner of the Lefka Ori - the road to Xiloskalo goes past here, and from there you can walk through the Gorge of Samaria. There are no trees on the Lefka Ori above 1000 metres, so the locals call it **Madares** (the bare mountains). The only vegetation is low bushes and a lot of wild flowers. There is luxuriant verdure and wildlife in the gorges, however. Here, the unique National forest of Crete, an area of 48.000 stremmata, surrounds the Gorge of Samaria - this forest has preserved a large part of the rich flora and fauna of Crete. Thick clumps of cypress trees, ever-green oaks and pine trees, springs with an abundance of water, steep rocks and inaccessible slopes - all these make up a place where the unique **Cretan ibex** (called the *agrimi* by the locals) still survires, as do the extremely elusive wild cat (felix silvestris agrius-the only known individual is a male, captured in May 1996) and significant populations of polecats, badgers, birds of prey, etc.

To the east, the precipitous slopes of the Lefka Ori have their final borders in the Imbriotiko Gorge and the Katre Lago (i.e. the Gorge of Katre). Further east again, the **Askyfou plateau** rises up, a bare and barren plateau with a semi-deserted village, Asfendou, and a single rough road that goes through it. This road begins just north of the village of Imbros and ends in the picturesque village of Asi Gonia. North of this road, the bare peaks of Agathes (1511 m) and Tripali (1494 m) can be distinguished, while to the south you can see many beautiful gorges that descend to the coast of the Libyan sea.

Continuing in an easterly direction, you cross a semi-mountainous landscape with many peaks (all under 1000 m) and many level cultivated areas with pastures between them. Throughout this region, there are many small scattered villages of farmers and animal breeders, totally uninfluenced by tourism as few tourists visit them. To the south there are the impressive Gorge of Kotsifou and the Kourtaliotiko Gorge, inside which are squeezed the roads that lead to the tourist beach at Plakia and to the historic monastery at Preveli.

From the beach at Plakia going east as far as Aghios Pavlos (St Paul), the massif of **Siderotas** (1136 m) protects from the deluge of tourists some of the most beautiful beaches in Crete that are hidden behind it - an example is Tripetra Beach. To the north-east of Siderotas, **Kedros** (1777 m), another massive grey rock rises up, and between them runs the main road from Rethimnon to Ierapetra. Both the road and the two mountains go in a north-west to south-easterly direction. The extremely beautiful **Amari valley** has exactly the same orientation - this opens up north-east of Kedro and is a very green, protected region that has been inhabited continuously since Minoan times. Today, about twenty or so of the most picturesque hamlets in Crete nestle here.

Immediately above these villages, the main **Psiloritis** range stretches out, having the same orientation (from north-west to south-east). It begins to rise smoothly at Moni Arkadiou and reaches its maximum height at the peak of Timios Stavros (the Holy Cross), 2.456 m, the **highest peak in Crete** (just a few metres higher than the peak of Pachnes in the Lefka Ori).

The small Chapel of the Holy Cross dominates the summit, a humble Christian continuation of the very ancient Minoan tradition of building peak sanctuaries. The impressive **of Nida plateau** stretches out to the east, at a height of 1.400 metres, enclosed by snowy peaks and bare mountain slopes. On one of these, the **Ideo Andro** is situated, the cave where, according to mythology, Zeus grew up, and a little further south is another Minoan sacred cave, the cave of Kamares. Apart from these, there are hundreds of explored and unexplored caves in Psiloritis, **a true paradise for speleologists.**

To the south, the mountain slopes of Psiloritis are steep at first and then come down smoothly to the plain of Mesara. The road goes by in the transitional stage; this comes from the villages of Amari and ends at the main road from Iraklio to Gortyna. This road passes through a dozen or so large and small villages built in the shadow of the precipitous mountain slopes, like the picturesque Lochria, Kamares and Vorizia, from where paths lead to the peak of Psiloritis, Zaros with its abundant springs and the head village of Yeryeri. A rough road ascends from the latter towards the north, and it ends in the **Rouva Wood**, a small island of thick wood with evergreen oaks, pine-tress, and huge cypress-trees; a poor sample of the vegetation once covering the whole of Psiloritis, as its ancient name bears witness to (Idi wooded landscape). On its north-east side, Psiloritis is a sea of both high and low peaks, with rocky bush-covered ravines between them, where one can follow some of the most impressive mountain routes in Crete. On the northern foot of the mountain and in the valley that opens up between Psiloritis an Mount Kouloukonas, there is a crowd of picturesque villages like the legendary Anogia, Zoniana with its interesting cave, Kalamos and Pasalites with their old neighbourhoods.

CRETAN LANDSCAPE

Nida Plateau, the yard in front of the cave where Zeus was born

The **valley of Mesara** begins south of Psiloritis, and stretches out towards the east - it is the biggest and most fertile plain on the island. It has a length of approximately 40 kilometres, a width of between 5 and 20 kilometres and most of it is covered with plastic greenhouses. It was formed by a tectonic earth submergence that left the **Asterousia Mountains** projecting as independent mountains. The Asterousia, which retain their Homeric name, is a small unexplored mountain paradise with few visitors and even fewer inhabitants but is full of outstanding mountain trails.

East of the Asterousia, after a small hilly area, the mountain slopes of **Dikti**, or the **Lasithiotika mountains** as the locals call them, rise up steeply. They stretch for a length of 10 kilometres and a width of 5-6 km in a horseshoe shape, and they hug the famous plateau of Lasithi. The highest peak is Dikti (2.148 m) and is followed by many others higher than 1.500 m. Between them, less well-known but much more beautiful plateaux than the touristy **Lasithi plateau** have been formed, like the Nissimo plateau to the north, the Katharos plateau to the east and the Omalos plateau to the south. On Dikti, the thickest woods in Crete have been preserved until today, through which pass many impressive mountain trails. Every summer, however, many fires are steadily reducing these beautiful woods, so visit them while they are still there.

The final mountain range in Crete at its eastern edge is **Thripti** with its peak of Afendis Estavromenos (1.476 m). Recently a dirt road was opened all the way to the summit, from which, at a glance, you can embrace the whole prefecture of Lasithi - the poorest and most barren but also the purest and most beautiful corner of Crete.

THE UNDERWATER WORLD

A large part of Unexplored Crete, and perhaps the most exciting, is to be found under the surface of the sea! To cross this border and get to know the beautiful landscapes and the inhabitants of the deep, all you need is a snorkel, a mask and a pair of flippers. Of course, if you have a diver's certificate, you can rent full scuba-diving equipment and explore the underwater world with much more ease and to a greater depth. If you haven't got a diver's certificate, Crete is the ideal place to get one. For a CMAS one-star certificate, or for a PADI Open Water certificate you need 25-30 hours of lessons (6-8' days). All you need is to be in good physical condition and of course to pay the required fees - the diving centre takes care of everything else. The diving centres in Crete that organise diving excursions, and offer educational seminars are the following:

HANIA
Blue Adventures
Spyros Papakastrisios
Daskalogianni 69 str.
tel/fax 0821 - 40.608

Crete Diving Center
Kalligeris Giorgos
Kissamou 121
tel. 0821 - 93.616 fax 0821 - 97437

Hania Diving Center
Stamatis Malefakis
Gef. Kladisou 1
tel./ fax 0821 - 96.582

IRAKLIO
Creta Mare Diving Center
Hegel Meers
Creta Mare Hotel
Limenas Hersonissou
tel. 0897 - 22.122 fax 0897 - 22.130

Coral Diving Center
Kostas Papadopoulos
Cretan Village Hotel
Limenas Hersonissou
tel. 0897 - 22.996 fax 0897 - 22.243

ScubaKreta
Giorgos Georgantas
Nana Beach Hotel
Limenas Hersonissou
tel. 0897- 24.915 fax 0897 - 24.916

RETHIMNO
Atlantis Diving Center
Giorgos Yioubakis
Rithymna Beach Hotel
7 km east of Rethimno
tel. 0831 - 71.002

PLAKIAS
Aegean Diving Shop
Isabela Papadaki, Ilse Stroud
Plakias Beach
tel. 0832 - 31.206 fax 01 - 8981.120

AGHIOS NIKOLAOS
Nikosub
Nikos Koutoulakis
Elounda Beach Hotel
Elounda
tel. 0841 - 41.576, fax 0841 - 41.373

Very many types of fish live in the seas off Crete. **Atherina** (smelt), **gavros** (anchovies) and **sardines** are small fish which live near the surface and move in shoals. You will often encounter them swimming in big shoals near the rocks on the shore.

If you see the shoal scattering in panic, it is probably being attacked by a **zargana** (garpike), a fairly small predator fish that swims near the surface; it has a lance-shaped body and a nose like a miniature swordfish, which you will also meet near the rocks on the shore.

If you go out further to somewhat deeper water near to a promontory, or above a shallow reef under which the water is very deep, you may encounter surface fish like the **kephalos** (grey mullet), a torpedo that moves in small shoals of 10-20 fish, or the

THE UNDERWATER WORLD

gopes (bogue), a very common species forming large slow-moving shoals that are difficult to approach.

If you are quite observant, you will notice, in the middle of the reef, at a depth of 5-15 metres, both large and small shoals of **melanouria** (saddled bream), with the characteristic black ring around the base of their tail - looking motionless and indifferent to what is going on around them.

If, however, a shoal of **synagrides** (dentex) appears from the deep, then they disappear in fright under the nearest rock. Synagrides are the queens of the deep, with their impressive colours and noble structure but they have sharp teeth that give away their predatory nature. They go around in small shoals of 5-20 and you will rarely be fortunate enough to see them hunting in the shallows.

An even rarer sight is a shoal of **magiatika,** large migrant fish with a hydrodynamic structure and a shimmering silver colour which appear in the waters of this country at the beginning of spring and stay until the summer. Sometimes they can be more than 50 kilos!

Fish like **tuna** and **swordfish** live and hunt for their food in much deeper waters in the middle of the open sea; these are big migrant fish that have used the same passages for centuries. Large fish like **fagria** (sea-bream) and **lithrinia** (common pandora) live in deep water, more than 50 metres down, in the so-called "benches" (flat areas of the deep with many rocks and seaweed).

If you find yourself above a reef or in rocks near the shore which shelve down smoothly to 15-20 metres, forming caves and crevices, swim as quickly as you can and observe the depths carefully to get to know the fish that prefer to live among underwater rocks. If you are lucky (and quite observant), you will see the squat **rofos**(dusky grouper), the king of rockfish, motionless in front of his hole looking at you with seeming indifference, moving his side fins slowly. But as soon as you go to dive to get near him, he will turn slowly and slip back into his rest, with the calmness and dignity of a king who is, alas, forced to retreat.

If you can hold your breath under the water even if only for 20-30 seconds and you know how to equalise the pressure in your ears so as to avoid the painful water pressure, try to notice an underwater dive to a depth where you feel comfortable. Hold on to the underwater rocks and look carefully into the inside of the crevices. If you are lucky, you will see the silver figures made by a shoal of **sargos** (white sea bream) which sway slowly in the depths of the crevice, some isolated **tsipoura** (gilt-head sea bream), the golden-yellow reflections of a shoal of sikios, or the antennae and armoured body of a **lobster.**

Outside of the rocks, you will certainly see **cheiloudes** (wrasse), **perkes** (painted comber), skorpios and many multi-coloured small fish eating tiny morsels of food, and clouds of black microscopic fish (called nuns because of their very black colour) staying suspended near the underwater rocks. You might even see a pair of **barbounia** (red mullet) searching the waters with their moustaches, a pair of multi-coloured **skaros** (peacock wrasse) going for a stroll like well-dressed, made-up ladies, or a shoal of **mourmoures** (striped sea bream) sinking their noses into the sand looking for their favourite worms.

Unfortunately, this undersea paradise is threatened by the continually increasing pollution that comes from industrial refuse, ships, oil slicks, pesticides which end up in the sea and much besides. It is also threatened by the overfishing that results from the use of methods which are destructive to the marine environment, like trailing underwater nets.

In Greece especially, very great damage is caused to marine life by illegal fishermen who use dynamite, and illegal amateur fishermen (mainly Greeks but also many Italian tourists) who fish with scuba diving equipment day and night. Unfortunately, the picturesque Kalymnos island sponge-divers cause significant damage -they have been more or less out of work since the time the artificial sponge was discovered. For social security reasons, the Greek state has granted them professional fishing licenses and since then, this small professional class has been turned into exterminators of underwater life, using professional automatic scuba diving equipment and spear-guns.

The harbour authorities make great efforts to enforce the law, but the means at their disposal are insufficient. But, the law on illegal fishing is strict, is enforced without exceptions and provides for confiscation of vessels and all the equipment used in illegal fishing.

While we're on the subject of **spear-guns,** Greek law lays down certain limits and prohibitions which you must certainly respect, otherwise you're in danger of getting into trouble. Spear-guns are strictly prohibited as follows: before sunrise and after sunset; used in conjunction with scuba diving equipment; inside harbours or close to organised beaches; used in conjunction with chemical substances of any type whatsoever; and during the month of May, when fish reproduce. You can catch up to **five** kilos of fish a day per person, or **one** big fish a day per person, regardless of weight. It is also most strictly forbidden to sell the fish you catch. If you are caught, you will be charged with a serious breach of the contraband law and, apart from having your equipment confiscated and being fined, you are also in danger of being sent to prison for some months. Finally for your own safety, **never go underwater fishing alone,** especially if you are an experienced deep-sea diver. The seas around Crete are full of big fish

THE UNDERWATER WORLD

where the water is very deep (20-30 metres) and it will certainly tempt you into doing deep dives; so it is a good thing to have someone equally experienced near you, and to look after each other. Every summer, at least five spear-gunners drown in Cretan waters. Most of them are experienced, but they go fishing alone...

Very few species dangerous to man live in Greek seas. Few sharks, usually following ships coming from tropical waters, have been sighted near the shores, and so far, there has been only one shark attack on a swimmer (in Pagasitikos gulf, central Greece). Other dangerous sea creatures are **moray-eels** (so don't put your hand into dark crevices), **jellyfish**, which cause a sharp pain in the area where they sting you, **drakenes** (small sand-burrowing fish with a poisonous spike on their back that stings bitterly if stepped on), and sea-urchins, whose spikes break off in your body. Of all these, the ones to be most careful of are the sea-urchins because they are everywhere (except on the sand), and if you step or sit on them, their spikes will sink into you and only a doctor will be able to get them out for you.

EXPLORING CAVES

By **Stephanos Nikolaidis**, speleologist, cave-diver

As you will certainly know from mythology, one of the most wonderful structures in Minoan Crete was the famous Labyrinth under the Palace of Knossos, an underground complex of passages in a chaotic architectural pattern where no-one who entered could find the way out. The person would wonder around hopelessly in the dark confusing passages and in the end would be eaten by the Minotaur, a monster with the body of a man and the head and strength of a bull.

Well, if you think that all this is just fantasy, you'd be wrong! Evans may not have found a Labyrinth at Knossos, but Greek and foreign speleologists have found hundreds of Labyrinths in the Cretan mountains. They are almost completely in proportion to the mythical Labyrinth at Knossos, if we discount the fact that most of the caves and sinkholes of Crete have an impressive arrangement of stalactites and stalagmites. But before you abandon the sunlight and enter the narrow mouth of a dark, cold cave, you should fix well in your mind the basic rules of safety (or rather, more correctly, of survival), the legal limitations and the basic principles of caving savoir-vivre. Otherwise you will be in danger of seeing the Minotaur himself or (in other words) death with your own eyes.

Safety Rules

- It is completely dark inside caves - you can't even see you nose in front of your face. If something happens to your torch and it goes out, you will be in a very unpleasant position. So you must have with you a spare torch with new batteries that will get you to the exit. It is also a good idea to have a candle and a cigarette - lighter with you, just in case. The only suitable torch is the one you fix onto your forehead, because this leaves both hands free. As for gas lamps, they are entirely unsuitable and dangerous.
- We are talking to you in the plural, because one person never goes alone into a cave. It is a good idea for someone outside the cave to know where you are, again just in case (but not your mum!)
- A piece of safety rope (5-6 metres) is useful for help on slippery descents and short climbs.
- Wear clothes that you don't mind getting dirty or torn, and shoes with lugged soles.
- Only at the cave entrance or under stones is there sometimes a likelihood of finding scorpions or snakes which my be poisonous, so be careful where you put your hands.
- It is absolutely necessary to wear a protective helmet, because caves are full of hard, sharp stalactites. Your motorcycle helmet is absolutely unsuitable. If you haven't got a mountaineering or bicycling helmet, you can make a rough helmet with a tight-fitting knitted cap or hat, inside which you stuff thick socks or your leather gloves.

Legal Limitations

- Under Greek Law, caves are considered protected natural and cultural monuments.
- Officially, you need a permit to enter every cave (apart from commer-

EXPLORING CAVES

The subterranean paradise of caves can become hell if entered with carelessness and lack of training.

cially developed ones); this you get from the Ministry of Culture, Department of Speleology and Paleoanthropology, in Athens.

• Naturally, removal of anything whatever from the cave (whether stalactites or archaeological objects) can get you into big trouble with the police, and not even Theseus will save you.

Savoir - Vivre

• When we enter someone's house, we wipe our feet or take off our shoes. This is an act of respect to the place. Most caves existed thousands of millions of years before man appeared on earth, and they have managed to bring into our modern times the secrets of their creation and remains of the creatures which lived and died inside them. It is not necessary to remove our shoes inside a cave, but we should be very careful indeed to **leave nothing behind us apart from our shoeprints,** and to take photographs and nothing else.

• There may be no wild animals or dragons inside caves but we will certainly run into bats that we try not to wake up or to frighten, and blind harmless insects that have adapted to the environment of the cave and they do not at all like to be stepped on or to go for a walk in the light.

PUBLIC RELATIONS
Approaching people

There is a very fitting word for the Greek attitude toward foreign visitors: *filoxenia* (hospitality). Throughout history, hospitality has been a typical virtue of the Greeks. In the Homeric epics there are scenes where a foreign visitor shows up at the door, receives the warmest welcome, and is treated like a "sacred person." The Greek gods (and especially Zeus) would frequently take the human form and show up at people's doors either to help them with some important matter or to take care of their own business (which was frequently of an amorous nature). The ancient Greeks knew that, so whenever a visitor knocked on their door they received him with the greatest honours and treated him with utter respect. They invited him to dine with them, filled his glass with exquisite wine, offered him a place to rest, and only when the stranger was well fed and rested did they dare to question him about his name and business.

Modern Greeks are quite different. Some of those who live and work in very touristy areas and who are proud of their glorious past are in fact totally ignorant of what hospitality means. The truth is, of course, that there aren't many Greeks working as waiters, receptionists etc in the first place! Blond tourist girls, who found a clever way to have a free or even lucrative holiday, serve you non-Greek drinks, which you enjoy while listening to non-Greek music along with many other non-Greeks. Foreign waiters hand you menus without a word of Greek in them, so that you can decide which non-Greek specialty to order. Foreign receptionists answer your questions in your own language, so that you can have an unforgettable stay at a non-Greek environment with all the comforts you would expect to find in your own country. In the midst of all this, the large poster on the wall of your room (which shows one of those delightful empty beaches nobody can exactly direct you to and has a huge GREECE on the bottom) may vaguely remind you of the country you are in...

Greece is not only sea and sunshine and gorgeous post-card landscapes; it is also the people who live here. And it is worth visiting it to find both, and perhaps even more for its people. But if it is difficult to find pure, unspoiled landscapes, it is twice as difficult to find pure, unspoiled Greeks. Look for them away from the much visited tourist places.

Cretans are particularly fond of motorcyclists. Children in villages will generally gather around you and cheer and gesture and ask you to do a tail spin (*soùza*) for them. They will look at your bike with admiration, observe your outfit, helmet and gear, marvel at the speedometer, and ask you what's the maximum speed you can reach (*pòsa piàni*). Let them touch their dream and give them food for endless talks with their friends. All it takes is sitting them in front of you on the bike and letting them touch the bars, press the starter or even turn on the gas. Needless to say, all this must be done when the bike is not in motion; avoid taking them on a ride, because you are assuming a serious responsibility.

Young boys and girls, on the other hand, will more likely stare at you from a distance, but they will have a more proud and reserved attitude. This doesn't mean you cannot approach them, though, and start a con-

PUBLIC RELATIONS

versation yourself; in fact, they are your best sources of information on local hang-outs and can help you to find your way around. If country youths are hesitant or even frightened at first, it is probably because they are afraid of seeming inferior in your eyes, so talk to them as an equal and do not try to impress them (they're already quite impressed with the fact you travel on a bike). Ask them about their life and plans, and let them reveal to you a side of modern Greece.

Unlike the reserved teenagers, the local motorcyclists are certain

If you know how to approach the locals there will always be a place for you at their table

to approach you and to invite you to join them at their table, or they will come and sit at your own table taking it for granted that they are welcome. Do not be offended if they seem a little proud; this only means they feel they know the ropes in their own area. In fact, their forward behaviour is nothing more than the expression of a friendly spirit, which is quite strong among motorcyclists in Greece and extends to all of "our own."

Finally, the old men in villages will be glad to see you, and they may get a bit nostalgic too. This may be because you remind them of their youth, when they would ride their horse and go work in the fields, or would travel on business or take part in war expeditions... Park your bike in front of the **kafenìo** (traditional café) at the centre of the village, greet them with a loud "hi" (**yàsas**), and sit at a table next to them. Before taking the first sip of coffee (or **kafè**) - which, by the way, they will most probably not let you pay for anyway - lift the cup and say "**stin ighià sas**" ("to your health"). If you like, you can do the same with water. This is enough to show that the sympathy is mutual and to establish a friendly ambience. One of them is likely to know some English or German and try to chat with you, but it would be very useful for you to know some Greek words or phrases too. In any case, wherever there is a friendly climate you are bound to find some way of communicating, even without too many words. A warm smile or handshake, a friendly gesture and an easy-going attitude will go a long way toward unlocking this special world - a world that is full of genuine feelings, traditional values and truly charming stories... a neglected world, too, which vanishes little by little.

Even the most out-of-the-way places are not **totally** deserted; some old man or woman is bound to have stayed behind at every abandoned

To you it's a stopover; to them it's their homeland. A little discreetness will be highly appreciated

village. The mountain dirtroad you took, which seems to be in the middle of nowhere, may in fact take you to a shepherd's sheepfold (or you may drive by one as you continue your exploration). The empty beach where you've set up your tent may be visited by a passing fisherman who leaves his boat and fishing nets and lays back waiting for his catch. The folks you'll meet are hospitable and warm, and they're always ready to give you something. They may offer you a glass of raki and a nice snack, or they may take you to their home and offer you a sumptuous meal. Be prepared, then, to give them some little thing in return, because you may never have a chance to visit them again and they will never visit your homeland. A bottle of wine or a nice dessert would be a small but symbolic contribution to their table. If, of course, after the first glass of raki you end up staying in their home for a day of two, enjoying delicious home-cooked meals and an experience to share with your grandchildren, you must think of something more suitable to thank them for their hospitality. If you are not prepared for this, do not hesitate to offer them something from your personal possessions; a small portable radio or a knife would make very welcome gifts. As for shepherds, a pair of binoculars is the most precious gift they could hope for. If you have a camera with you, take a few pictures of them and send them by mail. **Whatever you do, do not offer them money.** They may be gravely offended and consider your gesture as an act of charity.

Driving discreetly

Visiting an unspoiled landscape or a remote village is, by definition, a kind of **intrusion** into a place with a delicate balance.

To savour the beauty of the experience to its full extent, you must take care to approach the place as quietly and discreetly as possible and show **great consideration.** As far as driving is concerned, keep in mind that the most annoying form of pollution your bike can cause is noise pollution. This is why before leaving on your trip it is a good idea to check that the exhaust is in good condition. Also make sure you pay attention to some delicate situations such as the following:

When you drive on a dirt road and pass through an inhabited area, go as slowly as you can to avoid raising a lot of dust. Be especially careful when you see a peasant hanging her laundry to dry, a villager whitewashing his walls, a shepherd milking his sheep, or anyone sitting or walking by the side of the road.

When you see sheep or goats at the side of the road coming in your direction, stop, and wait until they have all passed you. Put 10-15 metres between you before you drive on to avoid scaring them and creating problems for the shepherd.

When you pass through inhabited areas late at night or during siesta time (that is, between the hours of 2:00 and 5:00 p.m.), drive as quietly as you can and avoid using the horn.

In **remote villages** and small places in general, traffic is so limited that people will often use the streets as walk zones and meeting places (and this is true even for the main street). Old women sit in front of their doorstep and chat, old (or young) men pull a table under the sun and play backgammon, farmers load and unload farm products and tools, kids run around in carefree play. The picture speaks for itself, so drive with extreme caution.

Little things you can do for tortured creatures

Shepherds, as you know, live on cream cheese, rusks and mountain greens and drink plenty of milk. Naturally, they think nothing is better for their dogs than what they eat themselves... On top of that, they praise them for eating so little: "See, I put all this bread and milk in his bowl and he just took a couple of bites"(!) The poor dogs munch their food with obvious resentment, eating hardly enough to survive. They drink so much milk that they've almost grown wool on their bodies and their barks start to sound like bleating... Keep that in mind as you enjoy your steak or chicken at the tavern and do not throw away the bones. It is so easy to give a hungry dog a taste of paradise...

In Crete, more than anywhere else, dogs are often tied up at some post in the middle of nowhere, guarding the sheepfolds, fields or abandoned homes behind them. Their masters visit them once a week and throw them some food, and they plant an iron barrel next to them to protect them from the heat. (Naturally, the poor dogs never use those barrel-shaped ovens). From the day they are born, these dogs are chained to the same post, wasting away in loneliness and misery and never knowing the joy of a good, long run. If you run into one of them (and see it can be approached), do something simple: give it the bones you have saved, and when it's fed **untie it.** It will run around for a while, but it will soon return to its base.

SAFETY MATTERS
The roads in Greece

Forget everything you know about the roads in your country and get ready for a completely new experience (one that may shock you unfortunately...)

The roads in Greece are plagued with all the problems you can possibly imagine (and with all those you can't...). The reason is that their construction is always allocated to the company that makes the lowest bid. Contractors will make very low offers to get the job, and then they will go on to build awful roads using the cheapest material they can get.

To make the asphalt they use limestone, the cheapest rock there is. After a year or two the limestone is totally smooth and the surface of the road **is glassy and slides like hell.**

They also use bitumen of the lowest quality and do not mix the asphalt ingredients in the right proportions. As a result, the asphalt may get softer in the scorching heat of the summer, or it may even **melt** in certain places, especially under the stand or your motorcycle!

To make things worse, they pave the roads with the thinnest layer of asphalt they can get away with. Naturally, the asphalt cracks and is eroded by water, and eventually it becomes full of **potholes**. They fix it and keep fixing it while new holes appear, until somebody decides that the road needs repaving and the bidding process starts all over again...

Another very objectionable practice is covering the new asphalt with white **gravel**. This is supposed to help the asphalt "stay in place," but in

---

Take a good look at this picture because it shows most of the problems you'll encounter on a typical country road. To start with, the asphalt is **worn,** which may make it difficult to have full control of the bike, especially if you try to take the turn at too great a speed. Very often, things are so bad that there are large and deep potholes in the middle of the road.

Notice the **gravel** by the roadside. Although this road was built many years ago, the gravel is still there, threatening to throw you off balance if you speed while taking the turn.

The **dark stains** on the road are a clear sign that it is used by sheep and goats, which of course know nothing about traffic rules. They may be lying in the middle of the road right after the next turn, or they may suddenly throw themselves in front of your bike in an apparently suicidal mood. When you see dung and wet spots, make sure you slow down.

There is a dirtroad starting right at the turn. It is difficult to see in the picture and even more difficult to notice when you are travelling at great speed. Keep your eyes open, though, because tractors and other farm vehicles have a way of suddenly appearing before you at such crossroads, running as if they own the road.

The curve of the road does not allow you to judge how sharp the turn is. After the rock you may suddenly discover you are at a U-turn, only a hair's breadth away from the precipice! If you think

SAFETY MATTERS

fact it's a way to cover up their sloppiness. After a while the gravel has disappeared from the middle of the road and gathered in heaps on both sides, especially at the turns. God help you if you miscalculate a turn and fall on these heaps! You can neither manoeuvre the bike nor stop.

Then again there are problems with the way roads have been designed. For instance, you will frequently encounter **turns with an outward inclination, pools of rain water in the middle of the road,** and **worn off edges** due to the lack of protective cement bars on the road sides.

You will also see a lot of signs warning you about "road works ahead," or a detour you must take, or the low speed limit you must observe, only the signs have been forgotten since the project in question finished some years ago. Conversely, when road works are actually in progress, or there is a serious problem (a landslide or a collapse of the road surface, for instance), warning signs are conspicuously missing.

Problems with problem-warning

Too much sloppiness, unfavourable weather conditions, and, worst of all, lack of programming and funds for road maintenance, are the primary reasons there are so many potholes and "traps" waiting out there for you.

The authorities charged with road maintenance usually remember to intervene after the twentieth accident or so. Meanwhile, it is the people living in each area that will try to warn you of any problems, or the victims themselves... This they do with whatever means

A PICTURE THAT SAYS IT ALL!

that all dangerous turns are marked by the triangular warning sign that you know, you are seriously mistaken. In Greece, the most reliable danger signal is an **icon stand** - like the one you see in the picture - dedicated to the memory of some unfortunate driver who died on that spot.

are available, so if you see any rocks, wooden boxes, trash bags, or cut barrels lying on the road, you should be alert to the possibility of a problem with its surface. Slow down and watch out for anything wrong; it could be a simple pothole or a total disaster!

The icon stands

Oftentimes you will see by the roadside some small, strange-looking iron boxes standing on four legs and having a cross at the top and the icon of a saint and a little oil lamp inside. These serve as shrines and are dedicated to the memory of loved ones who died in a car accident at that very site. Needless to say, it's always a site where something should have been fixed, where the road needed repaving or a protective bar or a warning sign...

Consider the icon stands as the most reliable danger signals. The more icon stands you see, the more dangerous the road is in that place...

The signs

There are over 500,000 hunters in Greece. They all know how to shoot, or else wild animals would not have become so scarce... Where do they practice? On signs, of course! In the countryside especially, if you see a sign that hasn't been shot chances are it was placed there the previous day or so...

Shot signs are particularly common in Crete, where it's practically a custom for every male over fourteen to have at least two guns (from small handguns to 45 Magnums). Here you will no longer see signs with a few holes in them, but holes framed with a bit of sign!

One rifle shot is enough. The sign becomes full of scratches and little holes and rusts in no time, the rust eats up the paint, and after a few months the sign has gone to pieces. Reading it then resembles reading an ancient inscription, since from a few surviving letters you try to figure out the words.

But it is not only hunters who damage the signs. Drivers, too, have a way of destroying them by falling right on them. If that happens their fate is to lie there, since the authorities very rarely care to fix or replace them. **Broken signs** are an incurable disease with lots of casualties.

Yet even if a sign survives all the above, it will not be of much use to you unless you can read some Greek (nine out of ten signs are **written in Greek,** you see). If, on the other hand, a sign is in English it may confuse you even more, because you will often see many different spellings for the same word.

Finally, reading Greek road signs requires a discerning eye and a healthy imagination... This is because many of them (especially those at crucial intersections by some dreadful coincidence!) **are handmade and found at the most incredible places.** You may see them against a wall, on beams nailed on trees, hanging from a fence, lying on some rocks, or dropped on the asphalt!

Road fences

Mountains, hills, or islands, it makes no difference; wherever you travel in Greece, you will frequently follow dirt roads only to stop suddenly in front of a wire fence.

SAFETY MATTERS

This fence is just for the sheep. You may enter freely

These fences do not mark the boundaries of private lands and are not there to stop *you* from passing. They simply enclose community pastureland and are there to stop the sheep and goats of the local shepherd. This means **you can pass freely,** although it's a pretty cumbersome procedure: You must get off the bike, open the fence, cross to the other side, get off again, shut the gate behind you, and then continue.

Two things to remember: First, these fences are usually made of thin wire, have no reflectors or other warning device, and **are not visible in the night.** Second, you are entering a pastureland that's visited not only by harmless sheep but by raging sheepdogs as well!

The sheepdogs

One hears terrible things about the sheepdogs that accompany the flocks on the mountain. They say that they are vicious and bloodthirsty; that their favourite food is the legs of motorcyclists; that they will jump on your motorcycle, grab you by the throat, and suck the marrow from your bones; and that they are the "piranhas of the mountains." Of course, all this is somewhat exaggerated...

The fiercer they look and the louder they bark, the more cowardly they actually are. Forced to spend several hours in the wilderness, they are bored to death with the quiet of the mountain and are looking for a bit of action. And what better action than chasing the passing motorcyclist? So what looks like a fierce attack is actually just a game. Up to a point at least! Because if they do manage to frighten you they sense it immediately, and the game gets bolder and more serious, and you may get bitten.

If you don't want to fool around with them **slow down as they attack until you almost reach a stop**. Dogs will typically respond by dropping the attack and leaving you in peace. If, however, they don't go away but keep bothering you, get off your bike and start yelling or... barking at them (and see what happens!) If nothing else works, pick up a stone from the ground and pretend to throw it (or go ahead and do it).

As the Greek saying goes, "a dog that barks never bites." However, just to be on the safe side, you may want to wear high leather boots and gloves when driving on the mountain!

Sheep and goats

Sheep and goats dominate the Greek countryside. You will see them almost everywhere in flocks that vary in size. If they are scattered about grazing not far from the road (say about 50 metres), or

Blind turns with shade may serve as... sheepfolds, so drive very carefully

if they move along its sides in a flock, we suggest you **slow down**. It's too difficult to predict their next move, and if it enters their sheep heads to cross the road they'll do it immediately no matter what. And don't be fooled: they may look like soft downy pillows from a distance, but if you collide with them it won't be a happy experience!

How do you know there's livestock in the area? Look for the warning signs with the cow and especially for the muck on the road.

Bees and bugs

In this country it is obligatory to wear a safety helmet. Those who make sure that the law is observed, however, are not the policemen (who will not only let you get away with it but sometimes don't even wear their own helmets...) but the bees and flies!

They are found everywhere, they fly in clusters or individually, and you don't see them except when they are already in your eyes! Flies are not really dangerous, but they are certainly annoying: You have to stop immediately and take the tiny thing out of your eye with a clean tissue. Do not rub your eye with your fingers while the bug is in there, or you'll get it all irritated and probably for a long time.

If you... collide with a bee the price is heavier, especially if it gets you at a sensitive area such as the face or neck. Should this unfortunate thing happen to you, stop immediately, make sure the sting has come out (if not take it out carefully with a pair of tweezers), and put some anti-allergic oint-ment on your skin.

The best way to protect yourself from bugs and bees is to wear your safety helmet all the time (this is advisable anyway, and for more serious reasons). If, however, you do not want to use it for short distances, you must at least wear a pair of glasses and a scarf around your neck. And one last thing: if you are riding your bike and feel like yawning, do not forget to put a hand over your mouth...

Tourists on rented mopeds

The happy tourists on the rented mopeds bear a striking resemblance to bees and flies: they are seen in large numbers during the summer, they move around like crazy, and they're suddenly in front of you before you have time to notice them. The difference is that colliding with them is much more painful!

Be careful, then, because most of the tourists who rent mopeds do not know much about them and drive dangerously. On top of that, the mopeds are often in a bad condition (worn out tyres and brakes). **Attention must be paid** especially on the islands during the night, because there are many drunk tourists driving and not always with their lights on.

If you see him as a motorcyclist, think again. He is just a moving threat

Turtles and hedgehogs

If you think that those irritating drivers who stick to the left lane and drive like turtles are the only slow users of the road, think again. You're probably forgetting the turtles and the hedgehogs, which live in this country in very large numbers, in spite of the countless victims they lose to the road every year. Their final speed (in the fastest models) is 1 km/h, and to cross a road that's ten metres wide they need about five to six minutes including the stops for rest! What's worse, their colour blends with the colour of the asphalt, so you need to be extra careful in case one of these cute little animals has decided to cross the street; if you run it over you may well lose control of your motorcycle.

Stolen motorcycles

"The swallows are back," say the innocent bright-eyed school kids when spring is around the corner and the lovely birds appear in the sky wishing to spend the next few months with us.

"The swallows are back," say the wicked motorcycle thieves when spring is around the corner and the lovely motorcyclists on the very expensive bikes appear in the country wishing to spend their holidays with us. And because of them, some of these tourists will return to their country earlier than planned and with their wings clipped...

Luckily, motorcycle thieves in Greece are few (far fewer, in fact, than their "colleagues" in Italy, Spain, or England) and they are also amateurs. Still, one should not ignore them.

Two basic reasons explain their preference for the bikes of foreign tourists: First, they are an easy target. Second, their victims will not stick around for long once their bike is stolen, but will take their helmet and whatever is left of their belongings and go back home, thousands of miles away. Your chances of finding your bike are **extremely poor,** unless it was taken by youngsters looking for a ride and was later abandoned somewhere out of the way.

On the whole, however, Greece does not have a very high crime rate. If you take some basic precautions there's nothing to be afraid of. These include a safe lock and a well lighted parking place.

WHAT TO TAKE ALONG
Camping gear

Ninety percent of motorcyclists travelling in Greece spend most of their nights in a tent. There is a number of reasons for this preference.

In the first place, Greece is known for its mild climate, which favours camping from early spring until the end of Fall. Also, the countless secluded areas make Greece a true paradise for campers.

With a tent and a sleeping bag, you can set up home any place you like

CAMPING GEAR CHECKLIST

- Small light tent
- Light sleeping bag (for the summer) or warmer feather sleeping bag (for the spring and fall)
- Mattress for the sleeping bag
- 2 x 2m plastic
- Camping lamp

The great demand for rooms during the high season is yet another reason to carry a tent as it may save you a world of trouble.

But camping is also a very practical solution in emergency situations, when a sudden storm or a problem with your motorcycle or any other unforeseeable circumstances force you to stay in the middle of nowhere.

Finally, a tent is one of the most economical ways to spend the night, since even the most expensive camping in Greece costs no more than 2500 drachmas a day (for two persons, a tent and a motorcycle).

CAMPING TIPS

- The biggest problem for campers in this country is the sun at noon. A tent with an aluminum sun roof will make your life easier, but it will not solve the problem. It will be much cooler if your tent has two openings to allow a current of air and if you set it up in a **shaded** area.
- Another big problem is mosquitoes. That is why your tent should come with a screen.
- If you are planning to camp on the beach you will need special pegs for the sand. Otherwise, you must use big stones to secure the regular ones. Place the stones on top of the pegs, or, better yet, use them to secure the ropes. There may well be a breeze, so unless you take precautions you may find yourself chasing your tent in the water!
- A **pillow case** stuffed with clothes makes a perfect pillow for a restful sleep, takes very little space and is easy to wash. Alternatively, you may use the case of your sleeping bag

Cooking utensils

For the travelling motorcyclist having good camping gear is not sufficient; certain cooking utensils are also needed. These will prove handy on many occasions. You can cook a warm meal when you get to the place where you are spending the night and all restaurants are closed. You can make tea or coffee or a hot soup at any time of the day without having to leave your room or tent. And you can cook

TIPS ON COOKING

- You can find standard-size camping gas cylinders even in the most remote Greek village.
- In provincial towns grocery stores stay open late, sometimes till midnight, so you can buy fresh vegetables and meat at the end of the day. However, a two or three day supply of rice, pasta or canned food (which travels well and is preserved outside the fridge) may come in very handy if you decide to camp somewhere and there is no grocery store nearby.
- Go for the light, compact cooking utensils and cutlery which you will find in good stores with mountain gear.
- Keep honey in the little plastic toothpaste-like tubes which you will also find in the same stores.
- Your grill will be clean only the first day you use it. After that it will be irreparably stained. But don't torture yourself cleaning it. Just let it "burn" over the fire for a while before you use it again, wipe it with a clean tissue after the use to get rid of the larger scraps of food, and make yourself a nice case of thick fabric in which to keep it wrapped in a newspaper.

WHAT TO TAKE ALONG

CHECKLIST OF COOKING UTENSILS

- ❑ Portable gas stove
- ❑ Boiler for coffee
- ❑ Cup
- ❑ Plate
- ❑ Spoon, fork and knife
- ❑ A few pots and pans
- ❑ Small grill
- ❑ Small plastic trash bags
- ❑ Dish-sponge and a small quantity of detergent (keep the latter in a safe bottle)
- ❑ Cooking essentials such as salt, pepper, spices, sugar, coffee, tea bags and olive oil (in a safe bottle)

your own meal at any place you choose to camp, whether it's the top of a mountain or an empty beach.

Lighting a fire

Few camping grounds have built barbecues for campers. But even if you can't find any, you can always ask the person in charge for a suitable spot to light a fire. Promise him a good share of your meal and he's almost certain to grant your request!

In case you are not aware of it, it is officially forbidden to light a fire outdoors (in fact not even free camping is allowed). You can find out more about free camping in the chapter ACCOMMODATIONS on page 106. Here we will only say that if you want to cook you should be **very careful** with the fire. Too much forestland is destroyed every year in Greece (in 1994 alone 135,000 acres were burned down), and part of the damage is caused by simple camp fires.

If you are camping on the beach start the fire at a spot **away from trees** and unclaimed by bathers. If there are signs of a previous fire there you can use the same spot. If there are other campers around you can light a single fire, gather around it and get to know each other...

If you are camping on the mountain **do not start a fire in a forest or near a forest under any circumstances.** Find a clearing and sweep the ground carefully. There should be no dry leaves and no weeds where you start the fire. So clear about two metres of land, fence the area with large rocks and keep some water close by the fire. Do not use much wood and do not walk away while the fire is burning. **If it is windy do not start a fire at all. It is an absolute no-no!** Last but not least: before you go to sleep or leave the area **put out the fire with water.** Do not be fooled if there is no flame; beneath the ashes the fire is still smouldering. The wind may carry dry leaves into the ashes and the fire may flare up, or it may create sparkles which travel long distances. So before leaving the place make sure you put out the fire **with plenty of water.**

Travelling essentials

Greece is a European country. The people and the landscapes should more or less be familiar and you won't feel like you are visiting another planet. Still, there are certain things which you should know about it and which you'd better take into account if you want a safer, worry-free trip.

The first thing you should take into account is that Greece **is a very hot country,** especially in the middle of the summer. Temperatures are quite high and sometimes they may even rise above 40^0 C in the shade! So be prepared for what you'll have to face.

Driving a motorcycle can sometimes be difficult! The hot air, the leather uniform, the helmet, the slow traffic of the towns, the waiting under the scorching sun, the jerk cutting into your lane, along with so many other things, cause you to sweat and get dehydrated. Make up for the damage by drinking lots of liquids with every stop you make; some cool water, or a soft drink, or - better yet - a refreshing iced tea with lemon will make a world of difference. And since there is no guarantee that there will be a vending machine or a creek around to quench your thirst, make sure you carry a **water bottle** and keep it where it's easy to reach. The best solution is a large-capacity collapsible flask (2L); the more you drink the smaller it becomes and the less space it takes among your belongings. If you plan to pitch camp in the middle of nowhere make sure you fill your bottle with water in advance, because if you find yourself somewhere where there is no spring or creek you'll need it to wash, shave, make coffee etc...

If you enjoy free-lance camping and plan to do a lot of it, what you need is a 10L **collapsible container.** This should give you independence for at least a couple of days. The obvious advantage, of course, as compared to your regular container, is that when it's empty it takes up very little space. Your best bet is to buy one that comes with a handle, a ring to hang it from and a small hose with which to shower.

If you love the sun and dream of... losing yourself in its warm caress, do not do it without precautions (as is true for anything you may fall in love with on your vacation...). You may get a sunburn or otherwise pay for it. What you need is a good **suntan lotion** with a high protection factor (15 SPF and above), preferably water-proof so that it stays on even when you perspire profusely. Use it not only on the beach but also when you're riding your motorcycle or hiking. A bottle with a screw cap is preferable, since flip top containers are likely to open and create a real mess.

Another serious problem is skin diseases, especially mycetomas, which you can get if you lie on a beach used by many people, cats, dogs etc. If you are not at an empty beach, you'd better lie on a **straw mat**, which you can buy practically anywhere at a low price. Some of these are particularly convenient for motorcyclists because they can be rolled and folded in two.

Mosquitoes are a real nightmare. Not only do they not let you sleep but sometimes they won't let you stand and will bite even through your clothes. If you plan to rent a room make sure you take with you some **insect-repelling tablets** and the small electric appliance needed for their use. If you prefer camping take a box of slow-burning spirals. In either case take a repellent in liquid form (such as Autan) as your last means of defence when, despite all other precautions, the enemy threatens to drink your blood.

It can happen even in the cleanest countries: traffic, especially trucks, can cause increased local pollution. Pass ten trucks and you need to take a shower and wash your clothes! What happens only in

WHAT TO TAKE ALONG

Greece, however, and is beyond all logic, is that there are almost no public laundries, not even where there is a lot of tourism! If you want to be safe and keep your clothes clean you better take along some **detergent** in a safe case.

Greece, as everyone knows, is a fun-loving country, and people stay up late. If you want to go to sleep when others are

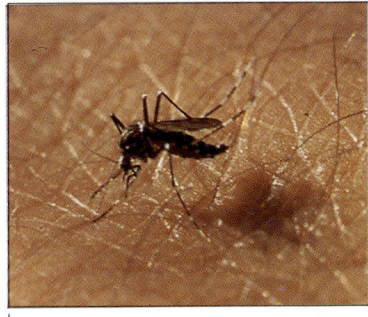

Do not let anyone drink your blood!

partying, or if you've been partying all night and want to go to sleep when others wake up, you've got a serious problem. Putting cotton plugs in your ears and an arm over your eyes will not get you very far. The best you can do is buy a set of wax **ear plugs** and an **eye mask.** They take up very little space and provide a deep, uninterrupted sleep even under the most unfavourable circumstances.

So far we've talked about certain special problems you may encounter in Greece and what you need to take with you to deal with them effectively. Let us now conclude this chapter with a brief reference to more basic equipment.

A good **pocket-knife** will come in very handy whether you want to cut a rope with it or open a can or do a number of other things. Avoid those showy Rambo-type butcher knives; they are heavy, bulky and entirely impractical. Also keep in mind that the Swiss multi-use pocket-knives are more useful as screw-drivers, mini saws etc than as pocket-knives. Go for a simple large pocket-knife with a folding blade and a sheath you can attach to your belt.

A good **flashlight** is the second basic tool you must carry with you. Forget the good old cigarette lighter and get organised. Get one of those aluminum compact flashlights with the halogen Maglite-type lamp.

For your camping needs you can use a butane lamp, which will give you bright light. The problem, however, is that these lamps tend to be large and fragile and do not travel well. Oil lamps are more romantic and an all-time-classic, but unfortunately they have a way of giving your things their unmistakable, all-time-classic smell! As for the neon flashlights, they're totally out of the question, because they spoil it all and will not let you escape from the city. In the final analysis, it might be best to buy a thick **candle**. It offers warm, diffuse lighting, costs very little, lasts long, and creates the right ambience!

A third "must" is a small **first aid kit.** This will help you to deal with most minor problems before they grow bigger. A small box with a few basic things is all you need.

A picture speaks a thousand words. If you want to capture those beautiful moments of your trip and share them with your friends you'll need to take a **camera.** When your trip is over you can fondly leaf through your memories...

Finally, you should take with you the following: Two **lighters** (one is as good as none since it has the magic quality of disappearing right when you need it and being in front of you all the time you don't); a strong **rope** about 10 metres long for heavy duty work (tying your motorcycle in the garage of the ferry boat, pulling to get it out of the mud, playing tug of war etc); some **string** (about 20 metres long) for dozens of daily uses (from

FIRST AID KIT.

- Aspirin
- Ointment for insect bites
- Ointment for sunburns
- Pills for diarrhoea
- Some basic antibiotics
- Liquid antiseptic for wounds
- Gauze, bandages, cotton-wool.
- Tweezers, pin

securing your tent to hanging your laundry); a role of **toilet paper** (common but indispensable); and **pen and paper** for your notes.

Personal items

The clothes and other personal items you take with you are of course a... personal matter! Each traveller will take along whatever he thinks best depending on his style and personal needs, the duration of his trip, the kind of holiday he has in mind, and the space available. However, the circumstances you will find in Greece will certainly affect your choices.

First and foremost, you must be well prepared for a **hot** climate. Light cotton clothes are your best choice, and you will feel very comfortable in them when you are not driving. Go for light-coloured, short-sleeved T-shirts and Bermuda shorts. The best pants for general use are, of

CHECKLIST OF TRAVELLING ESSENTIALS

- ❏ Collapsible 2L water bottle
- ❏ Collapsible 10L water container
- ❏ Pocket-knife
- ❏ Flashlight, candle
- ❏ Compass
- ❏ Cigarette lighter
- ❏ String, rope
- ❏ First aid kit
- ❏ Suntan lotion
- ❏ Beach mat
- ❏ Insect repellent: simple liquid, electric, burning spiral
- ❏ Detergent for clothes (powder)
- ❏ Toilet paper
- ❏ Ear plugs and eye mask
- ❏ Camera and accessories
- ❏ Walkman and tapes
- ❏ Paper, pen, books

course, blue jeans. They are fairly cool and sturdy at the same time, so they're also good to wear while riding your bike.

Your feet will be most comfortable in light shoes or sandals (when you are not driving of course). Good quality leather sandals can be purchased in any tourist area in Greece. As for socks, you will need them only when you wear your motorcycle boots, so be sure to take with you a few pairs of athletic socks, which are both comfortable and absorbent.

When you are under the sun, and especially at the beach, it is very important to wear a hat. Look for a wide-brim cotton one - which will al-

WHAT TO TAKE ALONG

so protect your eyes and the back of your neck - and preferably one with air holes. If you... reach boiling point the only thing that can save you is a dip in the sea, so don't forget to take a swim suit with you as well. You will also need a beach towel, and a towel for after the shower.

Though known for its hot climate, Greece may show you another face as well. If you visit it during spring or fall you are bound to feel **cold** - and that is true even in the heart of the summer if you're travelling on the mountains in the early morning or late evening. To protect yourself, take with you a light sweater, a woollen cap, and a woollen undershirt with long sleeves.

What you wear while driving seems to be a more complicated issue, and one could write pages on the different views expressed. The basic rule is that **one should always adjust to the environment.** Penguins cannot survive in the Sahara, and flamingos cannot survive in the Antarctic. As for motorcyclists travelling in Greece, they need clothes that will provide **both** comfort **and** a certain degree of protection. A good leather or Cordura jacket, a pair of jeans (preferably of those specially designed for motorcyclists that have protective pads around the hips), and a pair of leather boots or motorcyclist shoes (that offer extra protection for the ankles) are probably the best things to wear on your bike, as they provide the golden mean between comfort and safety.

Finally, don't forget to take along a good **helmet.** Greece is full of temptations, and of course being relaxed and giving in to some of them (always within the bounds of reason and safety) is what a holiday is all about. However, there are certain temptations you should definitely avoid, and one of them is driving without your helmet on. True, cops are generally flexible on this point, and high temperatures invite you to put your helmet aside. But don't. Make the use of a helmet an inviolable principle, and train yourself to resist temptation. If you need to feel cool use a jet-type helmet, but make sure it's of good quality, fits well and has a visor you can pull down (otherwise you must wear a pair of glasses). Still, we recommend you take a good full-face helmet, preferably with a front part you can pull up, because it offers the best protection for your head.

A good leather or Cordura jacket and a helmet are necessary for comfort and safety

Practical equipment

There is nothing worse than getting stuck with a dead bike at the side of the road because of damage you could easily have done something about if you had taken with you a screw-driver and a spanner. Imagine also that it is dark, you're up on the mountain

CHECKLIST OF PERSONAL ITEMS

1. ITEMS FOR RIDING
- Helmet
- Sun glasses
- Neck scarf
- Motorcycle jacket
- Motorcycle pants
- Motorcycle boots
- Waist belt
- Waist purse
- Short motorcycle gloves (without lining)
- Long motorcycle gloves (with lining)
- Rainproof outfit
- Rainproof covers for the gloves and boots

2. ITEMS FOR GENERAL USE
- Jeans
- Cotton T-shirts
- Shirt
- Sweater
- Socks
- Underwear
- Shorts
- Swim suit
- Beach towel
- Hat
- Woollen cap
- Woollen undershirt
- Town shoes
- Sandals
- Toilet articles

TIPS ON PERSONAL ITEMS

- Don't waste too much space on clothes. Take three or four sets of underwear with you and some cleaning powder to wash them at every chance.
- Don't take the largest towel you have at home. A small one will do the job and take less space too.
- Make sure the towel is completely dry before packing it away, or else it will mould.
- Hot air is very bad for your skin. Take a body lotion with you and some vaseline for the lips, and use them regularly before and after rides.
- If you wear contact lenses take along a second pair as well as a pair of glasses. In Greece you will find contact lens products at the optician's or the pharmacy, but mostly in larger towns or small but touristy areas. Available: AOSEPT, OPTIFREE, TITMUS H_2O_2 TE, OXISEPT, MULTIPURPOSE, LENSRINSE/LENSEPT.

WHAT TO TAKE ALONG

alone, you feel cold, your stomach is complaining and, why not, it is starting to rain (usually all these go together!)

To avoid similar situations you must take with you some practical equipment that may help you solve petty problems before they turn into big ones.

First and foremost, you must have some **tools** with you. Most motorcycles come with a small tool kit, but this usually consists of only a few basic tools of medium quality. It is best to replace these tools from the start with better ones, which will help you deal with problems effectively and will last you many years.

The basic tools you must have with you are mentioned on the checklist. However, it is important to consider which tools are necessary to perform a number of jobs **on your own motorcycle,** for instance to remove the front or rear tyre, to tighten the chain, change the clutch or gas cable, adjust the suspension, remove the spark plug screws, or tighten all vital bolts. Consider the matter carefully and make a list of the extra tools you may need.

For God's sake, **do not leave any tools behind.** If you are tempted to do so remember Murphy's law, which says that "the only tool you will need on your trip is precisely the tool you left behind!"

Secondly, you must have with you a number of "expendable" spare parts, especially those connected with vital functions. For instance, you must always carry along spare clutch and brake release levers, because even the simplest fall (for instance, when the stand fails to do its job) can cause great damage and leave you without front brake or clutch.

Thirdly, you must take along something to secure the bike. A special **motorcycle padlock** of very good quality will deter any prospective thieves. Also take a special case in which to keep it. Do not travel with the padlock attached behind the carburettor, because the vibrations may cause serious wear or damage to the frame or engine. Neither is it

You may not find shelter at the crucial moment, so take one along!

a good idea to tie it onto your bags; it is heavy and slippery, and sooner or later you are going to lose it.

Finally, a thin but tough **plastic sheet,** 2X2 metres in size, can protect your bike from the rain very effectively. This can also serve as an instant shelter for yourself in case of a sudden thunderstorm, if you will only put a ring on each corner and, through it, a rubber band with a hook.

Just before leaving

Once you have gathered everything you need you can load the bike and go on a weekend trip to check that everything is OK. Travelling two to three hundred kilometres on this last weekend should give you a good chance to find out if anything is still

PRACTICAL EQUIPMENT CHECKLIST

- ❏ Set of spanners, 8 - 16 mm
- ❏ Spark plug wrench
- ❏ Set of screw-drivers
- ❏ Set of Allen wrenches, 4 - 10 mm
- ❏ Adjustable wrench
- ❏ Pair of pliers
- ❏ Air pump
- ❏ Pressure gauge
- ❏ Tyre tube
- ❏ Levers
- ❏ Vulcanising foam
- ❏ Chain spray
- ❏ Extra cables
- ❏ Extra lamps
- ❏ Extra oil (for supplement)
- ❏ Extra fuses
- ❏ Spare clutch and brake release levers
- ❏ Extra straps and elastic tie-downs
- ❏ Insulating tape
- ❏ Wire
- ❏ Bolts, nuts, washers
- ❏ 2X2 plastic sheet

missing or if there are any problems with your equipment, so you can do something about it before leaving home. You may in fact discover anything, from the most trivial problems to the least likely ones: a tent eaten up by mice, missing pegs, a burnt lamp in the flashlight, a flash that isn't working etc.

You will also have a last chance to discover if anything is wrong with the bike, if there are any problems with packing and weight distribution, if your body can easily slip into its normal driving position (or if anything interferes with it), if your outfit is comfortable etc.

The day before your departure you can load the bike and lock it in a place where it's safe (such as your own garage - if one exists). The next day you will get up at your leisure, you will enjoy a good bath, have a royal breakfast, and wear your outfit slowly and ritually as if you were going to a wedding. Then you will ride the bike, start the engine, and... have a wonderful trip in Unexplored Crete!

WHAT TO TAKE ALONG

DEPARTURE CHECK

- Make sure you have taken your passport, motorcycle papers, wallet, boat ticket - if there is one - and a set of spare keys.
- Use the checklists in this guide to verify that you have taken everything you need.
- Make sure the tank bag is well fitted and doesn't block your view of the instrument panel.
- Make sure all luggage is well fitted.
- Check the headlight now that the bike is loaded and adjust if necessary.
- Do a last check of the engine oil and tyre pressure

WHEN TO COME

Each year Crete is visited by **2.5 million tourists.** Of those, 2.4 million come in July and August. Hence, it is not hard to imagine the crush at the beach, the squeeze at the restaurants, the rush for a hotel bed. During the rest of the year, the island is practically **empty,** although summer lingers on long after August and begins long before June. Just think that Crete lies at a latitude of 35.007 degrees, namely a lot more south than Tunisia or Algeria, and that tropical fruits like bananas and avocados thrive here! Why, then, does everybody come in those two months? **Simply because it is then most working people take their holidays.** If you belong to that category, you have no choice but to rub elbows with the crowds. Things, of course, are not desperately hopeless, as you will always find quiet, out of the way corners, but you shall have to look hard. Should you have, however, the luxury of choosing your holiday month, you are in lucky bliss. What will have been inferno for others, will look paradise to you, solely because you chose to come outside the peak season.

JULY, AUGUST
The worst time!

- Advantages

None, unless you like crowds.

- Disadvantages

Firstly, **it's horribly hot.** To survive you will certainly need a wide-

No advantages in July and August? Come on now!

brimmed hat that covers your neck too, quality sunglasses, sun lotion of high protection factor (15-20 SPF) and plenty of water. In the afternoon you should not expose yourselves to the sun and you should stay under shade, although even there the mercury may exceed 40°C. Riding a motorcycle becomes excruciating, your head simmering in the helmet and your body steaming in the leathers (the more so if they are black coloured).

Secondly, **you will have trouble with accommodation.** Hotels are full and so are the good rooms to let, not to mention the good spots in the camp sites. You will have to settle for rooms without view, remote hotels of lesser standards, or a small stretch of ground next to the campsite toilets.

Thirdly, **you will have trouble with food.** Waiters and cooks are humans too, and when they have to serve armies of hungry customers from morning to evening, it is expected that quality is sacrificed to quantity and speed.

Fourthly, **prices are high.** Greece is generally cheaper compared to other European Union countries, but the law of supply and demand works here as well. Indeed when demand exceeds supply, as is the case in summertime Crete, you will pay the highest prices without getting the best quality, either in food, accommodation or entertainment.

Lastly, **transportation is hellish.** Ports and airports are turned into a reign of chaos, where crowds of people, lack of organisation, strikes, delays and bad service will rack your nerves. On the roads, tens of thousands of hurried, incompetent or drunken car drivers and rented moped riders are a permanent menace.

SEPTEMBER, OCTOBER, NOVEMBER

After the tempest, the calm!

• Advantages

Firstly, **the heat wave is over.** Summer lingers on normally until the end of October, while the first rains will not appear before early November. The sea is not only pleasantly warm but calmer as well. The beaches that look like tins of sardines in August, now have much less people, if they are not totally deserted.

Secondly, **you will enjoy a pleasant stay.** Even the most centrally located hotels have vacant rooms, room owners will approach you with offers for rooms in the best quarters, campsites regain their relaxed and peaceful atmosphere.

Thirdly, **you will enjoy good food.** You may not find the variety of peak season, but the food will certainly be better cooked, portions will be bigger, service will be friendlier and prompter.

Fourthly, **you will move with ease.** Boats and planes depart on time and are not overloaded. Roads are not congested and you can enjoy the scenery as you don't have to drive defensively. Archaeological sites and museums are not jammed and, all in all, you will not feel choked.

In August, Vai is packed like sardines. A month later the whole beach is yours!

Lastly, **everything is discounted.** Hotels and rooms to let are at least 30% cheaper than the official summer rates, food is not as expensive, and even bars offer drinks at reduced prices.

• **Disadvantages**

Firstly, **the general slackness.** Many hotels, restaurants and tourist-oriented businesses close down so that their employees can rest. Many of those remaining open show the obvious signs of the invasion which occurred the previous months: battered rooms, slackening service, abandonment. The waves or the local cleaning crews have not yet removed the litter left behind by many unprincipled users of the beach.

Secondly, **the first signs of inclement weather.** The first days in November can also be the first days of winter. But if you are suitably prepared, not only will you be unaffected, you will enjoy it as well. You must carry rain-proof overalls, warm clothing, long gloves, lofty sleeping bags and waterproof tent.

Thirdly, **days are conspicuously shorter.** It gets dark early, so you must wake up very early to seize the day...

DECEMBER, JANUARY, FEBRUARY

Crete's most enchanting face.

• **Advantages**

Firstly, **you will see the Cretan's Crete.** Without its distorting touristy "make-up", Crete is a divine place. The rains and the wind clean the atmosphere, revealing unique natural beauty and highlighting the savage charm of gorges and steep mountain faces.

WHEN TO COME

Wild herbs emit their fragrant essence, colours become singularly deep. A sense of adventure comes alive, one without extremes or insurmountable obstacles. Winter sunshine, not rare at all, creates scenes from a fairly tale where everything appears so beautiful, cheerful and healthy. The natives welcome you as a traveller who seeks the real Crete, and offer you unforgettable hospitality and the treasures of their hearts, their land and their tradition. During these months there are no tourists in Crete, only its true lovers.

Secondly, **everything is at half price and even less.** The best rooms in the best hotels are at your disposal at incredible prices! Whereas in summer you needed very much luck (and money) to stay, now you are the honoured guest and you can see all the rooms before you choose, at rates that will thrill you.

Thirdly, **the whole Crete is yours!** In museums and archaeological sites you will be alone with the guard, who very probably will ac-

The colours and fragrances of wintertime Crete are unforgettable.

company you around as a personal guide and then will invite you to his tiny booth for a glass of raki with honey and a chat! You can pitch your tent anywhere, without bothering anyone or being bothered by anyone. Beaches are totally deserted, spotless and, on the south coast, water temperature is almost bearable for a swim.

• Disadvantages

Firstly, **you may hit very bad weather.** When it rains in Crete it pours, and it is very dangerous and unpleasant to be outdoors. Lightning strikes, rocks fall on the roads from cliff sides, torrents dig out ruts that make dirt roads impassable. Mountain passes are covered in snow and clouds block out the view. Usually, bad weather does not last for long but you cannot make a contract with the elements. It may be raining for two weeks non-stop; exactly the two weeks you chose to come! If you plan to visit Crete this period, it is advisable to have plenty of time available, as well as plenty of warm clothes and plenty of books to keep you busy in the hours (or days) you may be confined to a room.

Secondly, **the island's tourist infrastructure is at a standstill.** Most hotels, bars, car and motorcycle rentals, travel agencies, restaurants are closed. Everything designed to accommodate and transport tourists simply does not function. Of course, this is not a drawback for you, given that one of the reasons you are travelling this part of the year in Crete, is precisely to avoid the artificial face of the island. However, reaching a village and finding no place to eat or buy provisions, not a single inhabitant to ask for directions, no telephone and no service station for tens of kilometres, may cause you problems. Winter wandering may be much more exciting than summer tourism, but it is always an adventure more or less.

MARCH, APRIL, MAY, JUNE
Welcome to Paradise!

●Advantages
Firstly, **the weather is fine.** The last of winter weather is over by the first days of March and then a glorious sun illuminates and warms the mountain slopes, the beaches, the hamlets and the cities. Temperatures are high enough for you to drive without shivering, and yet low enough for you to stay dry under the leather overall. From late April on you can swim comfortably in an invigoratingly cool sea, and sunbathe without being scorched (but always use the proper sunscreens). The atmosphere is incredibly clear and the view from mountain tops and mountain routes is unlimited.

Secondly, **everything is in bloom.** Plateaux are turned into multi-coloured lakes of wild flowers. Gardens, road hedges, rock cracks are flooded with yellow daisies, scarlet poppies, white lilies and more than 300 other species of wild flowers, some of which are indigenous. The sea teams with life. Endless schools of fish frolic among the rocks and the eelgrass. Nature is a festival of colours and flavours.

Thirdly, **all is ready to welcome you.** Preparations for the new tourist season have been completed by mid April. Houses are freshly white-washed, rooms are painstakingly cleaned, shops have stocked their shelves anew, restaurants have put tables out in the sun. Early in April, the graders of each prefecture level the dirt roads that suffered in winter, and repair crews patch up the tarmac of the provincial and national road network.

Fourthly, **everything is cheaper than in summer.** Just like after the peak season, business is slow these months and prices are accordingly low. The natives' mood nevertheless is high and so is their

If you come to Crete in springtime, you almost don't need a travel guide; wherever you go is magical.

pleasure to serve the first customers of the season. So, they will treat you with the best rooms, hefty portions of food, special prices and a smile.

- **Disadvantages**

None!

ON WHAT MOTORCYCLE?

Crete is full of high mountains. Most roads are **mountain roads**: narrow, serpentine tarmac roads, badly designed country roads and, mainly, dirt roads. Most dirt roads are passable and pose no special difficulties. They connect isolated villages or rural areas with each other or with the main road network and , therefore, they are maintained regularly and, as a rule, they are in fair condition. They are being used by all kinds of vehicles (even buses) and you will not be troubled even on a street bike.

Yet, by a strange co-incidence, the dirt roads that lead to the most enchanting places, to the cosiest beaches, to the most thrilling terrains, to the most picturesque villages, are in bad condition, posing serious obstacles at certain points, such as steep gradients, protruding rocks, deep pot holes and ruts, loose stones and gravel (usually at bends), and all the like. In winter and springtime especially, the rains and melting snows aggravate the problem even more.

As a result, the demanding traveller who does not like getting stuck, will find **a lightweight enduro motorcycle between 400-600 cc ideal for the exploration of Crete.** If you do not own such a machine do not despair. Come to Crete on your motorcycle and, once here, rent a good enduro and roam on the mountains and the outback. In Iraklio and Limenas Chersonisou in particular you can rent **brand new enduro bikes (250-900 cc) at very reasonable prices.** Unless you are attached to your own motorcycle, renting such machines is a solution with advantages: **you save money** by avoiding significant expenses related to the preparation for a journey (tyres, oil, brake pads or shoes, service, accessories, etc.) and **you gain the comfort and security** of full insurance and free technical assistance in case the rented bike breaks down anywhere on the island. If you fancy this idea, here are the two largest and most reliable bike rental enterprises in Crete.

A super-sport bike will not enjoy such dirt roads

ON WHAT MOTORCYCLE?

1. TORNADO Rent a Bike, Trust S.A.
El. Venizelou 173, 70 014 Limenas Chersonisou
tel. 0897 - 22.821 fax 0897 - 21. 366
Branch Shops
1. Dimokratias 7, 70 014 Limenas Chersonisou tel. 0897 - 22.821
2. Ethnikis Antistaseos 2, Iraklio tel. 081 - 239.754

Enduro 125cc
Yamaha DT R
Kawasaki KMX
Suzuki TSR
Enduro 200/250cc
Kawasaki KMX
Kawasaki KLR
Honda NX, AX-1
Honda XLR
Yamaha Serow

Chopper 250cc
Yamaha Virago
Kawasaki EL
Honda CM
Enduro 400-650cc
Kawasaki KLE
Honda XLM
Honda Dominator
Street 500-600cc
Kawasaki EN

Yamaha Virago
Kawasaki ZZR
Kawasaki GPZ
Harley Davidson
Sportster
Dyna Low Rider
Heritage Softail
Fat Boy
Triumph
Tiger 900
Thunderbird 900

2. MOTOR CLUB Rent a Bike Sigma S.A.
Square of 18 Englishmen 1, 712 02 Iraklio Crete
tel.081 - 222.408,286.012 fax 222.862
Branch Shops :
1. Motor Club, Iraklio Airport tel. 081 - 223.310
2. Motor Club, Sophokli Venizelou 2, 741 00 Rethimno tel. 0831 - 54.253
3. Motor Club, Dimokratias Ave. 40, 700 07 Malia tel. 0897 - 32.033

Enduro 125cc
Yamaha DT R
Kawasaki KMX
Suzuki TSR
Enduro 250cc
Kawasaki KLR
Suzuki DR

Chopper 250cc
Yamaha Virago
Kawasaki EL
Enduro 350cc
Suzuki DR
Yamaha XT
Enduro 500-650cc
Kawasaki KLE 500

Yamaha XT 600
Kawasaki KLR 600
BMW F650
Chopper 500-650cc
Kawasaki EN
Yamaha Virago
Suzuki Savage

All bike rental shops are obliged to provide you with a helmet at no extra charge, but you will rarely find a good helmet to fit you. For the sake of safety, comfort, and hygiene you should bring along your own helmet, as well as gloves, jacket, boots and rain gear.

ACCOMMODATIONS
Hotels

According to extensive research we did in the summer of 1995, very few motorcyclists stay in hotels. This can partly be explained by the fact that at the places they usually go there are no hotels to stay in the first place! But it is also a question of the travelling spirit that characterises motorcyclists as a group, since they have very little in common with the tourists that go for travel packages and with the tourist industry that "processes" them massively and impersonally.

Of course, every rule has its exceptions. You will frequently see cosy little hotels with "character" in quiet out-of-the-way places, which offer a clean and hospitable environment you can enjoy. Whenever we found such a hotel we included it in the pages of this guide. There are also occasions when staying in a hotel seems to be the most convenient thing to do. Suppose that you're visiting a large town, for instance, or that you plan to use it as your base for day trips in the area. A hotel would certainly make such trips easier, because you wouldn't have to load and unload everything on your bike each morning. This is why on the city maps included in this guide you will also find a list of those hotels that satisfy our requirements. Hotels that are presentable, quiet and inexpensive and - most importantly - **have parking facilities for your bike.**

Depending on the kinds of facilities and services they offer, hotels are officially rated as Luxury, A, B, C, D, or E. Most of those we recommend in this guide are in the C category, and they will charge anywhere between six and twelve thousand drachmas for one night in a two-bed room. For larger towns we have also listed a few hotels in the A or B category in case you've had enough with mountains and camping and feel you need a change.

Boarding house or hotel, if you travel in the low season (April, May, September, October) you can get very **significant discounts** on the price of the room, sometimes even 50%. However, make sure you ask about the discount **before** taking the room.

Rooms to rent

Rented rooms are probably the most popular and inexpensive accommodations (besides camping of course). If you travel in Crete in the low tourist season, people of all ages, and especially old men and women, will stop you in the middle of the street or approach you at the cafeteria and ask: "Rooms?" Their first reaction if they see you're interested is to tell you "come with me." In this way they hope that they will get you to see how nice the room is, and then of course you'll rent it for the price they ask, or perhaps with a slight discount. But the low season is a period of huge offer and very little demand, so you can certainly benefit from the fact and rent for a very low price. Refuse firmly to follow them unless they tell you how much they want. **A good price would be 4000 drachmas for a single room, 5000 for one with two beds and 6000 for one with three.**

Starting with the tourist season of 1995 **every** rented room must

ACCOMMODATIONS

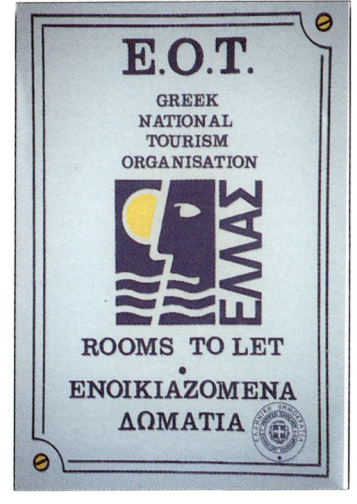

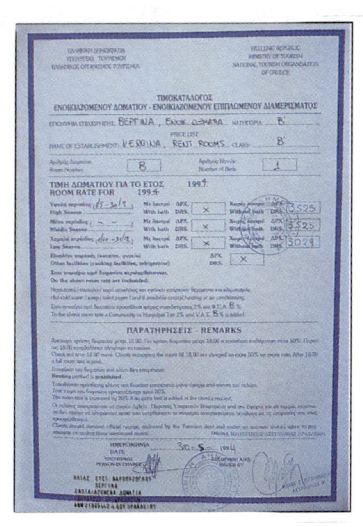

Check for the EOT sign outside your room and the validated price list behind the door

have the EOT sign somewhere where it's easy to see (the initials stand for the Greek National Tourist Organisation, in Greek "Ελληνικός Οργανισμός Τουρισμού"). If you don't see the sign, it obviously means that the rooms in question do not meet the requirements set by EOT, and it might be best to avoid them, so you don't have any unpleasant experiences.

Please note:

1. The price of the room for the high and the low tourist season as well as the exact dates marking the beginning and end of each season must be clearly written on a sign validated by EOT or the police and hanging behind the door of the room. The prices written on this sign are the **highest** the owner is allowed to charge and are fixed for the entire tourist season.

2. Prices are **final** and include all taxes and charges. If a room is rented for only one night the owner is allowed to raise the rent by 10%.

3. Each person is entitled to a bar of soap and a towel. Hot running water, heating and extra blankets **must be free of charge.**

4. Your room must be cleaned **every day** and bed sheets and towels must be changed twice a week (for rooms in the A category) or once a week (for those in the B or C category).

5. The price paid for one night entitles you to stay in the room until 12 o' clock the following day.

Needless to say, the above rules and regulations apply only to tourist areas. If you find yourself in some quiet, out-of-the-way village, do not look for the EOT sign and for the price list behind the door. Conveniences will most likely be minimal, but so will be the price; you can expect something like 3000 to 4000 drachmas for a double room. In such a place you will be treated more as a guest than as a client, so forget about the typical side of this and enjoy what's really essential: the family ambience, the landlords' company, and maybe some delicious home-made food.

REPORT ANY PROBLEMS

If you are asked to pay more than the price written on the sign behind the door, if the sign is not in place or looks like someone has tampered with the figures, if the room is dirty and the service unacceptable, or if you feel you're being deceived or insulted, report it. The Greek National Tourist Organisation (EOT) has started a campaign that aims to upgrade tourist service, so your substantiated complaints will cause violators to be heavily fined. Simply call the nearest police station - a list of them is provided in the practical information catalogue in this book - or dial 171 for the Tourist Police or 9515111 for the Complaint Service of EOT. Even better, write to them at the address: EOT 2b Amerikis St. Athens 10564

Camping grounds

There are approximately 15 organised camping grounds in Crete, and they are described in some detail at the chapters telling you "Where to Stay" in each area. The truth is, they are not of top-notch quality, but they certainly satisfy the basic requirements for comfort and cleanness.

Camping on your own

Officially, we have to inform you that free camping is forbidden **throughout Greece**. Unofficially, though, you can pitch camp **anywhere you choose** - or almost! Where camping is really forbidden, you will see a sign to that effect, and even then you can go ahead and ignore it if ten other campers have already done so. But if there is no sign, you should be aware of some "unwritten laws." **Discreetness** is a primary principle of free camping, so avoid setting up your tent beside an organised camping ground, in crowded beaches and touristy areas, or in the middle of an archaeological site...

It will be generally quieter if the place you choose is somehow sheltered and away from indiscreet eyes. Pitch camp at the far end of a beach rather than in the middle of it, inside the woods rather than at the clearing just beside the main road, at the slope of a hill rather than at its top, between the bushes rather than in the middle of a flat field, or at some suitable spot at the end of a meadow rather than on the path used by flocks or peasants.

If the beach of your dreams is crowded but you have still set your heart on spending your holiday there, the only way to secure some peace and quiet and avoid bothering others is to set up your tent late in the evening, when the crowds are gone, and to take it down early in the morning before the invasion starts.

Needless to say, discreetness must be coupled with **respect for the environment.** Most people love camping on their own precisely because it allows such close contact with nature. And it is this love for nature that causes them to sleep in the middle of the woods or an empty beach, not their desire for a free stay. If the issue was indeed the money, they could probably spend less by opting for one of those travel packages that promise ten days in a hotel, full board, and

ACCOMMODATIONS

plane tickets, all for 90,000 drachmas! But love for nature must also go along with respect. **It will only be possible to enjoy pure, unspoiled nature, if each camper makes a point of leaving the area as clean as he found it and without a mark of human presence.**

How can you do that? Just be careful with a few basic things. Collect all garbage in a plastic bag and throw it in the first trash can you

Free-lance camping? By all means! But also respect for the environment

will find. Also avoid wrapping wires tightly around trees or cutting off twigs, and do not throw chemical pollutants into the rivers or give your bike an oil change right in the middle of a field.

As for your bathroom needs, try to find a suitable spot away from where people walk or lie, for instance at the far end of a beach behind the bushes or where the waves break. In any case, **avoid soiling the small caves found at the rocks next to the water;** they are beautiful natural shelters and can protect you from the sweltering heat of noon or from a chilly summer night.

Finally, remember that the remnants of a fire also spoil the environment. Instead of lighting a fire at a different spot every time, find one that suits you well, fence it with large rocks to prevent the coal and ashes from being swept away with the wind, and make it a practice to light your fire there. More on the issue can be found on page 89.

Monasteries

It is a long-standing tradition of the Orthodox to put up travellers who have come to worship God. Also, monasteries are generally built in the most wonderful places, sometimes on steep mountain rocks overlooking breathtaking gorges, sometimes in beautiful woods with springs and rivers close by, and some times on empty sandy beaches. If you consider all this, you just might be tempted to retire in one yourself!

Of course, monasteries are no hotels or tourist attractions. As a rule, monks and nuns do not like the fact that most travellers today are not devout Christians but curious tourists, and do not appreciate the "see-and-photograph-everything attitude." They expect some regard for the sanctity of the place.

Needless to say, they will not let you enter in shorts or sleeveless shirts, because they feel it is inconsistent with that sanctity. Most monasteries provide their own solution to this problem as they have a stock of wide pants and skirts for men and women who visit the monastery.

Keep in mind that people living in monasteries usually go to bed very early, because they also have an early start in the morning. Monasteries close their door after sunset, so if you arrive late it is best to leave them alone.

While most monasteries will put up mixed company in the same or separate rooms, the feasibility of this depends on the rules set by each one; in some instances nunneries may not put up men and the opposite. The room where they will put you to sleep, whether large or small, is likely to have several beds in it (as many as it can take), so you will most probably sleep with others. The beds are exactly like their own, and with their rough pillows and heavy blankets they may not quite tie in with your idea of ultimate comfort, so a sleeping bag might prove handy. As for the food, you will be invited to eat what they eat, and no special fuss will be made over you. A simple but tasty meal, usually accompanied with good wine of their own production - or some local villager's production - is what you can typically expect. Also keep in mind that all monks and nuns are vegetarians. They usually eat casserole dishes cooked with oil, bean or chick pea soup, lentils, lots of greens - often handpicked - and pies, so if you insist on having meat you'd better open the can when you are alone in the guest room.

Besides food and sleep, monasteries also offer a wonderful opportunity to come in contact with an age-old religious tradition that goes back to the Byzantine times, and even earlier, to the first centuries after Christ. Wake up with the early morning bell, and go hear the liturgy leaving your camera behind (taking pictures in the church, especially during the liturgy, is forbidden anyway). Near the entrance of the church you will see a counter with candles. Throw a one hundred drachma coin on it and light a candle. Many monasteries have come to rely on candle money as their basic means of support, and on your part this is a symbolic gesture. Sit somewhere where you can see and hear well, and let your spirit take you far away. You may not understand a word of what you hear, but the chanting in the church, the smell of incense, the soft candlelight, the warmth exuded by the figures of the saints, every little thing that has remained unchanged for centuries of worship will take you back to the time of the first Christians. Regardless of your religious beliefs, the morning and evening service in a monastery is a unique experience and a fascinating trip in time, provided of course you open your mind and heart to it.

Chapels

While monasteries can be counted on to offer travellers a shelter for the night, they are not the only places you can seek refuge when you are in need. High up on mountain tops, at the far ends of mountain paths or meadows, in peaceful places near woods and springs or in the middle of a high plateau, there are hundreds of little chapels built by local villagers in memory of loved ones or as a token of their warm

ACCOMMODATIONS

In case of need, a mountain chapel can be the most welcome refuge

faith and deep gratitude for God's help at a difficult moment in their lives. Most of these chapels are made of stone and were built some time in the last century, but some of them are two or three or four hundred years old (or even earlier) and have wonderful samples of hagiography, fine wooden icon screens, old Bibles and priceless icons. Until about 1970 they were generally kept unlocked, but with the great spread of tourism and the first deplorable incidents of theft and vandalism the locals who kept them up put locks on their doors (or at least did so for the older chapels).

Chapels, especially those in the wilderness of the mountain, are an **excellent refuge** in case of need, as they generally have trees in front of their yard or a covered area in front of their door where you can lie down and sleep. If it is freezing or raining cats and dogs you could also sleep inside the chapel. Keep in mind, though, that you are in a sacred place and must do nothing that will offend the religious feelings of any locals who happen to pass by. Do not cook inside the chapel, do not move around the pews, the candelabra or the benches, do not smoke, and of course do not soil the place. It would be a good idea to wake up early in the morning, around 7:00 perhaps, so that you don't have any unpleasant encounter with any quick-tempered local who might misinterpret your intentions. Should you happen to run into an angry fellow or the local policeman or field guard, a very convincing excuse that will take care of the matter is that your motorcycle broke down on you and you were forced to spend the night.

BOATS TO CRETE

The connection of Crete to the Greek mainland is handled by five different shipping lines running a total of **eleven** big ferry boats that will take you to one of Crete's north shore harbours. Boats depart from Piraeus, Githio and Kalamata, and they arrive at Kasteli, Hania, Rethimno, Iraklio, Aghios Nikolaos and Sitia.

In spite of the heavy tourism in the summer and the huge profit of the ferry companies, the conditions at the ports and inside the ships are quite bad and keep getting worse.

Travelling by ferry during the months of July and August can indeed be a trying experience. The heat is often unbearable and ships and islands are swamped with millions of tourists. If you add to this the general sloppiness that characterises Greeks, there is only one word to describe the situation in the Greek ports and ships: **chaos!**

ROAD Editions is currently working on preparing an Annual Guide of Ferry Connections. It will be published soon and will contain valuable information on routes and prices and the quality of service in every ship, along with all the addresses and phone numbers of port authorities and shipping lines. But until we are ready to publish the guide, we hope that the following information will help you to survive.

Eating on the ferry

The trip to Crete lasts several hours, so you will probably feel the need to eat something. The bar or restaurant of the ship usually serves good quality food at reasonable prices. However, if you want to avoid the queues or want to enjoy your lunch on the ship's deck, try to get your own food and drinks before boarding the ship. Most restaurants in the port area will sell food in a package, so all you need to do is point to the dish you like and say *"se pakèto parakalò"* (package, please). In addition, you can buy some good quality snacks, or candy, bottled water and a few soft drinks from any street kiosk, or, alternatively, you can go into a supermarket and find everything your heart desires.

Sleeping on the ferry

As a rule, ferries leave for Crete some time in the late evening and arrive at the island the next morning. (In fact, day trips are almost impossible to find, though there is one from Githio and a couple from Piraeus). If you are travelling with at least one friend, your smartest move would be to book a cabin. (They come with either two beds or four). If you are alone, however, it might be best to avoid cabins altogether, because you never know who you'll be sharing it with, and you may end up having a dreadful night!

If you cannot afford to pay for a cabin, take along your sleeping bag and plastic mattress and look for a quiet spot on the deck or in one of the lounges. Such spots are unfortunately very hard to find and very quick to go, and motorcyclists in particular have little chance of finding one because they are always the last to board the ship. If the ship is too crowded, you may even have difficulty finding a place to sit!

These sad facts prompt us to advise you the following: If you are travelling with a group of friends go to the port early and park your bike near the place where the ship will moor. Send one person from the group to wait in line with the sleeping bags. As soon as passengers can board the ship, your friend will get in, run to the deck, find a good spot on which to lay the sleeping bags, and **stay there** to protect the place from invaders. This is why it is best to send the biggest fellow among you rather than a girl. As for the rest of the group, you must in no way relax your attention and scatter about the place, but should be alert so you can help your friend in case of emergency. If all this reminds you of a battle, well... this is exactly the case! Overcrowded ships in the high tourist season have unfortunately become a frequent phenomenon, and they can make your trip quite unpleasant.

Safety on the ferry

What suffers most during ferry trips is your motorcycle. The people at the garage could not care less for the fortune it may have cost you; they treat it like a sack of potatoes. They ask you to fit it in the gaps left between cars and trucks, or they squeeze all motorcycles together in front of the movable door or under the ramps leading to the second level of the garage. Of course, if something happens to your bike they never accept any responsibility.

Worst of all, insurance companies are well aware of the chaos prevailing in ferry garages and refuse to compensate you for any damages sustained in there. If there are witnesses you just may have a chance of compensation by the shipowners, but you must act immediately and with great persistence. Notify the person in charge of the garage and the captain of the ship, and show them that you are very angry at what happened and very determined to set things right. Otherwise, it will be impossible for you later to prove that the dint on the gas tank or the broken fairing had anything to do with the ship; so know it and act accordingly...

It is always best to park your bike near the garage wall, to put on a gear, to use the side stand

A boat's garage or a torture chamber?

rather than the middle one, and to secure the bike tightly with ropes tied against something immovable. If you use the wrong stand you may later find that the waves have rocked the boat so hard that they have caused it to fall; August, especially, is famous for its strong winds *(meltèmia)*, which create high waves that can rock even the biggest boat travelling in the Aegean. As for the ropes, do not expect to find any on the boat but bring your own.

A final note: **The best precaution you can take is to stay near your bike until everyone around you has parked and to go down to the garage every time the boat makes a stop.** In this way you will save your bike from any rough handling.

Tips for a pleasant voyage

All ships have air-conditioning, so the temperature on board may be slightly (or considerably) lower than you would like it to be. But since it is not possible to tell the crew to turn the air-condition down, it might be wise to take along a **footer** so you can keep yourself warm.

Lights never go out on a ship! Why should they, anyway, if no one pays for the electricity? If you have no cabin and plan to spend the night on the deck or in some passageway, be sure to bring along an **eye mask** like those distributed in airplanes.

Creaking and snoring and all kinds of sounds will go on **all night**. If you want to sleep in peace you must also bring along a pair of **ear plugs**.

For safety reasons, the garage of the ship will be locked all during the trip. Since in the havoc of the parking process you can easily get distracted by the shouts of the parking crew and the exhaust fumes of the truck right in front of you, you may easily forget to take with you half of the things you need. For this reason, we suggest you use the time you're waiting at the port to put those things in a shoulder bag.

BOATS TO CRETE

SHIPPING LINE	BOAT NAME	ROUTE
ANEK Piraeus: 01-4118611 Hania: 0821-51916 Iraklio: 081-222481	APTERA	Piraeus - Hania
	LISSOS	Piraeus - Hania
	KANTIA	Piraeus - Iraklio
	RETHIMNO	Piraeus - Iraklio
MINOAN LINES Piraeus: 01-4080006 Hania: 0821-45911 Iraklio: 081-22646	ΚΑΖΑΝΤΖΑΚΙΣ	Piraeus - Iraklio
	KING MINOS	Piraeus - Iraklio
	KNOSSOS	Piraeus - Hania
RETHIMNIAKI N.A.E. Piraeus: 01-417770 Rethimno: 0831-29221	ARKADI	Piraeus - Rethimno
	PREVELI	Piraeus - Rethimno
LANE A.E. Piraeus: 01-4274004 Aghios Nikolaos: 0841-26764	V.KORNAROS	Piraeus - Aghios Nikolaos -Sitia
MOIRAS FERRIES Piraeus: 01-4174459 Kalamata: 0721-20704 Githio: 0733-24501	THESEUS	Githio - Kasteli Kalamata - Kasteli

The routes

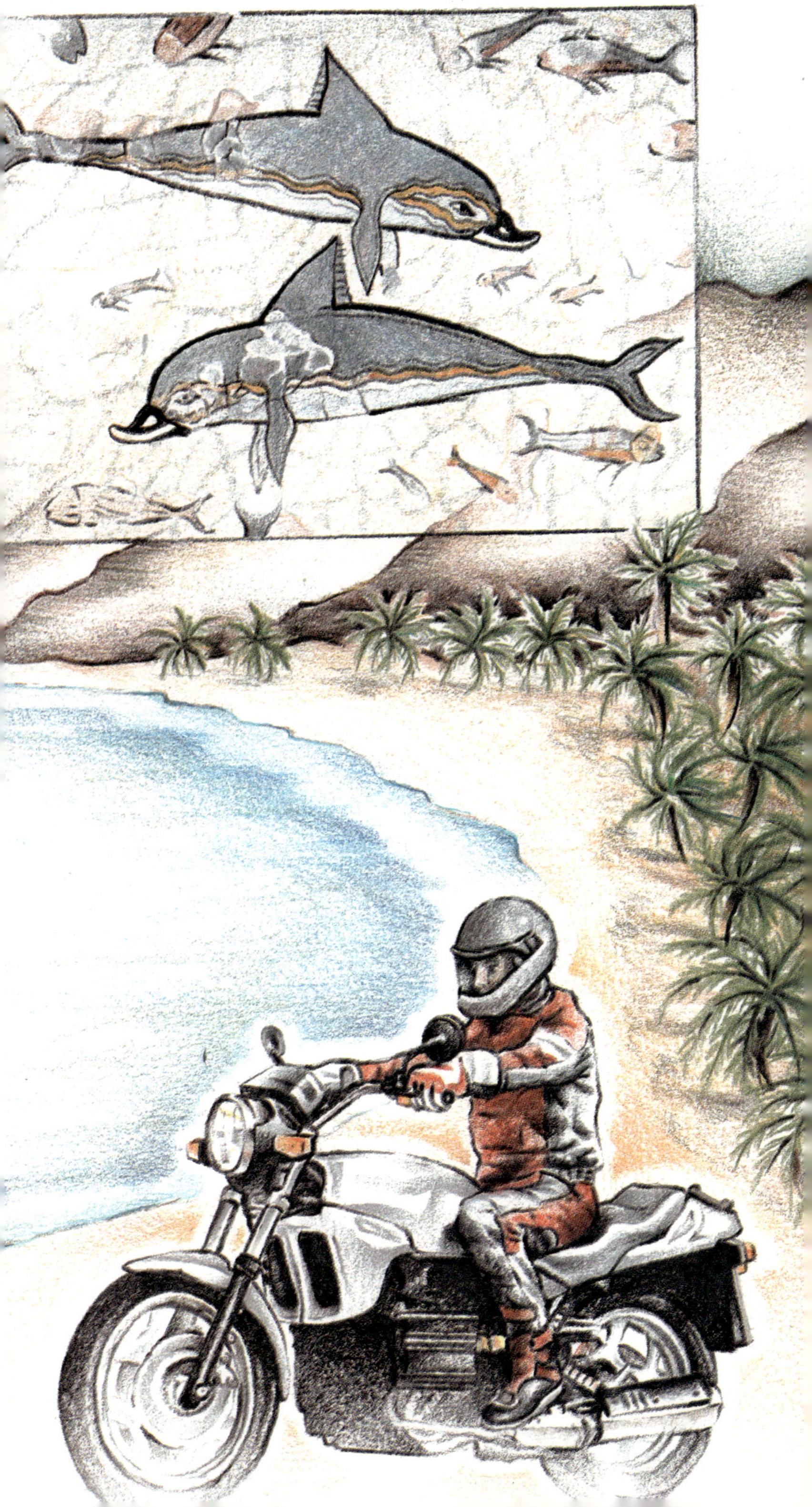

Hania

The Venetian harbour of Hania

ROUTES STARTING FROM HANIA

When you board a ship at Piraeus you probably expect that it docks at the port of Hania. Where you actually get off, though, is the port of **Souda** about seven kilometres away. To get to Hania simply follow the signs (Gr/E) and you will soon be at the heart of the town. The road you are on as you come from Souda (or Iraklio) at some point intersects with **Hatzimichali Giannari street** in front of the town market (you will also see the street lights). Here you turn left and drive for a couple of blocks, and at the third intersection you turn right. You are now on **Halidon street,** which takes you straight to the **Venetian harbour** at the heart of the town (see city map, red line). Halidon street can be recognised by the Gr/E signs pointing you to EOT / GNTO (the Greek National Tourist Organisation) and to the Museum. These signs, however, are easy to miss because they have been placed too high and are too small. But what you cannot miss is the Credit Bank branch right at the corner where you must turn.

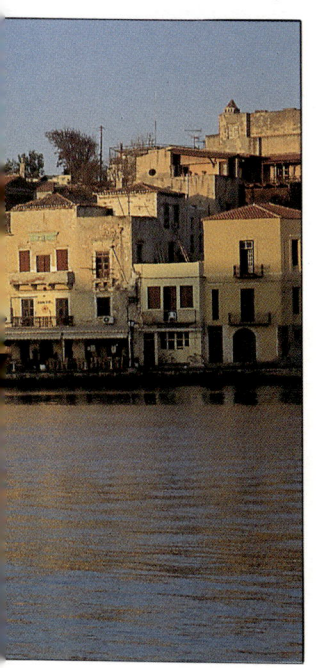

If you are coming from Kasteli Kissamou, you will enter the town from the west, driving on **Kissamou street** which then becomes **Kidonias.** Right after **Square 1866** you will see Gr/E signs directing you to the Old Town, the Museum and the City Hall. Here you must turn left in order to get to the beginning of Halidon street which, in turn, takes you to the Venetian harbour (see city map, blue line). The signs, however, are once again too high and too small and may be missed. A better mark is the big sign of HOTEL SAMARIA right on the point where you must turn.

As mentioned, Halidon street takes you straight to the Venetian harbour. If you wish to take a walk in the old part of town, you could pass (from the side) the chains blocking the entrance to the harbour and park your bike somewhere in the paved **Santrivani Square**. If you plan to stay for a few days, it might be wise to find a room first, so you can leave your motorcycle and luggage at a safe place. Keep in mind that Hania is a big town with lots of passing tourists and very close to the large port of Souda, too. This makes it unsafe to leave your bike loaded and unattended. The only place where you can do that is Santrivani Square, where you can take a walk and keep an eye on your motorcycle at the same time. The only other option if you want to leave your bike loaded is to take it to one of the two underground parking lots of the town **(44, 45).** They are open from 8:00 a.m. to 11:00 p.m., have a guard, and charge a symbolic fee of 200 drs. for 24 hours. Also keep in mind that during the period between April and October vehicles are not allowed in the old city after 11:00 a.m. and that this restriction applies until late at night.

As you stand in Santrivani Square facing the sea, there is a hill to your right which was once crowned with the citadel of ancient Kidonia **(the Kidonia *Akròpolis*).** The first inhabitants of the place, who arrived here sometime during the Neolithic age, chose to build their homes on this hill, not only because of the security it provided, but also because of the great view! (Climb the hill and check it out for yourself!) There was no harbour here at the time, but then again these people had no boats, so they didn't care! The need for a harbour arose later, toward the end of the period of the first palaces (ca. 17th century BC), when **an important Minoan settlement** was formed in this place, the most important in Western Crete. It was then that the first harbour was built, a harbour, it is true, that lacked the sophisticated design of later times. After that, the ancient town developed rapidly, and thanks to its artisanship and trade it soon acquired great wealth and power. It became so important among Cretan towns that it even minted its own coins.

Kidonia reached the height of its prosperity during the Roman period. In the year 30 BC the Roman emperor August Caesar granted it a status of autonomy under which the town really flourished. The good times continued for many more centuries, until one day in **824 AD**, when an Arabian fleet appeared in the Libyan Sea, driven away from Spain and looking for new victims. Like so many other Cretan towns, Kidonia was reduced to ruins...

In **961 AD** the Byzantines drove away the Arabs and rebuilt the town. To do this they used anything they could get their hands on, including stones from ruined buildings. They also decided to fortify the town and surrounded it with a large **fortress** which they named **Kasteli.** The only remnant of the Arabian rule is - according to one theory - the change of the town's name **from Kidonia to Al Chanea, Chanea, and finally Hania.**

But the story does not end here. In **1204** the island was conquered again, this time by the Venetians. The new rulers reinforced the walls of Kasteli and rebuilt the town, which had suffered once again from armed conflict. As you may guess, they used the same materials again, taking stones from ruined buildings and incorporating them in the new ones they built in their place.

The Venetians came to stay, and indeed they did stay for an awfully long time; the 400 years of their rule was the longest occupation Crete has ever known. Since they had such plans, they started building and building, and pretty soon the area inside the fortress had changed considerably. They put up many luxurious houses - among them the Commander's beautiful mansion - and a Cathedral, and when they were done they lay back comfortably to enjoy the lovely sunsets they could see from their porch. They thought that their strong navy and many soldiers would protect them from any danger, but they were fatally wrong. One dreadful evening in **1263,** as they were preparing to watch the sunset, they saw something that made their blood freeze; their sworn enemies, the Genoans, were almost outside their door... Now, the Venetian army was nowhere near - it was based in Handakas, the modern Iraklio - and the Venetians were totally off their guard. They were violently attacked before they had time to organise their defence and were consequently defeated. The Genoans stayed on for a while, and then they took whatever interested them and returned home. As a farewell present, they burned down the city.

The Venetians came back with their wings clipped and once again they rebuilt the town. They decided that they were not going to be in that position again, and they realised - somewhat late, it is true - that one fortress around the small hill of Hania was not enough to defend the town from a serious attack. Some years later they built a second wall, and this time they surrounded with it all the houses built outside Kasteli. It was a large square wall that took some twenty years to be completed, but when it was finally over in 1356 they felt that it was too low to protect the town and not well designed. For this reason Venice dispatched its best engineer, **Michele Sanmicheli**, to remedy the situation. Sanmicheli built a much stronger wall and in the process used any building materials from ancient buildings that could serve his purpose. The ancient theatre of Kidonia, which had survived so

All around Kasteli you can see parts of the city wall that were built at different times and with different stones.

many wars, was sacrificed for this wall, and so were many other public buildings and temples. It seems that the stones of these buildings had become like dominoes in the hands of fate, thrown down from time to time and always set up in a new formation...

The fort was equipped with 300 cannons and 30,000 cannon-balls and pretty soon more forts were built on the nearby islands of Thodorou, Souda and Gramvoussa. The Venetians were finally in control again, and western Crete was well fortified. It withstood all pirate attacks for many years to come, and even the legendary Barbarossa was unable to raid Hania.

After that Hania had a new period of prosperity. Many imposing public buildings were built, along with some equally imposing houses, and the town was planned according to the Venetian tradition which gave it a "European" character. The Venetian traders and battleships became a typical sight at the harbour and the bottom of the harbour was dug to accommodate them. In addition, seventeen dockyards were made **(49)** and ships were built or repaired in them. Seven of these dockyards survive to this day.

However, even the strongest fort cannot hold for ever. In August, **1645**, hordes of ferocious

Turks appeared before the town, determined to take it **at any cost.** And when the Turks say "any cost," they mean it. After two months of merciless siege and **40,000** dead, the ammunition and the strength of the attacked were exhausted and the 10,000 Turks who survived managed to get in.

The town was destroyed and built from the start according to the tastes and tradition of its new occupants. The Turks repaired the damaged wall and made it even stronger. Hania was now so well fortified that the Turks made it the seat of their administration of Crete.

In the two centuries of the Turkish rule of the island, the Greeks rebelled several times, but each time the fort provided protection to the Turks living in Hania and the surrounding area. But the revolution of **1897** was the last straw. The Great Powers of the time, England, France, Russia and Italy, decided that the Ottoman occupation of Crete could not go on any longer, and they intervened to have Crete declared **an autonomous state.** Sixteen years later, in December of **1913,** Crete was united with Greece and the Greek flag was raised at the fortress, on the western bastion at the entrance of the harbour where it can still be seen.

The extensive damage caused by so many wars and the endless recycling of building materials have wiped out the traces of the earlier periods of the town's history. From the Minoan Kidonia we have nothing but the scant ruins of a few houses and some clay tablets with writing in Linear A and Linear B. But the Minoan palace that undoubtedly stood in this place has not yet been found. The buildings and artefacts of the Minoan culture lie deep within the ground, below the foundations of modern-day homes, and they are inaccessible to the archaeologists. As for the priceless treasures of the Minoan palace, they may be right under your feet or the bed you are sleeping on...

The town's recent history, however, has yielded a lot more, and that, despite the extensive damages the town suffered. And even though it was bombarded by the Nazis in the second world war and the largest part of the old town was destroyed, there are still many buildings from the Venetian and Turkish occupation that have survived. Most of these buildings were maintained in very good condition, and today they house museums, bars, restaurants, hotels and public services. On the other hand, many old homes are still lived in. The Venetian harbour and the old town behind it, the narrow streets and the tall mansions, all create a feeling of nostalgia that takes the visitor many centuries back.

Due to its strategic location, Hania was often claimed by many peoples and became a crossroads where different nations and cultures came in contact. It also was - and still is - an ideal base for the Great Powers, which wanted a strong presence in the Mediterranean. The streets and squares of the town were once filled with English, French, Italian and Russian sailors as well as with locals, foreign merchants, and travellers from all over the world. Today, in these same streets and squares walk thousands of tourists, who mingle with the locals and with the American pilots and marines of the Akrotiri NATO base. As for the corsairs (the blood-thirsty pirates), they have long disappeared from the Cretan seas. The only corsairs to be seen nowdays are the invincible A7-Corsairs of the Greek Air Force. They take off from the Souda airport, and as you lie on the beach you may suddenly see them flying just above your head...

The boat arrives at Hania - or rather, Souda - at 6:00 a.m. This gives you the chance to see the old town and its Venetian harbour **at the best possible moment,** when the sun rises over the hill, dyeing the proud mansions and the tranquil sea with a deep red colour.

Until about 10:00 or 11:00 a.m., the time that tourists begin to wake, the town has an enchanting, serene feeling about it. This is your best chance to get a taste of the daily life of the locals. For the best taste - metaphorically as well as literally - go to the **Town Market (46).** It is a closed cross-shaped gallery that houses over 70 food stores, among them many with fresh fruit produced locally. You will also find meat, dairy products, bread, legumes, and anything else you need. The Town Market was built in the beginning of the century, following the demolition of the main rampart at the south of the city wall and the filling of the moat before it with rubble. Behind it is a park with benches and some coffee shops favoured by the locals. After you are through with the market, you could come here and take a rest.

If you continue your walk to the east, you will find yourself in **Splatzia.** This was the Turkish quarter of the town and it still has many old

ROUTES STARTING FROM HANIA

homes. Its alleys have been turned into pedestrian zones, so you can take a good long stroll. Here you will also see a couple of Venetian churches, the one dedicated to St. Rokkos **(52)** and the other to St. Nicholas **(51)**. The latter was converted to a mosque, but from that mosque only the minaret survives - and not for long! It has a quite dangerous inclination, and it is bound to come down with the first strong earthquake, possibly on the head of an unsuspecting passer-by... The town authorities have put a protective fence on one of the side streets - which is far from being adequate - and did not bother to put any warning signs. (But be warned and do not ever park your bike around here!) In front of St. Nicholas is the small square of Splatzia, once filled with Turks who would enjoy their nargilehs under the shade of the tall trees (or of the Christians that were hung on them...)

By eleven o' clock the cafeterias in Santrivani Square and all around the Venetian harbour are full of tourists who have just woken up and are having their breakfast. The harbour cafeterias are the best place to enjoy a good breakfast and to watch some action. Their prices, though, are quite high. If you are looking for something tasty and inexpensive, try **Iordanis' cream-filled pastries** (boughàtsa). They are always fresh - if you are lucky you'll buy them right out of the oven - and you can find them in any of Jordan's three bougatsa shops **(11, 12, 13)** from 6:00 a.m. to 1:00 or 2:00 p.m. As for sandwiches, the best place to go is the **Cafe Chiao,** opposite the Archaeological Museum on Halidon street. They have great baguettes with fresh vegetables, and their outdoor tables will certainly invite you to watch the crowds while sipping a fresh juice or coffee.

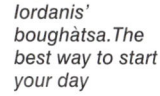

Iordanis' boughàtsa. The best way to start your day

By noon, the market looks very lively, especially on Halidon street and in the area around the Metropolis Square **(50)**. Try walking on **Skrindlof street;** it is very colourful and it has many small, inexpensive shops selling quality leather goods that are produced locally. Most merchants and small-time manufacturers in this area sell some very good things, but the "modern" and "tourist-catering" image which they try to project may end up working against them. Ignore the fancy display of goods and the tourist signs and look carefully on their shelves for the truly good folk art they produce. One of the interesting places is the **knife shop** of Apostolos Pahtikos on 14 Sifaka street.

THE CRETAN KNIFE

Apostolos Pahtikos has been making knives ever since he was thirteen. Fifty years now, he holds a chisel and a file in his hands and carves with superb mastery the bone and the horn out of which his knife handles are made.

He is in no hurry. He takes the horn softly and caresses it, as if it were alive. He sings to it. He ponders with which blade to make the match. And when he finds it, a slow ritual starts, which will eventually turn the hard material into a beautifully carved handle, a perfect match for the sharp steel blade.

His shop is a tiny hole, the customers are few, and time has stopped in the past. He sits there surrounded by a microworld of his own: a small furnace; a wheel; a vice; a counter with the tools for his work; an old wooden chest of drawers filled with knives in every shape and size; and a small window-case where the finest samples of his work are exhibited, real jewels made of bone, horn and steel. Indifferent to the tourist craze around him, old Apostolos pauses for a moment to watch the people rushing outside his door, and then he picks up his artwork and hums softly:

> "If you are five, go away
> And if you are ten, come close;
> Cause my Cretan knife blade
> Does not fear your approach..."

ROUTES STARTING FROM HANIA

Between 2:00 and 6:00 p.m. most tourists are at the beach, while many of the locals enjoy a good nap. The humming in the streets subsides for a few hours and everything seems peaceful. If you don't take a nap yourself or go to the beach, you can spend these hours visiting the town's museums; they are less crowded at this time and they also protect you from the scorching heat outside.

The **Archaeological Museum of Hania (47)** is closed on Monday and open Tuesday through Friday from 8:00 a.m. to 5:00 p.m. and Saturday and Sunday from 8:00 a.m. to 3:00 p.m. The building where it's housed is a sight in itself! It is an old Franciscan monastery, possibly built in the beginning of the 16th century, but it is the most important religious edifice to this day. In the course of the last few centuries this monastery had a history that was anything but dull! In 1645, the Turks converted it to a mosque (one can still see the foundations of the minaret and the beautiful Turkish fountain in the inner courtyard). In 1913 the Greeks converted it to a theatre and a movie house! In 1941 the Germans converted it to an ordnance depot (which they fortunately spared when they left the town). Then the building was left to its fate until 1968, when it was finally turned into a museum after undergoing extensive maintenance work. The museum houses a rich collection of archaeological findings from the area, dating from the Neolithic age to the Roman times. The most impressive exhibits are the Roman mosaic floors of the 3rd century AD, some classical statues, samples of Minoan pottery, and **clay tablets with writing in Linear A and Linear B.** Inside the museum you will find some very informative material including photographs of exhibits.

Just opposite the archaeological museum is a "live museum" where a rare, age-old tradition is practised. It is the **church-bell foundry** of the Papadakis family, housed - for a short while yet - in a building that once was a Turkish Bath.

The **Maritime Museum (48)** is open daily from 10:00 a.m. till 4:00 p.m. It is a small but interesting museum at the Venetian harbour and it has a rich collection of exhibits. You will see miniatures of warships, old navigation instruments, old pictures, an interesting representation of the Venetian town, and a sizeable collection of sea shells.

GOD'S VOICE

It is three generations now that the Papadakis family has been making bells for the churches and chapels of Greece. Nikos Papadakis learned the trade from his father, Apostolos, who learned it from his own father, Stelios.

"My grandpa went to Trieste in 1890 and picked up the trade. In 1903 he came back and started a foundry of his own in a historical building on 35 Halidon street, where the Turkish women had their bath. He chose it because the holes in its roof were very convenient for the furnace. Our foundry is still housed in this building..."

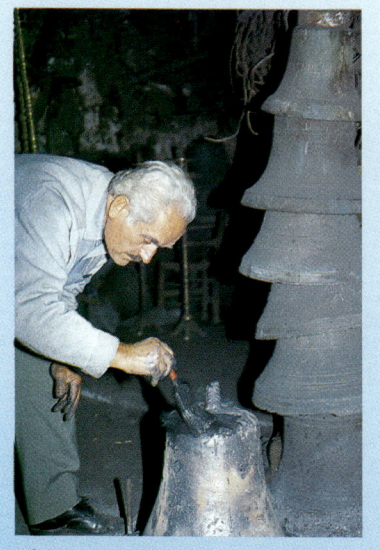

As you enter the foundry of the Papadakis family, you find yourself suddenly stepping into the past, at the beginning of the century. The furnace, the coke, the sooty walls, the equally sooty faces, the dirt floor, the primitive tools, everything reminds of times long gone. In the small furnace that is responsible for the tremendous heat of the room, the copper and the bronze mix in a secret ratio, a well-kept family secret that determines the "voice" of the bell, **"the voice of God,"** as Grandpa used to say.

Then the heated material is poured into the *mothélo*, the mould that gives the bell its shape, and it takes a solid form. "Solid," that is, only as regards the object. Because every time the bell sounds, it melts back into a flowing current, one that spreads over hills and valleys and fills the air with the same always devout call.

Grandpa Stelios' technique was improved by his son, Apostolos, and now his grandson, Nikos, is preparing a "modern" foundry of his own, just a short distance from the town. Life goes on with an ever-renewed face and tradition is slowly fading into history...

ROUTES STARTING FROM HANIA

Behind the Koundourioti Coast (*Aktì Koundouriòti*) is the heart of the **old town.** It is here that people come in the early evening, when they want to take a walk or eat something after a day at the beach. Zambeliou, Theotokopoulou, Angelou and Kondylaki are the nicest streets in the area, lined with old houses that have been turned into hotels, bars and restaurants. Of these, the **Renier Mansion** on Moschon street is the most interesting example. It was built in the early 15th century to house a Venetian family and today its surviving inner courtyard has been turned into a restaurant (SULTANA'S), where you can enjoy a delicious meal. Also surviving is the door with the Latin inscription and the Renier coat of arms as well as the family chapel which is dedicated to St. Nicholas.

A little later in the evening people begin to gather around the paved **Koundourioti Coast** and the **Tombazi Coast** (*Aktì Tombàzi*). As they stroll along the waterfront, they meet each other and exchange ideas for the night, then groups are formed and the evening plans are fixed. The action continues until the early morning hours, concentrated mainly around the western part of Koundourioti Coast with its many bars and discos and around **Enosseos Coast** at the eastern side of the harbour.

The town's **beaches** are all to the **west.** Most of them are sandy and clean, but of course you must not expect to find any isolated spots. They are literally covered with deck chairs and umbrellas and surrounded by countless hotels and restaurants and many businesses involving sea sports. If you are not bothered by crowds and development, you can enjoy a cool and clean sea and try your hand at canoeing, skiing or surfing.

The **municipal beach** of Hania is about a ten-minute walk to the west of the town (just take the street that starts behind the Maritime Museum). It has showers, cafeterias and restaurants, and of course it is the first beach to be filled with people. No time is too early to find it packed.

A little further lies the beach of **Aghii Apostoli**, which is also sandy and nice. However, it, too, is full of people, and you may feel as crowded as if you'd taken the bus during rush hour!

Your best choice is **Chrissi Akti** (Golden Coast), located 3.2 miles to the right of Square 1866, right after the EKO gas station. It is a beautiful sandy beach and large enough to accommodate the crowds.

The sea in the Hania area hides some

impressive reefs with very interesting marine life. If you would like to explore it together with the most experienced guides in Hania, contact **Blue Adventures Diving (32)** and ask for Spyros Papakastrissios.

In case of trouble with your motorcycle, you should be aware of the following: In Hania you will find agencies of YAMAHA **(27)**, KAWASAKI and PIAGGIO **(28)**, HONDA **(29)**, SUZUKI, DUCATI and CAGIVA **(30)** with authorised service stations and a large stock of genuine parts. Any spare parts not already available can be brought from Athens in a matter of 24 hours. In addition, there are four service stations for any type of motorcycle **(21, 22, 23, 24)**, a shop for electrical repairs **(25)** and a shop with accessories **(26)**.

If you need any help with service stations, or if you'd simply like to meet an interesting group of people, contact ΛΕΜΟΠΕΧ (*Lemopèch*), the Motorcycle Club of Hania **(31)**. Giorgos Roumbedakis, Argyris Karabinakis, Eftyhis Nikolouzakis, Antonis Karakis and the rest of the guys will be happy to meet you and give you any assistance you need. Members meet every Monday and Wednesday evening at about 8:30 p.m.

Contrary to what you will see in most maps and guides, the EOT (GNTO) information centre **is not** at the old Turkish Baths of the Venetian harbour.

Hania: A magical world awaits you at the bottom of the sea

Since 1992, it is on Kriari street **(36)**, next to Square 1866. Here you can be advised on where to stay and what to see and you can pick up information on the schedules of boats, planes and buses.

If you are more interested in the town of Hania, though, we suggest you contact the Town Information Centre **(37)**. Irini Michailakaki, who is

ROUTES STARTING FROM HANIA

there to help you, is also a member of the Hania Mountain Climbing Club (EOS Hanion), and she can provide you with info on hiking and mountain climbing expeditions as well.

EOS Hanion **(33)** is a very active club with 500 members and three refuges at the most beautiful sites of the White Mountain range. The members are very knowledgeable on the Cretan peaks and gorges and they can give you all the information you need. Offices are open from 8:30 p.m. to 11:00 p.m. and anyone who is a member of the international mountain-climbing family is very welcome. If you wish to participate in one of the club's organised expeditions ask for the schedule they publish every three months and let them know in advance. Information on the European Walk Path **(E4)** can be obtained from Stavros Badogiannis, who helped to mark it and knows it like his backyard.

WHERE TO STAY

Hania is by far the most picturesque town in Crete and yet it is the least crowded by tourists. This may be due to the fact that it is far from the major tourist attractions of Crete such as the Minoan palaces of Knossos and Faistos. However, the town is capable of accommodating large crowds - there are thousands of rented rooms and about a hundred hotels inside Hania as well as on the west coast - and even in the month of August you won't be left without a place to stay. If you wish to rent a room, there are some **wonderful traditional pension houses around the harbour,** but of course during the high season they are full and very expensive and there is a lot of noise from the bars close to them. (However, in early spring and fall, a time when Crete is quite warm, these same places are half-empty and will give you a room for half the price!) Another option is to find a room somewhere in the suburbs, where the prices are generally lower and the environment more quiet and where you also stand a chance of finding a courtyard for your bike. As for the large hotels, those inside the town are few and rather old and usually without garages, so you had better look for one a little further away. On the other hand, there are some very nice hotels just west of town, recently built and well looked after. Most of them are near the beach, offer peace and quiet, and have a safe place to park your bike. Finally, for those that prefer to camp, there is a camping ground about three kilometres west of Hania, and a second, much better one, at the Aghia Marina beach, about eight kilometres west of town.

BOZZALI, Pension
Class A. Open April -October.
7 rooms.
5 Gavaladon and Sifaka
Tel. (0821) 50 525
A little diamond in the quiet pedestrian streets in the heart of the old Turkish quarter. It is an old mansion, very well preserved and tastefully furnished. Next to the entrance there is a parking area for your bike.

CONTESSA, Pension
Class A. Open March - October.
6 rooms.
12 Theophanous St.,
Iel. (0821) 57 437

PANDORA, Suites
Class A. Open all year round.
11 rooms.
29 Lithinon St.,
Old Town of Hania
Tel. (0821) 43 589, Fax (0821) 55 213
A well preserved mansion, built on top of the Kasteli hill and having **the best view of the harbour.** Luxury rooms named after the ancient gods, wooden ceilings, bathroom, kitchen, sitting-room and large beds.
Best room: "Aphrodite"

AMPHORA, Pension
Class A. Open all year round.
20 rooms.
20 Theotokopoulou St.,
Old Town of Hania
Tel. / Fax (0821) 93 224
Built in 1300 (and kept in excellent condition), this pension has many Turkish and Venetian elements. Every room is different in size, furniture and equipment, but they all share the same classy quality. The rooms of the third floor have a wonderful view of the Venetian harbour.
Best room: No 7

KIDON, Hotel
Class A. Open all year round.
113 rooms.
Agora Square
Tel. (0821) 52 280, Fax (0821) 51 790

PORTO VENEZIANO, Hotel
Class B. Open March - October.
59 rooms.
Akti Enosseos
Tel. and Fax. (0821) 59 311

IRIDA, Hotel
Class B. Open all year round.
18 rooms.
8 Dekemvriou and Eleftheriou Venizelou
Tel. (0821) 51 888, Fax (0821) 46 060

NOSTOS, Studios
Class B. Open all year round.
12 rooms.
40 - 42 Zambeliou St.,
Old Town of Hania
Tel. (0821) 94 740, Fax (0821) 54 502
An old mansion, built in the year 1400 and kept in excellent condition. Independent studios consisting of different levels - the beds are on the upper level - and having a kitchen, bathroom and telephone. The ones at the front side of the house have a great view of the harbour
Best room: No 3 .

ARKADI, Hotel
Class B. Open all year round.
61 rooms.
Square 1866
Tel. (0821) 92 801, Fax (0821) 94 031

XENIA, Hotel
Class B. Open all year round.
44 rooms.
Firka Area,
Old Town of Hania
Tel. (0821) 91 238

ROUTES STARTING FROM HANIA

THERESA, Pension
Class B. Open April - October.
10 rooms.
8 Angelou St.,
Old Town of Hania
Tel. (0821) 92 798
A wonderful old three-storey house with a lot of character. Old objects, a wooden staircase that creaks under your feet, and cosy rooms with a very warm feeling about them. The furniture is beautiful and the beds have their own little nook on the upper level of the rooms.

CASA DELFINO, Apartments
Class B. Open all year round.
12 apartments.
9 Theophanous St.,
Old Town of Hania
Tel. (0821) 93 098, Fax (0821) 96 500

VILLA ANDROMEDA, Apartments
Class B. Open all year round.
8 apartments.
150 Eleftheriou Venizelou
Tel. (0821) 45 263, Fax (0821) 45 265

SAMARIA, Hotel
Class B. Open all year round.
59 rooms.
Square 1866
Tel. (0821) 71 271, Fax (0821) 71 270

APTERA BEACH, Bungalows
Class C. Open April - October.
46 rooms.
Aghii Apostoli Beach
Tel. (0821) 91 110, Fax (0821) 92 672
A recently built complex, quiet, well looked after and with a safe parking area for your bike. It is close to a very nice beach which, however, is too crowded.

OMALOS, Hotel
Class C. Open all year round.
36 rooms.
71 Kidonias St.
Tel. (0821) 95 215, Fax (0821) 98 510

ZEPOS, Hotel
Class C. Open all year round.
18 rooms.
29 Manoussou Koundourou St.,
Tel.(0821) 44 921, Fax (0821) 44 923

DHOMA, Hotel
Class B. Open March - October.
29 rooms.
124 Eleftheriou Venizelou
Tel. (0821) 51 772, Fax (0821) 41 578

CAMPING AGHIA MARINA
8 km west of Hania, next to the Aghia Marina beach.
Open April through October.
10,000 m^2, 80 spaces.
The south end of the camping has very few trees and a lot of noise, because it is next to the road that goes along the coast. The north end of it, though, is a true paradise. Situated next to a beautiful sandy beach opposite of the historical island of Thodorou, it is full of eucalyptuses and palm trees that give a nice shade. The thick grass and the serenity of the place also add to its charm.

CAMPING HANIA
3 km west of Hania on the way to Kasteli Kissamou.
Open April through October.
10,000 m^2 (or about 2.5 acres), 50 spaces.
The camping is usually full from the beginning of the tourist season. It is very close to Chrissi Akti (Golden Coast) and, although rather small, it is quite attractive, offers peace and quiet, and has plenty of olive trees for shade.

WHERE TO EAT

One of the greatest pleasures Hania has to offer is good food in restaurants "with character." Most taverns and restaurants have been around for several years and they have established a good reputation among the local "connoisseurs." Some of them are housed in old Venetian mansions, which create a very special ambience and somehow make the food taste better! The only restaurants it would be good to avoid are the tourist traps at the harbour, which you can distinguish by their fancy front and "predatory" waiters. The food they serve may sometimes be good, but their prices are always too high.

There are also many good taverns outside the town. These are generally favoured by the locals, because they are not addressed to tourists and they do not have the tourist prices of most restaurants in the town centre. Most of them are quite typical and very simply decorated - sometimes with bad taste, too - but they have the family atmosphere, tasty food and friendly service that go with any good Greek tavern.

PALATSO
36 Sourmeli St., Venetian harbour.
The best ouzo bar in Hania. It has many brands of ouzo and a great variety of snacks.

HIPPOPOTAMUS
A young people's hang-out among the busy coffee bars of Sarpidonos street. Tasty spaghetti and pizzas made with imagination.

SULTANA'S
2 Moschon St., Old Town.
Housed in an old Venetian mansion of the 15th century, SULTANA'S is a pricey but very good restaurant with tables in a quiet inner courtyard.

MATHIOS
3 Akti Enosseos, Venetian harbour.
The oldest fish-tavern in town. Great variety of fresh fish, done on the coals or fried. Try the broiled cuttlefish with the olives and fennel and the famous sea-urchin salad.

THOLOS
36 Aghion Deka St.
A good restaurant, housed in (what is left of) an old historical building. Excellent fillets, steaks cooked to order and many traditional specialties.

ANDREAS TSALIKIS
Terma Selinou, Nea Chora Hanion.
The best fish-tavern of Hania, situated at the western end of the town, right next to the sea. Great variety of fresh seafood, but also meat, salads, and a good selection of wines. **It is favoured by the locals.**

TAMAM
49 Zambeliou St., Old Town.
One of the most popular restaurants in Hania, housed in what used to be the Turkish Baths. Specialties: Vegetable patties, zucchini croquettes, soups, baked aubergines with feta cheese. If you want to find a table, go early.

ROUTES STARTING FROM HANIA

KALINTERIS
Akti Papanikoli, Nea Chora Hanion.
A restaurant at the western end of town with a great variety of dishes. However, you could easily satisfy your hunger with only the appetisers. Try the traditional pies, the stuffed potato, the Sphakian dish, the Sphakian honey pie and the wine that is drawn from the barrel.

ELA
47 Kondylaki St.
A nice restaurant housed in an old Venetian mansion without a ceiling... Casserole dishes and steaks cooked to order. Live Greek music.

KARNAGIO
8 Katechaki Square, Venetian harbour.
The locals think it may be the best restaurant in town. It has traditional Cretan cuisine and its specialties are the Cretan *bourèki* (a kind of small pie), the *skaltsoùnia* or turnovers (small pastries with dough made with almonds), and the sea-urchin salad.

KRONOS
A simple pastry shop at the west corner of the Town Market. Though it may not catch your eye, it serves the most wonderful loukoumàdes (bite-size donuts covered in honey).

MONTERNO
9 Tzanakaki St.
A take-away pastry shop. Though there are no tables, the ice creams are the best in town. Recommended: chocolate or caramel parfait and caramel cake.

APOKORONAS
Apokoronou St.
A barbecue house that caters to the most demanding clientele. Juicy steaks, mouth-watering lamb chops and good wine drawn from the barrel.

WATERPOOL
Opposite the Hania Swimming-Pool.
A student hang-out with huge, tasty, inexpensive souvlàki for starving folks.

TARTUFFO
16 Iroon Politechniou
Probably the best pizza parlour in Hania, Tartuffo is also known for its very tasty fillets and great variety of pasta dishes.

West of Hania, on the way to Kasteli:

STAVRODROMI
On the Stalos intersection.

DIOGENIS
In the village Platanias.

MYLOS
Also in Platanias.
Very good tavern at a pleasant country site. In its yard there is a little creek with ducks. Excellent service.

EFTYHIA
In the town of Kolimvari.
Cretan specialties. Try the *skaltsoùnia* and the meat pies.

ARGENTINA
Also in Kolimvari.
The best fish-tavern in the area with a great variety of seafood.

South of Hania, on the way to Omalos:

PANORAMA
In the village Malaxa.
The name says it all; it has the best view of Hania and the surrounding valley.

BIGAZA
5 km south of Hania, in the village Galatas.
It has traditional dishes of Constantinople, often with a hot taste and lots of spices. Specialty: **ghiaourtloù** (skewered pork meat with yoghurt and red sauce). The people of Hania often like to come here.

KOULOURIDIS
4 km south of Hania, in the village Vamvakopoulo.
Excellent Greek cuisine, fresh salads, very good meat done on the coals.

ENTERTAINMENT
Hania offers so many opportunities for quality entertainment that even if you stay until the end of your vacation you cannot possibly exhaust them all. The old town is full of bars, which may vary in size, but are always nicely decorated and have great music. It is hard to say which are the best ones, which is why people like to visit three or four of them every evening! After midnight the action continues in the large discos along the beach west of Hania.

FAGOTO
Housed in an old Venetian building at the harbour, it is the oldest bar in Hania, a small place with a lot of character. It is very tastefully decorated and plays soft jazz-rock music.

SANTE
A coffee bar in Akti Koundourioti. Nice environment, rock music, young clientele, a very good place for an afternoon coffee.

FOUR SEASONS
The best rock music in Hania, in an excellently preserved old building at the harbour.

TUTTI FRUTI
8 km south of Hania, in the village Aghia. An open-air disco-bar with a large swimming pool, cocopalms, loud dancing music and frequent strip shows. It stays open later than any other disco.

STREET
Situated in the harbour area. The owner, Giorgos Kanatakis, has a street bike (a Harley), but he welcomes all motorcyclists! Rock music.

PLAZA
A new dancing club at the Venetian harbour, very large and with loud dancing music.

DYO LOUX
A coffee bar on Sarpidonos street and a favourite hang-out of the young people of Hania for at least ten years. It has the best coffee in town and 20 different kinds of tea.

ANAGENNISIS
The largest disco bar in town. It is housed in an old harbour warehouse that is in excellent condition. Loud techno music, impressive light effects, explosive atmosphere.

MELTEMI
A coffee bar on a very convenient passage in Akti Koundourioti. There is a large parking area for your bike.

RUDY
24 Sifaka St.
The most exotic beer house in town. Though the place is small, it is run by a Belgian beer lover, Rudy, who brings from home an amazing variety of beers. Delicious snacks.

BABES IN 4/4
Aghii Apostoli, waterfront.
Loud trance music that attracts the budding youth of Hania, promising nights of wild dancing.

IDAION ANTRON
A nice hang-out on Halidon street with an inner courtyard.

TO AVGO TOU KOKORA
(The Cock's Egg)
On the corner of Aghion Deka and Sarpaki.
A restaurant-bar with a special ambience. Excellent pancakes, salads... made with imagination, and pleasant background music (jazz). Open all day long.

TZAMIA-KRYSTALLA
(Windows, Crystal)
35 Skalidi St.
The name alludes to the business that occupied the premises in the past. Two young people, Manoussos and Giorgos, turned the place into an art gallery, which includes a coffee shop with music.

SYNAGOGI
(The Synagogue)
15 Skoufon St.
Housed in a seventeenth-century Venetian building on the corner of Skoufon and Kondylaki (or rather a side street of Kondylaki), this cafe-restaurant offers a unique environment, the best rock music and delightful coffee. Since the German bombs at WWII turned it into... an open-air place, you can enjoy your meal and look at the stars above.

MYLOS
In Platanias.
The... temple of dancing and western music, MYLOS features a fascinating environment. Swimming pool with bar, palm trees, cool nights.

TO MIKRO KAFE
(Little Cafe)
6 Akti Miaouli
True to its name, this cosy little place features a nice ambience, walls covered with old advertising posters, magazines, newspapers, and great hot chocolate.

HANIA

LEGEND

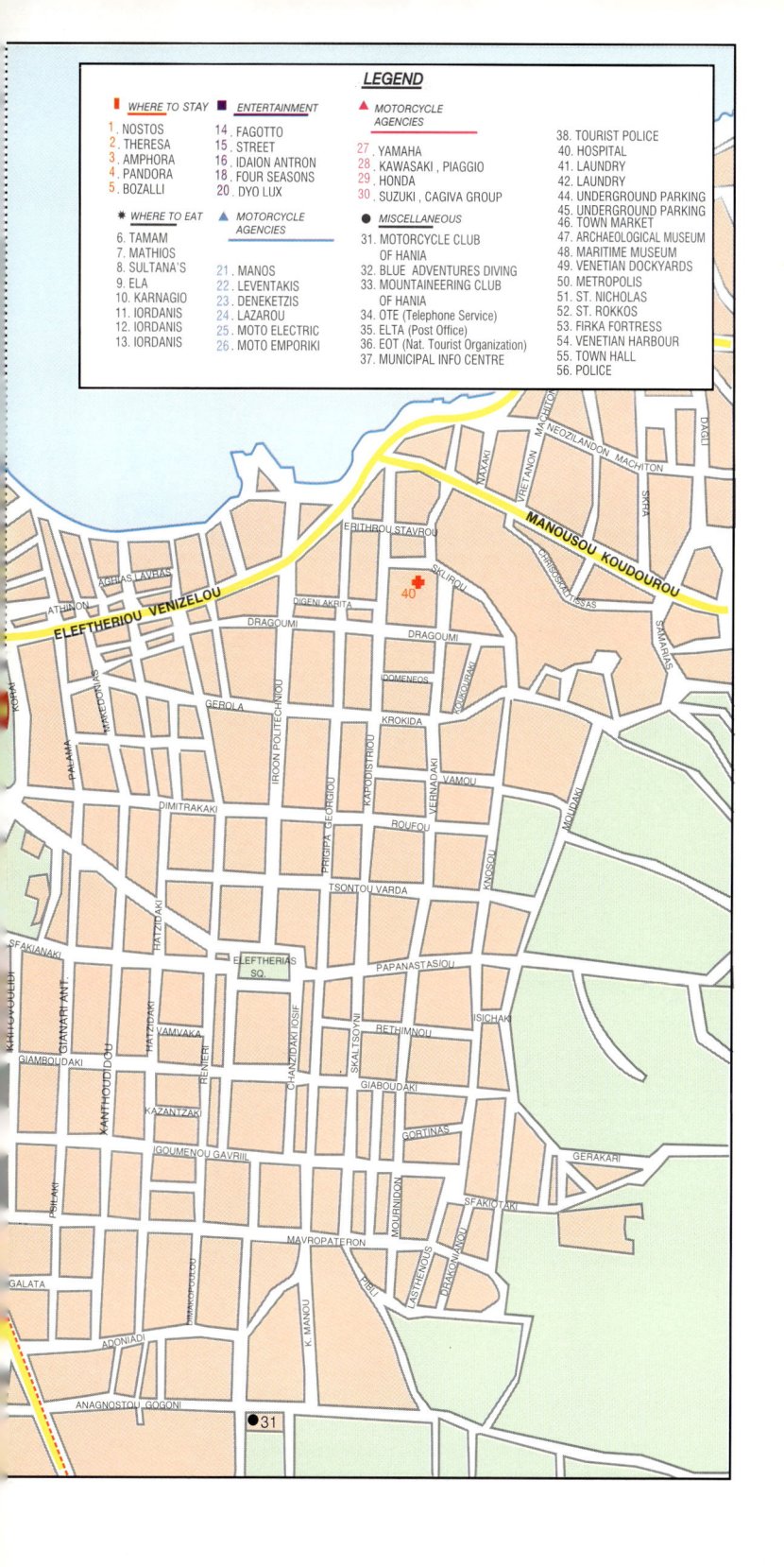

WHERE TO STAY
1. NOSTOS
2. THERESA
3. AMPHORA
4. PANDORA
5. BOZALLI

WHERE TO EAT
6. TAMAM
7. MATHIOS
8. SULTANA'S
9. ELA
10. KARNAGIO
11. IORDANIS
12. IORDANIS
13. IORDANIS

ENTERTAINMENT
14. FAGOTTO
15. STREET
16. IDAION ANTRON
18. FOUR SEASONS
20. DYO LUX

MOTORCYCLE AGENCIES
21. MANOS
22. LEVENTAKIS
23. DENEKETZIS
24. LAZAROU
25. MOTO ELECTRIC
26. MOTO EMPORIKI

MOTORCYCLE AGENCIES
27. YAMAHA
28. KAWASAKI, PIAGGIO
29. HONDA
30. SUZUKI, CAGIVA GROUP

MISCELLANEOUS
31. MOTORCYCLE CLUB OF HANIA
32. BLUE ADVENTURES DIVING
33. MOUNTAINEERING CLUB OF HANIA
34. OTE (Telephone Service)
35. ELTA (Post Office)
36. EOT (Nat. Tourist Organization)
37. MUNICIPAL INFO CENTRE
38. TOURIST POLICE
40. HOSPITAL
41. LAUNDRY
42. LAUNDRY
44. UNDERGROUND PARKING
45. UNDERGROUND PARKING
46. TOWN MARKET
47. ARCHAEOLOGICAL MUSEUM
48. MARITIME MUSEUM
49. VENETIAN DOCKYARDS
50. METROPOLIS
51. ST. NICHOLAS
52. ST. ROKKOS
53. FIRKA FORTRESS
54. VENETIAN HARBOUR
55. TOWN HALL
56. POLICE

1. Hania - Akrotiri

ROUTES STARTING FROM HANIA

The Akrotiri region is a flat peninsula east of Hania with a hill at its eastern side (528 metres high). If you are interested in the beauty that nature has to offer, you won't find much to see in Akrotiri. The entire area is cultivated and spoilt by the presence of a military airport and a NATO missile launching base. This is also where the dreary cement buildings of the Hania University campus are located as well as some factories and a number of country houses randomly built all over the place.

If you wish to swim, again this is not the best place to come, because Akrotiri has very few good beaches. The most charming sandy beach is at **Kalathas,** but it is surrounded by many Rooms to Let, Hotels, taverns etc.

A second beach, tiny but sandy, is that of **Tersanas**, which has much fewer buildings around it and is much more quiet. Only a hundred metres from the beach you can find the Studios to Let "Alianthos." These make a very cosy place to stay, as they are surrounded by many trees, offer peace and quiet, and have balconies with an exquisite view and sheltered parking. Nearby you will find a nice tavern.

A third beach, the largest of Akrotiri, is also sandy and lies west of **Stavros.** However, only a hundred metres behind the beach - and right over your heads - there is a huge military radar, which is not only disturbing but may also pose a threat to your health. The village itself consists of many large country houses, a few huts, and a couple of taverns featuring plastic tents, plastic chairs and plastic signs. The small sandy beach of the village must have been quite beautiful a century ago, but today it's covered with plastic deck chairs.

Still, **a few of the most beautiful monasteries of Crete** are located in Akrotiri and it's worth making a trip just to see them.

The **St. Trinity Giagarolo monastery** is perhaps the most impressive monastery of Crete. It was named after its founders, **Jeremiah and Lavrentio Giagarolo,** two brothers from a wealthy Venetian family who had converted to Orthodoxy. As they faced problems with other monks, perhaps because they were ex Catholics, wealthy, handsome and young, they decided to leave the monastery of Aghios Ioannis (see further ahead) where they

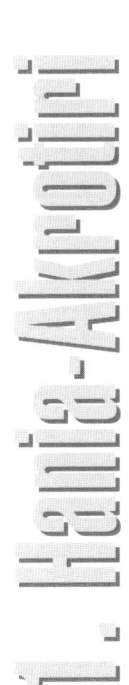

The Giagarolo monastery

were leading their ascetic life and to move a few kilometres to the south, where they built their own monastery to avoid being disturbed! They had money, courage and faith, so nothing was lacking. And since they were going to build a monastery, they decided to do it right. One of the brothers, Jeremiah, dashed to the Holy Mount Athos to bring the best architectural designs he could find, while Lavrentio started gathering stones and other building materials. Construction began in **1612**, but the plans Jeremiah had brought were so ambitious that 30 years later the monastery still was not completed, despite the hard work they put into it from dawn till dusk. And then, in **1645**, appeared our dear friends, the Ottoman Turks, who had the bad habit of entertaining themselves by burning monasteries and slaughtering monks. During a rare moment of generosity the Turks pitied the two monks and decided to spare the monastery. They didn't burn it, but they didn't allow its completion either, so our poor Giagarolo brothers had to pray in a domeless church, in direct contact with Heaven above! Their prayers, and those of the monks that lived after them, were granted two centuries later when, in **1834,** after a grand dinner given by the monks, the Turkish lord of the region allowed them to build the dome and to complete the construction of the monastery. In the same year, the British explorer **Robert Pashley** visited the place and was impressed by its wealth and exquisite wine.

The monastery church is of Byzantine style, and it is dedicated to the Holy Trinity. It has an impressive front, a high bell-tower (built in 1864), and two chapels, one dedicated to the Zoodochos Pigi (The Source of Life) and the other to Ioannis Theologos. Most of the monastery cells are locked, and the buildings are in desperate need of maintenance, but they have kept their grandeur intact. Inside the church you will find some beautiful wall paintings, but they cover only part of the church.

The surrounding landscape is also very beautiful. A thick olive grove (where you can comfortably camp) spreads around the monastery, while the road leading to its gate is lined with tall cypress trees.

A Gr/E sign outside the monastery directs you to the **Gouverneto monastery** in the north. For the first five hundred metres the road (D1) goes through the olive groves, then it ascends (A4) through a landscape full of rocks and bushes, passes through a beautiful small **gorge**, and ends at a small plateau where the monastery is located. Its pale earthy colours blend perfectly with the savage beauty of the desert landscape. The road to this place was built in 1980, and it has definitely had an impact on its serenity.

Above the main monastery entrance an excerpt from the Mathew gospel has been inscribed:

"ΣΤΕΝΗ Η ΠΥΛΗ ΚΑΙ ΤΕΘΛΙΜΜΕΝΗ Η ΟΔΟΣ Η ΑΠΑΓΟΥΣΑ ΕΙΣ ΤΗΝ ΖΩΗΝ"

(Narrow and sorrowful is the path leading to the afterlife)

The monastery was built by monks of the Aghios Ioannis monastery (see further ahead) for whom the "path leading to the afterlife" was very "sorrowful" indeed. As if the sacrifices and suffering of the ascetic lifestyle were not enough, pirates made things even worse. So at some point in time - nobody knows exactly when but most researchers place it during the first years of the Venetian rule - the monks abandoned their monastery and moved to a safer place in the south, where they built a true **monastery - fort!** This was surrounded by a thick rectangular wall, 40 x 50 metres, whose four corners feature square towers with embrasures and scorchers. Scorchers were particularly useful for the

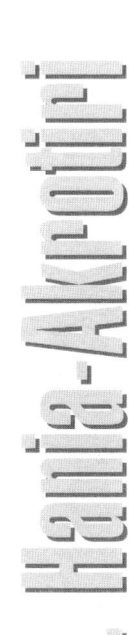

The Gouverneto monastery

Gouverneto monastery, sculpture decorating the front of the church

defence of the place, since boiling water could be poured on the attacking enemy!

In the centre of the monastery yard stands the church, dedicated to **the Mistress of the Angels**, the Virgin Mary. Its front is very impressive, decorated with sculpted monster heads of Venetian craftsmanship. There are also two chapels, one dedicated to St. John the Hermit, founder of the Aghios Ioannis monastery, and the other to the "Aghii Deka" (The Holy Ten). Unfortunately, there is very little to see inside the church, because all the valuable relics and icons were destroyed in 1821, when the barbaric Turks burned the monastery down and butchered the monks. Today only two monks live at the monastery and they are only threatened by the hundreds of tourists that arrive here daily, in July and August... If, however, you visit the monastery in the spring or autumn, you will feel most welcome. **The monastery is closed daily from noon till 3 p.m.**

From the Gouverneto monastery a path leaves to the north and enters an impressive and majestic gorge called Avlaki. After about a half-hour walk you will arrive at the abandoned Aghios Ioannis monastery, better known as **Moni Katholikou**. Built during the

ROUTES STARTING FROM HANIA

6th or 7th century on a steep gorge side in the heart of the rough-looking landscape of Akrotiri, Moni Katholikou is probably **the oldest monastery of Crete.** Its founder is allegedly none other than **St. John the Hermit,** who spent his life in this area. The monastery church is carved into the rock, and only the western side is made of stone. An imposing stone bridge about 50m long and 15m wide extends in front of the monastery, uniting the two gorge sides at a height of 30 metres. This bridge also serves as the monastery's yard.

In the early Christian era, and long before the monastery was built, the caves around it, still visible today in the steep sides of the ravine, were inhabited by hermits. In the largest of these (which has a depth of 135 metres) St. John the Hermit spent a life of seclusion and passed away quietly. Its 2 x 1.8-metre opening is situated at the left of the monastery church, and it can be easily explored with a good torch.

If you wish to explore the area even further, you can continue after the bridge and follow the rough path, which after twenty minutes will take you to the rocky shore where the monastery's small harbour was once located. Though there is no sand to lie on, the water is crystal-clear, ideal for a quick dive.

If it's afternoon when you return to Hania, you can make a small detour at the western corner of Akrotiri (2-3 kilometres before you

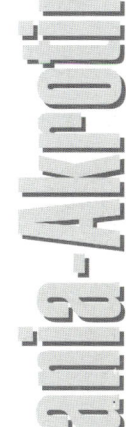

With such crystal-clear water, who needs sandy beaches?

1. Hania-Akrotiri

145

ELEFTHERIOS VENIZELOS

"...it's man that shapes the generation; the generation doesn't shape the man...."

Written about Eleftherios Venizelos, this folk Cretan serenade expresses perfectly the feelings of Greeks towards this leading Greek politician, who dedicated his life to the service of his country during the most critical phase of its recent history. Born in Mournies (just outside Hania) in 1864, he lived a troubled childhood full of revolts, wars, exiles and suffering. From a very young age he became involved in politics; at the tender age of 23 and shortly after graduating from the Law School of Athens, he was elected as a Member of Parliament representing the Kidonia district. It was the time that Crete was still under Turkish rule, but the Berlin treaty of 1878 (which followed a successful Cretan revolt) had forced the Sultan to allow Cretans to have their own parliament and to share extensive governing responsibilities. This was the first step of Eleftherios Venizelos in his long and extremely difficult political - and even armed, when needed - struggle for the liberation of Crete, Macedonia and Thrace from Turkish occupation and for their unification with the rest of Greece. The treaties of London, Bucharest, Neigy and Sevres, which consolidated Greece's borders as they are today, all bear his signature. Behind his accomplished diplomatic skills, his mastery of rhetoric, and his political insight and daring, lay a burning love for his homeland and his vision of a Greece so powerful that she could claim effectively what was rightfully hers, so grand as she was during the most glorious periods of her history, and so well governed as to become once more the model of a democratic and progressive country. He served repeatedly as Prime Minister of Greece and during his entire life he was the main protagonist of the nation's political arena. After his death in Paris in 1936, his body was carried over to Hania where the entire population turned up at the funeral. His grave at Akrotiri (lying next to that of his son, Sophocles) is a site of national pilgrimage.

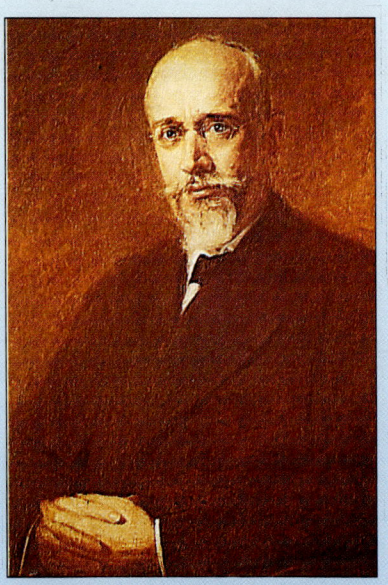

enter the town) and head for the **Profitis Ilias** hill, where you can enjoy the sunset and a wonderful view of the entire town and valley of Hania. This is also where the plain stone **graves of Eleftherios and Sophocles Venizelos** are located.

2. Hania-Paleochora

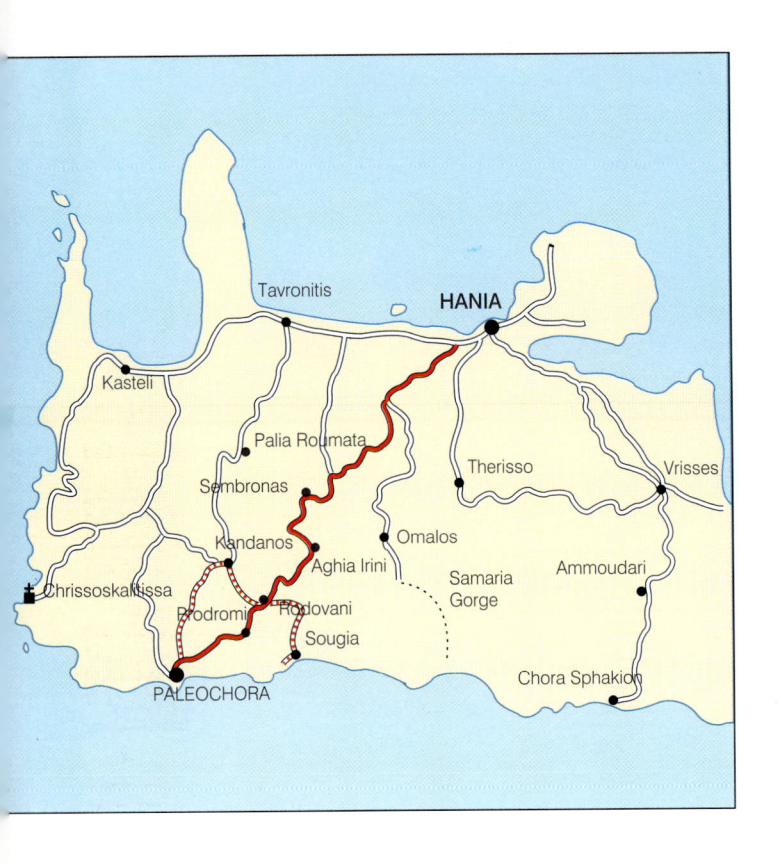

ROUTES STARTING FROM HANIA

2.1 HANIA - AGRILES

From Hania you head to the south, taking the road (A2) to **Omalos,** and after 13 kilometres you turn to the west (toward **Alikianos)**.

If you happen to be a beautiful Italian girl (especially from Venice) on the lookout for a suitable husband, you couldn't have come to a worse place on earth. About four centuries ago the beautiful Venetian princess **Sofia,** daughter of the local feudal lord **Francesco Da Molin,** was engaged to wed Petros, son of the Cretan rebel **Giorgos Kantanoleos.** This wedding took place at the initiative of the Kantanoleos family and was intended to reconcile the two enemy sides. But Francesco Da Molin considered this to be his best opportunity to get rid of his opponents once and for all. During the great feast following the wedding, he made sure that Kantanoleos and his three hundred men were so drunk with wine that they finally fell asleep. Then he gave a sign for a two-thousand-men Venetian army force to come unexpectedly from Hania. They caught the rebels and during the next few days they hanged them in the streets as a warning and a threat to the local people. After that the Cretans learned their lesson well: if you want to be a rebel, better forget about marriages and stay in hiding in the forests!

This tragic affair is the theme of a 17th century chronicle (the Trivan chronicle) and a 19th century novel (Cretan Marriages by Sp. Zambelios), and it seems to be based on historical facts. In the orchards outside Alikianos you can still find the ruins of the Da Molin castle. You can touch them but you cannot make them speak. Still, one of the stones, once found at the main entrance lintel, has an inscription with the moral of this story, a moral that may easily apply to any state of affairs:

OMNIA MUNDI FUMUS ET UMBRA
(Everything in the world is smoke and shadow)

This great truth was probably unknown to the young German parachutists who left the warmth of their wives and their grandmothers' delicious "Apfelkuchen" to land on this valley on the 21st of May, **1941,** armed to the teeth. This was the only form of sightseeing round the island that made them entirely unwelcome, when they could have simply come as tourists, archaeologists or merchants at any time they chose (and even bring the family along). The local people became furious and stormed the valley with knives, rakes,

The ruins of the Da Molin castle

old guns, relics of the revolution, whatever they could find. Still, the German Mausers proved to be superior. Most of the population of Alikianos was killed during the fighting, and those that survived were later executed... A monument has been erected in their memory just outside the village, close to the intersection with the main road.

Today Alikianos is again the lively country village it once was. Nested in the middle of a fertile valley, which is irrigated by Keritis - the ancient river Iardanos - and covered with orange and lemon trees, the village stands proud, pleasing the eye with its beautiful orchards. In the middle of these orchards, opposite the Da Molin castle, stands a Byzantine church, built in **1243** and dedicated to Aghios Georgios, which is worth visiting. Inside, the icons of the saints, painted by **Pavlos Provatas** in 1430, have been very well kept. Another Byzantine church with impressive arched gates and beautiful wall paintings undergoing maintenance is the church of **Ai-Kyrgianni**, to the north of Alikianos, five hundred metres before the village of Koufos.

After Alikianos you continue to the south, taking the road that crosses the Keritis valley with its vast orange tree plantations. You pass a large village called Skines, and you start climbing the smooth northwestern side of the White Mountains (**Lefkà Ori**). The vegetation of the area consists of olive, chestnut, and oak trees, and the villages are often small and half-ruined.

If you wish to enjoy a **dazzling mountain route** in the remote areas of Kidonia and Kissamos, turn to the west at the intersection with the Gr/E sign leading to Sembronas (you will see the

ROUTES STARTING FROM HANIA

The Byzantine church of Ai-Kyrgianni

intersection about two kilometres after Prasses). This route (D3/7km) will lead you one kilometre outside Kakopetros, while a sideroad (D3/11km) will take you to the north, to the village of Voukolies. Whichever way you choose, you can later continue southward and head for Paleochora, if you follow Route 9 (see page 226).

About three kilometres to the south of this intersection (and three kilometres before the village of Aghia Irini) there is another junction, allowing you to reach the Omalos plateau and the Samaria gorge. This road is asphalt-paved during the first kilometre (A2) and then becomes a passable country road (D1/8km). It takes you through the western side of peak Tourli (1458m), at an altitude of about one thousand metres, and it offers a startling view of the Hania Gulf, the Libyan sea and the White Mountain tops.

If walking the Samaria gorge seems too much for you, you have another opportunity to try your hiking abilities and to enjoy the savage beauty of the Cretan gorges. Just after the village of **Aghia Irini** you will find a fairly easy path, which is hard to miss. Stretching for about seven kilometres, this path goes through the fairly smooth **Aghia Irini gorge** and ends just north of Koustogerako. The hikers of the group could perhaps start their walk from Aghia Irini and the rest could continue on bike and wait for them at Koustogerako.

Finally, if you decide to forget about the gorges of Samaria and Aghia Irini - two very interesting side trips - and if you continue southwest instead, you will arrive at **Agriles,** a village 500m above sea level. Until recently, this village offered a great view of the White Mountains. Unfortunately,

2. Hania-Paleochora

though, a great forest fire, which broke out in August of 1994, destroyed the entire area south of Agriles (and all the way to Sougia) and nearly threatened to burn the Aghia Irini gorge. One kilometre to the south of Agriles, at a village called Rodovani, the road splits.

2.2 RODOVANI - SOUGIA

If you choose the eastern direction (toward Sougia), about 100 metres after the intersection you will see to your right a hill crowned with a church. Turn to the right on the narrow road that climbs the hill, and after a while you will arrive at the top, where once the ancient city of **Eliros** was situated.

The next village on your route is **Moni**, where you can visit the Byzantine church of Aghios Nikolaos with its beautiful wall paintings, among

ELIROS

However much you look around you, you will only find some traces of the ancient city. The couple of column drums, the few carved stones and the scattered pieces of ceramics make it difficult to believe that at this place stood the **largest city of the southwest of Crete in the classical times**. It was a city of 16,000 people and it became wealthy through... arms trade!

Eliros was famous for its quality bows, arrows, knives, catapults and other weapons, which it sold all over Crete. It also exported these weapons, and used for this purpose no less than three harbours, Lissos, Syia, and Pikilassos! At the same time, the townsfolk cultivated the fertile valley to the east and south of the city and kept bees. In fact, Eliros had become so wealthy that it minted its own coins on which the two symbols of its wealth were represented: on the one side an arrow in the side of a goat (although those who bought the arrows used them for other targets than goats) and on the other side a bee.

The homes of the ancient Elirians were luxurious and had a grand view of the Libyan sea to the south and the White Mountains to the east, as you will be able to see for yourself. But although these people were great arms merchants, they were not masters of the weapons themselves. As a result, they vanished from the face of the earth, probably as victims of the invasion of the Arabs who conquered the whole island during the early 9th century BC. Never has an archaeological excavation taken place on this hill and what remains of ancient Eliros probably lies some feet under the ground.

which the outstanding painting of St. Nicholas, the work of Ioannis Pagomenos.

About two kilometres to the south of **Moni** a road (A3) heads to the east, passes through Livadas, and ends at the legendary **Koustogerako**. If some members of the group have decided to walk through the Aghia Irini gorge this will be the best place to wait for them. As you enter the village you will see a **monument** dedicated to the memory of the tragic events that took place here during the second world war and to the heroic resistance of the local people. The Koustogerako people have a long tradition of rebellions and restlessness, and they fought hard against the Nazis (this is where the illustrious rebel Kantanoleos came from, see page 149). The Nazis surrounded the village but the armed men managed to escape. They left their women and children behind assuming the Nazis would not harm them, but they were totally wrong. Ten of these men, hidden behind a rock, witnessed how the Nazis gathered the women and children together in the village square and set up a machine gun. Still, the incredible cruelty did not make them lose their readiness; they aimed well and a few seconds later the machine gunner and another nine Nazis fell dead. Then they charged and chased them until Moni, killing and wounding many of them. The next day a more powerful Nazi death squad entered the deserted village and blew everything up. This was the fourth time that Koustogerako was reduced to ruins (it was twice before burned by the Venetians and once by the Turks), but the heroic Koustogerako people rebuilt it from scratch after the war was over.

Today, two *kafenia* are located at the beautiful village square, where you can enjoy a good cup of coffee and a great view of the White Mountains and the rock from which the Koustogerako fighters shot the Nazis. It's worth paying a visit to the small Byzantine church of Aghios Georgios at the edge of the village; it was built in the 10th century and has many impressive paintings of the 15th century made by **G. Provatopoulos.** If the hikers of the group have not shown up by now, it may be wise to start looking for them!

Two interesting mountain-hiking routes begin at Koustogerako. The most popular one, which takes five hours, heads to the northeast, continues smoothly and at a relatively low altitude (below

1000 metres) through the western side of Mount Psilafi, and ends at the small chapel in the western entrance to the Omalos plateau, at Seliniotikos Giros. The other route is more demanding (six hours) but far more interesting. It goes east passing through a gorge and suddenly gains height climbing the southern side of Mount Psilafi. After only eight kilometres from Koustogerako, the road has climbed 1200 metres, taking you to an altitude of 1700 metres at the Linosseli pass, the highest point of the route. Here you can enjoy a **dazzling view of the Libyan sea** and quench your thirst at a cool spring that refreshes the traveller all year round. After two kilometres of descending you will reach Xiloskalo at the beginning of the Samaria gorge. For both these routes it's advisable to request info and maps from the Hania Mountain Climbing Club (see map of Hania, **33**). Part of the second route, the first six kilometres, can be done on bike and will offer you the most enjoyable mountain ride in the area. The road (D3) passes through a forest and stops suddenly at a place with a beautiful view of the southern coast of Crete and the surrounding area.

If you return to Koustogerako on the central road and continue to the south, you will arrive after three kilometres at **Sougia**, a relatively new settlement built on the site where once the ancient city of **Syia** was located. In front of the village is a wide and beautiful pebbly beach, the cause of the tourist development in the area. Fortunately, only few hotels have been built here, but the buildings are randomly situated and many people have built homes only to rent rooms during the tourist season. It would be a good idea to make this quiet place your base for two or three days and to explore the region on foot or bike. You can walk to the west taking the seaside path to ancient Lissos (see further ahead) or you can take the boat to Aghia Roumeli and walk through the Samaria gorge (see page 172). If you decide to stay here, your best choices are the **Santa Irini Hotel** (Tel. 0823 - 51 342) and the **Lotos pension** (Tel. 0823 - 51 142) in front of the beach. There are plenty of other Rooms to Let and small hotels in Sougia, so you shouldn't have any trouble finding a room even during the high season. If, however, you wish to camp, you can set up your tent at the eastern side of the beach, at any place you choose. For your shopping we recommend the SOUGIA mini

ROUTES STARTING FROM HANIA

Lie on the most comfortable mattress: the pebbles at the Sougia beach.

market. Its owner, Giorgos Falagaris, is a member of the Hania Motorcycle club, has many stories to tell you about his adventures on his bike in Northern Africa, and will provide you with all the information you need about the Sougia area.

From ancient **Syia**, the seaport of Eliros that flourished during the Roman and early Byzantine time, very little has survived. This consists of a few wall ruins at the east corner of the beach and the floor mosaic of a 6th century basilica on which the village church was later built.

If you wish to enjoy an impressive hiking archaeological exploration in the footsteps of the famous British explorer of the 19th century **Robert Pashley,** just follow the path at the back of the Sougia harbour that heads to the west. You will pass through a beautiful gorge, reach the crest of the hill side, and finally descend toward the sea. After about one hour you will reach the ruins of the ancient city of **Lissos**.

Lissos used to serve as the port of Irtakina and Eliros and seems to have flourished from the classical times till the 10th century AD. Most of its inhabitants were sea merchants and fishermen, but the greatest source of wealth was...tourism! In fact, it was a curious form of tourism with a... clearly medical nature, since the **Asclepieion** of Lissos - a religious shrine of the healing god Asclepius with a famous healing water spring - attracted visitors from all over Crete. So wealthy was Lissos, it even minted its own **golden coins**.

The area was largely unexplored until 1957, although the position of the ancient city was known. That year one of the locals, wishing to find the source of the water, dug exactly on top of the sanctuary of Asclepius and found about

2. Hania - Paleochora

twenty statues portraying Asclepius, Hygeia, Pluto and a few devout patients. Fortunately, it was not an illicit dealer but a lover of antiquities, so he informed the Ephor of Antiquities of the island, Mr. Nikolaos Platonas, who immediately started an excavation of the area. This brought to light the Lissos Asclepieion with its **magnificent mosaic floors,** some graves dating from the Roman period, the foundations of houses and public baths, as well as traces of the aqueduct and the city theatre.

Except for the Asclepieion, it won't be easy to identify the other ruins of the ancient city, because not only have the excavations not been completed, but the place has been left to its fate as well; there

The rocky south shore where Lissos was built

is only one temporary guard, and by now thick bushes cover everything. If you walk through the rocks and bushes, you will find indications of ancient Lissos in each step you take. As for the statues our friend found some decades ago, you can see them exhibited in the museums of Hania and Iraklio.

The two Byzantine chapels of the 13th and 14th century that are built on top of two earlier basilicas (of the 4th or 5th century) are also worth seeing. The first, close to the guard's hut, is the chapel of **Ai-Kyrkou** (Aghios Kyriakos) with pale fading wall paintings. In this chapel Robert Pashley and his group spent the night of 27th April, 1834. The other, close to the shore rocks, is the chapel of the Virgin Mary, built with materials from an earlier time.

2.3 RODOVANI - PALEOCHORA

If you head west of Rodovani, after about a couple of kilometres you will find a very picturesque village called **Maza**. Make a stop here and visit the Byzantine church of Aghios Nikolaos, decorated with beautiful paintings that tell the story of the saint. These were made by **Ioannis Pagomenos,** the well known Cretan artist of the 14th century who combined the Byzantine icon-painting tradition with many elements of the local Cretan school.

After Maza continue west (toward the village of **Temenia**). The road goes through thick olive groves covering the hill sides, occasionally interrupted by vineyards that give a tasty red wine. Just before Temenia you will have to choose between two routes.

The first one is for street motorcycles and goes north toward **Kandanos** (A3). On your way there you will pass through a couple of charming villages, **Vamvakados and Anissaraki,** with three Byzantine churches, and you will cross some large olive groves and small fields with vegetables and vines.

The second option is for off-road motorcycles and allows you to reach Paleochora driving on a country road that offers beautiful scenery (D3). Turn left at the crossroads before Temenia and take the dirtroad going to Prodromi (you will see a Gr/E sign that says "Prodromi 6"). The steep rocky hill right in front of you was once the homeland of the **Irtakinians.**

Irtakina was an ancient town with an apparently great fear of enemies. In fact, it was more like a military camp than a town except for the fact that it also had a life beyond military concerns. Built on the side of a steep hill, it was immune against any attack from the north or east, but the citizens were still afraid and they built **two Cyclopean walls** around their town to protect it further. They lived there with their wives and kids, and whenever they were not busy defending their town they cultivated the fields to the southwest of it (in the direction of Paleochora). Whether out of deeply rooted insecurity or because of the major threats they faced, at some point they decided to seek an alliance with their neighbours, so together with Eliros, Lissos, Syia, Pikilassos and Tara they

The road that joins Prodromi and Paleochora

formed a coalition known as **To kinò ton Orìon (the Mountain-People League,** 3rd century BC). However, they were not a truly warlike people (like our friends, the Spartans), or at least that's not what the few remaining monuments seem to tell us. Apart from the few surviving parts of the walls, which testify to the city's great need for defence, the most important remnant from the ancient times is a temple dedicated to **Pan,** the protector of flocks and shepherds... Let us also note that the hill was excavated in 1939 and it was then that the temple was brought to light.

Irtakina is a fine example of a ruined ancient town exciting the imagination, and the entire island echoes with memories from the past. These will spice your journey with a sense of travelling through time and they will give you something interesting to think about. But of course Crete's charm comes from everything about it, history **as well as** people, scenery and adventure. If you are hungry for beautiful scenery or exciting adventure, the crossroads one kilometre after you turn for Prodromi will invite you to choose.

Two ways lead to Paleochora from this crossroads. The one is to turn left (east) and go through Prodromi - a route promising **adventure and exploration** - and the other is to go right (west) and go through Platanes to enjoy **a scenic ride.** On the crossroads you will see a Gr/E sign pointing you to Prodromi via a small country road (D3). Whether you take this road or go through Platanes, you are in for a great experience.

ROUTES STARTING FROM HANIA

If you select the first option you turn left on the dirtroad and continue until **Prodromi.** Prodromi is a colourful village with many old houses and a Byzantine church dedicated to Panagia Skafidiani and decorated with the paintings of Ioannis Pagomenos (**1347**). Exactly 1600 metres from the sign at the northern entrance of the village, you will see a white icon stand and a small cement-paved path which immediately turns into a dirtroad. Take this path, make a left turn at the first intersection you will hit, a second left turn at the second intersection, and a right turn at the third (all other roads are dead-ends, anyway, and stop suddenly before a field). You will pass through a barren landscape and go through a fence gate. After that starts **a truly magnificent route through the steep southern shores of Crete, a route that's great for enduro bikes and exciting in its wilderness.** At some point the road intersects with the Sougia - Paleochora coastal path (E4) and a little further it stops suddenly at some distance from the shore. Needless to say, you can camp anywhere you like in this area, but there is no water, no shade and no reason to do so! Those of you that like to hike can continue on foot to Paleochora (a two-hour walk you will certainly enjoy). The rest can return to Prodromi by the same road and from there continue to **Anidri,** a little further to the west. There you will see the beautiful Byzantine church of Aghios Georgios, also decorated with the paintings of Ioannis Pagomenos. After the village the road goes through an impressive gorge full of plane trees and caves, and shortly before you leave the gorge it turns into an asphalted road (A3) that leads to Paleochora.

Your second option at the crossroads (the one with the view) is to forget about Prodromi and go right. The road (D3) takes you to a pretty high altitude from where you have an enchanting view of the south coast, then goes through the half-deserted villages of Platanes and Asphendiles and turns north following the eastern slope of a gorge in the bottom of which flows the Azogirian river. This route offers you a great view of **Azogires,** a very beautiful village on the other side of the gorge surrounded by thick forests. A little later the road crosses to the other side taking you to the village. The attractive scenery brings quite a few tourists to this place and so do the Harakas cave and the Monastery of the Holy Fathers, which is built about two kilometres away on the top of the hill (however, the monastery and the cave are nothing special). If you wish to stay in Azogires, you will find a few Rooms To Let and a couple of taverns. A wide, uninteresting dirtroad (D1) will take you south of Azogires and join the main road about three kilometres north of Paleochora.

PALEOCHORA

Paleochora has long ceased to be the quiet fisherman village it once was. The reason for its tourist development is the **gorgeous sandy beach** with the crystal-clear water at the west side of the peninsula where the town is built. Another nice beach (but with large pebbles) lies east of the town, while many smaller and quieter beaches are found in small coves on either side of it.

In **1282** the Venetians built a fort on the tip of the peninsula, which they named **Castel Selino** (the Celery Fort), possibly because of the large quantities of celery, a wild plant that grew everywhere in the area! The idea was to use the fort to impose their dominion over this

Paleochora

rebellious area. As it turned out, the fort was very vulnerable, not only because it was poorly designed from the start, but also because it was cut off from the main centres of Venetian authority and from all supply stations. As a result, even a group of... amateurs could assault it successfully, and the fort was conquered, destroyed and rebuilt several times in its history. Its last occupants, the Turks, finally decided that it was futile to try to preserve it and they left it to its fate. The irony, though, is that the fort is much more effective now in protecting the area than it was when it was first built! Since 1940, a time still untainted by excessive tourist development, the entire peninsula on which it is built has been declared a historical site, so the building frenzy and exploitation of the area stopped right outside the city walls. Although mercilessly besieged, the fort holds stubbornly!

Today Paleochora has many small hotels and many pubs, taverns and restaurants catering to the needs of the tourists, but it still has that special feeling of an out of the way place about it. After 5:00 p.m. the narrow alleys of the town close for all vehicles, and they turn into pedestrian streets that are often filled with the tables of taverns or with playing children. At night these same streets are filled with music from the pubs and people having fun. In the morning, the action shifts toward the beaches, but there is plenty of room for everyone. If you are looking for a more quiet spot, though, there is a very good beach east of Paleochora. Go past the camping ground and after a couple of kilometres park your motorcycle somewhere and walk for another ten minutes till the end of the cape.

WHERE TO STAY

Many hotels have been built in Paleochora in the last eight years, but they are still not enough to accommodate the ever increasing number of tourists. July and August are the worst months of the year and unless you book early you will have a hard time finding a room.

Still, the town has over two thousand beds in rented rooms (by official records), so if you look around you are bound to find something in the end. Many of these rooms are in cosy, one-storey houses that also have a yard, so you can park your bike with safety. The quietest and cheapest rooms are toward the north of the town, while the more fancy and expensive ones are concentrated at the south and closer to the fort. If you feel more like camping, there is a very nice camping ground just outside the town.

KALYPSO, Apartments
Class A. Open April - October.
7 rooms.
Tel. (0823) 41 429
Just opposite Diktamo. An old mansion that has been turned into a hotel. Each apartment has a bathroom and a kitchen of its own and attention has been paid to detail. There is no parking lot.

DIKTAMO, Hotel
Class B. Open April - October.
22 rooms.
Tel. (0823) 41 569
A nice hotel, recently built and well designed. It has a marble-paved inner courtyard surrounded by the quietest rooms. There is no parking lot.

AGHAS, Hotel
Class B. Open all year round.
13 rooms.
Tel. (0823) 41 155
Your best choice. A hotel of two storeys, recently built, situated at a quiet place at the northern part of town. It has great balconies and a courtyard where you can safely park your bike.

GLAROS, Hotel
Class C. Open April - October.
16 rooms, parking for bikes.
Tel. (0823) 41 613

REA, Hotel
Class C. Open March - November.
12 rooms.
Tel. (0823) 41 307

PAL BEACH, Hotel
Class C.
Open April - October.
54 rooms.
Tel. (0823) 41 512, Fax (0823) 41 578

CAMPING PALEOCHORA
At the beach, 1 km east of the town.
Open April - October.
10,000 m^2 (or about 2.5 acres)
45 spaces.
It is an **olive grove** turned into a primitive, clean, quiet camping ground; just pick your favourite olive tree and set up your tent! Trailers are too big to get in and the campers are exclusively hikers, bicyclists or motorcyclists. There are toilets and showers with hot water available and a small restaurant that serves a nice breakfast. The beach in front of the camping has pretty big stones, but 1.5 km to the east there is a **great beach** with sand and small pebbles.

WHERE TO EAT

Paleochora has plenty of good restaurants, which are concentrated in two places: on the waterfront at the eastern part of town (where you have a great view but are in danger of having your food swept away by the frequent southeast winds, the siroccos) and on the main street of the town where all the action is.

RENA
One of the best restaurants in town. Rena serves home-cooked meals made with the best ingredients. Try her meat casserole and her mousaka. The sign outside does not say "RENA" but "RESTAURANT, SMALL GARDEN INSIDE, ΕΥΤΥΧΙΟΣ ΑΡΧΟΝΤΑΚΗΣ"

ROUTES STARTING FROM HANIA

PELEKANOS
Nice restaurant at the south end of town, next to the sea. It has a great variety of cooked meals, which are spread out behind a window-case outside the kitchen, so you can see them and choose. There are also tables inside in case of wind.

DIONYSOS
Possibly the best tavern in town and at the same time the cheapest! Very tasty steaks done on the coals, fresh seafood, **great peasant salad** (*choriàtiki*), and lots of cooked meals which you can see and choose for yourself if you visit the kitchen. Also very good selection of wines.

THE THIRD EYE
A very good restaurant for vegeterians, situated in the west part of town. Pleasant environment, soft music and outdoor tables. Its dishes are very tasty, made with fresh vegetables and a lot of spices.

NIKI
A small and ugly place in the centre of town. It has no tables outside but it serves good and inexpensive pizza that is baked in an oven heated with wood fire.

GALAXIAS
Typical nice restaurant by the water-

3. Hania - Samaria

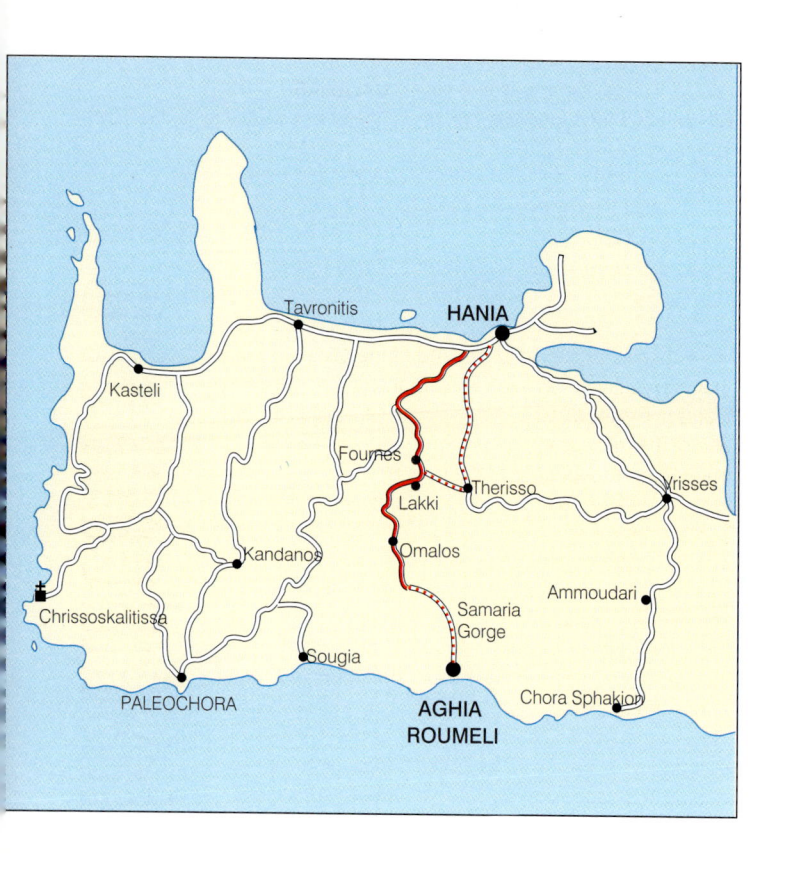

ROUTES STARTING FROM HANIA

There is one main way to get from Hania to the Omalos plateau and the Samaria gorge and that is to take the road southwest of Hania (A3/25km) that will take you to **Fournes** (from where you can continue to Lakki and then to the village of Omalos, your last stop before the gorge). As you travel on the Hania - Fournes road, you will cross a rather indifferent valley with orange groves and face some heavy traffic. This traffic is because the road is used not only by tourists but also by the local farmers.

If, however, you want to avoid this dull trip, you can get to Fournes by an alternative route, longer but far more inviting, which will take you through the **Therissiano gorge** (A3/23km and D3/7km). You will pass a village called Perivolia and then enter the beautiful Therissiano gorge, which has a total length of about six kilometres. The road follows a stream, occasionally crossing from one side to the other, and the landscape, full of planes, locusts, olive trees and bushes, is a true feast for the eyes.

In July, **1821,** a military force of 5000 Turks led by Lati Pasha was crossing the gorge, determined to get to Therisso and stifle the revolt of the locals. When they reached the south end of the gorge they were attacked by 300 Therissians led by the **Halides brothers,** whose name was later given to one of the main streets of Hania. The battle was in many ways reminiscent of the famous **Thermopylae battle**, some 2300 years earlier, in which Leonidas and his 300 Spartans got killed as they were trying to hold back a much larger Persian army, which, having also started from Asia Minor, was crossing a similar pass in its effort to conquer Southern Greece. This time, however, the invaders were defeated, and they soon retreated after suffering heavy casualties. But not for long. They gathered reinforcements, returned to the village, and burned it to the ground. Such acts, of course, increased the hatred in the hearts of the Cretans and they fostered even more rebellions, which eventually led to Crete being declared an autonomous state (1897). In **1905** Eleftherios Venizelos (page 146) led the **revolution of Therisso,** which resulted in the resignation of Prince George the Second and opened the way to Crete's union with Greece some years later. The house that served as Venizelos' headquarters has survived, and today it can be easily distinguished by the many buses that come here daily and by the noisy children swarming in and out of it. If you are hungry and want to make a stop, try the tavern "O ΑΝΤΑΡΤΗΣ" (*o andàrtis*, the rebel) on the main street, just opposite the school. The owner, Manolis Roumeliotis, serves delicious sausages, *ghravièra* and *mizìthra* (Gruyere and cream cheese), and *sìnglino* (smoked pork meat cut up in small pieces), **all of his own production.** He also makes great *choriàtiki* (peasant salad) with juicy tomatoes and pure olive oil.

As you continue to the south of Therisso, the road (D3) passes through a barren landscape and takes you to **Zouvra,** then turns into asphalt (A3) and goes a little to the north again until the village of **Meskla**. Built among large orange groves, Meskla looks so serene and pretty that it

SINGLINO

In the old times, when there was no electricity and no refrigerator, pork meat was preserved **sìnglino**. The family would slaughter the pig, cut up a few chops to be eaten on that same day, and store the rest in a large earthen jar, after cutting it up in small pieces which were smoked on a charcoal grill. The jar was filled with the pig's own fat, which preserved the meat for a period of five to six months. When it was time to consume it, they cooked it in a frying pan, either by itself or together with eggs. Today, in many Cretan villages, folks continue to prepare the meat in the old traditional way.

is hard to think it was twice destroyed in the past. But it was. The Venetians, first, and the Turks later, laid everything waste, and it is indeed very fortunate that two Byzantine churches managed to survive, even though they were seriously damaged. The church of Christ the Saviour has some wonderful wall paintings by the hand of the Veneri brothers (1403), but unfortunately they suffered severe and irreparable damage. The **church of the Virgin Mary**, a little further to the north, is particularly interesting, as it contains parts of earlier buildings including a temple of Aphrodite that was once built in this exact place. It is also worth noting that the mosaic covering part of the present church floor was once the

ROUTES STARTING FROM HANIA

mosaic floor of a fifth century basilica. Finally, around the village one can see many ancient ruins of homes as well as parts of a city wall. Although it is not certain which city that wall surrounded, the ruins are thought to belong to the ancient town of **Rizinia.**

After Meskla you continue a bit further to the north (on an A3 road) until you reach Fournes (this completes the alternative route from Hania which we proposed earlier). Your next destination on your way to the gorge is Lakki, a village lying southwest of both Fournes and Meskla. This village can be seen from Meskla, but it cannot be easily reached unless you go through Fournes first. However, if you have an off-road bike you can also go straight from Meskla to Lakki, simply by following the narrow dirtroad that starts about ten metres before the bridge at the north exit of Meskla. (This dirtroad passes through some olive groves and then takes you to the main asphalt road connecting Fournes and Lakki, which it intersects at a point just north of the village). Alternatively (if you do **not** opt for the off-road route, but choose to go through Fournes instead), you can reach Fournes in two ways: by the A3 road we mentioned earlier or by a nice dirtroad. This dirtroad starts from the same point at the north exit of Meskla, and it heads north following the course of the Keritis river.

Lakki is built on a slope full of chestnut and olive trees and it gives you a great view of the White Mountain range. It is the last village before the Omalos plateau, so if you intend to walk the Samaria gorge or do some mountain climbing it would be wise to buy supplies here. For all those that want to avoid the crowds at Omalos and the Kallergi refuge, the taverns and boarding houses of Lakki are the last chance to eat a decent meal and have a good night's sleep.

The landscape after Lakki is no longer "human." There are no orange groves and no cultivated lands, nothing to remind one of how man "tames" nature. The road (A3) climbs suddenly through steep mountain slopes with tall cedar trees and thick bushes, and as it climbs it offers a spectacular view. Be careful, though, because **it has many dangerous hairpins.** About 15 km south of Lakki, at a height of 1200 metres, the road goes through a pass from which you have a sudden view of the Omalos plateau some

3. Hania-Samaria

The Omalos plateau

200 metres lower. From early fall until the end of spring, the mountain peaks surrounding the plateau are covered with snow.

In the spring the snow melts and the plateau is turned into a huge swamp or even a lake. Those parts that are not covered by water are full of wild flowers. In the summer, most of the flowers are gone and the mountain greens have been eaten by goats or collected and made into herb-pies. In the past people grew potatoes in this place and they took pride in their delicious taste that was known all over Crete. Today there is nothing cultivated and the few people staying at the small settlement in the middle of the plateau are all into the tourist business. There are a few hotels, each with its own restaurant, and rooms are booked in advance even for the low season; as for the high season, they are all taken. If you want to book a room, your best choice is probably the recently built **Neos Omalos Hotel** (tel. 0821 67 269). It has a shelter for your bike, a common area with a fireplace, and rooms with double windows that protect you from the night cold.

After Omalos the road (A3) continues south for another 4 km, ending in an asphalt-paved square full of parked vehicles. You are at the entrance of the Samaria gorge, in a place called **Xiloskalo.** Here you will find an information table of the Forest Authorities, which tells you briefly about the gorge, and a stone-built restaurant with a great view and not so great prices. A word of advice: it might be best to walk or hitchhike to Xiloskalo rather than come by bike, because once you are here you will find out there is no safe place to park.

If you are not interested in walking the gorge, there are other things to do. One option is to take the dirtroad (D2) that starts about 400 metres before Xiloskalo and goes west. This road goes through the plateau and takes you to a small shepherd settlement called **Seliniotikos Giros**. From here you have the option of following another dirtroad which heads east and takes you back to Omalos (this completes your tour of the plateau). A better option, though, is to turn west instead of east and to go for a spectacular ride on the south and west slopes of Mount Tourli (1453m). This ride promises **a wonderful view of the Hania Gulf, the Libyan sea and the White Mountain peaks**. It finally takes you to the Hania - Paleochora road at a point about three kilometres north of Aghia Irini, and from here you can either head for Hania or go south in the direction of Sougia and Paleochora (see Route 2, page 148). An interesting alternative here would be to turn west (right) on the dirtroad (D3) that you will find about two kilometres **before** you get on the road leading to Sougia (you can't miss it; it is the only dirtroad in the area). You will find yourself crossing **a beautiful thick forest of chestnut trees,** and eventually you will get back on the Sougia road, only this time at a different point, the village of Prasses.

Finally, another alternative from Omalos is to go to the Kallergi refuge (tel. 0821- 54 560, height 1675 metres), a base for many mountain climbing expeditions. To do this, take the dirtroad (D3) that starts 400 metres before Xiloskalo and goes **east** (in other words, take the dirtroad that is almost exactly opposite of the one going to Seliniotikos Giros). After a four-kilometre ride through spectacular scenery, you will reach the refuge. From here you can go on a two-day expedition to Anopolis and Loutro (the most popular among many other options). You will find detailed maps and info at the Kallergi refuge (and of course at the Mountain Climbing Club of Hania), but keep in mind that to try this expedition you must have considerable experience in mountain climbing. If, however, you do not want to walk, there is a dirtroad you can take, which goes pretty deep into the White Mountains (see page 192). You will find this dirtroad on the way to Anopolis.

THE GORGES OF THE PREFECTURE OF HANIA

There are fifty-four gorges in the Hania prefecture alone! Some of them can be crossed by bike, some can be very easily walked through, and some can be explored only by experienced mountain climbers. Do you know which is the most beautiful? No, it isn't the one you think! The **Samaria gorge** is the most famous in Crete (and Greece, actually), but it isn't the most beautiful. It has become very popular because it is **practicable** and yet **quite demanding.** It is true, of course, that it is a very beautiful gorge with high vertical walls and narrow passes, and it is also true that crossing it is quite difficult because it is long (16 km) and drops about 1200 metres from one end to the other. At the same time, though, there is a whole infrastructure meant to facilitate the visitor: organised transport to and from the gorge, places to eat and sleep at either end of it, a smooth path, bridges at all difficult points, a first-aid station etc. **Yet the most spectacular gorges of Crete, far more imposing than that of Samaria and truly unspoilt, lie west and east of the gorge, only a few kilometres away.** They are not mentioned in any tourist guide, nor marked on any map, because they are hard to cross, have no infrastructure to help the visitor, and lie outside the area of organised business interests. Crossing them is an adventure that calls for all your strength, endurance and skill and will take you to your limits. It is a hard struggle against Nature, an experience that will sharpen all your senses. **Strict warning: do not attempt to cross these gorges unless you are an experienced climber, have detailed maps and information from the Hania Mountain Climbing Club, and are accompanied by an experienced guide.**

The **Klados gorge** is the first one to the west of Samaria. The path leading to its north entrance starts from the Linosseli pass west of peak Gigilos. It is not marked except by a few "domes" - piled up rocks - at the most dangerous points, and it is evidently very infrequently crossed as the path is often blocked by bushes. A little before the entrance to the gorge there is a **very dangerous** spot with a **chalasè** (loose gravel on a steep slope) and a nine-hundred-metre precipice. Crossing the gorge requires descending by rope in three different places (70, 25 and 15 metres deep), and when the snow melts in the spring there are cascades in these places too. Needless to say, before attempting to cross the gorge you should get a detailed weather forecast, because the sudden rainstorms create sweeping torrents, which in the narrow parts of the gorge may be as deep as fifteen metres! (Incidentally, almost the **entire gorge** is very narrow...) On the other end of the gorge there is a beautiful beach called Tripiti, where you can find water to drink by digging in the sand. To return to civilisation, take the coast path that goes east and leads to Aghia Roumeli (a five to six hour walk). The shores are very steep and the path climbs the mountain to a height of seven hundred metres. From Aghia Roumeli you can take the boat to Chora Sphakion.

The **Tripiti gorge** is the second one to the west of Samaria and, as with the Klados gorge, the path leading to its north entrance also starts at Linosseli. A little before the entrance there is a **very dangerous** passage where you risk getting stuck (so that you can neither walk on nor turn around and go back). Two people were killed at this point and many others were in serious danger, so do not attempt to pass it without an experienced guide. The gorge is truly amazing with its high steep walls and its rich flora and fauna.

The **Eligia gorge** is the first one to the east of Samaria. The path leading to its north entrance starts from the Katsiveli refuge, but it can also be reached from the refuge of Kallergi. It's fairly walkable and marked with small "domes," but you must have very specific instructions or be accompanied by an experienced guide, because there are also many secondary paths in the area and they all lead to sheepfolds. The gorge is very narrow and very deep from one end to the other, and even its exit is too narrow to distinguish from the sea. Its special characteristic is that it descends very sharply and has lush vegetation. In the winter the torrent coming down the gorge sweeps away large tree trunks, which block certain narrow passages and make the gorge as forbidding as a jungle! To return to civilisation, take the coast path to Aghia Roumeli. It is a fairly easy one-hour walk.

The Samaria Gorge

Having a total length of sixteen kilometres, this gorge is the **largest in Europe** and certainly the most famous and visited among the many gorges of Crete.

Until about the middle of the century it was a wild landscape with a totally undisturbed ecosystem and home to a great number of wild birds and mammals as well as to a small population of woodcutters and shepherds who lived in Aghia Roumeli or in the village of Samaria inside the gorge. Today this village has been abandoned, but the steep slopes of the gorge and the thick forests in the surrounding area are still populated with many rare species. These include over fifty species of wild birds - among them, the extremely rare **harrier eagle** (Gypaetus barbatus) and **golden eagle** (Aquila Chrysaetos), both threatened with extinction - and about ten species of mammals among which the famous Cretan wild goat otherwise known as **kri kri** and the Cretan polecat known as *zourìdha*. As for the flora of the area, it is abundantly rich and includes many wild flowers native to this land.

In 1962, the gorge, together with a small area to the west and east of it, was officially declared a **National Park,** so that its delicate ecosystem could be protected. The park extends over an area of 5100 hectares and, unlike its quiet days in the past, today it is visited by some **300,000** people a year, all of them determined to walk the gorge. Visits are allowed between May and October, but in July and August the tourists are so many that it is impossible to be alone even for a minute. On the other hand, if you can come between

May and early June, or between the middle of September and the end of October, you will certainly enjoy it a lot more.

A good time to visit the gorge (in fact, a time before it is officially opened to the public) is the first weekend of April, when a two-day festival is held in Samaria in honour of **Osia Maria**. The liturgy in the small Byzantine church is chanted by father Giorgis Chiotakis of Sphakia, an amazing priest who likes a good feast as much as anyone else and yet is a truly holy man. This is followed by a feast featuring traditional goodies (such as sardines and cream cheese) and some genuine fun. If you want to spend the night in the gorge, this weekend is your one and only chance. However, you must first contact the Mountain Climbing Club of Hania (city map, **33**) and let them know of your plans.

As mentioned, there are several signs of human presence in the gorge - shaping of the entrance, fire stations, first-aid stations, waste baskets, explanatory signs, toilets, tables and chairs - and all these take something away from the beauty of it. Yet the gorge still remains **a landscape of unique beauty** and walking through it will be an experience to remember.

Most visitors take the early morning bus from Hania, arrive at Xiloskalo, walk down the gorge, reach Aghia Roumeli on the other side, and then take the boat to Chora Sphakion where they catch another bus for Hania.

This procedure has many disadvantages, especially in the high tourist season. In the first place, you must make a **very early start;** there are three to four bus departures every morning, between the hours of 6:00 and 8:30 a.m. Second, you will get squeezed both at the bus terminal and inside the bus, and this will spoil your fun. Third, you will find yourself walking in the gorge along with another hundred people. There will be someone passing you all the time (or someone that you'll bump into if you walk too fast), and no matter how discreet their presence you won't be able to lose yourself in the landscape. Fourth, you will be cold in Xiloskalo and hot in Aghia Roumeli, because Xiloskalo is at an altitude of 1200 metres (plus, you'll be there in the morning), and Aghia Roumeli is at sea level (plus, you'll be there in the early afternoon). Finally, you will arrive in Aghia Roumeli at rush hour, and after a tiresome and crowded journey you will have to give a battle to secure a plate of food. And of course it will not be the cheapest meal you can remember...

Well, guess what! We suggest you walk against the current! Go up the gorge (instead of down), and enjoy the many advantages of a route that's less difficult than you think. This will save you from many unpleasant things, among which:

The crowded bus. In the morning, you will start your journey from Aghia Roumeli feeling the cool sea breeze on your skin (so start early!) In the afternoon you will be almost alone in the bus going to Hania.

SAMARIA GORGE: INFO AND REGULATIONS

The gorge is open to visitors from May 1 to October 31. These dates are not fixed but can be moved forward (or... backward) depending on weather conditions. The most important criterion is the level of the water in the gorge, which is particularly high in early spring (when the snow melts) and in late fall (when there are many sudden downpours). It is, however, up to the guards to decide whether they will let you in the gorge during the period that it's closed for the public, depending on your capacity and the prevailing conditions.

The National Park is open daily from 6:00 a.m. to 3:30 p.m. The gorge must be crossed during those hours. **It is strictly forbidden to spend the night there.**

On entering the gorge you buy a one thousand drachma ticket with the current date on it. This ticket must be shown at the control station on the other side. If you lose it you must pay again, and if the date is not current they will conclude that you have stayed overnight.

The following are strictly forbidden: swimming in the river; cutting flowers; hunting or disturbing the animals; lighting a fire or smoking; creating noise pollution (radios etc); walking outside the marked path; littering the place.

Inside the gorge you will see signs informing you about the designated rest areas, the water sources, and the location of first-aid stations and fire stations. There are staff members that have been trained to deal with health emergencies, and there are mules for the transportation of patients as well as heliports for emergency cases.

ROUTES STARTING FROM HANIA

The crowds in the gorge. By noon you will practically have walked to the other side. The gorge will be all yours, because the crowds from Xiloskalo will not have had the time to get as far as **you** did.

The early afternoon heat. By that time you will be walking the last few kilometres to Xiloskalo, which is 1200 metres above sea level.

Still, we must warn you that during the last three kilometres you climb 700 metres, so this last part is quite demanding and calls for good physical condition. However, the path is pleasant, and instead of climbing vertically it winds up the mountain in many smooth turns.

If you are two people with two bikes you can completely avoid the bus. The one that gets less exercise (or doesn't care for much) goes to Xiloskalo and walks down the gorge. The other one goes to Chora Sphakion, takes the boat to Aghia Roumeli, and then goes up the gorge. Then the one takes the bike of the other and in the evening you meet at Hania. But there is one little thing to pay attention to: When you meet inside the gorge, do not forget to exchange keys...

Finally, if you are alone, or if everyone in the group wants to enjoy the trip up the gorge, the best solution is to take route 5, lock up your bikes in Chora Sphakion, and then take the boat to Aghia Roumeli and walk to Xiloskalo on the other side of the gorge. From Xiloskalo you catch the bus to Hania and from Hania you catch another bus to Chora Sphakion. Here you pick up your bikes and continue your trip to the east.

3. Hania-Samaria

4. Hania-Sphakia

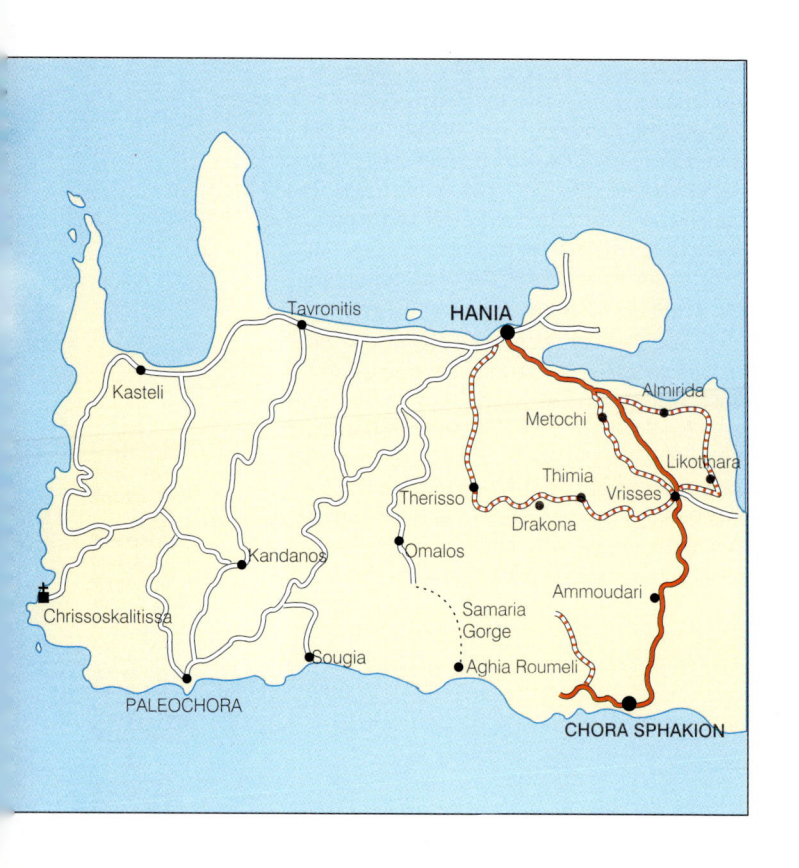

ROUTES STARTING FROM HANIA

4.1 HANIA - VRISSES

As you leave Hania behind you and head for Rethimno, the first thirty-two kilometres of your journey, up to the intersection leading to **Vrisses**, are on a beautiful wide road - here called the National Road - that will invite you to speed. If you go too fast, though, you will miss the chance to see many interesting sights along your way.

The National Road stretches for two hundred kilometres along the coast of Crete. It connects Hania and Aghios Nikolaos and it is practically the only highway on the island allowing you to ride at full speed. Many foreign bikers, after spending an exhausting few days on the winding country roads of the island and tiring of the appalling low speeds, take this road from end to end just to get it out of their systems. The people of Hania know the road like the back of their hand. From time to time they stage Dragster races on it, proving that they are indeed **very fast** drivers. Their fellow cyclists from Rethimno, Iraklio and Sitia also enjoy driving here, and the latter often entertain themselves by making all other vehicles look... motionless in comparison to their superbikes. If you and your motorcycle want to let off steam because of the dreadfully slow rides in the Hania countryside, you might feel the irresistible urge to imitate them and drive as fast as possible until the road will allow you to go no further. Do not hesitate to satisfy your desire. Pop down to Rethimno or Iraklio and return to Hania feeling relieved. And now you can calmly start Route number 4!

About twelve kilometres east of Hania, you will reach an intersection with a road leading to the south (Gr/E sign to **Megala Chorafia** and **Aptera**). Turn right on this road (A3) and follow it up the mountain, then turn left at Megala Chorafia. You will shortly arrive at the **Aptera** archaeological site, situated just east of Metochi.

If you want to enjoy the best view of the Souda Bay (to the north) and the valley of Kiliari with its many olive groves (to the south), continue on the road which leads to the northeastern part of the hill and stops just outside the **Itzentin Fort.**

ITZENTIN FORT

After the Ottoman Turks put an end to the Cretan revolt of 1866, the Turkish commander Reouf Pasha, believing that the Turkish rule would last a long time, decided to reinforce the defence of Hania where the administration was based. He made up his mind to build the fort in **1867** and gave it the name of his son, **Itzentin**.

It is one of the best preserved Turkish forts, not only because it is the most recently built, but also because it served as a Greek prison

Once you stand on the spot where ancient Aptera was situated, you will understand that the reason the Dorian settlers chose this location to build their town was the magnificent view! Built at a height of two hundred metres above the sea on a steep hill, with the entire Souda Bay at its feet, this important west Cretan town looks like it has taken off; why on earth they chose to call it Aptera ("the non-winged one") remains a mystery!

The prevailing interpretation derives from Greek mythology: a musical contest between the Muses and the Sirens is said to have taken place on this spot. The Muses excelled in creating beautiful music; indeed so splendid was their music that they even gave this art form its name! (music < Muse). Still, the audacious Sirens, the sea goddesses that were half woman and half bird, had the nerve to challenge them to a musical contest. Their impudence was due to the fact that they had no rival in their territory, a rocky island somewhere in the Mediterranean sea from where they bewitched those sailing by and led them to wreck their ships on the treacherous rocks of the shore. As you may remember from the Odyssey, the only one who escaped that dreadful fate was Odysseus, because he had the intelligence to put sealing-wax in his companions' ears and to have them tie him on the ship's mast... But the Muses were no mere sailors who could not resist their mellifluous songs.

And it so happened that the competition took place and the Muses won. After their victory they grabbed the Sirens, pulled out their wings and feathers, and threw them in the sea as a punishment for their rude audacity. In commemoration of the event, the Dorian settlers decided to call their town Aptera.

The striking landscape always delights the heart, and delight gives the artist wings. On the other hand, the city's position on top of the hill greatly contributed to a feeling of security. These facts allowed the people to... take off and reach the height of achievement. Their craftsmanship was famous not only in Crete but also on the Greek mainland and even as far as Southern Italy. Their workshops turned out the most beautiful masterpieces. They had their own fleet of ships and two handy ports at the Souda bay, and they built up a lively trade. The city pros-

until 1971. Although on the outside the architecture has remained intact, the inside has been changed radically and often reinforced with cement in order to serve as a prison. Today it stands abandoned and unguarded, and it is full of rubbish nobody seems to care about.

APTERA

pered during a long period of time, during which no less than seventy-two different coins were minted!

Some of these precious coins were discovered in 1834 by Robert Pashley, a British traveller who happened to dig the ground around the city ruins and thus determined its exact location. By that time ancient Aptera had vanished into thin air. It was destroyed by the Arabs in 832 AD and no one heard much of it ever since...

Since Pashley's days, only a few excavations have taken place in the large area where once the ancient city stood. Those few that took place brought to light some significant findings, many of which you can admire at the Hania Archaeological Museum. Most of the treasures, though, remain buried under the ground awaiting the government subsidy that will allow the archaeologists to find them.

A notable part of the city wall, which once had a perimeter of approximately four kilometres, still stands in good condition, as do two large vaulted cisterns dating from the Roman period, the ruins of a theatre, the foundations of many houses and temples, some vaulted tombs, and the mosaic floors of some old Christian basilicas from the last period of the city's existence. At the centre of the archaeological site there is a guarded area surrounded by a fence, where you can see the foundations of a small temple dating from the classical period (5th century BC) and an arched Roman building that probably housed the parliament. But the greatest part of the town, once full of ancient houses and streets, is now below the olive groves and barren fields.

4. Hania-Sphakia

The Itzentin fort

Once you have explored the area leave ancient Aptera behind you, return to Megala Chorafia, and turn south (toward Stilos). You will cross a rural area full of olive trees and streams which join to form the Kiliari river. Settlements have existed in this fertile land since the Minoan period. In fact, one such settlement was recently brought to light when a hill was excavated in the area near Stilos, just after the crossroads leading to Malaxa. You will certainly find that the road you have taken - the old National Road which connects Hania and Rethimno - does not have much traffic, since everybody seems to prefer the new road. After a quiet ride, you will arrive at **Vrisses**.

From **Vrisses** you can go just about any place (including Sphakia), as you will soon discover. The village has some Rooms to Let and a small hotel, and on the main street there are lots of coffee shops, restaurants and super markets, so this is a good chance to replenish your supplies. In the super markets you will also find fresh fruit, refrigerated and delicious.

4.2 HANIA - VRISSES (MOUNTAIN ROUTE)

If you are considering exploring the White Mountains from the northwestern side, you can choose to avoid the National Road altogether, and instead of following the coast you can reach Vrisses through the mountain. Head to the south of Hania toward Therisso, riding through the beautiful **Therissiano gorge** (see page 181). Just after Therisso you will find a dirtroad (D2) with a Greek... hand-written sign directing you to Δρακώνα (Drakona). Turn left and climb the mountain. From the very first kilometres, an imposing view of the northwestern side of the White Mountains will unfold before your eyes. Continue for a while until you see a second dirtroad (D3) to your right, which also climbs the mountain. This road stretches about 8.5 kilometres and takes you to an altitude of 1350 metres, only to stop suddenly at the foot of the Kaloros peak. But even though it leads nowhere, the road is worth taking since it will reward you with **the most beautiful scenery any route on the White Mountains has to offer. The entire northern coast of the Hania prefecture lies before your eyes,** from the Gramvoussa peninsula in the west to the Vamos peninsula in the east, while on very clear days you can see as far to the north as the coast of the Peloponnese! As you climb the mountain you will see large grey rocks, and between them thin clumps of cedars, pine and oak trees, low bushes, marjoram and sage. There are no intersections to confuse you on this road, except for one at 4.5 kilometres, where you turn left - a right turn would take you right to a sheepfold(!) - and there are no places to pitch camp, except for a few level spots by the roadside. It would be wise, though, to avoid camping here, because you will be exposed to the very strong gusts of wind coming down the mountains around you.

When you have fully enjoyed the view, you will want to get back to the main route. Once back, you must keep on it for a couple of kilometres, until you see an intersection where you turn right, closely followed by a second one, where you turn **left** in order to get to **Drakona** (please ignore the badly placed Greek sign which seems to point you to the right). After taking a break to walk through the picturesque alleys of Drakona, take the asphalt-paved road which leads to **Gerolakos**, and turn right shortly before you get there in order to visit the picturesque **Thimia**.

The people in these villages continue to live with the traditions and customs of their forefathers, and technology, though beneficial, has not brought significant changes to their characteristic way of life. Each family produces its own basic goods: milk; cheese (***ghravièra*** and ***mizìthra***); top quality butter made of cream (appropriately called ***stakovoùtiro*** or "cream butter"); yoghurt; meat (especially that of the ***fouriàrika katsìkia***, wild goats that taste delicious);

bread; biscuits; vegetables; eggs; olives and olive oil; wine; raki; and a lot more. If you are lucky enough to be invited to their table **you will never forget the experience.** It is not only their mouth-watering food and the irresistible smells that will delight you; it is also the birds chirping above your head, the beautiful sight of the slopes around you, and the fresh mountain air on your skin. Above all, it is the warm hospitality of these people and their sunny smile that speaks volumes about their heart. They will treat you to the most sumptuous meal and then they'll ask you to forgive them because they didn't have the time to prepare everything as they should! They will clink glasses with you and say something like *kalòs ìrthate ke òpos mas evrìkate* (welcome, no matter how prepared you find us) or *lìgha pràghmata, polì aghàpi* (little food, much love). They will make you feel that you are really special, and they will do it because they "exude" warmth, not because they are interested in your money. If you can afford to spend some time with them you will discover a whole new world, one that has **nothing to do** with the tourist world of the Cretan coast that's just a few kilometres away...

If you are invited to have lunch with peasants you will never forget the experience!

After you have visited Thimia, take the dirtroad to the east of the village, which climbs the mountain slope (if you get a little confused in the village streets, keep going and you will certainly find the way). When you reach the col that lies ahead and pass a cement cistern, you will see an intersection where you turn right. The road then descends and takes you again to the asphalt at the north entrance of **Kambi**. Turn right when you get there (that is, head south) and cross the green slopes until you reach **Tsakistra**. Here you have one more opportunity to climb the mountain again; simply turn right on the road going to **Madaro** and keep going. The road you are on (D3) stops after ten kilometres at a height of one thousand metres. However, it offers **a magnificent view** throughout those ten kilometres, so it is again worth the trouble. When you return to Tsakistra, turn left on the dirtroad (D3) that will take you to the asphalt road a little north of

ROUTES STARTING FROM HANIA

The Vothonas plateau on the Tzitzifies - Vafes route

Kiriakoselia. Our route continues southward (to the right), but we highly recommend a short break from it; just turn left, go past Kiriakoselia, and after 1.5 km you will see Aghios Nikolaos, **one of the most beautiful Byzantine churches of Crete.** Built around the end of the 11th century or the beginning of the 12th, it has some very impressive wall paintings which are in excellent condition. To see them, however, you must first go to Samonas and ask for the key at the *kafenio*.

If you now get back to our route and continue southward, you will pass through **Ramni** and head for Kares. Don't continue until Kares, but turn left just before you get there. You will pass through a couple of very picturesque villages, **Melidoni** and **Pemonia**, where you should really make a stop in order to walk their alleys. Then turn right in order to see the equally charming **Fres** and **Tzitzifies** (there are Gr/E signs in all intersections). In Tzitzifies you will see a large pink church before which starts a dirtroad going right (D3). This is your last chance to enjoy a route through the northern side of the White Mountains, one that does not stop in the middle of nowhere (for a change), but makes a half circle and takes you to **Vafes**. If it was pretty late when you left Hania, or if you took your time along the way and find that it will soon be dark, **you can camp at an excellent spot** at the middle of the route. We are talking about the Vothonas plateau, found at a height of six hundred metres and having everything you need: thick grass, shade-giving trees, and a cistern with drinkable water. To get to Vafes, simply cross the plateau, ignoring the road you will see to your right (this seems to go up the mountain, but in fact stops after five hundred metres in front of a shepherd's hut). From Vafes you continue on an asphalt-paved road (A3), which will take you straight to **Vrisses**.

4: Hania-Sphakia

4.3 THE VAMOS PENINSULA

In contrast to the "tourist craze" prevailing on the entire coast west of Hania and the equally crazy situation in Georgioupoli, which is fast spreading to the Almiros bay area too, the Vamos peninsula will delight you with its peaceful beauty and unique landscapes. The lack of beaches to swim and the new national road which cuts the peninsula off from the rest of the island are the two main barriers that have kept the hordes of tourists away and have made it possible to save the region from tourist development. As a result, the traditional ways of the Cretan farming community have remained intact.

On this low rocky peninsula, some twenty small villages are nested, truly charming with their stone-built houses and narrow cobbled streets, and full of the wonderful smell of home-cooked food and the sound of playing children. Yet many houses have been abandoned and neglected by their "modern" owners who preferred the profitable tourist beaches to the exhausting farm labour and the isolation of the village. Fortunately, many of these houses have been bought - often at bargain prices - by foreigners who seem to appreciate them more, and instead of lying in ruins they have been carefully and lovingly restored.

To enter this beautiful area, exit the National Road twelve kilometres outside Hania and turn left at the junction leading to **Kalami** and **Kalives**. If, however, you decided to visit ancient Aptera first (a wise choice!) you can continue south of Megala Chorafia to **Neo Chorio** (the name means New Village, but the village was actually visited by Pashley in 1834) and from there you can head east towards **Armeni** on a road lined with huge eucalyptus trees. You will at some point encounter the National Road and cross under it. When you arrive at **Kalives** you'll see that all roads crossing the peninsula begin here.

Kalives (the word is Greek for "huts") is exactly the opposite of what the name suggests. It's a large noisy village with a lot of traffic, much like Kalami which lies three kilometres to the west. These two places are the only ones that have been infected by "tourist fever," mainly because they are situated to the right and left of a long beach, which happens to be the only good place to swim in the peninsula.

Somewhere along this beach, or perhaps a little closer to **Almirida** in the east, stood the ancient town of **Ippokoronion**, one of ancient Aptera's two harbours. This is also where the Arab conquerors of Crete landed their troops in 826 AD, a "performance" repeated some thousand years later by the Egyptians, Turkey's allies. During the latter attack, the local people fought back with iron determination and the beach was filled with dark corpses. Today the beach is filled with dark bodies every summer, which the locals also "attack" with iron determination.

The floor mosaic of the early Christian basilica in Almirida.

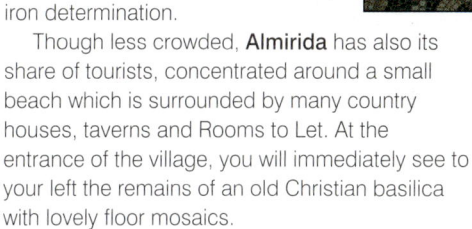

Though less crowded, **Almirida** has also its share of tourists, concentrated around a small beach which is surrounded by many country houses, taverns and Rooms to Let. At the entrance of the village, you will immediately see to your left the remains of an old Christian basilica with lovely floor mosaics.

From here on starts an interesting route (A4), which will take you through the charming villages of **Plaka** and **Kokkino Chorio** and all the way to cape Drepano, the tip of which is inaccessible due to the presence of an army camp. Continue to the south towards the attractive **Drapanos, Palialoni** and **Kefalas**, and make a stop at the **Likotinara** village square to enjoy an impressive panoramic view of the Almiros bay and Rethimno. Then take the road to Selia and Amigdali and continue until Vrisses. From here you can head for Sphakia.

Vrisses is the starting point of an impressive route (A3) through the eastern side of the White Mountains, which goes through the Sphakia mountain area and ends at the southern coast of Crete and the Libyan sea. This route is popular and very scenic, and the road is asphalt-paved and quite decent, but one needs to be careful of the many sharp U-turns and the heavy traffic.

Approximately four kilometres south of **Vrisses** you will spot a road (A3) heading east (toward **Alikambos**). It's worth making a detour and following this road. At Alikambos you will see a dirtroad (D3), also heading east. This stops suddenly after a while, but it is worth taking if only to enjoy a magnificent view of Lake Kourna and of

"It was Crete's fate to challenge Death and to wear on its head the black veil..."

Old Ieronymos was born in 1913, the year that Crete regained its freedom after seven hundred years of Venetian and Turkish rule. The smell of gunpowder, the gunshots and the black colour of mourning have been part of his existence as far back as he can remember.

"Crete wears the black veil for mourning and sorrow. Crete has always been oppressed. There were Venetians, Turks, the Nazis..."

He did not just experience war and occupation through the stories of his father and grandfather but lived through them himself. In the second world war he found himself fighting against fascist Italy on the Albanian front.

"The hunger and the cold, that's what beat us. For eighty days we were on the 1600 hill to the right of Klissoura. And then that bastard officer commanded my company to take position five kilometres further to the north, more snow fell, and they lost our tracks. For four days we were stuck there, they didn't give us anything, they didn't even know where we were! The fourth day they found us and they gave us some sea biscuits. You opened the pack and the biscuit would be full of insects. So we wiped the insects off and ate them. They dated from 1920! But what could we do? This was all we had, this is what we ate.

We dug a trench, threw two pieces of canvas on top to stop the snow storm hitting us, and inside we laid a few Italian blankets 'cause we had none of our own... So I tried to go to sleep and there was something bumpy under the blanket. I lift the blanket and what do I see: the knee of a poor Italian soldier that was buried in the snow! There must have been more than a thousand dead bodies lying on that hill under the snow, Italians and Greeks alike...

I left the battlefields suffering from frostbite... yes, me, a shepherd and a hunter who's used to the cold. There were 160 of us in our company, but only 27 survived...

And today young people serve in the army, they have a better time than at home and they want to commit suicide! They are all a bunch of sissies, that's what they are!"

the entire bay of Almiros with its sandy beaches. On your way back you will also enjoy a great view of the eastern side of the White Mountains.

Halfway the distance to Chora Sphakion, and about seven hundred metres above sea level, lies the Askifos plateau with four small villages surrounding it. Of these, **Ammoudari** is the most "advanced," having a gas and tyre station as well as a few restaurants and Rooms to Let. Since very few people wish to spend the night here, you shouldn't have any trouble finding a room. Your best choice, however, is the rooms of "barba" Ieronymos Gialedakis, located right above his tavern near the gas station (and note that there is also a shed for bikes!)

"But why stay at Ammoudari?" you may ask. Well, there are plenty of reasons. You can stay for the cool, refreshing nights and the star-studded sky. You can stay for the great walking routes: one to the west, leading to the Agriokephala peak and the Tavri refuge at a height of 1200 metres; one to the east, taking you to a fortress and peak Halara at about 1100 metres; one to the north, crossing the impressive Katre gorge; and one to the south, leading to Asphendou, and from there to Frangokastelo through the Asphendiano gorge. Finally, you can choose to stay for the great *sfakianès pìtes* (Sphakia pies) and the mountain tea with *piperòriza* (ginger root) that "barba" Ieronymos makes, or, above all, for the wonderful stories that he and the other old men share over a bottle of *rakì*.

The most impressive part of the journey is from Ammoudari to Chora Sphakion. The road, carved on the western side of the impressive Imbrian gorge, is narrow and full of bends and U-turns. It goes through a rough and barren landscape with steep grey rocks and high cedar trees and offers you an amazing view of the gorge below and the Libyan sea to the south. Although it could be characterised as dangerous, keep in mind that it was made in the middle of our century for travel by mule and not for vehicles, and treat it as a sight in itself... As for the old stone parapets, they are ideal for a short break from the journey or for a quick picnic! So drive slowly, enjoy the view, but beware of other vehicles too.

About two kilometres before you enter Chora Sphakion you will see a road (A3) to your left and a GR/E sign at the crossroads pointing you to

The Imbros - Chora Sphakion route

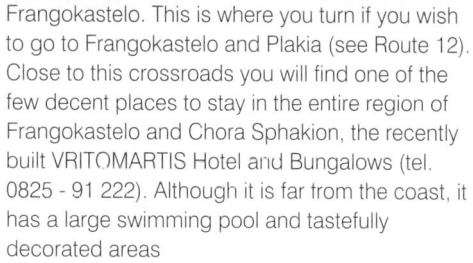

Frangokastelo. This is where you turn if you wish to go to Frangokastelo and Plakia (see Route 12). Close to this crossroads you will find one of the few decent places to stay in the entire region of Frangokastelo and Chora Sphakion, the recently built VRITOMARTIS Hotel and Bungalows (tel. 0825 - 91 222). Although it is far from the coast, it has a large swimming pool and tastefully decorated areas

SPHAKIA

Only two kinds of mammals have been able to survive on the isolated mountain slopes: wild goats and the Sphakia people. The Arabs and the Turks - both members of the carnivorous feline family(!) - conquered the island, but they hardly ever set foot in these places. And though the people of Sphakia suffered occasional raids, they never faced true slavery. Isolated on these mountains with the dozens of gorges and the countless paths and caves, keeping their primitive customs and their strict tradition of marriage within the family, they have managed to a considerable extent to retain their physical characteristics. They are generally blond, tall, and well built, and they have light-coloured eyes. The elderly as well as many of the younger people continue to dress in the traditional way (with boots, breeches and a headband), and **most of them carry guns!**

They live on a steep and barren rock, and the land, for the most part, is not fit for cultivation. Yet these people not only managed to survive, but they even became wealthy. How? **Piracy**, of course! They were the most feared and unscrupulous raiders and they terrorised the entire southern coast of Crete. They made no distinction

ROUTES STARTING FROM HANIA

as to the nationality of their victims, although they did show a distinct preference for Turkish ships... And whenever they were out of ships to loot they simply lowered the pirate flag and practised the honest trade of sea transport instead.

Today, the Sphakia people continue to make money out of sea transport. And although it is tourists that are being carried to and from the Samaria gorge and the surrounding beaches, their small shipping company, ANENDYK, still operates on a pirate mentality, threatening to sink any boat a competing company might dare to sail. You see, the stakes in this area are quite high: 300,000 passengers each season at 1200 drs. a person equals about... 360,000,000 drs. ANENDYK was founded in 1975 and today it has six ships, among which a couple of ferries that carry passengers like sheep in a truck! (Conversely, they will take no vehicles). Info on their timetables can be obtained at the following telephone numbers : (0825) 91 221 (Chora Sphakion), (0825) 91 251 (Aghia Roumeli) and (0821) - 44 222 (Hania).

Despite the threats, a small competing company, the A.N.E. SELINOU, was founded in 1993. Its base is in Paleochora, and it has one ship on the Paleochora - Aghia Roumeli line. Departures and arrivals take place during hours other than those of the ANENDYK boats (info tel. 0823 - 41 180), and of course the company would not even dream of touching Chora Sphakion although it has every right to do so. After all, how could the independent state of Sphakia, which did not surrender to Venice and Turkey, possibly bow to the laws of the Greek state and to the rules and regulations of the free market economy?

Today the Sphakia region still has an air of roughness about it, and this roughness characterises not only its people but also **its landscapes, which are the most exciting and least spoilt in Crete.** The infertile ground, the steep mountain sides with the deep gorges, and the fact that the area is far away from the north beaches and the famous archaeological sites, all seem to suggest the same thing: Sphakia will probably remain a fairly quiet place for many years to come.

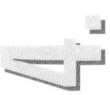

Chora Sphakion, however, is extremely disappointing. Abandoned during the difficult years of the Cretan revolution at the end of the 19th century, it succumbed to the destructive force of Time and saw its beautiful stone houses reduced to ruins. When during the early 70's tourism developed at the Samaria gorge, the Sphakians returned to this village to do business with the tourists who arrived by boat after crossing the gorge. But in the place of the old mansions they built tasteless hotels and restaurants, perhaps because they tried to do it overnight. They destroyed every traditional building, let the old neighbourhoods and the picturesque harbour go to pieces, and threw cement on the pebbly beach in front of the village. Today, Chora Sphakion, the once proud capital of this isolated region, is a chaotic mish-mash of buildings that have no character at all. Unless an effort is undertaken immediately to smarten up the place, even the most tired and starving tourists will pass through it without making a stop.

Sphakia: An unspoilt landscape of unique beauty

But do not let this ugly place get to you. Just keep going westward and smile, because just a little further you will see landscapes of sheer beauty, picturesque villages with all the authentic Sphakia characteristics, and **some of the loveliest mountain routes on the island.**

One kilometre east of Chora Sphakion you will find a pebbly beach - the only one you can reach by road - and a small bay, where you will see the ILINGAS BEACH (a quiet hotel with no phone). We recommend, though, that you go up the mountain and stay at a Room to Let in the picturesque **Anopolis,** which is an ideal base for exploring the southern side of the White Mountains.

The road (A3) from Chora Sphakion to Anopolis climbs the bare mountain side with plenty of 180º turns, so you will have a change of view from east to west as you ride. It's **a truly**

ROUTES STARTING FROM HANIA

enjoyable mountain route, and it will suddenly take you from the sea level to an altitude of six hundred metres.

Anopolis is a shepherd settlement with many stone-built houses and people that insist on wearing the traditional costume. There are a few olive groves around the village, but the rest of the region is full of **landscapes of unique beauty that have no sign of human presence.** If you wish to stay here for a few days - a smart idea, by all counts - you will find a few Rooms to Let and a tavern at the village to accommodate you. From here you can make several trips - whether on foot or by bike - and explore the beautiful White Mountains.

For the hiking trips, it will be necessary to obtain maps and information from the Hania Mountain Climbing Club (see the map of Hania, **33)**. Here we will simply give a sketchy description of the best options available. The easiest one is a two-hour walk to **Loutro**, a small seaside settlement in the south with quite a few taverns and Rooms to Let. (Note that this can only be reached by boat from Chora Sphakion and not by bike). A better idea is to reach the beach through the **Aradena gorge** which is no less impressive than that of Samaria (count on a five-hour walk). As you come out of the gorge, the mountain path descends to the very beautiful beach of Marmara. However, a little further to the east (as you head for Loutro), you can find more quiet beaches with a few Rooms to Let and one or two small taverns. Although these beaches are often visited by all those who take the boat or walk here from Chora Sphakion, they are large enough not to be crammed. If you wish to continue walking, you can follow the coast path to the west and reach Aghia Roumeli. This should take you about five hours, including a short break for a swim at the heavenly Aghios Pavlos beach. Needless to say, from Aghia Roumeli you can cross the Samaria gorge (8 hours, see page 172) and from Xiloskalo at the other side you can walk to the Kallergi refuge (2 hours). From here you can cross the White Mountains going southeast and be back in Anopolis in two days.

For those that do not want to give up their bike, there are two motorcycle routes: the first one to the north, to the heart of the White

4. Hania-Sphakia

Mountains at a height of 1800 metres, and the second to the west, to the picturesque Aradena and Aghios Ioannis. **Both of these routes are indeed beautiful**.

To take the first route follow the road (D3) that starts from the tiny Anopolis square with the tavern and heads north. This passes through some olive groves and then climbs the mountain side with many sharp turns. As it climbs it goes through a thick pine forest, which gradually gives way to a beautiful cedar one with remarkably tall trees. As you leave the pine forest behind, you will spot a road (D3) heading towards the east. If you decide to follow it, you will see that it ends at Mouri after only four or five kilometres. **Mouri** is a very large village that has unfortunately been abandoned. Over two hundred houses stand in ruin, and the only buildings in good condition are two shepherd huts and the small village church.

If you now return to our main route (the first D3 road), you will climb steadily towards the heart of the White Mountains, passing through a beautiful wild landscape with large grey and white rocks. The road suddenly stops at a ravine some 1800 metres above the sea. On the west side of this ravine a small path continues to the north to the White Mountain refuges.

For the second route, head west from Anopolis and after three kilometres you will reach the **Aradena gorge bridge,** an iron structure which will leave you breathless as a gap of 150 metres opens under your feet! Next to the bridge you will notice an old cobbled road which goes down the gorge and climbs up the other side. This was the only link of Aradena and Aghios Ioannis to the rest of the world until the bridge was made in 1986.

The route that starts at Anopolis and takes you to the heart of the White Mountains.

ROUTES STARTING FROM HANIA

Aradena, Sphakia: The Byzantine church of Michael the Archangel

The Aradena gorge is among the most impressive in Crete. Starting at the foot of the southern part of Mount Kedrokephala, it ends at the Phoenix Bay seven kilometres away and is characterised by its extremely steep and tall walls (over 100m). Crossing it is a truly unique experience, and one that is free of the many constraints and rules connected with the Samaria gorge. If you are planning to walk a gorge while in Crete, this is definitely your best choice.

The village of **Aradena**, on the other hand, is almost entirely abandoned. What will probably draw your attention is the church of Michael the Archangel, built in the 14th century and having a peculiar high dome and many beautiful wall paintings. From here the road (D2) continues to Aghios Ioannis, which has more inhabitants, a few Rooms to Let and a charming tavern. From **Aghios Ioannis** it continues to the north (as a D3) for another three or four kilometres, then stops suddenly in the middle of nowhere at a height of 1200 metres. Here it becomes a small trail leading to the higher tops of the White Mountains.

4. Hania-Sphakia

5. Hania - Kasteli

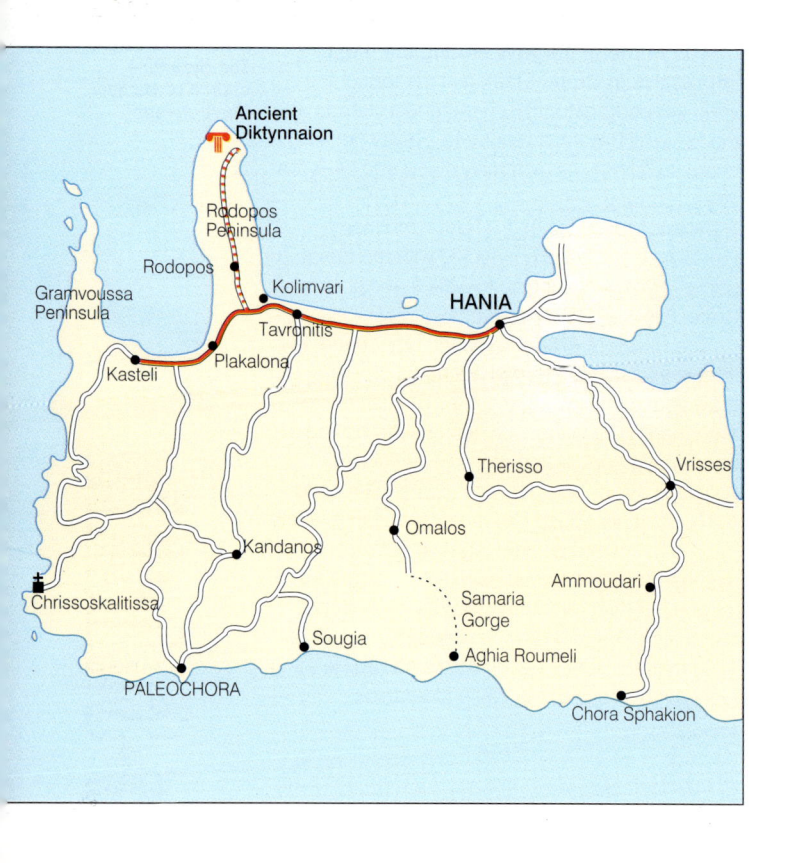

ROUTES STARTING FROM HANIA

The entire northern coast of Crete is quite even and often sandy, and for this reason it has frequently served as a landing point for both visitors and conquerors throughout the ages.

The coastline from Hania to Kolimvari has been especially attractive to invaders. This is where the Turkish army landed in **1645** (and based on this area it went on to conquer almost the entire island which it kept under its rule for 250 years). On this very same place a Greek army force landed in **1897**, marking the beginning of the Greek-Turkish war that led to the liberation of the island from the Turks and its subsequent union with Greece. This is also where in May of **1941** the terrible **battle of Maleme** took place after the sky started raining German parachutists determined to set foot on the island. Both sides suffered heavy casualties in this battle and the land was filled with corpses of Germans and allies - Brits, Australians and New Zealanders - lying side by side. Today another huge invasion takes place every summer, as tourists "storm" the hotels, the taverns and the scarce sandy beaches of the area, causing a frightful strain.

On the other hand, if you want to get to the most heavenly places, you must first endure the torments of hell! Indeed, the shortest route to the wonderful peninsulas of Rodopos and Gramvoussa is the coastal highway. **This road is lousy, slippery and narrow, and it usually has a lot of traffic.** It passes through an area suffering from chaotic and tasteless "tourist development" and full of plastic signs inviting you to Rooms to Let, Hotels, Apartments, Studios, Villas, Handicraft and Souvenir shops, Taverns, Souvlaki Stands and agencies renting cars or organising Tours of Crete. This lasts all the way to Kolimvari, so travel these twenty-four kilometres carefully and without stopping, and as soon as you have passed the village turn to the north to enter the Rodopos peninsula. From here on your trip will become more pleasant.

THE RODOPOS PENINSULA

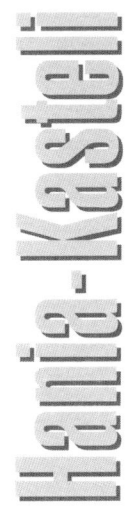

The roughness of the Rodopos peninsula is visible from a great distance. A bare brown rock with steep shores, without water, without trees, without even land for cultivation, it has never been inhabited - and will never be inhabited - because it cannot sustain life. On the other hand, since the early antiquity, the isolation and the magnificent wilderness of the landscape were the ideal environment for worshipping the gods.

The only exception to the emptiness of the place is the few small hamlets situated at the very beginning of the peninsula, and that's because of the small patches of arable land that allow people to have some fruit and olives. In fact, the **olive oil** of this area is of outstanding quality and it is sold in standard packaging under the name "Kolimvari, Extra Pure Oil" (it comes in a handy glass bottle of 500 ml, which does not leak and is highly recommendable). Until 1960, these villages were completely cut off from the world - the mule was the only means of transportation - but today they can all be reached by an A3 road. **Afrata** has two *kafenia*, which also serve a quick meal. **Astratigos, Aspra Nera** and **Ravdoucha** are small, poor villages with stone-built houses and elderly Cretans with the traditional black headband. As for **Rodopos**, it is the largest village in the area. It has a bakery, a grocery store and a butcher shop, so before you explore the peninsula you can stop and do your shopping.

Rodopos is also the starting point of a country road (D3), which was recently built on the track of an old path. This road takes you to the northeastern end of the peninsula, exactly before cape Spatha, where there is a small bay, Menies, with a magnificent sandy beach. **This was the location of the temple dedicated to the Cretan Goddess Diktynna.**

The dirtroad leading to the sanctuary of the Cretan goddess Diktynna

THE ANCIENT DIKTYNNAION

Diktynna was an ancient Cretan Goddess who had a lot in common with Artemis. She was the goddess of hunting and was young, beautiful and a virgin by conviction. For this they had given her the name **Vritomartis,** which means "sweet virgin." She was worshipped all over Crete but especially in the western part of it where most of her sanctuaries were located. The most famous and wealthiest one was Diktynnaion of Rodopos, where during the Hellenistic and Roman period worshippers kept coming with rich offerings from all over Greece as well as from other parts of the Mediterranean. Custom required them to arrive barefoot, in order to be in direct contact with the earth and the nature which the Goddess personified. During the dark ages following the collapse of the Roman Empire the sanctuary was abandoned and looted, but the foundations of a temple and a sacrificial altar, both dating from the reign of Hadrian, remain intact. In the valley west of the temple, close to the sea, there are more ruins, including those of a Roman aqueduct which probably provided the priests and visitors with water. Also, a few ruins of older temples can be seen, dating from the 7th and 6th century BC.

Today the area has been deserted and there are only some ruins of recent buildings to be seen. The only building that remains intact is a small chapel, built by the local fishermen who come here to find shelter from the storm or to rest before pulling their nets. In August many tourists arrive, either by boat from Hania or with rented cars or bikes, but in May, June, September and October, the area is a true paradise. You will have at your disposal a wonderful sandy beach, an almost unexplored archaeological site, a solitary place for long walks and all the tranquillity you could hope for. Among the ruins there are plenty of pine and cedar trees offering a welcome shade, and the patches of thick grass growing around them make **ideal spots for camping.** You will also find lots of wood on the beach for your camp fire, and a well, close to the chapel, which can provide you with fresh water for your shower. It might be better not to drink from it, though, as it is not certain that it's potable.

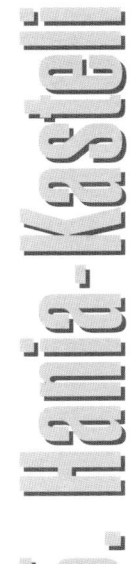

The secluded beach at the bay of Menies

About three kilometres before the Menies bay a small country road will lead you to the ruins of a monastery of the ninth century. The parts of it that have survived to this day are the church, dedicated to Aghios Georgios, and a few cells. In the only cell that has a roof, a goat herder has set up his household and his few goats animate this barren landscape. There is also an impressive tower, the remnant of the strong fortification the monastery needed to defend itself from the frequent attacks of pirates who terrorised the region. It seems that after some time the monks, tired of fighting rather than praying, decided to transfer their monastery from the lion's mouth to a safer place. Acting on this decision, one beautiful morning in **1618**, they packed their belongings and left to set up a new monastery at the south end of the peninsula.

In this endeavour they were prompted by *Osios Vlasios*, who came to live with them somewhere around the beginning of the 17th century. One night, the story has it, as Osios Vlasios was praying, he saw a vision of the Holy Mary, who **led him** to the place where she wanted a monastery built in her honour. It was this vision that gave the monastery its name, **Moni Panagias Odigitrias,** as it was Panagia Odigitria - the Guiding Mary - that dictated where it should be built. Construction started in 1618 and finished in 1634, as the sign on the church dome informs us. The monastery then grew rapidly, acquiring some very large estates that gave it substantial wealth. It was exquisitely decorated with paintings of saints and had a rich library.

ROUTES STARTING FROM HANIA

The remmants of the Aghios Georgios monastery

Yet, once again, the monks found themselves in grave danger: on the 13th of June, **1645,** fifty thousand terrifying Turks landed a few yards from the monastery, starting a fierce attack that resulted in the occupation of Crete. The scenes that followed are too horrible to describe. From that time and until the liberation of the island in 1897, Moni Odigitrias Gonias suffered endless raids, cannon shots, massacres, and fires. (In one of these, in 1867, the whole library was burned down and thousands of rare books and manuscripts were turned to ashes). Each time, though, the monks had the good sense to hide as many treasures as they could, and with their faith and endurance they kept the monastery alive.

Today, in the church of the monastery and in the small museum **(closed from 12:30 to 4:00 p.m.)** you can admire many of these treasures that have survived, among them priceless post-Byzantine icons such as The Crucifixion (painted by Konstantinos Palaiokapas in 1638), the icons of St. Nicholas (Palaiokapas, 1637) and St. Anthony(1772), The Assumption of the Virgin Mary (1728), and the triptych "Last Supper - Birth - This is the Man" (painted by Dimitrios Sgouros in 1622). You can also see a few manuscripts, early printings of books, silver vessels and pontificals and, most important of all, an invaluable **tomb stele of the 3rd century BC,** originating from the ancient Diktynnaion. It bears a relief representation of Efploia Aphrodite with a ship and Diktynna - Vritomartis with a Cretan wild goat.

Approximately five kilometres north of Rodopos a country road (D3) goes west and a

The rocky shores of Rodopos and Gramvoussa are a feast for the eyes

sign (Gr) directs you to the chapel of Άγιος Ιωάννης Γκιώνας **(Aghios Ioannis Gionas)**. This is where every year, on August the 29th, a grand three-day festival takes place gathering hundreds of people from the nearby villages. During the rest of the year, though, the area is secluded - only a few shepherds bring their flocks to graze - and you can camp during the night in the chapel's yard. The road continues for another two kilometres to the south (D4) and stops three hundred metres before the isolated **Aghios Petros chapel.** The entire west coast of the peninsula is nothing but steep rocks.

If you now continue westward (from Kolimvari to Kasteli) there are two roads to choose from. If you prefer to enjoy a speedy ride choose the National Road (A1/15km), which has good asphalt and the right inclinations. But if you are looking for a more interesting ride you'd better choose the old road (A3/20km), which winds up and down the hill sides, passing through huge olive groves and hamlets with stone-built houses. Be careful, though, because the road is very narrow and slippery and has many dangerous turns. At one of these turns, at the western exit of **Plakalona**, you will have a wonderful view of the entire Kissamos Gulf and the peninsula of Gramvoussa. If you happen to pass by at sunset, the view will be an unforgettable experience.

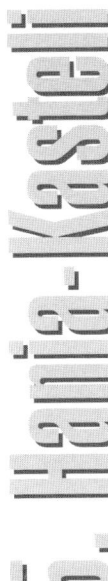

5. Hania-Kasteli

Kasteli Kissamou

Kasteli Kissamou, seen from the hill of ancient Polirrinia

ROUTES STARTING FROM KASTELI

Kasteli, officially **Kissamos** or **Kasteli Kissamou** (Kasteli of Kissamos), is the major town of the Kissamos county and has developed into a fairly large place with plenty of conveniences. This development is due to the fruit and juice canning industry, the vineyards, the well-selling olive oil as well as other agricultural products. It is also due to the many tourists it attracts without even having sights or beaches. The reason for this is its **harbour** and the boat lines to and from Githio and Kalamata at the south end of the Peloponnese. Most foreign tourists who arrive from their countries to the port of Patras, and especially the German bikers, find it very convenient that they can board a ship in the Peloponnese and get off in Crete. In this way they do not only avoid the unpleasant journey to Piraeus and the jungle of Athens, but they also get to explore Crete without having to go back and forth, because the ship docks at the westernmost port of the island.

The town has a history of at least **2500** years behind it. In antiquity it was called **Kissamos** and it served as the seaport of ancient Polirrinia. It flourished from the classical times till the Roman period and was a close ally of the Romans, which is why they did not only spare it when they conquered other Greek towns but they even adorned it with many public buildings. These included a large theatre, public baths, and a large aqueduct which provides the town with water to this day! In addition, the Romans built many luxurious villas.

Today, foundations of Roman villas are quite frequently discovered in the town's building sites, and many of the finest floor mosaics have come to light, dating from the 2nd and 3rd century AD. One of these is in the archaeological site right behind the Health Centre of the town.

Kissamos has been well fortified throughout its history, because its close proximity to the sea and its considerable wealth invited many attacks. Those who built the strongest walls, though, are the Venetians, who were masters in the art of fortifying a town. The Venetian Rule spanned the period between 1204 and 1664 AD, and the

Scattered all over Kasteli are parts of the city wall, now a prey to the destructive force of Time

Castelo, built from the very first days of it, became a landmark of the town, which was thence called **Kasteli.** (They also named it **Kasteli Kissamou** in an effort to distinguish it from the dozens of other Kastelis all over Crete). During its long history the town was besieged countless times, so the famous Castelo was often destroyed and rebuilt. What survives of it today is a jumble of parts built at different historical times. These can be seen just about anywhere, and unfortunately they have been left to their fate without the least provision for maintenance.

The port of Kasteli is situated about three kilometres to the west of the town. As you get off the ship and walk on the pier toward the shore, you will see the Rodopos peninsula to your left (west) and the Gramvoussa peninsula to your right (east), where you can also distinguish the country road that runs along the east side of it (see Route 6). People tend to get off the ship and immediately start their exploration of Crete, which is why Kasteli has **very few hotels** and even fewer restaurants! On the other hand, there are plenty of grocery stores, since everyone buys supplies before leaving for the big journey...

If, however, you want to spend a few days at Kasteli to get a rest and make short day trips in the area (see Routes 6 and 7), your best choice is Vista Del Mar Villas (tel. 0822 - 22 008). You will see the villas on your way to the town about 1.2 kilometres after the port. They are very cosy, inexpensive and comfortable, and they come with a bedroom, sitting room, bathroom and kitchen, and a balcony overlooking the sea. You should also know, however, that they don't like to rent them for less than three nights, so if you are planning on making a one-night stop you'd better look elsewhere. A very decent alternative is the Helena Beach Hotel (tel. 0822 - 23 300), built right next to an attractive beach. As you approach the town, you will see it on your left hand side.

Camping is another interesting option you have. A few kilometres to the east of Kasteli you will find two good camping grounds, so avoid the Kasteli camping, which is noisy, neglected and situated at the... backyard of a factory! Take the new road to Hania and after five kilometres you will see an intersection. The sign at the intersection points you to the **Mithymna Camping** (tel. 0822 - 31.444), a rather primitive establishment with few luxuries, but with beautiful trees, lots of shade, peace and quiet, and a large sandy beach in front of it with a very nice restaurant. In fact, this business was recently expanded to include... a newly built apartment complex, so if you change your mind about camping you can always rent an apartment instead! The second option is **Nopigia Camping** (tel. 0822-31.111), which is about 1.5 kilometres further to the east. It, too, has peace and quiet and nice trees for shade. It also has flowers, common areas that are well looked after, and a large swimming pool. As you may guess, however, the swimming pool exists because the beach in front of the hotel is covered with fairly large stones and is rather uninviting.

If you are not particularly fond of organised camping we have still another suggestion. Continue to the east on the dirtroad going along the beach, and right after you pass Nopigia Camping you will run into a fenced pastureland that blocks your way. Open the door, get in, shut it behind you, and keep going. After a while you will see a chapel with a covered yard and a small pebbly beach in front of it. **This entire area is ideal for camping;** it's full of trees, it has a drinking fountain next to the chapel with cool, refreshing water, and the ground is quite level allowing you to set up your tent comfortably. For your camp fire try to use the same spot as the people who were there before you. Finally, collect your garbage in a plastic bag and take it with you when you leave, because there are no barrels around.

6. Kasteli - Gramvoussa

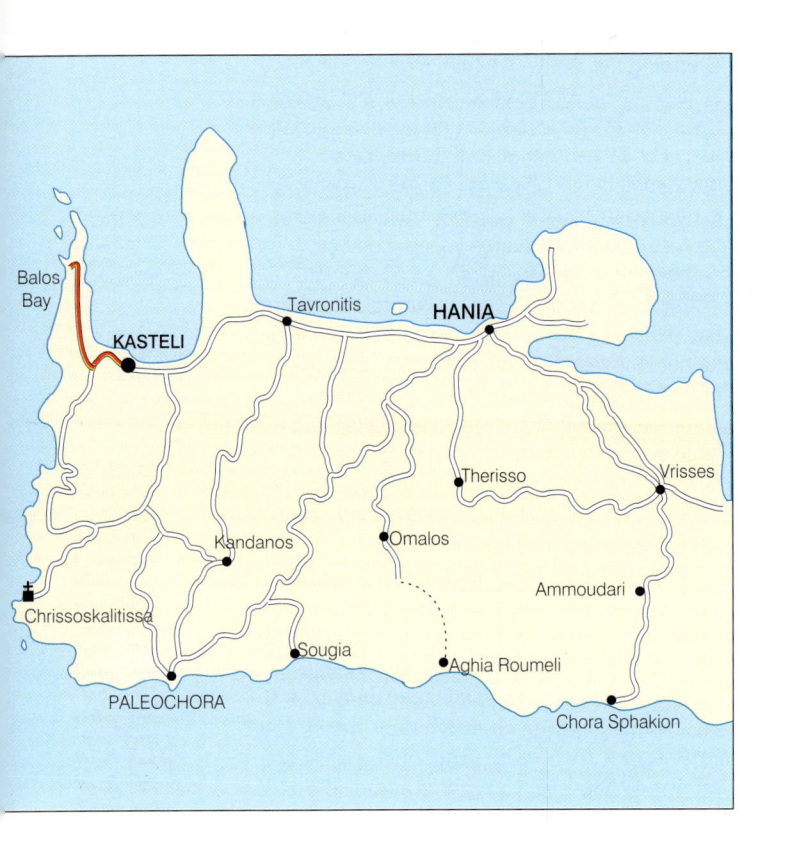

ROUTES STARTING FROM KASTELI

You take the road going west and after Trachilos you turn toward **Kaliviani**. The asphalt stops and a sign (Gr/E) directs you to "Balos / Gramvoussa Peninsula" in the north.

The **Gramvoussa peninsula** is a large piece of rock that sticks out into the sea and is covered with thorny bushes, marjoram, sage, thyme and thousands of wild flowers. A dry and barren place with steep rocky shores, **it hides at its northwestern part one of the last paradise lands of Crete.** In cape Tigani there is a very wide beach with fine white sand, which is known as **Balos Beach.** Behind it is the steep slope of Mount Geroskinos (762m), while in front of it lie two desert islands, Agria and Imeri Gramvoussa, which look like two pirate ships turned into stone. The water is shallow and warm, and the sea floor is covered with the same white sand, which gives the sea an emerald green colour like that of the tropical Pacific Islands...

This place is ideal for camping, provided of course you have taken with you everything you need. At the one end of the beach there are two fishermen huts. Every summer their owners turn them into tavern-bars that serve a few basic dishes and soft drinks. However, it is best not to have to rely on them, because it is an amateur set up and they may close for days without prior warning.

The dirtroad (D1) going to this place was built recently on the track of an earlier path. It starts from Kaliviani and follows the eastern slope of Mount Geroskinos, offering a great view of the steep Gramvoussa shoreline and of the Rodopos peninsula just opposite to it. About two kilometres before the beach the road suddenly stops - thank God - and it doesn't look like they are planning to continue it. Then a path starts, easy to see and follow, which takes you all the way to the beach. If you want to enjoy an **enchanting view** of the entire northwestern side of the peninsula, do not follow this path but climb the smooth mountain slope west of the point where the road stops. If you keep going northwest you will eventually get back on the path.

There is also a side path that goes north. This takes you to the chapel of Aghios Sostis, which is built among the ruins of **Agnion,** an ancient

Balos Beach

Roman town, where according to the ancient writers there was once a temple of Apollo. Finally, another historical chapel, dedicated to Aghia Irini, is at the east side of the dirtroad, just before it ends.

Some of the most beautiful places of Crete can be reached neither by bike nor on foot. One such place is the **desert island of Imeri Gramvoussa,** which can only be reached by boat from Kasteli.

Imeri Gramvoussa (Tame Gramvoussa) is anything but what its name implies. In reality, it was a site of hard battles and a pirate nest. The story starts in **1579**, when the Venetians, rulers of Crete, decided to build a fort to protect their ships which sailed these waters on their way to and from Venice. Three years later, on the top of the steep rock stood a well-built fort that was **unassailable** indeed. Its water supply came from two wells and five large cisterns and it was soon filled with weapons and ammunition; in 1630 the list included 24 cannons of different bore, 4000 cannon-balls and 40,000 pounds of gunpowder.

When Crete was conquered by the Turks, the Morozini Treaty provided that this fort, together with the forts of Souda and Spinaloga, would remain under Venetian control. But the Turks had other designs, and they used the only effective means they had to conquer it. **They bribed the**

officer in charge, who opened the door for them, turned over the keys, said "Welcome to Gramvoussa," and then boarded a Turkish vessel for Constantinople where he lived to be a very old man, dishonest but rich!

The Turks stayed in the fort for 130 years during which there was no need to fire a single cannon shot! They simply sat in this desolate place and watched the seagulls flying by...

Then one day, in 1821, the Greek Revolution broke out and the Cretans decided that they needed a safe base of operations. They chose the fort in Gramvoussa because it was exceptionally strong, there was a harbour for their ships, and it was close to the Peloponnese where the people had also rebelled against the Turks. In December of **1823** the Turkish garrison numbered only fifty soldiers. One night a body of five hundred men came quietly ashore. Their leader, **Bouzomarkos,** climbed up the wall, jumped in, went straight to the gate guard post, and stabbed the guard who was innocently sleeping in the arms of his sweetheart. Gallant as he was, though, he pitied the woman and spared her life. This, of course, turned out to be his fatal mistake. The woman escaped, woke up the guards with her screams, and Bouzomarkos was killed before he had a chance to open the door. **(Moral: Never underestimate the power of a woman!)**

The Cretans left the fort alone for a few years, until the Turks forgot the episode and returned to their usual deep sleep. Then one afternoon, in July of **1825**, seven hundred men, determined and fearless, rowed their boats to the east shore of the Gramvoussa peninsula and hid themselves in the chapels of Aghios Sostis and Aghia Irini. Three of them, who knew the Turkish language, disguised themselves as Turks, lit their pipes, and fired two shots in the air (a signal that they wanted the boatman to come from the fort and take them to the island). This was standard procedure and the boatman did as asked without ever suspecting them. The sentry at the fort, equally unsuspecting, opened the gate, received a grateful "thank you," and was promptly stabbed in the heart. Thus, our brave lads took the fort without ever spilling a drop of Greek blood!

Imeri Gramvoussa, the island with the Venetian fort

The rebels took hold of the fort and made it a base of operations in their war of independence. Soon, though, it became a base for a... different kind of operations, by which we mean "a pirates' lair." The pirates treated all ships passing in the area with equal fairness, although they did show a distinct preference for the British and French merchant ships. You see, there were three thousand souls in the fort and they had to be sustained. They did so well in piracy, though, that they soon had far more than their daily bread; **they gathered fabulous riches** and hid them in secret caves in Gramvoussa. Finally, the situation became unbearable and the victims decided they had to do something about it. One day the British and the French joined forces and a naval squadron appeared suddenly before the island. The attackers seized all the ships in the harbour, bombarded the fort, and finally took it. Then they forced everyone to leave the island (empty-handed, of course), and they tore down the houses and a part of the wall.

If during your walks you happen to come upon the mouth of a dark and narrow cave, take your flashlight and walk right in. For all you know, when you come out you may have a chest of gold with you...

ROUTES STARTING FROM KASTELI

6. Kasteli-Gramvoussa

7. Kasteli-Elafonissos

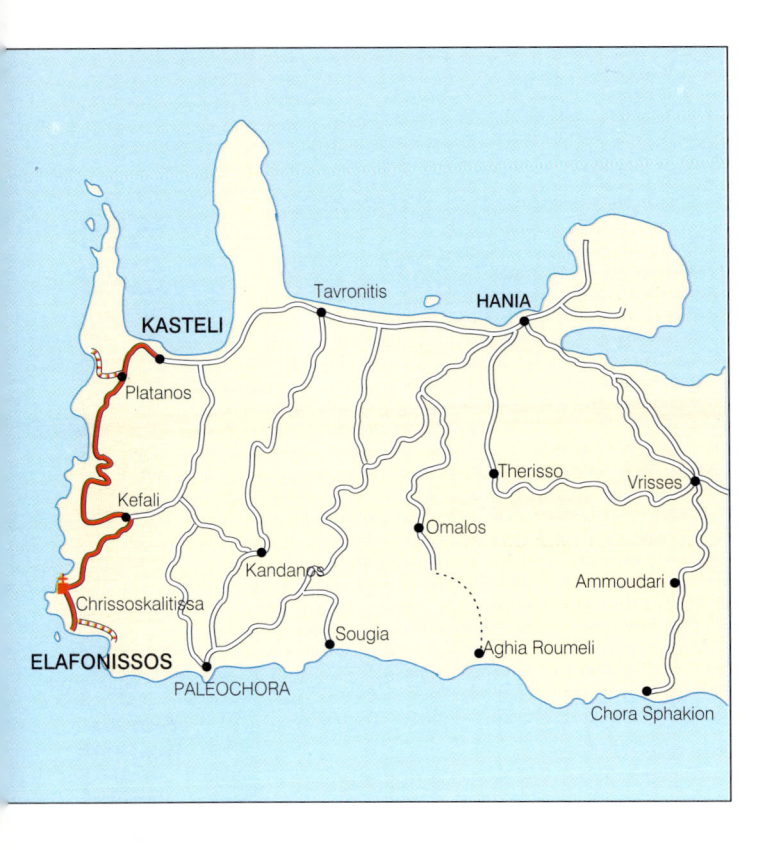

ROUTES STARTING FROM KASTELI

7.1 KASTELI - PLATANOS

This is a rather quiet route that goes through cultivated fields and small rural villages without particular interest.

Platanos is the largest village in the area with 1500 people who make a living out of olive trees and olive oil. Most houses are new and colourless, featuring walls made of concrete, but there are also some old stone-built houses concentrated mainly around the foot of the hill at the east of the village. If you walk through the village you will see an odd mixture of the old and the new lying peacefully side by side: courtyards with age-old **equipment used to make** *raki*, traditional bakeries, old-time coffee shops where the elderly sip Greek coffee and have heated political discussions, and next to them modern cafeterias filled with young people who spend their energy and pocket money on electronic games.

Should you feel like staying for an evening and catching a glimpse of life in a Cretan village, the Rooms to Let **Photopoulos** are the most convenient accommodations. The number is (0822) 41 052, and there is a very handy cement yard where you can park your bike under your window. The restaurant next door is quite good and it belongs to the same owner.

7.2 PLATANOS - FALASSARNA

As you leave **Platanos** from the south you will see an intersection with a Gr/E sign pointing to **Falassarna.** If you follow it, after five hundred metres you will have a beautiful panoramic view of the Falassarna beach, the cape where the ancient town was built, and the valley south of it which today is full of olive groves and greenhouses.

If you are thinking about taking a swim, there is a small pebbly beach right in front of the ancient town, and a second quieter beach a little further to the north, behind the acropolis rock. **A third beach, one of the best in Western Crete,** with very fine sand, lies south of the town and is three kilometres long. Its most beautiful part, empty and clean and without "development," is Pachia Ammos ("Thick Sand"), right in the middle of it. You will reach it if you take one of the many trails

Falassarna beach

that go through the valley with the olive groves and greenhouses.

South of the archaeological site are a few pension houses and small hotels. These are fairly close to the beach, but not at its best part. Among them, we recommend the Hotel FALASSARNA (0822 - 22 003), the Rooms to Let STATHIS (0822- 41 480), the Rooms to Let PETALIDA (0822 - 41 449) and the Bungalows SUNSET (0822 - 41 209). Needless to say, there are many quiet spots for camping all along the beach.

The fertile valley at the south of the Gramvoussa peninsula has always been the area's chief source of wealth. The Falassarnians chose to build their town at the north end of it, and throughout their history they fought hard to defend it from all those who wanted it for themselves. Falassarna was built right next to the sea, but the gradual rise of the west shore of Crete (and the sinking of the east shore) changed the topography of the area, so that today the town's ruins are about three or four hundred metres away from the water. To get there simply follow the sign as mentioned. The road actually goes north following the coastline, and at some point the asphalt stops and a dirtroad (D1) begins, which takes you further to the north. Take this dirtroad and you will soon see to your right an impressive **throne made of stone.** A little further you will see an imposing wall made of limestone, which once surrounded the town, as well as a small harbour. Although the only parts of it that have survived are a few large blocks of stone once serving as foundations and a few segments (which at places are

7.3 PLATANOS - ELAFONISSOS

If you leave Platanos and head south toward **Sphinari** you will travel on a very nice road (A3) that was recently paved. About a couple of kilometres before the village the road intersects a dirtroad (D3), which takes you down to the Red Cliffs Beach (Kokkina Gremna), a nice place that invites camping or swimming. In Sphinari you will find a few taverns and Rooms to Let, which accommodate the tourists travelling to Elafonissos (also known as Elafonissi). There is no special reason to make a stop here, except perhaps for a swim at the small beach south of Sphinari or for a nice lunch at the cosy little tavern next to the water.

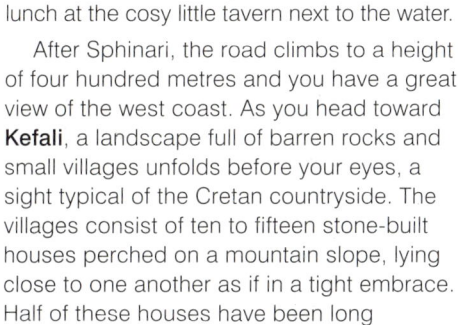

After Sphinari, the road climbs to a height of four hundred metres and you have a great view of the west coast. As you head toward **Kefali**, a landscape full of barren rocks and small villages unfolds before your eyes, a sight typical of the Cretan countryside. The villages consist of ten to fifteen stone-built houses perched on a mountain slope, lying close to one another as if in a tight embrace. Half of these houses have been long abandoned and the rest are inhabited by a few old people that insist on staying at the village and taking care of the few vines, olive

---

FALASSARNA

as high as three metres), you can tell it used to be a harbour because there are **holes carved in the wall to tie up the boats.** Also surviving are the foundations of a temple and of some homes as well as the stone-paved streets of the town and a few cisterns. A recent excavation of the Department of Marine Antiquities, which is responsible for the Falassarna area, revealed a bathing complex with four **clay bathtubs.** Finally, at the top of the hill are the remnants of the Acropolis wall and the ruins of a temple that came down with an earthquake and has not yet been excavated.

or fruit trees which they grow on the terraced land surrounding it. (As for the terraces, they are a permanent feature of the landscape and are meant to keep what little soil there is from being washed away by the rains). One of the villages you will pass through is **Amigdalokefali,** where it is worth making a stop to visit the Byzantine chapel that is dedicated to Michael the Archangel. The church bell is Venetian and it dates from 1628.

THE CRETAN BISCUIT

Nikos Tsatsaronakis of Platanos Kissamou was born in a baker's family, and his first images of the world included bread loaves and biscuits and barley flour, which to him had the aroma and the flavour of Life itself. This is why when he grew up and took over the family business he named it "The Manna."

"Since 1952 I've been baking biscuits in the old traditional way. The barley is ground between two millstones, and the dough is baked in an oven heated with wood fire. Then it is sliced by hand and the slices go back into the oven and are baked some more. This is how my grandma used to make biscuits, this is how I make them too."

Biscuits come in many different kinds and shapes. There are the barley and the rye biscuits, made of at least 85% pure barley and rye flour respectively, which are most people's favourites. There are the classic biscuits, biscuits that come in rings or half-rings, and biscuits in bite-size that make a perfect snack. The latter are the base for a very tasty appetiser known as "tako." You will see it quite often in Crete (as well as other places in Greece), and it is so nutritious that it can even substitute a meal! To make it, you simply dip a biscuit in water so it gets softer, put a little olive oil on top, cover it with a chopped tomato and some feta cheese, and sprinkle it with oregano and salt.

Biscuits are a good snack by themselves, but they can also be dipped in tea or coffee, or eaten with feta cheese and olives (or with anything your heart desires). They taste great, cost little and are quite nutritious, which explains why people like them so. As Nikos Tsatsaronakis puts it, "if God truly loved His people, then the manna He sent them from heaven must have been biscuits."

ROUTES STARTING FROM KASTELI

The next stop you must make is at **Kefali**, which used to be the largest village in the area. Today its few remaining inhabitants cultivate their olive trees and do business with the passing tourists. There are two or three taverns on the main road and a few Rooms to Let, and there is also a small mini market for your shopping needs. Of course, we suggest you visit the two Byzantine churches of the village. The Metamorphosis church has an inscription informing the traveller that it was restored and decorated with wall paintings in the year **1320.** The church of Aghios Athanassios was built in 1394, and on the wall facing south you can see an impressive painting of two ladies in elegant, low-neck dresses. In case you are wondering, these ladies were the owners of the church.

Right after the east exit of Kefali, you will see an intersection with a sign (Gr) directing you to Χρυσοσκαλίτισσα **(Chrissoskalitissa)** and Ελαφόνησος **(Elafonissos)** in the south and to Χανιά **(Hania)** in the northeast. The route to the Chrissoskalitissa monastery follows the north side of the small ravine of Xiropotamos, then goes through a couple of half-deserted traditional villages, **Vathi** and **Plokamiana**. In the wider area around the monastery there are several country homes, three or four tourist taverns, and a few Rooms to Let. Of these, we recommend the newly built GLYKERIA (tel. 0822 - 61 292).

Moni Panagias Chrissoskalitissas, "the Golden-Step Monastery of the Holy Mary," is a historical monument built on a low rock by the sea, in the same place where the monastery of Aghios Nikolaos was situated. According to the legend, one of the ninety steps of the monastery is gold, but it can only be seen by those who have the purest heart (we can assure you we saw nothing of the kind!) If you come late in the day, though, you will see a golden sun dive into the sea...

It is not quite certain when the monastery was built. The icon of the Holy Mary, which is devoutly worshipped, is allegedly a thousand years old. Our first verifiable information comes from 1855, when the Reverend Manassis Glynias, a monk consecrated bishop, came to live in the area and gave the monastery new life. Under his guidance new cells and storerooms were built and some fifteen nuns from nearby retreats came to live here. In 1894,

The Chrissoskalitissa monastery

a new, large church was built, the same one we see today, and it was promptly decorated with paintings of saints. Then, in 1900, the monastery ceased to exist officially and its property was sold. Yet the candles never stopped burning, thanks to the faith and patience of some nuns that never gave it up. Since 1955, an amazing priest, **Father Nektarios,** has put in a lot of personal work and, together with the only nun that lives there today, has kept up the buildings and the tradition of the monastery. Though the monastery itself has nothing special to show, it is worth visiting it if only to meet Father Nektarios. It would be best, though, to avoid the high season (July and August), or you will get lost among the two or three hundred tourists that visit the place daily...

A little before you get to the monastery there is an intersection with a half-faded sign (Gr/E) pointing you to **Elafonissi.** A fairly smooth dirtroad (D3) takes you through an open area planted with olive trees and... country homes and ends just before a sandy beach opposite of Elafonissi. Today this beach has been turned into a huge parking lot, and it is filled with hundreds of cars that come here every day.

Elafonissi is a small island that can be reached by... walking, since it is only separated from the shore by a body of water that is about 100 metres wide and 0.5 to 1 metre deep! Because the water is so shallow, it is also very warm and has a sparkling deep colour that reminds of tropical islands. The island's beaches are covered with a fine white sand, very pleasing to the eye, but to see them you must come quite early in the summer, because in July and August there are **at least a thousand visitors a day.** They arrive by bus from Hania or by boat from Paleochora or in their own private vehicle, and the beaches disappear under thousands of towels and umbrellas!

Twenty years ago this island was a little paradise, but today, especially in August, it is more like hell. "Hell" also describes the situation around the turn of the century, when the lack of a lighthouse made the island a real death-trap for all the ships that were caught in the storm. Finally, it is an apt characterisation for what took place here in 1824, when 850 people in hiding, men, women, and children, were discovered and slaughtered on these very beaches by a barbarian Turkish-Egyptian force led by Ibrahim Pasha. All around them, the water and the sand were dyed red...

At about three fourths of the way between the monastery and Elafonissi, the road widens considerably and on your left-hand side you see some fences followed by an intersection. If you turn left here you will soon reach a much quieter beach lying at the end of an impressive **cedar forest.** This is a great spot for camping, but unfortunately there is no fresh water available. A second road (D3) starts here and goes north, climbing the mountain with many sharp turns. This leads to **Maniatiana,** from where you can either continue for **Paleochora** or take Routes 8,9, or 2 backwards and return to the north coast.

7. Kasteli-Elafonissos

8. Kasteli-Paleochora

THROUGH TOPOLIANO GORGE

ROUTES STARTING FROM KASTELI

Take the old road to Kolimvari in the east of Kasteli, and when you get to Kaloudiana turn south (in the direction of **Topolia**). This route is a classic for most people who wish to get from Kasteli to Paleochora, because it promises a first encounter with the famous Cretan gorges. And indeed, the **Topoliano gorge,** through which it takes you, is quite impressive; a deep ravine stretching over an area of 1.5 km, it has very steep limestone walls (sometimes as high as a hundred metres) full of

The route through the Topolian gorge

small and inaccessible caves, while its floor is covered with beautiful plane trees. The road (A3) is carved on the west side of it and it is very narrow. (At one point there is even a tunnel, which is one of two or three on the entire island). It also has many turns without visibility, so although the scenery in the gorge is indeed very attractive you should always keep an eye on the road!

Many tourist guides mention **the cave of Aghia Sophia** as an impressive sight. In reality, it is a rather shallow cavity in the rock without much interest, and it is full of garbage thrown by the deceived tourists and never collected by the Greek authorities. There is also a small

8. Kasteli-Paleochora
THROUGH TOPOLIANO GORGE

church at the entrance of the cave which looks more like a decrepit hut.

At both ends of the gorge there is a village - **Topolia** in the north and **Koutsomatados** in the south - with many Rooms to Let and even more restaurants. These are concentrated on the main street in order to attract the passing tourists, but they are not worth much. After Koutsomatados you have two options. You can take Route 8.1 and travel on an asphalt-paved road (A3), or you can take Route 8.2 and travel mostly on dirtroads (D3). Both routes will take you to Paleochora.

8.1 KOUTSOMATADOS - VOUTAS - PALEOCHORA

The road (A3) from Koutsomatados to Strovles goes through a typically rural area full of olive groves and small hills. Approximately one kilometre after Strovles you will see an intersection with a sign (Gr) that says "Βουτάς 15" (Voutas 15). Turn right (south) on the road (A3) that climbs the mountain and keep going. The asphalt is excellent, the turns are great, and you will be tempted to drive fast. Although there are no signs, the turns are not dangerous and there is always a protective bar by the roadside. You can ride all the way to Archondiko with excellent conditions - **the road is one of the best mountain roads in Crete** - and you will have the chance to see some beautiful White Mountain scenery. Right after the pass at the

The road to the Sklavopoula villages

north side of Mount Kendoukles, at a height of eight hundred metres, a wonderful picture appears before your eyes: at your feet the valley of the Pelekaniotis river, which is covered with olive trees, and in the west the villages of Sklavopoula. When you reach Voutas, the largest village in the area, you have again two options. If you want to drive on asphalt, follow the Gr/E sign directing you to Paleochora and turn left; you will go down the mountain, driving through the olive groves at the east side of a ravine, and you'll arrive in Paleochora in no time. But if you want to visit the charming Sklavopoula area and do not mind driving on good dirtroads (D1 / D2), follow the Gr sign that says "Σκλαβοπούλα 7" (Sklavopoula 7) and turn right. You will see many mountain villages - **Kalamios** (at the end of an asphalted road), Sklavopoula, Sphakia, **Maniatiana** (the starting point of a dirtroad leading to Elafonissi in the west), Vathirrouma, Azogires and Aghii Theodori - and they are all very picturesque and full of hidden charms awaiting a discerning eye. The route is also very pleasant, taking you through beautiful mountain slopes and offering some lovely scenery. After Aghii Theodori the road continues southward, going downhill, until it takes you to a seaside village, **Koundouras,** planted in the middle of an area with very large greenhouses. Here you turn east on the main coastal road (A3) and follow it all the way to Paleochora.

8.2 KOUTSOMATADOS - SASSALOS - PALEOCHORA

Once in Koutsomatados, turn left (east) on the road that leads to **Sassalos** (you'll see a Gr/E sign at the intersection). The road goes downhill, passing through several olive groves, and takes you straight to the heart of the village. It is a very picturesque village, built at the bottom of a ravine with lush vegetation, but its only inhabitants are unfortunately a few old people that have refused to leave their homes for a larger town. At the two **kafenìa** of the village, the old men gather and tell stories. It is worth stopping here for a simple meal and a glass of raki or red wine. (The latter, by the way, is produced locally and has an excellent taste).

A chat with these simple mountain people will certainly make your day.

After Sassalos, the road (D2) continues southward, following the course of the river that

RAKI (ALSO KNOWN AS "TSIKOUDIA")

It is impossible to visit Crete and not be treated to a few glasses of raki! Raki is the national drink of the Cretans. It is produced in practically every household, with a ritual that takes place at the courtyard, and despite the fact that it's a family thing rather than an industry **the production is massive!** There is no home without a pitcher or a small barrel of raki, and all through the day people drink small glasses of it, usually with friends. The custom is to accept the first couple of treats, to raise your glass and say **stin ighià sas** ("to your health"), and to **toss it down.** If you are not used to it, though, or if you are on an empty stomach, do not drink more than two glasses, or you are going to find yourself in a state of tipsiness (or downright intoxication!)

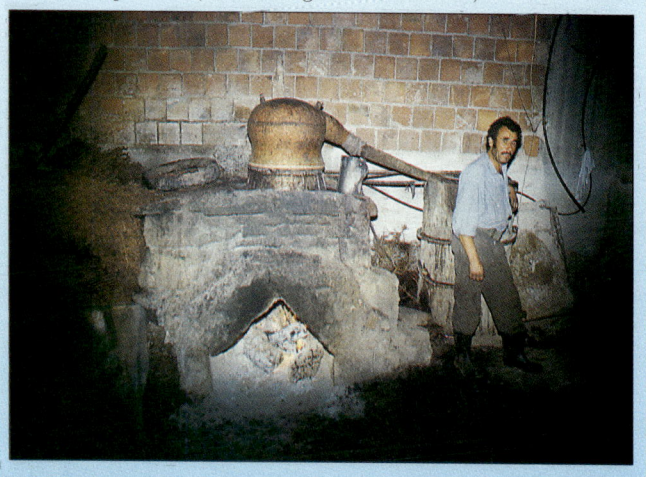

The distillation ritual usually takes place in the evening. They light a big wood fire and heat an old copper cauldron in which they place the **stèmfila** (the left over parts of the treaded grapes whose juice has been made into wine) along with **aromatic herbs** collected from the fields. The vapours are channelled into a spiral tube that goes through a barrel of cold water, they are condensed, and the raki drips into a ceramic jar that is half buried in the ground.

The peasants gather in big parties around the cauldron, and they sing and dance. They also consume large quantities of raki, freshly produced and tempting. The ritual has remained unchanged through the centuries, and if you happen to run into a group of folks engaged in it you should consider yourself welcome and prepare for a really... intoxicating experience.

ROUTES STARTING FROM KASTELI

One of the most picturesque villages at the Kakodikian stream

8. Kasteli-Paleochora THROUGH TOPOLIANO GORGE

flows through the gorge. **It goes through a beautiful area full of plane trees** and takes you to a small village called Milones. There are no sharp inclinations, so this entire route is good for walking or bicycling. If you like, you can pitch camp in many places, as the whole area invites camping. About one kilometre after Milones the road splits. Turn left and you will soon be on the main road, at a point just north of Dris. A couple of kilometres after Dris you will see a dirtroad (D2) to your right - there is a Gr sign at the intersection that says "Κοπετοί" (Kopeti). Turn right, and as soon as you cross the river turn left. This will give you the chance to enjoy **a very pleasant route** alongside the west bank of the Kakodikiano stream. The scenery includes thick olive groves and a dozen hamlets with beautiful stone-built houses. Unfortunately, most of these houses have been recently abandoned, and it is only when the olives are picked that people come and stay. All the other months, they are completely deserted.

The dirtroad you are on will eventually take you to **Vlithias,** a small village with a Byzantine church in its cemetery. This dates from the 14th century, and it is dedicated to Christ the Saviour (*Christòs Sotìras*). It has some beautiful wall paintings that are worth seeing, so follow the sign (Gr/E) on the main road and you will soon be there. From here on you simply continue on the main road (A2) that leads to Paleochora.

9. Kasteli-Paleochora

THROUGH EPISKOPI

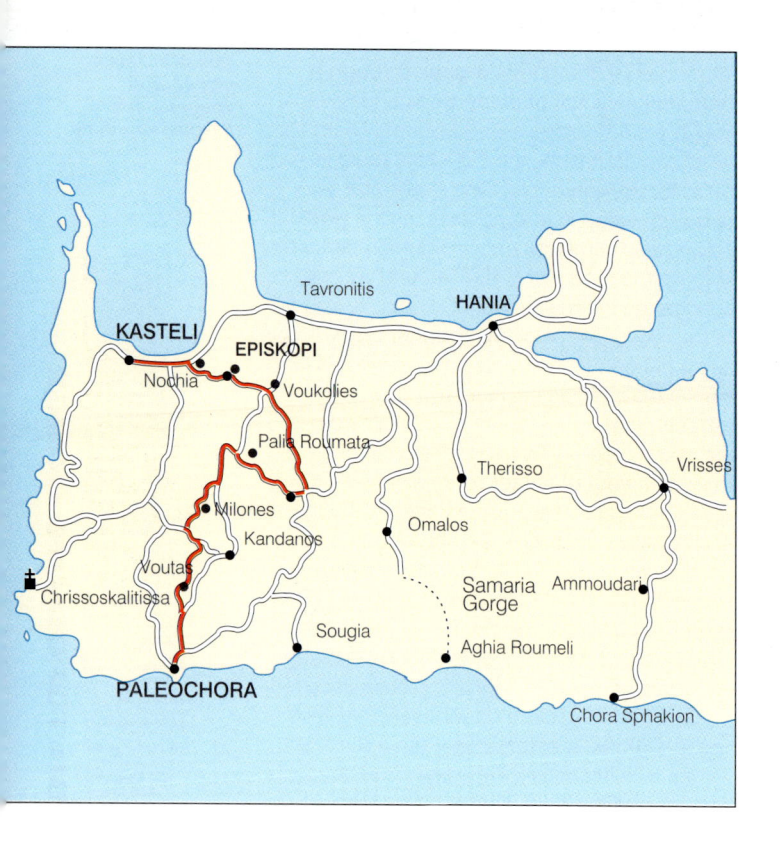

ROUTES STARTING FROM KASTELI

Head east and as soon as you are out of Kasteli turn right in order to get on the old road (A3) that goes to Kolimvari (there is a Gr/E sign at the intersection that says "Hania Old Road"). About a couple of kilometres after **Plakalona** turn right, following the direction of Nochia. (You will see a Gr/E sign at the intersection pointing you to the village). About 1500 metres after the intersection - and a little after you have passed Nochia - you will see another intersection with a Gr sign directing you to

The Byzantine chapel of Aghios Stephanos

"Γερακιανά, Δρακώνα" (Gerakiana, Drakona). Turn left, and follow the road (A3) as it winds up and down some small hills covered with olive groves and vineyards. When you get to **Drakona** you will notice that the village itself has nothing special to see. Yet 200 metres after its south exit there is a very narrow path - so narrow, in fact, that a bike can hardly follow it - which leads to the **chapel of Aghios Stephanos,** just 150 metres away. This is a small Byzantine chapel that's certainly worth visiting. Built in the beginning of the 10th century on the side of a small ravine that today is full of plane trees, it has thick stone walls

9. Kasteli-Paleochora
THROUGH EPISKOPI

The Byzantine chapel of Michael the Archangel

and a vaulted roof and it is decorated with some exquisite wall paintings that are quite well preserved.

As you continue southward, you will see a Gr/E sign just before **Episkopi,** which directs you to the Byzantine church of Michael the Archangel (otherwise known as "**The Rotonda**"). It is a very imposing church, which once served as an Episcopal seat (2nd Byzantine period, 961 - 1204 AD), and **it is like no other in Crete.** Its unique architectural feature is its dome, built in five successive levels. Judging from the few surviving parts of the paintings, such as the face of the archangel, its decoration must have been very impressive. Also impressive is the carved marble font with the two seats. The excavation of the area has revealed that religious worship in this place must have been an ongoing practice for at least 1500 years; the church was apparently built on the ruins of an earlier basilica, possibly of the 5th century, whose foundations (as well as a part of a floor mosaic) have survived to this day. Currently, the Rotunda is undergoing extensive restoration work, both on the inside and on the outside. Despite the fact, the people from the surrounding villages continue to visit it, and they never leave without lighting a candle.

If you plan to spend a night in the area, the best place to camp is the **plateau at the east side of the impressive Rokka gorge.** To get there, go through **Astrikas,** and take the

ROUTES STARTING FROM KASTELI

An excellent nook for camping above the Rokka gorge

dirtroad (D3) which you will see about 400 metres after the south exit of the village. (It is just opposite the Panethimos intersection and it goes west). The road goes through some olive groves and ends before a steep precipice just above the gorge. The place where it stops will charm you with its serenity and **panoramic view,** especially in the direction of the Kissamos Gulf and the village of Rokka. For those that would rather stay in a room, there is a new **guest house** in Astrikas that is appealing and has a safe parking area for your bike.

To continue your trip toward Paleochora, you can take one of the many fairly smooth dirtroads (D3) that start from Glossa, Vassiliana or Zimbragos and take you to the main (asphalted) road. The most interesting one starts at Zimbragos. You will probably have a hard time finding its beginning, so ask someone *pou ìne o chomatòdhromos ghià Kakòpetro* (where is the dirtroad leading to Kakopetro). That road goes through a beautiful small gorge and takes you to the main road just east of Kakopetro. From here you can continue south on the main road (A2), and you will get to Kandanos and then **Paleochora**. However, you must **drive very carefully;** even though you are on the main road, the asphalt is very slippery, the signs are totally inadequate, and the road is too narrow to accommodate the heavy traffic.

The above route is recommended for **street** bikes. But if you have an **off-road** bike, you can take an **alternative route** after Episkopi, one that **will take you through the mountains and offer you the most wonderful panoramic view of the entire Hania prefecture.** The Voukolies - Sembronas - Palia Roumata part of it could in

9. Kasteli - Paleochora THROUGH EPISKOPI

The Voukolies-Sembronas route

fact be rated **among the best three mountain routes in Crete.** The desolate landscape, the incredible scenery almost during the entire trip, the great places to camp along the way, and the very good condition of the dirtroad (D2 / D3), all contribute to this rating.

To follow this route, go east once you get to Episkopi and take any of the roads that will take you to **Voukolies.** In Voukolies you will see a road (A3) to your left, which goes toward Sirili in the northeast. (There is a Gr sign at the intersection that says "Σιρίλι 4"). This is the starting point of our route, so reset your counter in order to follow **Road Book 1.** Turn left on this road and **after 200 metres, in fact right after a small cement bridge, turn right** on the narrow concrete-paved road that you'll see. (There is no sign to direct you). This road goes through an area with orange and lemon trees, and after about 1 km it turns into a dirtroad (D3), climbs through the olive groves, goes through the half-deserted **Kafouro,** and offers a great view of the Tavronitis valley. All around, the mountain slopes are covered with bushes, and there are gorges with thick clumps of plane and chestnut trees. After 9 km you will be at an altitude of 800 metres, at the highest point of the route, and you will be driving just a few metres below the

ROUTES STARTING FROM KASTELI

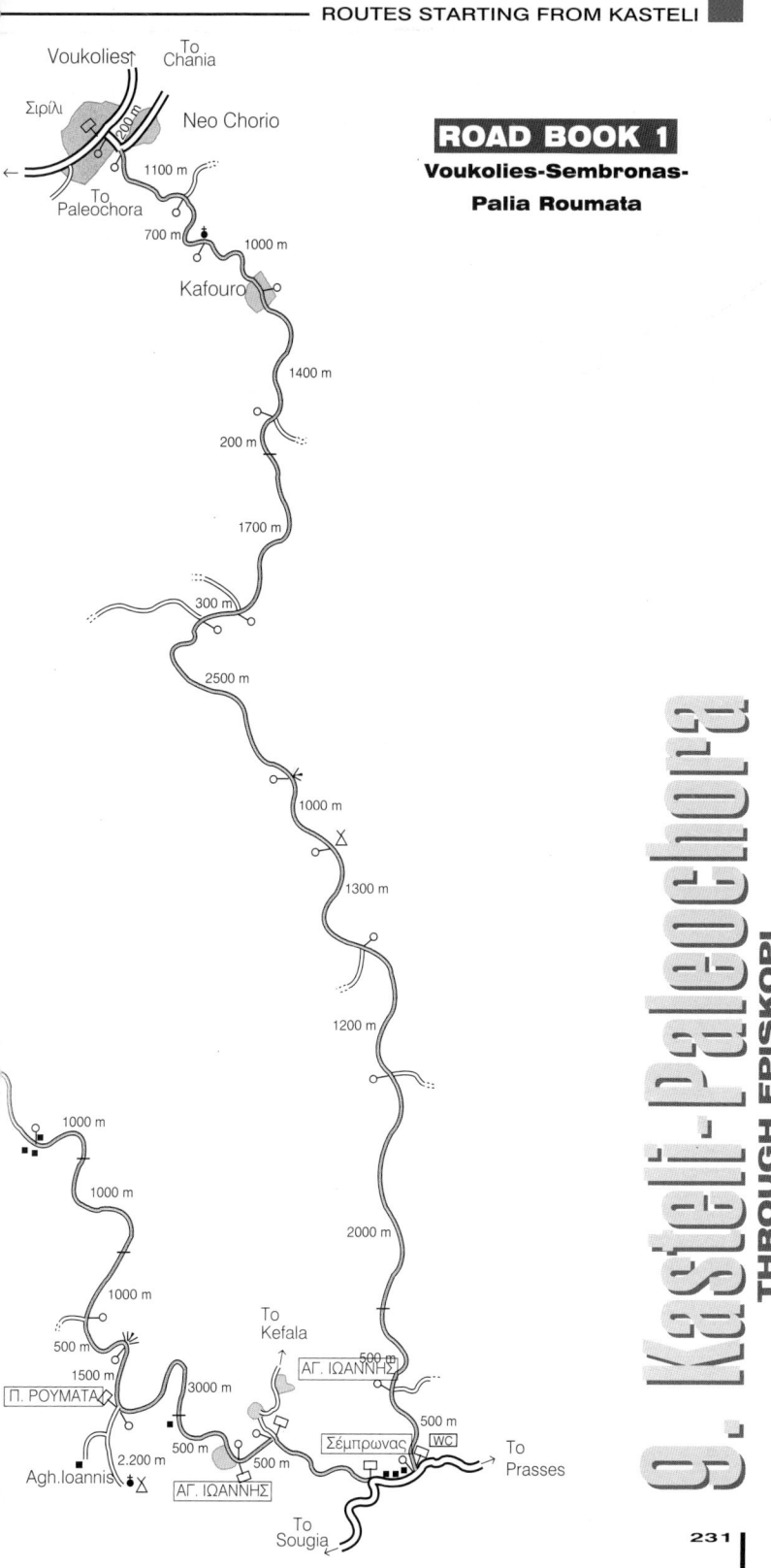

ROAD BOOK 1
Voukolies-Sembronas-Palia Roumata

9. Kasteli-Paleochora
THROUGH EPISKOPI

231

The chapel of Aghios Ioannis

peak of the mountain and enjoying the truly panoramic view. **The view to the north is particularly charming; you can see the entire Gulf of Hania,** the Akrotiri peninsula to the east and the Rodopos peninsula to the west. And if you feel like an eagle, you won't be the only one; just look around, and you may well see a family of four eagles flying slowly and majestically around the Plataniani peak (900 metres) where they have their nests... **If you feel like camping here, there is a wonderful small plateau** just a little bit further on the way, at an altitude of 750 metres. After the plateau, the road **goes along the mountain ridge, offering the most spectacular view.** It eventually leads to the Hania - Sougia road, which it meets right where the first of the area's three roadside coffee shops is (the one furthest to the north). Unfortunately, there is no sign at the intersection for those that would like to do this route backwards and to get on this dirtroad as they travel from Sougia to Hania. The only mark that could help you is a small white building. It is situated exactly where the dirtroad starts, and on the wall it has a big "WC" written with green paint...

This concludes the first part of this beautiful mountain route. About 200 metres further, you will see a Gr sign directing you to "Σέμπρωνας" (Sembronas). Turn right and prepare for the second, equally impressive part of the route. Just before the first of the five spread out settlements that make up Sembronas, you will see a dirtroad to your left with a small handwritten sign. The sign says "Δρακουλιανά, Αγ. Ιωάννης, Αποπηγάδι, Παλιά Ρούματα" (Drakouliana, Aghios Ioannis, Apopigadi, Palia Roumata), and in English it says "Palia Roumata." Here you turn right and reset your counter once again. For the next 500 metres the road goes through a cultivated area, climbing to Drakouliana. When you get to Drakouliana turn right. (There are two Gr signs at the intersection pointing you to Aghios Ioannis and Palia Roumata). After the last house of the settlement - at kilometre 1 - you will run into the gate of a fenced pastureland. Open the gate, go right in, and close it behind you. The landscape from here on becomes increasingly wild, and it is full of shrubs and gorges with thick clumps of plane trees. The road (D3) is generally "decent," with the only exception of two or three sharp turns with gravel. It goes uphill and at some point - kilometre 4, altitude 800 metres (the highest in the route) - it splits. At the intersection you will see a handwritten sign that's written half in Greek and half in English. One arrow points left, towards "Αγιος Ιωάννης" (Aghios Ioannis), and another arrow points right toward "Palia Roumata."

As mentioned, our route goes through Palia Roumata, so here you must obviously turn right. However, if you happen to arrive at this point when it's about to get dark, **there is no better place to spend the night than the chapel of Aghios Ioannis.** It is a beautiful stone-built chapel at the edge of a cliff, only 2.2 km from the intersection, and it has a paved courtyard with a wooden roof and wooden benches, offering the weary traveller a spectacular view of the White Mountains. If you'd rather not sleep outdoors, there is also a small room with a bed right next to the chapel, which is all yours (unless of course somebody was there before you). Finally, there is a fountain with ice-cool water, straight from the spring!

To continue toward Palia Roumata, you make a right turn at the Aghios Ioannis - Palia Roumata intersection, and you follow the road as it goes downhill. At kilometre 5.5 you will pass a col from where you have a great view to the west, a view reaching as far as the Gramvoussa peninsula. At kilometre 9 you will start passing through some small rural settlements, and at kilometre 11 you will encounter the concrete-paved road that connects Palia Roumata and Micheliana, where you must turn right. The main square of the village is only 1 km away.

Like all villages in the area, **Palia Roumata** is unaffected by tourism because it has nothing to do with the classic itineraries of most tourists. Its economy is clearly based on farming, and more specifically on the production of olives and olive oil. There is a good *kafenìo* hidden in a small alley, where you could try some very tasty Cretan specialties, but do not confuse it with the *kafenìo* at the main square. When you have walked around the village, get back on the road - no longer a dirtroad but an A3 - and follow it till the place just outside Kakopetro where it meets the main road that leads to Paleochora.

Whipping the olive trees

As you continue southward on the main road, you will pass through the large village of **Kandanos** with its many taverns and coffee shops. If you visited the place in the summer of 1941, the only thing you would see here would be a marble column informing the world - in both Greek and German - that:

> "At this site stood the village of Kandanos. It was destroyed in compensation for the murder of twenty-five German soldiers."

In no other instance of the second world war did the Germans show such a raging desire for revenge. They destroyed an entire village and shot every person arrested, because the peasants put up a fight. A second sign went even further:

> "Because the men, women, children and priests dared to resist the Great Reich, Kandanos was levelled to the ground and will never be rebuilt."

The Great Reich was of course nothing more than a Great Group of Psychopaths, a dream that burst like a Big Bubble, leaving behind it a

ROUTES STARTING FROM KASTELI

trail of destruction and chaos. Kandanos was rebuilt and grew into a beautiful small town. Yet its main square still has the column with the Nazi inscription, a permanent reminder of human stupidity and beastliness.

After Kandanos you continue southward through the Kakodikian ravine and as with the street route you reach **Paleochora**.

If, however, you cannot get enough of off-road routes and have refused to drive on asphalt, there is **still another option** before you reach Kandanos. When you get to **Floria,** you will see a dirtroad to your right and a Gr sign at the intersection that says "Σάσαλος 7" (Sassalos 7). If you turn here and follow the road to Sassalos, you can continue until Paleochora following route 8.2 (page 223). Here is a quick outline of the Floria - Sassalos route so that you don't get lost: At kilometre 2.2 you will see an intersection where you have three options. Here you turn left and go down the west side of the mountain. At kilometre 3 you pass a small village called **Selia.** At 4.3 you will see a dirtroad going up the mountain, but you ignore it and continue straight. At 4.8 you will pass another small village called **Maneriana** (this is in fact one of the Sassalos settlements) and you will see Sassalos, which is built in a ravine. At 5 you will see an intersection, where you turn left and go straight to Sassalos. (The dirtroad on the right leads to the picturesque **Pirgos,** another one of the Sassalos settlements, and from there to the asphalt road just north of Sassalos).

9. Kasteli-Paleochora
THROUGH EPISKOPI

10. Kasteli-Sirikari

In the town of Kasteli you will see an intersection with a Gr/E sign directing you to **Polirrinia.** The road (A3) goes south, climbing some small hills full of olive groves and vineyards. **Drive carefully because there are many potholes and dangerous turns.** The problem with the potholes gets even worse after the village of Grigoriana (where, incidentally, you can find a few Rooms To Let). It gets so bad that the road has... more potholes than asphalt, but luckily this doesn't last long. The asphalt ends at the centre of **Polirrinia,** where you will see a restaurant and some Rooms To Let; just north of the village is a hill (417m high) with the ruins of the ancient town. The foot of this hill can be reached in two ways: you can walk through the cobbled streets of the village, or you can turn left on the dirtroad that you'll see about a hundred metres after the sign at the village entrance. This road will take you to a cemetery, where you can leave your bike and continue on foot. At the cemetery you will see the church of the Holy Fathers, which is partly constructed with ancient building materials.

THE ANCIENT TOWN OF POLIRRINIA

Two cocks in the same hencoop are bound to fight, and two powerful towns in the same area cannot be the best of neighbours. Ever since the Achaeans settled in this area in the 8th century BC and built the town of Polirrinia on a tall, well fortified hill, they were in constant fight with their more powerful neighbours, the Kidonians, who had settled just a few kilometres east of the town, on the site of modern Hania. Judging from the name of the town (Polirrinia < Gr. poly, many and ren[e]a, sheep), one would think that the settlers were peaceful shepherds. In reality, they were a warlike people that survived mainly for being good warriors. Many of the town's coins depict Athena as a warrior-goddess, wearing a helmet and bearing a spear in her hand. Athena and Artemis, it seems, were the two patron goddesses of the town, and apparently they did a good job at protecting it since during the entire classical and hellenistic period the town and its two seaports, Falassarna and Kissamos, managed to survive without any major war catastrophes. When the Romans appeared on the scene, the Polirrinians quickly entered into an alliance with them - before the Kidonians could do the same - and with a sweeping attack they managed to teach their age-long enemies a good lesson. All during the period of the Roman rule, Polirrinia was a prosperous town, well protected behind its high walls. After the 3rd century AD we have no reference to it, but in the 10th century it is once again mentioned in the literature, this time as an important Byzantine town. Today one can see the ruins of the city wall, which belong mainly to the Byzantine period, as well as a couple of aqueducts from the Roman times, carved into the rock and preserved in very good condition. From the earlier periods of the town's history only few things have survived, such as the foundations of some temples and houses and a number of inscriptions. Also, close to the two aqueducts above the town is a small cave dedicated to the Nymphs, in whose walls one can still see the carved niches that contained the Nymphs' statuettes. If you are wondering what happened to the hundreds of stone-built houses and the temples and big public buildings of the town, you should know that they didn't disappear, but they simply

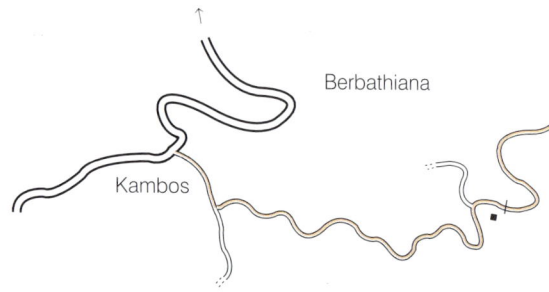

Scattered all around the hill are the ruins of the ancient town of Polirrinia

ROUTES STARTING FROM KASTELI

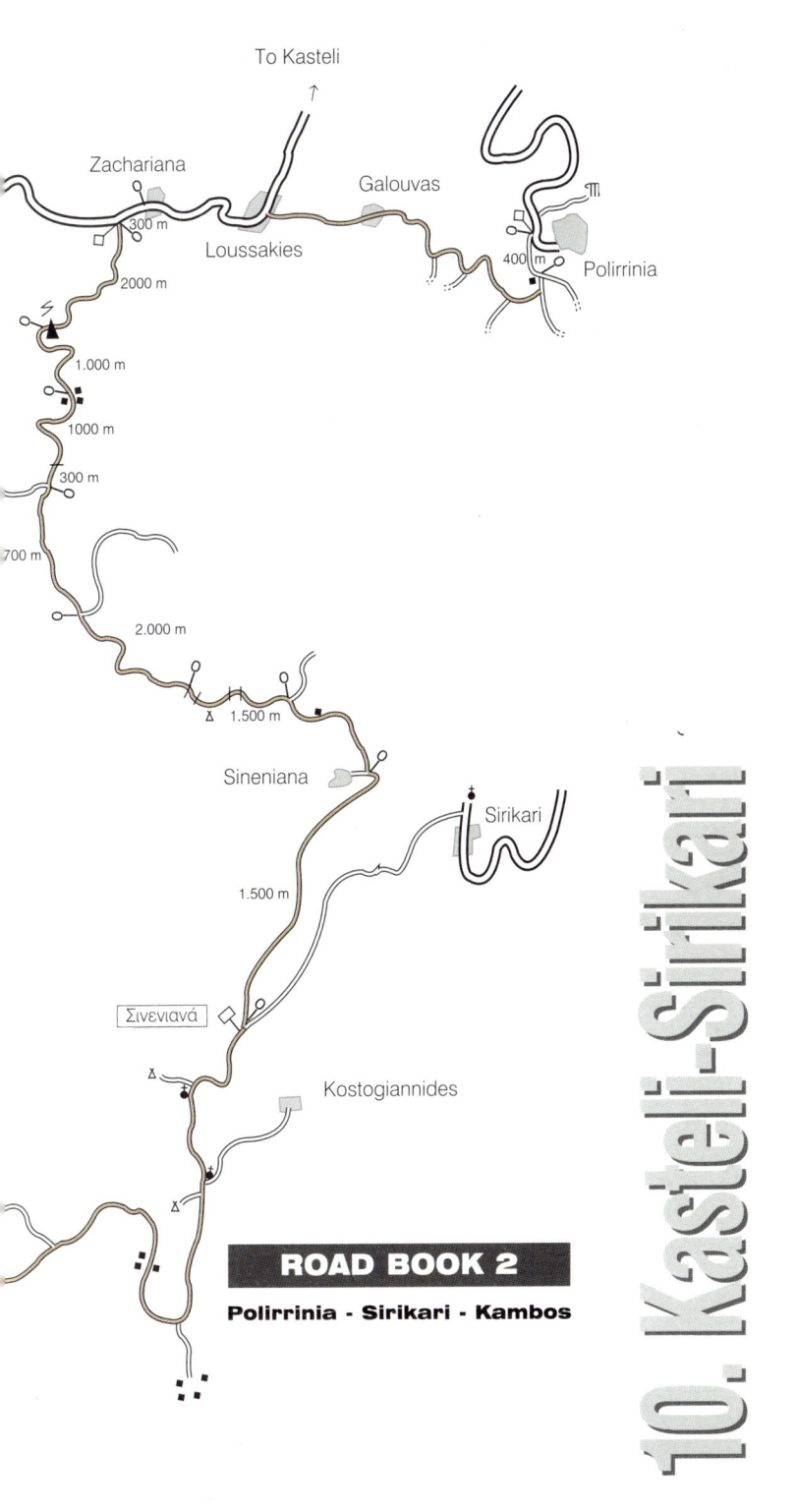

To Kasteli

Zachariana
300 m
Loussakies
2000 m
Galouvas
400 m
Polirrinia

1.000 m
1000 m
300 m
700 m
2.000 m
1.500 m

Sineniana
Sirikari

1.500 m

Σινενιανά

Kostogiannides

ROAD BOOK 2
Polirrinia - Sirikari - Kambos

10. Kasteli-Sirikari

changed form; the modern village of Polirrinia has inherited not only the name of the town, but also all building materials that were still of use. Recycling, one could say, in its purest form!

About 150 metres before the sign with the village name you will see a dirtroad (D3) to your right with a small sign marking the European Path (E4). Turn right on this dirtroad, and after 400 metres you will see a building with a tiled roof, which houses the elementary school of the village. Turn right and follow the E4 diamond-shaped signs: make a right turn 50 metres past the school and a second right turn after another 100 metres, and at the next two or three intersections that you'll see keep turning right. The road goes through a desolate landscape with low hills covered with bushes, passes through the small village of Galouvas, and takes you to Loussakies where it meets the main road. Go left at this point and continue until you get to **Zachariana.** About 300 metres after the sign west of the village, turn left on the dirtroad (D3) which you will see climbing the mountain - there is an E4 sign at the intersection - and reset your counter in order to follow **Road Book 2.** Until the village of **Sineniana,** you will be travelling through a rocky area with many chestnut and olive trees, while at some point you will cross a small plateau where you could pitch camp. (This lies about 550 metres above sea level). After Sineniana **the scenery becomes immensely enjoyable and you pass through a gorge full of plane, chestnut and oak trees** that has some very inviting spots for camping right next to the river. At about 1.5 km after the village you will see a dirtroad (D2) to your left, which leaves the gorge and joins the asphalt road just a few metres north of **Sirikari.** After Sirikari, the road (A3) goes downhill through the olive groves, and all you have to do is follow the signs that will take you back to Kasteli.

If you do not want to return to Kasteli, you have two options. One, you can turn right at **Kalathenes** so that you get to follow Route 8. Two, you can simply ignore the road that goes to Sirikari and keep going straight. A few kilometres down the road you will see a chapel followed by a dirtroad on your left-hand side. This dirtroad leads to the picturesque **Kostogiannides,** but we suggest you ignore it

ROUTES STARTING FROM KASTELI

and go straight. If the night is falling and you are tempted by the idea of camping in the area, **there is an excellent spot by the river, where you can camp in the shade of huge plane and chestnut trees.** (Just turn on the dirtroad that you'll see to your right about a hundred metres after the chapel and you will find it). When you get back to the route, follow the dirtroad as it turns to the west and climbs the mountain. You will travel through **a very beautiful forest of giant chestnut trees** and then through a pass at an altitude of eight hundred metres. This is the highest point of the route, and it offers a spectacular view of the west coast of Crete, especially at sunset. From here on the road winds down the mountain through the woods and takes you to the village of **Kambos** from where you can follow Route 7 to Elafonissi.

10. Kasteli-Sirikari

11. Sphakia-Rethimno

TRAVELLING INLAND

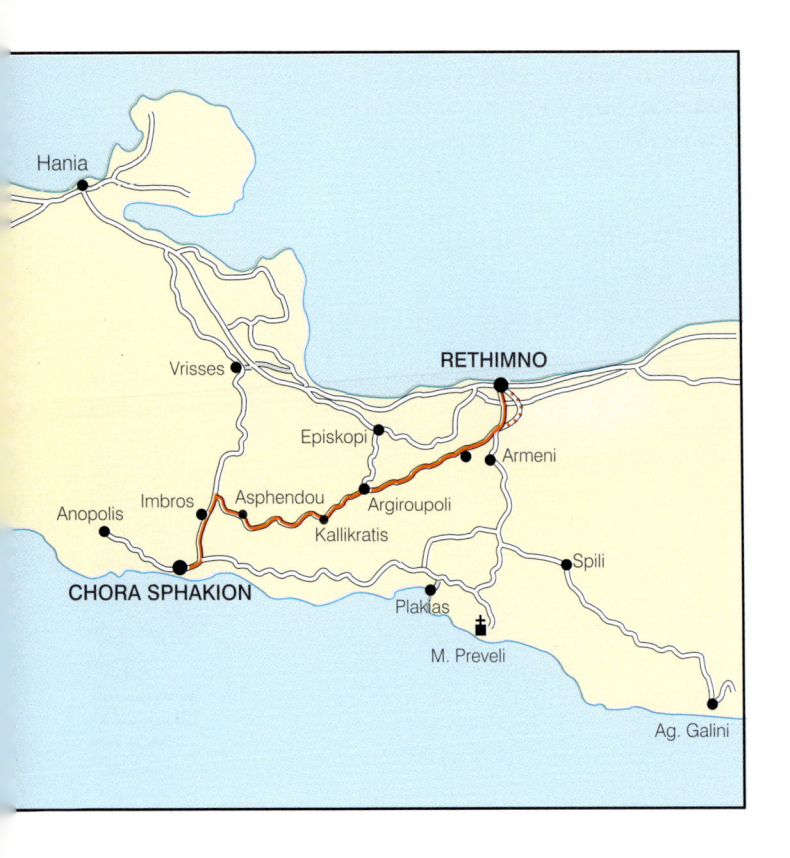

ROUTES STARTING FROM SPHAKIA

This route allows you to explore the inner region of the Rethimno prefecture, possibly the poorest and most primitive area of all Crete. For the most part, the roads in this area are fairly smooth dirtroads (D3), the villages are small settlements of shepherds or small-time farmers that have nothing to do with tourism, and the land is barren and rocky.

Head east of Chora Sphakion on the road leading to Vrisses, and as soon as you pass Imbros turn toward **Asphendou**. (There is a Gr/E sign at the intersection with "Ασφένδου" written on it). The road (A4) is very narrow, and it would certainly not be asphalt-paved if it didn't lead to the antenna of the Greek Telecommunications Company (OTE) on the nearby peak of Akones (1240 m). Keep in mind that about 900 metres before the antenna, at the point where the asphalt ends, you must turn on the dirtroad (D3) that you will see to your right (east).

The road goes through a desolate landscape of steep mountains, small rocky hills, and small fields full of stones. The first villages you will encounter are **Asphendou** and **Kallikratis.** They are both almost entirely deserted, but their stone houses still hold, probably because they are maintained by the shepherds who continue to bring their flocks in the area. Oddly enough, if these two villages have suffered from Time, the twenty or so hamlets in the area east of them are in much better shape, and they offer a typical example of the traditional ways of small Cretan communities dependent on the land. Needless to say, there are very few Rooms To Let (and very simple, too, with just the bare essentials), and only the larger villages have a few small taverns. The people, on the other hand, are very friendly and hospitable. If they detect in your eyes or voice a genuine interest for their homeland and a friendly attitude like their own, they may treat you to some tasty snack or offer to put you up for the night.

If you are lucky enough to receive such an offer, **you will have a rare opportunity to travel through time** and experience things like those we read in the journals of 19th century travellers: straw mats on dirt floors, food cooked in primitive pots, *mandinàdhes* (rhyming couplets) improvised that very moment for your pleasure and sung by the old man or woman of the house, tasty barley biscuits and freshly made

11. Sphakia-Rethimno — TRAVELLING INLAND

The Imbros-Kallikratis route

cheese of their own production, and plenty of wine from the barrel to make the experience even more intoxicating...

Right after Kallikratis the road splits in two. If you head southeast (right) you will get to **Miriokefala,** but you will have to drive on a road (D4) that is almost entirely neglected and at places dangerously narrowed by landslides. Rather than do that, take the northeast direction and after 5 km you will be at the beautiful **Assigonia.** The name of the village was aptly chosen: -Gonia ("corner") because it is built at the south corner of the Moussela valley, and Assi- ("rebel" in Arabian) because, like most peasants in this mountainous region, the people were in a constant uprising against the Turks who ruled the island.

Isolated in this out-of-the-way place, Assigonia has retained its traditional character; its economy is based on stockbreeding, its houses are made of stone, and its customs are deeply rooted in tradition. The most impressive custom is the **blessing of the livestock,** which takes place on April 23, the day of St. George. The people bring their flocks to the church to have them blessed by the priest, and they milk them right in the churchyard. Then the peasant girls boil the milk and offer it to everyone present, villagers as well as visitors.

After Assigonia the road (A3) continues to the north through a beautiful wooded gorge, and after a few kilometres you reach an intersection with signs (Gr/E) pointing you to all directions: to **Episkopi** in the north, to **Kato Poros** in the east, and to **Argiroupoli** and **Ancient Lappa** in the south. Here you have two options. If you are in a hurry to get to Rethimno, turn left (north), go through the rather indifferent village of Episkopi, get on the coastal highway (the new National Road), and head east for the town. Do not drive at full speed, though, because thanks to the endless sandy beaches and the many hotels the road between Georgioupoli and Rethimno has too much traffic. Whatever you do, **avoid the old National Road between Episkopi and Rethimno, because it is dangerously narrow and slippery.** Also avoid Lake Kourna and the town of Georgioupoli in the west. Most tourist guides consider them a "must," but in reality they are both "fake." Georgioupoli is presented as an attractive sea resort, but it is nothing more than a tasteless mish-mash of hotels and restaurants crowded around a narrow beach with constantly wet sand that shows it has been stepped on. Lake Kourna is visited by thousands of tourists "herded" to "Crete's unique lake," but you haven't come to Crete to see lakes! Admittedly, when seen from the mountain tops it may look attractive. But any European lake is better than this shallow hole; it is constantly filled with dozens of small plastic boats that carry the happy tourists who were brought massively by the Hania and Rethimno travel agencies, and it is simply a staged attraction.

If you are in no particular hurry and would like to do some exploring, you can follow a much more interesting course that will take you to Rethimno after some travelling through the region. In what follows we describe a cyclical route that is your most interesting option. When you reach the intersection we mentioned earlier, turn right instead of left and head south towards **Argiroupoli.** The town is built on top of a hill, on the site of ancient Lappa.

After Argiroupoli keep going south for about 1.5 km and then turn left (southeast) to get to Vilandredo and from there to the many other hamlets scattered in this desolate area. (At the intersection you will see a Gr/E sign pointing you to Vilandredo and Alones). You'll be following a beautiful cyclical route and driving on an asphalt-paved road (A3) that climbs the northern side of Mount Krioneritis (1312m). **Alones** is a quiet shepherd settlement built on a plateau surrounded by mountain peaks and steep ravines.

When you get there you will see two roads (D3) going east and crossing a small cultivated plateau with many nooks that are good for camping. Both of these roads will take you to **Kali Sikia.**

Once in Kali Sikia, you have again two options. If it's late in the day and you feel like heading for Rethimno, take the road east of the village (A3), which will take you through Kanevos, Angousseliana and Aghios Vassilios and then meet the Aghia Galini - Rethimno road (A2) where

---

According to the legend, Lappa was built by Agamemnon, King of the Mycenaeans. The fact is that whoever built it chose its location very wisely; to the north of the town lay a large and fertile valley through which flowed the river Mousselas, to the south and west of it lay steep mountains that protected it from behind, and there was also a safety distance from the sea so that the town was not threatened by pirates or every passing invader.

The Lappans soon acquired wealth and power and they prospered throughout the classical and hellenistic period. They had a strong army, but what really did the trick was their **cleverness and diplomacy**. They formed the best alliances and saw to it that they had good relations with everyone. When there was war they had the information and the astuteness that they needed to guess which side was strongest, and they always allied themselves to it. However, after the war, they also showed their sympathy to the defeated! As Polybius, the historian, tells us, when Knossos destroyed Littos in 220 BC (with the aid of Lappa), the Lappans accepted the ragged and homeless Littaeans in their town and offered them hospitality!

But even these clever diplomats could not avoid destruction. In **68 BC,** when Crete was a Roman province and inner strife was beginning to tear the Romans, the Lappans welcomed the army of Octavius which they considered stronger. And indeed it was stronger, but at the time it was defeated by another army force led by the Roman general Metellus. As they left, the winners did not forget to level the town to the ground...

Yet thirty-seven years later, when the Aktion sea battle marked Octavius' decisive victory over Marcus Antonius and Cleopatra, Octavius remembered his former allies, and he gave them their freedom and helped them to rebuild their town. Lappa was once again a flourishing town and it even surpassed its former glory. Many mansions and splendid public buildings were erected, among which a large aqueduct

ROUTES STARTING FROM SPHAKIA

you turn north to get to the town. Though the road is pretty wide and allows you to reach your destination after a quick drive, we suggest making a small side-trip to the seaside village of **Plakias** south of **Kanevos**, and back, so you can drive through the **impressive Kotsifos gorge** with the high vertical walls that seem to press against the road and the stream between them. Also, we propose making a stop at the **Minoan cemetery**, just one kilometre north of **Armeni** (see page 278)

LAPPA

that supplied the famous **Roman Baths** with water from mountain springs. The town's prosperity was also indicated by the fact it had its own mint, which during its operation produced thirty-six different coins. However, the town did not survive the Arabs' sweeping attack. In the year **824 AD,** it was stripped of all its wealth and glory, and **whatever could** not be taken was turned into stone and ashes...

The ruins of ancient Lappa must be buried underneath the homes of the modern town that was built in its place, but no one seems willing to tear down his house - built, in all likelihood, with many ancient stones well hidden under the plaster - in order to let the ancient ruins come to light. A recent excavation in an expropriated building site revealed a **wonderful floor mosaic** dating from the Roman period when the town was at the height of its glory. If you want to see it, you may find the following instructions helpful: Leave your bike by the side of the road near the church at the village entrance. Follow a sign that says "TABEPNA" (tavern), walk under a stone arch, turn left at the first alley after it, walk for another fifty metres, and you will see it in front of you, protected by a wooden roof. Such an important finding and there isn't a single sign that mentions it! When you leave the place, drop by the local cultural society and, if you find anyone there, complain of the situation...

11. Sphakia-Rethimno
TRAVELLING INLAND

The gorgeous plateau south of Kali Sikia

If, however, you still have the time and the energy to continue your exploration, do not head east after Kali Sikia, but take the road (D3) that goes north and continues the circle you have started. The idea is to get on the old National Road connecting Hania and Rethimno, but in order to do that you have several options. The best one is to follow the road (which, incidentally, starts west of the village but heads north taking you through the desolate countryside) until it

The route through the Kotsifos gorge

meets a second road (A3) about 1 km east of Velonado. Here you turn right (north) and follow the road as it goes downhill, passes through a beautiful gorge followed by the villages of Moundros, Roustika and Kaloniktis, and takes you to the old National Road, about 1km west of Aghios Andreas. As you get near the coast, it may attract you irresistibly and you may be tempted to drive straight to Rethimno. Don't rush, though, because there are still great places to see!

A little before the entrance of **Aghios Andreas** you will see an intersection. Turn right (south), following the Gr/E sign that says **A. Varsamonero,** and just before entering the village turn left and head for **Kastelos.** As you drive you will have a **great view** of the entire bay of Almiros. When, after a turn, the village of Kastelos appears before your eyes, stop for a minute and get oriented. Behind the village is the impressive Minoan cemetery of Armeni (see page 278). Somewhere around it was the site of the (still undiscovered) ancient town to which the cemetery belonged. At the top of **Mount Vrissinas** - the mountain you see behind the village - was an important Minoan sanctuary (see page 322). If you have the time, visit everything!

Finally, if you want to get a bird's eye view of Rethimno and the coastline, turn on the road (A3) opposite to the Minoan cemetery and drive on the north side of Mount Vrissinas, taking the opposite direction of the one we propose in Road Book 3 (see page 320).

12. Sphakia-Rethimno

FOLLOWING THE COAST

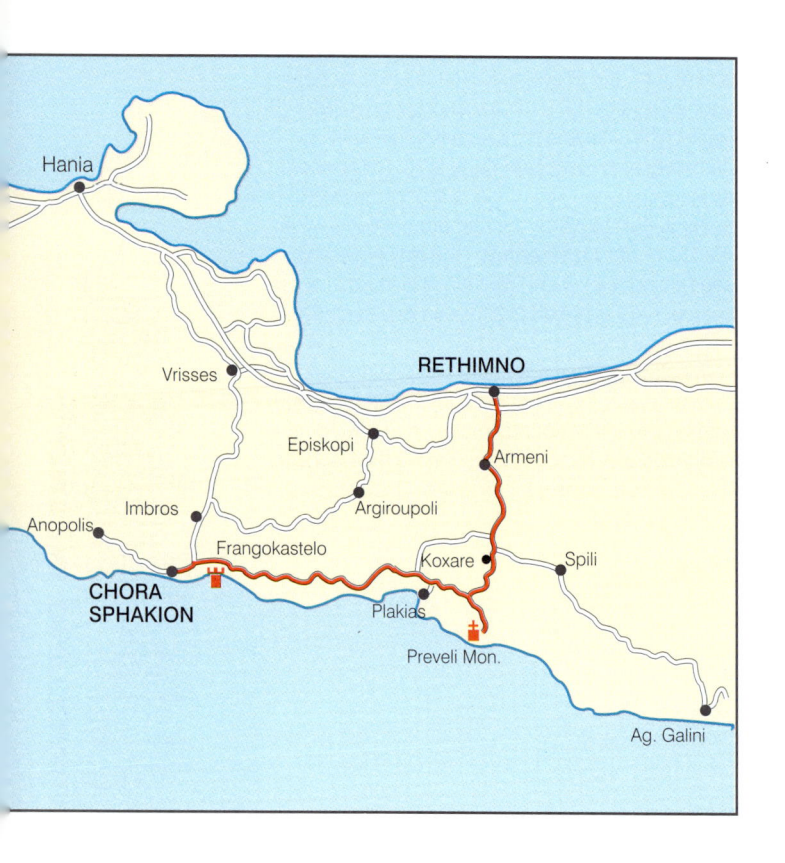

ROUTES STARTING FROM SPHAKIA

About two kilometres east of Chora Sphakion you will see a road (A3/25km) that leads to **Frangokastelo.** It is a narrow road with many turns and potholes, carved on mountain slopes full of olive groves and following the coastline from a certain distance. Though it doesn't climb too high, it allows a **wonderful view:** to the south you can see the Libyan sea, and to the north a succession of high mountain peaks (all over 1000m), which are often separated by deep gorges.

Three of those gorges are very good for walking. If the length of the Samaria gorge or the crowds visiting it have discouraged you from walking through a gorge, this is your chance to change your mind. All three gorges are quite as beautiful, and yet much smaller, quieter, and easier to cross. The first, the **Imbriotiko gorge,** is 3 km long, and the path for climbing it starts from Komitades and ends in Imbros (total route length: 4 km). The second, the **Aghios Nektarios gorge,** is 2 km long, and the path for climbing it starts from Aghios Nektarios and ends in Asphendou (total route length: 3.5 km). The third, the **Kallikratiano gorge,** is 1 km long, and the path for climbing it starts from Patsianos and ends in Kallikratis (total route length: 4 km).

As mentioned, all three gorges are quite small, so you can start early in the morning and walk through them without great effort. In the process you will also enjoy the gradual change of scenery as you move from the sea to the desolate Sphakia countryside with its typically poor villages. No matter how slow your pace, you will certainly have enough time to rest, to walk leisurely back - you should be at your base no later than early afternoon - and to cool off with a good swim.

Certainly, you can lock up your bike at the village from where your hike begins and go as far as your strength and desire takes you. But if you can do it, we think it is worth walking to the village at the other end of the gorge. Imbros, Asphendou and Kallikratis are all very picturesque with their traditional stone-built houses, and if you do not visit them by following Route 11 you ought at least to hike there on a break from Route 12.

As you drive on the main coastal road, you will see many dirtroads - or even asphalt ones - branching off toward the sandy beaches to your right. The first one on your way is the large sandy beach in front of the famous **Frangokastelo.**

12. Sphakia-Rethimno FOLLOWING THE COAST

Frangokastelo is just one more fort that testifies to the Venetians' vain desire to impose their rule even in those parts of the island where they had nothing to gain. It was built in 1370, thanks to the insistence of the feudal lords of Rethimno, but it was never used, at least not by the Venetians! The locals paid no attention to this isolated and harmless fort, and they kept on living unsubdued... taking their rebellions just a little bit further. The decline of its glory started from its very first day. The Venetians grew tired of sitting around in a remote fort doing nothing, the garrison was reduced to very few men, and the guards napped on their posts, lulled to sleep by the waves and by the sound of the bells of the local shepherds' goats. How can you play the part of the defender of a place if no one is willing to attack you? The cannons soon grew rusty from disuse, and the fort, gradually abandoned, started falling apart.

It took another 450 years before there was some action to justify the fort's existence. We are speaking of the amazing **Frangokastelo battle** (1828), which took place between the Turkish army, led by Moustafa Pasha, and a Greek army force from Ipiros, led by **Hatzimichalis Dalianis.** Now, what business did an army force from Ipiros have on the island of Crete is quite a long story. But to make it short, let us simply say that those designing the tactics of the Greek War of Independence (which broke out in 1821 and ended with the liberation of Roumeli and the Peloponnese) felt that the Cretans lacked in tactics and performance and were in need of support. Yet the Cretans knew very well what they were doing. They took advantage of their inaccessible mountain peaks and deep gorges and fought a war of quick assaults and safe retreats in their hide-outs. Still, the generals from the Greek mainland felt that killing ten to fifteen Turks each time was not the best way to eliminate the Sultan's countless Turkish, Albanian and Egyptian soldiers. As a result they sent an army force of 600 infantrymen and 70 horsemen, led by Hatzimichalis Dalianis, to free Crete with large scale, face-to-face battles. Moustafa Pasha rushed out to meet them, starting with a... moderate 8000 and 400 men respectively. As you may guess, Dalianis and his troops did not live to give many battles...

The Cretans advised Dalianis to follow their own tactics, but he did not listen to them. He called them "cowards" and proceeded to do things his own way. Ignoring the insult, the Cretans wished the brave Ipirian leader "good luck" and retreated to their mountains. Dalianis, on the other hand, ranged his men in the valley in front of Fran-

FRANGOKASTELO

gokastelo and waited for the Turks to show up. When they did, a fierce battle started, which resulted in twice as many deaths on the part of the Turks. After an hour or so, 200 Greeks had been killed - their leader included - compared to 400 Turks. If things went on like that, the remaining 400 Greeks did not have much future in the fight against the 8000 Turks opposite them. They wised up at the last moment, saw an empty fort behind them, and quickly barricaded themselves in it.

And so it happened that for the first time in 450 years the fort fulfilled its purpose! And in spite of being abandoned it did its job very well! The besieged managed to keep the Turks away for seven days. By that time, Moustafa Pasha had begun to feel threatened by the quiet reinforcements he saw gathering up around him, and he chose to withdraw his men discreetly. As a gesture of good will, he allowed the exhausted warriors to leave the fort, promising he would not harm them. Then he tore down a big part of it and started retreating toward the northeast. But the Sphakians who had come to the aid of Dalianis waited for him at the gorges. They were not used to gestures of good will (and why should they be?) so they viciously attacked him and destroyed his army.

If you want to get an idea of the terrible condition in which the besieged soldiers were when they left the fort, come here on June 4, 5, or 6 at the crack of dawn. You will see the **Drossoulites,** the sad ghosts that each year appear before the walls, floating about gloomily. This vision or mirage has not yet been explained, and it is certainly very interesting.

Frangokastelo survives in very good condition, thanks to the last repairs made by the Turks in 1866. Above the gate one can still see a somewhat worn stone, on which are carved the Lion of St. Marcus and two coats of arms belonging to Venetian feudal lords.

Next to Frangokastelo one can see the abandoned monastery of Aghios Haralambos. Unfortunately, only its church has survived, while all the other buildings have fallen apart. Just east of the monastery lies a beautiful beach with big sandhills.

Although the area around Frangokastelo has just begun to be developed, most hotels and Rooms to Let are ugly, because they were designed and built quickly and without any aesthetic concerns. The only exception is the guest house at **Patsianos,** which was built very recently and doesn't have a phone yet. If you'd like to camp, the beach of Frangokastelo is all yours, and the taverns all around will help to cover your needs.

The next attractive beach as you go east is the sandy **Korakas Beach.** This can be reached by the dirtroad (D3) that you will see a few kilometres after Frangokastelo or by an asphalt road (A3) that passes through **Rodakino.** Needless to say, it, too, is surrounded by several small hotels, Rooms To Let, taverns and restaurants. If you'd like to stay, the best place is the POLYZOS HOTEL (tel. 0832 - 31 334), which is next to the sea.

When you reach Selia you will see a dirtroad (D2) that goes south. A little before it reaches the shore another road branches off to the west and takes you to Souda, a wide beach with palm trees. At the edge of it is a small tavern and a quiet, newly built hotel, the SOUDA MARE, which offers a great view of the beach.

If you continue eastward on the coastal road, you will soon be at **Plakias.** This was a tiny seaside settlement, built around the turn of the century by a few fishermen from the nearby Sellia. Until 1970 it had no more than ten permanent residents, but today it has about twenty hotels, five hundred rooms that are rented out to tourists, and many restaurants, bars and discos that serve the needs of the huge crowds that arrive here every year (and we are talking about five-digit numbers). The main attraction is the large sandy beach of the village, but unfortunately this is usually covered with rented umbrellas and deck chairs. (However, you *will* find a few quiet and clean corners at the west and east end of it). If you absolutely must stay here, your best choice is the Plakias Bay Bungalows (tel. 0832 - 31 215), a well looked after complex at the east end of the beach, away from the noise of this cosmopolitan

ROUTES STARTING FROM SPHAKIA

Plakias Beach

resort. (If you are hungry, by the way, there are plenty of taverns on the main road of the village, but we recommend Sunset, the fish-tavern at the west end. Despite its banal name, it serves fresh fish that are very well done as well as many other tasty dishes). An alternative to the bungalows type of accommodation is the Plakias camping. It is a big site at the village entrance that should give you plenty of space, but the truth is you must look hard for a quiet spot to settle. For true camping, away from the tourist crowds, head east of the village, in the direction of Lefkogia.

The road (A3) is intersected by a second road that leads to the Damnoni beach (which was very beautiful once but has now been spoilt by the sight of a huge, rich-people's bungalows complex that was built here by a Swiss company). Pass the intersection, and a little before Lefkogia turn right on the road (A3) where you will see a sign that says "HOTEL RESTAURANT **AMMOUDI**." This road ends **at a wonderful sandy beach,** full of shade-giving trees, a secluded place that is ideal for camping. About two hundred metres to the back is the very good "Ammoudi Hotel & Restaurant" (tel. 0832 - 31 355 / 31 756), a small and elegant building that belongs to the Daskalakis family. Other than that, the beach is empty of buildings, and it still has great natural beauty (but for how long?) It is ideal for relaxing - though you can always visit Plakias when you want to see some action - and it is also a great base for small trips in the area. The Amari valley in the east and the Sphakia region in the west are among the places to visit.

12. Sphakia - Rethimno
FOLLOWING THE COAST

After Lefkogia you will see a road (A3) to your right, which goes to a hamlet called **Gianniou.** Turn on this road and follow it to the village. From here on you continue on a dirtroad (D3), which takes you to a pass between two hills. Right after the pass you get a view of the Libyan sea and soon afterwards the **Preveli monastery** (Moni Preveli) appears before your eyes. To be precise, this is the Pisso Moni Preveli, to be distinguished from the Kato Moni Preveli that is close by.

Pisso Moni Preveli

It is not certain when exactly and by whom the monastery was founded. The countless raids, the looting, and the destruction it so often suffered - like all Cretan monasteries - resulted in the loss of precious historical documents that could shed light on its past. Carved on the monastery fountain is the year 1701. Yet the church bell of the "twin" monastery Kato Moni Preveli, a couple of kilometres to the north, suggests a different time of foundation, since the inscription on it reads "1594."

The monastery was built at a secluded place with an excellent view of the Libyan sea (as you can see for yourself), but the serenity of the landscape around it sharply contrasted with its - mostly - turbulent history. Like most monasteries in Crete (or Greece, for that matter), it frequently served as a refuge for rebels or even as their base of operations. During the second world war it offered protection to the allies; it was here that they found refuge, and it was from here that their departure from the island was organised. Today, the monastery's small but well organised museum contains many interesting exhibits, precious relics that the monks were able to save from destruction. Among them is a silver-plated cross, which, as the story has it, is made of wood from the Holy Cross and has the power to work miracles.

ROUTES STARTING FROM SPHAKIA

About 500 metres north of the abandoned Kato Moni Preveli is a road (D3) that goes east. At the intersection you will see a misleading E sign that says "Palm Beach 2 km," but points you in the same direction you came from. Ignore the sign and turn right (east). You will pass a brook with a small bridge, and after 6 km you will be at the coast, at a small parking area next to a couple of taverns. Leave your bike in front of whichever tavern you like best so that the tavern

MONI PREVELI

The buildings you see at the monastery are not the original ones. Those were destroyed, rebuilt or modified so many times that nothing is left from them. The church was built in 1835. It has a beautifully carved wooden icon screen with **wonderful icons,** some of which come from the church before it. Especially noteworthy are the icons of Christ the High Priest and of Adam and Eve in Paradise, at the left door-leaf and the lower right corner of the icon screen respectively. The latter catches the eye with its great variety of birds, fish and animals painted in bright colours, and both are works of Michail Prevelis and date from 1750. The works of this monk as well as the other treasures of the monastery and its exciting history are a good reason for visiting the place. And if you go in early spring or late fall, when there are not so many visitors around, Father Kallinikos and Father Chryssanthos, the two monks that live there, will be glad to show you around. Incidentally, Father Chryssanthos speaks very good English.

Kato Moni Preveli

This monastery is in a terrible condition, and little by little it falls apart. The cells still have walls, but they have no roofs. The church, which is dedicated to John the Baptist, has a roof, but it has suffered great damages and it was both abandoned and vandalised. Yet the fountain at the entrance can still quench your thirst.

owner can keep an eye on it - needless to say, you'll promise him that you will eat there after your swim - and continue on foot (**Palm Beach** is only ten minutes away). The sight you will see is indeed beautiful: lots of palm trees growing alongside a river that divides the beach into two parts and flows into the sea. Yet the famous beach attracts too many visitors and campers, and especially in the high season it is extremely crowded and filthy.

If you are looking for empty beaches with crystal-clear water, take the dirtroad (D3) that you'll see about two or three hundred metres before the taverns. This goes east and takes you to the road (A3) that connects **Kerames** and the Aghia Irini beach in the south. **The beaches** between Aghia Irini and Aghios Pavlos in the east **are the best of Crete** (see Route 13 and Road Book 5).

The river with the palm trees and Palm Beach

If you get back to the route and follow the road (A3) north of the abandoned Kato Moni Preveli, it will take you to **Assomatos.** After the village the road continues through the impressive **Kourtaliotiko gorge** with the high steep walls. At the north end of the gorge there is an intersection. If you want to complete Route 12 and to get to Rethimno, continue straight (in the direction of **Koxare**). After a while, you will hit the main road (A2) that connects Aghia Galini with Rethimno, and from there it's only a matter of fifteen to twenty minutes till you reach the town.

If, however, you have no desire to go to Rethimno, turn right (east) and follow the road to the picturesque **Frati.** If you keep going east, the road (A3) will take you to Aghia Pelagia and then to Mixorrouma, and from here you can either continue eastward, following Route 13, or cross

ROUTES STARTING FROM SPHAKIA

the main road and continue toward **Karines** in the north (from where you can follow Route 14). A third option, for those that have off-road bikes and enjoy beautiful scenery, is to follow the dirtroad (D2) that starts at the east exit of Frati and takes you to **Mourne.** You will pass through a wooded area with plenty of chapels and places suitable for camping, then get to the village and continue on the asphalt-paved road that leads to **Spili.** Here you have again two options: continuing south towards Aghia Galini (see Route 13), or taking the dirtroad (D3) northeast of Spili in order to get to **Patsos** and take Route 14.

12. Sphakia-Rethimno
FOLLOWING THE COAST

Rethimno

The Venetian harbour

ROUTES STARTING FROM RETHIMNO

Working slowly for millions of years, Mother Nature made at this part of Crete one of the most beautiful sandy beaches of the island that stretches over an area of 12km.

Working feverishly for twenty years, the modern Homo Touristicus inhabiting the island adorned this beach with countless hotels, restaurants, bars, discos, Rooms to Let, car rental offices and other tourist businesses which he planted alongside the coast.

With such extensive exploitation, it is hard to imagine what this place must have looked like in 1500 BC, the time when the first people came to live here and built their homes - in all likelihood - on the small hill at the west end of the beach. Who they were, where they came from, and how they lived are questions that may never be answered, since the only remnant we have from this first Minoan settlement is a small grave carved on the rock. The name of the settlement, though, must have something to do with the name **Rithimna,** which was given to the town that flourished here in the Post-Palace and the historical period.

Rithimna existed throughout the classical, Roman and Byzantine period, but it was not an important town and we have very few references to it. When the Venetians came in 1204, they felt that the place was suitable for building a harbour that would protect their ships when they sailed along the north coast of Crete and would enable them to swim at a place protected from the winds. So they built a very simple harbour and quickly fortified their small town. Life went on without any major problems, until one day in **1538** the legendary pirate **Barbarossa** attacked the town hoping for some loot. The good God and the stubborn resistance of the guard saved the town, but the Venetians realised that they needed a stronger wall if they were to survive similar attacks in the future. In 1540, they began building a wall, which started from the east end of town (where the EOT / GNTO offices are located, **26**) and extended to the west end of it (to the main gate, the Porta Guora, **38,** which has survived intact and is the only remnant we have of that wall). Then they locked and bolted the gate as

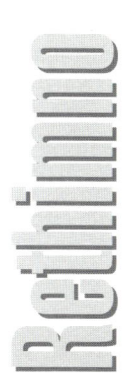

For twenty-two days the Venetians were barricaded inside the impregnable Fortezza and fought against the Turks

well as they could, and they planted their guards on the bastions.

The building lasted thirty years, and it finished just in time. Barely had the mud between the stones dried up, when the enemy appeared... but not where he was expected! It was a poor Algerian pirate, **Oloutz Ali,** and his men, and... like any original pirate he attacked the town from the side of the sea! The Venetians understood how stupid they were to leave their town unprotected from that side, but it was too late. Oloutz Ali landed on the beach, took the town in a flash, plundered it and burned it.

This time the Venetians became wiser. After licking their wounds for a couple of years, they got over the shock and the humiliation and started building **a fortress** on the hill **that was the largest and strongest ever constructed on the island.** The building lasted only ten years, but it took the combined work of all the people in the Rethimno area, who put in a total of 77,000 days of compulsory labour. The Venetians fortified the wall by adding four bastions and giving it three sharp edges, and they filled the fortress with cannons and ammunition. When they were done, they put Venice's emblem, the St. Marcus lion, over the main gate at a prominent position and sat back to admire their work. The famous **Fortezza** was now complete. Today it survives in excellent condition.

The fortress created a feeling of security, even though there were not enough houses within the walls to accommodate everyone in case of attack. In the next years the Venetians constructed many public buildings, and they gave the town a new splendour. Many of those buildings have been very well preserved.

But Fate often shakes the foundations of human works and makes even the strongest forts look like sand castles. It was only sixty years that the Venetians enjoyed the safety of their fortress. In **1646,** the famous Venice lion was crushed like an ant under the giant paw of an elephant, and the Turkish army of Hussein entered the acropolis after twenty-two days of siege. Power is the most fragile illusion of man. It is gained with much effort, and it is lost with a blow of the wind...

The lazy Turks followed their usual practice and they built almost nothing in the town. They simply repaired the damages to the wall, made a few fountains to drink and keep cool, and added a few minarets to the existing churches, turning them into mosques. They also managed to reduce the Greek population of Rethimno very quickly. While during the Venetian rule the town's population was predominantly Greek, during the Turkish occupation it was just the opposite. As Robert Pashley reports, when he visited the town in 1834, there were 3000 Turks living in it and only 80 Greek families.

What has always divided the Greeks and the Turks is their religious convictions. The Turks were outraged by the resistance they met in matters of religion, much more than they could be by any war confrontation. Even the war prisoners had a chance to save their lives, if they only renounced the Christian religion publicly and became Muslims. Faced with this dilemma, most people chose to live as Muslims rather than die a martyr's death, although secretly they still worshipped their own God. But one day four young men from Melambes - Manouil, Nikolaos, Georgios and Angelis Retzepis - were taken prisoners, and they chose the path of holiness. Taken to the execution site outside the Guora gate, with their hands all tied up, they saw their executioner holding his sword, and they heard him ask the typical question: "Will you adopt the Turkish faith?" This, of course, was a question posed to each and every prisoner, and the standard answer was a humble "Yes, my Lord." But instead of following the standard procedure, the first man in line surprised everyone with a scornful "No." And a few seconds before his head was cut off, he added: "I was born a

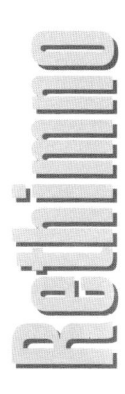

Christian and a Christian I will die." One by one, the others did the same. After their death a number of miracles were reported, and the people decided to build a small church to honour their memory. This was later replaced with a much bigger one, the Church of the Four Martyrs which you can see today at the place where they died **(42)**.

The biggest miracle, however, which happened mainly thanks to the Great Powers of the time - England, France, Russia and Italy - but must have surely also been the work of every saint worshipped on the island, was the final departure of the Turks from Crete.

All the streets leading to Rethimno take you to the Four Martyrs Square, just outside of the Porta Guora **(38)**. Behind this gate lies the old town, but if you come any time between May 1 and October 31 you won't be able to ride your bike in it. The largest part of the old town is inaccessible to all vehicles, twenty-four hours a day, due to a strict prohibition (see the area marked with the dotted blue line on the city map).

Just south of the Four Martyrs Square is an outdoor parking lot. However, this is not the safest place to leave your motorcycle if it is loaded. Your best choice is the parking lot on Melissinou street **(33)**, under the Fortezza, which is outdoors but guarded. It is open 24 hours a day and costs 300, 500, or 700 drachmas for two, six, or twenty-four hours respectively. Of course, if you intend to stay in Rethimno, it is best to find a good hotel first and to unload the bike, so you can have greater freedom of movement. And if you happen to find a room in or near the old town, you won't be needing your bike at all, because the beach, the bars, the restaurants and all the sights will be just a few blocks away.

Leave the shutters and the windows of your room open so that you can wake early and enjoy the cool breeze and beautiful colours of the dawn. The town at this time is wonderfully inviting as it wakes from its sleep, and the only people at the **Venetian harbour** are the few fishermen mending their nets and the tavern owners sweeping their floors. Take a stroll at the harbour and then sit at the "VENETSIANIKO" Cafe Bar **(20)** to enjoy a good breakfast or a simple cup of coffee in the company of the harbour ducks that will gather around the crumbs of bread you throw them.

ROUTES STARTING FROM RETHIMNO

Very little has changed in the harbour since the Venetians built it in **1300** hoping to protect their galleys. The lighthouse, the cobbled area along the waterfront where people stroll, and many of the houses overlooking the harbour are from the time of the Venetian rule. But the Turkish cannons that once aimed at the enemy's ships are today part of the mole, and they look downwards and are used to tie up the fishing boats.

After the Venetian harbour - and while it's still early - go see the Venetian fortress, the famous **Fortezza (37).** It opens at 8:30 a.m., and until 10:00 a.m. there are very few visitors to break the stillness. After ten, though, and until the fortress closes at six, it is usually full of crowds that won't let you explore it quietly. Apart from the walls and bastions, which are excellently preserved, there aren't too many things to see in the fortress. Still, it is worth walking along the wall and on the embrasures, and going back to the past, some 350 years ago, when the raging Turks attacked the fortress and the Venetians defended it. On the north side and close to the wall are the remnants of the old Administration Building, an amazing mansion with 49 doors and 81 windows. Next to it is what is left of the old storerooms that were once here, and underneath the storerooms are the cisterns of the fort that survive in good condition. Somewhere at the centre you can see the church of Aghios Nikolaos, which was later turned into a mosque with the addition of an impressive dome (that survives intact) and a minaret (that has tumbled to pieces). Finally, on the east side there is a small, Russian-built church dedicated to Aghii Theodori, the only thing that reminds of the Russian army's short and friendly stay (1897 - 1909).

Just opposite the Fortezza gate you will see a large building made of stone. This used to be a Turkish prison, but since 1989 it houses the **Archaeological Museum of Rethimno (30**, open Tuesday through Sunday from 8:30 a.m. to 3:00 p.m), probably the most handsome and well organised museum in Crete. On the outside, the building has kept its original imposing appearance, but on the inside it has been very carefully modified so as to highlight the archaeological treasures exhibited. There are tables with good explanatory texts in both Greek and English, photographs, and drawings of the

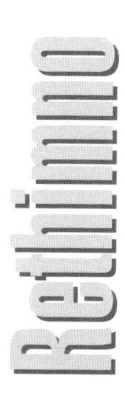

The Fortezza

excavation sites. In this way the exhibits are no longer cold and incomprehensible, but they become small "windows" through which the visitor can travel to another place and time and gain a well rounded perspective of it. Inside the museum's modern showcases, as well as outside of them (placed right next to you), are some unique masterpieces of craftsmen that lived in times long past: statuettes, jewellery, weapons, tools and pottery from the Neolithic age; ritual axes, seal stones, golden jewels, stone coffins and statuettes from the Minoan Kingdom; and glass vases, pottery, statuettes, coins and statues from the classical, hellenistic and Roman times.

This small and pleasant museum cannot have tired you very much. If you wish to continue with more, you have the option of visiting two very good museums, which are also small and pleasant and will not tire you.

The **Historic and Folklore Museum (31)** has collected with great care and sensitivity hundreds of items of folk art, textiles, old photographs, musical instruments, traditional tools and other objects of everyday life, all exhibited in a very lively manner. A little further down the street is the **Folklore Collection of the Lykeion Ellinidon (32)** with some very interesting embroideries, woven fabrics, local costumes, and a variety of household items.

A few steps further is the **Petichaki Square,** which is at the very centre of things. It features the famous **Rimonti Fountain (39),** a Venetian fountain of historic significance with three lion heads. Water is still running from their mouths, offering the worn out traveller relief from the heat of the day. Some of the best coffee bars in town are concentrated here, and from the break of day till late at night they are never empty of their young clientele. All around the square, the streets are full of shops and, more than any place in town, they are bustling with activity.

East of the Petichaki Square, at the end of Palaiologou street, is the **Venetian Lotzia (40),** an elegant building of the end of the 16th century where the Venetian lords met and had fun or carried on their business.

South of the Petichaki Square, at the end of Vernardou street, is the **Nerantze Mosque (43).** The building started out as a Venetian church dedicated to Santa Maria, but in 1657 it was converted to a mosque and acquired a roof and three wonderful domes and the highest minaret in town. (The minaret survives to this day and must certainly offer the best view in town, but unfortunately you can't go up there, because they say it isn't very stable!) In 1925, the building was christened "the St. Nickolas church" - though it was never used as such - and today it houses the Rethimno conservatory. If you happen to pass by and catch a few notes from a practising musician, go inside and take a seat. You will enjoy some fine music at a place designed to create an out-of this-world sensation.

West of the Petichaki Square, on Nikiforou Foka street, is the **Church of the Mistress of the Angels (47).** It was built by the Venetians in 1609 and was initially dedicated to Mary Magdalen. When the Turks took over they gave it to the Greeks, who dedicated it to the Mistress of the Angels. After a while, though, they changed their mind, took it back, and turned it into a mosque. Her Holiness was very displeased with this move, so She made Her icon disappear and did not let the minaret go up. Desperate of ever seeing it stand, the Turks left the minaret incomplete, but they still didn't give the church back. Yet the sacrilege was continued even after their departure from the scene, only this time it was committed by the Christians; instead of using the place as a church they turned it into army quarters! This time Her Holiness lost Her patience. In 1917, about two hundred and seventy years after the church was first taken, She appeared in two soldiers' dreams and revealed where Her icon was hidden. The

RETHIMNO

LEGEND

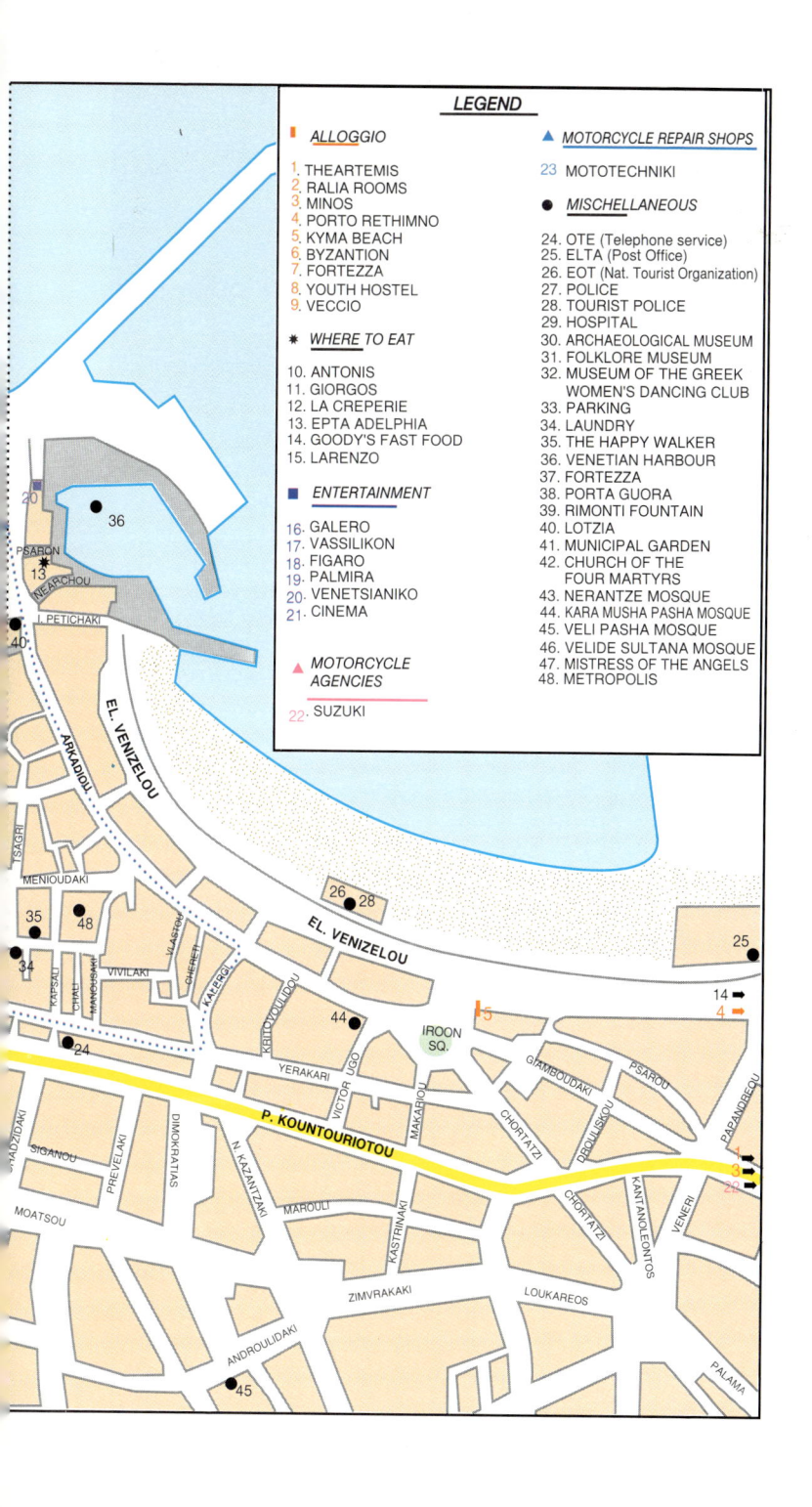

ALLOGGIO

1. THEARTEMIS
2. RALIA ROOMS
3. MINOS
4. PORTO RETHIMNO
5. KYMA BEACH
6. BYZANTION
7. FORTEZZA
8. YOUTH HOSTEL
9. VECCIO

WHERE TO EAT

10. ANTONIS
11. GIORGOS
12. LA CREPERIE
13. EPTA ADELPHIA
14. GOODY'S FAST FOOD
15. LARENZO

ENTERTAINMENT

16. GALERO
17. VASSILIKON
18. FIGARO
19. PALMIRA
20. VENETSIANIKO
21. CINEMA

MOTORCYCLE AGENCIES

22. SUZUKI

MOTORCYCLE REPAIR SHOPS

23. MOTOTECHNIKI

MISCHELLANEOUS

24. OTE (Telephone service)
25. ELTA (Post Office)
26. EOT (Nat. Tourist Organization)
27. POLICE
28. TOURIST POLICE
29. HOSPITAL
30. ARCHAEOLOGICAL MUSEUM
31. FOLKLORE MUSEUM
32. MUSEUM OF THE GREEK WOMEN'S DANCING CLUB
33. PARKING
34. LAUNDRY
35. THE HAPPY WALKER
36. VENETIAN HARBOUR
37. FORTEZZA
38. PORTA GUORA
39. RIMONTI FOUNTAIN
40. LOTZIA
41. MUNICIPAL GARDEN
42. CHURCH OF THE FOUR MARTYRS
43. NERANTZE MOSQUE
44. KARA MUSHA PASHA MOSQUE
45. VELI PASHA MOSQUE
46. VELIDE SULTANA MOSQUE
47. MISTRESS OF THE ANGELS
48. METROPOLIS

The Nerantze Mosque, today housing a music school

icon was indeed found beneath the floor of the church, and ever since then this has been the favourite church of the faithful.

Whichever street you take in the old town, you will be taking a walk through History. Dozens of Venetian and Turkish buildings and monuments and more than seven hundred Venetian facades are scattered in every alley and corner. Buildings that have stood the test of Time and today house the restaurant that you will eat in, the bar where you'll spend the evening, and the hotel where you will go to rest.

After all this walking, the well looked after **Municipal Garden (41)** will revive you with its cool shade and comfortable benches (a function very different from its previous use as a Turkish cemetery). Better still, take your sunscreen lotion and beach towel and go straight to the municipal beach next to the harbour. Though it is usually full of people, it is also very clean. For more quiet, you have twelve kilometres of sand to the east, and they are all yours to choose where you will lay your towel!

WHERE TO STAY

Even if half of Europe came to stay here, there would still be enough room for everyone! The hotels of Rethimno are... practically countless. They are spread over a large area, measuring eight kilometres in length and one kilometre in width, and they form an uninterrupted line connecting Rethimno with Perivolia and Platanias. At the first and second row are the most expensive hotels of the A and B class, while at the third - or even behind it - are the lower rated hotels, primarily C class, which may be smaller but are also well looked after. The first-row hotels offer great view and immediate access to the beach (where each of them has planted its own rented umbrellas and deck chairs), but of course they charge too much and are also noisy because of the coastal road. Those of the back rows are generally new, housed in small, elegant buildings with spacy parking areas, and they are also cheaper and quieter. A good rule of thumb is that the more you go to the east and away from the beach, the better hotels you will find.

The hotels and pension houses in the old town are the first to go, and if you find a clean and quiet room here it means you are very lucky (as for cheap, you might as well forget about it!) But if you come before May of after October (when temperatures in Crete are still quite high), everything will be at your disposal and for half the price.

Since it is impossible to offer an exhaustive list of all the places to sleep, we are providing you here with a very small selection of the best accommodations you can find, a list including different types of accommodations and different hotel categories.

RITHYMNA BEACH, Hotel
Class A

Open March - November.
450 rooms and 120 bungalows!
7 km east of Rethimno, right on the beach.
Tel. (0831) 71 002, Fax (0831) 71 668
This isn't a hotel; it is a small town excellently equipped to answer your every need! Unparalleled class, luxury, and endless opportunities for sports and recreation. There is also a perfectly equipped diving centre.

PORTO RETHYMNO, Hotel
Class A

Open March - October.
200 rooms.
52 Venizelou
Tel. (0831) 50 432, Fax (0831) 27 825
The largest seaside hotel so close to the town centre. It features a great view of the town and an outdoor parking lot behind the hotel, which, however, is unguarded and unsafe. Still, you can park your bike on the pavement in front of the reception.

THEARTEMIS PALACE, Hotel
Class A

Open March - November.
175 rooms.
30 Portaliou St.
Tel. (0831) 21 991, Fax (0831) 23 785
A very luxurious hotel just a step away from the heart of town. It has balconies with a beautiful wooden railing and top-notch service.

BYZANTION, Pension
Class A. Open all year round.
14 rooms.
24 - 28 Vosporou St.,
Tel. (0831) 55 609

FORTEZZA, Hotel
Class B.
Open March - November.
54 rooms.
16 Melissinou St.,
Old Town of Rethimno
Tel. (0831) 55 551, Fax (0831) 54 073
A wonderful, modern hotel, housed in an excellently kept up Venetian building overlooking - what else? - the Fortezza. Safe parking in a guarded outdoor parking lot a hundred metres from the hotel. Your best choice for a comfortable stay.

KYMA BEACH, Hotel
Class B. Open all year round.
34 rooms.
Iroon Square
Tel. (0831) 21 503, Fax (0831) 22 353

MINOS, Hotel
Class B.
Open March- November.
150 rooms.
5 Machiton Scholis Chorofilakis St.,
Perivolia Rethimnou
Tel. (0831)53 921, Fax (0831) 23 544

RALIA, Rooms to Let
Open all year round.
Rethimno has thousands of Rooms to Let, and if you take the trouble to look for them in the alleys of the old town you will certainly find one. A very good option is the Rooms to Let of Mrs. Ralia (*Ralia*) at the intersection of Salaminos and Diakou streets. It is an old three-storey building with clean and inexpensive rooms. At the small square near it there is a fairly safe place where you can park your bike.

YOUTH HOSTEL
41 Tombazi,
Old Town of Rethimno
Tel. (0831) 22 848
A large, clean and very inexpensive place on a quiet street in the old town. If you like a good team spirit you will enjoy staying here. Very nice inner courtyard, restaurant, laundry, small library.

ELISABETH, camping
3 km east of Rethimno, next to the Missiria beach.
Open May through October.
10,000 m^2 (or about 2.5 acres), 80 spaces.
A very quiet and well looked after camping ground next to the beach. The road ends there, so there is no noise from passing vehicles. Lots of trees and shade, clean toilets, showers with hot water, level ground with thin grass, and a simple mini market and restaurant. Mrs. Elisabeth, the owner, can give you a lot of information on the area.

WHERE TO EAT

In every corner of Rethimno and in every big hotel - or just next to it - you are sure to find restaurants for every taste and wallet. The most popular ones, always full of tourists with rather thick wallets and a poor sense of taste, are the ones on the waterfront, especially on the east side of it. A certain sign by which to recognise them is the huge, lighted plastic menus next to the entrance and the aggressive waiters who speak ten languages each (but only ten words of each language...) The more you go to the east the worse it gets, with the restaurants of Platanias being the worst.
The wisest thing is to go to the old town. Most good restaurants are concentrated between four

ROUTES STARTING FROM RETHIMNO

streets - Minoos, Nikiforou Foka, Arabatzoglou and Xanthoudidou - that form one block. In the early evening these streets are closed to vehicles and filled with restaurant tables. If you want to enjoy a well laid table, soft music and romantic candlelight, coupled with good service and a delicious meal, this is the place to come. It may still be a little expensive, but at least you will get very good value for your money. Let us also note that the restaurants at the old harbour are somewhat more expensive.

ANTONIS (fish-tavern, 10)
The temple of traditionally cooked seafood, housed in an old Venetian building on Markou Botsari street, behind the Rimonti Fountain. Under the arched roof of the tavern, Antonis the fisherman and his wife serve the best *kakaviá* (fish soup), crunchy fry, bogue, red mullets, whatever is caught in Antonis's fishing nets. Small place, loyal clientele, low prices and a unique experience. If he feels like it, Andreas, the owner's nephew (born in... 1990), may entertain you with his terrific singing.

FANARI (tavern)
An excellent tavern on the outskirts of the town, near Plastira Square. It is favoured by the locals and serves a great variety of appetisers, fresh seafood, steaks done on the coals, and a tasty red wine that is drawn from the barrel. Opens at noon.

GIORGOS (restaurant, 11)
A typical restaurant with cooked meals, which opens at noon. It has the great advantage of being on Petichaki Square where you can enjoy some very hot action. Bon appetit!

PLATEIA (snack place)
Located at the small Plastira Square at the north end of town, this friendly place has quick service and a great variety of goodies to choose from.

LA CREPERIE (pancake house, 12)
Pricey but tasty pancakes created with imagination. The place is open from early morning till late at night, so you can go whenever you are hungry.

GOODY'S (fast food restaurant, 14)
Located next to the Porto Rethymno Hotel, GOODY'S is probably your best option among the dozens of restaurants built by the waterfront in the east part of town. Unlike the other restaurants, it does not pretend to be something fancy, and it serves decent food at reasonable prices. It is part of the largest chain of fast food restaurants in Greece, which can be counted on for quality and pleasant, air-conditioned premises.

EPTA ADELPHIA (restaurant, 13)
An old restaurant at the old harbour, which offers not only a nice view but also some tasty meals. It has great steaks, cooked to order, and some delicious seafood (octopus, squids etc). If you think of its location, the prices are quite reasonable.

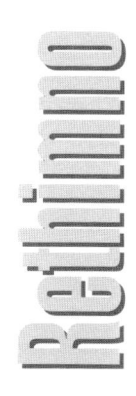

ENTERTAINMENT

Like food and sleep, entertainment needs are covered by two very different kinds of businesses. On the one hand are the big discos and the noisy dancing bars that are concentrated mostly along the beach in the east part of town, attracting crowds that want cheap drinks, loud music and packed rooms. On the other hand are the several small pubs at the heart of the old town, housed - for the most part - in old Venetian buildings and having a lot of character.

GALERO (16) and VASSILIKON (17)

"Twin" coffee bars at the small Rimonti Square, right in the heart of things. From morning till afternoon they serve coffee to their many young clients, who stay here for hours and gossip, play *tàvli* (backgammon) with their friends, and watch the action around them (= choose their "targets" for the evening). From the moment it gets dark till the early morning hours they serve refreshing cocktails to the hottest young people in town and play some really good music.

FIGARO (bar, 18)

Nice rock music in a beautifully decorated environment. The spaces of the old Venetian building housing the bar have been very cleverly used.

CINEMA (disco club, 21)

An ex-movie theatre that has been turned into a big disco with a capacity of over one thousand people. Completely packed after midnight!

MILO (bar)

A small bar on Arkadiou street with great ambience and impressive wall paintings with scenes from the life of Adam and Eve (no, it isn't a church!)

BAROQUE (bar)

A youthful place housed in a building that shows its age. It features dancing music and popular Greek late-night hits that excite the spirits.

VENETSIANIKO (coffee bar, 20)

The best place for your morning, noon or afternoon coffee. Pleasant interior but also lots of outdoor tables at the old harbour pier.

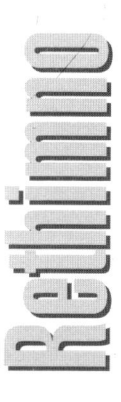

13. Rethimno - Ierapetra

FOLLOWING THE SOUTH COAST

ROUTES STARTING FROM RETHIMNO

Between Rethimno and Spili (30 km) there is a nice open stretch of road with good asphalt (A2) that will certainly invite you to speed. About 9 km south of Rethimno, though, slow down a bit and look for the big Gr/E sign that says "Minoan Cemetery of Armeni." Turn right following the sign, park your motorcycle next to the guard's hut, take along a torch and a camera with a flash, and prepare yourself for a sight worth seeing: **the most impressive Minoan cemetery of Crete** (see next page).

As you continue southward on the main road you can drive fast, because unlike so many other roads this one has been carefully designed. After 15 - 30 minutes (depending on how fast you go!) you will arrive at **Spili**. What you see from the main road does not do justice to this large, yet picturesque village. If you want to see it as it really is, follow the OTE sign and get off the main road. Park your bike outside the police station (for safety reasons) and then take a walk through the cobbled streets of the upper neighbourhood. (These go uphill and are lined with aristocratic,

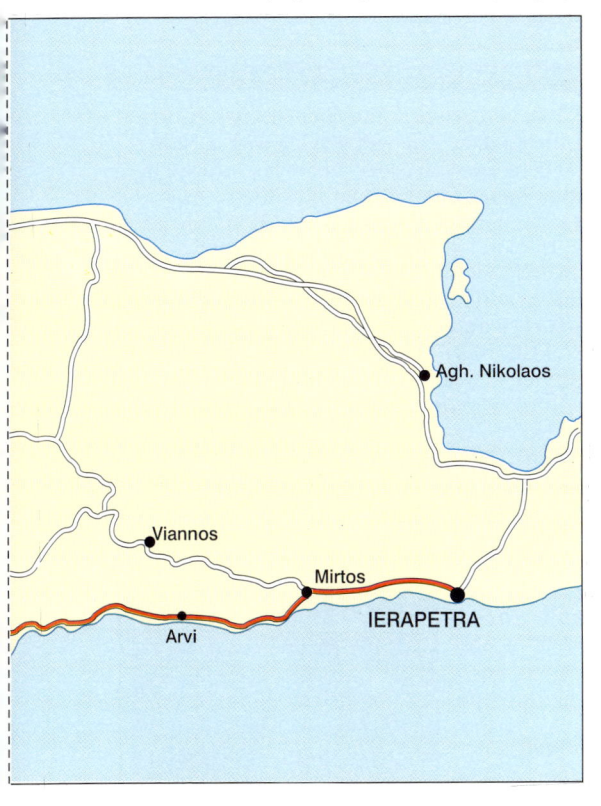

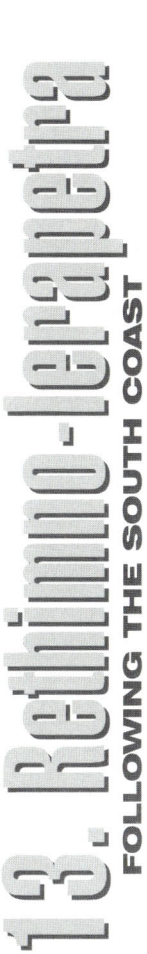

13. Rethimno-Ierapetra
FOLLOWING THE SOUTH COAST

stone-built houses that are fortunately still lived in). On the main street you will see a small square with seventeen lion-head fountains that make an impressive sight. If your walk has tired you and your stomach starts complaining, your best option is Mr. Tzourbakis' restaurant at the north exit of the village. Right above it are some rooms for rent, air-conditioned and carefully looked after.

Between Spili and Aghia Galini the road is also good (A2), with nice turns, good asphalt and clear views during the entire route. It goes through two bald mountains with grey rock, **Kedros** in the north (1780m) and **Siderotas** in the south (1660m). Behind Kedros lies the Amari valley surrounded by beautiful mountain villages, but

THE MINOAN CEMETERY OF ARMENI

In the spring of 1965 a teacher at the elementary school of Somatas saw a little fellow who was playing with a rather unusual object. He took a closer look and to his surprise he saw it was a **Minoan vase**! The kid told him where he had found it and the teacher notified the authorities. When the archaeologists came, the kid led them to an oak-covered slope where his father usually took his flock. The excavation that started immediately revealed **over three hundred graves, carved into the soft rock and dating from the Late Minoan III period (1450 - 1100 BC). Most of them had not been looted** and gave us many treasures: numerous vases, weapons, decorated clay coffins, jewellery and miniature artefacts. (Some of these findings are exhibited in the Archaeological Museum of Rethimno). The graves were family-owned and had a square room and a long passage carved into the rock, and a few of them were of "royal size." Certainly, a cemetery as large and as well designed as that must have belonged to a big town, but to this day this town **hasn't been found.** In spite of the many excavations that have taken place in the surrounding area in an effort to discover the lost town, the only findings so far are a stone-paved street near **Kastelos** and an ancient copper mine four kilometres to the west of it. Even the largest and most renowned cities can disappear from the face of the earth, and under the weight of the centuries their names are easily forgotten...

obviously you're not interested or you would have chosen Route 14! If, however, you change your mind, your last chance to switch routes is to turn on the road (A3) that starts a little before the north entrance of Spili. (There is a Gr/E sign at the intersection that says "**Gerakari**"). Once in Gerakari, turn to page 323 for the rest.

If you haven't turned to page 323 it means you are a beach lover! Sure enough, behind Siderotas you will find **the largest, cleanest, emptiest, nicest beaches in all of Crete** (Road Book 5, page 280). The coastline between Aghia Irini (the beach south of Kerames) and cape Melissa (at Aghios Pavlos) is a true paradise. After Aghios Pavlos, you can find good beaches - small, for the most part, but sandy and quiet - behind the Asteroussia mountain range, and more specifically on the coastline between Kali Limenes and Maridaki (the beach near Tsoutsouros). After that, there are still some clean beaches, but the landscape has been spoilt by the huge, plastic-covered greenhouses of the farmers' villages that are in the area. To reach all these beaches you need an off-road bike, since you will be frequently driving on quite difficult dirtroads (gravel, steep inclination etc).

For the first beaches (the ones behind Siderotas) you need to get off the main road at Kambos Kissou. When you get there, turn right (in the direction of **Aktounda**) and follow the road as it climbs the north side of the mountain, goes through Vatos, Adraktos, Drimiskos and **Kerames** (all of which are rather indifferent villages without much character), and takes you to the picturesque - but almost completely deserted - **Agalianos.** Even before Kerames you have a view of the coast below with its truly wonderful beaches. After Agalianos you need to continue on a dirtroad (D3). Road Book 5 marks the basic route to help you distinguish the road you must take among the maze of dirtroads that end in the olive groves. However, what will really help you is a good sense of orientation, coupled with persistence and luck, and the knowledge that you should never lose sight of the coast. The first beach to the west (at the end of an asphalt-paved road that goes south of Kerames) is **Aghia Irini,** while the last beach to the east that can be reached by a path branching off the Kerames - Aghia Paraskevi road (and the best beach of them all) is **Triopetra,** named after the characteristic three rocks at its east end that jut out into the sea. Needless to say, you can camp at any beach you like. Your water needs could very likely be covered by one of the wells in the area, and if not, you can certainly find water in Aghia Paraskevi. Though the village has been abandoned, there are five or six wonderful stone houses under construction, and they will be available for renting from the summer of 1996.

Yet **the most impressive beach of Crete,** a real masterpiece of Nature, **is the beach of Aghios Pavlos** further to the east. This is not

ROAD BOOK 5

The beaches behind Mt. Siderotas

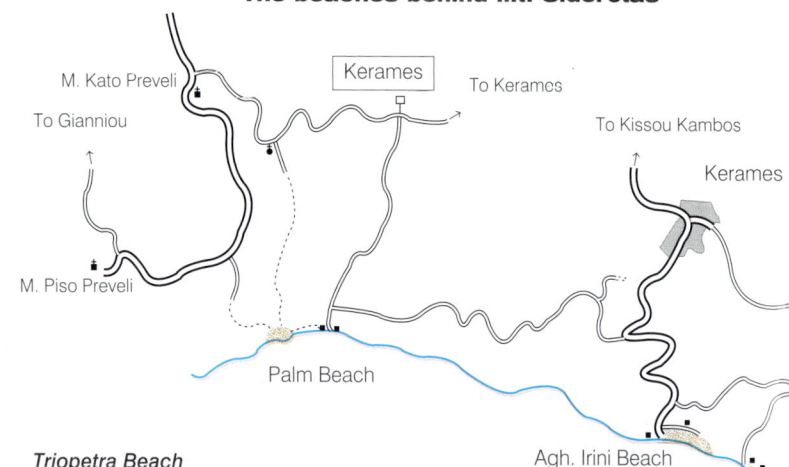

Triopetra Beach

accessible from Aghia Paraskevi, since the coastal road connecting Aghia Paraskevi and Aghios Pavlos has been abandoned and is no longer serviceable. It can be reached if you get back on the Rethimno - Aghia Galini road at Kambos Kissou, continue southward until Nea Kria Vrissi, and then turn right. The sand at Aghios Pavlos is very rich. The beach is separated into three coves divided by large rocks, and of these the west and middle one are **totally empty** of buildings (and can be reached with a five to ten minute walk from the top of the hill where you will leave your bike). At the east cove you will see two or three Rooms to Let, which are quite nice and have balconies with gorgeous views. Their taverns are also nice, serving good meals at low prices. Your best choice is the tavern and Rooms to Let of Aris and Carol. Since there is no phone available, the only way to book a room is by mail, so write early at the following address: Carol and Aris, Taverna "To Koutali," Poste Restante Aghia Galini, Crete.

Whatever your maps show, there is no coastal road between Aghios Pavlos and Aghia

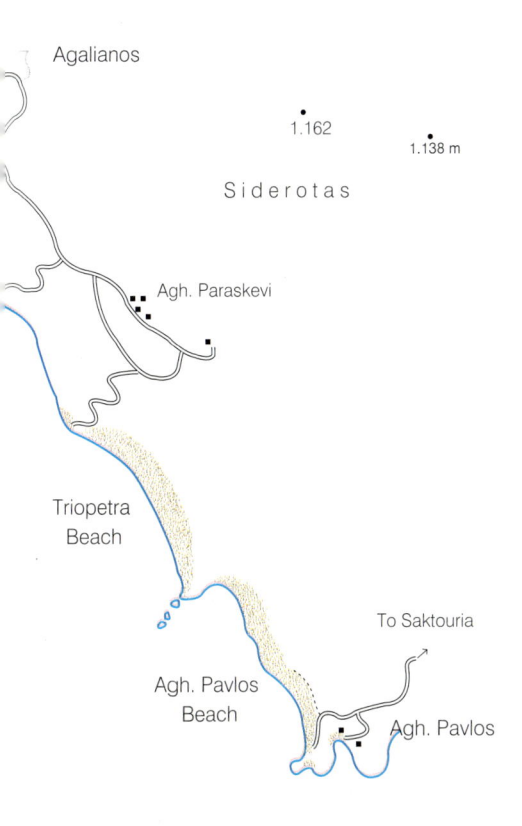

Galini. The two dirtroads that seem to lead to Aghia Galini, one starting south of Sachtouria and another intersecting the Sachtouria - Aghios Pavlos road and heading east, are in fact misleading, and they end in olive groves and steep cliffs above the shore. To continue Route 13 and head east again, you must first go back to Nea Kria Vrissi. From there you can either go down the main road to **Aghia Galini** or take the road that takes you there through Melambes. The latter is very slippery, though, so it is best to avoid it.

AGHIA GALINI

At the beginning of the century a few families from Melambes, among which the Mamalakis, came to the peaceful and empty bay of Aghia Galini and built a coffee shop and a few huts to facilitate the Sphakian tradesmen who unloaded their lumber. (This was in turn loaded onto donkeys and carried to Iraklio). As the years passed, a few cottages sprang up, followed by a warehouse, then a tavern, then... Today the scenery is completely changed, and the place is full of all sorts of tourist businesses: **about fifty luxury hotels** one next to the other, many restaurants, car rental offices, tourist shops, jewellery shops, pubs, everything you can imagine. So dramatic was the change in fact that, to be accurate, the name of the place should change from Aghia Galini (Holy Serenity) to Demonismeni Anastatossi (Demonical Madness...) The beach in front of the hotel-

Aghia Galini: An incredibly crowded town

avalanche is very small and ugly, and there is a horrible wire fence on the slope behind it that's meant to protect bathers from landslides. Of course, a little further to the east there is a better beach as well as a camping ground, but the truth is that in the high season the crowds and the noise can be very annoying.

After Aghia Galini continue eastward on the main road that leads to **Timbaki**. You will drive on the lower part of a mountainside full of olive groves, and after a turn you will suddenly face the **Messara valley** that spreads out to the east as far as the eye can see.

The Messara valley covers a huge area of land along the south coast, and it is **the most fertile valley of Crete.** It is irrigated by two big rivers, Geropotamos and Anapodiaris, and numerous tributaries, and it is protected from the winds due to the mountains around all but the west side of it. (The latter stretches till the Gulf of Messara). The first thing that crossed people's minds when they saw the valley was something like: "Oh, my God, this is the nicest place on earth; I want to live here!" It was this thought that led the first settlers to set up their Neolithic homes here, and it was this thought that led the Minoans to build the Faistos and Aghia Triada palaces and the Romans to make Gortina the capital of Crete. But when you see the place from above, the first thought that will cross your mind will be: "Oh, my God, what a hellhole!" Unfortunately, a very large part of the Messara valley is buried under the plastic roofs of the Cretan greenhouses and polluted with countless yards of loose plastic lying around everywhere. It is impossible to describe the harm done to the landscape by the overexploitation that the land has suffered in the farmers' hands.

If you have a street bike, you can visit the important archaeological sites of Faistos, Aghia Triada and Gortina and then follow **an impressive mountain route** (A3), which starts from **Apessokari** and gives you a taste of the Asteroussia wilderness and the sandy beaches behind the mountains. The road winds up the mountain with spectacular and dangerous turns, passes through the villages of Miamou and Krotos, and eventually takes you to **Lendas** (to the east of which lie some nice beaches among which the gorgeous and sandy **Loutra**). To continue, you must first return to Apessokari from the same road, because to the east and west of Lendas there are only dirtroads. Once there, the best way to cross the Messara valley is the road (A2) that passes through the villages at the foot of the northern side of the Asteroussia. This will take you to **Martha** at the east end of the valley, where it meets the Iraklio - Ierapetra road. All you have to do now is turn right and go straight to **Ierapetra**.

If, however, you have an off-road bike, **this place is your paradise!** The Asteroussia mountains offer a wonderful chance to enjoy **some of the greatest mountain routes in Crete.** A number of dirtroads will take you to empty beaches, out of the way monasteries, picturesque hamlets that seem untouched by Time, archaeological sites unknown to most, and breathtaking landscapes full of wild beauty and nooks ideal for camping. The routes we suggest are mapped out in Road Books 6a, 6b, 6c and 6d. But before you disappear on the mountains, go see the archaeological sites of Faistos, Aghia Triada and Gortina, which are really worth visiting. If you start early in the morning, you will have visited all three by noon, and then you can take

A dirtroad on the Asteroussia Mountains

the first Asteroussia route and find a good camping site or a room for the night.

As mentioned, the first relatively large place you see as you come from Aghia Galini and enter the Messara valley is **Timbaki,** a town without character but with many shops for the provisions you need before starting your mountain trip. The road passes outside a small military airport built by the Germans, which has long ceased to function as an airport and was until recently used for motorcycle races.

About a couple of kilometres after Timbaki you will see a Gr sign that says "Αγία Τριάδα" **(Aghia Triada).** Turn right on the narrow dirtroad at the intersection, go through a gorge... filled with heaps of trash, turn left after the gorge, climb the... burned hillside that follows it, and you will find yourself at the parking area outside the archaeological site of Aghia Triada. If, however, you are not so crazy about the idea of travelling in the middle of junk - an unpleasant experience caused by the lack of sensitivity on the part of most Greeks and by their inability not only to create a new civilisation but even to respect their ancient monuments and keep the area around them clean - you can choose to ignore the sign directing you to Aghia Triada and continue on the main road. About one kilometre later, turn right on the road (A3) that leads to the palace of Faistos. From here you can either follow the road (A4) that leads to Aghia Triada in the west, or decide to see Faistos first (since you are already here). The latter option is preferable, but you should know that there is no safe parking area for your bike and that you will have to leave it at the unguarded outdoor parking lot about two hundred metres from the archaeological site. This is why you should take all valuables with you.

THE PALACE OF FAISTOS

(Guarded archaeological site, open daily from 8:30 a.m. till 3:00 p.m.)

There was a time when our distant ancestors - or perhaps not so distant, just ten or twelve thousand years in the past - survived on what the good God provided them. They hunted (delicious) wild boars and deer, gathered juicy fruits from the trees, and slept in cool and quiet caves. The only things they produced with their hands were a few stone tools and weapons which made their lives a bit easier. Then one day between the years 10,000 and 8,000 BC, an idea suddenly sprang in their primitive minds: "Instead of exhausting ourselves hunting wild beasts, why don't we catch a few, build a wall around them, tame them, and eat them whenever we are hungry? Why put so much effort and do such dangerous things?" So they stopped wandering around in search of food and sleeping in caves, and they built the first pens for

The magnificent main entrance to the Faistos palace

the animals and the first huts for themselves at places that made them feel secure. Then they thought: "Why tire ourselves gathering fruits and vegetables from wherever God made them grow? Why not grow them ourselves near our homes to cover our needs?" And so it was that humankind took a big step forward - though perhaps in a less simple manner than we seem to suggest - and from the Palaeolithic wandering hunters and fruit gatherers evolved the farmers and shepherds of the Neolithic age.

The places where people chose to build their settlements were usually hilltops surrounded by fertile valleys. The hills were not very low (so as to function as good look-out posts), but they were not very tall either (so as to afford easy access to the fields).

It was on such a hill (100 metres tall) at the west side of the Messara valley that a group of people chose to build a settlement somewhere around 3000 BC. (Today the hill is known as **Kastri**). At their feet was a fertile valley with a big river (today known as Geropotamos) and at a short distance in the west was the sea. The people had a magnificent view of the valley from their courtyards, which must have given them a feeling of security and euphoria. (If you happen to be here at sunset you will understand why). The excavations that took place here revealed vestiges of their huts, the hearths where they gathered to warm themselves or cook over the fire, and many beautiful clay vessels with a unique for the time decoration. This was characterised by the use of a red colouring substance on a polished black surface.

The human presence on the hill was uninterrupted until the early Byzantine period. The first Neolithic settlement was succeeded by a very powerful and wealthy Minoan town built on the same site, which flourished especially in the period between 1900 BC, when the **first Minoan palace** was built, and 1400 BC, when the **second Minoan palace** was destroyed. The name of this town, **Faistos,** survived thanks to the ancient writers and the Linear B tablets found in Knossos. If we had to rely only on the archaeological findings we have from the place, we would not know its name today, just like we don't know the names of so many other Minoan settlements, large or small. The craftsmen of the time spent years and years building magnificent palaces and towns, but they never thought of putting in a few hours in order to carve a name somewhere...

The exact site of Faistos was determined for the first time in the middle of the 19th century by the British admiral T.B.A. Spratt. Yet the excavation of the area did not start until 1900, when the Italian School of Archaeology sent a team led by Professor Federico Halbherr. In 1909 it was interrupted, in 1928 it was resumed for another four years (1928 - 1932), and in 1952 it was once again resumed, always by the Italians, who continue the excavation to this day. The findings brought to light are quite important but, as they date from the entire period that there was a settlement on the hill, the non-expert gets easily confused in a maze of ruins spanning several centuries. In an 18,000 square metre area you will see, built one on top of the other, the ruins of: the first Minoan palace that was built in 1900 BC and destroyed by an earthquake in 1700 BC; the second Minoan palace that was built right after the destruction of the first and was also destroyed, sometime around 1400 BC, either by an earthquake or by invaders who came suddenly and razed everything to the ground; the settlement that was built on top of the palace ruins and flourished during the Mycenaean and Geometric period (1400 - 700 BC); and the buildings of the Hellenistic and the Roman times. To explore the area, take out your map and enter bravely. We shall see how well you do with labyrinths!

As you walk on the paved passage that leads to the archaeological site, you will pass the EOT

THE PALACE OF FAISTOS

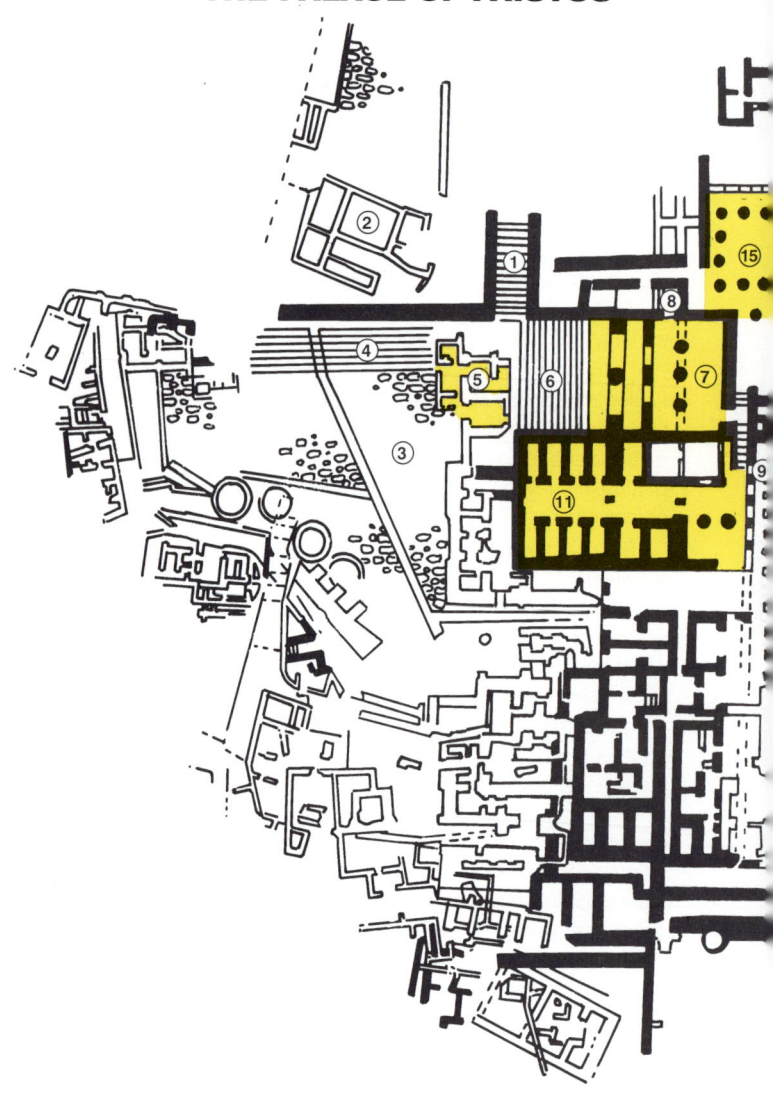

(GNTO) kiosk and the window where you pay the inevitable thousand drachmas, and then enter the site from the norhtwest. You will go down the steps **(1)** that belonged to the first palace, passing on your right-hand side the ruins of a house **(2)** of the hellenistic times (ca 200 BC), which was built on the ruins of a Neolithic house of approximately 3000 BC, and you will find yourself at the **West Court (3)**, which belonged to the first as well as the second palace! Now go to the seats **(4)** at the north end of the West Court and sit down to figure our where everything is.

ROUTES STARTING FROM RETHIMNO

■ First palace
☐ Second palace

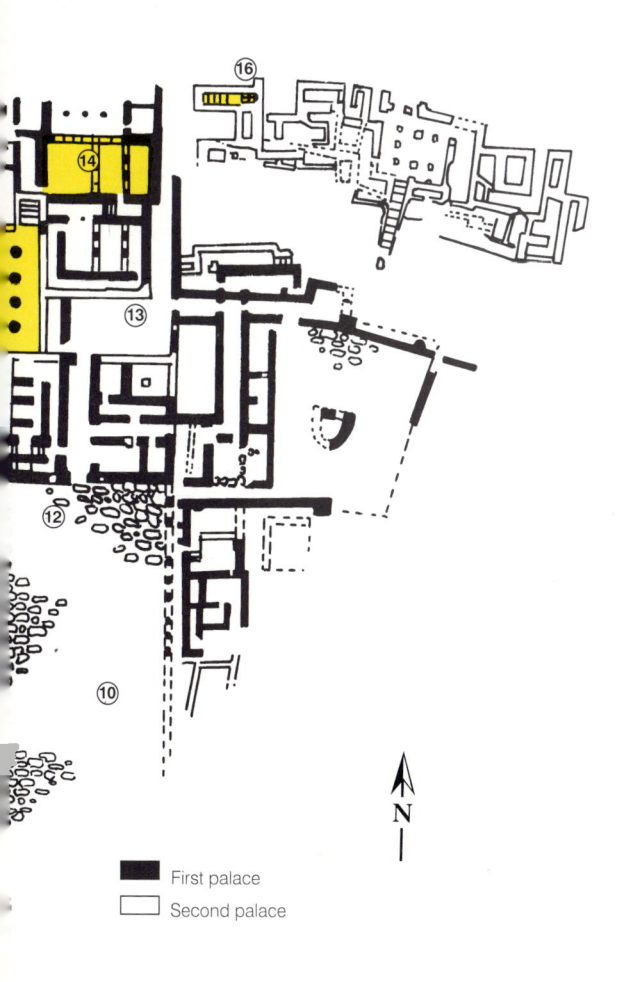

13. Rethimno-Ierapetra
FOLLOWING THE SOUTH COAST

Take a few deep breaths, relax, and let your eyes wander over this well built court. Imagine that you are watching the ***tavrokathàpsia*** (bull-leaping shows) that took place here in which the Minoan athletes grasped the bull by the horns and vaulted or somersaulted over him. Imagine the lords of the place speaking to an audience and the priests proceeding out of the Sanctuary **(5)** in order to conduct a religious ceremony. Imagine dainty Minoan girls from the cream of the aristocracy taking their walk in the twilight and people passing by the merchants' stalls. In front of you and to the left, picture the west front of the first palace, rising two or three storeys high, and seven or eight metres behind it that of the second palace, with a length of about a hundred metres and impressive alcoves and projections. Exactly to your left is the **Main Stairway (6)** with twelve steps, 13.5 metres wide, that end before the majestic-looking entrance **(The Propylaea, 7)**. What makes the stairway seem so impressive? If you observe the steps for a minute, you will see that they are thicker at the centre than at the ends! Now that you have observed them, go up the steps in a slow ritualistic manner, pass (from the right or left) the big column that supported the front part of the Propylaea - with your eyes you can see only the base of it but with your imagination you can see it whole - and enter the main room from the right or left gate respectively.

At the north wall of the Propylaea was a gate leading to a wide, well built stairway **(8),** at the top of which were the **Royal Apartments** of the second and third floor. These have not survived, unfortunately, but you can still stand on the same steps that the all-powerful Minoan King walked on when he retired to his quarters.

Much further and to the right is a small stairway **(9)** leading to the **Main Court (10),** which was common for both palaces. It was here that everything took place. Judging from the representation on the famous Aghia Triada *ritò* (a type of ritual vessel), which shows athletic games taking place in front of colonnades, athletic games must have indeed taken place here. This was also where the carts with the palace provisions passed as evidenced by the wheel marks on the south side of the court **(11)**. Finally, it was the place where the storerooms of the first palace were built. In these storerooms, the archaeologists found a **huge collection of clay sealings** (over 6500 clay balls with impressions from approximately 300 different seals), as well as many clay tablets with inscriptions in Linear A, a syllabary that has yet to be deciphered.

The facades of the buildings surrounding the Main Court must have been very impressive and elaborately decorated, although we have no traces of frescos. At the north part of the court is a gate **(12)** leading to a paved passageway decorated with half columns and niches. This takes you to an inner court **(13)** from where you can visit two of the **most beautiful places of the second palace** frequented by the King and those around him. One is a room **(14)** that had two open sides, the east one leading to an open yard and the north affording a wonderful view of the slopes of Idi. The other is a peristyle court **(15)** which was open from the north side (also affording a view of the mountain) and which was at the centre of the royal apartments from where it could be reached.

At the north side of the archaeological site were several apartments of the first palace. In one of these **(16)** the Italians discovered the famous **Faistos Disc,** a clay disc with a text on both sides of it. This includes 241 symbols in a sort of spiral arrangement and it is still a puzzle to the experts.

After the second palace was destroyed the place continued to be inhabited, although there was never a third palace. Faistos lost its old glamour, but it managed to remain a self-governed city that lived on for at least another thousand years and had a fairly large population. At about the middle of the 3rd century BC it came under the power of Gortina, and at about 160 BC the Gortinians, God knows why, destroyed it entirely. This was the final blow for one of the most splendid centres of the Minoan civilisation...

The few inscriptions we have from Faistos are all in Linear A, the undeciphered code, and there are none in Linear B to reveal the town's history and the names of its great lords. As a result, the only names that have come down to us are that of **Radamanthys,** a mythological king of Faistos and brother of King Minos, and **Epimenides**, a philosopher that was born here in the 6th century BC and was one of the seven wise men of ancient Greece. The latter was supposed to have slept for 40 years straight and to have lived 150 years! But as long as he may have lived, he, too, succumbed to the fate of humanity. Like the rest of his fellow citizens and the town itself, he died, and Time enveloped him in utter darkness. Maybe this darkness will be partly dissolved when the archaeologists find the lost graveyards or the royal burial site of Faistos.

The Faistos Disc

THE MINOAN MANSION OF AGHIA TRIADA (=HOLY TRINITY)

(Guarded archaeological site, open daily from 8:30 a.m. till 3:00 p.m.)

Giving a Christian name to a Minoan mansion can only sound like a stupid joke. And yet it's true. The Italian archaeologists that excavated the place (1902 - 1905, 1910 - 1914, 1935) did not find any clue about the name of the mansion, so they named it after the deserted village nearby. They could at least have borrowed the earlier name of the village, **Pirgiotissa** (loosely translated as "The Tower Lady"). The Minoan mansion of Pirgiotissa. Doesn't it sound better? But a place can only be named once.

The mansion of Aghia Triada is not as old as the first Faistos palace, nor is it as big. It was built at about the same time as the second palace of Faistos (ca 1700 BC) and was in fact very much in its shadow. It might have been the summer residence of the Prince of Faistos, or, more likely, the base of some independent landowner of the region. Yet the treasures found here are every bit as magnificent as the findings in Knossos and the other important Minoan settlements, and they have greatly contributed to our image of the superb civilisation that flourished in Minoan Crete.

The settlement next to the Aghia Triada mansion

Today you can see them at the Archaeological Museum of Iraklio.

Since 1902, the Italian archaeologists have brought to light everything you can imagine! At the **Reception Room (1)** they found some of the most impressive naturalistic frescos of Minoan art. Their graceful elegance is evident in the picture of the priestess standing in front of an altar in an idyllic landscape full of wild flowers. Somewhere around, a hungry cat stalks a pheasant with utmost concentration. Right next to this room is the **Lord's Office (2).** Here the archaeologists found many clay seals, apparently used on the lord's... business mail and on the parcels he received. At the **Treasury (3)** they found nineteen big **tàlanda,** large bronze pieces weighing twenty-nine kilos each and used in business transactions. Inside the **Bedroom (4)** they found a bench made of plaster, which served as a kind of bed frame, and the oil lamps that once gave the room their soft light. At the west side of the **Altar Court (5)** and close to the **Royal Apartments** (which were on the second floor, right above the Reception Room), the archaeologists found two *rità* (ritual vessels) made of steatite (a soft rock mineral). These bore some relief representations of everyday scenes that have now become famous. On the first, a group of men return home after the harvest to the sound of music, and on the second a group of athletes practise wrestling, boxing and bull leaping. At the **Servants' Quarters (6),** a wonderful steatite cup was brought to light, depicting a lively children's game: the King and his soldiers. The **Main Storerooms (7)** were full of large jars with carved or engraved decorative themes. (These were used to store away the wine,

13. Rethimno-Ierapetra
FOLLOWING THE SOUTH COAST

the oil, and all the tasty things that went into the meals that the occupants of the mansion enjoyed in their *symposia*). Finally, the **Sanctuary (8)** gave us three ritual vessels with snake-shaped handles and traces of a wonderful floor mosaic with octopuses and dolphins which the archaeologists have managed to preserve.

But the most amazing finding, which told us the most about the Minoan religion, is the box-shaped **Sarcophagus** (stone coffin) found in a rectangular grave at the cemetery near the house (about 150 metres to the northwest of it). This is covered on all four

THE MANSION OF AGHIA TRIADA

■ First Palace
□ Second Palace

sides with painted representations, not yet fully interpreted, concerning the rituals and beliefs of the Minoans when it comes to death. On one of its long sides you can see two priestesses sacrificing a bull to the sound of music. The bull is tied on the altar and his blood is carefully collected in a vessel. On the other side you can see a priestess making a libation to the gods. She is accompanied by a musician and a second priestess carrying sacred vessels, and she is surrounded by several sacred symbols related to the beliefs of the Minoans about the afterlife and to their funeral customs (these include the double axe, a vessel with fruit, an altar and a tree). At the other end the deceased receives the presents of three youths: a ship (on which to travel to the "Islands of the Happy Ones") and two calves (to eat during his voyage). Finally, on the two smaller sides there are some strange chariots. They are driven by women and pulled by griffins, the mythological animals that had the body of a lion and the wings of an eagle. Obviously, inside the sarcophagus must have been a very important person. Yet the artist who decorated it never thought of carving the name of its occupant...

The after-harvest scene on a ritual vessel

The Aghia Triada mansion was destroyed at the same time as the palaces of Knossos and Faistos, and obviously by the same cause. It was replaced with a considerably smaller **Mègaro** (mansion) of the Mycenaean type, which must have been some sort of cult centre since it was full of votive statues.

The settlement north of the Aghia Triada mansion, however, continued to exist even after the mansion was destroyed (see the area marked by the dotted line on our sketch). At its east side you can still see a row of eight **shops (9)** that served the needs of the people. Then the place was abandoned for many centuries, and it was once again inhabited during the Hellenistic years, at which time a temple was built here in honour of Zeus Velchaios. During the Roman years some art lover built his villa at this place and it seems there was also a settlement. During the Venetian and the Turkish rule there was a village of 150 people, mostly Christians, but in 1897 the Turks attacked the village and slaughtered its entire population. In our modern era, especially in the last ten years, the place is "attacked" by the one thousand people that come here daily. Welcome to Aghia Triada!

THE TOWN OF GORTINA

(Guarded archaeological site, open daily from 8:30 a.m. till 3:00 p.m.)

As King of the Gods, Zeus had everything in the world that he needed, and he had it just for the asking: plenty of ambrosia and nectar for his feasts, wonderful smells from the sacrifices offered in his countless sanctuaries on earth, a whole bunch of previously mortal friends who were given immortality and taken to Olympus because he enjoyed their company (Hercules and Ganymedes being two prime examples), an inexhaustible stock of thunderbolts to throw on the heads of his enemies, and a lovely and faithful wife called Hera. Yet he also had a weakness that tortured him, because it was not as easy to deal with as everything else: **he liked women!**

First of all, he had to steal away from his wife, who knew what an incorrigible womaniser he was and always kept a watchful eye on him. (In fact, she often caught him in the act). Then he had to fool the lovely chosen one, so that she would not realise who he was and would not spoil everything with her screams. But he was so resourceful and obstinate that he always found a way to achieve his goal.

One day he spotted **Europe,** a lovely princess who was playing with her friends at the beach of Sidona in what today is Lebanon. (Imagine the range of his vision; nothing got away!) He appeared in front of her as a harmless white bull and started rolling on the sand like a playing kitten. When Europe went near him and sat on his back, the bull started walking around carefully and quietly, because he did not want to scare the lady. Then, at the right moment, he plunged into the sea, and started swimming off the shore with great speed. The poor girl apparently didn't know how to swim, so the only thing she could do was to hold on tightly and cry her heart out. The cruise ended a few hours later on the empty Cretan beach that today belongs to Lendas. Zeus changed his form (though in his heat he was still like a bull), and he took the girl to the most idyllic place of Crete. (And when Zeus chose a love nest he knew what he was doing, especially on this island that was also his birthplace!) The place he chose was near a small creek by the bank of the Litheos river and it was covered with plane trees. Some years later **Gortina** was built on this same site.

If this was Zeus' first choice for a love nest, imagine how beautiful the now ugly valley must once have been. This fact also explains why Gortina never suffered any great catastrophe during its long history - its end excepted - but was instead such a prosperous town. As a token of gratitude and respect, the Gortinians established a yearly celebration in honour of Europe, the **Ellotia,** and they put on their coins the picture of the princess as she sat on the bull.

It is true, of course, that Gortina was not a great town from the start. At the time of the Minoan palaces (2000 - 1400 BC), it was only a small village on a hill by the west bank of the Litheos that was under the power of Faistos. As the years passed, however, the town grew quite rich and powerful, and it spread over a large part of the valley at the foot of the hill. What remained on the hill, protected behind walls, was the town's acropolis, but its religious or military significance was rather small.

By the 5th century, Gortina was the largest and richest town in the valley. But if you think that its wealth came from cultivating it, think again! Instead of growing cucumbers or getting all muddy trying to make vases, the Gortinians preferred to practise another fascinating trade: piracy! Their base of operations was the harbour town of **Levin** (the modern Lendas) and their territory included the entire south coast of Crete.

The main rivals of Gortina were Knossos in the north and Littos in the east. On the other hand, Kidonia, which lay west of Gortina, was also a powerful town, but it was too far away to be any kind of threat.

What is certain is that these powerful Cretan towns must have had their share of fighting over the years. However, we do not have much information on the subject, because the great

The Roman music school in Gortina

historians of Greece (Thucydides, Xenophon etc) did not write much about Crete as it never played a part in the developments on the mainland. As for the local historians, they had the unfortunate idea of writing their works on... palm leaves, which some years later fertilised the soil under the Cretans' flowers. The only thing we know is that the Gortinians and the Knossians were alternatively at war or allied against other common enemies. In 220 BC, during one of the periods when they were allies, they conquered and burned Littos, the No 3 powerful town in the region, and they turned it into... No 0 for ever!

But before the inevitable showdown between Knossos and Gortina another enemy appeared on the horizon: the Romans. Now, the Knossians joined forces with other Cretan towns to deal with the enemy, but the shrewd Gortinians immediately realised the hopelessness of the situation and, instead, they chose to become Rome's allies. Not that they didn't mind having a "boss" over them, but since the Romans were there to stay they thought it would be best to be on their good side. Indeed, in 68 BC the Romans conquered Crete without much difficulty, and they destroyed Knossos along with many other towns that resisted them. But for their ally, Gortina, they reserved special treatment. Not only did they not touch anything, but they even made the town the capital of their new province, and they set about adorning it with beautiful - and needed - public buildings.

Of course, they started with a very luxurious **Praetorium (1)** for the needs of the Roman praetor (the governor of the province); fancy offices and conference rooms, comfortable bedrooms and a spa were all thought to be indispensable parts of it. Then they built an **Amphitheatre (2)** in which to enjoy their... graceful shows that ended with the loser's death (beast and gladiator fights). But to these they added two **Theatres (3, 4)**, a **Music School (5)**, a **Stadium (6)**, a large **Public Bath (7)**, and many **temples**, including the one of Isis and Serapis **(8)**, two imported deities that were "made in Egypt."

From the pre-Roman Gortina we have the splendid **temple of the Pythian Apollo (9)**, one of the most important temples of the town, dating from the 7th century BC. On the base of it the Gortinians carved their laws and the treaties they signed, because they wanted to place them under the protection of the god. The large blocks of stone at the Music School which are inscribed with **The Laws of Gortina** must in all likelihood have come from this temple. No other Greek inscription has been saved that is that big: in 12 columns, 600 lines, and a total of 17,000 letters - carved one very close to the other and forming lines that are alternatively read from left to right and vice versa - is the longest and most difficult legal text we have in the ancient Cretan dialect. It dates from the 5th century BC, and... no matter how good your ancient Greek, you will have a hard time reading it! After years of study, the experts inform us that it is a kind of civil code, dealing with matters of property, dowry, inheritance, marriage, divorce, adoption etc., as well as with the rights and obligations of slaves.

A second temple of the 7th century BC is the **temple of Athena (10)** on the acropolis. Here you will see traces of the wall that protected the first settlement, as well as the foundations of a Roman building of unknown use which is known as "Kastro" (The Fortress).

When the Christian religion started spreading in Crete, Gortina, following its standard policy of going along with the nation or trend that seemed strongest, was the **first** town to adopt it. As a result, the archbishop of Crete and student of Paul, Titos, had his base in Gortina. The Metropolis, dedicated to **Aghios Titos (11)**, was built much later (around 500 AD), and it has been preserved in pretty good condition. However,

GORTINA

To Faistos

To Iraklio

Mitropolian River

Aghii Deka

Metropolis

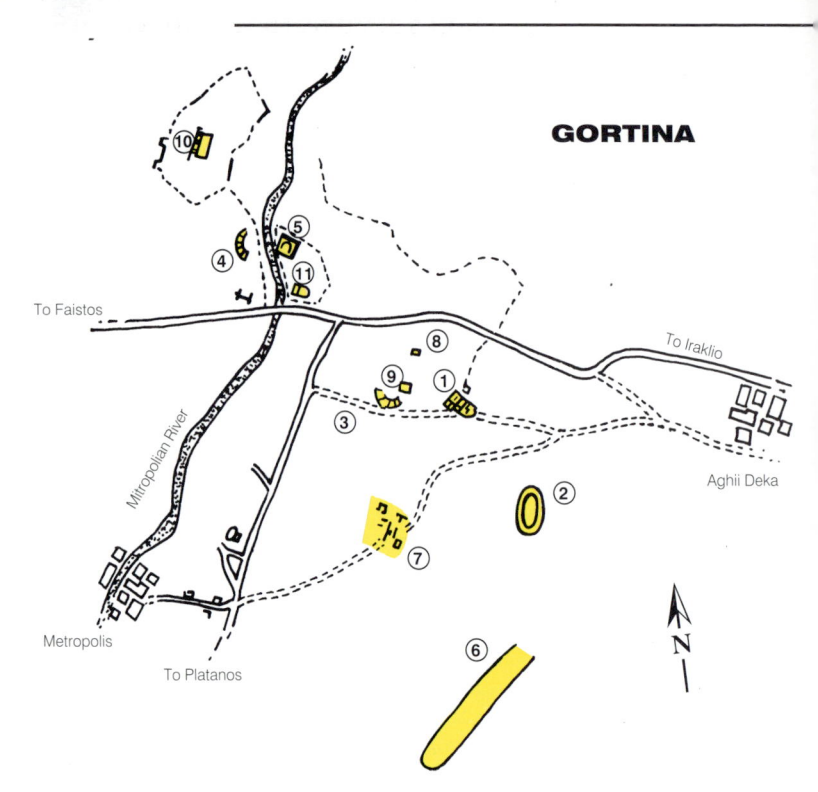

To Platanos

N

The "pieces" of the ancient town of Gortina, scattered in the fields around it

Christianity did not win immediately. The Romans did not like the new religion, and at first they reacted with violence. During the reign of Emperor Decius (249 - 251 AD), ten young Christians were put to death here. In their memory, the modern village that was built near the ancient town was named **"Aghii Deka"** (The Holy Ten). To honour the ten martyrs, let us also mention their names: Saturninos, Efporos, Gelassios, Theodoulos, Evnikianos, Zotikos, Pompios, Agathopous, Evarestos and Vassiliades.

But apart from the Romans, there was somebody else who was mighty displeased with the Gortinians' change of religion: Zeus Himself. After giving them a grace period of six to seven centuries in which to repent, he sent them a huge Thunderbolt (with a capital T) and laid everything waste. The thunderbolt came in the form of the Saracens in **828 AD.** The town could not resist the Arabian attack and it disappeared from the face of the earth for ever. Its glory and splendour were gone, and its shattered pieces can be seen today scattered all over the fields and olive groves surrounding it...

THE ASTEROUSSIA ROUTES

After visiting all those interesting archaeological sites the time has come for a good ride on the Asteroussia Mountains. If you want to take things from the start, it is best to return to Faistos from the main road, continue south (toward **Matala**), and then head eastward, following the routes shown in **Road Books 6a, 6b, 6c and 6d.**

The beaches of **Matala** and **Kalamaki** and the villages near Faistos have suffered from the massive tourism in the area. Matala, in particular, has always been a crowded place thanks to its large sandy beach with the caves at its north end. These were inhabited by the primitive people of the Neolithic age, and they were also inhabited by the primitive hippies of the 60's. But if you wish to stay in Matala forget about the caves; they have been closed by the archaeologists. Instead, look for a room (there are plenty around) or set up your tent in the camping ground.

At Sivas you will see a dirtroad (D3) heading south toward the picturesque **Listaros.** Unfortunately, most of the houses in this village are not lived in and they've been allowed to fall apart. At the centre of the village there is a Gr sign, which points you to the right and informs you that after four kilometres you will be at "Μονή Οδηγήτριας" (**Moni Odigitrias,** the Monastery of the Guiding Mary) and after eleven at "Καλοί Λιμένες" (**Kali Limenes**). Follow the road (D3) as it goes up the east side of a small ravine, and soon you will see to your right a little chapel dedicated to **Aghios Eftychianos the Cretan,** a Christian man who was put to death here because he refused to convert to the religion of the Turks. (Outside the chapel you can still see the axe-mark on the rock where he was beheaded). As you continue southward you will pass through a desolate place and at some point you will see **Moni Odigitrias** by the roadside.

When you first lay eyes on the monastery from afar it will seem like an old fortress. Although it was far away from the pirate-infested coast, the place was as vulnerable in the 16th century as it is today, and its only defences in the wilderness against those who threatened it (robbers, Turks etc) were its high walls and lion-hearted monks.

As the story goes, one of the monks who lived here was the legendary **Xopateras** or **Xepapas**, as Ioannis Markakis (or Father Ioasaph) was called after his unfrocking by the archbishop. (The name roughly translates as "he who is no longer priest"). The unfrocking was because he killed a Turk who spoke offensively about his sister, and it was only the start. From that time Xopateras began wandering around the monastery together with his wife and child, his sister, and a few loyal companions, killing every Turk he found in his way.

The Turks set a price on his head and began a raging manhunt that lasted for a long time. In February of 1829 they finally managed to corner him at the monastery. Xopateras and his companions barricaded themselves in the tower that still stands outside the church, and they put up a fierce fight against the hundreds of Turks that besieged it. After three days their ammunition was exhausted and they finally fell into the hands of their enemies. Their death surpassed in cruelty anything the Turks had ever done before.

The monastery was plundered and laid waste on several occasions, but many of its treasures have survived in spite of everything. It has an impressive collection of 15th century icons and on the church walls there are several parts where you can see paintings dating from the same period. Although abandonment has caused great damage to the monastery's buildings, restoration works have recently begun.

Right next to the monastery you will see an intersection. A handwritten Gr/E sign points straight, toward **Kali Limenes,** while a second sign points right, sending you to **Martsalo** and **Vathi** (Road Book 6a). If you are in a hurry to get to the beach, follow the first sign and ride straight to Kali Limenes (you'll be driving on a nice wide D1 road). But if you are in the mood for an interesting ride through desolate places get out of your way for a while and you won't regret it. The route to Martsalo is full of intersections with smaller dirtroads leading to sheepfolds, but it is also strewn with countless small signs, so you

ROUTES STARTING FROM RETHIMNO

The tower at the Moni Odigitrias (the Monastery of the Guiding Mary) from which Xopateras fought against the Turks

won't get lost. As you keep seeing those signs, you will probably wonder: What is Martsalo? Is it a beach? A mountain? A fortress? A village? When you get to the end of the dirtroad (D3), the only thing you'll see is a new chapel dedicated to Efmenios and Parthenios, two monks that were ordained as priests. Then a new sign points you to the path that leads to the ravine and repeats again: Martsalo! Finally, after a fifteen-minute walk you will arrive at Martsalo, which is a truly **impressive hermitage,** an eagle nest carved into the soft rock on the ravine wall. This was home to two monks who once lived here, and today it lies there with its door unlocked, exciting the imagination. If you want to get a taste of how their life must have been, turn on your flashlight and go right in. After the hermitage, you can also explore the exotic ravine and enjoy the stillness and the palm trees, and after the ravine it is only 15 - 20 minutes till you get to the beach.

Now return to Moni Odigitrias from the same road and continue south. You'll be driving on a smooth dirtroad that goes through a desolate place and takes you to **Kali Limenes** ("Good Harbours"), a small seaside settlement with some Rooms to Let. Unfortunately, the Good Harbours are often visited by Bad Ships (meaning

13. Rethimno-Ierapetra
FOLLOWING THE SOUTH COAST

303

"tankers"), since the islet two hundred metres off shore is an oil supply station...

After the Good (but Poor) Harbours, the road (D1) continues east following the coastline. It goes through Platia Peramata, a large area entirely covered with tomato fields, and it takes you to **Lendas,** a well known settlement built next to the sea (Road Book 6b). Incidentally, a few kilometres before you get there you will see a large sandy beach, taken over by nudist campers and having three or four taverns whose owners rent rooms as well. This is a great place to be, but try not to come later than the middle of July, or you are bound to get crowded.

Lendas is a rather ugly village and the beach in front of it is not so great either. The main reason why the place is well known is because it is at the end of the popular route that starts from Apessokari. A second reason is that here you will find the ruins of the ancient town of **Levin.**

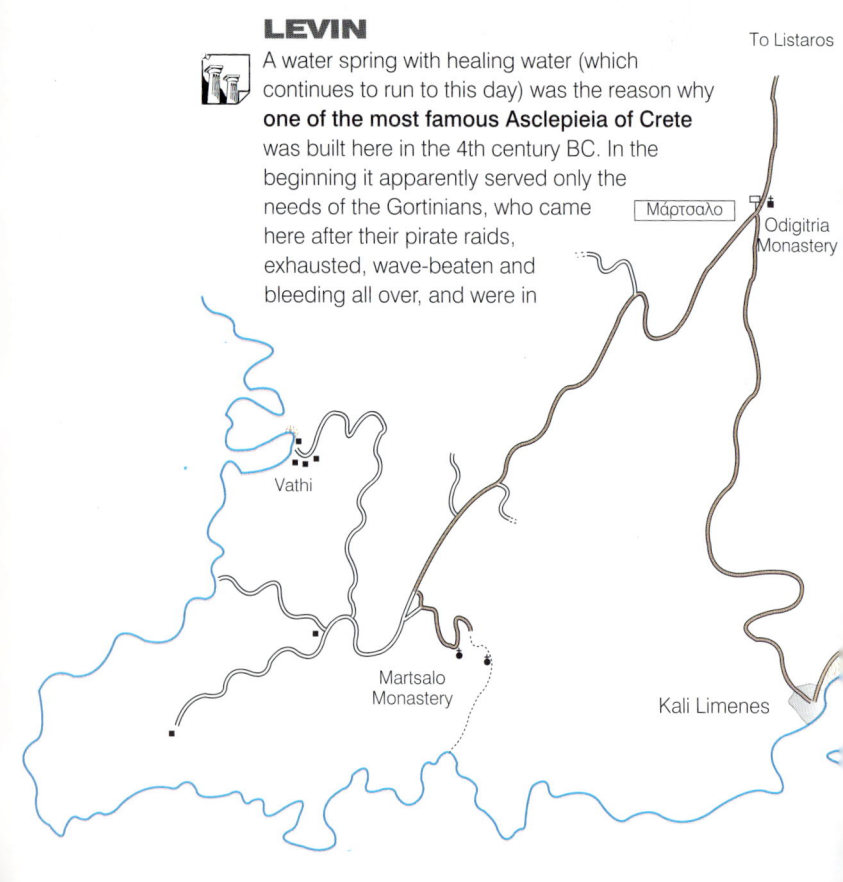

LEVIN

A water spring with healing water (which continues to run to this day) was the reason why **one of the most famous Asclepieia of Crete** was built here in the 4th century BC. In the beginning it apparently served only the needs of the Gortinians, who came here after their pirate raids, exhausted, wave-beaten and bleeding all over, and were in

To Listaros

Μάρτσαλο

Odigitria Monastery

Vathi

Martsalo Monastery

Kali Limenes

ROUTES STARTING FROM RETHIMNO

need of therapeutic treatment. Soon, however, its fame grew, and people started coming from every corner of Crete, from the Greek mainland, and even from the shores of North Africa! In the Roman times it reached the peak of its glory and it was completely renovated and decorated with marble statues and a wonderful floor mosaic with sea themes. It was also expanded to include guest houses and other secondary buildings.

Apart from a set fee, the cured visitors offered Asclepius - the healing god - valuable presents in order to express their gratitude. These were stashed away in the **Thesaurus,** a two-metre deep, square-shaped well, which was hidden in the northeast corner of the temple under the floor and was sealed with a specially carved stone that opened with some kind of key. The Italian archaeologists who dug here in 1884 and 1913 found a hole in the floor, a broken cover, and an empty well. Whoever the looters were, they got here before the archaeologists (maybe even a thousand years earlier), and they probably became rich enough to treat themselves to a lifetime vacation at the most luxurious ancient "health club"!

At the east end of the bay of Lendas you'll see a beautiful sandy beach called **Loutra.** Three hundred metres behind it is a tavern with a few rooms above it which are rented out to tourists. At the end of the beach a level tree-shaded area invites you to camp, while five hundred metres behind is a beautiful gorge with high steep walls

ROAD BOOK 6a

Mt. Asteroussia / Kali Limenes

To Pigaidakia
To Andiskari
LASSEA
Platia Peramata
To Lendas (see Road book 6b)

Fuel tanks

13. Rethimno-Ierapetra
FOLLOWING THE SOUTH COAST

that tempt you to walk through it. Incidentally, this is quite feasible.

The next stop is at the beach of Tripiti. To get there, you can take the dirtroad that heads toward Krotos in the north and then turn right at the intersection that you'll see about two kilometres later. (Marks: a stone hut and a Gr/E sign that says "Tripiti, 3 km"). However, these two kilometres until the intersection are very rough as the road has a steep inclination and some very difficult parts (D4); the earth has been washed away by the water, leaving some deep ditches, and as the road winds uphill there are several hairpins with gravel! This is why, if your bike is heavily loaded, it might be best not to take this road at all. Instead, return from Loutra to Lendas, take the asphalt road (A3) to Krotos, and from Krotos take the dirtroad (D3) that goes south. After 2.5 km you will find the intersection for Tripiti and turn.

The road (D2) to the beach of Tripiti is carved on the west side of a ravine. The ravine gets narrower toward its end and turns into a beautiful small gorge. The road turns before the gorge - though you can always leave your bike somewhere and visit the gorge on foot - and then

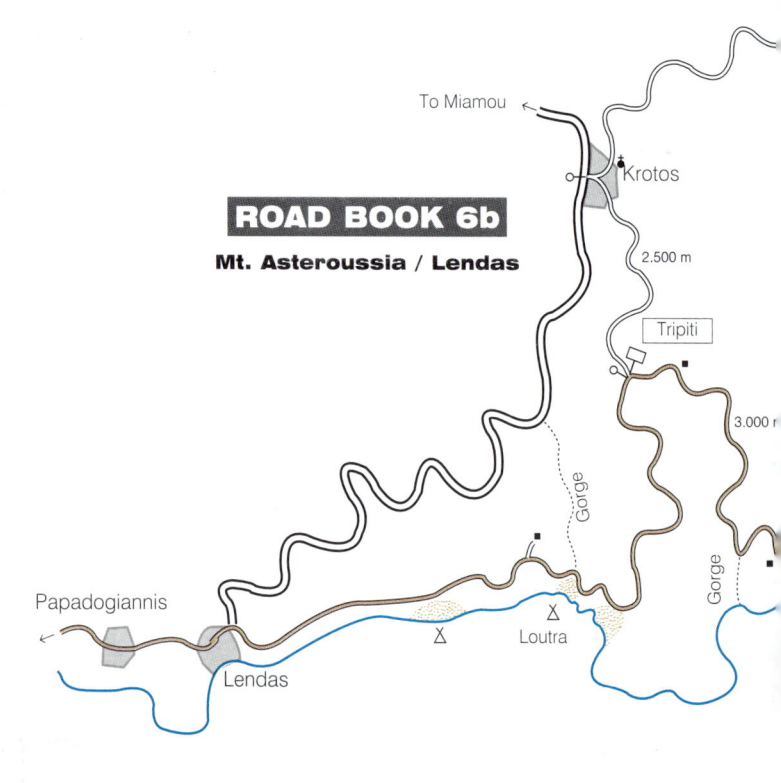

ROAD BOOK 6b

Mt. Asteroussia / Lendas

ROUTES STARTING FROM RETHIMNO

it follows the rocky shore and takes you to the **wonderful beach of Tripiti** (3 km after the intersection). The beach is not empty (in fact, there are four or five huts there), but you can still camp without any problem.

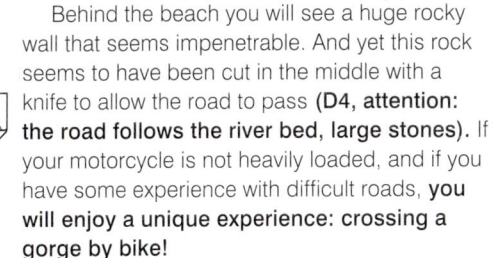

Behind the beach you will see a huge rocky wall that seems impenetrable. And yet this rock seems to have been cut in the middle with a knife to allow the road to pass **(D4, attention: the road follows the river bed, large stones).** If your motorcycle is not heavily loaded, and if you have some experience with difficult roads, **you will enjoy a unique experience: crossing a gorge by bike!**

After the gorge the road climbs the east side of the ravine that opens up behind it, and it offers a wonderful view of the west side of it with its almost vertical wall and its many caves. When you are out of the ravine you will see a small "stockbreeding

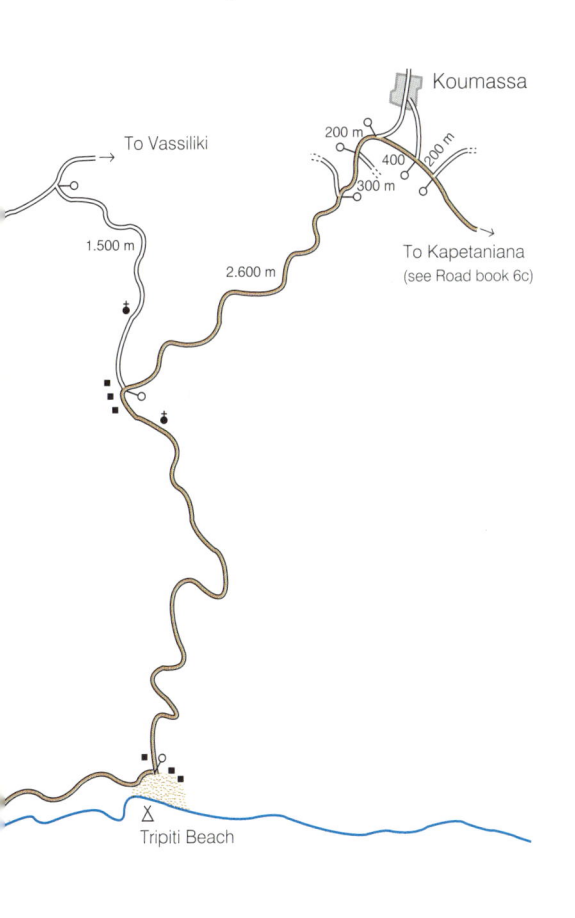

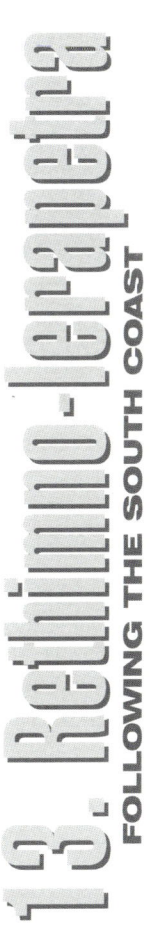

13. Rethimno-Ierapetra
FOLLOWING THE SOUTH COAST

The Loutra beach east of Lendas

unit," opposite of which is a dirtroad (D3) heading east. Turn right on this road, and a little before you get to Koumassia turn right again on the dirtroad that goes up the mountain (Road Book 6c). **It is here that the best part of the mountain route starts.** The road goes through barren, rough-looking places that are home to many vultures and other large birds of prey. As you ride on the

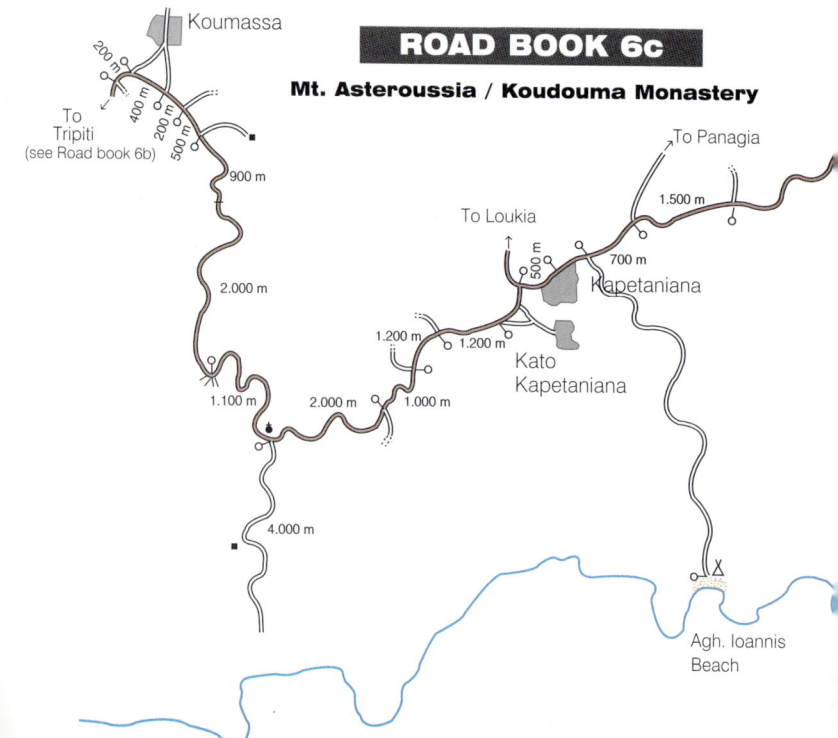

ROAD BOOK 6c

Mt. Asteroussia / Koudouma Monastery

ROUTES STARTING FROM RETHIMNO

mountain, you will see them above your head, proudly weighing themselves in the air. All around, the landscape seems to be untouched by time and civilisation, and it has a wild, intoxicating beauty that will take your breath away. The one village that is perched high up on the mountain, **Kapetaniana,** also seems to cling to the past. Many of its houses have been deserted, but already there are two or three German and British families that have chosen to live here for the biggest part of the year, and they have bought and restored a few houses. The village suddenly appears before your eyes, as you come out of a mountain pass, set against **Kofinas,** the highest peak of the Asteroussia Mountains **(1230m)**.

South of Kofinas lies the beautiful beach of Aghios Ioannis with the country homes of the people of Kapetaniana. There are no Rooms to Let in the area, but tourists can camp at the beach. The road that goes there starts at Kapetaniana and heads east. However, instead of going to Aghios Ioannis, it is best to continue straight toward Kofinas and then turn right in order to get to the **Koudouma Monastery** (Moni Koudouma). More than the monastery itself, it is the route there that is really worth the trip: **sixteen kilometres on a winding road, without ever**

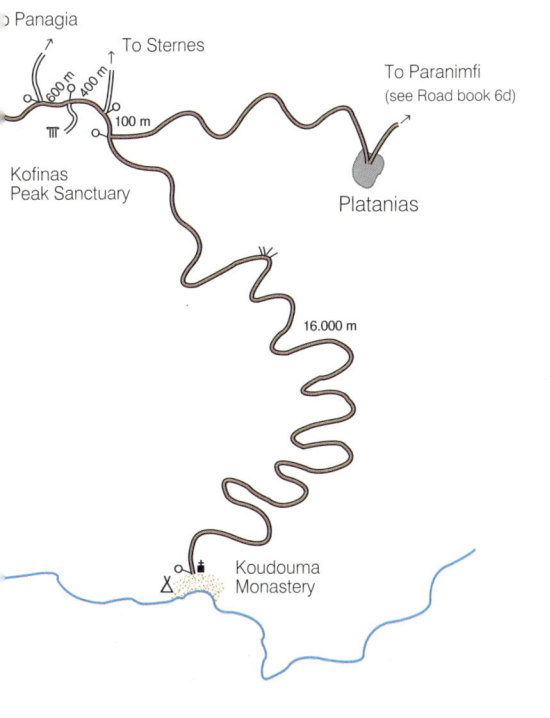

13. Rethimno-Ierapetra
FOLLOWING THE SOUTH COAST

309

losing sight of the Libyan sea and of the south shore of Crete that fades away in the distance. At the highest point of the route, and very close to the peak of Kofinas (before you start going downhill), there is a spot with an **amazing panoramic view,** where you can turn your head and see, at one and the same time, the peaks of the White Mountains and Psiloritis and Dikti! At the end of the route, you will find a pebbly beach (even better than Aghios Ioannis), an old monastery with three or four aged monks, and a fountain, next to the monastery, that will refresh you with its cool water. Keep in mind that the monks will certainly offer you food and shelter; the food is very tasty (so take them up on their offer), but the room is miserable (so refuse it politely).

About 4 km east of the monastery there is a **great pebbly beach** near the village of Tris Ekklissies (Three Churches). However, there is no coastal road going east of the monastery - nor west, for that matter - so you will have to go back the way you came (Road Book 6d). At the intersection behind Kofinas turn on the road (D1) that heads east and leads to Platanias and Paranimfi. As you approach Paranimfi, you will see from above two roads that continue from there. The one goes southwest and stops in the middle of nowhere, at a place with grey rocks, a chapel and a fountain (an ideal camping site). The other goes southeast and takes you to Tris Ekklissies. The entire route to Tris Ekklissies (where the road ends) is a feast for the eyes: ten kilometres on a D3 road, carved on steep mountain slopes separated by ravines and stretching along the rough rocky shore. At the village you will find a few

The route leading to the Koudoumas monastery. In the background you see Mt. Dikti.

The Tripiti gorge

Rooms to Let and two or three taverns. However, it is really worth it to camp at the huge empty beach west of it, a move that will allow you to combine the pleasures of camping in the wilderness with the comforts of the village close by (food, entertainment etc).

When you head back, turn right (north) at the first intersection you'll see a few kilometres before Paranimfi. The road will take you to **Mournia,** a poor country village in the midst of barren hills that seems forgotten by the world. After Mournia, the road continues north, climbing the hills until a place with a great view of the entire Messara valley. Then you reach a T-junction where you turn right, and you follow the road to the villages of **Ethia** and **Achendrias.** Achendrias is without signs, so you will have to rely on your instincts to get on the road (D1) that you'll see from above as you get near the village. (This goes east and crosses a small plateau.) Five kilometres after the village you'll see a second road (D3) to your right and a Gr sign at the intersection that says "Μαριδάκι" (Maridaki). If you turn, it will take you to the last nice beach in the area. If you continue, you will go downhill and get to the shore, and from there you will

The wonderful beach west of Tris Ekklissies

follow the coast all the way to Ierapetra. The landscape is full of farmers' settlements and greenhouses, and although you can still find a few "decent" beaches, you won't be so thrilled to swim next to the greenhouses and the pieces of torn plastic that are everywhere around.

The uninviting landscape is a good reason why you can cover the entire distance to Mirtos (and from there to Ierapetra) with very few stops - and detours - along the way. The first thing that's worth seeing is the **impressive Arvi gorge,** at the end of a country road that starts from the village of **Arvi** (where you turn left following the E sign that says

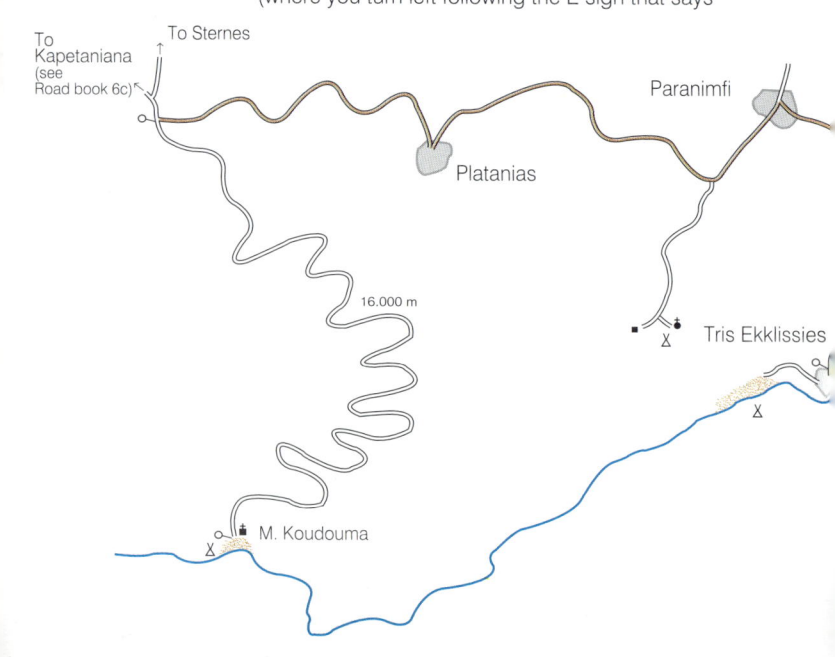

ROUTES STARTING FROM RETHIMNO

"FARANGI, MONASTERY SAINT ANTONIOS"). The distance to the gorge is quite short and the sight is very rewarding: a narrow pass between two vertical walls of rock that are three hundred metres tall and look like they've been cut apart with a knife! If you want to walk in the gorge you'll have to wet your feet because there is a small river that runs through it.

A little further on the coastal road you will find the only picturesque village on the entire coast between Tsoutsouro and Ierapetra: **Psari Forada.** The village has a beautiful beach, but unfortunately it is not allowed to camp there. Still, you can camp at another beautiful beach a little further east; it is two kilometres before Mirtos, it is covered with pebbles, and it is "undiscovered." If you'd rather stay in a room, you will find several Rooms to Let and three or four small hotels at **Mirtos,** a nice village that has also a few taverns and a good pebbly beach of its own.

Between Mirtos and Ierapetra there is nothing much to see. It is twenty long kilometres, the worst of the route, through places that have suffered from overexploitation: greenhouses to your left, greenhouses to your right, greenhouses before you and greenhouses behind you!

The only thing worth seeing in this area is an **archaeological site** east of Mirtos. It is a Minoan settlement of the Early Minoan period (2500 - 2200 BC), named **Fournou Korfi** after the hill on

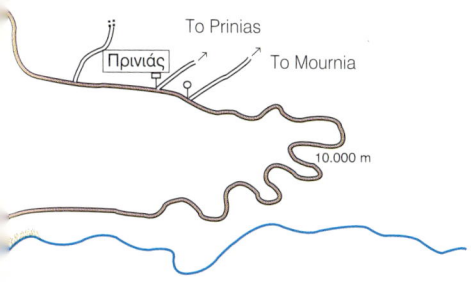

To Prinias
Πρινιάς
To Mournia

10.000 m

ROAD BOOK 6d
Mt. Asteroussia / Tris Ekklissies

13. Rethimno-Ierapetra
FOLLOWING THE SOUTH COAST

The Arvi gorge

which it is built. As you drive on the main road you will see a Gr/E sign that says "Mirtos Fournou Korfi, Archaeological site." Unfortunately, the sign has been placed... only at the opposite side of the road, so it can only be seen by those coming from Ierapetra! If you have the eye of an eagle and spot it in time, turn on the dirtroad where it sends you and leave your bike a few metres after the turn. Next to the road is a footpath that will take you to the top of the hill. It is here that the settlement was discovered in 1967, when the British School of Archaeology conducted a two-year excavation of the place under the leadership of Peter Warrer. The British team brought to light over one hundred rooms and found a host of things that indicate there was considerable production of handicrafts: parts of a weaving machine, over seven hundred vases and items of everyday use, lathes etc. In one room, which must have been a place of religious worship, the archaeologists found a clay statuette of a goddess holding a vessel. Today, this and other findings from the site are exhibited at the Archaeological Museum of Aghios Nikolaos.

After this visit you can head straight to Ierapetra. But if you do not want to go there and prefer to see Aghios Nikolaos instead (a wise choice by all counts), there is a very pleasant route (A3) that takes you there, which starts from the village of **Stomio.** Until Anatoli the landscape is quite dull (greenhouses at first and then a burned mountain slope), but after that it changes radically. The road goes through thick pine forests and picturesque villages (Kalamafka, Prina, Kalo Chorio) built at the foot of Mount Dikti's southeast

ROUTES STARTING FROM RETHIMNO

side, and then it meets the coastal road connecting Aghios Nikolaos and Sitia. Here you turn left (north) and continue to Aghios Nikolaos. If, however, you have an off-road bike, there is **a still more impressive route,** which takes you to the town through mountains and plateaus (see page 340-342).

13. Rethimno-Ierapetra
FOLLOWING THE SOUTH COAST

14. Rethimno-Ierapetra

TRAVELLING INLAND

ROUTES STARTING FROM RETHIMNO

If you want to avoid the crowds and the "tourist face" of most villages on the north and south coast of Crete, drive between them on the mountains and plateaus of the hinterland. This is the paradise of the true traveller, a land full of traditional hamlets, historical monasteries, important and yet unknown archaeological sites, spectacular mountain routes, and countless nooks for camping, all waiting for you to explore. Very few tourists ever make it to these places; most of them simply travel from coast to coast, "glued" to the main traffic arteries, never taking the time to explore out of the way places. As a result, the hinterland has kept its authenticity and peacefulness. When people are not blinded by the prospect of making an easy profit through the tourist industry, their traditional economy, based on farming and stockbreeding, proves healthy enough to support them. Most inland villages of Crete, whether large or small, are healthy communities with sufficient resources, a balanced social life, and a considerable number of young people who want to continue their fathers' work and to uphold their traditional

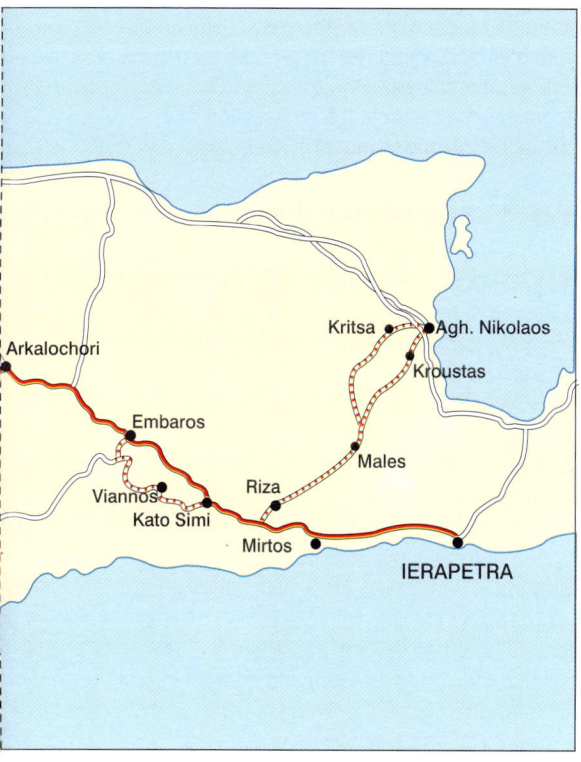

14. Rethimno-Ierapetra
TRAVELLING INLAND

values. This is the hidden beauty of Crete, the face that you can't see in the post cards and the tourist agency advertising pamphlets. Come and see it for yourself.

Take the road that starts from the centre of Rethimno and goes east toward the village (or rather suburb) of **Perivolia.** You will see an intersection with a Gr sign that says "Αμάρι" **(Amari)** and "Ηράκλειο Παλαιά Οδός" **(Iraklio Old Road).** Turn right when you get here, and when you pass under the New National Road turn right again, following the Gr/E sign that sends you to Amari. Right after the turn there is another intersection, which offers you two options as you start Route 14. If you have a street bike, follow Route 14.1 and keep straight (in the direction of Prassies). If you have an off-road bike and would like to travel on some very nice dirtroads, follow Route 14.2 and turn right (there is a Gr/E sign at the intersection that points to **Chromomonastiri).**

14.1 THROUGH PRASSIES

The road (A3) to **Prassies** goes through a small gorge full of olive trees. The landscape is quite attractive, but please drive carefully because the road is narrow and slippery and it has many turns and a lot of traffic. After Prassies, a picturesque village with many old houses, the road goes downhill toward a very green valley irrigated by the Pelopidas river. As you travel, you have great views of the Psiloritis mountain peaks.

About 300 metres after the intersection for **Mirthios** you'll see a road to your left that goes north. During the first 100 metres you drive on cement and then you run into a fenced pastureland. Open the gate and go right in (but don't forget to close it behind you). You will drive on a D3 road, which ends at a very beautiful place you can walk through: the **Prassiano gorge.** The area is quiet and peaceful, and as it is full of big plane trees with great shade it is a true campers' paradise.

When you get back on the main road and continue south you'll cross a valley full of olive trees. About 5 km after the intersection for Mirthios you'll see another intersection and a road leading to the village of **Patsos** in the west. If you wish to visit the impressive **Patsos gorge,** turn right. A short distance west of the village you will see the signs leading to the gorge (page 321). After the visit, you get back on our route from the same road.

The next stop is at the village of **Aghia Fotini** in the east. To get there, you leave the Potamidas valley behind you and travel on the west side of a beautiful ravine covered with olive trees. The village offers a beautiful view of the Amari valley, which is framed by two mountain slopes. Choose which one you prefer in order to continue Route 14 (see pages 322).

14.2 THROUGH CHROMOMONASTIRI

The road (A3) to Chromomonastiri climbs through some olive groves and then follows the west side of a small gorge. The first village on your way, **Mili**, has no classic tourist sight, but it is certainly worth a quick stop in order to walk its alleys and get a taste of a typical country place that insists on following its own pace of life. On the east side of the gorge, right opposite of Mili, is **Old Mili** (Παλιό χωριό Μύλοι), a village that was deserted some thirty years ago when a series of dangerous landslides scared the people away. However, the big landslide that was supposed to destroy it never came, so the Milians still come from their new village and take care of their old homes and orchards (although they have built nothing new there). Incidentally, this is a good opportunity to see how Cretan villages were at the beginning of the century.

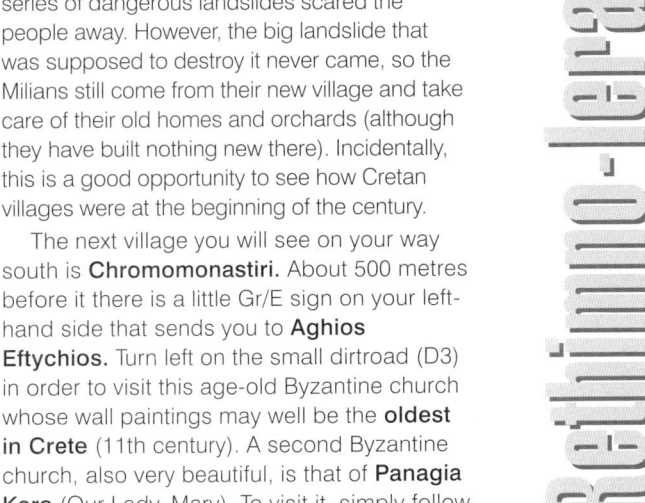

The next village you will see on your way south is **Chromomonastiri**. About 500 metres before it there is a little Gr/E sign on your left-hand side that sends you to **Aghios Eftychios.** Turn left on the small dirtroad (D3) in order to visit this age-old Byzantine church whose wall paintings may well be the **oldest in Crete** (11th century). A second Byzantine church, also very beautiful, is that of **Panagia Kera** (Our Lady, Mary). To visit it, simply follow the Gr/E signs around you: turn left at the square that's at the village entrance, then right after 600 metres, and then left again after another 500 metres (see Road Book 3 as well). But before setting off, it is worth making a stop first, so you can explore this very beautiful place and drink something refreshing at the cool village square.

Once you've seen the chapel of Panagia Kera, get back on the road you turned from (now a D3), reset your counter, and follow the road as it goes south climbing the north side of Mount Vrissinas. Soon you will be five hundred metres above sea level, admiring a **spectacular view** of Rethimno and the north coast.

The Byzantine church of Panagia Kera (Our Lady, Mary)

But what is really worth admiring is at the very top of the mountain; follow **Road Book 3** and you will soon be there.

The Vrissinas dirtroad will eventually take you to the main road connecting Rethimno and Aghia Galini, and more specifically to the intersection from which you go to the Minoan Cemetery of Armeni. When you get there go south, and after about 5 km you will see a second intersection and take the road that heads east (toward **Ambelaki**). Twenty metres further you will see a dirtroad (D3) that goes southeast. Take it, and at the first fork you'll encounter (after only 20 or 30 metres) go left. After driving

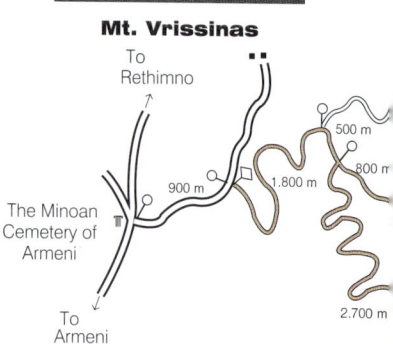

ROAD BOOK 3

Mt. Vrissinas

ROUTES STARTING FROM RETHIMNO

through a desolate area you will find yourself at a small shepherd settlement named **Karines** from where you continue eastward on the road (D3) that leads to **Patsos**. A little before the village you will cross a small cement bridge. Five hundred metres after the bridge you'll see a small dirtroad and a couple of Gr signs: a wooden one that says "Φαράγγι Αγίου Αντωνίου Πατσού" **(The St. Anthony of Patsos gorge)** and a small blue one that says "Άγιος Αντώνιος" (St. Anthony). Turn left and follow the dirtroad (D3) till the south end of the gorge. From here on you can continue on the footpath that the Forest Authorities of Rethimno have so tastefully formed, building wooden steps and small bridges where needed. Getting to the other end should take you less than two hours and the walk is indeed pleasant; the small river that flows through the gorge and the plane trees growing along its sides make it a real treat. But before setting out to cross the gorge you might pay a visit to the small cave-church of Aghios Antonios very close to its south end. Outside it you will see wooden tables for picnics. These were apparently put there quite recently, and at that time the workers found a few vase fragments and part of a statue of the goat-legged Pan. All of

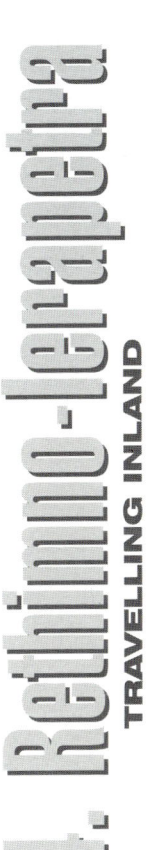

14. Rethimno-Ierapetra — TRAVELLING INLAND

them point to the conclusion that the cave must have been used as a place of worship since the ancient times.

The villages in this area, including Patsos, are small and picturesque and they do not have many luxuries for visitors; one or two coffee shops, some small grocery stores for your basic supplies and a few taverns and Rooms to Let is what you can typically expect.

THE PEAK SANCTUARY OF MT. VRISSINAS

On the sharp rocks of the **peak of Mount Vrissinas** the ancient Cretans living in a nearby settlement had built a **sanctuary.** This was discovered in 1962, although the place was not systematically excavated until ten years later. The numerous findings that came to light show that this cult centre was **one of the largest and most significant on the island.** Stuck in the crevices of the rocks were hundreds of clay statuettes of worshippers or oxen as well as many other ceramic objects (as is usually the case). In addition, the archaeologists found a fragment of a stone vase with an inscription in Linear A, which is exhibited at the Museum of Rethimno. To reach the sanctuary you must leave your bike and walk for an hour. However, it is really worth the trouble, if only to enjoy the **panoramic view from coast to coast.**

THE AMARI VALLEY

A few kilometres south of Patsos lies the **Amari valley,** which is irrigated by the Plati river. Framed by two mountains, Kedros in the west and Psiloritis in the east, the valley is full of olive and cherry and apricot trees and surrounded by some forty attractive hamlets perched on the mountain slopes, **possibly the most beautiful ones in Crete.** This protected area has been continuously inhabited ever since the Minoan times. Important Minoan settlements have come to light, while every village has at least one Byzantine church of the 14th or 15th century and sometimes even earlier, always with amazing wall paintings. The valley is crossed by three roads: one (A3) going through the hamlets on the east slope, one (A3) going through the

ROUTES STARTING FROM RETHIMNO

ROAD BOOK 4

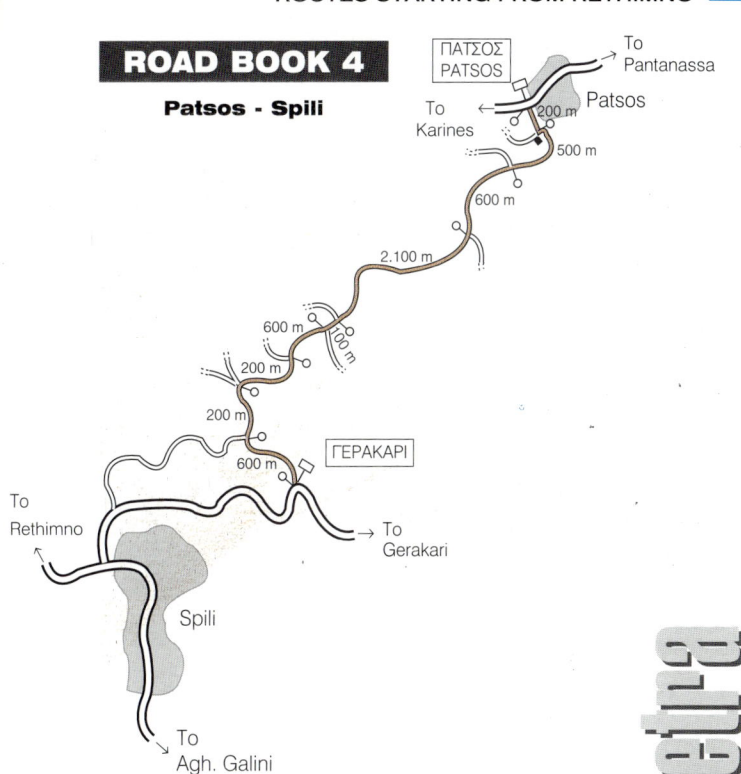

Patsos - Spili

(Map labels: ΠΑΤΣΟΣ / PATSOS, To Pantanassa, Patsos, To Karines, 500 m, 200 m, 600 m, 2.100 m, 600 m, 100 m, 200 m, 200 m, 600 m, ΓΕΡΑΚΑΡΙ, To Gerakari, To Rethimno, Spili, To Agh. Galini)

hamlets in the west, and one (also A3, but larger and faster) that goes through the heart of the valley. Of course, it is worth taking all three and exploring every corner of the valley, but if you are pressed for time we recommend the first one, which starts from the village of **Aghia Fotini**.

There are two ways to get from Patsos to the east side of the valley. If you'd rather ride on a dirtroad (D3), turn right (south) at the west end of Patsos. This way you'll get on the dirtroad that climbs on the side of the Katsonissi peak and finally meets the Spili - Gerakari road (A3, **Road Book 4**). At the intersection turn left and head for **Gerakari** - unless of course you'd rather turn right, go to Spili and switch to Route 12 or 13 - and from Gerakari head north on the road (A3) that takes you to **Aghia Fotini**. If, however, you prefer to ride on asphalt, go northeast of Patsos, pass the villages of Pantanassa and Voleones, get on the Rethimno - Amari road, and turn right (south) in order to get to Aghia Fotini. The last part of the trip is particularly beautiful as you'll be following the west side of a ravine that's full of trees.

14. Rethimno-Ierapetra

TRAVELLING INLAND

The Byzantine church of Panagia in Thronos

One kilometre northeast of Aghia Fotini is a picturesque village called **Thronos** (The Throne). True to its name, the village seems to be sitting on the mountain slope as if on a throne, **and it offers a unique view of the Psiloritis peaks and the Amari valley.** The truth is, however, that the name of the village comes from the "Episcopal Throne of Sivritos." What survives from the magnificent metropolis of that time (7th century AD) is a part of a floor mosaic, which can be seen outside the Byzantine church of the Holy Mary that was built here in the 14th century.

In its turn, the Byzantine diocese inherited its name from the Minoan town that was built

THE MINOAN PALACE OF MONASTIRAKI

The traces of the Minoan palace that was once on the low hill southeast of Monastiraki were first discovered in the mid 40's. Yet the systematic excavation of the area began only in 1980 under the direction of the University of Crete. The findings are very similar to those of the Faistos palace, and they include some interesting pottery and the foundations of some large storage rooms and workshops. The numerous seal stones point to a sophisticated administrative and economic structure and the clay model of a sanctuary indicates the existence of a place of worship. Everything proves that during the Middle Minoan period (2000 - 1700 BC) a significant palace existed at his site. Apparently, it was destroyed by the big earthquake of 1700 BC and it was never rebuilt

ROUTES STARTING FROM RETHIMNO

here first. **Sivritos** was built on a well protected site offering a great view, and as its pre-Hellenic name suggests it had many trees and a lake or river close by (Si<**Sy**, water, Vritos<**Vrity**, sweet, fresh. Cf. **Vritomartis,** sweet virgin). During the Roman and the first Byzantine period the town really flourished and it even minted its own gold and silver coins. In 825 AD, however, it was destroyed by the Arabs along with most Cretan towns. But soon it was rebuilt and all through the second Byzantine period and the years of the Venetian rule it was quite prosperous. In the last few years the area north of Thronos is being excavated and a part of ancient Sivritos has come to light. To visit the archaeological site follow the Gr/E signs that say "Ancient Sivritos. Greek - Italian excavation."

If you continue north of Thronos you will pass through a small village called Klissidi. A **very beautiful route** (D2) starts from here, a route that goes through green mountain slopes and low mountain passes and finally takes you to the historical monastery of Arkadi (**Moni Arkadiou,** page 420). If you so desire, from the monastery you can switch to Route 16.

Our route, however, continues to the south. The road (A3) after Thronos passes through the village of Kalogeros, then goes downhill through the forests. When you get to the Assomaton monastery you'll see an intersection and a road (A3) that goes south. This is your chance to visit three villages in the area: **Monastiraki,** where the ongoing excavations have revealed an important Minoan palace, **Amari,** the largest village around here, and **Vizari,** where you can see the foundations of a 7th century basilica. If all these sound interesting, make a small detour to visit them, and when you are in Vizari turn left in order to get to **Fourfouras** and continue with our route.

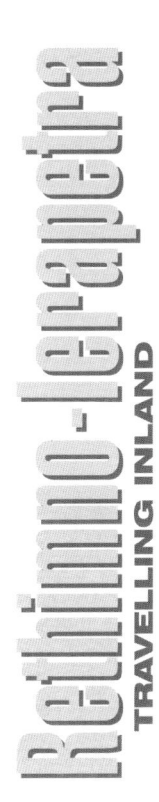

If instead of the detour you continue to the east of the Assomaton monastery, you will climb a green slope, go through some olive groves, and end up in **Vistagi, one of the most beautiful villages on the island,** built on a mountain and spread along the two sides of the road (A3). The village is not on the classic tourist routes, so it has very few tourists and no infrastructure to accommodate them. It is large and peaceful and very pleasing to walk through. Most of its houses have been whitewashed but some are painted in earth colours and especially ochre. The Amari valley and the snow-capped Psiloritis peaks all around complete the **scenery** that you can enjoy from here.

After Vistagi continue to the south (toward Fourfouras) and prepare yourself for **one of the most beautiful routes on asphalt in all of Crete,** which takes you to the town of Aghia Varvara some 60 km away (on the road that connects Iraklio and Gortina). Although it cannot exactly be described as a "mountain route," it follows the west and south side of Mount Psiloritis and sometimes takes you to a pretty high altitude from where you can enjoy **a great view wherever you look.** If the night finds you travelling in this area, you have very few chances of finding "decent" accommodations. Apart from some shabby Rooms to Let in Platanos, Kamares and a few other villages, there is no place to rent. The only really good place in the area is Hotel Idi in **Zaros** (tel. 0894 - 31 302). It has a nice swimming pool and a spacious parking lot for your bike.

If, however, you are no longer interested in mountains and would like to ride to the coast, turn right when you get to **Nithavris** - there is a Gr/E sign at the intersection that says "Aghios Ioannis" - or else turn right just after **Apodoulou.** You can now switch to Route 13.

After the village exit you'll see an intersection where you go left (east). You'll pass through

APODOULOU MINOAN SETTLEMENT

A small blue sign in the village of Apodoulou informs you that 2 km to the west you will find the **Apodoulou Minoan settlement.** Like so many other cases, this settlement was conventionally named after the modern village close to it, since there was no clue as to its actual name. The first excavations took place in 1934 under the direction of Professor Marinatos. They revealed an important building complex dating from the end of the Middle Minoan period (1600 BC), complete with its large storage rooms and artists' workshops, whose walls still stand, sometimes even two metres high. Among other things the archaeologists found inscription-bearing libation vessels, a small golden axe, and numerous vases including a steatite one inscribed in Linear A. Apart from the main building complex they found ruins of other buildings, scattered all over the surrounding area and dating from the same time.

The village of Vistagi

some picturesque villages built at the foot of the south side of Psiloritis, but you need to **concentrate on the driving because the road (A3) is narrow and full of potholes and it has worn edges.** When you get to Lochria you'll see a dirtroad (D3) winding up the mountain. After 14 km it stops before a few *mitàta* (shepherd huts) at a site with a beautiful view of the south coast. A little further on the main road, before entering Kamares, there is an amazing gorge that cuts the mountain in two. At the point where it meets the road, the Kamares Community has built a small path, which takes you to a place from where you can really admire this magnificent gorge.

If you continue eastward you'll get to **Zaros,** the largest village in the region, where you have the best chances of finding a good place to sleep and eat. In the village you'll see a Gr/E sign that sends you to a recreation area called **Votomos,** a short distance to the north. Here you'll find a spring whose water is bottled and sold throughout Crete. Whatever is left of it forms a nice small lake that mirrors the wooded mountain slopes around it. Behind the lake is a path leading to the Zaros gorge and around it is an ideal picnic site with wooden tables. Though there is nothing better than enjoying your own food, we suggest trying the (local) trout and salmon served at some of the nice taverns you'll see on your way to the lake. Next to them is IDI, the comfortable hotel we mentioned earlier, and next to the hotel is the age-old mill of Michalis Frangiadakis, which still works!

PSILORITIS: CAVES AND MOUNTAIN ROUTES

No matter how many stones the proud Hanians pile up on top of their own mountain, **Psiloritis is still the tallest mountain in Crete** (2456m), even if only with a three or four metre difference from the White Mountains! This is one of the reasons why it is visited by so many climbers every year, although it cannot compare in beauty with the White Mountains. But if you are not a determined climber that will settle with no less than the highest mountain peak, you have still two very good reasons to wear your

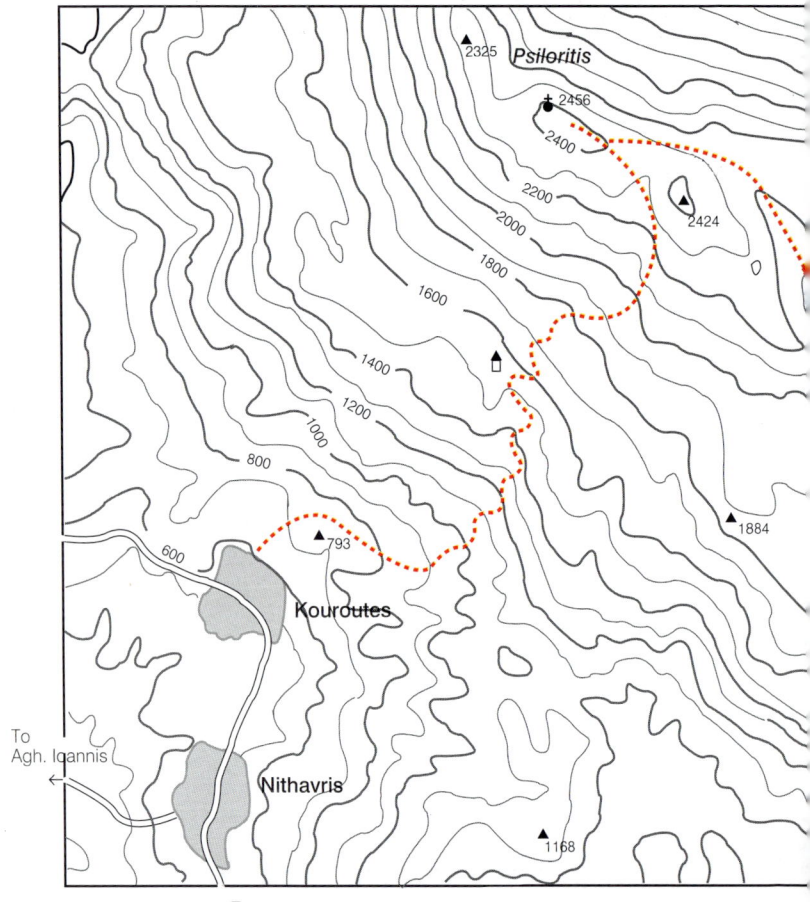

ROUTES STARTING FROM RETHIMNO

mountain shoes and climb it: the cave of Kamares and Ideon Andron. The former is at a height of 1524 metres and has given us some wonderful vases of 2000 BC, and the latter is at a height of 1495 metres and is allegedly the birthplace of the mighty Zeus.

There are many paths leading to the top. One of them starts from the village of Fourfouras, another from Kouroutes, and a third one from Lochria. Yet the most popular paths, which will also take you to the caves mentioned, start from the villages of **Kamares** and **Vorizia.**

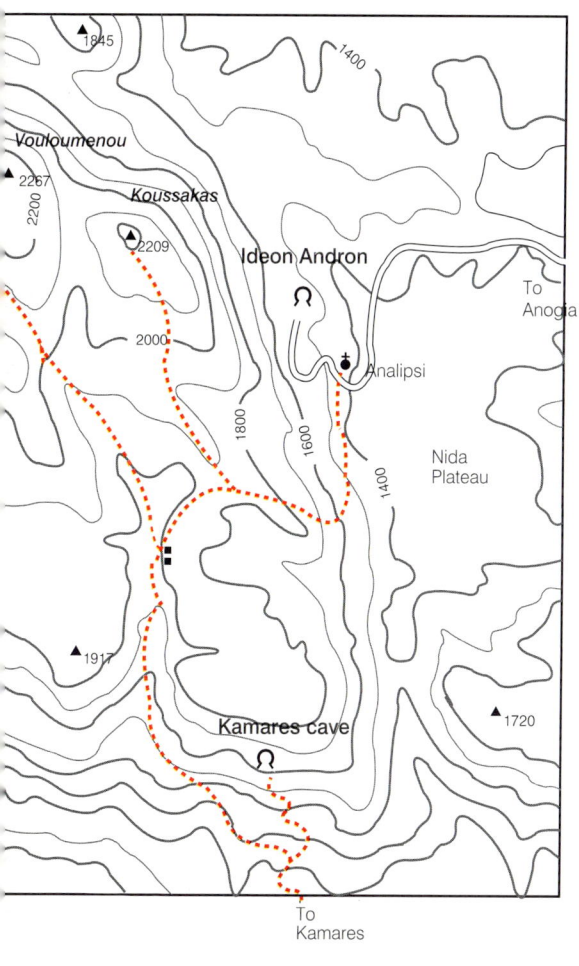

The **Kamares cave** was discovered in 1890 by some local shepherd, but of course he was not the first one to go there. Ages earlier, around 3000 BC, it was discovered and inhabited by a group of people of the Neolithic age. Around 2000 BC, it was apparently used by the Minoans (most probably of Faistos) as a site of worship, possibly of the goddess of labour Eileithyia. The **lovely colourful vases** that were offered to the goddess were found during the excavations of the Italians (1894 and 1904) and the British (1913) and are exhibited at the Archaeological Museum of Iraklio. The only thing left to admire up here is the wonderful view of the Messara valley below. The path that starts from the village of Kamares has a steep inclination that may tire you, and to get to the cave you'll need at least three or four hours. Fortunately, though, the path is well marked with red paint, so you will not lose your way.

The **Ideon Andron** (The Idi Hide-out) is another three or four hours to the north (if you walk), but you can also get there by bike from the north side of the mountain; in fact, you'll be mostly travelling on asphalt (see Route 18, page 409). The cave was Zeus' home for the first years of his life, and according to one tradition it was also his birthplace. In any case, his mother, Rea, hid him here to protect him from his father, Kronos, who had the bad habit of eating his children! This was not because Kronos believed in cannibalism, but because he wanted to protect his power; according to the oracle he was to lose it to one of them. "And what is more natural than being succeeded by your son?" you might ask. Nothing, of course, but when you are the absolute ruler of the universe you don't want to give your place to anyone. The baby-sitters of little Zeus were two cave nymphs, Adrasteia and Idi, who fed him with honey and goat milk supplied by the goat Amalthia. But the child cried desperately for his mummy and he was in danger of being heard by his daddy and eaten for dessert. To avoid this terrible prospect, the demons *Kourites* covered his screams by clashing their huge bronze shields. Yet when Zeus became King of the Gods he forgot their precious service, and he killed his faithful bodyguards for a trivial offence.

Of course, Zeus was not born in this cave, nor in any other cave, but in the imagination of the ancient Greeks. Yet he was enthusiastically worshipped throughout the Greek antiquity, from the Early Minoan period till the time of the Roman Empire. Among the countless worshippers that went past the mouth of the Andron, as you are doing today, were the philosophers Pythagoras and Epimenides. (Incidentally, the back of the cave was full of humble offerings). When Zeus "died" and Christ was born, the cave was forgotten for centuries, and it was only in 1885 that it was rediscovered, this time by the Italian School of Archaeology. The various excavations which have been carried out since then (and which are still being carried out today under the direction of Ioannis Sakelarakis) have brought to light numerous findings that are very important and span the entire period of Zeus' worship. These are exhibited at the Archaeological Museum of Iraklio, and among other things they include: the famous **ritual bronze shields** that conjure up the image of the mythical, shield-bearing Kourites (ca 750 - 650 BC); ivory artefacts from about the same time; seal stones; parts of bronze statues; clay statuettes; golden jewellery; and many painted vases.

If you want to get to the top of the mountain (to the chapel of the Holy Cross at a height of 2456 metres) and to return to the same place, you will need another seven or eight hours of walking. This means that you must pitch camp at some convenient spot in the Nida plateau and start climbing early in the morning. The footpath that leads to the top starts from the second hairpin of the road between the half-finished Nida refuge and the cave. It is well marked and generally easy to follow, and after the first twenty-five or thirty minutes of going south it turns to the west and climbs the south side of a ravine. After about two hours of walking you should arrive at a mountain pass 1900 metres above sea level. Here you will find a stone hut and a trail that leads to a peak in the north. **Do not** follow this trail - it will only take you to peak Koussakas at a height of 2209 metres - but **head south instead and go downhill** for about ten minutes. When you are down to 1800 metres you will see a place with a spring, two or three huts, and several paths. Take the most worn path (in the northwest), which obviously leads to the top. After two hours or so you will be at the peak of the mountain, and if you are lucky and there is no fog or haze you can enjoy **a truly wonderful panoramic view.** At the top

A typical sight at these hillsides south of Iraklio, the vineyards of Archanes and Peza are quite famous

you will find the small chapel we mentioned - an excellent refuge too - and a cistern with potable water.

ON THE WAY TO MT. DIKTI

Between the mountains of Psiloritis and Dikti there is very little to see. The landscape is an indifferent blend of low barren hills, fields and country villages, and it is not until you get to Lasithi and the south side of Mt. Dikti that it gets interesting again. Therefore, choose the fastest route to **Embaros** (just north of the town of Martha) and prepare for the **amazing mountain route to the Omalos plateau** that starts from that village. Still, if you have a little time to spare it might be worth making a small detour to the north in order to visit two places: the Byzantine fortress **Temenos** and the **Monastery of Epanossifis.**

To get to the former, go north after Aghia Varvara (following the road that leads to Iraklio), and after 13 km turn right (east) at the intersection you will see upon entering **Venerato.** (There is a Gr/E sign there that says "Paliani nunnery"). Three hundred metres after the turn you will see a nice painted E sign that sends you to the right to enjoy the "Nice Route to Kiparissos." If you ignore it and keep going straight, the road will take you to the nunnery (where it ends) after only 800 metres. This is a very old convent, possibly of the 7th century, but it has nothing special to show. The actual 7th century building was completely destroyed by the Turks in 1866, and what you see today is just the new church and the new cement cells and handicraft shops that were built here after that. If you do follow the sign and turn, the

"Nice Route to Kiparissos" will not leave you breathless. Still, it is a pleasant route that takes you through the countryside; the road (A3) winds up and down the cultivated hills, between olive groves and vineyards, and stops before the abandoned village of **Pirgos** - or rather, it is the asphalt that stops, only to start again at **Kiparissi**. On your way to Kiparissi you will see the village of **Profitis Ilias** at the foot of a hill in the northeast. If you look at the hill more carefully, you'll notice the **ruins of the Byzantine fortress known as Temenos.** Kiparissi may be somewhat confusing, because there are no signs to direct you to Profitis Ilias. In any case, do not turn left at the intersection that is at the heart of the village. Keep going straight until the end of the road, then turn **right** and continue until you see a war memorial. Turn left when you reach it and you will soon be in Profitis Ilias. Good luck!

Once there, you will again have a hard time trying to find the path that leads to the fortress. There is **not a single sign** to help the visitor. What is worse, the beginning of the path has disappeared under extended courtyards and illegal buildings, an unmistakable sign of the total indifference of the locals for the treasure they have right next to their homes. If this were in any other European country, the villagers would have cleaned and kept up the archaeological site on their own initiative. They would have opened paths, placed signs in and out of the village to encourage people to visit the place, put spotlights to make the walls impressive at night, printed maps, pamphlets and post cards to tempt and facilitate the visitor, told the monument's history with texts, diagrams and representations, and done everything in their power to highlight their treasure. But for most Greeks the only treasure they know is what they have in their bank account...

Just a few kilometres northeast of Profitis Ilias you can see some very impressive archaeological treasures: the Minoan settlement in Archanes, the sanctuary "Anemospilia" on the top of Mount Youchta, the Minoan mansion of Vathipetro, and of course **Knossos,** the most splendid Minoan city. All of them are described in detail in Route 20. But if you are not going to follow that route, it is indeed worth it to make a detour at this point and to continue with Route 14 later. There is a dirtroad (D2) that connects Profitis Ilias and Houdetsi (from where you can continue northward to visit all these sites), but if you'd rather ride on asphalt you can go to Iraklio instead and then turn on the road for Knossos and head south. After seeing these important archaeological sites (page 439), continue southward in order to visit the **Epanossifis Monastery** and to get back on route 14.

If you choose not to make the detour after Profitis Ilias but wish to go straight to the monastery, you will need to return to Kiparissi and take the road that passes through Galeni, Roukani and Karkadiotissa.

The high hill (500m) with the twin peaks south of Profitis Ilias has been inhabited since the ancient times. During the Minoan period there was a town here whose name was **Likastos**. Apparently, the town prospered greatly thanks to the well protected site on which it was built and the fertile fields around it. This is evident from the fact that during the Trojan war it contributed ships and men to the Greek expedition force, as Homer tells us in his Iliad (B, 647). Unfortunately for Likastos, the neighbouring town of Knossos became even more rich and powerful, and Likastos was inevitably conquered and destroyed. (Ever heard about the small fish being eaten by the larger one?) After that sad event Likastos went through centuries of defeat and humiliation, being constantly subjugated to one town or another.

In **961 AD** things seemed to turn around. This year marked the beginning of the second period of the Byzantine rule (961 - 1204), made possible by the glorious victory of General **Nikiforos Fokas** over the Arabs, whom he forced out of the island. At that time the Byzantine General was looking for a good place in which to build the new capital of Crete, since the existing capital, Handakas (which later became "Iraklio"), had been destroyed in the war against the Arabs. He wanted this new place to be at a safe distance from the sea and to provide a natural advantage over any attacking enemy.

The General's advisers recommended this hill, and the General liked it immediately and decided to build the new capital here. However, he did not bother to ask the people of Handakas how they felt about his decision, and he turned a deaf ear to all their protests, which were not very loud in the first place. Determined to go on with his plans, he ordered them to

ROUTES STARTING FROM RETHIMNO

THE EPANOSSIFIS MONASTERY

From the moment you step through the courtgate, the **Epanossifis monastery** will impress you with its **great wealth.** As known, monasteries do not get rich from the work of the monks but from the **generous offers** of the faithful, whose faith increases in direct proportion to the miracles performed by the saint or his icon - and the more they believe, the more generous they become. In this case, St. George, the patron saint of the monastery, started performing miracles very early, and they say he has never stopped. This is why he has the most **impressive icon** you will see on the

TEMENOS, THE BYZANTINE FORTRESS

start carrying and hewing stones immediately. Then one bright day in 968 the fortress was finished and Nikiforos Fokas was urgently called back to Constantinople as the new Emperor chosen by the army and the people. The very next day the people of Handakas returned to their ruined town, and sighing with relief they began to rebuild their homes. As a result, there were never any homes built behind the walls, and the fortress remained an empty shell. During its history it came into the possession of several Byzantine dukes and Venetian lords, and it occasionally served as a refuge in moments of crisis. It was repaired from time to time but without much care, and the building materials frequently came from the ancient town of Likastos. Today you can see them incorporated in the fortress wall.

Though the fortress was not destined for glorious moments, it is still a precious monument. If you touch the stones on the wall and let your spirit wander, you may "connect" with the ancient Likastians that fought in the Trojan war and with the people of Handakas who hewed the stones with their own hands.

14. Rethimno-Ierapetra TRAVELLING INLAND

island, an icon full of precious offerings.

Until the year 1600, all that St. George had in this place was a poor chapel in the midst of the olive groves belonging to the rich lord Langouvardos. Then one night the chapel was visited by a wandering monk, Father Paissios, who had been kicked out of the Apezanon monastery on the Asteroussia Mountains because of his unacceptable behaviour. Apparently, the saint saw in him a unique opportunity to have a better church built in his honour. He visited him in his dream, fierce-looking on horseback, and ordered him sternly to build a splendid church in the place of the chapel without any delay! The very next day the God-fearing Paissios, whose secret desire happened to coincide with the saint's order, gathered some men from the nearby villages, appropriated several hectares of Langouvardos's land, and began building the church. When Langouvardos heard of this, he got really angry and ordered the building to stop, since it was completely illegal. But that same night the saint miraculously appeared in his dream. What the saint told him remained between him and Langouvardos, but the effect of the dream was a complete turnaround in Langouvardos's behaviour. From the next morning, the landowner not only permitted the building to go on but even took it upon himself to cover the expenses and to offer the monastery some more land as support. In a similarly miraculous manner, the rider-saint convinced many more lords to offer a part of their land, and pretty soon the Epanossifis monastery - named after a shepherd called **Sifis** who had his hut *edhò epàno* (up here) - became **tremendously rich.** When Robert Pashley visited the place in 1834 he was treated like royalty, and he had the most unforgettable stay and the most sumptuous meal of his life. So did all the other travellers of the time who crossed the threshold of the monastery. Today

The icon of St. George at the Epanossifis Monastery

there is no more fuss made over visitors, but if you happen to come here on April 23 or November 3, the days that the monastery celebrates in honour of its patron saint, you will be certainly impressed with the festivities. As for your own secret desires, kneel piously in front of the saint's icon and tell him all about them. Being a rider himself, he will probably like you and grant you your wishes.

FROM THE EPANOSSIFIS MONASTERY TO MT. DIKTI

As mentioned, between the Epanossifis monastery and the first villages at the foot of Mt. Dikti there is nothing much to see. But the road is good, so you can at least travel the distance to the southwest end of the mountain without much delay. Though the route is rather indifferent, Mt. Dikti will reward you for the trip.

After you have visited the monastery, continue eastward, following the Gr/E sign that says "Iraklio." When you get on the Iraklio - Pirgos road turn right (south), and after about 3 km turn left (east) on the dirtroad (D1) that goes to Amourgeles. After Amourgeles, the road, once again asphalt-paved, continues through **Panorama,** a village that offers a truly panoramic view of the valley below it, and then it meets the main road leading to **Arkalochori.** Contrary to what one might expect, this road is **narrow and dangerously slippery** and it has no signs and no marked traffic lanes.

Arkalochori (-chori meaning "village") could well be called Arkalopolis (the Arkalon town) because it has indeed become a town. It is possible that you may get lost here. Do not continue straight through the village, because you will end up on the road to **Partira,** but **turn left** at the main square in order to get on the road to Viannos. (Unfortunately, there is no sign at the intersection). A few kilometres later you may again get confused when you reach a point where four different roads radiate in four different directions. (But the one you want passes from Nipiditos and has a Gr/E sign that sends you to Viannos). After passing Panagia, follow the Gr/E sign that sends you to Embaros and turn left (east). The road will take you to Embaros, Xeniakos and Katofigi, three very

Three shepherds, the Stavrakakis brothers, at the Omalos plateau

and are totally unaffected by tourism. (Incidentally, the same holds true for **Miliarades,** which is close but not on your way). These hamlets are not on the classic tourist routes, so they are still authentic. Maps often do not include them, much like they don't include some truly great routes that you'll find on the ROAD maps. Among them, the **amazing mountain route** that will take you to the secluded **Omalos plateau.**

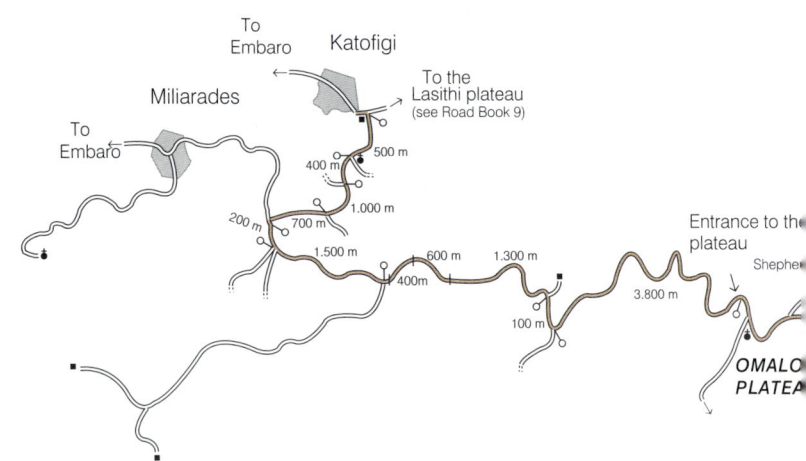

ROAD BOOK 7

Katofigi - Omalos plateau - Kato Simi

From Mt. Dikti to Ierapetra via the Omalos plateau

The route to the Omalos plateau is the most impressive one on Mt. Dikti. It starts right after the east exit of **Katofigi**, where you must reset your counter in order to follow **Road Book 7**. The dirtroad is generally good (D2 / D3), except for two or three kilometres shortly before the plateau where it has a steep inclination. The plateau is 1300 metres above sea level and it is truly beautiful. It has a small lake at its centre, a little chapel, and a primitive stone hut that is the home of three shepherds, the Stavrakakis brothers. Needless to say, you can pitch camp anywhere you like; the best idea would probably be to set up your tent at a nice spot and then pay a visit to the shepherds. They will offer you raki and wonderful cream cheese of their own production, and they will be very happy if in return you give them three or four packs of cigarettes, which for them is a precious little gift since they rarely leave the mountain to go down to the village. If you have a warm sleeping bag and sleep outside your tent, and if you are lucky and the night is cloudless and moonless, you'll have an experience to remember all your life. The stars are so bright and the stillness is so deep that you'll have the magic feeling of being on a spacecraft travelling through the galaxies...

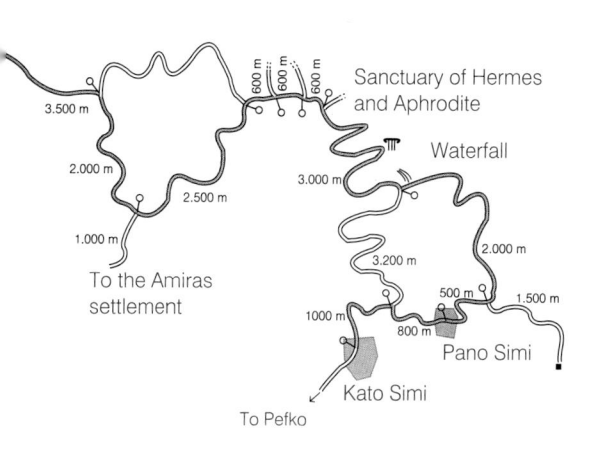

The road crosses the Omalos plateau from west to east and then goes downhill. It winds through the **thickest and most beautiful pine forest of Crete** and takes you to the abandoned (Ep)ano Simi and to the very lively Kato Simi. Since it is fairly easy, it allows quick off-road driving and will not tire you. If you get hot, you can take an ice-cold shower at the small waterfall that you'll find just before Kato Simi. About one kilometre earlier, you will see a fenced area next to the road. This encloses what's left of the **Sanctuary of Hermes and Aphrodite,** which has an uninterrupted history spanning the years from the Middle Minoan period till the third century AD. It was discovered very recently (1972) and was excavated systematically by Mrs. A. Lembessi. Among other valuable items, she found many clay and bronze statuettes, tiles of the temple engraved with the names of donors, and several sacred vessels. Some of these findings are exhibited at the Archaeological Museum of Iraklio.

At the village of Kato Simi you will see a war memorial. This was built to remind the world of the five hundred men executed here in 1943, when the Germans decided to punish the locals for the murder of two German soldiers. Their rage was such that they also burned six villages to the ground...

By now you may have had enough of driving on the mountains and you may be dreaming of a refreshing swim. As you follow the main road leading to Ierapetra you will see many intersections where you can turn right (south) and head for the beach. If you decide to continue on the main road it will take you to **Mirtos** (see page 313), a seaside village with a nice pebbly beach where you can also take a swim. If you are looking for a nice beach to camp, there is one two kilometres west of Mirtos, although the best beaches lie west of Keratokambos, many kilometres away (see Route 13). East of Mirtos there is little to see, except for the Minoan site between this village and Nea Mirtos which we mentioned earlier (page 313) From Mirtos all you have to do is follow the coastal road until you reach Ierapetra.

Travel to Aghios Nikolaos (via the Katharos plateau)

If you do not want to go to Ierapetra (where there is very little to see anyway) and feel like driving more on the mountains and visiting

ROUTES STARTING FROM RETHIMNO

ROAD BOOK 8a

Riza - Males

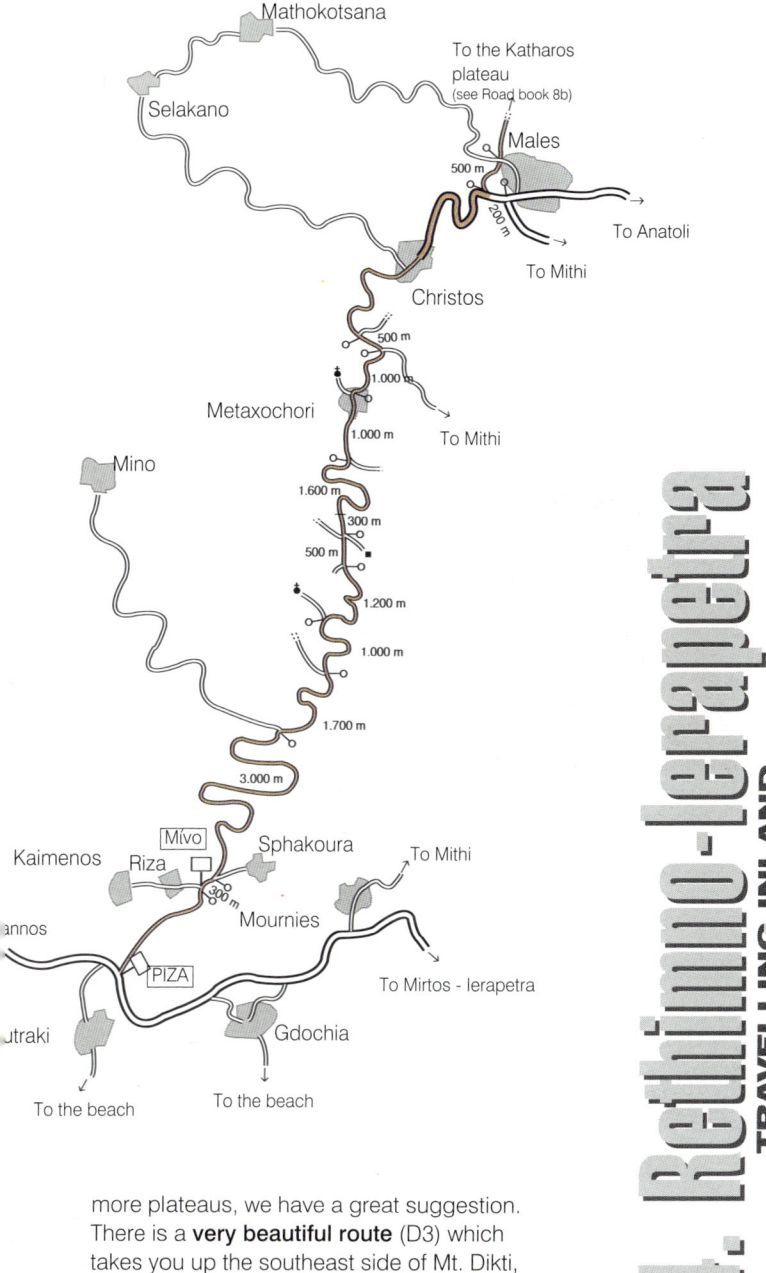

Mathokotsana

To the Katharos plateau (see Road book 8b)

Selakano

Males

500 m

200 m

To Anatoli

Christos

To Mithi

500 m

1.000 m

Metaxochori

1.000 m

To Mithi

Mino

1.600 m

300 m

500 m

1.200 m

1.000 m

1.700 m

3.000 m

Mívo

Sphakoura

Kaimenos Riza

To Mithi

300 m

annos

Mournies

PIZA

To Mirtos - Ierapetra

utraki

Gdochia

To the beach

To the beach

14. Rethimno-Ierapetra — TRAVELLING INLAND

more plateaus, we have a great suggestion. There is a **very beautiful route** (D3) which takes you up the southeast side of Mt. Dikti, goes through some very picturesque villages, then takes you through the Katharos plateau, goes downhill in an easterly direction and finally

341

ends in **Aghios Nikolaos,** a town where there is certainly more to see and do.

To follow this route, take the same road that leads to Mirtos and turn left on the A3 road that you will see near the intersection for Loutraki. (There is a Gr sign at the point where you must turn which sends you to "PIZA"). The road ends at a T-junction where you must turn right - a left turn would take you inside the village - and reset your counter so you can follow **Road Book 8a.** From the start, you have a great view of the Mirtos and the Ierapetra valley, even though the pine forest that once covered the mountain slope was

---

A TASTE OF PARADISE

What are we made of? The things we eat, the air we breathe, what we see and hear. Giorgos Tzanakis, shepherd and cheese maker at the Katharos plateau, was born between the sheep in the fields sometime in winter. The first bed he lay on was a warm sheepskin, the first sounds he heard were the bleating and the bells of the sheep, and the first smells he ever knew were those of sage and marjoram.

When we arrived at his small hut we found him chopping wood for the stove. It was the beginning of December, and the weather was cold and rainy.

"Welcome, lads! Come in and have a raki with me to warm up a bit. But you must be hungry too."

By the time we had taken our helmets and raincoats off, he had unearthed five or six potatoes, cut a couple of tomatoes from his small greenhouse, fetched two eggs from the hencoop, cut a large piece of hard cheese of his own production, taken out some barley biscuits, olives and raki, and filled the table with goodies...

He shook the earth off the potatoes, cut them in large pieces and threw them in the pan with the sizzling olive oil. The wonderful smells of the French fries, the freshly sliced tomato with the oregano and the burning wood became the incense that turned the poor shepherd's hut into a chapel. This was no lunch he was offering us; it was like a Holy Communion. We got a taste of his personal paradise and continued with our own trip and lives...

ROUTES STARTING FROM RETHIMNO

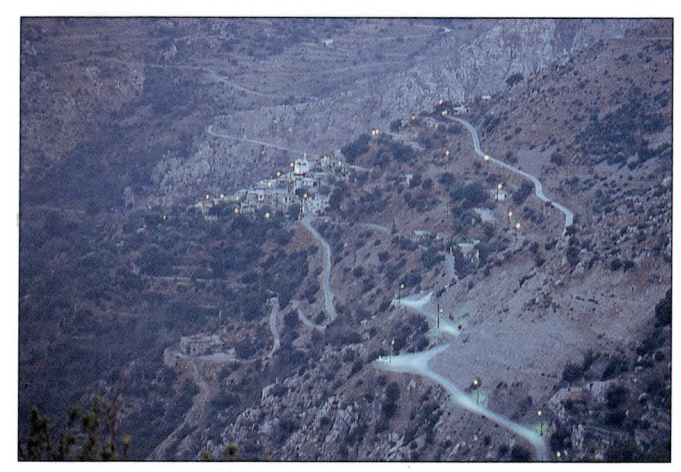

The village of Christos

burned in 1990. After 2 or 3 km the sad sight of burned trees disappears and you find yourself in a very beautiful landscape with steep mountain slopes and ravines just above your head and pine or cedar forests or tall bushes all around you. A little further a road branches off to the west and takes you to an almost abandoned village called **Mino.** Our route, though, continues straight and leads to **Metaxochori,** a village well worth making at least a short stop. Very few people have stayed at the village, but its traditional architecture will earn your admiration with its many virtues. The houses are solid, wisely designed, practical and very tasteful, as you can easily see since most of them are open and abandoned. In Metaxochori you will see a T-junction where you must turn right. (A left turn would take you to the fields). After a while the road will take you to **Christos,** a very beautiful village with many old churches. Christos, like **Selakano** and **Mathokotsana** (which are even more secluded), will satisfy the traveller who has a taste for traditional, old, unspoilt things.

After Christos you continue on an asphalt-paved road (A3). About 200 metres before the intersection west of **Males,** turn left on the small cement road that climbs the mountain. After 500 metres you will see an intersection. (This is at the north end of the village and can also be reached if you go through it, but you may easily get lost in the village alleys). Once here, reset your counter in order to follow **Road Book 8b** and go

14. Rethimno-Ierapetra — TRAVELLING INLAND

right, following the road that goes up the mountain. (The one to the left leads to Mathokotsana and Selakano). The road (D3) passes through a beautiful pine forest and goes uphill. It finally takes you to the **Katharos plateau,** which is much higher and quieter than the neighbouring Lasithi plateau with which there is no direct contact. The plateau belongs to the Kritsa community and the locals have each appropriated a small - or large - part of it. Scattered all over the place, you will see small houses, shepherd huts, sheepfolds, storage rooms and chapels, as well as a couple of primitive taverns that serve mostly the needs of the locals (since very few tourists come this high). If you are hungry, look for the tavern-hut of Giorgos Tzanakis, the shepherd. It is at a settlement called Avdeliakos near the intersection for Kritsa and it will give you a taste of another epoch.

· If you'd like to camp in the Katharos plateau you will find many quiet nooks to set up your tent, especially toward the northwest end of it. Keep in mind, though, that you will need a warm sleeping bag because up here it is cold even in August. In the spring the plateau is covered with a multi-coloured

ROUTES STARTING FROM RETHIMNO

carpet of wild flowers, and it is like a beautiful tableau.

From Avdeliakos to Aghios Nikolaos

Avdeliakos is the starting point of a good dirtroad (D2), which winds down the mountain for 16 km, offers spectacular views of Aghios Nikolaos and the Mirambellos Gulf, and takes you to **Kritsa**, a large village known for its very good woollen clothes and textiles that are

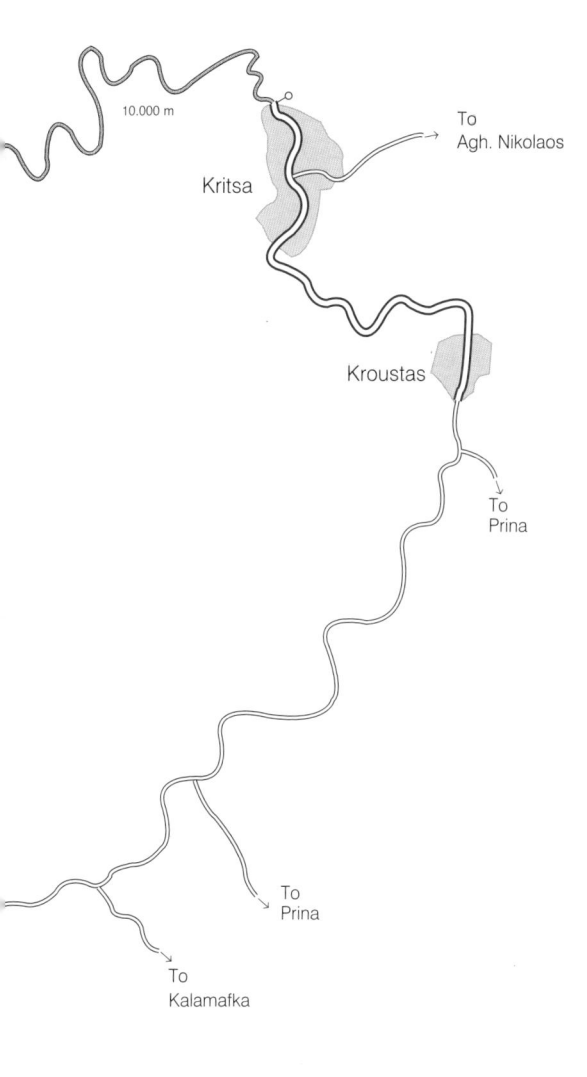

14. Rethimno-Ierapetra — TRAVELLING INLAND

ROAD BOOK 8b
Males - Katharos plateau - Kritsa

345

produced locally. We suggest that you avoid the stupid patterns with the windmills and the small boats, which are made to appeal to those who don't know better, and that you look for the traditional geometric patterns and the natural colours of wool: beige, brown, grey and white.

If it is earlier than 3:00 p.m. you can visit the church of **Panagia Kera** (Our Lady, Mary), one kilometre after Kritsa, on the way to Aghios Nikolaos. This church is full of wall paintings of the 13th and 14th century that are very well preserved. The uniqueness of the themes, the richness of the colours and the diversity in expression, the interesting thematic details that give valuable information on the time the paintings were made, and the details of style and execution will certainly impress you.

After Panagia Kera you simply continue for another ten kilometres and you will reach Aghios Nikolaos. However, if you have the time, you may want to return to Kritsa first and to make a small detour before Aghios Nikolaos in order to visit the Minoan town of **Lato** in the north. It is certainly worth the trouble.

LATO

(Guarded archaeological site, open Tuesday through Sunday from 8:30 a.m. till 3:00 p.m. Free entrance)

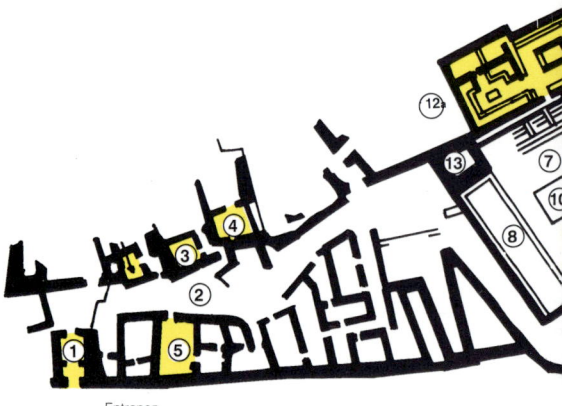

Entrance

ROUTES STARTING FROM RETHIMNO

One beautiful morning somewhere around 700 BC, some Dorian settlers, looking for a new homeland and tired of their long voyage, decided to pull their boats on the small sandy beach that later became the site of Aghios Nikolaos. We don't know what need or desire led them to this God-forsaken place, but we feel they must have been impressed at the sight of the lake and the vertical rock behind it which they named **Kamara.**

Used as they were to build their towns in hard-to-assail positions in the mountains, they merely built a small settlement here so that they could have a seaport. Then they took their stuff and continued inland in a westerly direction, looking for a suitable hill on which to build their town. Their goal was to find a hill that would offer them protection from enemy attacks and a great view. Indeed they made the best choice possible, especially as concerns the view, which you can admire for yourself. As for the town that was born here marking their new life, they gave it the name of the goddess of labour Leto, which in the Dorian dialect changes to **Lato.**

Like a true warlike people, they surrounded their town with a wall and built a very strong **gate (1)** that could not even be passed by an enemy mosquito! After you pass through it (fearlessly!) you can follow the steep path that used to be the main road **(2)** of the town. On

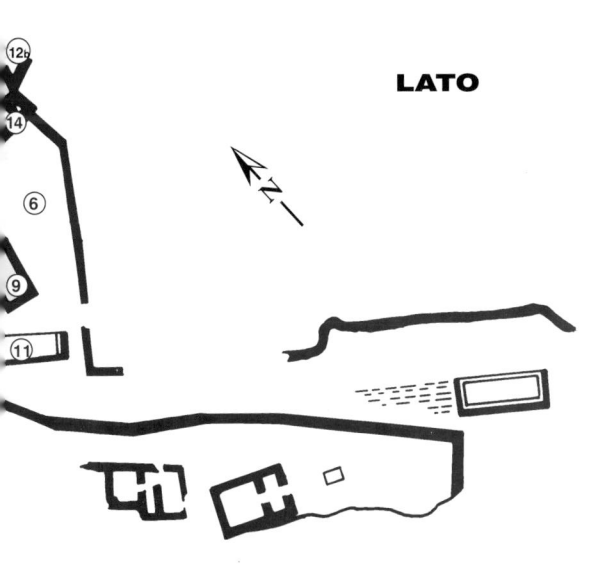

LATO

the left (north) side of the road were the people's homes and a couple of defence towers **(3,4)**, and on the right (south) side of it were the shops and the workshops of the craftsmen. One of these **(5)** is believed to have been the workshop of a textile dyer, because the water cistern and the other paraphernalia found in it suggested a similar kind of use. The main road will take you to the main square of the town, the **Agora (6)**, a large open area that served the needs of public life. When the weather was good the citizens would sit on the steps **(7)** at the north end of the Agora and they would listen to political speeches or watch art shows or religious ceremonies or other public events. When the wind or the great heat made it inadvisable to sit there, they probably gathered in the roofed **gallery (8)** at the west end of the Agora. At the centre of the Agora was their **temple (9)**, which was apparently without a roof. Numerous clay statuettes were found here, but unfortunately they did not have any distinctive features that would allow the archaeologists to decide safely which deity was worshipped in the temple. The water supply of the town came from large underground cisterns, one of which **(10)** is right in front of the temple. Behind the temple you can see a three-sided platform **(11)** carved into the rock, with two steps on each side of it. This platform was also used on public occasions.

The major decisions and the administration of the town's affairs, however, were in the hands of the Prytaneis, a group of wise elderly men who spent their time in the **Prytaneum (12a, 12b)**. This was a well made building behind the steps (seats) at the north end of the Agora, and it was framed by two towers on its left and right side that were more effective in giving it a monumental character than in offering any kind of protection. In this building the Prytaneis received the envoys of other towns and all important visitors that came from other lands. As a visitor from a foreign land, you, too, have every right to enter the Prytaneum. Start with the **Banquet Room (12a)**, where you can take a rest from your trip and have something to eat. (If you do not find those in charge of the banquets just make do with your own sandwiches!) Then proceed to the **Conference Room (12b)**, choose the stone bench that you like best, and lie back comfortably; the prytaneis are "away on business," and it is not certain when they will be back...

In the middle of the Conference Room is an altar that stands right before your eyes. It was here that Lato's sacred flame once burned, a flame that was never put out and had come to symbolise the uninterrupted life of the town. However, this life was terminated only five hundred years after the town was founded. No, it was not any violent attack from the outside that caused the flame to go out; it was rather the "lack of fuel." The Latoans at some point grew tired of living in a well fortified mountain town that was never threatened by anyone, and they decided that it was time to move closer to the sea. So they abandoned the old Lato, which by that time had become less important and was called "The Other Lato," and they moved to their seaport, **Lato near Kamara,** which had already taken the place of the old town.

Ierapetra

ROUTES STARTING FROM IERAPETRA

The modern town of Ierapetra is built on the exact same site as the ancient Dorian town of **Ierapitna**, which grew big, powerful and rich thanks primarily to the trade with the most significant harbour towns of the eastern Mediterranean, and especially those on the African, Greek and Sicilian coast.

Like all rich people from the beginning of the world, the Ierapitnians were not satisfied with what they had, and they did everything in their power to acquire greater wealth. In this endeavour they followed a primitive but effective way, which has never ceased to be popular throughout the world: appropriating their neighbour's property by force. After long and hard wars, they managed to conquer the neighbouring town of **Praisos,** thus expanding their power over almost the entire eastern part of the island. The poor Pressians, who were the last of the Minoans and had sought refuge on the mountains of eastern Crete after the Dorian invasion, were literally wiped out; those that were not killed in battle or executed were sold as slaves. The Ierapitnian merchants took no account of the fact that they were the No 1 species in danger of extinction, and together with their vases and jewellery and wine and olive oil they exported Pressian slaves. In fact, they probably got a very good price for them, because they sold them to the last one! And so it happened that the last descendants of the Minoans, the people whose forefathers created one of the most splendid civilisations, had a truly inglorious end...

Now that the Pressians were out of the picture, the last rival to deal with was **Itanos** (page 502). "Cornered" at the northeast end of Crete, Itanos stubbornly resisted the Ierapitnians' attacks, much like the Galatian village of Asterix put up a fierce resistance against the Roman legions! Yet the town was a "small fish," and it would inevitably be eaten by Ierapitna which was a much bigger one. It **would** be - but it wasn't, since a third, giant

Greenhouse tomatoes: the jewels of Ierapetra that made the whole town rich

"fish" gulped down both of them with one swift move. This happened in **67 BC** and the third fish was the Roman Empire.

However, Ierapitna did not suffer under the Romans. Instead, it prospered greatly, in fact more than any other time in its history. It soon spread out over a larger area than the one taken up by the modern town, and it was filled with magnificent public buildings: theatres, baths, aqueducts, temples etc. Until about the 10th century there were plenty of ruins to be seen from the Roman town, but today there is almost nothing above ground. Under the ground and the modern apartment buildings, however, there must still be plenty of precious historical monuments, probably doomed to stay there for ever.

In 824 there was a new sweeping invasion that left nothing standing: the Arabian one. Plundering and destroying everything in their path, the Arabs did not spare Ierapitna. Soon, however, they regretted its destruction and built it from the start, because they realised it was a very convenient base for their sea raids. When the Venetians took over the island they built a small square fortress, the **Castel Gerapetra,** which was meant to protect their galleys in the harbour. The fortress underwent restoration work under both the Venetians and the Turks, and, more recently, under the care of the Greek authorities, and today it is almost intact.

The modern town of Ierapetra has about 12,000 inhabitants. Although you might not guess it, it is the richest town on the island and ranks quite high among rich towns in the entire country. Its wealth does not derive from tourism, however, but from... cucumbers and tomatoes. Until 1965 it was a rather poor place with an economy that was based on farming and stockbreeding. Then something happened and its fate changed; a young Dutchman by the name of **Paul Coopers** came to Ierapetra, armed with some precious knowledge. Coopers was a member of a poor and large family, who had studied agronomy with the support of the Church and was under the obligation to offer his services free of charge in some underdeveloped area. He chose Ierapetra because he foresaw that its mild climate and fertile ground would be excellent for the greenhouse crops that were becoming so popular. The locals did not pay much heed to his advice and they were even mistrustful. But Coopers was not one to get easily disappointed, and he persisted in spite of their narrow-mindedness. He built a greenhouse and showed them how lucrative it was to produce juicy red tomatoes in the heart of winter! In the next twenty years the entire south coast of Crete was covered with greenhouses, and the farmers' pockets were filled with earnings. Ironically, Coopers did not live to see the fruits of his success. He died in 1968 in a car accident and was posthumously honoured by the locals with a splendid statue, which they erected among the greenhouses, at the same place where he once planted the "seed" of their present wealth.

In spite of its wealth, Ierapetra is a town full of eye sores: ugly apartment buildings that stifle it with cement, narrow streets full of potholes, and debris lying around everywhere. The municipal beach at the east side of town is not so ugly, but you will certainly find better beaches a few kilometres to the east. Near the harbour you can see a part of the old town which has survived, but as the fronts of the houses have not yet been restored and there are no pedestrian zones it gives the impression of a rather shabby old neighbourhood. At the west part of the old town you can see a Turkish mosque and fountain, the most obvious reminders of the Turkish presence in the area. As for the time of the Venetian rule, it has left behind several landmarks, especially small churches. Among them, the church of **Afendis Christos** (Christ, Our Lord), which dates from the 14th century and is situated just west of the fortress, the **Panagia tou Kale** just opposite of the fortress gate, and the church of **Aghios**

Nikolaos. Though the churches are usually locked, there is always somebody around who knows where to find the keys.

Another thing worth seeing is the **archaeological collection,** housed in an old building opposite the town hall at the main square. (Incidentally, the building once served as a Turkish school). The place is open Tuesday through Sunday, between the hours of 8:30 a.m. and 3:00 p.m. Among other exhibits, one can distinguish the marble statue of the goddess Demeter, dating from the 2nd century BC, and a clay Minoan sarcophagus of the 14th century BC, which was found in Episkopi and bears some wonderful representations of chariot processions, hunting scenes etc.

Although you have no particular reason to stay in Ierapetra, if you decide to do so your best choice is the PETRA MARE HOTEL at the east exit of town (tel. 0842 - 23 341, fax 0842 - 23 350). This is a large A class hotel next to the sea, which was recently redecorated and has a spacious parking area for your bike. A second A class hotel, the ASTRON (tel. 0842 - 25 114, fax 0842 - 25 917), which is also a good choice, is on 56 M. Kothri St. (the main street just behind the waterfront). On no 42 of the same street you will find a C class hotel named EL GRECO (tel. 0842 - 28 471), which is also very good and considerably cheaper. Both ASTRON and EL GRECO have a few rooms offering a view of the sea, but none of them has a parking place for your motorcycle. Finally, at the centre of the town you will find another C class hotel, LYGIA. It is on 12 Saridaki street, in a nice quiet area behind the post office, and it is your least expensive choice without making a great compromise in quality. In addition, it has a convenient area next to the entrance, where you can easily park your bike.

If you are hungry, go straight to Stratigou Samouil street next to the sea. This street starts from the fortress wall in the old harbour, continues behind the municipal beach, and ends at the main square of the town. Here you will see most of the restaurants and ouzo bars in town and rows of tables right next to the sea. Your best option, which is also the absolute choice of the locals, is NAPOLEON on number 26, which serves fresh seafood as well as a great variety of cooked meals and local specialties. (We recommend the mousaka or the rabbit with potatoes). A little further on the same street (at no 10) is a bakery with delicious chocolate-filled croissants and a variety of sandwiches, which are especially good for breakfast.

If your motorcycle breaks down in Ierapetra it means you are very unlucky; there is no large authorised repair shop. For tyre jobs you can go to the shop on 45 Kostoula Adrianou street near the town exit that leads to Mirtos. Here you will find a small stock of motorcycle tyres and a helpful owner, Kostas Marangakis, who is himself a motorcyclist and will help you with minor repairs. Mr. Marangakis can also bring any tyre you need within a matter of twenty-four hours.

15. Ierapetra -Zakros

COASTAL ROAD

ROUTES STARTING FROM IERAPETRA

From the centre of Ierapetra take the road to Sitia and after passing the hospital at the northern exit of the town you will reach a fork (no road signs posted) where you turn right (east). The road continues along the coast, which for the first two kilometres from Ierapetra is pebbly and with enough trees to offer shade. The beach is wide and clean, but not the best choice for a swim, as the busy road running alongside it causes a lot of noise. Even more disturbing is the ugly landscape beyond the coast that has suffered horrible defacement from the agricultural over-exploitation and the vulgar and haphazard tourist development. The ugly scenery continues for many kilometres to the east until the village of Analipsi. Hence it is better to ride through without stopping.

In the village of **Makrigialos** you will see a sign that says "Minoan Villa". If you wish to get a good idea of the meaning of **utter negligence** on the part of the local authorities, the neighbours and, certainly, of the Ministry of Culture, turn left (north) at this point and visit this archaeological site. We are not dealing here with a medieval chicken coop or a broken Roman column, we are dealing instead with a wonderful **Minoan villa of 1600 BC,** miniature of the Knossos Palace, the residence of the local lord. The elementary steps that the local authorities or the Ministry of Culture should have taken, is to pave the 300 metres of road to the site and spend a pittance per year to keep it clean.

Carrying on eastward from Makrigialos you pass the likewise miserable village of Analipsi, immediately after which you turn right onto the coastal road (there is a Greek/English sign at the junction that reads: Kapsa Monastery, Goudouras, Kalo Nero). From here onward the landscape is rocky, desolate and increasingly interesting. Up to the village of **Kalo Nero** the road is very good (A2), but also the dirt roads traversing the landscape beyond this point until Zakros are generally very good (D1, D2). Eastward from Kalo Nero the road runs very close to the rocky coast. On your left (north) you have a nice view of the precipitous craggy hills with their countless large and small caves. Shortly past Kalo Nero you will unexpectedly encounter the **Kapsa Monastery,** perched on the cliff at the mouth of the narrow and impressive Perivolakia Gorge. Below the monastery there is a small sandy beach with coarse pebbles and shady trees, a very good spot for rough camping.

Following the Kapsa Monastery the road is asphalted (A3) until Goudouras village, which is a small community within a plastic sea of greenhouses covering the entire plain behind the coast. In front of Goudouras there is a large beach with coarse pebbles, totally unsuitable for a swim. A road begins at this beach (an English sign at the crossroads reads: Aghia Triada, Apidia, Ziros) and initially winds through the greenhouses, to turn later into dirt (D2) in an easterly direction. About 2.3 kilometres from Goudouras beach you will run into a junction without signs. Continuing straight leads to the village of Aghia Triada, while turning right also leads to Aghia Triada but via a much more

---

We do not know exactly when the monastery was founded (it is conjectured that someone called Kapsas built it in 1450), but we do know when it began to flourish. It was in the spring of 1841, when its owner, Hatzinikolis Zaphiris (who had bought it from the Turks together with all its land), granted it to a small-time crook, Yiannis Vincentzos or Gerontoyiannis, from the village of Lithines. Gerontoyiannis had been using the ruined monastery for some time as a hideout, as he had done with the inaccessible caves of the Perivolakia Gorge, and he lived off petty theft. One day, while sitting in the monastery garden, he thought of a wonderful way of becoming rich not by plunder but by means of voluntary contributions by his victims! So he spread it around, with the help of several of his trusted friends, that he had been visited by Divine Grace

ROUTES STARTING FROM IERAPETRA

No, this is not a rubbish tip; it's the minoan villa at Makrigialos

interesting coastal route through a deserted landscape. Now then, here turn right and at the next crossroads, some 300 metres ahead, turn left (the right branch stops at a storehouse). One kilometre after this junction there is a

THE KAPSA MONASTERY

which had made him a saint capable of working miracles. He could make the sign of the cross over sea water and render it drinkable, sit on his overcoat and float over to the islands opposite, and of course, with God's help, cure the faithful of all illnesses (if he failed, this was not his fault, but that of the believer whose faith was not as strong as it should have been and so God had refused to cure him). It was then that Zaphiris granted him the monastery and soon the (over-gullible) faithful were forming queues outside his cell for him to cure them, bringing with them, naturally, the richest gifts they could afford, as proof of their faith and a token of their gratitude to the good God and to his earthly representative.

The monastery very quickly became famous and acquired a clientele from all corners of Crete. With a small part of the wealth he had amassed, Gerontoyiannis renovated the monastery, built new cells and added a second chapel (which was dedicated to the glorious Holy Trinity) next to the original chapel (which was dedicated to the humble John the Baptist). He decorated both chapels with ornate wooden iconostases made by the Lasithian craftsman Hatzi Minas, and with beautiful icons, the work of the Irakliot iconographer Antonis Alexandridis. He appointed heir to this fraudulent racket his grandson, Iosif, who carried on the work faultlessly after his grandfather's death in 1874. Indeed, he had an ornate reliquary made, where he placed the bones of Gerontoyiannis and on top, in a special case, he put his skull for the people to make pilgrimages to. As you can see for yourselves from the size of the skull, Gerontoyiannis really had a lot of brains!

15. Ierapetra-Zakros COASTAL ROAD

second junction where you turn left again (right will lead you over a very bad road to a spot of no special interest on the coast, called Atherinolakos). At the next (third) junction turn left again and, following a few kilometres of enjoyable ride in a desolate landscape, you will run into the main dirt road just before Aghia Triada village (formerly called **Tsou!**). Unfortunately, no coastal road exists from Atherinolakos to Xerokambos and therefore you are obliged to take this detour north. Carry on northward from Aghia Triada until you come to the main road (A3), a bit south of the village of Ziros. With the exception of the small church of Aghia Paraskevi, boasting beautiful frescoes dating from 1523, there isn't much to see at Ziros, so head left (south) on the road that climbs to the Air Force installation.

At some point along this road you will see large signs warning that you are approaching a military zone and prohibiting further advance. Exactly at that point you will also see two unmarked roads (D1) branching off to the right. The southernmost of these roads (i.e. the one on the right as you face them) goes to Kalo Chorio. You follow the northern one (left) to Xerokambos. From this point onward to Xerokambos and from there to Zakros lies **the most enjoyable part of Route 15.** An excellent dirt road traverses an utterly desolate rocky landscape covered in bushes and wild flowers, unchanged for centuries. Equally unchanged through time is the small hamlet of Chametoulo, **perhaps the most authentic village of Crete,** which you will encounter at some point of this route. The short detour that leads to Chametoulo stops a short way out of the village, at the church next to the cemetery, and just after that start the houses, two score all in all, whitewashed and clean, clinging to each other, with narrow cobble alleys between them. The poor villagers living here keep a few flocks and tend a few barren fields on a small stretch of flat ground that holds a little earth among the craggy hills. Visiting this village and riding the stretch from here to Xerokambos are reasons enough to try Route 15.

Past Chametoulo the road descends towards the coast offering a splendid view of

ROUTES STARTING FROM IERAPETRA

On the Ziros-Xerokambos route.

the Libyan sea. The best time to enjoy it is late in the afternoon when the sun's slanted rays create sharp shadows on the rocks and paint the sea in vivid blue hues. For many kilometres you will not come across either houses, fields or any trace of humans whatsoever. When you reach the seaside settlement of **Xerokambos** you will be greeted by two of the most beautiful beaches in Crete, spacious, sandy, serene and spotlessly clean. Here you will find three very good tavernas and a few rooms to let. On Xerokambos' west side beach there are (alone in the open) the brand new rooms to let owned by Constantinos Takakis (tel.: 0843-91206 and 31792), all with private kitchen and bathroom. In the same complex there is a mini market with a maxi choice of goods where you can buy provisions and cook in your room. If you are seeking a quiet spot for quiet holidays you cannot find a better or cheaper place than Xerokambos.

Beyond Xerokambos the road (D3) continues northward to Zakros, crossing very impressive rocky scenery full of large and small gorges, perhaps the most virgin corner of Crete that keeps a lot of beauty concealed from all but those willing to walk and explore. You will come across many secondary roads intersecting the main route and leading to incredible places! If you stay on the main dirt road you will end up eventually on the asphalt road connecting Ano Zakros to Kato Zakros, only a few metres from the last houses of Ano

15. Ierapetra-Zakros COASTAL ROAD

Zakros. Exactly at that junction you will see the foundations of a Minoan house, which came to light during the road construction works in 1965 and is the first example of the Minoan settlement that flourished in this isolated part of Crete.

Ano Zakros is the head village of the region. Here you will find a small old hotel (tel.: 0843-93379), few rooms to let, tavernas and food stores. The inhabitants are mainly farmers, taking advantage of the plentiful waters available locally, while the limited tourist flow to the Minoan palace of Kato Zakros (that mandatorily passes through their village) has left them indifferent so far. Hence you are not going to witness here the misery of haphazard tourist development so prevalent east of Ierapetra.

The name of **Zakros** sounds pre-Hellenic and most likely it has remained unaltered since extreme antiquity. Although the area has been inhabited continually until the present, there is no reference of Zakros in the works of ancient historians, or in the censuses conducted by the Venetian and Turkish conquerors. It is mentioned for the first time in the census taken by the Egyptians in 1834. Such oblivion shows how isolated this area was, an area which still receives very few visitors.

From Ano Zakros a new road (A3) descends to Kato Zakros where the Minoan palace was discovered. Here is a wonderful pebbly beach dotted with several tavernas and rooms to let, open from May to October. The spot is ideal for quiet holidays and as a base camp for hiking excursions to the surrounding hills, or for rides to the magnificently desolate Ziros Plateau west of Zakros, as well as for exploring the entire eastern end of Crete, a land still retaining plenty of its authentic beauty.

If you have hikers amongst your group, a good idea would be to let them off at Ano Zakros in order to walk to Kato Zakros through the impressive Zakros Gorge or **"Gorge of the Dead",** named after the numerous Minoan burials discovered in the caves that line its vertical walls. The footpath is passable and well marked; it starts at the southern end of the village and if you can't find it just ask the natives. It is much easier to find the path if you set off from Kato Zakros.

ROUTES STARTING FROM IERAPETRA

THE PALACE OF ZAKROS
Guarded archaeological site.
Open: Tuesday-Sunday, 8.30am-3.00pm, Fee: 400 Drs

In the summer of 1901, **David George Hogarth,** a young English archaeologist who was working with Sir Arthur Evans at the excavations at Knossos found himself (in an interval of the excavations) in the sandy beach at Kato Zakros. When the villagers who had their fields on the small plain behind the beach found out that he was an archaeologist, they told him that they often found ceramic and various ancient objects every time they ploughed their land. They showed him fragments, from which Hogarth immediately concluded that there was a Minoan settlement somewhere in the area. Judging from the other Minoan habitations which were built on hillsides, he assumed that the habitation must be situated on the hillside north-east of the small plain of Kato Zakros. Indeed, in the excavations which were carried out, he discovered the foundations of a number of Minoan habitations and he found important artefacts of the period I600-I500 BC, mainly tools, weapons and an impressive number of seals (500), perhaps the remains of commercial correspondence. From the wealth of the discoveries, he concluded that here was a very important settlement. He worked systematically and very intensively despite the limited means he had at his disposal, but he stopped just ten metres short of the amazing palace....

Sixty years later, in 1961, the experienced Greek archaeologist **Nikolaos Platon** had the inspiration to excavate the flat area at the base of the hill where Hogarth had excavated. From almost the first blows of the archaeologist's pickaxe, one of the most important Minoan palaces came to light - the palace of Zakros - and after this, an extensive settlement which climbed the hillside north and north-east of the palace.

There is not the slightest reference to the name of this palace in any literary source or archaeological finding. Neither indeed do we know the name of the King who lived here. We can, however, walk through his bedroom **(1)**, refresh ourselves with the water which still bubbles up from his round swimming-pool **(2)**, walk around the central courtyard of the palace **(3)**, sit and eat our fruit in his dining-room **(4)** and have a soft drink in his banqueting-hall **(21)**.

The first part of the palace to come to light after 3,500 years of undisturbed sleep under the ground were the store houses with their earthenware jars **(5,6,7,8)**. A little further south, the **Royal Apartment (9)** was discovered, a

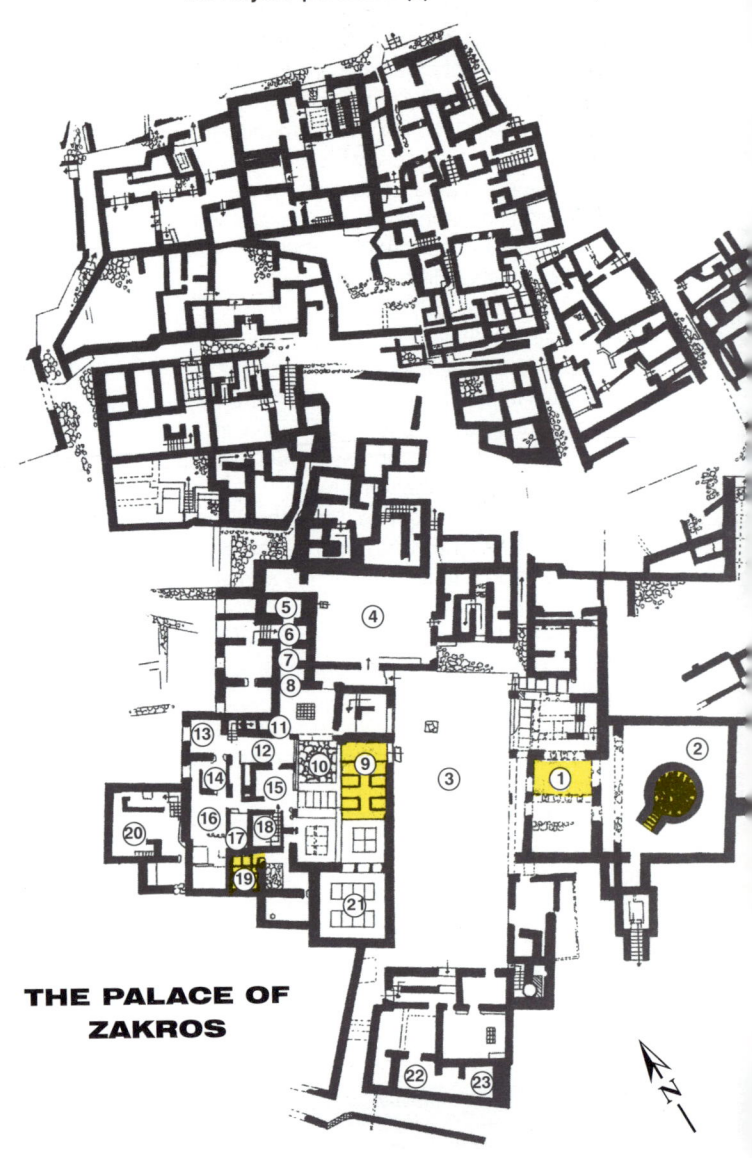

THE PALACE OF ZAKROS

The palace of Zakros

wonderful room divided into two by an internal colonnade, which had a paved internal courtyard/skylight **(10)**. There was also an internal staircase here **(11)** that went up to the second floor of the palace (some steps have been preserved) which must have been the **Treasury.** Many of the priceless treasures which were kept here (swords with gold hilts, ornate cups, fruit bowls, etc.) were found scattered on the ground floor **(12, 13, 14, 15)** directly beneath the Treasury. Room **16** must have been the **Archives.** Whole chests were found here containing tablets where the palace secretaries had recorded accounting details in a language (Linear A) which archaeologists still have not managed to decipher.

The most exciting moment of the excavation, however, was when the Altar of the Palace (17, 18) and the Treasury of the Altar (19) were found. In the latter, more than 100 ceremonial vessels were found - of stone, clay, metal and rock crystal - the most impressive which have been found to date

This wing of the palace also contained the main workshop areas **(20)**. Here, precious objects were made in elephant bone, ivory, stone and glazed earthenware. There were also workshops in the east wing of the palace **(22, 23)**. The copper boilers which were probably used for the preparation of perfumes were found here.

Water coming down the Gorge of the Dead reaches the palace of Zakros

Who were the people who lived here, who their King was, where they came from and what happened to them we shall probably never know. The life of the settlement was exceptionally short - its building begun in 1600 BC and in 1500 BC it collapsed in ruins, due either to a natural disaster or to an attack by invaders. In this short period of 100 years, however, industry and trade brought great wealth to the palace. The palace treasures were preserved intact (not having been robbed), well protected under the earth for many centuries. Today you can admire them at the Iraklio museum. (Room VIII).

ROUTES STARTING FROM IERAPETRA

15. Ierapetra-Zakros
COASTAL ROAD

16. Ierapetra -Zakros

INLAND ROUTE

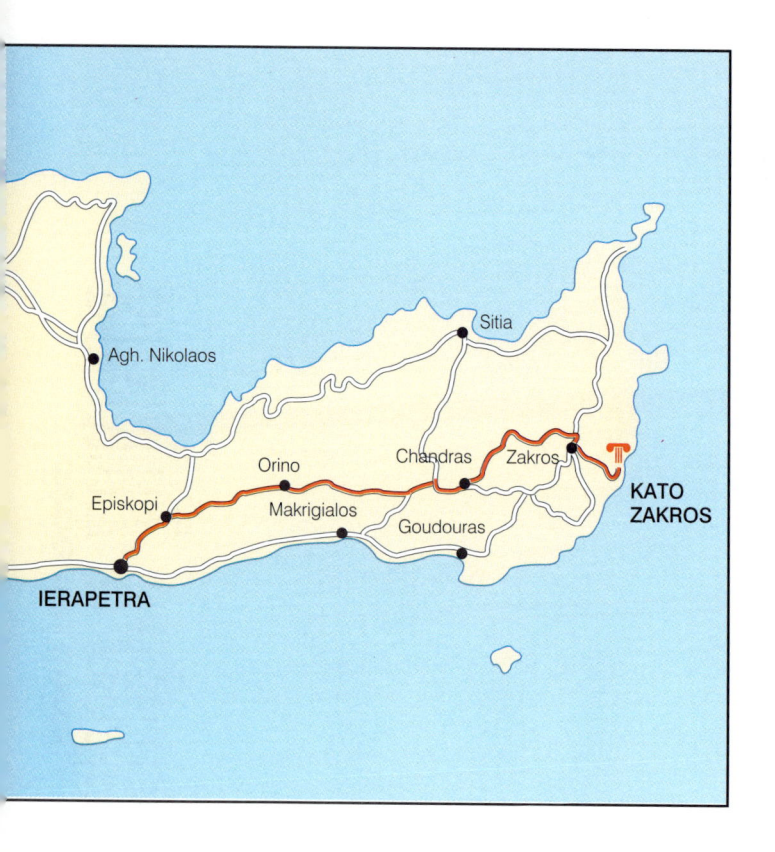

ROUTES STARTING FROM IERAPETRA

If you take a look at the map of Crete, you will see a central circular route at the eastern end of the island. The route starts from Ierapetra, crosses a plain replete with olive trees that opens to the north (the narrowest point on Crete) until it reaches the northern coast and then turns eastward to Sitia, where it turns again southward coming to the southern coast at the village of Analipsi and continues along the shore returning to Ierapetra. This circular route attracts most of the traffic, **but the interesting part is precisely the mountainous region enclosed by it.** Here lie two rocky massifs, Thripti with its summit at Afentis Estavromenos (1,476 m) and Orno with its summit at Askordalia (1,237 m). Their slopes are covered in bushes, herbs and wild flowers with a few surviving islands of pine forest that once thrived everywhere. On the highlands formed between the peaks are nested a score or so of poor hamlets that subsist on animal breeding and small-scale farming (mostly grapes) on the limited, terraced ground. Most of the roads connecting these villages are unpaved (D3), although a good tarmac road does exist. Let's see them from the start.

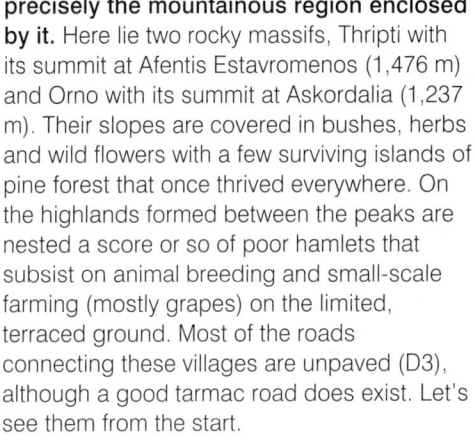

You set out from Ierapetra on the road to Aghios Nikolaos and 6 kilometres later you leave the main road by turning right and heading for Ano Chorio. Once in this village you may be confused by the maze of minor roads, but try to reach the village's eastern end, where a little church marks the beginning of our route. If you get lost, ask a native for the road to Thripti. Having managed to find the start of the dirt road set your trip odometer to zero and follow Road Book 11. Beyond Ano Chorio the road climbs abruptly to 500 m and offers a panoramic view of the vast olive grove covering the isthmus between Ierapetra and Pachia Ammos. Farther on you ride through one of the last remaining pine woods in Crete and soon you enter the mountain village of **Thripti**. To be exact, you come to a crossroads at the village's south and where you see a large walnut tree and a small blue sign bearing a white arrow that instructs you to turn left. If you wish to visit the village, heed the sign, otherwise keep on straight ahead to continue

16. Ierapetra-Zakros INLAND ROUTE

Route 16. The few dwellers of Thripti migrate up here in spring and summer to tend their vines, and in winter time they return to the lowlands, leaving their village totally uninhabited.

One of the rare permanent residents of this area is the large family of shepherd Manolis Vardas, who keep their hut and sheepfold two kilometres east of Thripti village, on the road to the village of Orino. Two parents, ten children, a hale and hearty grandfather, twenty beautiful sheepdogs and a flock of 400 sheep make a whole village by themselves! If you have room to spare in your luggage, stop and buy a head of **galotyri** (hard salty sheep's milk cheese that is cured for a month in small wicker baskets) or soft **mizithra** (low fat fresh white cheese made, naturally, of sheep's milk).

About 800 metres beyond this sheepfold (to the east) you will see a passable dirt road branching off to the right (south). This road was opened in 1993 and climbs to the peak of Thripti, Afendis Estavromenos (1,476 m). If you are lucky to be there on a clear day, **the view from the top is unlimited in all directions.**

ROUTES STARTING FROM IERAPETRA

Resuming your journey eastward you will soon reach the mountainous village of **Orino**. The cindery remains of the pine forest that once flourished here scar the landscape and your soul until you come to the village of **Stavrochori**. Here you head north on the asphalt road (A3) which offers enjoyable riding through the picturesque villages of Chrisopigi, Skordilo and Achladia, and ends at the village of **Piskokefalo**.

If you prefer to continue on tarmac, you can turn north at this point toward Sitia and proceed eastward following Route 21. Should you prefer, however, to enjoy dirt road routes on the magnificent Ziros Plateau, turn south. Until you reach the beginning of the dirt road you can enjoy sporty riding on the well-designed road (A2) up to the village of **Epano Episkopi**. Here you turn left (east) at the cross-roads that is posted with an English/Greek sign which says Ziros. This road (A4) is very dangerous as it is

Little Georgia was born, and now grows like a wild flower, on the mountains of Thripti

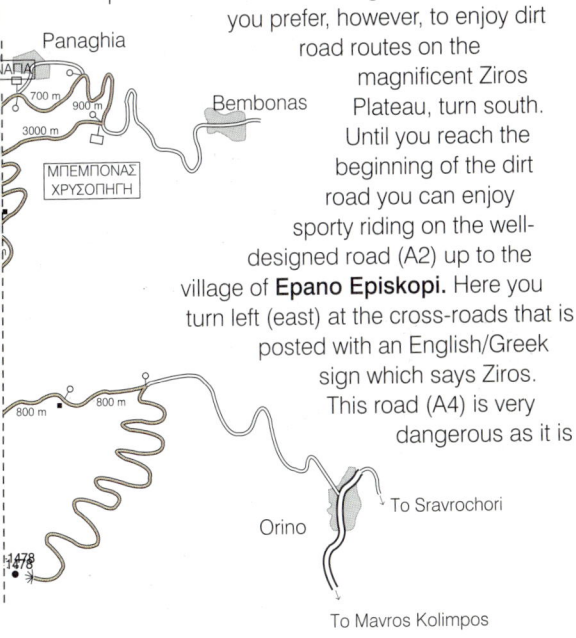

ROAD BOOK 11
Kavousi-Ano Chorio Mt. Thriptis

16. Ierapetra-Zakros INLAND ROUTE

narrow and full of tricky bends. As soon as you arrive at the village of **Nea Presos** you will see a large English/Greek sign marked "Praesos Archaeological Site" and pointing to a dirt road in a northerly direction. Ride through the village fields (small signs mark all junctions) and 1,800 metres later you will come upon a sign informing you that you have reached the archaeological site of Praesos.

Resuming your trip south from Nea Presos on the road (A3) toward **Chandras**, shortly before entering the latter village you will notice on your left the remains of a medieval settlement. Some 500 metres before Chandras a dirt road (D1) branches off to the left and

When the Achaeans came down to Crete in around 1450 BC, initially they clashed with the local Minoans but the two peoples were quickly reconciled and learned to live in harmony with each other. They tried, of course, to avoid intermarriage but in the end the two peoples influenced each other and in this way the Cretomycenaean civilisation developed. Around 1100 BC, however, the Dorians, a Greek race who knew how to use iron, began to invade Crete in waves. When we say 'use iron', we mean basically that they knew how to make deadly spears and swords with which they skewered their enemies, i.e. all those who were not Dorians. The Minoans realized that these invaders were not joking, like the last ones, and so they all packed their bags and moved to the most isolated corners of eastern Crete, hoping that the Dorians would not pursue them. Indeed, the Dorians left them in peace for many centuries and so, these final descendants of the Minoans, the so-called Eteokrites (i.e. authentic Cretans - eteos means true) got on with their lives enclosed in their traditions and their fortified towns.

The biggest Eteocretan city was Praisos. Built on the slopes between three hills (which were its acrop-

then left again at the next junction and leads directly to the ruins, although you can get to this point by riding through Chandras proper. Most houses of this medieval settlement have collapsed, but amongst them still proudly stands a tower, whose vaulted gate and first floor survive today, although not for long, as it has been abandoned to the ravages of time without the slightest maintenance. The only building that has enjoyed maintenance is the church of St. George (15th century) at the hilltop, with enough visible traces of its original frescoes. A bit north of the ghost village, next to the dirt road, lies its monumental stone fountain, cool water still flowing out.

ANCIENT PRAISOS

olis) with a strong wall completely surrounding it and with a fertile plain at its feet that was watered by a river with abundant waters (then called Didymos and today named Stomio), Praisos not only survived but also became stronger and gradually expanded the boundaries of the land it controlled. When at some stage these boundaries met the boundaries of Ierapetra, the biggest Doric city in eastern Crete, the conflict happened. The centre of the bitter claims was the Temple of Diktaios Dias (Zeus at Diktaio) (near the Palekastro of today, see page 504) which was claimed by a third city, Itanos (see page 502). This bickering of the three cities did not have a favourable ending for the Praisians. In 155 BC, the Ierapetrians captured their city and levelled it without a second thought. Those Praisians who were caught were sold into slavery in the slave markets of the East, while those who had time to get away settled in the area which is Sitia today.

The first person to excavate in the ruined city was the Italian archeologist, Federico Halberr, in 1884. Without much effort, since everything was there as the fleeing Praisians had left it, he found dozens of earthern idols, pots, tools, utensils and the first eteocretan inscription, a text written in the Greek alphabet but with completely incomprehensible words.

More extensive excavations were done later (in 1901) by the English School of Archeology under R.C. Bosanquet, and brought to light many houses and graves with valuable finds. Despite the importance of the site, only a very small part of ancient Praisos has been excavated. As you walk between its three acropoleis, at every step you will come upon fragments of pots strewn over the earth since the time when the Ierapytnian invaders broke them and scattered them 2,000 years ago.

From Chandras follow the only dirt road (D1) coursing in a north-easterly direction, in order to enter the **Ziros Plateau,** an isolated highland region hosting ten or so poor hamlets, ideal for off-road explorations. The road passes outside the village of Katelionas but it is worth detouring briefly just to travel back a century in time! Then you pass through the village of Sitanos, where again it is worth detouring on the dirt roads (D3) branching off to the east just to travel even further back in time to the era of Venetian rule, when villagers used to live isolated and self-reliant in the most inaccessible places, seeking peace and quiet. A little before the village of Karidi turn east. Following a wonderful landscape of strange solitary brown rocks, you will arrive at **Adravasti** village, destitute but proud of its traditions, from which you continue south towards Zakros (see page 506)

Four hundred years of history are supported by a crumpling

ROUTES STARTING FROM IERAPETRA

16. Ierapetra-Zakros
INLAND ROUTE

Iraklio

ROUTES STARTING FROM IRAKLIO

It is said that the fate of a city is determined by its geographical position. Fertile land, a protected natural harbour, a strategically important location are all factors that favour the establishment and development of a city. In the case of Iraklio, none of these factors apply, not even the basic ones like a water source or a fortified position. It was, however, the nearest point on the coast to Minoan Knossos, and this is why the Knossians founded a seaside settlement and a small harbour here, which they called **Iraklio**, obviously because there was a Temple of Heracles here. The wealth and merchandise which were loaded and unloaded here were simply passing trade, to and from Knossos. The unfortunate Iraklio remained throughout ancient times a poor, insignificant settlement which concerned nobody; no historian wrote about it, no important event happened here, and it was always in the heavy shadow of Knossos and of its other harbour, Amnisos.

After the destruction of Knossos, Iraklio continued to be inhabited but it never exceeded the size of a poor settlement. Perhaps this was the reason why it seems not to have been in the sights of the very many pirates who existed all those ancient centuries until the end of the First Byzantine Period (824 AD). Even its ancient name was forgotten and in some unknown period, probably at the beginning of the first Byzantine period, the name **Kastro** predominated.

All this applies up to **824 AD.** Because in that year, the Saracen Arabs, having conquered the whole of Crete, chose Kastro as their capital and base for their attacks, for what reason it is not known. They built a strong wall around the city and dug a deep trench on the outside. Their capital was named **Rabdh el Khandak** after this trench, as the words mean in Arabic 'The Castle with the Trench'. And so, totally unexpectedly, this tiny village which not even its neighbours knew became **the most renowned centre of piracy in the whole Mediterranean.** Tens of thousands of seamen and islanders who had been taken prisoners by the Saracens were sold into slavery in its slave market. Untold wealth accumulated in its treasuries and storehouses, the spoils of the greed of the bloodthirsty Saracens, who continued their robbing activities for 137 whole years!

In 961, after various unsuccessful attempts, the Byzantines, under their distinguished general **Nikiforos Fokas,** finally managed to free Crete from the Arabs and to corner them at the fortified **Chandakas** (as Rabdh el Khandak was called in the local language). The siege lasted for almost a year and ended in the triumphant entry of the besiegers, general slaughter of the besieged and total levelling of the city.

After his victory, Nikiforos Fokas decided arbitrarily to move the capital of now Byzantine Crete several kilometres to the south, to the safety of the hinterland. But the Cretans did not like the hill he chose and had started to build the new city on. As soon as Fokas returned to Constantinople, they returned to Chandaka, rebuilt it, repaired its walls and harbour ad persuaded the Byzantine colonists and the Administration to settle there themselves.

During the Second Byzantine Period (961-1204), Crete was a **Thema** (Byzantine province) and its governor had the title of **Duke.** The Byzantines made great attempts and actually managed to heal the wounds of the Arab conquest. Many Byzantine nobles came to settle in Chandaka (and throughout Crete); they made close ties with their new country and became the heads of the local Cretan aristocracy, acquiring enormous economic and political power as the years passed.

When the Crusaders overthrew the Byzantine Empire and divided up its lands (in 1204), Crete passed into the hands of the Venetians who appreciated the strategic position of Chandaka and there established the capital of the **Kingdom of Crete,** as they named their new province. Giacomo Tiepolo was appointed as the first Duke of Crete and his first job was to repair the Byzantine walls of Candaka, which was now called **Candia,** a name that soon prevailed throughout Crete. The biggest threat to the new rulers was the old Cretan aristocracy, which was not prepared to give up its privileges. When the Venetians pushed things very hard, the aristocracy stirred up the people to rebellion which was almost always successful. The Venetians then barricaded themselves inside Candia, negotiated peace terms (mainly the granting of privileges to the aristocrats) and life then continued normally.

Two hundred and fifty years passed in this way, during the course of which Candia became a big European city with splendid public buildings. The **Palazzo Ducale** was built at this time (the government house where the Duke and his Councillors were installed, based on the Venetian model) as were the **Church of St Mark,** and **Loggia** (the centre for the social events of the Venetian aristocracy), paved squares, fountains and much besides. Candia was called the **Venice of the East** and became the centre of the political, economic and artistic life of the Island. At the end of the sixteenth century, the Academy of Stravaganti was founded at Candia; this was a society of writers headed by Andreas Kornaros, who was possibly a relation of Vincenzo Kornaro who wrote the Erotokritos. Top artistic personalities of Candia were the painter **Michael Damaskinos** (the top representative of the Cretan school in iconography) and **Dominicos Theotokopoulos,** or **El Greco,** who was already a famous painter when he left his birthplace to work in Europe.

When the Turks appeared on the scene, however, and especially when they captured Constantinople, the Venetians realised that the threat was very serious and that the Turks would not be long in attacking Crete. Candia had already expanded a long way outside the Byzantine walls, which in any case were not capable of withstanding a serious siege. So they sent their best engineer, **Michele Sanmicheli,** who designed the most imposing and fortified walls ever built in any European city up to that date. Building of these walls began in 1402 and lasted for more than 100 years! To make possible the building of this gigantic wall, which was 3 kilometres long and had seven ramparts and four gates, all Cretans between 14 and 60 years of age who lived in the greater area of central Crete, worked like slaves for one week a year each, carrying stones from the quarry of Katsomba and also from the ruins of Knossos.

In 1645, the Turkish army landed in Crete (in the Chania area) and gradually captured the whole island except for the Capital. When they arrived in front of the mighty city walls, in May 1648, the Turks realised that it would not be an easy job to capture it, but they could never have imagined that they would have to struggle quite so hard; the siege lasted for **21 years without a break.**

On the one side, i.e. on the castle battlements, were lined up the Venetians, the Cretans and every so often various European armies and individual volunteers who were driven by religious zeal to join the fight against Islam. Around the walls was lined up the large mass of the Turkish army which threw itself into a merciless war to bring glory to the name of Mohammed by conquering and violently converting to Islam as many people as possible. From the early years of the siege, the Turks built an outside wall around the wall of Candia. Protected behind this fortification, they bombarded the city and undertook frenzied attacks on the walls. The walls were of course very strong, but their defenders were few and without many supplies. Their calls for help took a long time to be heard, as the Venetian motherland was also exhausted and had very little margin.

In 1660, i.e. in the twelfth year of the siege, the King of France, Louis XIV sent an expeditionary force of 4,000 men, but this was diverted to Naxos and Paros where it busied itself with terrible plunder! When it at last arrived in Crete, it avoided clashing with the powerful Turkish army outside the besieged capital. It shot a few cannons near

ROUTES STARTING FROM IRAKLIO

the castle of Chania just to look good and departed for France loaded with spoils from the plundered islands.

In the following year, 1661, the Venetians sent reinforcements of 3,000 men and a lot of supplies of armaments and food, and this raised the morale of the besieged people. In 1666, the Sultan furiously recalled the commanding general of besieging Forces, Hussein Pasha, and beheaded him for being responsible for the disgrace of the Turks in not being able to take the city all these years. In his place, he appointed his best general, **Ahmed Kioprouli Pasha**, but the Venetians also charged the defence to their best general, **Francesco Morozini**.

Kioprouli realised that he would never take the castle with his cannons alone, and that if he did not get results quickly, his head would also finish up on a stake because of the Sultan's anger. So he used the most effective weapon to have been invented until today - **gold.** "Since I cannot beat them with my cannons" thought the cunning Turk. "I shall buy their desertion and betrayal." Indeed, the wretched besieged people, who had on top of everything remained helpless, jumped from the walls one after the other, formed a queue outside Kioprouli's counting-house, took their reward and went their way! Some of them were seduced by the fat rewards which were offered for the giving of information (common betrayal) and revealed to the Turks where the weak spots in the wall were, where exactly to direct their cannons, etc. One of these, **Andreas Barotsis,** a colonel in the Engineers, became a permanent employee of the Turks and he was chiefly responsible for the final fall of the castle. Kioprouli spent money like water (around 700,000 gold coins!), but on 28 September 1669, he entered Candia in triumph. In a rare moment of magnanimity, he allowed the final remaining defenders to pack their bags and embark on the Venetian ships which had come to fetch them. The final blow, however, which did not come from the Turks was dealt by merciless Nature - a terrible storm sank most of the refugee ships with all hands, in the narrow strait between Crete and Kythira...

The Turks took possession of a ruined city without a living soul. Despite this, they decided to establish the capital of their new province there for the safety (tried and tested!) which the city's Venetian Walls would afford them. So their first job was to repair the damage to the wall; this work was done by - who else? - the wretched Cretans from the countryside. They later rebuilt the city based on the eastern concept of city planning, i.e. without any planning! The city, which was now called **Megalo Kastro** (Big Castle), was full of narrow alleyways and small houses clustered together and built in the way that suited each Turkish householder. Those churches which remained standing were converted straight away into mosques; anything Greek or Christian was frenziedly persecuted; anyone who persisted in resisting conversion to Islam ended up bound hand and foot in the squares where the executioners despatched them with various tormenting and degrading methods (they usually skinned them alive); and generally a thick darkness of misery covered the city where once arts and sciences had flowered. The first census taken by the Turks showed that only 800 Greeks lived in Megalo Castro.

When the 1821 Revolution broke out, the Turks replied with the mass slaughter of Christians, without discrimination as to age or sex, throughout Crete and of course in Megalo Kastro. The Great Slaughter however took place on **25 August 1898,** i.e. in the last year of the Turkish occupation of Crete. On that fatal day, the Turks pulled out their yataghans (sabres), they spilled out into the streets of Megalo Kastro and indiscriminately killed all the Christians they could find. In their rush however they made the Big Mistake - they also killed 17 British soldiers and the British Consul on the island. Only then were the Christian British moved (up to that point and right throughout Turkish Rule in Crete they had followed with indifference the slaughters of the Christian Greeks) and at last turned their guns on the Turks, putting an end to the dark period of Turkish Rule in Crete. Right from the early years of the period of the Autonomous Cretan State, the remaining inhabitants made serious attempts to restore the life of the city to normal. For a start, they restored its ancient name. **Iraklio,** although it was no longer the capital, was the centre of the biggest trading activity and of the most important intellectual and artistic life on the island. The energetic 'Educational Society of Iraklio' started off the first archaeological researches in the Knossos area, tried to preserve as many treasures as it could and laid the foundation for the establishment of the Archaeological Museum. A prosperous urban class gradually developed in Iraklio, many jobs were created (mainly in factories) which attracted people from the poor countryside. The city became full of people and a serious housing problem was created which was dealt with by arbitrarily building on every square centimetre of available land within the walls. Neighbourhoods rapidly expanded over a large area, outside the walls as well, and already by 1940, Iraklio had a population of 40,000.

It was then that the last invaders appeared from the skies, the crack German parachutists of the 7th Division who took only a few hours to capture Iraklio, which had previously been mercilessly bombed by the Stukas. When they left after four years (which is nothing compared with 460 yeas of occupation by the Venetians and 230 years under the Turks), they left behind them many dead Cretans and great destruction. Fortunately however, they cut down the chaff with the wheat as the German bombs destroyed the arbitrary housing that had been strangling the city, creating many open spaces which today have become roads and squares

The city was rebuilt more carefully this time, but again it was impossible to avoid the ugliness of the big city - dense housing, few parks, even fewer parking areas, noise and crowds. Despite all this, Iraklio is a neat, clean city with quite a lot of pedestrian streets and many signs in both Greek and English, which is a great help to visitors. The street signs even have an explanatory legend beneath the names! Iraklio today is the fifth biggest city in Greece (with a population of 120,000) and since 1971, it has been again the capital of Crete.

Eleftheriou Venizelou Square, which the locals call **Liondaria** (Lions), is the best point

to begin your tour of the city. In the centre of this small triangular square, the **Morozini Fountain (13)** has been preserved in its original position - this is the famous fountain which was built in 1628 by the Venetian Governor of the city, Francisco Morozini (a different person from the man who defended the city against the Turkish siege). This is the heart of the city, a meeting-place and the centre of traffic 24 hours a day. Most of the shops around the square are patisseries and cafeterias that are always full. Here you will find the celebrated bougatsa (a sweet pie) shop "Kir-Kor" which, truly, makes excellent bougatsa but serves tiny portions and charges a lot for. In the far part of the square are the little bars frequented by young people.

Directly opposite the Liondaria is the **Loggia (12),** the Society of Venetian nobles which today has been restored and houses the Town Hall's Council Chamber. **The Town Hall (4)** itself is housed in the restored building of the Venetian Barracks, next door to the Loggia.. Enclosed within the northern wall of the Town Hall is a sculpture which in the old days adorned another of the Venetians' fountains, the **Sangrento Fountain** that was situated at the north-west corner of the Loggia. Many years ago, opposite the Loggia and facing the Morozini fountain was the **Palazzo Ducale** (Ducal Palace), the seat of the Venetian Duke and his Council, a most elegant building of which nothing remains. The third building that completed the nucleus of Venetian Cadia was the **church of St. Mark (14)** built in 1239, i.e. in the very early years of Venetian rule. The Patron Saint of the Venetians had a very elegant church here in Candia, adorned with remarkable frescoes which of course the Turks destroyed while converting the building into a mosque. But, in 1915, Mohammed was evicted and the new owner (the Borough of Iraklio) restored it to its original form. Today it is used as a hall for exhibitions and functions.

Behind the Town Hall lies a lovely paved square, in the centre of which is the **church of St. Titus (15).** St Titus was a disciple of St. Paul, the first Bishop of Crete and patron saint of the island (but not a very effective one, judging by the sufferings the Cretans endured during the last fifteen centuries!.) The first church to be dedicated to him was in Gortyna, but the Arabs destroyed it in 824. When the Venetians threw out the Arabs and Chandaka was reborn, a magnificent church to St. Titus was built here at the end of the 10th century, as a replacement for the church that had been destroyed at Gortyna, where the seat of the Diocese of Crete and the relics of the Saint were transferred. When the Venetians came, they gave the Saint equal honours with their own official patron saint, St. Mark, in accordance with the proverb "don't put all your eggs in one basket!" Indeed, in 1363, they dared to give him fist place of honour - they lowered the flag of the Republic of St. Mark and raised onthe bell tower of the church the flag of the **Republic of St. Titus.** St. Mark and his faithful representative on earth (Venice) did not stand for this and they crushed such rebellion with terrible bloodshed. From that time on, St Titus moved into second place until 1670, when Turks dealt with him and made him unrecognisable. He kept his new name and role **(Vizir Mosque)** until 1923, when he passed again into Greek hands and all the Moslem alterations were removed. In 1966, after being given 300 years of hospitality in Christian Venice, the head of St. Titus returned to the church (and is exhibited today at a popular shrine.)

Opposite the Liontaria is the pedestrian Daedalus Street which has the best clothes shops in the city. This pedestrian road ends in Plateia Eleftherias (Freedom Square) where the **Archaeological Museum of Iraklio (8)** is situated. This museum was built between 1937-1940 on exactly the spot where the Catholic church of St. Francis used to be. This church was the jewel of Iraklio, the most magnificent ecclesiastical edifice built by the Venetians during all the years of their presence in Crete. It sustained great damage in the earthquake of 1508, but the Venetians restored it immediately. But when the Turks came, they allowed the church to fall into ruins and later took its stones to rebuild the Vizir Mosque (today's St. Titus). One part of the Church building remained standing, however, which was thoughtlessly demolished by the Greeks so that they could build the new museum. At the time it was built, the arhaeological museum of Iraklio was a building of high specifications. Today, it is a heavy, dark and graceless building, a real grave for the treasures it houses. Meagre lighting from neon lamps on the ceiling, antiquated show-cases with dusty exhibits, only a few inadequate explanatory plaques, no photographs, no reproductions and no drawings. The only answer is to knock it down and build another in its place, one worthy of housing the treasures of the Minoan civilization. If you come here in July or August, the thing that will tire you most are the crowds, every day and hour that the museum is open (Tuesday - Sunday 8am - 7pm; closed on Mondays). Even if you come here in a quieter month, you will need at least three visits and very good preparation to be able to see these treasures in the way you should. A good guide book is also absolutely essential (you wil find many in the museum shop), otherwise you will feel lost.

Directly opposite the museum is the **EOT (3)** (Greek Tourist Organisation) Information Office. From the Archaeological Museum, Beaufort Street takes you to the jetty where the coastal steamers dock **(7)** and the coast road, while Democratia Street comes out east of the walls and is the main road to Knossos. In the opposite direction from Democratia Street lies Dikaiosyni Street where the tourist police **(6)** and the police station **(5)** are situated. Behind the police station, on Zographou Street, is the Central Post Office of Iraklio. **(2).** 25th August Street goes past the front of the Liondaria; this street was so named in memory of the hundreds of Irakliots massacred by the Turks on 25th August 1898. If you follow this road, you come out on the **Square of 18 Englishmen** (also victims of the Turks that sad August) and now you are in the **Venetian Harbour (10).** The Venetian fortress **Rocca al Mare** stands proudly at the northern edge of the harbour. It was first built in the middle of the 13th century, but was destroyed in the earthquake of 1303. The building you see today was constructed in 1523, as the inscription over its entrance bears witness.

North of the Liondaria, diectly behind the shops on the square, is **Theotokopoulos (El**

ROUTES STARTING FROM IRAKLIO

Greco) **Park,** one of the few green corners inside the walls of Iraklio. The central offices of the OTE (Greek Telecommunications Organisation) **(1)** are here, and these are now used only by the locals to pay their telephone bills as, to make telephone calls (even long-distance) there are dozens of card phones in every corner of the city. Minotavrou Street begins here which, after a circuitous route, brings you to the **History and Folklore Museum** of Crete **(9)**.

The History museum is housed in a wonderful neoclassical house donated for this purpose in 1952 by **Andreas Kalokerinos,** a rich, distinguished Irakliot. This exceptional museum is a treasury of extremely precious historic objets d'art, which are exhibited in beautiful showcases with correct lighting and many explanatory plaques in both Greek and English. In direct contrast to the suffocating wretchedness of the Archaeological Museum, here you can take an exciting journey through history, from the first Byzantine years in Crete (330 AD) to the Second World War. You do not need a guide for this Museum. Just come as early in the morning as you can (it is open Monday - Friday from 9am to 5pm and Saturday, from 9 am to 2pm) to enjoy at your leisure this journey through history.

If you are interested in iconography, apart from the wonderful portable icons and the frescoes (removed from the walls) that you can see at the History Museum, it is worth seeing the icon collection of the Cretan School at the **Church of St. Catherine (16)**, which contains six works by the most famous iconographer of the 16th century, Michael Damaskinos. The church was built in the 15th century and it belonged to the Sinai monastery. It has great estates, thanks to which it was able to maintain a very active shool of Higher Education right throughout Venetian rule, And this turned out important theologians, philosophers, writers and painters. Vitzentzos Kornaros (the author of Erotokritos), Michael Damaskinos and Dominicos Theotokopoulos studied here.

In the same square you can see the bulky and rather graceless church of St. Minas, which is the seat of the Diocese of Crete. It was built at the end of the last century and it is said to hold 8,000 people. A rather nice little 17th Century church, also dedicated to St. Minas, continues to live in its heavy shadow, but unfortunately this is locked most of the time.

South of the Liontaria, 25th August Street ends after a few metres in Nikiforou Foka Square (it is not exactly a suare, but a traffic hub). From here you can walk to the pedestrian shopping street, **1866 Street**, to buy fresh fruit and Cretan products from the popular greengrocers and grocers, while on the neighbouring precincts (on the Grousouzadika as the loals call them) you can find many popular tavernas open from morning until late at night and serving charcoal-cooked meat and dishes stewed in flat pans. On the southern edge of 1866 street is Vitzentzou Kornarou Square. You can drink water here from the oldest fountain in Iraklio, the famoun Bembo Fountain (18), the work of the Venetian architect Zuanne Bembo in 1588, in which is embedded a headless statue of the Roman Period from Ierapetra. If you prefer a coffee or a soft drink, there is a monumental Turkish fountain next door that has been converted into a refreshment bar!

The most impressive monument in Iraklio, however, is its **Venetian Walls.** You can make your first visit on your motorcycle, by riding around the internal ring road which is made up of Beaufort, Pediados, Plastira and Makariou Streets. But it is better to leave your motorcycle and walk around or on top of the walls, to be able to see at close hand this gigantic work which has been preserved in excellent condition despite the savage waves of attaks it received for centuries. Stand for a little while on its south-west rampart (17), the Martinego rampart, as the Venetians called it, in front of the grave where **Nikos Kazantzakis** is buried (one of the top Greek writers, known throughout the world mainly for his novel "The Life and Times of Alexis Zorbas"). The following words are engraved on his plain gravestone column: "I hope for nothing, I fear nothing, I am free"

Paradoxically, to date there is no motorcyclists club in Iraklio, although the motorcycle market (repair shops, dealers,

ROUTES STARTING FROM IRAKLIO

accessory shops, etc.) is big and the city is full of motorcyclists. A group of motorcyclists, whose main activist is Dimitris Nikolidakis, has drawn up the charter of a club which is in the process of being formed, but up to now everything is "at the planning stage". The small cafeteria "Passatempo" performs the temporary functions of a club - this is on the first bend in Demokratias Avenue, immediately after you come out from the walls, two hundred metres from Eleftherias square. Most afternoons, you will find here Dimitris Nikolidakis, Yannis Ioakimidis, or Yannis Malliarakis, who will advise you about their area and help you with whatever you need. During shop-opening hours, you will find Yannis Ioakimidis in his shop (see list of helpful information, Triumph Dealer).

The offices of A.M.S. Iraklio (the Iraklio Association of Mountaineers and Skiers - Tel: 081-227-609) are at the third floor of 53 Dikaiosynis Street. Before you attempt an ascent to the summit of Psiloritis, it is better to ask for information and maps from the experienced Iraklio Mountaineers, who gather at their Association meeting-room daily between 8:30 - 10:30 pm except for Saturdays and Sundays. If you are lucky and happen to choose the days of one of their organised excursions, you will have the chance to use their new Refuge, "Prinos", on the eastern slopes of Psiloritis at a height of 1,100 m (the path starts at the village of Ano Asites). If you are a big hiking group, get in touch with them ten days in advance, so they can give you keys to the refuge and relevant instructions.

WHERE TO SLEEP

Iraklio is the biggest city in Crete, has the biggest harbour and the biggest airport on the island and is the main gate of entry and exit for visitors to the island. And yet it has less hotels than any other city or tourist area on the island. It seems that the famous archaeological museum of Iraklio and neighbouring Knossos are not sufficient reasons for anyone to stay in Iraklio. All the tourists, immediately after their arrival, go straight to the developed tourist resorts on the north coast, with their huge hotel complexes, mainly east of Iraklio at Limena Chersonisou and at Malia. As for the archaeological museum and Knossos, most people spend half a day, or at the most one day, just enough to say they have seen the wonders of the Minoan civilisation, and then return to their resorts and their bars. So very few are interested in staying in Iraklio that only few businessmen have invested their money in building hotels here. For this reason, most hotels in Iraklio are old, in bad condition and not worth the money. Rented rooms are almost non-existent and as for camping, the nearest site is 7 km west of the city.

ASTORIA Hotel
A class, open all year
141 rooms.
Eleftherias sq. 11
Tel: 081-229-002, fax: 081-229-078
The most expensive and luxurious hotel in the city, directly opposite the archaeological museum. No guarded parking.

ATLANTIS Hotel
A class, open all year
164 rooms.
Yghias 12
Tel: 081-229-103, fax: 081-226-265
The biggest luxury hotel in Iraklio, in a quite spot, with big rooms, a large lounge and facing a big park, but not the slightest parking space.

GALAXY Hotel
A class, open all year
140 rooms.
Demokratias Avenue 67
Tel: 081-238-812, fax: 081-232-157
A big hotel with luxury rooms and the largest swimming pool in Iraklio, but not the slightest parking space.

ATRION Hotel
B class, open all year
65 rooms.
K. Palaiologou 9
Tel: 081-229-225, fax: 081-223-292
Your best choice in Iraklio.
A newly built hotel in a very quiet street, although very near the city centre, with clean spacious rooms fully air-conditioned. The only hotel in town with underground garage.

ASTERION Hotel
B class, open all year
46 rooms.
Ikarou 50
Tel: 081-227-913, fax: 081-227-957

VERGINA Rooms to Let
Open all year
4 rooms
Chortatson 32
Tel: 081-242-739
If you manage to find a room here, you've hit the bull's eye!
These are neat, clean rooms in an old house, with a courtyard to park your bike in! It is very cheap, in a very quiet street, and in the city centre.

WHERE TO EAT

Iraklio is a large city of 120,000 people that is alive all year round and not just during the tourist season. If finding a good hotel is problematic here, the opposite is true of tavernas and restaurants; they are plentiful because they serve a lot of people, and they are good because they cater to demanding local clientele. All you need is a hearty appetite and Iraklio will satisfy even the most peculiar palates!

ROUTES STARTING FROM IRAKLIO

GIOVANI, restaurant
Korai Pedestrian Street
Only the name is Italian. The cuisine is international, the service is European and the delicacies are traditionally Cretan! Try lahanodolmades (stuffed cabbage leaves), arnaki klefliko (lamb baked in wood fire), fresh charcoal grilled fish, sea-urchin salad and the excellent saganaki (fried cheese). The owner, Yannis Katsarakis (known as Giovani), is personally responsible not only for the superb food but also for the exemplary renovation of the neo-classical building housing the restaurant.

TO KENTRIKON, all-night eatery
El Greco Park, on the first floor of the corner block of flats opposite the Loggia.
The night birds end up here for a hearty and cheap meal. Speciality: lamb's head, spaghetti, lettuce salad.

NIKOLOUDIS, all-night eatery
Corner of Papandreou and Knossou Streets
Steaming patsas (tripe) and boiled goat to soothe your stomach after the alcohol of the evening's revelling. For the night birds of western suburbs, Nikoloudis maintains a second eatery on the 3rd kilometre of the Iraklio-Rethimno road.

TRES JOLLIE, creperie
Aghiou Titou Street opposite the Loggia
Large, filling savoury crepes and rich sweet crepes served to standing customers.

IONIA, restaurant
Corner of Evans and Hatzimichali Yannari Streets
One of the oldest popular restaurants in town, open in the morning. You choose a favourite dish from the pans behind the glass display-case and in no time a good portion is on your table.

YAKOUMIS, restaurant
Fotiou 5 Street, in the market place
Casserole dishes are served here, too, but everybody comes to Yakoumis for the fantastic lambs' ribs and the tenderly succulent steaks.

LA BUSSOLA, Italian restaurant
Kyprou Square
Housed in a well-preserved neo-classical building, it serves excellent pasta dishes at reasonable prices.

NEW CHINA, Chinese restaurant
Korai Pedestrian Street
Typical Chinese restaurant; you will always find a table, you will be served promptly, you will eat well and you will get a reasonable bill.

EL AZTECA, Mexican restaurant
Agiostefaniton Street
The ambience is not the best, but the food is good, inexpensive and adequately Mexican!

IGLOO, ice creams
Eleftherias Square
From 9 a.m. to late evening, ice creams in a large variety of flavours and warm croissants.

KYRIAKOS, taverna
Dimokratias Ave. 53
This is a rather luxury restaurant than a tavern. Fillet of veal is the speciality

CHIAO, fast food restaurant
Directly opposite the Lions.
Good local fast food restaurant in the town centre.

TARTUFFO, pizzeria
Dimokratias Ave. 83
Simply, the best pizzeria in town.

LOUKOULOS, Italian restaurant
Korai Pedestrian Street
Housed in a brilliantly restored neo-classical building, this is the most luxurious restaurant in town. Expensive china, classical music, impeccable service, a rich cellar and delectable Italian cuisine. Pricey, but certainly worth the money.

MALANDRIS, taverna
Gr. Lambraki Square
Traditional tavern with large variety of casserole dishes. Renowned for charcoal grilled meats.

GOODY'S, fast food restaurant
Psaromiligon and Kantanoleon corner
The well-known and trusted national chain of fast food outlets in a large air-conditioned hall.

ENTERTAINMENT

Anyway you look at it, Irakliots are the cosmopolitans of Crete. Their city is full of beautifully designed bars, hangouts of the local young generation that enjoys itself with good music and lively spirits. Entertainment here is not industrialised as in the vast holiday resorts, i.e. no enormous discos playing deafening music here. Those desiring late night hubbub and squeeze go to Chersonisos, 20 km east of Iraklio, where they get plenty of that of course. In Iraklio, evening entertainment is based on agreeable ambience and quality music, not on pandemonium!

GUERNICA, bar
Andreou Kritis 2
The best rock music in town, in an old two-storey house that retains its elegance: wooden staircase, wooden ceiling, handmade tiles on the floors, spacious patio and balconies full of people in the summer, fireplace for the winter, marble topped tables, even a vintage telephone set!

NOTOS, AVGO, TO MILO TIS ERIDOS
Three cafe-bars next to each other, in the small square at the end of Korai Pedestrian Street.
Open morning to evening, with cool music. Here is the eastern end of the night life hub (the western end lies at the bars of Chandakos Street, while the centre is at Venizelou Square and the Lions).

ODEON, bar
Kantanoleon Street, at El Greco park.

BABEL, dancing club
Agiou Titou and Idomeneos Streets
Large continuous indoor space in two levels. Black colour everywhere, three bars, huge screen on which old films and videoclips are projected non-stop. Big crowds and lively dancing music.

TAKE FIVE, bar
Arkoleontos Street, at El Greco park

IDAION ANDRON, cafe-bar
Korai Pedestrian Street
Very well decorated space with an air of old-fashioned "kafeneio" in an old mansion.

ODYSSEIA, cafe-bar
Corner of Chandakos and Kalimeraki
Outdoor tables on a plot among blocks of flats. Open from morning for coffee, to late night for a quiet drink.

ROUTES STARTING FROM IRAKLIO

DE FACTO, cafe-bar
At the Lions
Its basic advantage is that it is located at the heart of the bustle, at Lions' Square, which becomes Iraklio's fashionable catwalk in the evening. Secure a good seat on time and watch the city's cream stroll by you!

TRAPEZA, dancing club
Dukos Beaufort 7
Huge building, easily accommodating 1,000 persons. International dancing music until midnight and then Greek music that makes all hell break loose!

JASMIN, tea shop
Agiostefaniton 6
Good variety of teas, pleasant jazz and rock music, relaxing atmosphere with many magazines to read and backgammon to play.

INDRIGA, UTOPIA, MAGEMENOS AVLOS
Three of the cafe-bars concentrated on Chandakos Street.
Very attractive ambience, good rock and jazz music. Open in the morning for a delicious (but very expensive) coffee, until late night when the crowds come! In summertime Chandakos Street is jammed with people.

TRIA TETARTA, dancing club
Theotokopoulou 1 and Sof. Venizelou
A neo-classical building on the corniche, full of frescoes, offers magnificent view to the port and dancing revelry each night with Greek music mainly. In the summer it moves to an open site on the opposite side of the street.

IRAKLIO

ROCCA AL MARE
11
10
SQ 18 AGLON
SOF. VENIZELOU
SQ KOUNTOURIOT
KOUNDOURIOTI
MITSOTAKI I.
MONIS ARKADIOU
LACHANA
MARINELI
KALOKERINOU
THEOTOKOPOULOU
THALITA
VIRONOS
GAZI ANTH.
GAZI ANTH.
GREVENON
CHANION
LOGIOU
AVGERI
CHORTATSON
KALIMERAKI
PALEOLOGOU
MINOTAVROU
KIDONIAS
EROTOKRITOU
ALMIROU
SQ PIREOS
25 ης AVGOUSTOU
PATER ANTONIOU
EVROPIS
KOTZIA
EPIMENIDOY
SAPFOUS
KORONEOU A.
KORONEOU A.
SQ EL GRECO
CHORTATSON
CHANTAKOS
AGHOSTEFANITON
ODOS 1770
KRITIS
VLASTON
CHARALAMBI
CHANDAKOS
KADANOLEON
SQ EL. VENIZELOU
TITOU
EVROPIS
IDOMENEOS
ARIADNIS
PASIFAIS
MALIKOUTI
IGIAS
BEAUFORT
MIRABELOU
ARETOUSIS
MELIDONIOU
XANTHOULIDOU
CHATZIDAKI
PERDIKARI
KORAI
MILATOU
DEDALOU
SQ FOKA NIK.
AGH. DEKA
ZAMBELIOU
GRAMVOUSIS
ABGIRAKI
MONIS ODIGITRIAS
DIKEOSSINIS
ELEFTHERIAS SQUARE
IKAROU
GIANNARI
FOTIOU
ODOS 1821
EVANS
KOSMON
ODOS 1866
KATECHAKI
KARTEROU
TSIKRITZ
SMIRNIS
KOZIRI
GOURDOU
ZOGRAFOU
SQ DASKALOGIANNI
AMALTHIAS
SQ ARKADIOU
BIZANIOU
SQ VITS. KORNAROU
AVEROF
RENIERI
ANOPOLEOS
DIMOKRATIA
PEDIADOS
VIKELA
GIANIKOU
MOUSOUROU
ALBER
LASITHIOU
VIANOU
EVANS
MILIARA M.
NOKOUSIOU P.
KRITOVOULIDOU
MACHERIOTI
GIABOUDI
GEROLA
ACHARNON
KALONADON
CHALIDON
PAGEOU
MITSA
PEDIADOS
LEBATOU
PLASTIRA
MICHELOGIANNI
CHAR. TRIKOUPI
DRAKONTOPOULOU
ATHINAS
DIMOKRATIAS
GERONIMAKI
TIRNAVOU
DIALIANI
ATH. DIAKOU
ATH. DIAKOU
MISONOS
CHAR. TRIKOUPI
ZERVOUDAKI
CHRISOSTOMOU
KARAGIANNI
MILIARAKI
KASTRINAKI
SGOUROMALINIS
STAVRAKAKI
KASOU
PETRAKI NIK.
PAPANDREOU G.
FOTAKI
GALI
ETHNIKIS ANDISTASI
ZALOGOU
SQ GR. LABRAKI
PAPANDREOU
APOLLONOS
MONIS ARETIOU
MAGANARIDON
KNOSSOU
SOLOMOU
DIMOKRATIAS
ITANOU
KAPODISTRIOU
SOLOMOU
NEAS IONIAS
KAPODISTRIOU
KONSTANDINIDI
APOLLONIOU RODIOU
PRAKTIKIDOU
MAVILI
FOKON
KASTRINAKI
SKOULA
SBOKOU

SQ KOUNTOURIOT

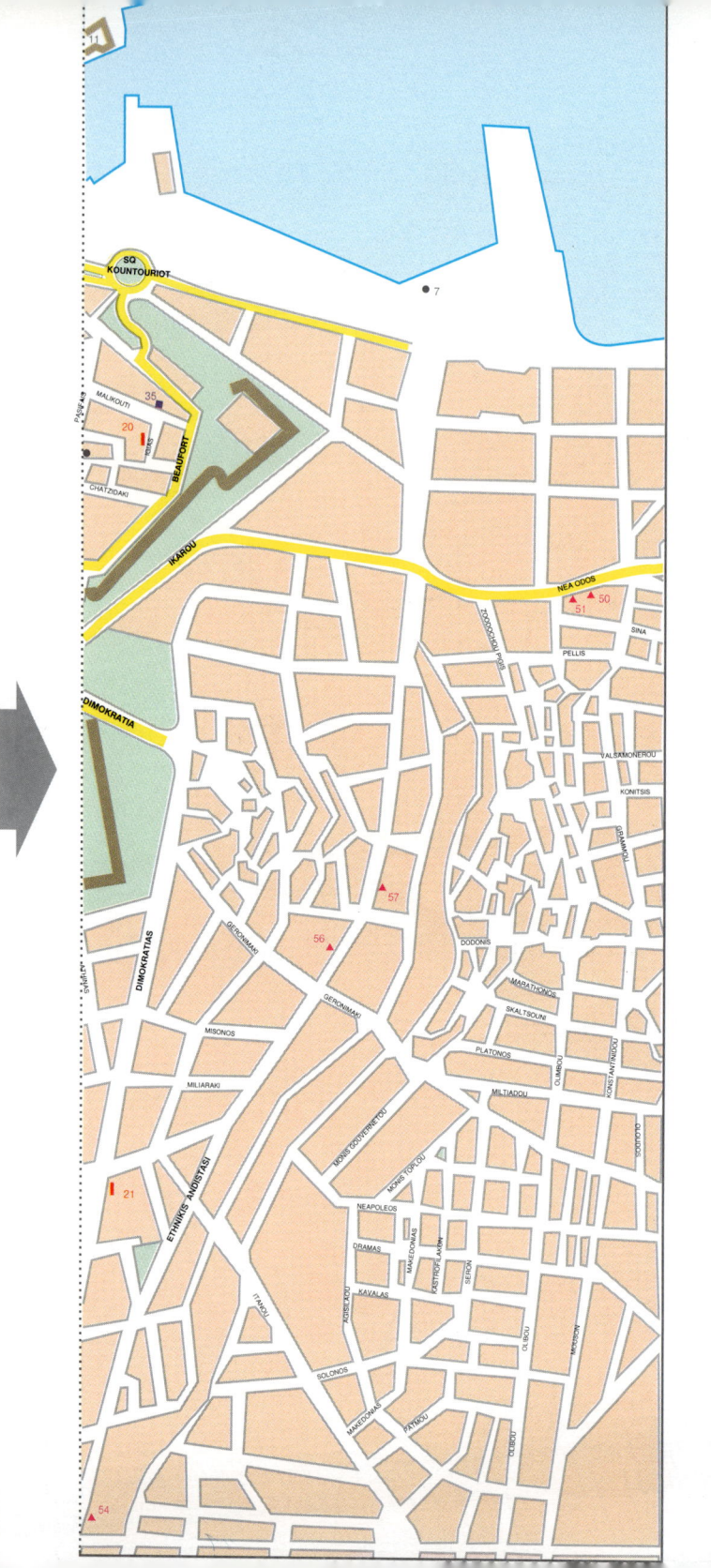

PASIFAI
MALIKOUTI
35
20
IDAS
CHATZIDAKI
BEAUFORT
IKAROU
NEA ODOS
51 50
SINA
PELLIS
TOSSOSKAI PYER
VALSAMONEROU
KONITSIS
GRAMMOU
DIMOKRATIA
57
56
GEFONIMAKI
DODONIS
MARATHONOS
SKALTSOUNI
STEFANOU
DIMOKRATIATTAS
MISONOS
GERONIMAKI
PLATONOS
OLIMBOU
KONSTANTINOU
MILTIADDOU
MILIARAKI
OLIMBOU
MORIS DOUVERNETOU
MORIS TOPLOU
21
ETHNIKIS ANDISTASI
NEAPOLEOS
MAKEDONAS
KRISTOPLAKIN
SIEROU
DRAMAS
ITANOU
AGISSILAOU
KAVALAS
OLIMBOU
MENEXION
SOLONOS
MAKEDONAS
FATINOU
OLIMBOU

54

KEY TO MAP

● MISCELLANEOUS

1. OTE (Telephone Service)
2. ELTA (Post Office)
3. TOURIST ORGANIZATION
4. TOWN HALL
5. POLICE
6. TOURIST POLICE
7. FERRY DOCK
8. ARCHAEOLOGICAL MUSEUM
9. HISTORICAL MUSEUM
10. VENETIAN HARBOUR
11. ROCCA AL MARE
12. LOGGIA
13. MOROZINI FOUNTAIN
14. ST. MARKO CHURCH
15. ST. TITOS CHURCH
16. ST. EKATERINI CHURCH
17. KAZANTZAKIS TOMB
18. BEBO FOUNTAIN
48. LAUNDRY
59. HOSPITAL

■ ACCOMODATION

19. ASTORIA
20. ATLANTIS
21. GALAXY
22. ATRION
23. VERGINA ROOMS

✱ WHERE TO EAT

24. LOUKOULOS
25. GIOVANNI
26. IONIA
27. GIAKOUMIS
28. NEW CHINA
29. EL AZTECA
30. NIKOLOUDIS
31. KEDRIKO
33. GOODY'S
34. IGLOO
35. CREPES TRES JOLLIE

■ ENTERTAINMENT

36. GUERNICA
37. ODISSIA
38. VAVEL
39. INDRIGA
40. OUTOPIA
41. MAGEMENOS AVLOS
42. IDEON ANDRON
43. NOTOS
44. AVGO
45. TO MILO TIS ERIDOS
46. DE FACTO

▲ MOTORCYCLE DEALERS

49. HONDA
50. YAMAHA
51. SUZUKI
52. KAWASAKI
53. HARLEY
54. TRIUMPH
55. CAGIVA
56. PIAGGIO
57. BMW

17. Iraklio -Rethimno

COASTAL ROAD

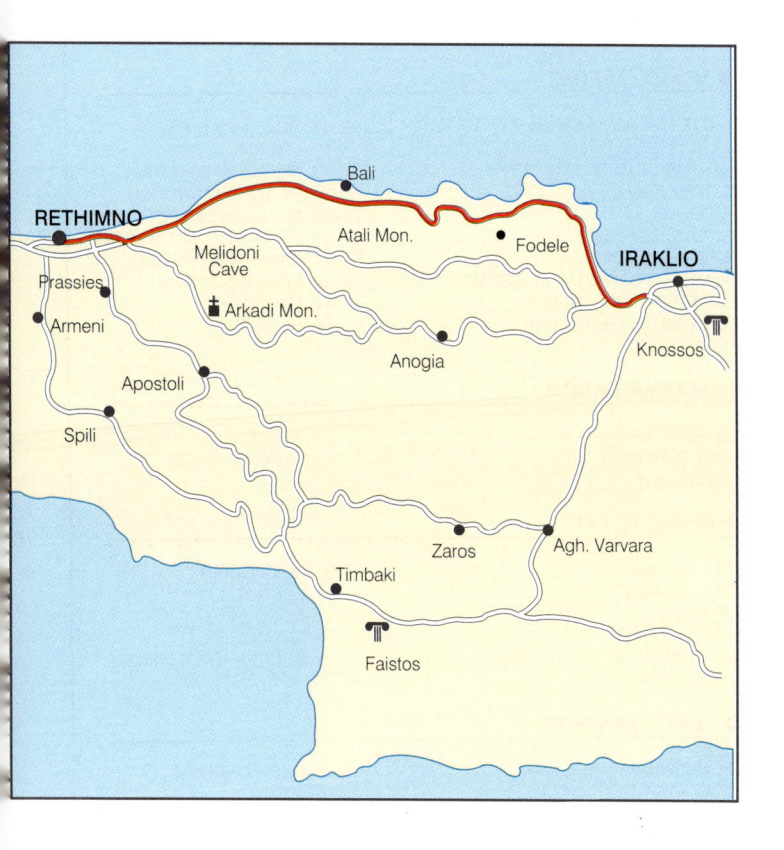

ROUTES STARTING FROM IRAKLIO

For those that love sport touring, Route 17 is the best Crete has to offer. The road (A2) is quite well designed; it does not suddenly get narrower, it has no dangerous turns or blind spots, and you can follow it without having to make detours. Admittedly, it is quite narrow - one main and one side lane per traffic direction - and has no parapet in the middle, but it still has what's essential for sport driving: **excellent asphalt and helpful signs.** The approximately 80 kilometres between Iraklio and Rethimno can be travelled in much less than 60 minutes. How much less depends on your motorcycle and the way you ride, but, in any case, do not test your limits if you have never travelled on this road before, because there are certain parts that may be dangerous if you do it.

Besides the thrill of speed, you will enjoy a very scenic ride between rows of oleanders with charming pink or white flowers. But though you drive very close to the coast, you will not find a single beach that's great for swimming. Nor will you see any remarkable sights, except perhaps for two or three places worth a stop, so you can turn up the gas and enjoy the feeling.

Leave Iraklio from the Hania gate and follow the Gr/E signs directing you to Hania and Rethimno - or leave from the gate of Knossos, follow the Knossos signs, and when you find the New National Road turn right and head for Rethimno.

As soon as you pass Cape Panagia, you will encounter the first of three roads branching off the main road and leading to the beaches of Aghia Pelagia and Ligaria. Ignore them and keep straight. Aghia Pelagia has lost its natural beauty, as year by year it was filled with hotels and restaurants crowded behind a narrow stretch of sand. As for Ligaria, the once peaceful beach that was the Iraklians' last hope for a nice swim, it is smaller than the Aghia Pelagia beach, and already it has been taken over by a large company that has dug up the hill behind it and is putting up a luxurious building complex with a 1200 room capacity...

The next intersection you will encounter has a Gr/E sign directing you to **Fodele** ("Fodele 3, Achlada 7"). The road goes through some orange groves and ends at the small village square which is usually full of buses and rented

17 - Iraklio-Rethimno COASTAL ROAD

cars. Fodele is visited by large crowds of tourists, because it is said to be the birthplace of the painter **Dominicos Theotokopoulos**, the famous **El Greco.** With so many visitors, the villagers should normally be rich. Wouldn't you be tempted by an old time coffee shop with a yard full of trees and orange juice squeezed out of fresh village oranges? Wouldn't you like to sit at a small restaurant with small hand-painted signs, chairs of straw and wooden tables covered with a simple check tablecloth? Wouldn't the idea of a well cooked mousaka or a refreshing peasant salad with fresh tomatoes appeal to you? And wouldn't you visit a small museum at the home where the famous El Greco was born? (Imagine an interesting collection of the painter's personal items, or at least an exhibition of typical everyday objects of his time). Well, instead of all this, here is what you are going to see: restaurants with plastic chairs and plastic signs; cafeterias full of idle old and young men sipping cafè frappè, practically the only thing served; and dozens of balconies with rows of cheap T-shirts with stupid slogans reaching almost down to the street, or with a "parade" of carpets with pink dolphins and other similar folk art items made in Hong Kong. The house where the painter is supposed to have been born is permanently locked, and the El Greco Museum that travel guides advertise is nothing but a room in the community office, also locked, containing a hastily put together collection of cheap, low-quality copies of El Greco's works together with some miserable-looking books spread out on a table. (If you wish to see it you must first pay a visit to *Kirà Marìa*, the lady who holds the key; her shop is about 100 metres away). Even the sign directing you to El Greco's home is rusty, and his name has been written with a spray! Just think: these people are supposed to live in a village honoured by a world-renowned painter of the 16th century, and they didn't bother to put a tasteful, painted sign outside his home. This fact alone is sufficient proof that **El Greco was not born here.**

Why come to Fodele then? For the wonderful **Byzantine church of the Holy Mary.** It dates from the 14th century, and it is built on the foundations of an earlier Christian church of the 8th century, which has also provided some of

ROUTES STARTING FROM IRAKLIO

The Byzantine church of the Holy Mary, dating from the 14th century

the building materials that went into the later church. You will see it on your right-hand side as you enter the village, situated next to the El Greco house and framed by orange trees. Unfortunately, this church is also permanently locked. However, you can see its excellent wall paintings from the window of the sanctuary, a window that belongs to the 8th century church and has two marble arches.

After the visit take the same way back and continue west on the National Road. At the next intersection that you'll see there is a road leading to **Sisses**, but the village is not worth visiting and neither is the beach at the end of the dirtroad

17. Iraklio-Rethimno COASTAL ROAD

(D3) that goes north of Sisses. Continue then to the west and treat yourself to a wonderful view of the north side of Mt. Koukoulonas and the rocky shore. The next intersection is to your right and if you turn you'll reach a seaside settlement named **Bali**. Bali in Turkish means honey, and the name reminds of old times when the area was known for its wonderful **honey.** Contrary to the sweet associations it brings to mind, the village has no exotic beaches or magic beauty; it is, in fact, a mish mash of hotels and restaurants lining a rather ugly beach. In classical antiquity this was the site of **Atali,** the seaport of Axos, a town of which nothing has survived.

A few hundred metres after the Bali intersection you'll see a road branching off to the left and a sign directing you to the "Holy

(closed between 12:00 and 4:00 p.m. and all day Friday).

We do not know exactly when the monastery was built. We do know that the first reported renovation was in 1635, when the Venetian rule of the island was almost at its end. Being in the middle of nowhere, the monastery served as an excellent refuge for rebels and outlaws all during the Venetian and Turkish rule. After the failure of the 1866 revolution, however, the Turks caught on, and they launched a fierce attack against all monasteries in the region. The historical Arkadi monastery went up in flames, and the Turks destroyed the monastery of John the Baptist and killed the monks. Half-ruined and forgotten, the monastery

ROUTES STARTING FROM IRAKLIO

Monastery Atalis Bali". The **monastery is dedicated to John the Baptist** and it is the first sight on our route that is worth visiting.

Once back on the National Road, continue straight for 1.5 km and turn left on the dirtroad that you'll see after you get out of a mountain pass and have a sudden open view to the west. There is no sign at the intersection to direct you, but the road leads to **Exandis**, the village you'll see to your left. At the heart of the village, opposite to the *kafenio* (where they serve fresh orange juice), turn left again on the road (A3) that leads to **Melidoni.** When you get there you'll see a sign directing you to the historical "Melidoni Cave"; turn right and follow the narrow cement path all the way to its entrance. The local guy that will try to sell you flashlights

HOLY MONASTERY ATALIS BALI

went on "living" until 1941, when the last of its monks died. In the forty years that followed, it was looted by men and ruined by the forces of Nature, so that it was no longer recognisable. In 1983, though, Father Anthimos came to live here, and aided by the Department of Byzantine Antiquities, the EOT and the faithful who never gave it up, he restored the monastery. Twelve years later, the outcome is incredible. Not only is it impossible to tell what condition the place was in, but the visit will charm you, especially if you treat yourself to a nice picnic in the shaded yard behind the church. Bring a snack, sit at the wooden table, and let your eyes wander over the sea. Father Anthimos will offer you cool water and refreshing apricots right from the tree.

17. Iraklio-Rethimno COASTAL ROAD

The monument in honour of the 350 who died in Melidoni Cave

and a personal tour is not worth the money he is asking, so refuse politely and proceed on your own. (You might want to give him two or three hundred drachmas, though, to keep an eye on your motorcycle). Do not get disappointed by the first one hundred metres and the rotting electricity wires that the Melidoni Community decided to hang inside the cave; a little further it gets really wonderful. The first hall you will find has a monument erected in honour of the **350** men, women and children who died in the cave in 1822, after the Turks discovered their hide-out and lit a fire to make them suffocate. From here you can continue either to the right (you'll reach the end of the east chamber that has a length of 35 metres) or to the left (until the end of the 30-metre chamber to the north).

Between Melidoni and Rethimno there is nothing special to see. After your visit to the cave you can simply continue southward, reach Perama, and turn right (west) on the Old National Road connecting Iraklio and Rethimno. This will take you to the coastal road, near the village of Stavromenos, from where you can continue straight to the town. Your best option, though, is to go back to Exandis, make a stop for another one of those great cheap orange juices, and get back on the coastal road at the same point you left it. From here to Rethimno, it is one fast, enjoyable ride without stops or detours.

ROUTES STARTING FROM IRAKLIO

17. Iraklio-Rethimno
COASTAL ROAD

18. Iraklio -Rethimno

TRAVELLING INLAND

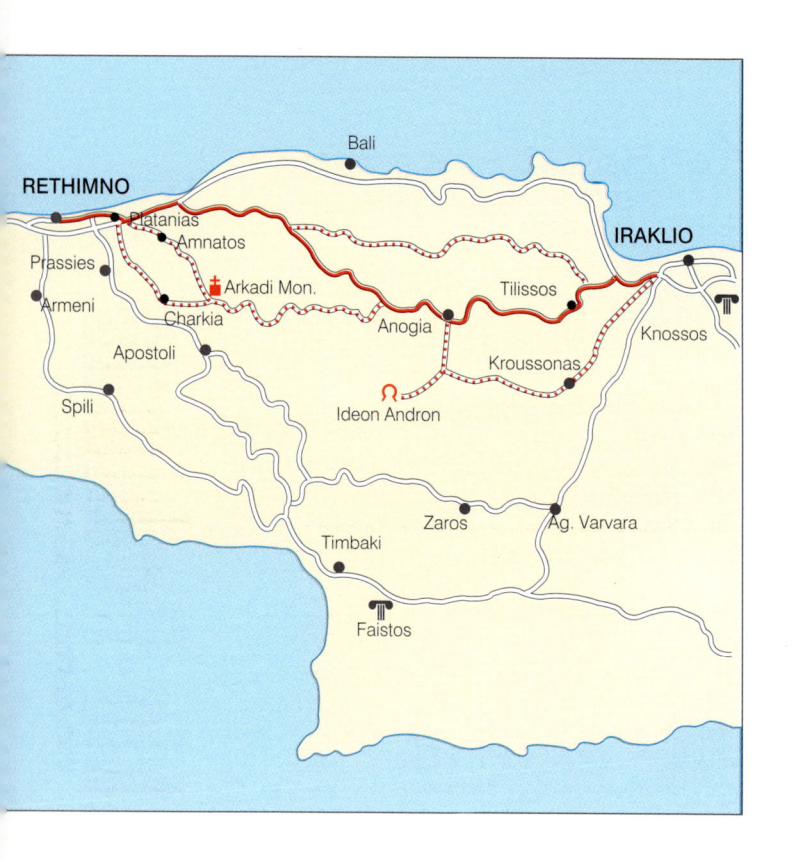

ROUTES STARTING FROM IRAKLIO

Between Iraklio and Rethimno there are hundreds of villages, small or large, perched on the north side of Mt. Psiloritis and connected with a rich network of roads (both asphalt and dirt). They offer many interesting opportunities to explore the area, and if you are not in a hurry you can treat yourself to some leisurely trips. (Speed lovers are reading the wrong chapter. Please go straight to Route 17!)

A classic and popular choice is the **Old National Road connecting Iraklio and Rethimno** (Route 18.1, A3/70 km). If you'd like to see more mountains, you might want to take the route that goes through Tilissos and **Anogia** (18.2, A3/85 km). Finally, for those that love dirtroads there is a third route (D2 - D3) which starts from Kroussonas and goes through the **Nida plateau** in the heart of Psiloritis. Just take your pick!

18.1 IRAKLIO- RETHIMNO (OLD NATIONAL ROAD)

After the construction of the New National Road connecting Iraklio and Rethimno one would expect that the old road would be left to its fate. Oddly, though, it was just the opposite; the State, to its credit, paved it with high-quality asphalt and keeps it in good condition, repairing it at regular intervals. The road is narrow and full of sharp turns and steep inclinations, which discourages most drivers of cars and tour buses from using it. For motorcyclists, however, it is a real pleasure, especially if your bike has a good grip on the asphalt. Of course, you cannot travel as fast as you would on the New National Road, but the route will reward you with many more sights and more interesting scenery.

Leave Iraklio from the Hania gate (west), pass Gazi, and go under the New National Road, following the Gr/E signs to "Rethimno, Old Road." You'll find yourself going uphill on a pleasant ride (A3) on the side of Mount Stroumboulas (800m). At a certain hairpin of the road you'll see on your right-hand side the *Voulismèno Alòni* ("sunk in threshing floor"), a crater with a one-hundred-metre diameter that was apparently formed by a meteorite crash or the collapse of a cave roof. Incidentally, the late Manos Hatzidakis, famous Greek composer, had proposed that the place be turned into an open-air theatre.

About 1 km later you'll see on your left-hand

The Stroumboulas plateau

side a dirtroad (D3) without any sign, which climbs toward the peak of Mount Stroumboulas. If you follow it you'll soon be at the idyllic **Stroumboulas plateau**, at an altitude of 500 metres, where you can pitch camp and enjoy the absolute stillness of the place. If you cross the plateau you will get back on the main road at Marathos or Damasta. However, you can also get back from the same road.

Approximately 1.5 km after Marathos you'll find a dirtroad (D1) which leads to Fodele in the north (see page 399). If you keep straight you'll travel through some beautiful mountain land and after a while you'll go down to the Milopotamos valley which is covered with fruit-bearing trees and vineyards. When you get to **Perama,** the largest village in the valley, you'll see a road that leads to the historical **Melidoni** cave in the north (page 403). This cave has beautiful stalactites that have remained almost intact, and it is easy to explore, even if you are a beginner, provided you have a couple of good flashlights and shoes that aren't slippery.

After Perama the road goes through the cultivated valley, taking you to Stavromenos where it meets the coastal road that leads to Rethimno. About 2 km west of Perama there is another road that goes to **Margarites** (a village known for its pottery), ancient Eleftherna and the monastery of Arkadi. This, however, is quite a big detour, and it is described in more detail in Route 18.2. If you are interested in archaeological sites and picturesque villages, you better take this route from the start.

18.2 IRAKLIO - RETHIMNO (THROUGH ANOGIA)

Start in the same way as Route 18.1, but about 4 km after the New National Road bridge turn left following the signs toward Tilissos and Anogia. After a trip through a fertile valley planted with vineyards and olive trees, you'll enter **Tilissos**, a village with a name that goes back 3500 years. To visit the ancient settlement that once stood here, follow the Gr/E signs that you'll see at the entrance of the village.

As you continue your trip to the west and leave Tilissos behind, you'll find yourself on a winding road that climbs the north side of Mt. Psiloritis. After going through the picturesque **Gonies,** a hamlet with a beautiful old neighbourhood, you will arrive at **Anogia,** a large, humming mountain village spread between two hills. Most visitors pass through this place on their way to Rethimno and Ideon Andron, and they see nothing more in it than a village with rather ugly houses and a lot of tourist shops. But Anogia is a place with history and character, with warm people and an excellent cuisine. It is indeed worth it to spend a night here, so you can have a chance to enjoy all this.

But it is also worth it to spend a night at the **Nida plateau,** 1400 metres above sea level, at the heart of Psiloritis. It is one of the largest and most secluded plateaus on the island and certainly the most beautiful. If you come around the beginning of spring you'll see it in all its glory, **covered with wild flowers in full bloom!** You can set up your tent anywhere you like and spend a truly magical evening under the light of the Galaxies that seems to caress the snow-capped mountain peaks. To get here, drive to the east entrance of Anogia and turn on the road (A3) that goes south and climbs the mountain. (There is a Gr/E sign at the intersection that says "Ideon Andron 21"). **The route itself offers a wonderful opportunity to travel on the mountains,** and though it has many sharp turns the asphalt is quite good.

The next morning you can get up and visit the **Ideon Andron,** the cave where Zeus grew up according to mythology (page 330), or, even better, try to get to the Holy Cross on the top of Psiloritis. (This is at a height of **2456 metres,** and

Some time around the turn of the century a farmer was digging his vineyard. Suddenly he struck something metal. Digging around the thing, he unearthed a huge bronze pot that weighed 50 kilos! Of course, such a large object could not have gone unnoticed. The news spread to the entire village and pretty soon the Department of Archaeology also got word of it. The archaeologists took over where the farmer left off, and, under the direction of Iossif **Hatzidakis,** they brought to light two more pots, large jars with colouring substances (red, yellow, blue, black etc), a bronze talent (ancient coin), and some clay tablets inscribed in Linear A. Here, then, was the treasury **(1, 2, 3)** of a Minoan home, the storeroom where everything precious was kept. The rest of the excavation revealed a building of impressive architecture, a **mansion** that must have served as the home of the local lord.

The mansion dates from about 1700 BC, the same time when the second palaces of Faistos and Knossos were built, and it was destroyed at about 1450 BC, apparently by the same cause that destroyed the palaces of these important Minoan cities. Scattered all over the island, the mansions of this period reflect a change in the social and political structure of the Minoan society. It seems that after the destruction of the first palaces in 1700 BC, the kings started to co-operate more closely with local lords in order to make their power more secure. These lords had their mansions around the important palace towns and on the streets connecting these towns between them and with their seaports.

House C

House B

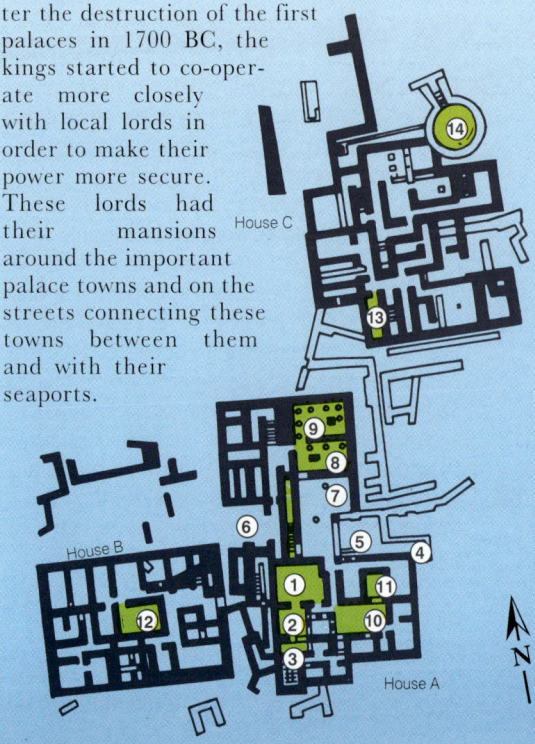

House A

THE MINOAN SETTLEMENT OF TILISSOS

The lord of Tilissos lived in a comfortable - even luxurious - house, apparently with two (or three) storeys. We can walk on the same stones as he did and follow his progress from the main gate **(4)** to the paved inner courtyard **(5)** and the staircase **(6)** that led to his private quarters in the upper floor. (The first seven steps have survived to this day). Based on evidence found on the ground floor, we can picture these quarters with large windows and beautiful wall frescos.

As we go around the place we can visit the lord's storage rooms **(7, 8, 9)** and touch the large jars he touched whenever he checked his provisions in oil, wine etc. We can sit at his living room, the so called *Mègaro* **(10)**, which due to the hot climate did not have a fireplace in its centre, and then go down the steps to his lustral basin **(11)**.

This mansion, labelled **House A,** was not the only one in the area. Just west of it, I. Hatzidakis discovered the foundations of a second mansion, **House B**, which was somewhat smaller but had an equally impressive architectural design, including of course the typical Megaro at the centre **(12)**. A third mansion, **House C,** situated north of House A, gave us fragments of remarkable frescos with floral designs **(13).** At the north end of House C there is a cistern **(14)**, which was used to collect the water that was transported there from a spring in Aghios Mamas (the same spring in fact on which the modern village relies!)

After the mansions were destroyed in 1450 BC, the place was inhabited by the Dorians, who arrived here and built their own, self-governed town. The town was named **Tilissos**, and in the following centuries it became so rich that it even minted its own coins. Unfortunately, we don't know yet where the ruins of the ancient Tilissos are buried, because there are no funds to continue the excavations and the entire region is covered with vineyards. Maybe one of the reasons why the red wine they produce tastes so great is that their roots are wrapped around the hidden treasures of the past...

you should count on eight hours to get there and walk back). Several dirtroads start from the plateau. One of them (D3) goes south, climbing down the mountain, but stops suddenly - and probably with no prospect to continue - just 1 km away from the road that starts from Vorizia, a village at the foot of Psiloritis' southern side. A second dirtroad (D3) goes northwest, leading to a ski resort, and at some point splits in two. A branch of it (D4) goes north, taking you through wooded mountain slopes and pasturelands, and meets the asphalt road a few kilometres east of Zoniana. However, it is not certain that you will find it in good condition, because it is used very little (having practically become a sheep path!), it is rarely repaired, and it can easily become impassable if there is a heavy downpour. It might be best, then, to return to Anogia the same way you came.

On your way back, you will see a dirtroad (D3) on your right-hand side, which starts about 1 km after the plateau and climbs Mt. Schinakas (1750 metres). A second road branches off to the right and takes you through the **wonderful Rouva forest** with its big holm-oaks, which seem to have been a permanent feature of the landscape since the ancient times. Unfortunately, the road stops here; had it continued for another two kilometres it would have met the road that starts from Gergeri and climbs to the south side of the forest. In general, you should know that there is no road starting from the plateau that can take you to the villages at the foot of the south side of the mountain.

The Nida plateau

ROUTES STARTING FROM IRAKLIO

Anogia

If you spent the night in your tent and the next day you climbed to the top of Psiloritis, you should treat yourself to a well deserved rest. In Anogia you will find many Rooms to Let, which, though far from being luxurious, will give you that "homey" feeling for a very low price. (This is especially true of the rooms in the lower neighbourhoods with the narrow alleys). The village is about 700 metres below the Nida plateau, but keep in mind that the nights are just as cool and you will need a blanket even in the heart of summer. If you've spent several days at the beach and have had enough of the heat, you may wish to stay here for a few more nights and enjoy the mountain temperatures.

What you're certain to enjoy more, though, is the villagers themselves. The Anogians form a closed mountain community with a traditional economy based on stockbreeding. Social structures have remained the same as in the past, and the people have their own distinct dialect and culture. They speak in their own curious way, with l's sounding more like r's, they use plenty of ancient Greek words, and they even swear in the name of Zeus! They receive their visitors with the same hospitality that Homer describes in his epics, they sing and dance and play music, and they have big parties that create a feeling of elation, second only to the celebrations of their ancient forefathers. The greatest Cretan singer, perhaps the greatest Greek singer, **Nikos Xylouris,** was born in this village. As for the local cuisine, it will offer you a unique glimpse of a world of Primeval Delight.

18. Iraklio-Rethimno TRAVELLING INLAND

Mt. Psiloritis features countless caves, sometimes with underground waters that form a marvellous decor

To get a good taste of it, go to the tavern of Manolis Pasparakis on the main road. It is called **Ο Αετός (The Eagle)**, and it is the first tavern you will see on your left-hand side as you enter the village from the east. The small wooden sign of the tavern is not so easy to spot, but the Greek "barbecue" out on the pavement will tell you that you're at the right place. The way Manolis cooks the meat must not be very different from the way it was prepared by the cave dwellers of the past. He cuts (or tears!) the meat in large chunks, spits it, secures the spits around the three sides of the barbecue, and allows it to cook slowly over the fire that he lights in the centre with dry holly wood. (Incidentally, the meat is of his own production). Even the poor chicken taste like wild pheasants, while the steaks are a true delight and the lamb chops will be a memorable experience. As for the sausages (also of Manolis's own production), you will need many glasses of strong red wine to recover from their "explosive" taste and aroma. Along with the meat, you will be served crunchy French fries, cucumber-and-olive salad with aromatic olive oil, and **apaki,** smoked ham kept in brine and vinegar and served slightly fried. Admittedly, during the high season a big part of the magic is lost, because Manolis has to cope with too many hungry tourists demanding service at the same time. But if you happen to come off-season you will have an experience to remember all your life.

ROUTES STARTING FROM IRAKLIO

If you are interested in caves, Psiloritis is a true paradise. Besides the well known tourist sights - Ideon Andron and the Kamares cave (page 330) there are hundreds of other small or large caves and chasms on the limestone body of Psiloritis. For detailed speleological info, look up Lykourgos Vrentzos in Anogia. The son of a shepherd and a member of the Speleological Society of Iraklio, Lykourgos knows the caves in the area like the back of his hand.

The road (A3) after Anogia goes down the bare mountainside. As you continue your trip and head west, you will find a second road to your right after a few kilometres, which leads to the village of Axos. (There is a Gr/E sign at the intersection directing you there). Axos is visited by all tourist groups that come here in buses or rented jeeps, so you can expect a good many restaurants and tourist shops with "folk art" that spoil the picture. If, however, you happen to come in the off-season, you will get to enjoy a picturesque hamlet with many Byzantine churches that go back to the 13th or 14th century. At the south entrance of the village, right behind the Byzantine church of Aghia Irini, you will see a footpath. If you follow it for 400 metres or so (5 - 6 minutes of walking), it will take you to the scarce ruins of the ancient town of **Axos.**

Axos was founded by the native Cretans, the **Eteocretans,** who fled to the mountains under the pressure of the Dorian invasion that took place around 1100 BC. The Italian archaeologists who excavated the area in 1899 found a wonderful bronze helmet (now at the Archaeological Museum of Iraklio) and the foundations of an archaic temple that was probably dedicated to Athena, the war goddess with the helmet. With such relentless pressure they had to face, the poor Eteocretans may have even **slept** with their helmets on!

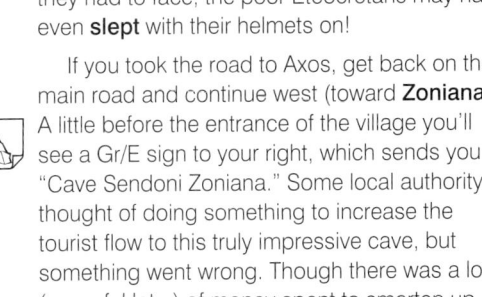

If you took the road to Axos, get back on the main road and continue west (toward **Zoniana**). A little before the entrance of the village you'll see a Gr/E sign to your right, which sends you to "Cave Sendoni Zoniana." Some local authority thought of doing something to increase the tourist flow to this truly impressive cave, but something went wrong. Though there was a lot (an awful lot...) of money spent to smarten up the area outside the cave and build a nice kiosk, everything has been left to its fate and is now falling apart. What's worse, this is not due to any understandable reasons but to red tape and miscommunication. Apparently, the community felt that it had to get a certain price from whoever rented and operated the new facilities, but no one offered to pay such a price. As a result, the community decided to close them down and let them fall apart, thus making it evident for one more time that the Greek Authorities are **totally incapable** of managing effectively the country's "capital" (be it its natural beauty, or the archaeological treasures that have come to light, or any other asset).

The Sendoni Cave served as a hide-out for the Greek fighters during the years of the Turkish rule, but luckily only the entrance area was used. In the largest part of the cave the stalactites have survived intact, offering a truly wondrous spectacle. The cave is one of the most beautiful on the island (at least among those that have been explored), but if you want to see it you

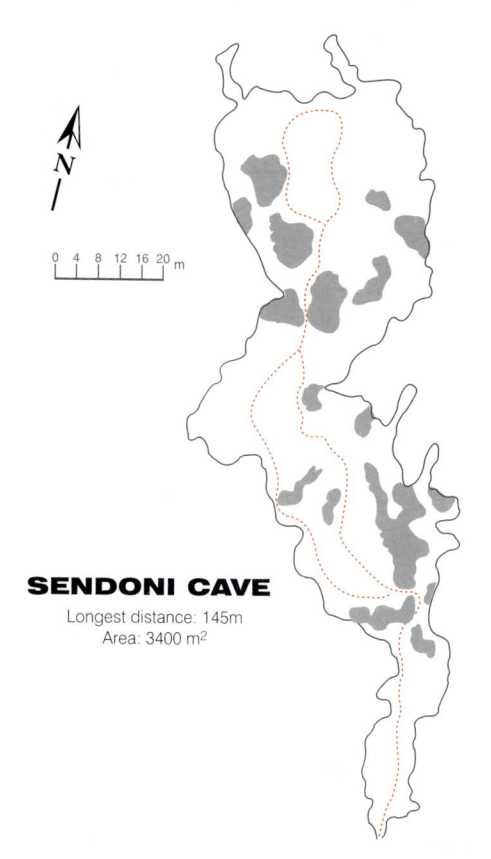

SENDONI CAVE

Longest distance: 145m
Area: 3400 m^2

must be very careful because it has several galleries and many slippery passes.

After Zoniana the road (A3) passes through some fifteen villages (practically one every one thousand metres). Some are large and ugly (like Livadia), some are large but attractive (like Kalivos and Aghios Ioannis), some are small and picturesque (like Kalamos and Passalites), and some are almost abandoned (like Kalandare). If you drive slow and make a few short stops on the way to visit some old churches and pottery workshops, you will see everything there is to see in the area. The next long stop is at the village of **Ancient Eleftherna,** where you can see the ruins of the ancient town after which the village was named. As you enter it you'll see a small square with a fountain and a road that starts there and goes to the right. (There is a Gr/E sign at the intersection that says "Antiquities"). After 200 metres or so the road stops before a tavern. On the right side of the tavern there is a footpath with a rusty old sign directing you to "Ancient Eleftherna." Take it and in three or four minutes you'll be walking among the ruins of the ancient town (see next page).

As you continue west of Ancient Eleftherna, you pass the ugly modern village and then turn left at the intersection with the signs directing you to the **Arkadi** Monastery (page 420). After the monastery you'll see a road (A3) on your right-hand side, which goes north, passes through some small villages - Amnatos, Kirianna, Loutra, Adele - and takes you to Rethimno, which you enter from the east. If you'd rather not follow this course, there is an alternative route to Rethimno that goes over the mountain, but this is part of route 18.3.

18.3 IRAKLIO - RETHIMNO (THROUGH THE WILD MOUNTAINS!)

If you like mountain dirtroads and have an off-road bike, Route 18.3 is the best way to get from Iraklio to Rethimno. It combines the best part of asphalt route 18.2 (Anogia - Arkadi monastery) with impressive rides on dirtroads at the beginning of the route (Kroussonas - Anogia) and at the end of it (Arkadi monastery - Rethimno). Incidentally, these rides can make excellent daytrips from Iraklio or Rethimno respectively.

Like an excellent sculptor, working patiently over a period of several millenniums, Nature has carved two deep ditches on the left and right side of a large rock of limestone. Her work was done with the use of two streams and the outcome was indeed spectacular. Highlighted between the two ditches, the rock projects against the sky like a huge Stone Boat. Its shape is oblong (with a length of 800 metres and a width of 200) and it has two pointed edges that are only 4 metres wide. No doubt, it must have seemed like a boat to the **Dorian** settlers who arrived here in their own ships some day in the early 10th century BC. These people left their boats at the north shore of Crete and walked through the valley until they came to this hill. Their decision to build a town here proved very wise, since the Stone Boat gave them a safe voyage through the centuries. At least it was safe until the 8th century AD, when the boat was sunk by the most blood-thirsty pirates ever to show their face in the Mediterranean, the Saracens.

The first people to inhabit the area, however, were not the Dorians. Much earlier than the Dorian settlement, in the Early Minoan period, it was inhabited by some people who built their huts here (but left nothing behind except for a few vase fragments). When the Dorians came along they built their own town, which they named **Eleftherna.** The name seems to reflect their great love for Freedom (*Eleftheria*), which they tried to safeguard with a strong wall made with large blocks of stone cut for this purpose. Thus they fortified their hill - which could not easily be taken in the first place - and made it almost immune to enemy attacks. At the south end of the hill, the only access to the fortified acropolis, they built a tall tower that has survived to this day, though its original form was altered during the Roman and Byzantine rule. The Dorians built their houses on the west and east side of the hill and in the valley with the two rivers that lies at its foot. At the time of its glory (that is, throughout Antiquity), the town was spread as far as the opposite hill, where the modern Eleftherna is built.

Most visitors simply walk around the level top of the hill. However, with the exception of the (admittedly) impressive tower and the passageway that's carved into the rock and leads to the acropolis entrance, there are very few things left to see here. To visit the most interesting ruins of the ancient town, take the narrow path that starts behind the chapel of Aghia Irini (at the west side of the acropolis), and walk toward the valley. The first thing you'll see is a couple of large and very impressive cisterns, which used to hold the water brought by a large aqueduct. Further down and close to the river bed, underneath the highest part of the acropolis,

ANCIENT ELEFTHERNA

Professor Nikos Stamboulides discovered an **archaic cemetery.** The evidence found here suggests that the townsfolk burned their dead, together with their personal items (jewellery, weapons etc) and the votive objects that accompanied them to the tomb. On certain special occasions, the burial ritual may have included human sacrifices, as suggested by a knife with a thirty-centimetre-long blade that was found in an unusual position, next to the neck of a dead person. After the archaic cemetery the footpath continues northward. About 500 metres later you'll see a big stone bridge with a triangular arch, which dates from the hellenistic period and reminds of similar Mycenaean structures.

These scattered - but significant - ruins of the ancient town are the most certain signs that, underneath the vineyards and olive groves of the fertile valley around the Stone Boat, there are many treasures to be found. Somewhere around here lie the foundations of the house of the famous **Diogenes the Physicist**, the ancient scientist whose views on Nature and cosmogony were so ahead of his time that they caused him to be exiled from his hometown. Somewhere around here lie the ruins of the ancient Agora, where the famous sculptor **Timochares** had his workshop. And it was in this same Agora that a nice young man named **Ametor** recited his love poems and played his guitar. Only twenty centimetres of soil cover the twenty centuries of glory of one of the most important Dorian towns in Crete...

THE ARKADI MONASTERY

As you continue west of Ancient Eleftherna, you pass the ugly modern village and then turn left at the intersection with the signs directing you to the Arkadi **Monastery.** This monastery is the most sacred symbol of the Cretan fight for independence. On November 9, **1866,** a Turkish army force of 15,000 men, led by Suleiman Bey and having ~30 cannons, besieged the monastery. Inside it were 350 armed rebels along with their wives and kids, a rough total of 1000 people. The battle that followed was entirely uneven and the rebels were doomed from the start. Still, they put up a fierce resistance against the Turks, who suffered heavy casualties. When the cannons knocked down the gate and the Turks rushed into the monastery, the rebels, along with their wives and kids, shut themselves inside the powder magazine. Hundreds of Turks gathered outside, never expecting what would happen next. When the courtyard was filled with Turks, one of the rebels set the powder barrels on fire, and the building went up in flames, sending some 1500 Turks to the Muslim paradise. Many of the street names you'll see in the Cretan towns and villages, especially on the main roads, belong to the protagonists of that tragic event. Among them were Hatzimichalis Giannaris, Gabriel the Abbot *(Ighoùmenos Ghavriìl)*, Giamboudakis, Yannis Demakopoulos and Giorgos Daskalakis.

After the liberation of the island, the monastery was rebuilt according to its original design, so what you see today must not differ much from the way it was then. In the small museum of the monastery you can see some wonderful icons and precious relics from the time of the holocaust. The architecture of the place, which reminds one of a fortress, the excellent maintenance of the buildings, and of course the History behind these walls are the primary reasons why the Arkadi monastery is at the top of all the travel offices' list. This is also the only drawback in visiting it: no matter what time you come, the monastery will be full of visitors.

Start as in Route 18.2, but right after the New National Road bridge turn left (south) following the Gr/E signs to **Kroussonas.** Keep following those signs at all the intersections you'll encounter as you travel through the fields. When you get to the village - or rather town(!) - of Kroussonas, pass through it, heading for its east exit where the road forks. Here you'll see a Gr/E sign that says "Ideon Andron" (Ιδαίον Άντρο) and "Holy Monastery of Aghia Irini" (Ιερά Μονή Αγίας Ειρήνης) and sends you to the right. Take the right road, then, and reset your counter, so you can follow **Road Book 10.**

Three kilometres past Kroussonas, after the indifferent monastery of Aghia Irini, the asphalt road ends before the gate of some institution for children. Here you'll see a dirtroad (D3), which goes left and climbs the mountain. One kilometre later (and after you've passed two more crossroads as shown in the Road Book), you'll find an intersection where you must make a choice. The road to the right climbs on the north side of Mt. Gournos (1295 metres) and offers a great view of the ravine below and the town of Iraklio in the north (at the end of the horizon). The road to the left goes inside the ravine and along the foot of Mt. Gournos (the south side of it), eventually taking you to a second intersection 3 km later, where you'll see a nice stone fountain. Here you have again two options.

The road to the left offers **a truly charming ride through the natural passes of a rocky and wooded area.** You will follow it for about 3.5 km, pass a couple of sheepfolds, and stop in front of a permanently locked fence gate, which marks the beginning of some community pastureland. Of course, you can bypass it from the right and keep going, but there is no reason to do so because the road stops anyway about 700 metres later, right in front of a shepherd's hut. On the other hand, the place where you run into the fence gate is indeed beautiful. Right next to the street, you'll find **a wonderful nook for camping, in fact one of the best in Crete.** In the heart of a quiet and secluded gully, with Mt. Schinakas (1750m) towering above it and plenty of trees shading it, is a nice area with a carpet of soft grass. The Forest Authorities have landscaped this area, adding some low, tasteful stone walls and a "barbecue corner." Wood is plentiful all around, water can be found at the fountain we mentioned earlier, and milk and cheese can be provided by the local shepherds.

Your second option at the intersection with the fountain is to go right. The road climbs the ravine that's at the foot of Mt. Gournos - at the southwest side of it, to be precise - and eventually meets a second road that comes from the north side of the mountain. The point where the two roads meet is at a cultivated plateau where you'll see two or three farmhouses and a few chapels. Then the road (always D3) continues in a westerly direction, passing through some mountain pasturelands with an occasional *mitàto* (traditional shepherd hut made of stone). It finally meets the Anogia - Nida road (an asphalt road) at a point marked by a shepherd hut and a nice stone chapel dedicated to Aghia Marina.

Here you have three options. No 1: You decide you have plenty of time to spend in the area, so you turn left and go to the **impressive Nida plateau.** You pitch camp, visit the Ideon Andron, and, why not, attempt to climb to the top of Psiloritis, 2456 metres above sea level. (For the above scenario see page 328). No 2: You are an

ROAD BOOK 10

Anogia-Kroussonas   Mt. Psiloritis

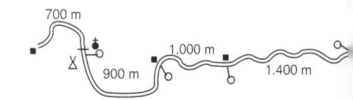

ROUTES STARTING FROM IRAKLIO

The Kroussonas - Anogia route, taking you through the ravine

experienced off-road driver with a light bike and an appetite for wild mountain rides, so you turn right, only to kiss the asphalt good bye after 200 metres and take the dirtroad that you'll see to your left. (You've certainly had enough of the asphalt!) The dirtroad will lead you to the **beautiful forest of Lake Roussa,** and from there on you'll try to find the road that takes you just out of Zoniana. (No, you cannot see it in the Road Book, because what good are the mountains without some adventure?) No 3: It is getting dark and you are starving to death, so you turn right and follow the asphalt road all the way to Anogia, where you go straight to the tavern ΑΕΤΟΣ (The Eagle, page 414).

From Anogia to the Arkadi monastery, Routes 18.3 and 18.2 are exactly the same, so follow the directions on pages 409-420. At the Arkadi monastery you'll see a road (A3) that goes north, passes through Amnatos, and takes you to Rethimno. This is the main artery

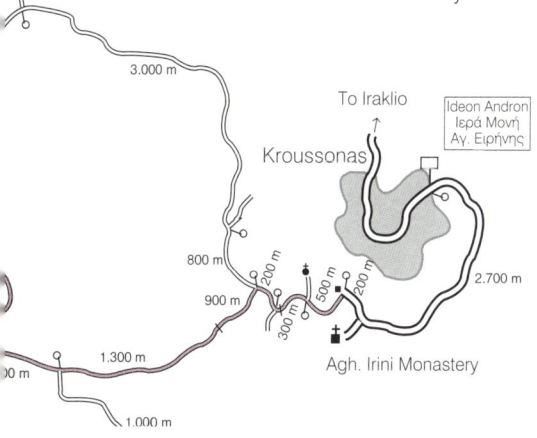

18. Iraklio-Rethimno TRAVELLING INLAND

The gorge to the north of the Pelopidas river, on the Arkadi - Charkia - Rethimno route

connecting Rethimno with the Arkadi monastery, and it is always full of buses and rented jeeps. You, however, do not like... consorting with buses, so you'll smartly avoid this road and turn left on the nice dirtroad (D3) that goes south (left) of the monastery. This scarcely used dirtroad, which at some point turns into a narrow asphalt strip, crosses a scarcely visited but very beautiful area covered with shrubs, and takes you to a couple of scarcely known but very picturesque villages, **Kavoussi** and **Charkia**.

About 50 metres before the south entrance of Charkia, turn left on the dirtroad (D3) that goes up the mountain. After 1000 metres you'll see an intersection where you turn right. (The left road stops in the middle of the fields). The road follows the south side of Mt. Gargani (650 metres) and offers a **spectacular view** of the fertile Pelopidas valley. About 2800 metres later, you'll see a second intersection. The left road goes down the mountain and over the river and meets the main artery connecting Rethimno and Amari (A3). The right one heads north and offers a very nice view of the valley from an approximate height of 500 metres. After 5 km or so it turns into a narrow, cement-paved road that goes downhill. This takes you to Platanias, which is practically the east suburb of Rethimno.

ROUTES STARTING FROM IRAKLIO

18. Iraklio-Rethimno
TRAVELLING INLAND

19. Iraklio-Agh. Nikolaos

COASTAL ROAD

19. Iraklio-Agh. Nikolaos COASTAL ROAD

The coastal national road from Iraklio to Aghios Nikolaos is wide, well-designed and ideal for fast riding. As far as Malia, it follows the coast closely and serves the island's biggest tourist area - this means that there is a lot of traffic and you shouldn't go too fast on this section of the road. It would also be better to avoid riding on this road at night, because it is full of Irakliot and foreign drivers going to Chersonisos for a night out or coming home from there, usually rather 'merry', if not inebriated, after a few drinks.

From Malia to Aghios Nikolaos, there is much less traffic on the road so you can accelerate with no trouble. Just after Malia, the road leaves the coast, going in a south-easterly direction, and runs along with the old Iraklio-Aghios Nikolaos road in the verdant Selinari ravine where you will enjoy a very spectacular route. At some point, you will see in front of you a huge wall of rock blocking the ravine on its south side. The old road climbs over the top, while the new one goes through the rock via a tunnel. As soon as you come out of the tunnel, you face the cultivated valley of Neopolis through which the road winds like a stream as it descents towards Aghios Nikolaos, crossing the old road over bridges and then running directly alongside it. Five or six kilometres before Aghios Nikolaos, you will see two European style petrol stations, the best in Crete, where it is worth making a stop for supplies and a bike check before entering the town.

If you don't want to ride all the distance in one go, there are many places along this route, worth at least a short visit, and some very interesting diversions.

First of all, there is **Amnisos,** one of the two harbours of Minoan Knossos, built on the coast at the foot of Mesovouni Hill, approximately 8 km east of Iraklio (there are Greek/English signs on both the old road and the new motorway that will lead you to the archaeological site). On the eastern slope of the hill, archaeologist Spyros Marinatos discovered in 1932 a luxurious Minoan villa dating back to 1600 BC, which was called the **Villa of Krinon** after the well-known fresco that was found here and is on exhibition today at

427

the Iraklio museum. At the foot of the hill on the north side, he found a smaller building which he called the Port Authority, and a little further to the west, an open-air temple with a large round altar, dedicated to Zeus. Due west of the altar are the remains of the jetty of the Minoan harbour, and today, these are sunken beneath the surface of the sea. King Idomeneas set off from here with his ships for the Trojan War, and Odysseus stopped here during his adventurous journey on his way back from Troy (Homer's Odyssey, T.188-89).

After 26 km is **Chersonisos,** the biggest and most organised summer resort in Crete. If you haven't been to Chersonisos, you don't know what chaos is. Mykonos is a girls' school, Rhodes a hermitage and Corfu a cemetery, by comparison! Just to list the bars and hotels in Chersonisos would take ten pages. But you don't need a guide or suggestions to find your way around in Chersonisos - **all** the buildings here are either bars, discotheques, hotels, restaurants or tourists shops. The choice is endless! There is also a wide, sandy beach at Chersonisos, but most of the people lying on the sand are not sunbathing but have simply fallen there flat out at dawn after the evening's revelries. All this is of course only in July and August, well, maybe up to the middle of September. After this, Chersonisos is like a deserted town.

It is rather improbable that you should want to visit Chersonisos for its history, but if you are interested in such things, you can see on the east side of the harbour right in front of the seaside bars, the remains of the jetty of Greco-Roman Chersonisos, then called **Cherronisos.** Only a few coins and scattered foundations of houses have been saved from the even older town (Cherronisos started off as the port of Lyttos). At the end of the small peninsula (chersonisos) (from which the town took its name) you can also see the foundations and the mosaic floor of a large basilica of the 5th century, and also the marble Christian Altar which was the lid of a Roman sarcophagus before it was recycled!

From an archaeological point of view, there are much more interesting things for you to see a few kilometres along the road at **Malia.** A huge

ROUTES STARTING FROM IRAKLIO

Drink flows endlessly at Chersonisos

tourist resort the same size as (and perhaps a little bigger than) Chersonisos has developed around the big sandy beach at Malia and is an open shrine to the goddess Enjoyment, with orgies of feasting and ecstatic dancing until morning! On its east side, however, far away from the noise and the crowds, are the ruins of an important Minoan palace whose name is not known and so it is called by convention **"The Palace of Malia"**.

THE PALACE OF MALIA
(Guarded archaeological site, open from 8.30 a.m. - 3.30 p.m. Closed on Mondays.)

One day around 1850, a villager from Vrahasi ploughing his field here, in the narrow fertile plain stretching between the sea and the mountain peak of Selena, saw something glittering in the freshly-turned earth. He picked it up and looked at it carefully. He may not have understood that it was a piece of Minoan jewellery, but he realised immediately that it was **gold** and therefore valuable. So he took it to the town and sold it to a goldsmith, who melted it down to make his own jewellery with the gold...

The villager became rich overnight, but the secret got out just as quickly. The place, which was named **Hrisolakkos** (golden hole) after the treasures it was hiding, filled up with illegal excavators. The gold objects they found had a value for them that was totally financial and not at all archaeological. So most of them ended up in the goldsmiths' furnaces as a raw material, although a few were sold to foreign antiquities smugglers who, in this particular case, must be considered as benefactors as

19. Iraklio-Agh. Nikolaos COASTAL ROAD

they saved unique treasures from certain destruction. It is considered probable that the "Treasure of Aegina", today to be found in the British Museum, originated from here.

Sixty-five years later, when not even a stone was left in its place at Hrisolakkos, the Archaeological Service learned the news. It purchased the violated land in 1915 and immediately began excavations under the leadership of the archaeologist I. Hatzidakis. After seven years of systematic work, a wonderful Minoan Palace came to light, totally plundered but in good condition.

The Palace of Malia (whose ancient name remains unknown) has absolutely the same proportions as the palaces of Knossos and Phaestos. It was built in around 1900 BC,

The palace at Malia

suffered great damage in the earthquake of 1700 BC but was rebuilt more splendidly than before, and was completely destroyed in around 1450 BC. It developed around a large, paved Central Courtyard **(1)** with an orientation from north-east to southwest. The main entrance to the palace was to the south **(2)** and you too will go in this way, but there were also entrances to the east **(3)**, north **(4)** and west **(5)**. Of course it had large storehouses **(6)** where wine and oil were stored in enormous jars, whereas grains and other cereals were probably kept in eight circular storehouses at the south-west corner of the palace **(7)**. The dining-room must have been on the upper floor, on the northern side of the Central Courtyard, above the area with the six big bases of the columns **(8)**. A narrow passage led to the northern courtyard **(9)**, from where another passage ended up at the Royal Apartments Complex **(10)**. A spacious room on the west side of the Central Courtyard **(11)** must have been the feasting area while directly behind this was the Temple of the Palace **(12)**, and further back still was probably one of the kitchens **(13)**. Directly north of these rooms was the magnificent staircase **(14)** which ascended to the apartments on the upper floor. In the south-west corner of the Central Courtyard, you will see the first four steps of an even wider staircase **(15)** that probably served in sacred ceremonies because next to it was found a **kernos,** i.e. a round, wide stone with 34 sculptured cavities of various diameters where they probably placed (as an offering to the deity?) the first fruits of the harvest.

A large and seemingly rich city grew up around the palace, with many craftsmen,

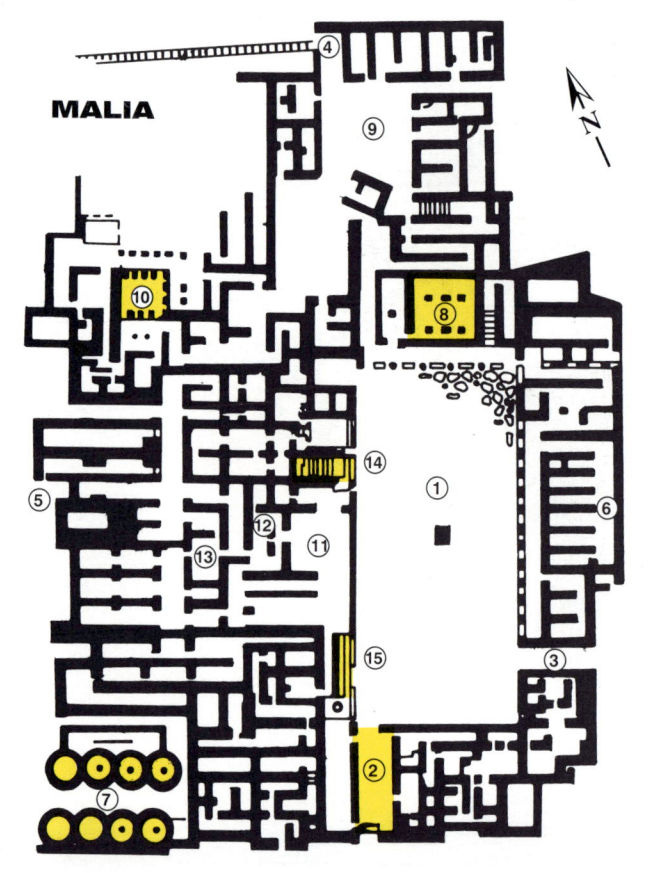

MALIA

ROUTES STARTING FROM IRAKLIO

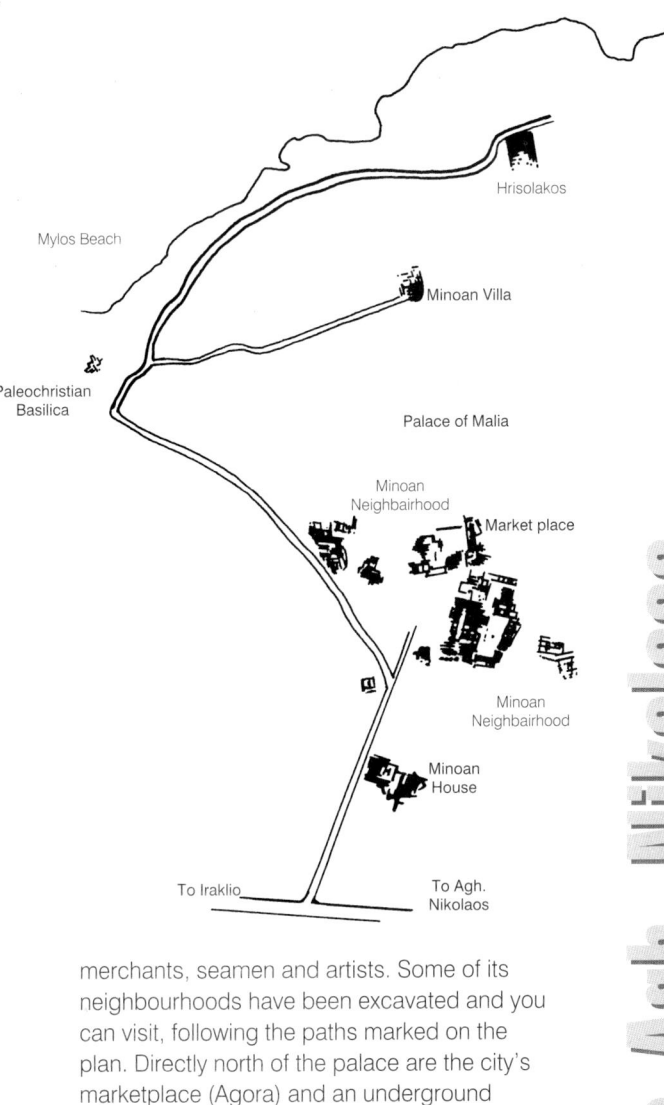

19. Iraklio-Agh. Nikolaos COASTAL ROAD

merchants, seamen and artists. Some of its neighbourhoods have been excavated and you can visit, following the paths marked on the plan. Directly north of the palace are the city's marketplace (Agora) and an underground building of unknown use which was named the Hypostyle Crypt, and was possibly a place for secret meetings. At the north-east edge of the archaeological site, isolated from the city's neighbourhoods, is the graveyard, the famous Hrisolakkos of the antiquities smugglers. A piece of jewellery that escaped them (the juxtaposed bees, see page 51) and was found by the French archaeologists who have been digging here from 1922 onwards, is enough to show the marvellous skill and aesthetics of the Minoan goldsmiths. You can admire them at the Iraklio Museum but you will also feel sad if also feel sad if you think how many other similar masterpieces were melted down in the furnaces of the antiquities smugglers...

West of Malia as far as the cape of Aghios Antonios and from there to Aghios Nikolaos, the coast is rocky and often precipitous and the hinterland behind is one of the few 'islets' where the real character of the Cretan soil survives. Just like the Vamos peninsula in the prefecture of Hania, this big triangular piece of land north of the road from Malia to Aghios Nikolaos has avoided tourist development because it is lucky enough not to have beaches and archaeological sites and to be situated in a corner outside the tourist routes. There is of course the jet set resort of Elounda on the east coast, but this is an isolated complex that does not affect the rest of the region. There are also the ruins of an important Minoan city, Driros, but this is near to Neopolis and most visitors don't go any further inland. Whichever road you take, you will go through picturesque villages, most of which are unfortunately semi-abandoned, and see impressive monasteries like the restored Moni Aretiou north of the village of Karidi, the ruined Moni **Xera Xyla,** whose cells have been taken over by a shepherd to use as a sheepfold (!), and the Monastery of Aghios Antonios on the Cape of Drepani. You will find few rooms to let in the poor villages, but you can stay at the village coffee-house for a

Elounda and Spinalonga, in the background. An extreme combination of luxury and wilderness

ROUTES STARTING FROM IRAKLIO

The Xera Xila Monastery

coffee or a very tasty plate of fried potatoes, and it is very likely that the taverna owner will find a room to put you up in for one night.

Elounda is the most 'jet set' holiday centre in Crete but without there being any special reason for this. The place is very dry, the coast is rocky, there is no airport or port nearby, neither is there any traditional or historic village that would act as a magnet. Just a few poor villagers lived here and struggled all year round with their olive trees, and they supplemented their income by extracting from the neighbouring hill a type of fine-grained emery, the so-called whetstone from which they made knife sharpeners. These poor people saw their barren fields acquire enormous value from the one day to the next when the first big hotel complexes started to be built. Today, some ten luxury and 'A' category hotels are gathered here, where the cheapest double room costs 30,000 Drachmas a night, and to stay in the most expensive, you will have to sell your motorcycle in order to walk over the threshold! It is completely improbable that you will want to stay here, but in the rare event you are on honeymoon or you've just won the lottery, we will mention some of them. Astir Palace Elounda (0841-41580), Elounda Mare (0841-41102), Elounda Ilion (0841-41703), Elounda Beach (0841-41412), Elounda Village (0841-802), Elounda Marmin (0841-41513). Elounda may not have even ten metres of beach worth speaking of, but it does have dozens of swimming pools, tennis courts and golf courses where you may meet

19. Iraklio-Agh. Nikolaos
COASTAL ROAD

select members of the financial and political aristocracy or even the Prime Minister in person! If you are an ordinary mortal, there are also some cheap rooms in Elounda, but it is not necessary to tell you how marginalised you will feel staying in these!

Directly opposite Elounda is the deserted island of **Spinaloga,** which many years ago was not an island but a peninsula that was joined by a narrow sandy isthmus to the opposite shore. The Greco-Roman city of **Olous** was built on this isthmus, but land subsidence sent it beneath the sea. Archaeological excavations have never taken place here and the only things you can see from ancient Olous (on a day when there are no waves) are some foundations of houses in the shallow water. The harbour at Spinaloga was the safest harbour in Crete not only because it was not hit by bad weather, but also because its only (at that time) northern entrance was protected by an impregnable fortress built by the Venetians in 1570. But at the beginning of this century, French seamen dug the canal which you can see today, separating Spinaloga from the mainland without there being any important reason for so doing, except perhaps their vanity in creating an island! Today there is a small bridge joining Elounda to Spinaloga. The only road on the island is a rough dirt road (D4) which goes through the bushes and ends up at a small pebbled beach on the east side, a rather inconvenient but quiet spot for rough camping. In order to see the fortress of Spinaloga (which is not actually on Spinaloga but on the small rocky islet of Kalydona, north of Spinaloga) you have to take a boat from Elounda or Aghios Nikolaos.

ROUTES STARTING FROM IRAKLIO

19. Iraklio-Agh. Nikolaos
COASTAL ROAD

20. Iraklio-Agh. Nikolaos

TRAVELLING INLAND

ROUTES STARTING FROM IRAKLIO

Since Evans discovered the ruins of the palace of Knossos, at the beginning of the century, there has not been a single visitor to Iraklio who has not gone up the hill to the archaeological site, if only for a short visit. With so much that has been written about Minoan Crete, everyone wants to see Knossos, the most important centre of the Minoan civilisation.

So leave the centre of Iraklio in a southerly direction, following the **narrow, slippery** road to Knossos (there are Greek/English road signs everywhere and you can't miss it). Ignore the various parking areas you will see some hundreds of metres before the archaeological site and park your motorcycle, free and safely, right outside the entrance to the archaeological site.

THE PALACE OF KNOSSOS

Close your eyes for a moment and try to imagine the palace of Knossos. A palace that surpassed in magnificence and luxury all other buildings in the whole of Europe of the Bronze Age. A palace of 22,000 square metres with 1,500 rooms and five floors at some points, two big paved courtyards, a theatre, an altar, storehouses and workshops. A palace built by clever architectural design which ensured coolness in the summer, warmth in the winter and abundant light in all its living quarters. A palace decorated with impressive frescoes, its columns and walls painted in bright colours.

Well, don't tax your brain too much because not even the most daring imagination can easily compete with the architectural inspiration of the people who designed this palace 3,500 to 4,000 years ago. If you could go back in time and see the palace from high up, what you would be faced with could not be too far removed from what you will see when you turn the page.

As with all palaces of all ages, so it is here, inside the luxurious bedrooms, the brilliant banqueting - rooms and the underground passages, scandals took place, compared with which, even present-day palace scandals pale into insignificance!

The first king to live in this palace was the fabulous, **Asterionas** and his wife **Europa** (whose adventures with Zeus we have referred to in the description of Gortyna, see page 296). The legendary **Minos** was born from the first sexual intercourse Europa had with Zeus. It seems that Zeus continued to be in love with Europa even after her marriage to Asterionas and he visited her whenever he had a chance. From these erotic meetings were born **Radamanthys** and **Sarpidonas.**

While they were young children, the three princes (whom Asterionas believed to be his own children) played happily in the courtyards and gardens of the palace. When they grew up, however, and the time came for one of them to take the throne after the death of Asterionas, they were at each other's throats!

The palace of Knossos

ROUTES STARTING FROM IRAKLIO

Minos, being the first-born, argued that he was the gods' favourite and consequently the kingdom belonged to him. And in order to prove it, he maintained that the gods would give him whatever he asked for. His brothers gave him a difficult one, to push him into a corner: 'Ask the gods to send you a white bull from the sea!' Minos prayed with all his heart to Poseidon, the god of the sea, to send him the bull, and promised that he would sacrifice it in his honour as soon as he took over the kingdom. Poseidon had no particular reason to grant Minos' request, but Zeus supported his first-born son by Europa at that critical moment and ordered Poseidon to send up immediately the most beautiful bull he had in his

20. Iraklio-Agh. Nikolaos
TRAVELLING INLAND

underwater stables. And so, before the amazed eyes of all who were sitting waiting on the rocks on the seashore, a very beautiful bull with a strong body and shining horns emerged from the sea and went to stand beside Minos. After this undoubted proof of divine favour, everyone went to his place - Minos to the royal throne of Knossos, Radamanthys and Sarpidonas into exile and the subjects to their houses. But the beautiful bull, instead of going straight to the altar to be sacrificed, was taken to the royal stables.

This obvious breach of promise on the part of Minos enraged Poseidon, who took the cruelest and craziest revenge - he made Minos' wife, **Pasiphae,** fall madly in love with the bull! Poor Pasiphae, who after all was not to blame for anything, was tormented for a long time unable to be released from her passion. In the end she sent for **Daedalus,** that clever craftsman and inventor from Athens who was then working at the Palace of Knossos, and begged him to help her get over the 'technical' difficulties of having sexual intercourse with the bull! Indeed, Daedalus made a wooden cow which was so perfect that it managed to fool the bull. After several trials (to make sure of the attractiveness and robustness of the construction!), Daedalus placed Pasiphae inside the hollow likeness and so the queen's passion was satisfied. Unfortunately, however, not without consequences - she became pregnant and after a while gave birth to the terrible **Minotaur,** a carnivorous monster with the body of a man but the head and strength of a bull. Minos tore out his hair in despair when heard the events he had caused to happen, but it was too late. He locked the Minotaur inside the dark **Labyrinth** (also the work of Daedalus), an underground complex of passages where no one who entered could find the way out. He imprisoned Daedalus and his son, Ikaros, in the palace; as for Pasiphae, he never wanted to see her again and took to pederasty and a debauched life with other women.

Despite all this, Minos was especially loved by his subjects thanks to his renowned justice and his wise laws. Personally, he

ROUTES STARTING FROM IRAKLIO

Baby Minotaur in his mother's arms, when he was still suckling milk and devouring Athenian youths

cannot have been particularly wise or just (judging by his behaviour to Poseidon), but his father, Zeus, helped him as much as he could. Every nine years, Minos met his father on Idaio Andro, where he took new laws and accepted instructions on the policies he should be following. So all Cretans feared him and respected him and agreed (voluntarily or by coercion) to submit to his authority. During the years of his rule, Crete knew its greatest prosperity. Under his leadership, Cretan ships plied the Mediterranean and expanded the power of Crete to many Aegean islands and to the opposite coast of Karia on the Asian continent.

Minos had many children by many women, but he had only eight legitimate children by Pasiphae. One of these, **Androgeos,** was an athlete of exceptional prowess. Having swept off all the prizes in all the local games, he went one day to Athens where he repeated his athletic triumphs and won all the events. He thought that nothing could stop him and he set off to go to neighbouring Thebes to take part in the games scheduled to take place there. But the defeated and humbled Athenian athletes stopped him in the most

20. Iraklio-Agh. Nikolaos

TRAVELLING INLAND

dishonourable way - they ambushed him just outside Athens and killed him.

When Minos was informed of the death of his beloved son, he went crazy. He immediately organised an expedition against Athens, laid siege to the city and eventually, with the help of the gods, he captured it. He then punished the barbarity of the Athenians with an even worse barbarity - he forced them to send seven young men and seven young women every year to Knossos, whom he threw into the Labyrinth to be eaten by the Minotaur.

One year, a brave volunteer went with the young people that were being sent for the Minotaur's dinner - it was **Theseus,** the son of the King of Athens, **Aegeas.** Theseus had great success in the difficult feat of exterminating wild beasts and all kinds of destructive forces and he was determined to go and kill the Minotaur and to release Athens from this unbearable tax. His father, naturally, was very worried and tried to deter him, but it was impossible to dissuade Theseus. He promised his father to be careful and that, if all went well, he would take down the ship's black sails on the journey home and hoist white ones.

Theseus did indeed manage to kill the Minotaur but he owed his achievement less to his strength (which was truly great) than to his blinding beauty! As soon as he set foot in the Palace of Knossos, one of Minos' daughters, the very beautiful **Ariadne,** saw him and fell in love with him. She ran immediately to Daedalus (who, as we have seen, was under house arrest) and asked him how she could save her beloved from the darkness of the Labyrinth and the jaws of the Minotaur. Daedalus told her to give him a ball of thread, the famous **Ariadne's Thread,** which he would unravel as he advanced through the tortuous passages and when, with the help of the gods, he had killed the Minotaur, he would wind it up again and would find himself at the exit (every pot-holer in the world still uses this self-same sure and simple tactic!).

So Theseus managed to kill the Minotaur, get out of the Labyrinth and set sail for Athens, taking with him Ariadne (whom, however, the ungrateful young man abandoned on Naxos several days later). When Minos heard about all this, he went crazy again. He realised that

Daedalus was once more responsible, and gave orders for him to be executed. But Daedalus suspected what was in store for him and did not sit around with his arms folded. He made wings for himself and for his son, Ikaros, and they escaped through the only available exit - the sky! Ikaros, excited by his first experience of flying (he was the first aviator on earth) made the stupid mistake (pilot error, we would say today) of flying very high, too near the sun, with the result that the wax holding his wings onto his back melted and he fell, broken, into the sea near the island which has borne his name ever since (Ikaria). Daedalus took a westerly route and landed at a secret base on Sicily, at the palace of King Cocalo.

When the guards announced Daedalus' spectacular escape to Minos, the king nearly went out of his mind with anger. He left the palace and his luxurious apartments, equipped ships and began an unprecedented manhunt to catch Daedalus and strangle him with his own hands. After a prolonged systematic search, he arrived at the city of Camico in Sicily, at the palace of king Cocalo where Daedalus was hiding. While the two kings were dining, Minos put into action the trick he believed would locate Daedalus - he placed on the table an empty snail shell that had a hole in the top, and asked Cocalo if he knew anyone who could pass a fine thread through the spirals of the shell. Cocalo took the shell and went to Daedalus' room to set him the problem. The unsuspecting Daedalus (for whom riddles like this were just a game) caught an ant, tied the thread onto it, put it into the hole and shortly afterwards, the ant came through the other side with the thread. Joyfully, Cocalo took the shell with the thread passed through it, to Minos. Minos was even more joyful, however, as he immediately realised that Daedalus was hiding nearby (he was the only person capable of solving such riddles so easily).

Daedalus heard Minos shaking with laughter and was terrified, but he kept his cool. When Minos went, after the meal, to have a bath, freshen up and think how to kill his hated enemy, Daedalus (who had fixed the plumbing) channelled hot tar down the pipes and killed Minos.

This was the black and inglorious end of the legendary king of Knossos. The end of King Aegeas (the father of Theseus), was nevertheless, equally black; he saw his son's ship returning from Crete with the black sails hoisted (because Theseus forgot to change them for white ones) and he fell into the deep black waters of the sea which was therefore called the Aegean sea, and was drowned.

These exciting stories about Minos, and many others that would require volumes to tell, were preserved in many ancient literary sources and have come down to us today, but until 100 years ago, everyone believed that they were sheer myths. Yet, an inspired and charismatic English archeologist, **Sir Arthur Evans,** had a feeling that there must be some historical truth surrounding king Minos. He came to Crete in 1894, located the area around the village of Makrytoichos (built on top of the ruins of Minoan Knossos, and so called because of a long stone wall which had been preserved since the time of Roman Knossos), bought a very large piece of land and, in **1900,** began excavations. By 1906, the ruins of the magnificent Minoan palace and many Minoan treasures had come to surface - you can admire these treasures today at the Archaeological Museum in Iraklio. The excavations continued until 1939 and, from then until today, many supplementary excavations have been carried out by famous archaeologists like Duncan Mckenzie and J.D.S. Pendlebury, who have uncovered sections of the great Minoan city built around the palace, as well as sections of the city's graveyard.

Although the excavations went very deep, as far as the levels of the first habitation of the region, which it is estimated dates back to 6000 BC, the legendary **Labyrinth** was not found. However, when you walk among the ruins of Knossos, you will feel completely lost and you will agree that the Labyrinth was the palace itself, with its hundreds of rooms and its endless passages. The ancient Cretans themselves gave the name of Labyrinth to the palace of Knossos, a name etymologically associated with the word **Labrys,** which means Double-Headed Axe (the holy symbol of the Minoans,

ROUTES STARTING FROM IRAKLIO

The snake goddess, found at Knossos and now housed at the Iraklio Museum.

20. Iraklio-Agh. Nikolaos
TRAVELLING INLAND

with which the palace was decorated). Even in Minoan times, when the palace was at the height of its glory, it was impossible for a stranger to visit without an experienced guide. Today, when the ruins of many floors coexist on the same site with the various stages of architectural development of the palace, only if you are accompanied by an experienced archaeologist and after serious study, can you walk through the archaeological site and understand what you are seeing and where you are. If, of course, you come here in July and

August, the intense heat and the crowds will make your movements even more difficult.

On the pretext of preserving the ruins, Evans gave in to the temptation of doing extensive restoration and reconstruction work, using concrete and other modern materials, a fact that provoked much comment about arbitrary and unscientific interference in such an important archaeological site. Evans, however, was a pioneer and (as happens with all pioneers) it is natural that wrong choices were made, which in no way lessen the total contribution and the enormous work of this man. It is a fact, nevertheless, that this restoration work will help you get an idea of the magnificence of this palace, much better than if you were just faced with the ruins.

In a few years, this time the business genius of the English, will make Evans' vision of the rebirth of Knossos materialise in the most impressive way. A company has already been formed under the name of "Minoan State", which will build an exact full-size replica of the palace and of the Minoan settlement at Knossos, on a 200 stremmata plot of land, not far from the real Knossos. The inspirers of and main investors in this fantastic project are famous archaeologists, architects, university professors, set designers, and big businessmen. As for the Greek businessmen and Government, once again they have proved

The archaeological site of Knossos.

to be coldly indifferent to investing in the cultural heritage and archaeological treasures available in their country. Actually, the 'Minoan State' company should have been a great investment, if not for the Ministry of Culture, then at least under its aegis, as part of a complete programme that would have included a corresponding "Mycenean State", "Macedonian State", "Byzantine State", etc.. Instead of this, the Government is not in a position to do even the basic, self-evident things in the real Minoan State - in the archaeological site of Knossos, **there is not even a toilet for visitors,** and the staff are insufficient even for the most elementary protection of the site.

So until the "Minoan State" has been built, where everything connected with the Minoan civilisation will be intelligible even to small children, walk as you will through the archaeological site of Knossos and try to understand as much as you can, with the help of the reproduction, the topographical plan, and the short guide that follows.

Today's entrance brings you into the paved West Courtyard **(1)** which was first constructed around 2200 BC. In this courtyard, there are two "roads" separately paved. The north "road" **(1b)** used to lead to an entrance to the palace which was later closed, while to its left there are three pits **(2a, 2b, 2c)** where the Minoans used to throw their broken pots and other useless objects. Before the courtyard was built, there where several houses here which were levelled to the ground and covered up. You can make out their foundations on the floors of these pits. The south "road" **(1c)** leads you to the West Entrance **(3)**, from where the magnificent Processional Corridor **(4)** started - this used to lead to the interior of the palace and was decorated with wonderful frescoes depicting young men and women in ceremonial procession carrying offerings to the king/deity (the remains of the real frescoes are exhibited in the Archaeological museum of Iraklio). The biggest part of this corridor has disappeared due to land subsistence at this point. One leg of this corridor **(4b)** turned left and led to the Central Courtyard **(5)**, while just before this, another of its legs also turned left and led to the South Entrance **(6)** which was decorated with frescoes (the ones you see are copies), and from there to a wide staircase **(7)** which ascended to the luxurious apartments on the second floor.

On the second floor, immediately after the staircase, there was an Antechamber **(8)** that had two doors leading into the large Reception Room **(9)**. A small room on the south-eastern side of this room must have been the Central

THE PALACE OF KNOSSOS

ROUTES STARTING FROM IRAKLIO

Treasury of the palace **(10)** because on the ground floor below, many valuable vessels (rhyton) and other sacred utensils were found, which had obviously fallen from this room. An imposing staircase **(11)** to the east led to the Central Courtyard while a long open-air corridor **(12)** to the west led to two large rooms that were probably the Central Accounts Office of the palace **(13, 14)**, because on the ground floor area below, a very rich archive was found lying, comprising 1,400 tablets with accounts and commercial inventories in Linear B script.

Under the corridor of the upper floor was the long, dark corridor of storehouses **(15)**, west of which were the 21 Central Storehouses of the palace **(16)**, also dark and cool, where supplies of oil, wine, grain, olives and other products were stored in large earthware jars. Directly north of the Corridor of Storehouses, is a large Room **(17)** in the centre of which there a Purification Basin. Here, foreign visitors to the palace who came along the northern Royal Road **(18)** washed their bodies with water and anointed them with oil (the earthware vessels which held the oil were found at the spot). If they were official guests or nobles, they must have organised some sort of welcome for them in the open-air theatre **(19)**. After this, they went through the North Entrance **(20)** from where a long corridor **(21)** which was decorated with wonderful frescoes led into the Central Courtyard.

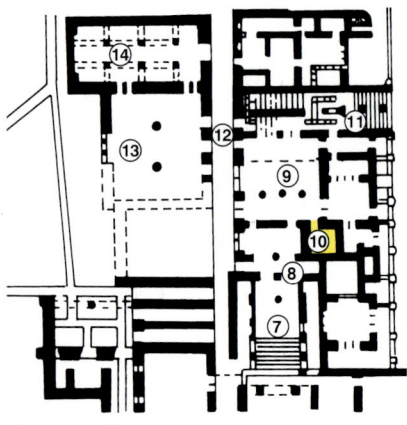

The second floor of the Palace of Knossos

The heart of the palace and a sacred place right throughout its existence was the **Throne Room (22)** where you can see the plaster throne of the King/Archpriest and opposite it, the Purification Basin which they used for their solemnisations.

East of the Throne Rooms was an Antechamber **(23)** and to the west, a small altar **(24)**. Directly south of the staircase which led to the upper floor was a three part altar **(25)** that looked onto the Central Courtyard, and behind the Altar was the ground floor Treasury **(26)**. Two hiding places were found under the floor of the Treasury. In one of these, Evans discovered a stone chest in which was kept, among other valuable objects, the renowned **Goddess of the Snakes** that is exhibited today at the Archaeological museum of Iraklio. The stone chest, once in the other hiding place, had been robbed long ago, and the few traces of gold found in the hole, bear witness to the fact that some extremely valuable treasures have been lost forever.

In the centre of the palace's east wing, a truly masterly staircase **(27)** led to the upper floors, which in that part of the palace were four or five. This staircase was one of the most admired works of Minoan craftsmen, especially designed in accordance with the human footstep to be relaxing, and with abundant light from the peristyle skylight **(28)** on its east side. One of the most splendid rooms of the palace was found in this wing - the Room of the Double-Headed Axe **(29)**, so-called because it was decorated with this sacred symbol and with shields, and it also had a wide L-shaped peristyle balcony **(30)**. The Queen's Apartments **(31)** were also in this wing, and these were full of frescoes, such as the famous fresco with dolphins, quite a large area of which was preserved in good condition, and today this is exhibited, together with the other Knossos frescoes, on the top floor of the Archaeological Museum of Iraklio.

YOU HAVEN'T SEEN THE BEST YET!

After their visit to Knossos, most visitors return to Iraklio, pay a quick visit to the Archaeological Museum and immediately afterwards, make for the tourist resorts on the north coast to enjoy their holidays, feeling that they have seen what there was to be seen of the Minoan civilisation. In reality, however, they have seen few things (and more probably understood even fewer).

If you are especially interested in the Minoan civilisation and you want to get to know it better, there are, a few kilometres to the south of Knossos, several archaeological sites of exceptional interest, of equal importance with Knossos, and with the advantage that you will probably be alone with the ancient remains (there are not even any attendants). You can visit them any time of day, for no charge, at your leisure and without limitations.

So, after Knossos, continue south on the road to **Archanes,** but ride very carefully because this is **the most slippery and dangerous road in Europe** and probably in the world! The criminal contractor who built this road couldn't have done a better job if he'd tried. Even wet glass has better road-holding. So go **very slowly** until you reach the village of **Patsides** and immediately after the village, turn right (there is a Greek/English sign at the junction that reads 'Kato Archanes'). Go through the small village of Kato Archanes and after a kilometre you will be in Ano Archanes (or just Archanes).

ARCHANES

The name of the Cretan town **Archanes** appears for the first time in a 5th century inscription which was found at Argos in the Peloponnese. Etymologically, the root 'ach' is Indo-European and is associated with water (we meet it in many names of rivers and lakes like Acheloos, Inachos, Acherousia, etc.). Truly, the abundant water which gushes up from the surrounding hills and waters the fertile basin of Archanes was the factor that brought human settlement here, way back in Neolithic times (6000 BC). The first habitations developed in Archanes in that period are lost, and only some sporadic finds (jewellery, stone tools and idols) bear witness to the high level of their civilisation.

When the great palaces of Knossos, Phaestos and Malia were built around 1900 BC, a large palace was also built at Archanes. We still do not know exactly how big it was because today's village is built right on top of it. Excavations by archaelogists Yiannis and Efi Sakellarakis have been completed only at certain points where expropriations have taken place on open plots or ruined houses, but the trial excavations at various points of the habitation have shown that **the Palace of Archanes was equally luxurious and magnificent as the great Minoan palaces.** For the sections and bases of the columns, they used marble in a great variety of colours (white, grey, black, brown) and red or blue slate. Its walls were built of well-shaped limestone and many of them were decorated with frescoes. It can be concluded from their thickness that the palace had three storeys at many points.

What such a big palace was doing so near to the palace of Knossos (just 10 kilometres) has not yet been explained. Evans' opinion that it was the summer palace of the King of

ROUTES STARTING FROM IRAKLIO

Knossos is completely improbably, anyway. All the archaeological finds reinforce the view that the palace of Archanes was an autonomous and powerful administrative centre around which an extended settlement had developed, but there were also many other settlements and isolated farms scattered all over the Archanes basin, which were dependent on this palace.

The palace of Archanes followed the fate of the other palace centres of Crete. It was destroyed by the strong earthquake of 1700 BC, but it was rebuilt to be even more brilliant. It suffered damage in the earthquake caused by the eruption of the volcano on Santorini in around 1600 BC, but it was immediately repaired and it reached its peak in the period 1600-1450 BC. It was destroyed by some unexplained violent cause in 1450 BC, but it was reconstructed immediately after (like the palace of Knossos) and it became the seat of a Mycenean noble. A new peak period then began which lasted some three hundred years, until 1100 BC when the Dorian invaders captured the whole of Crete. Life in Archanes has continued uninterrupted from ancient times until today. Today, Archanes is a lively town of 4,000 inhabitants that has maintained its traditional character quite well. One of the houses in the village (the old junior school) has housed the **Archaeological Museum of Archanes** since 1993, where mainly ceramics exclusively from the Archanes area are exhibited. Despite its small size and its humble exhibits (the gold and other valuable finds continue to be 'buried' in the Iraklio museum), the Archanes museum offers you the most exciting, comprehensible and relaxing journey into the history of the Minoan civilisation, and from this point of view it is a model museum. If all local authorities were as responsible as the municipality of Archanes, if all Greeks appreciated the cultural treasures of their country as do the inhabitants of Archanes, and if there were more charismatic and dedicated scientists like the archaeologists Yiannis and Efi Sakellarakis, who designed the Archanes museum, then Greece would be much more beautiful.

When you enter the village of Ano Archanes, you will notice on your right, just before the central square, a big stone building which is the junior school. Immediately before the school, you will see a narrow street going off to the right (there is an English sign at the junction that says 'Ancient Fourni'). Follow this road to

Archanes, as seen from the Minoan graveyard at Fourni

its end (it stops 400 metres along, outside a sheepfold), leave your motorcycle and climb up the slope, following the easily distinguishable path to the top of the hill which the locals call **Fourni,** where the **Minoan graveyard of Archanes** is situated. The archaeological site is fenced in, but the fence has fallen down at many points and you can easily get inside. There is an attendant's kiosk but no attendant, so you must undertake his role, i.e. you must be careful not to walk on the walls of the ruins, not to drop litter and, of course, not to move even the smallest thing.

THE MINOAN GRAVEYARD AT FOURNI

From the time of Venetian Rule and perhaps even before, the farmers of Archanes had planted vineyards on the slopes of the low hill north of their village. They called this hill **Fourni** because on the top there was a vaulted stone building like a village baker's oven (fournos), which the vinegrowers used as a storehouse for their tools. Nobody remembered when this stone hut was built, neither did they ever attach any significance to its strange shape. When the

The vaulted tomb at Fourni where the first unlooted royal burial in Crete was found.

archaeologist Yiannis Sakellarakis ascended this hill in 1964, he realised immediately that this hut was a **vaulted Mycenaean grave!** What the villagers used as a door was the hole which had been made by grave-robbers (probably in Roman times), near to the roof of the grave. Earth had fallen inside through this hole, and a new floor had been formed over the years, some metres higher than the original floor of the grave.

When the excavating workmen had taken away all the earth from the inside of the grave, Yiannis Sakellarakis ascertained that the grave had been looted. In one corner, he found the bones of a horse which had been sacrificed in honour of the dead person, a fact indicating that it must have been some prominent person. The experienced eye of the archaeologist (more experienced than that of the ancient grave-robbers) noticed a peculiarity in the structure of the wall on the south side of the grave, which made him suspect that perhaps there was a side room behind, as was well-known in similar vaulted graves in Mycenae and Orchomenos. Taking away the stones carefully, he made the first important find, the head of a bull that had been sacrificed in honour of the dead person, a find interpreting the bull sacrifice scene in the famous sarcophagus of Aghia Triada - bull sacrifices in Minoan Crete were solemnisations not only in honour of the gods but also in honour of dead kings and priests. The decay of the monument did not allow him to take away any more stones and so he continued the external excavations. Before his astonished eyes, the **first unlooted royal grave in Crete** was revealed!

The jewellery made of gold and precious stones which was found in that grave was more than all that found in all the vaulted graves in Crete put together! They also found ten bronze vessels of excellent quality, the ivory decoration on a wooden chest, eight earthenware pots, and of course the earthenware sarcophagus with the remains of the dead person who was certainly a royal figure. The most valuable of these finds are on display at the Archaeological Museum of Iraklio, while most of them remain buried in its warehouse. Ordinarily, they should be transferred from this wretched museum to their natural place, the brand new Museum of Archanes.

After 17 years of excavations, Yiannis Sakellarakis has uncovered the majority of this Minoan necropolis which was in use for more than 1400 years, from 2400 BC until 1000 BC approximately. North of the vaulted grave with the unlooted royal burial chamber **(1)**, he discovered a Mycenaean burial enclosure **(2)** with seven dug graves, in

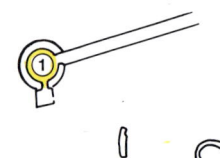

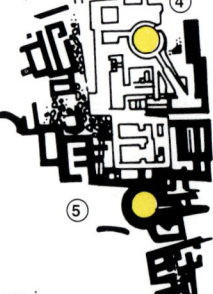

The Minoan graveyard at Fourni

which he found burial chambers with rich funeral gifts (stone pots, seals, bronze vessels and decorative artefacts made of ivory). On the south side of the necropolis, he found another unlooted vaulted grave from 1350-1300 BC **(3)**, where a young woman was buried with all her jewellery made of gold and precious stones, while in her left hand, she was still holding her mirror. Three more vaulted graves, one from 2100-2000 BC **(4),** one from 2200-2100 BC **(5)** and one from 2400-2300 BC **(6),** held dozens of well-protected burials in sarcophagi, earthen casks, or free in the ground, with rich funeral gifts that demonstrate the high cultural and living standards of Archanes.

Twenty six buildings in total have come to light so far at Fourni, some of which are not graves as, for example, the big rectangular building **(7)** in the centre of the graveyard. This must have been a workshop where they made the artefacts necessary for funeral ceremonies. Other finds include the weaving weights of the looms on which they probably wove the materials worn by the dead, a "tortoise" (i.e. a solid piece of bronze) which was the raw material for the manufacture of bronze objects, numerous pots in which food must have been stored, stone colanders, whetstones and other tools. One of the rooms **(7a)** was a wine-press, where they made the wine they used in the funeral libations. You can still see the special formation of the ground for treading grapes and for collecting the must.

If, during your tour of Unexplored Crete, you notice some strange stone hut poking out of the bushes, inform the archaeological department immediately. One of the dozens of unknown Minoan cities and graveyards might come to light thanks to your being observant!

THE SACRED MOUNTAIN OF JUHTAS

Just five kilometres south of Knossos is a large limestone rock 811 metres high, which to the eyes of the ancient Cretans looked like the figure of Zeus lying on the ground. **Juhtas,** as it is called today, was the sacred mountain of the Minoans where they founded four temples. On its western slope, at a height of 720 metres, is the small cave of **Chosto Nero** (Deep Water)

which was a place of worship back as far as the Prepalatial Period. On the south-west slope, at a height of 400 metres, is the **Cave of Stravomyti,** which was in use (initially as a habitation and later as a graveyard and a place of worship) since the Neolithic Period. Both these caves were known to travellers (from the 15th century onwards) who were searching here for the Grave of Zeus, according to the rumours of the impious Cretans who dared to maintain that the king of the gods had died and was indeed buried on their island!

At the beginning of the century, Sir Arthur Evans pointed out and excavated a **Peak Sanctuary** on the top of the highest summit of Juhtas, where he found bronze double-headed axes and a multitude of earthenware votive idols of animals and humans.

But the most important discovery at Juhtas and one of the most important in the whole of Crete, which caused a commotion among archaeologists and archaeophiles throughout the world was the **Temple of Anemospilia,** located in 1979 by the archaeologists Efi Sapouna-Sakellarakis and Yiannis Sakellarakis. Excavations began in the summer of the same year and brought to light a rectangular building with four rooms - three of these were next to each other and in front of them was an oblong ante-chamber. In this ante-chamber, excavations uncovered a multitude of pots (around 150) and the skeleton of a man who had fallen head down to the ground, having been hit by the stones that fell from the roof during the very strong earthquake which destroyed not only that temple but also all the palace centres of Crete in around 1700 BC. From his position and from the fractures in his bones, it seems obvious that he tried to run out of the temple when he felt the earthquake, but he did not have time. Next to the man was found the pot he had been carrying (broken), a typical ceremonial pot which the Minoans used in their bull sacrifices to collect the blood of the sacrificial animal. A lot of ceremonial vessels were found in the east room, and in the central room, apart from the vessels, were found two earthenware legs which obviously belonged to the wooden statue of the deity that was worshipped here. Advancing the excavations into the west room, the two experienced archaeologists were certain, from the evidence in front of them, that they would find the bones of the bull being sacrificed at the time of the destruction of the temple. Astonished, however, they found **three human skeletons.** One belonged to a man aged approximately 37 years, who had on his left hand a very valuable ring and a cameo made of agate. Next to him was the skeleton of a woman approximately 28 years old. And in approximately the centre of the room, on a stone altar, was the skeleton of a young man, approximately 18 years old, turned over on his right side in a position that strengthens the supposition that he was bound, with a big ceremonial knife resting in his stomach. The most probable interpretation of all these findings is that it is a case of **human sacrifice,** which the priests of the temple carried out in a final attempt at atonement to the deity when the preseismic tremors threw the island into confusion, just before the manifestation of the big earthquake in 1700 BC

To visit the ruins of this temple, follow the sign that says Anemospilia, immediately after the Junior School, in the central square of Archanes (it is the next road after the one which leads to the graveyard at Fourni). Of course, all the finds have been moved to the Iraklio museum and the site is fenced off, but even from a distance it is worth seeing the building where this prehistoric drama unfolded. And if you come up here in the afternoon, you can enjoy the superb view towards Knossos and Iraklio.

The asphalt road (A3) which continues south from Archanes passes through well-cared for vineyards and olive groves which covering these low hills. The landscape you see around you cannot have changed much since Minoan times. Even the cultivation was the same! Among the vineyards, on a hill a little farther north of the abandoned village of **Vathypetro,** the archaeologist Spyros Marinatos discovered a big Minoan villa dating back to 1600 BC, in which there was an intact wine-press and olive-press (there is a Greek/English sign on the main road which will direct you to the archaeological site). All the relevant equipment was also found in its place in such good condition that you think the farmer is about to come in with his grapes and make must! Unfortunately, the excavator gave in to the temptation and restored and roofed the two most important rooms in the villa with a cement ceiling. There is no attendant at the site, and the gate in the fence has fallen down, but unfortunately the two rooms with the wine-press and olive-press are permanently locked.

TOWARDS THE LASITHI PLATEAU

South of the archaeological site of Vathypetro, you continue along a dirt road (D1) which divides into two after a while. Whichever leg you choose, you will come out at the village of Choudetsi, where you take the main road (A3) which comes from Iraklio. From here on, you have to cross on indifferent farming landscape until you arrive at the plateau of Lasithi. The quickest way of covering this distance is to turn north of Choudetsi towards the village of Kalloni, immediately after which you turn right (east) towards the village **Aghies Paraskies.** From Aghies Paraskies you can already see in the distance the impressive western slopes of Dikti, behind which is the plateau of Lasithi, but don't get carried away with riding fast, because the road is slippery asphalt and is full of dangerous bends.

When you arrive at the entrance to the village of **Kasteli,** you have two choices. If you want to ride only on asphalt, turn left (to the north), following the Greek/English signs which say "Chersonisos" and "Iraklio", and after 9 kilometres turn right onto the main road (A3) which crosses the lush valley of the River Aposelemis. Having passed through the picturesque villages of Potamies and Avdou, you climb the main road towards the Plateau of Lasithi with dozens of tourist coaches and rented jeeps for company. If, however, you don't mind riding over dirt roads for a while, you have a much better choice; turn north out of the village of Kasteli, following the Greek/English signs reading "Chersonisos" and "Iraklio" and another 400 metres along, turn right at the junction where you will see a

ROUTES STARTING FROM IRAKLIO

The country church of St. George on the hill of Lyttos, built entirely with materials from the ancient town

Greek/English sign saying "Xydias" and "Mathia". You will soon enter the large, picturesque village of **Lyttos**. About 400 metres after the village sign, you will see a small rusty sign in English which says "Aski", "Avdou", "Tzermiado". Turn left here onto the road (A3) that climbs with very enjoyable horseshoe bends on the vine-planted hillsides.

Just before you arrive at the highest point of the route, you will notice to your right on top of a hill some ruined windmills and two old country churches. On top of this hill, **one of the most powerful Doric cities in Crete, Lyttos (or Lyktos)** was built. To arrive at the top of the hill, turn right (south) onto the dirt road you will see hiding among the vineyards just 100 metres before the highest point of the main route from where you have the first view down into the valley of the River Aposelemi and the village of Avdou. This dirt road stops at a small opening between the two churches, which are almost completely built of ancient materials. At exactly the opening where you have parked your motorcycle, and as far as the northern church (of the Holy Cross), was the **Agora** (market), the heart of the ancient city. Its ruins were found buried just a few

20. Iraklio-Agh. Nikolaos
TRAVELLING INLAND

metres beneath the soil, waiting patiently for the archaeologist's pick-axe, which has made only a few investigatory cuts in this most important city.

At the summit of the hill to the south, where the church of St. George stands, is the **council chamber** of the city. The city itself was built like an amphitheatre on the hillside, and occupied a very large area. Its theatre was the biggest in Crete. It could still be seen in 1583, when the Venetian archaeophile, Onorio Belli (the personal doctor to the Venetian Duke of Crete) saw it and marked it with remarkable accuracy, but in the course of time it has been filled with earth and covered up and its exact position is unknown today. The Venetian doctor sent the statues and other sculptures which he found here to his master and since then, of course, their fate has been unknown. The only visible traces of the city are the ruins of a habitation of the Hellenistic Period, and parts of the wall of the Byzantine Period, and you can see these on the hillside due west of the church of the Holy Cross. But if you walk among the vineyards and the wild grass, you will see many pieces of marble and, of course, many fragments of pots from ancient Lyttos.

When exactly the first settlement was built up here is unknown, as no archaeological research has yet taken place. The historian Polyvios, however, mentions (IV, 53-5) that Lyttos is the most ancient city in Crete.

The village of Aski

ROUTES STARTING FROM IRAKLIO

Homer in the Iliad (p 605-616) tells us of the self-sacrifice of the brave soldier Koiranos, from the well-built Lyttos, who sacrificed himself in order to save the King of the Cretans, Idomeneas, from Hector's spear. It is certain that, from the time when the Dorians settled here, around **1000 BC,** Lyttos knew a long period of prosperity which lasted until the Roman era. Its military power was greater than that of Knossos and its rule spread over the greater part of eastern Crete. Lyttos was one of the few Cretan cities which did not have walls, because it considered its worthy army and its fortified position a powerful shield. For many centuries it was a thorn in the side of the Knossians, who had allied even with their enemies, the Gortynians, to subdue it but every time they were defeated. In 220 BC, however, the Lyttians made their big mistake. They attacked Ierapytna with their whole army, leaving behind a small guard, but they had some difficulty in the battle with the Ierapytnians and were late in returning. The Knossians found the opportunity they had been waiting for centuries, and with the help of the Gortynians, they dominated the undefended Lyttos without difficulty. Without delay they plundered it, pulled it down to the ground and burned it. When the Lyttians returned home and saw their destroyed city, they fell into deep melancholy. They dragged themselves in despair to the hospitable Làppa, where they settled temporarily. Many years later, when they had got over it a bit, they returned to their devastated city and rebuilt it with the help of the Spartans. They had, however, lost their old power for ever and chiefly their self-confidence, and so they allied themselves with neighbouring cities which had once been under their rule, in order to survive. They resisted the Romans in 68 BC, but to no avail. However, under Roman domination, Lyttos went through a new period of prosperity. When the life of the city was finally snuffed out and from what cause, what were the daily occupations of its inhabitants, what their houses and their public buildings were like - Lyttos has kept all these and many other secrets to itself up to this day, buried a few metres below the earth.

20. Iraklio-Agh. Nikolaos
TRAVELLING INLAND

After the village of Aski, the dirt road (D1) continues through the olive groves which cover the valley of the River Aposelemi. What makes this route so very enjoyable is the fact that at every junction there are clearly marked brand-new English signs which guide you in all directions. Following steadily the signs towards **Avdou,** you can ride without stopping, and indeed at a spanking pace if you want, as the road is perfect. The route from Aski to Avdou is an example of how enjoyable and relaxing a tour through Greece would be if all the local authorities had the elementary sense to place road signs at junctions.

The village of Avdou and the next village, Gonies, are big villages which owe their vitality to the fact that they are built on one of the biggest tourist routes in Crete - the Iraklio-Lasithi Plateau route. Here, of course, you will find many restaurants and rooms to let on the main road, but the genuine character of a Cretan village is maintained in the neighbourhoods behind the road: children running on the pavements, the fat grocer carrying sacks into his warehouse, the old men sunning themselves in the small yard of the coffee-house; and if you can find a free table and if the coffee-house owner likes you, he might make you a plate of mouth-watering fried potatoes!

The Monastery of Kera

ROUTES STARTING FROM IRAKLIO

After the village of Gonia, the road (A3) climbs steadily up the western slopes of Mount Dikti, which are covered with low vegetation (bushes and wild flowers) and with sparse trees. Just before the village of Kera, you will see on your right, next to the road, the **Monastery of the Virgin Mary of Kera** (closed between 1.00-3.30 p.m.). This is a very old monastery, also known as the **Moni Kardiotissa,** probably built at the beginning of the 14th century. Its chapel is fully embellished with exceptional frescoes of that period and its architecture is strange - the result of its various renovations. The unfortunate thing is that it is situated next to the main road, and it is included in the sights visited by the endless batches of tourist coaches going towards the Plateau of Lasithi. You will be very lucky if you manage to go when there are only a few visitors.

A few metres before (north of) the monastery you will see a cement road that descends into the ravine and after a while ends at the old village of Kera, built at the edge of a ravine and literally smothered in greenery. Not only do tourists not visit it, but even its inhabitants have also abandoned it; they have all moved together to **Epano Kera,** next to the main road, in search of a better income in the small shops which serve the passing tourists. In the old Kera, you will see that time has stopped at the end of the last century and there will be two or three almost indestructible old men sunning themselves in the grassy yards or slowly dragging themselves along the pavements. This place is an abandoned paradise, with water running everywhere, an amazing view to the Valley of Aposelemi and a ravine full of birds whose song is heady.

A few metres before you enter old Kera, you will spot on your right a dirt road (D3) descending the northern slope of the ravine through the wood. This dirt road ends at the country church of Zoodohos Pigi built in an amazing landscape. The absolute silence, the absolute isolation and a well with drinking water make this an ideal spot for a free overnight stay.

After the Monastery Kera, the narrow road (A3) ascends the steep mountainside, offering a lovely view of the plain to the west, but you'd better just look straight ahead because this road has the worst c.p.h. rate (coaches per hour)! In August, especially, the average is 75 c.p.h., and this is exceptionally dangerous because of the narrowness of the road: on sudden and blind hairpin curves, the coaches take up all the road in order to turn. When you see a big parking area with dozens of coaches and hundreds of camera-toting tourists standing even in the middle of the road, then you've arrived at the highest point of the route (900 m) and at the entrance to the plateau. Park your motor bike next to the cafeteria and climb a few metres up the northern slope to the place where you will see some old ruined windmills, so as to avoid the scrum. Even better, climb to the summit at Papoura (1,025 m high) some 100 m higher than the windmills, from where you will enjoy a superb view of the plateau.

THE LASITHI PLATEAU

The Lasithi Plateau is situated at a height of 820-850 metres and is one of the biggest plateaux in Greece. Precipitous mountain peaks, all more than 1,000 metres high, surround it, forming a strong natural fortification that has only eight relatively accessible passes. The waters that run from everywhere each spring, when the mountain snows melt, enrich

The Lasithi Plateau.

the earth with their minerals and then drain off into the swallow-hole on the southwest corner of the plateau, near the village of Kato Metohi. Much of this water however remains in the extended water table at a depth of 8-10 metres. Its naturally fortified position and its extremely fertile land attracted human habitation to the plateau very early on as it is natural.

The **Cave of Trapeza** (also known as Kronio), outside the village of Tzermiado, was used as a place of burial during the Prepalatial period (2500-2000 BC), while in the Neolithic period it may have been used for habitation, as the excavations of the English archaeologist, John Pendlebury, revealed in 1936. On the hill of **Kastelos,** east of Tzermiado, the English archaeologist found the ruins of a settlement which seems to have been flourishing right throughout the Prepalatial period (2000-1700 BC). And on the top of the slope at the plateau 's western entrance which the locals call **Papoura,** John Pendlebury and his team found the ruins of a settlement of the Neo-palatial and Post-palatial period (1700-1100 BC), while yet another important settlement from the same period was excavated by the English archaeologist R.M. Dawkins near to the village of Plati. The invaders who destroyed all the palace centres in Crete in around 1450 BC seem not to have had a desire for mountaineering, and so they did not disturb the settlements on this plateau. They may however have attempted to conquer the area, but without success. Sir Arthur Evans, who also researched the area, discovered the remains of strong fortifications at all the passes/entrances to the plateau. **Diktaio Andro,** however, near to the village of Psychro, has special importance on the Plateau of Lasithi; this is where Cretan mythology placed the birth of Zeus. For more than 1,000 years, from the beginning of the Neo-palatial period (1700 BC) to the end of the geometric period (700 BC), the Cretans ascended to the sacred Diktaio Antro to worship, presenting valuable votive offerings. In the excavations carried out by the English archaeologist, David Hogarth, in 1899-1900, many bronze idols of humans and animals, weapons, tools and sacred double-headed axes were found.

When those wild men, the Dorians, invaded

Crete in around 1100 BC, the Minoans and their co-inhabitants, the Achaeans living on the plains, ran like hunted men for refuge in the inaccessible mountainous areas to the east. A large wave of refugees came and settled on this plateau. Indeed, for even greater safety (imagine how scared the poor things must have been!), they preferred the most inaccessible peaks around the plateau. Pendlebury and his team found such a settlement in 1937-39, on a small flat piece of land near the summit of **Karphi,** almost 2 kilometres northeast of the summit of Papoura. Its ancient name is unknown and so it is conventionally called "the Minoan settlement at Karphi". In order to visit it, there is a passable signposted path which starts at Papoura peak (an hour's walk) but there is an even better one that starts at the plateau of Nisimos (see below).

The refugees spend approximately 150 years holding on in their eagle's nest. In the end, they became sure that the Dorians were not about to go to the trouble to climb all the way up here to fight then, so they came down to more level land, nearer their fields on the Plateau of Lasithi. It was then that the settlement at Papoura started to develop, and this seems to have been inhabited without interruption until Roman years; indeed, it knew great prosperity. It remained, however, in absolute isolation and for this reason is not mentioned by any ancient writer.

During the difficult years of the Byzantine period, when the pirates were ravaging the coasts of Crete, and in the dark period of Arab rule, the mountain-dwellers of Lasithi lived undisturbed in their safe refuge. During the period of Venetian rule, when the whole of Crete suffered from suffocating feudal oppression, the Plateau of Lasithi became the rebels' hideout. When the problem became serious for the Venetians, they made a decisive mountain attack in **1263** and captured the plateau. They cut down the trees, uprooted the crops and drove out **all** the inhabitants. They installed guards at the passes and strictly forbade anyone (on pain of death) to come up here for whatever reason. So the Venetians freed themselves from this thorn in their side, although the rebellions continued from other bases. This uprooting had positive results from an ecological point of view, however; in the two hundred years that the blockade lasted, the plateau was transformed into thick forest and a rich living landscape. Its swallow-hole blocked the water, which drained off slowly with the result that the plateau was transformed into a lake every spring when the snows melted.

But difficult years came for the Venetians and their new nightmare was famine. They were then forced to cultivate all available fertile land, including the Lasithi Plateau. Having stripped it, they sent some experienced hydraulic engineers who opened up drainage ditches (the so-called linies) still furrowing the plateau to this very day. The farmers who rented this land built rough and ready huts on the fringes of the plateau, and these gradually became big villages, the same ones you see today. They dug wells to water their fields, and they pumped the water with small windmills of which there were more than 10,000!

Today the Lasithi plateau is a big tourist playground. Most of the fields certainly continue to be cultivated, mainly with potatoes and fruit trees, but the chief income comes from tourism. The 21 villages on the plateau have lost their genuine character and have been turned into unsightly, cheap bazaars where they trade in materials, rugs, T-shirts and all kinds of souvenirs hung on every available stone fence. Jerry-built rooms to let and garish restaurants complete the scene, while the only windmills you will see are plastic imitations in the form of key-rings in the tourist shops. Diktaio Andro is today the den of arbitrariness. The road that ascends from Psychro is bedecked throughout its length with cheap Taiwanese kilims hanging from the fences. It ends at a flat piece of land used for parking where all visitors are obliged to leave their vehicles to take a ten-minute walk to the cave entrance. But a heavy, irascible local appears, apparently the owner (?) of this field and demands that you pay him 500 drachmas for parking!

There's nothing to see on Diktaio Andro (the finds that were made there are exhibited at the

Archaeological Museum in Iraklio) and you'd be wise to avoid the crush and its arbitrariness. The ring road that goes through the villages also has nothing worth seeing to offer you. There are however two very good (and totally unknown) routes which start at the plateau and cross very interesting landscapes.

The first starts at the village of Tzermiado. At the western entrance to the village, you will see a dirt road going off to the north (there is a Greek/English sign at the junction which says "To Timios Stavros Church"). Initially there is a small problem on the road (loose gravel on an uphill part) but afterwards it is very passable (D2) to the end. After a climb of 2 kilometres, you enter the deserted and very beautiful **Nissimos plateau,** where you can get an idea of what the landscape must have been like in the B.T. (before tourism) period. Two hundred metres down the road, you will see a junction where a Greek/English sign tells you to the right is the way to the church of the Holy Cross (Timios Stavros) from where you have a lovely view of the Lasithi Plateau. If however, you want to visit the **Minoan settlement at Karphi,** take the road to the left. After two hundred metres, you will find yourself at a trifurcation. The road to the right and the middle road cross the plateau and end at its northern edge, at a shepherd's fold. You will take the road to the left, which stops after 500 metres at the base of

The Karphi mountain peak, where the persecuted Eteocretans built their settlement. Malia in the far background.

ROUTES STARTING FROM IRAKLIO

The settlement of Eteocretans at Karfi.

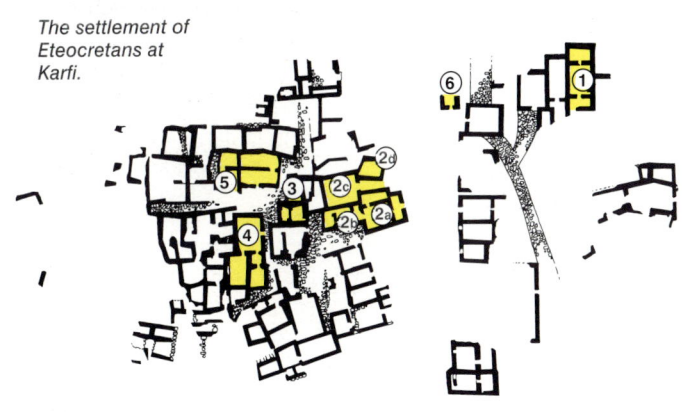

the mountain top. Leave your bike in the shade of the only tree at the side of the road and get ready for a pleasant and easy climb (45 minutes) by the marked path that starts to your west, at the point where the road ends. We should warn you, however, that not many things from the Minoan city have been saved for you to see. The excavators, having completed their research (in 1939) abandoned the ruins without doing any reinforcement work so that most of the walls of the houses today are shapeless piles of stones. Two or three more heavy winters and a few careless visitors and nothing of the ancient city will remain standing. If you have a good imagination, and with the help of the diagram, you will be able to locate, on the northeast edge of the settlement, a typical house of the period **(1)** with its prodomos in the front (something like a hall), the "megaro" (i.e. the sitting room) with the hearth in the centre, and the thalamos (the bedroom) at the end. In the centre of the settlement, a large house **(2a)**, which had storerooms **(2b)**, a courtyard **(2c)** and a stable **(2d)**, must have been the residence of the governor. The governor's neighbour was the baker **(3)** and a little further along was the big, comfortable house of the priest **(4)**. The commercial stores **(5)** were all clustered together in the upper-class neighbourhood, in an eminent position, while the poor neighbourhood was on the west side of the settlement. If you can't manage to make out much, go to the sentry's observation post **(6)**, from where you will certainly enjoy the unlimited view to the west!

Your second choice is a very nice enduro

20. Iraklio-Agh. Nikolaos

TRAVELLING INLAND

On the Kaminaki-Katofigi route.

route which begins at the village of Kaminaki, crosses the wild mountainside of southwest Dikti at a great height and finishes at the village of Katofigi. From here you continue on an even more impressive route towards the Plateau of Omalo and Kato Symi (see Road Book 7, page 338) and come out on the coast road to Ierapetra. To start off on this route, go to Kaminaki and turn left (south) on the asphalt road you will see in the centre of the village, 300 metres after the sign giving its name and is pasted at the eastern entrance to the village. The road climbs the slope and after 1,200 metres becomes a good dirt road (D2). Turn your trip odometer back to zero and follow **Road Book 9.**

If you want to continue from the Lasithi Plateau towards Aghios Nikolaos, there is only one road, as you can see from the map. All tourist traffic goes down this road, so don't expect to see anything exceptional. A good alternative would

ROUTES STARTING FROM IRAKLIO

be to go to Aghios Nikolaos via the Plateau of Katharo, situated south-east of the Lasithi Plateau, but only hikers can do this, since to date (1996), no road has been opened up to join these two plateaux.

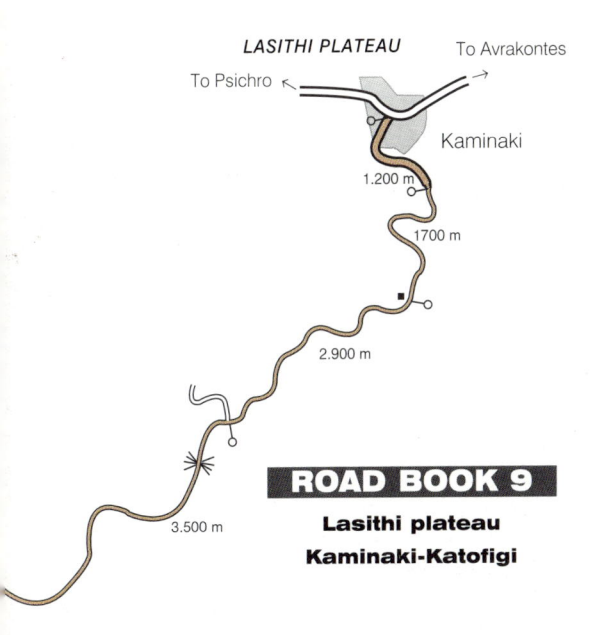

LASITHI PLATEAU
To Avrakontes
To Psichro
Kaminaki
1.200 m
1700 m
2.900 m
3.500 m

ROAD BOOK 9
Lasithi plateau
Kaminaki-Katofigi

20. Iraklio-Agh. Nikolaos
TRAVELLING INLAND

Aghios Nikolaos

ROUTES STARTING FROM AGHIOS NIKOLAOS

A kilometre to the north of the present town, at the spot where the luxury hotel, the Minos Palace, now stands, a small, protected harbour is formed which was used by experienced seamen to tie up their ships as far back as Minoan times. When the Byzantines threw the Arabs out of Crete and the second Byzantine Period (961-1204) began, this small harbour became the centre for commercial traffic in east Crete. In today's world of laws and statutes and means of protecting citizens' lives and property, it is difficult for us to realise the anxiety and insecurity that tormented the people in that not so remote period. Constantinople was a two month journey away, and the Byzantine fleet travelled at a snail-like pace. Who would protect their lives and their property if pirates suddenly appeared at that small isolated harbour? Their only comfort and hope was God and his saints, and especially **St. Nicholas,** the patron saint of seamen. So the pious Cretans built a humble church at the entrance to their harbour which was dedicated to St. Nicholas and which they decorated as well as their limited finances would allow.

Unfortunately, when you are attacked by enraged pirates, your faith operates more as a comfort after the destruction than as a protection against it. The Venetians, who knew this very well, preferred to strengthen their defences with castles rather than with churches when they conquered Crete. In order to protect the **Porto di San Nicolo,** as they called this small harbour, after the church which stood at its entrance, they reinforced the castle that the Genoan pirate Enrico Pescatore had had time to build (but not to enjoy for very long) in 1204 on the hill between the lake of Aghios Nikolaos and today's marina. The small, insignificant Doric town of **Lato Pros Kamara** was built on the same spot, of which very few traces are left.

The castle of **Mirabello,** as they called it after the wonderful view it had over the whole bay, was not so strong after all and so Turkish pirates captured it in 1537 and plundered it. A century later, in 1645, when the Turks mounted a campaign with their whole army against Crete, the Venetian governor, thinking logically, abandoned it without a fight and took refuge in the much stronger fortress of Spinalonga, on the island of the same name a few miles to the north. It seems that all its inhabitants abandoned it, as no source since then has referred to Aghios Nikolaos at all.

Only at the beginning of the 19th century did some villagers from Kritsa come and build their huts here, using stones from the completely destroyed fortress. Their small settlement, **Mandraki,** grew gradually by serving trade and sea transport in east Crete, and by the end of the 19th century it was already a big town spreading around the **Voulismeni Limni,** a lake whose waters are so deep that popular imagination believed it to be bottomless! This myth was dispersed by the English admiral, Spratt, in 1853 when he sounded it and found its bottom at an impressive depth of 64 metres. It ceased to be a lake in 1870, when the small canal was dug which to this day joins it to the sea and which turned it into a sheltered harbour for fishing boats in the heart of the town. This lake, the creation of nature from the epoch of great geological wonders (the Miocene, 25 million years ago), was the exotic factor that started to attract tourists in the beginning of the 1960s.

Aghios Nikolaos today is a big town of 8,000 inhabitants, the capital of Lasithi prefecture, with a lot of tourist traffic during the summer months. It has no airport, but it is connected by a regular ferry service to Pireas, on board the wonderful vessel, "Vincentzos Kornaros", the best ship plying the Aegean today. Unfortunately, the disorganised and sudden expansion of Aghios Nikolaos destroyed to a large extent the traditional character the town had maintained until the 1960s. The picturesque fishing village is now full of inelegant blocks of flats encircling the Voulismeni Lake and covering all the surrounding hills. Scattered through the town, in the shadow of the blocks of flats, some traditional mansions still exist, having by some miracle escaped demolition, and they are today preserved buildings which usually house restaurants or luxury guest houses. Most of these are situated on the hill south of Voulismeni Lake, where the Venetian fortress, Mirabello, once used to be.

Nothing remains of the Venetian monuments of Aghios Nikolaos. Not even the fortress Mirabello exists any more, and only its name survives in the name of Mirabello Bay. As for the small Byzantine church of St. Nicholas which gave its name to the town, this at least has managed to stay upright and indeed it has preserved its frescoes. Now that the restoration and maintenance work has been completed, you can visit this small chapel (ask for the key at the reception desk of the Minos Palace Hotel) and admire the 14th century frescoes, underneath which much older decorative plant and geometric motifs of the 8th-9th centuries have been found. Another very interesting Byzantine church, the church of the Virgin Mary **(6)** is preserved in excellent condition two blocks behind the Cathedral of the Holy Trinity **(7)**, but it is permanently locked and it is difficult to find anyone to open it for you (ask at the cathedral).

A real adornment of Aghios Nikolaos is the **Archaeological Museum (5),** at 68 Palaiologou Street, near the Voulismeni Lake (open from 8.30 a.m. - 3 p.m. every day except Monday). It may not be very big, but it has exceptionally interesting exhibits and it is worth going early in the morning so you have plenty of time before you. In its seven well cared-for rooms, you will see important treasures from the Neolithic Age up to the Roman Period which have been found in east Crete. In **Room 1** you will see burial gifts from Neolithic graves (3000 - 2300 BC) found in Aghia Fotia, near to Sitia, and many pots, among which one Early Minoan pot stands out - it has many triangular holes and is probably a brazier or a censer. In **Room 2,** the outstanding exhibit is the anthropomorphic libational pot, the so-called "Goddess of Myrtos", which was found in the Minoan settlement of the same name; it is a masterpiece of the Early Minoan Period. **Room 3** is full of finds from peak sanctuaries, burial grounds and cities of the post-Minoan Period. In **Room 4** you will see funeral gifts from various burial grounds of the post-Minoan Period, but the outstanding exhibit is a child buried in an earthenware pot from Krya, outside Sitia, which was brought to the museum and exhibited exactly as it was found. In **Room 5,** many idols of the Geometric and Archaic Periods are exhibited, while in **Room 6,** large busts of women predominate, which were found in Greco-Roman Olous (the place where present-day Elounda is situated). In **Room 7,** you will see burial gifts found in graves of the Roman Period. The most impressive is a skull adorned with a gold wreath and with a silver coin between its teeth, the fare which the dead had to pay to Charon to ferry them in his boat to the Underworld.

Aghios Nikolaos does not have any notable beaches, neither does the Mirabello Bay generally. If you don't want to be crowded on the public beach of Kitroplateia or of Almyro, the best and nearest answer is the fairly large sandy beach approximately one kilometre outside Aghios Nikolaos on the road to Elounda. All these beaches are naturally full of umbrellas and sun-beds, and it is unlikely that you will find a free piece of sand to spread your towel out on.

There are few motorcyclists in the town and, naturally, there is no motorcyclists' club. You will however, find garages and some shops that sell oil, brakes and motorcycle tyres (see the list of practical information at the end of the book). It is a good idea to find a sheltered place away from the harbour and the town's tourist roads

When the tourist season is over, the beaches of Aghios Nikolaos regain their natural beauty.

and lock your motorcycle, because many incidents of damage and theft caused by drunken tourists have been reported. The only open-air parking area in the town, opposite the Archaeological Museum, **illegally** refuses to accept motorcycles, with the disgraceful excuse that they may fall off their stands and cause damage to neighbouring cars!

WHERE TO SLEEP

According to EOT (Greek National Tourism Organisation) statistics, Aghios Nikolaos offers more than 80 hotels of various sizes, ranging from Luxury to C class, as well as 2,000 beds in rooms to let. Nevertheless, if you arrive here in July or August you will not find even a public bench to lie on! In all other seasons, however, you will not have trouble finding accommodation at prices lower than those of equivalent lodgings in western Crete.

MINOS PALACE Hotel
Lux class, open March-October
142 rooms, 9 bungalows
3 km north of Ag. Nikolaos on the road to Elounda.
tel. 0841 - 23.801, fax 0841 - 23.816

MINOS BEACH Bungalows
Lux class, open March-October
132 bungalows
2 km north of Ag. Nikolaos on the road to Elounda.
tel. 0841 - 22.345, fax 0841 - 22.548
This hotel, as its sister one above, is the greatest luxury you can offer yourself in Ag. Nikolaos. Park your bike outside your bungalow, sip your drink and enjoy cool afternoons by the pool. Magnificent buffet breakfasts, posh restaurant, exemplary service, and impeccable attention to detail.

MIRABELLO VILLAGE Hotel
Lux class, open all year
131 rooms
1 km north of Ag. Nikolaos on the road to Elounda.
tel. 0841 - 28.400, fax 0841 - 28.810

LITO Hotel
C class, open March-October
38 rooms
2 km north of Ag. Nikolaos on the road to Elounda.
tel. 0841 - 24.332, fax 0841 - 24.330
A comfortable and elegant hotel at a quiet spot just outside the city, near the beach, with safe parking for your bike.

MARILENA Pension
Open all year
12 rooms
Erithrou Stavrou 4
tel. 0841 - 22.681

ARGIRO Pension
Open all year
6 rooms
Solonos 1, across from the Prefecture building
tel. 0841 - 28. 707
The sweet Mrs. Koula has converted her early century house into a spotless and very hospitable pension. Quiet, with a garden and a neighbourly atmosphere.

MANTRAKI Apartments
B class, open April-October
20 apartments
Kapetan Tavla 1, behind the Aghia Triada church.
tel. 0841 - 28.880
The most convenient and quiet place to stay in the heart of town, especially if you are a group (4 to 6 persons). All apartments with fully equipped kitchen, private bath and balcony overlooking the sea. You can park your bike under your balcony.

KATERINA Pension
Open all year
6 rooms
Stratigou Koraka 33
tel. 0841 - 22.766
This is your best choice for budget accommodation is Ag. Nikolaos. An old detached house with a beautiful garden (absolutely safe parking for your motorcycle) in a quiet neighbourhood just beyond the city centre.

STEFANAKIS Rooms
Open all year
8 rooms
Pasiphaes 18
tel. 0841 - 23.381
A modern block of flats converted into rented rooms of satisfactory standard. Its advantage lies in that it is situated on a dead end street where you can park your machine quite safely.

WHERE TO EAT

Your choices of good food in Aghios Nikolaos are surprisingly limited! There are of course the restaurants in the expensive hotels but these cater mainly to their guests. There are also many tourist restaurants around the Voulismeni Lake and around the Kitroplateia beach, but most of them serve mainly good views rather than good food, and at high prices indeed.

PELAGOS, Fish-tavern
Corner of Koraka and Katehaki streets. Housed in a perfectly preserved old house, with tables in the large open yard. Enjoy fresh fish, a vast variety of seafood, impeccable service and quiet ambiance without paying a fortune. By far **the best restaurant in town.**

ROUTES STARTING FROM AGHIOS NIKOLAOS

DU LAC, Restaurant
At the Voulismeni Lake.
Located in the most touristy area or Ag. Nikolaos, with touristy prices, but a big variety of very tasty dishes (international cuisine) and proper service.

ROUMELI, Tavern
Metamorfoseos 3 and Sof. Venizelou
No tables outdoor but spotless in every detail. Traditional Greek and local Cretan cuisine, beautiful tablecloths, straw chairs, good music.

PORTES, Tavern
Corner of Anapafseos and Hortatson
A small indoor space with few tables but very well cooked food at very reasonable prices.

SARRI'S, Eatery
Corner of Kyprou and Modatsou
Opens in the morning for a rich breakfast (omelettes, sandwiches, etc.) until late in the evening, with tables on the sidewalk and the courtyard under the trees, in a quiet neighbourhood. Good inexpensive food.

LAMBROS, Bakery
Corner of Metamorfoseos and Sof. Venizelou
The best bakery/pastry shop in town. Bread, croissants, rolls, biscuits, Cretan sweets like kaltsounia and kserotigana. Always very fresh. Ideal spot to start your day! For coffee, exactly opposite there is 'To Vassano', a pretty, traditional Greek kafeneio.

ENTERTAINMENT

From the night-life point of view, Aghios Nikolaos is the Chersonisos of eastern Crete. Chersonisos certainly can boast of many more bars, but in Aghios Nikolaos too the streets are full of fun that lasts till morning. Don't be misled by the city's name which sounds like a church; every night in summer time Aghios Nikolaos is turned into a vast bar! Large and small groups of Europeans, mainly Italians and British, dance from one bar to another and after midnight the streets of the harbour and the lake become a multi-coloured, rip-roaring fashion show. There are of course a few quiet neighbourhoods (the farther away from the port the quieter), but if you are after peaceful relaxation, Aghios Nikolaos is certainly not the best choice!

It is impossible to list all the bars of Aghios Nikolaos, not only because of their great number, but also because each year new ones open while existing ones either close down or change name. Treat Aghios Nikolaos as a wide-spread bar and look for the most cheerful spots in the alleys near the port. Have fun!

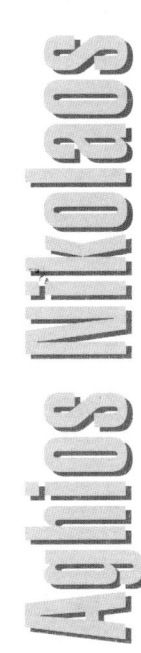

AGH. NIKOLAOS

LEGEND

● *MISCELLANEOUS*

1. OTE (Telephone Service)
2. ELTA (Post Office)
3. EOT (Nat. Tourist Organization)
4. TOWN HALL
5. POLICE
6. TOURIST POLICE
7. HOSPITAL
8. ARCHAELOGICAL MUSEUM
9. MUNICIPAL PARKING
10. FERRY DOCK
11. BYZANTINE CHURCH OF PANAGIA

▌*WHERE TO STAY*

12. MANTRAKI APARTMENTS
13. MARILENA PANSION
14. ARGIRO PANSION
15. KATERINA PANSION

✶ *WHERE TO EAT*

16. PELAGOS
17. DU LAC
18. ROUMELI
19. SARRI'S

▲ *MOTORCYCLE AGENCIES*

20. SUZUKI
21. KAWASAKI

21. Agh. Nikolaos -Zakros

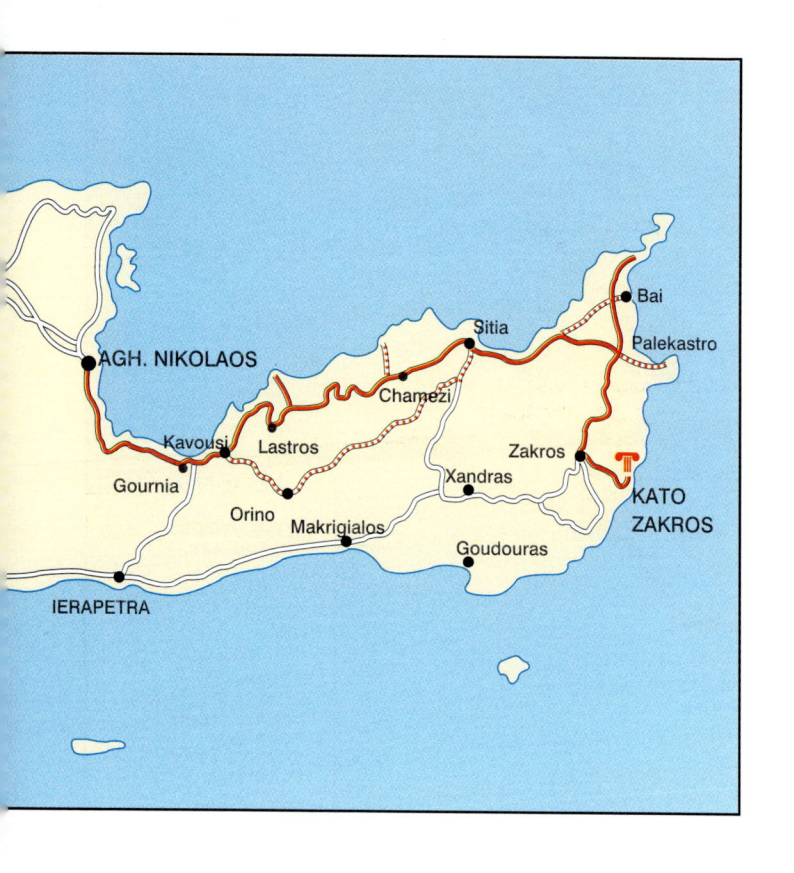

ROUTES STARTING FROM AGHIOS NIKOLAOS

Now that tourist development has covered all the areas north of Aghios Nikolaos as far as Elounda, it is starting to spread towards the south. The first 5 km as far as the village of Ammoudara are full of holiday homes and all kinds of tourist business gathered around the small sandy beaches. After Ammoudara until Pahia Ammos (an ugly village built behind an ugly beach), there are many inlets in the coast with sandy creeks, where many hotels, both large and small, and a camping site have sprung up, but the noise from the main road that goes right by them is a disadvantage. You can of course stop just for a swim, ignoring the illegal fences put up by many of these businesses. Remember that in Greece, **all beaches are public** and private property stops where the sand begins. The owners of land next to beaches are **obliged** to provide access paths to them, and if they don't do this, you can open their garden gate, cross their land and threaten to call the police if anyone dares to stop you.

The coastal route to the village of Kavousi is not particularly interesting. But the mountainous landscape to the south of this road hides some noteworthy places. The first is the **Minoan settlement at Vrokastro,** on a hill 1,500 metres south of the village of Istro. It was here that the American archaeologist Edith Hall excavated in 1910-12 the ruins of a late-Minoan period settlement which seems to have been inhabited until the Geometric Period (11th-8th centuries BC). There is no road leading to the archaeological site, so if you want to climb up here (300 m high), you will have to leave your motorcycle and take the path that begins just before the small sign marked "13 km" along the road from Aghios Nikolaos to Sitia. The climb is not as tiring as you might think, and you will certainly enjoy a beautiful view from up here, and a solitary tour of the (rather poor) ruins of the ancient city.

Almost 17 km along the road from Aghios Nikolaos to Sitia, you will see a dirt road (D3) going off to your right (there is a Greek/English sign at the junction marked **"Faneromeni Monastery"**). Even if you are not especially interested in monasteries, it is worth making this small diversion to enjoy the breathtaking view from the monastery down to the Bay of Mirambelo. This monastery was built in the middle of the 15th century and was dedicated to the Virgin Mary, whose icon manifested itself (thus the name of Virgin Mary Faneromeni, or Manifest) in a small cave on this spot.

Approximately one and a half kilometres east of the junction to the Faneromeni Monastery, you will see a road (there is a Greek/English sign at the junction that says "Gournia Archaeological Site") which branches off to the south and goes to the archaeological site of Gournia.

After Pahia Ammos, the road begins to climb steadily to the northern slopes of Mount Ornos, and the route starts to get interesting. As soon as you arrive at the village of **Kavoussi,** you have two choices, both wonderful!

They say that it was a small engraved stone found by a villager on this low hill on the east side of the Bay of Mirambelo that led a young and insignificant (at that time...) American archaeologist, Harriet Boyd Hawkes, to dig here in 1901. During the next four years, a fantastic Minoan city of the Neopalatial Period (1700-1450 BC) came to light; its street plan was wonderfully preserved. Its streets were rather narrow (1.5-2 metres wide) but well-built and cobbled with wide pebbles from the sea. The houses had only one entrance which gave onto the road; many of them had two floors, with stone walls on the ground floor and brick ones on the upper floor and a flat roof that was supported by wooden columns. It seems that the city prospered and occupied itself with peaceful pursuits (it did not even have walls) until it was destroyed by fire in around 1450 BC, the same period that the other Minoan centres on the island were destroyed. The inhabitants then abandoned it in a hurry, leaving behind their possessions, many of which were found intact in their place. The workshop of a metal-worker **(1)**, a potter **(2)** and a carpenter **(3)**, with many of the trade tools and work materials in their place, exactly as the Minoan craftsmen had left them, have given us important information about everyday life in Minoan Crete. Among them lived the lord of the settlement, who had his luxurious house on the top of the hill **(4)**, a miniature of the Minoan palaces of the period. As with so many other Minoan settlements, this one too keeps its ancient name secret...

ROUTES STARTING FROM AGHIOS NIKOLAOS

Choice Number 1: take the **south road,** i.e. turn south at the village of Kavousi immediately after the last (furthest east) house in the village (see Road Book 11, page 370) on the passable dirt road (D3) to Bembonas and Chrisopigi, and after Chrisopigi, follow the asphalt road (A3) that goes north-east and ends in the village of Piskokefalo, just south of Sitia. This southern road crosses a landscape of wild beauty, covered in low bushes, mint, thyme, dittany, oregano and sage that fills the air with perfume. A few poor mountain villages are hidden on these slopes, on the smooth highlands formed between Mounts Orno and Thrypti, and these are inhabited only during the summer months, as isolation and the heavy winters are intolerable even for the hardened locals.

Choice Number 2: continue on the **north road** (the main road from Aghios Nikolaos to

THE MINOAN SETTLEMENT AT GOURNIA

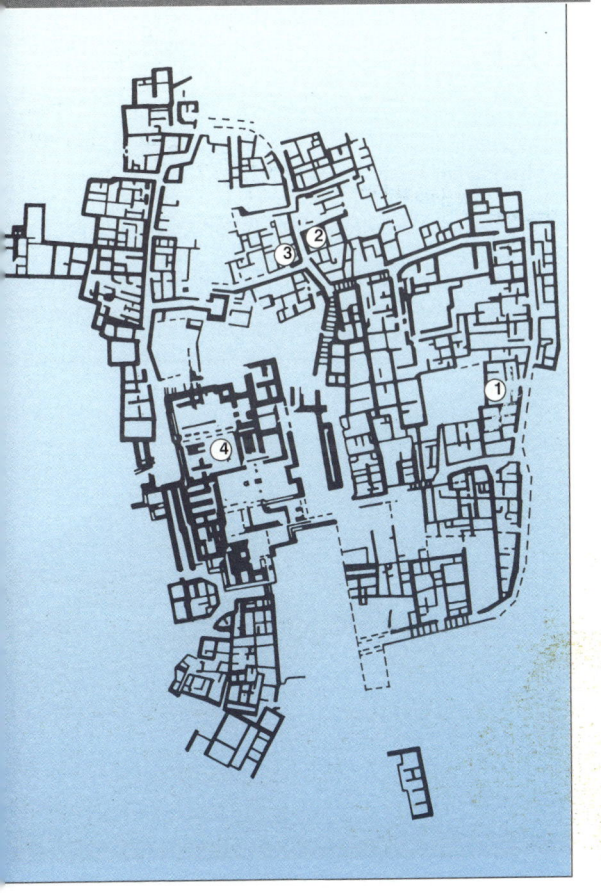

21. Aghios Nikolaos-Zakros

489

Sitia), which crosses the infertile and precipitous northern mountainsides of Mount Orno with many bends but with a good road surface that allows you to ride at a fair pace. The road goes through or next to the most beautiful villages in Crete, like **Lastros,** Sfaka, Mirsini, Exo Mouliana, Mesa Mouliana and **Tourloti.** In Tourloti, the biggest village in the area, there are two traditional coffee-houses. In one of these, the coffee-house of Michali Papadaki, you can eat local specialities like *khohlious* (snails) and *lahanopitia* (little pies made of wild greens).

> "Whoever has a beautiful daughter
> Should marry her off in Lastros
> Where it gets dark early And gets light late!"

Built on the edge of a ravine between two high mountain peaks rising to a height of 1000 metres, Lastros spends most of its daylight hours in the cool shadow of the mountains. So the Lastrians leave late for their fields and gather early in their homes, enjoying the delights of family life. They sit for hours around the lighted fire where they roast chestnuts or corn-on-the-cob, they enjoy a late meal around a laden table and of course they spend many hours in bed. Perhaps this "luxurious" life of the poor Lastrians is the reason why the neighbouring villages have given Lastros the nickname of **"the Paris of Crete"!**

ROUTES STARTING FROM AGHIOS NIKOLAOS

At many points on the road, you will see diversions leading to fantastic landscapes and archaeological sites on the north coast. From Kavousi itself, there is a road (D3) that goes north towards the sandy beach at **Tholo,** where you will find a taverna and a few rooms to rent, although you can easily camp rough. A little way down the main road you will meet the junction (A3) that goes to **Mochlos,** the seaside village where the mountain villagers in the area come down to spend their summer holidays. For visitors, there are two hotels and many rented rooms in Mochlo, which are

THE PARIS OF CRETE

One of these "Cretan-Parisians" was **Nikos Hatzidakis,** who was born in the spring of 1914, just six months after the Union of Crete with Greece. Poor and fatherless from a very early age, he walked through life with quiet and humble steps, with his pockets empty but with his stomach always full of the well-cooked food which his wife, Krystallia, made for him. He was neither handsome, nor tall or well-educated. But the sun shone out of his heart and this showed in his warm eyes and in his smile. He knew very well that warmth is an internal matter, just like the lighted fire in his home in his shadowy village. He could see God's work in the most improbable small objects, which he kept and took pleasure in, as if they were valuable treasures. When he was sad, he cried like a small child, and when he was happy he laughed from the bottom of his heart. He was one of those rare people who enjoyed Paradise on earth. He tasted it in every mouthful of fresh bread, he smelled it in the oregano and thyme that he rubbed between his fingers, he heard it in the voice of his only daughter, Venetsiana.

When he died in the summer of 1993, they found in his jacket pocket a small piece of paper on which he had written in his calligraphic handwriting:

"Whatever kindness passes through my hands, let me do it now. I mustn't put it off until tomorrow, nor must I neglect it. Because I shall never pass this way again..."

usually full of the archaeological teams who dig here every summer, and of the people who are gradually discovering this beautiful place. If, however, you cannot find a room to stay in, there are many quiet corners where you can pitch your tent. As for food, you have many good things to choose from. In the taverna **"Ta Kochylia"**, owned by Michalis Frangiadakis, you can eat *dolmades* (stuffed vine leaves), fantastic *athoulenious* (courgette flowers stuffed with rice), stuffed vegetables, moussaka, and really fresh fish (if it's available, try grilled skaro with tomato sauce). In the taverna **Mochlos**, owned by Yiannis and Elli Zervakis, underneath the hotel of the same name, you can eat extremely tasty rabbit. You can have the best bouillabaisse and also fresh fish cooked on charcoal at the **"Ta Kavouria"** taverna, owned by Spyros and Maria Galanakis. If you are lucky and they have made *fasoulopatates* (an oily dish with potatoes and fresh beans) that day, you'll lick your fingers as well. Just down the road is the **"Sophia"** taverna, owned by Yiannis and Giorgos Petrakis. Mrs. Marika, their mother, who works in the kitchen, makes a wonderful sea-urchin salad, grilled baby octopus, and all the fish is cooked on charcoal. Five hundred metres to the west, outside Mochlos, the **Limenaria** restaurant has very good fish.

On the small island of Aghios Nikolaos, just 150 metres opposite the coast of Mochlos, and on the island of Pseira three miles to the west, a Greek-American team headed by archaeologists Konstantinos Davaras and J. Soles have, from 1988 to the present time, been excavating the ruins of a Minoan city and of its graveyard, continuing the excavation that was begun in 1908 by the American Richard Seager. You can admire finds from this Minoan city (whose ancient name is also unknown) at the museums of Sitia and of Aghios Nikolaos.

Continuing east on the main road, 3.8 km after the eastern sign of the village Exo Mouliana, you will see a big new sign that says **"Chamezi Middle Minoan House"** and it tells you to turn right. "Fine!" you think, "here is the local authority urging me on and helping me visit this unique Minoan monument." Fifty metres further on, however, there is a junction,

ROUTES STARTING FROM AGHIOS NIKOLAOS

but this time without any sign to tell you where to go! If you feel like it, play the game that the local authorities make all visitors play, the one called "Orienteering in the olive-grove labyrinth"! Try to find the Minoan settlement without instructions. If you manage it, congratulations - you don't need this or any other Guide, as you are a born tracker! If you get lost, see below how to find the road. On your way, however, stop off at the village of Chamezi and deliver a letter of protest to the Chairman of the village, in the name of the thousands of travellers who have gone through the ordeal caused by the indifference on the part of the authorities in placing three silly signs at as many critical junctions, which shows their **complete contempt towards visitors.**

So, at the first junction, if you chose the wider road on the right, you're lost! Forty metres on, you will see a narrow road going off to the right. The most reasonable thing would be to continue straight on the wide road, right? Wrong, you're lost again! You should have turned right here. Six hundred metres on, there is a third junction. Without doubt, you choose the road on the right which climbs the hill, as you know that the Minoan habitation is built on the top of a hill. And you're lost for the third time! Because you should have turned left at the road going downhill, then right at the next fork and left at the one following and - phew! - you're there.

On top of the hill the locals call Souvloto Mouri, archaeologist Stephanos Xanthoudidis discovered in 1903 **the only circular Minoan house that has been found up to the present time.** At first, archaeologists assumed it was a peak sanctuary due to its strange architecture and because of four earthenware idols for worship found here, along with a well in the centre of the structure that resembled a circular depository. They later assumed it was a fortress because traces of stairs were found, which means that the building had a second floor.

But in 1971, archaeologist Konstantinos Davaras made supplementary excavations here and found a second entrance to the building, thus excluding the possibility of its being a fortress. He also found a waste water duct at the bottom of the well, which means that it was a tank for collecting and disposing of rainwater, and not a reservoir. As for the idols for worship, they must have belonged to a private temple that was housed in one of the rooms of this house. Its owner must have

The Minoan villa at Chamezi

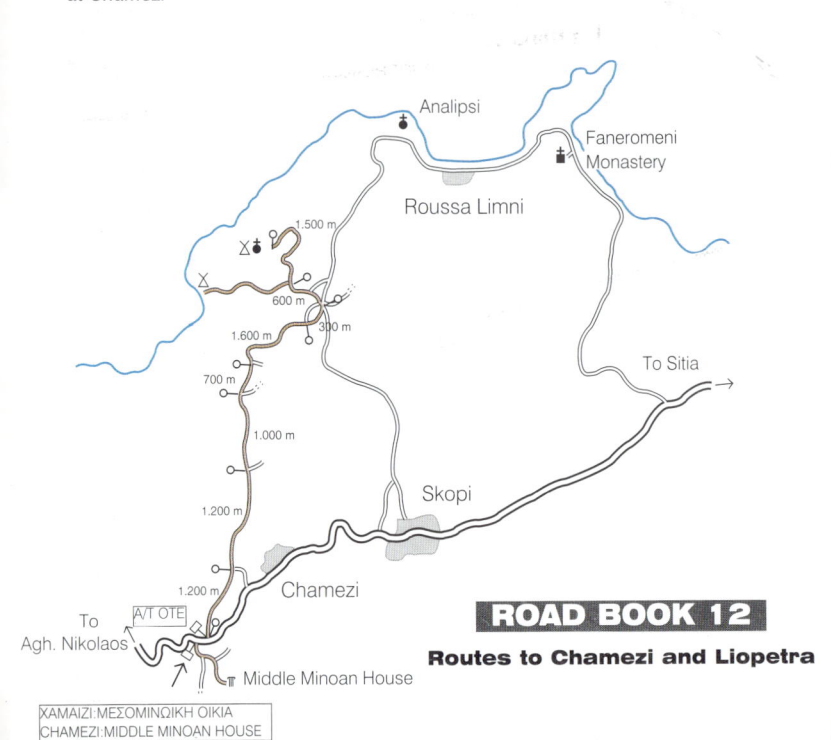

ROAD BOOK 12

Routes to Chamezi and Liopetra

been some local landowner who oversaw his fields from here. Now that he's away and he's left his house unlocked, you might feel the desire to sleep in his bedroom. Although sleeping in a genuine Minoan house must be an exciting experience, it's better not to try it as there are poisonous and sleepless guards. Not, of course, the local police (who probably don't even know the place exists) but the many **snakes** making their nests in the cracks of the walls.

Well, back on the main road and fifty metres along (to the east) from the sign showing the Minoan house at Chamezi, you will see a narrow cement paved (at first) road going off to the left, i.e. to the north (there is a small sign in Greek at the junction reading: "A/T OTE"). Turn here and set your trip odometer (kilometre counter) back to zero so you can follow Road Book 12 and go to **Liopetra, perhaps the best freelance camping site in Crete.** Liopetra is a high hill (430 m) near to the coast. Its eastern slope is quite smooth and the (D3) road climbs here up to the summit, where there is the well-kept country church of the Prophet Elias and the **impressive ruins of the Venetian settlement** built by the hunted inhabitants of Sitia just before the Turks captured their city in 1651. Most of the houses still have their walls and their vaulted roofs and you can easily sleep in whichever one you like! But it's better to pitch your tent on the flat balcony formed by the rock on the west side of the hill, with a sheer cliff 400 metres below it, and with an amazing view of the sea to the north and as far as Aghios Nikolaos to the west!

If you want to do everything, it is a good idea to go towards Sitia by the north road and to return from Sitia by the south road. If you prefer to do a combination, take the south road as far as the village of **Paraspori** (approximately 8 km before Piskokefalo), turn north onto the dirt road that begins in this village and come out again onto the main road from Aghios Nikolaos to Sitia at the village of Skopi. From Skopi, ride a few km westward to visit the Minoan house at Chamezi and to take the northern diversion towards Liopetra (see above).

SITIA

As is the case with most protected bays, the one on which Sitia is now built has been the scene of human habitation from a very long time ago. Many small Neolithic settlements were scattered behind this sandy coast, while in the Minoan era a large settlement grew up on the hill of Petra, about 2 kilometres east of the centre of Sitia. The English archaeologist Robert Bosanquet was the first to make excavations on this hill in 1901, and he maintained that the traces of buildings which he discovered belonged to the Minoan City of **Itia.** His hypothesis has been confirmed by the extended excavations that have been carried out here by the Greek archaeologist Metaxia Tsipopoulou since 1985 and which have revealed the foundations of a palace-like building at the highest point of the hill, and of a large city that grew up around it during the Neopalatial Period (1700-1450 BC). **Myson,** one of the seven sages of ancient Greece, was born in this city. Its harbour was used as a port by the ancient Praisians, who came and settled here in 155 BC (those who survived, that is) after the destruction of Praisos by the Ierapytnians. Most of the finds from the excavations at Sitia and the surrounding area are exhibited at the Archaeological Museum of Sitia (open Tuesday - Sunday, 9 a.m. - 3 p.m.) which is

Sitia: Here the Cretans outnumder the tourist

situated at the east end of the town, on the road to Ierapetra.

Down on the coast, at the point where Sitia is now, there was already a city from the end of the Roman era. It was one of the cities the Genoans fortified with walls in around 1204, but it soon passed into the hands of the Venetians, who strengthened its walls. During Venetian rule, the city was destroyed twice by earthquake and, in 1538, it was razed to the ground by the worst pirate of that time, Chairentin Barbarosa. Despite these numerous catastrophes, Sitia not only survived but also became a strong artistic and intellectual centre. It was here that **Vincentzos Kornaros** was born and worked in the middle of the 17th century; he was the poet who wrote **Erotokritos,** a long narrative love poem of 10,000 lines which has been so widely read and so loved by the people that many popular Cretan "bards" learned large parts of it by heart and recited it at folk festivals.

In 1648, when the Turks were at its gates, the Venetians had already moved its inhabitants to a castle which they built on the steep hill of **Liopetra,** about 10 kilometres west of Sitia. In 1651, after a spirited defence of 3 years, the Turks captured Sitia and reduced it to a pile of ruins. It remained in this condition for two centuries, until 1869, when it was rebuilt by the Turks.

Nothing has been preserved of Turkish Sitia except for the town's street plan. Today Sitia is a very beautiful town, the only town on the island that has managed to maintain a peaceful atmosphere and its authentic Cretan character. Don't imagine that it is some poor neglected town - on the contrary! Its 8,000 permanent residents are **the most cheerful and friendly Cretans you could hope to meet,** people who love their town and keep it clean and tidy, not so much to attract tourists but more because they themselves take pleasure in it and are proud of it.

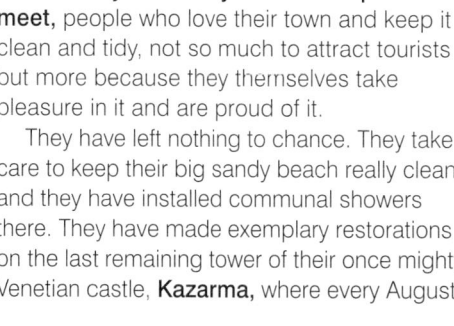

They have left nothing to chance. They take care to keep their big sandy beach really clean and they have installed communal showers there. They have made exemplary restorations on the last remaining tower of their once mighty Venetian castle, **Kazarma,** where every August they organise the "Kornareia", a very interesting cultural festival. With respect to the appearance of their town, they have the necessary infrastructure to offer visitors a pleasant stay, treating them as friends and not as walking wallets. In any case, tourism is not their main source of income. They maintain their own social and economic life, in which visitors are welcome. It is the only town in Crete where the locals outnumber the foreigners, even in August. You will see them bringing vitality to the commercial streets behind the park, from early in the morning until late in the afternoon. When evening comes, they dress in their best and go out for the 'statutory' **volta** or walk on the pavement next to the harbour, where most of the restaurants, coffee-houses, patisseries and bars are grouped. From the very first day of your stay, these cheerful people will make you feel especially welcome.

If we exclude the rather inelegant hotels situated by the harbour, you have many good places to choose to stay at in Sitia. The most luxurious and most expensive is the **Sitia Beach Hotel** on the east side of the town, next to the beach (A class, easy parking, two swimming pools, air-conditioning, etc., tel: 0843-28821, fax: 0843-28826). Convenient hotels in the town are the **Dennis** (B class, tel: 0843-28356), the **Crystal** (C class, tel: 0843-22284) and the cheap but clean **Nora** (D class, tel: 0843-23017). There are also many rooms to rent on every corner of the town. Absolutely the best you can choose (and indeed at an exceptionally low price) are the newly-built **Kazarma** rooms owned by Yiannis Angelidis at 10 Ionias Street, near the castle (A class, all rooms with refrigerator and balcony, common sitting room and kitchen, somewhat cramped but safe parking for your motorcycle, tel: 0843-23211).

For food and entertainment, all you have to do is take a walk to the small harbour and the streets around it, and all the choices open up in front of your very eyes. For well-grilled fresh fish you can trust the **Remetzo,** the **Zorbas** and the **Kastro,** all three of which are on the Sitia waterfront. A very good traditional taverna is the **Neromylos** in the neighbouring village of

Aghia Fotia, which is housed in an old watermill and, apart from the fantastic charcoal-grilled meat, it offers a very lovely view of Sitia (especially at night). Late at night (or early in the morning, if you prefer!) all the night-owls end up in the two traditional night restaurants on the north side of the harbour, the **Pharo** and the **Karnagia,** for a steaming hot dish of patsas (tripe), boiled goat, omaties (lamb's intestines stuffed with rise and finely-chopped offal) and all the typical casserole dishes.

There is not much choice of evening entertainment in Sitia. The outstanding place here is the **Planitario,** a huge discotheque with a sliding roof for crazy fun under the stars! It is situated 500 metres outside the northern edge of the town, which allows it to play its music to whatever decibel level it likes. In the town there are about ten bars, all in the same style and all playing more or less the same music - rock and jazz to start with, then techno and dance music and, after 2 a.m. Greek music. People gather first at one and then at the other bar, so you have to go to all of them (they're all near each other anyway) to see which one has the people.

Sitia does not have a motorcycle club, but it does have a big group of motorcyclists. Michalis Zervakis, Nikos Tsimpidakis, Ippokratis Misantonis, Giorgos Papadakis, and many others whom you will find in the town's motorcycle shops and workshops (see the list of helpful information at the end of this Guide), are eager to help you find your way around their home territory and to assist you in whatever you need.

If you decide to start your holidays in Sitia, you can come straight here from Pireas on the ferry **Vincentzos Kornaros,** the best ship sailing between Pireas and Crete, and one of the best Greek coastal liners. You can also come by air on the small Olympic Airways propeller aeroplanes that land four times a week in the small airport north of Sitia. When you arrive in Sitia, you can hire a motorcycle from the two local motorcycle rental offices, the **Knossos** (Yamahas XT 660, XT 350, DT 125; tel: 0843-24114) and **Petras** (Yamahas XT 250, XT 350, DT 125; tel: 0843-24849). If Sitia is the end of your journey, you can take the boat to Karpathos, Kassos and Rhodes or straight to Pireas.

EAST OF SITIA

The coastal road (A3) that goes off east of Sitia is the only one in the area with traffic because it leads to the two popular sights in east Crete - the Toplou Monastery (Moni Toplou) and the palm tree forest at Vai. If you want to cut off from the main road a little, about two kilometres after Sitia you will see a road (A3) going off to your right (south) and climbing towards the plateau of Ziros (there is a Greek/English sign at the junction marked "Roussa Ekklisia"). At the centre of the picturesque village of **Roussa Ekklisia** there is an enormous plane tree next to which runs the cold water of a spring. An iced coffee made from the water of this spring and the deep shade of the plane tree give you the coolest stop you could make. Returning to our main route, continue east on the coast road where there is not much to see, until you arrive at the historic **Toplou Monastery.** You must take great care on the road from Sitia to Toplou Monastery as it is narrow with many badly-designed bends.

Alone in the middle of nowhere and built at a time (around the middle of the 15th century) when pirates and bandits of all nationalities were ravaging Crete, the only way the Toplou Monastery could survive was to have strong fortifications. So the monks built a thick 10 metre high surrounding wall of stone, complete with small windows like arrowholes, a heavy castle gate, murder holes for pouring out boiling oil onto the heads of attackers, and they placed a cannon on the rampart of the door! (It was after this that the Turks called the monastery Toplou - 'Top' in Turkish means cannon ball.) Despite its strong fortification, the monastery was captured and looted twice, first by the Knights of Malta in 1530 and later by the Turks in 1646. It kept its fortifications however, and right throughout Turkish rule it was a refuge for rebels, which was the reason for the many disasters it suf-

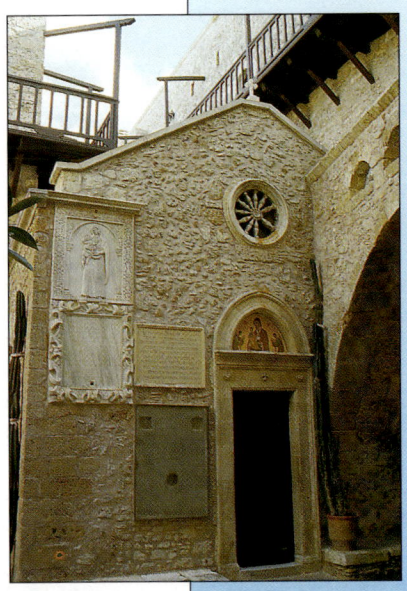

ROUTES STARTING FROM AGHIOS NIKOLAOS

After the Toplou Monastery, the road (A3) continues through an isolated landscape and meets the main road from Palaikastro to Vai at right angles. Turn left here and right at the next junction, following the Greek/English signs for Vai, in order to see a landscape unique in the whole of Crete. Vai is a big sandy beach like so many others in Crete but with the special feature that behind it there is a **thick palm tree forest** (more than 5,000 trees, said to have sprung up from the stones of the dates spat out by the pirates who were hiding here!). As you descend the road towards the beach, you have the impression that you are in an oasis in the African desert! As soon as you reach the beach, however, you will have difficulty in finding a parking place even for your motorcycle. There is an even greater jam on the beach, where the crowd is a fact of life from early in the morning, and it is the same thing in the taverna and the bar, where the prices are

TOPLOU MONASTERY

fered. Even during the German occupation, the monastery took part in the resistance with a wireless set installed here.

Unfortunately, most of the monastery's heirlooms were destroyed by the Turks. In the centre of the surrounding wall is a small chapel dedicated to the Birth of the Virgin Mary; this is distinguished by a wonderful icon dating back to 1770, the work of the icon painter, Ioannis Kornaros. The most important heirloom of the monastery, however, is not ecclesiastical; **it is an epigraph of the 2nd century BC,** engraved on a stone plaque, which comes from ancient Itanos. It contains the first 80 lines of the **Treaty of Magnisia,** a treaty signed by the Cretan cities of Itanos and Ierapytna under the arbitration of the Asia Minor city of Magnisia. The English traveller, Robert Pashley, in 1834 found it functioning as the altar in the chapel of the monastery's cemetery, and under his recommendation, the monks enshrined it in the external wall of the chapel where it is still to be found today. The Toplou Monastery today has only three monks, but it continues to own an enormous amount of land that earns a lot of profits for it, as you can see for yourself by the very luxurious work on improvements, maintenance and extensions being carried out at the monastery.

daylight robbery. Vai is a very beautiful place, but to enjoy it you have to come here after the end of September and before July. In the high season, it's better to try and see if you can find more space on the beach directly south of Vai, ten minutes away on foot by the path that starts behind the taverna.

Vai may steal the show, but if crowds annoy you, there are other lovely beaches in the area with much less people. Take the road (A3) that goes north towards Cape Sideros and leads to the small village of Erimoupoli. There are three wonderful beaches here next to each other. The best is the most southerly one, directly south of the ruins of the ancient city of **Itanos.** An even quieter beach, ideal for rough camping, is Chochlakia beach, one kilometre northwest of Erimoupoli. The dirt road that continues east from Erimoupoli towards Cape Sideros is cut off a little further along by the gate of an army camp which unfortunately takes up all the beautiful area of the cape.

ANCIENT ITANOS

Once, when the inhabitants of ancient Thera (Santorini) became too many, they decided that half of them had to leave and go establish a colony. So they sent a delegation to the Oracle at Delphi to ask Pythia, the priestess, about the most suitable place to colonise. The mischievous Pythia replied: Libya! The poor Therans had never heard of Libya and thus they set out in search of someone who could show them the way. While searching, they eventually came to **Itanos** where they found, at last, someone who had been to Libya. Well, he hadn't exactly navigated there but rather had been blown there by a storm at sea that lasted for days, and he had managed to return intact! He was **Koryvios,** a murex fisherman. The maze-like sketches he drew on the sand to help the Therans find their way were too complicated and so the latter convinced him to lead them to Libya, for a very handsome fee of course.

The story (preserved by Herodotus) provides a first valuable piece of information regarding the occupations of the residents of ancient Itanos. Much more evidence was unearthed by the French archaeologists who dug here in 1950, but have not yet published their findings officially! According to all indications, ancient Itanos was built (the exact time is anybody's guess) by **Phoenician** merchants on the site of a pre-existing Minoan settlement. The Phoenicians brought products of their country, sold them in Crete, then bought Cretan products and shipped them back to their homeland. Later on, however, they developed a local cottage industry for the production of **porphyropsin,** a bright purple pigment extracted from the sea-shells harvested in Cretan waters. Besides the porphyropsin workshops, Itanos also claimed (in Roman times) many glass-making workshops.

The Itanians worshipped their own Phoenician gods, naturally, but their most palpable profits came from a Cretan god, **Diktaios Zeus.** The famed temple of Diktaios Zeus (east of present day Palekastro) was situated in the region occupied by the Itanians and, consequently, the generous offerings made by the faithful ended up directly into their treasury! Yet, two other cities in the area, the Eteocretan Praisos and the Doric Ierapytna had had an eye on the temple for quite some time, not for religious reasons of course. Sometime around 160 BC, the Praisians managed to occupy the temple, but the Itanians recaptured it with the assistance of King Ptolemy of Egypt. A few years later (in 155 BC) Praisos was razed to the ground following a decisive attack by the Ierapytnians, who then started pressing heavily on the Itanians. Finally, the Romans intervened and destroyed the quarrelsome Ierapytna. Itanos on the contrary sided with the Romans and flourished during the entire period of Roman rule, as well as during its successor, the first Byzantine period. Nevertheless, it suffered great destruction in the earthquake of 795, never to recover since. Whatever was left intact by the quake was levelled by the Arabs in 824. Today, you can see only scattered stones around the two hills where the city once stood. As a tribute to those clever "manufacturers" who embellished their era with their bright pigments, do wear something purple as you tread through the ruins of their city!

Continuing south from Vai you will cross a barren rocky landscape and roughly 6 kilometres later you will reach the fairly developed and attractive village of **Palekastro,** frequented by tourists precisely because it is very close to the famed Vai. Here you can find plenty of rooms to let, as well as 4-5 hotels, the outstanding one being the Marina Village Hotel (C class, quiet location, swimming pool, safe motorcycle parking; tel.

In 1904, at a time of excavation fever in all corners of Crete, a team of English archaeologists headed by R.C. Bosanquet, came to dig the area exactly behind Chiona beach, at a point where surface findings were very promising. Indeed, they discovered the ruins of the **largest Minoan city after Knossos,** estimated to have covered a surface of 300,000 square metres! Its ancient name remains unknown. It is presumed to have been the ancient **Dragmos,** but for want of documentary evidence it was named after its modern-day place-name of **Roussolakos.**

Already in the first year of excavations a highly valuable finding came to light and helped to make a positive identification: it was the fragments of a limestone which was found among the remains of a totally ruined temple. Here therefore was the famous **Temple of Diktaios Zeus;** a temple that attracted many pilgrims and accordingly many treasures, to the extent that three cities, Itanos, Praesos and Ierapytna fought to gain control over it.

In more recent excavations between 1987 and 1990, English archaeologists discovered here the pieces of a gold and ivory statue, approximately 50 cm in height, known as the Kouros of Palekastro, which you can admire today at the museum of Sitia. Many archaeologists relate this statue with the worship of Diktaios Zeus.

The houses of this ancient city were built in neighbourhoods separated by wide flagstone paved streets. The rich findings bespeak of an affluent city with many workshops and brisk commercial activity. Such a city would certainly have had a king or a lord, who would have resided in a palace of some sort. Yet, until this day, no trace of such palace has been unearthed. In the hope that it has not been destroyed by the bombs dropped here in the Second World War, or by the careless villagers who used to

0846-61284). There are also a few good restaurants and tavernas, such as the **Mythos** that serves Cretan cuisine, **Basiakos** in the neighbouring village of Angathia, and three excellent fish taverns at Chiona, the beach of Palekastro.

The beach at Chiona is spacious, clean and sandy and attracts a good number of bathers. At its southern end, nevertheless, you will find many secluded sandy coves

THE ARCHAEOLOGICAL SITE OF ROUSSOLAKOS

exploit Roussolakos as a source of building materials, the English archaeologists carry on their excavations so speedily and diligently that they have laid themselves open to criticism by the suspicious locals (recently they were accused by the village of Palekastro of serious irregularities and lack of transparency in their diggings).

Apart from the Temple of Diktaios Zeus, which was the focus of religious life in this town for many centuries (from the Geometric to the Roman period), particularly significant was also the **Peak Sanctuary of Petsophas,** named after the present day hillock (215 m) at the headland south of Palekastro on which it stands. The dozens of clay figurines of humans and animals that were found here and are now exhibited at the museums if Sitia and Aghios Nikolaos, had been votive offerings of Minoans who came up here for their devotions. What would have been their deepest wishes and their greatest fears? What impressions and what dreams went through the bare skulls now unearthed by the archaeologists? The contact with the remnants of humans that lived so long ago reveals principally the unbridgeable gulf between us and them.

The village of Adravasti

among the rocks, where you can even pitch a tent. Directly behind Chiona beach lies the archaeological site of Roussolakos.

The narrow prefecture road (A3) south of Palekastro traverses a landscape of weird brown cliffs blotched by low thorny bushes and wild flowers. The gentle eastern slopes of the Ziros Plateau are the nesting grounds for half a dozen hamlets whose very inhabitants cling to their traditions and busy themselves mainly with the cultivation of olives. Langada, Azokeramos, Chochlakies, Kelaria, Adravasti, Klisidi, make one wonder how they managed to survive after all the calamities that befell them. The worst one happened in June 1824 when the bloodthirsty janissary Housein Lagoudoglou rounded up all the Christian men of these villages in a storehouse in Chochlakies on the pretext of reading to them some sultanic firman, and then took them out one by one and had them slaughtered to the last...

Inside Chochlakies you will see an English/Greek sign urging you east toward the **Chochlakies Gorge.** The road (D3) continues for about 2 km through olive groves and then becomes a foot path all the way to the coast where lies the exquisite and serene sand of Karoumbes beach.

South of Chochlakies, at the northern end of Adravasti village you will come upon a dirt road (D3) that goes west and ascends towards the Ziros Plateau. This is a very good choice if you want to return to Sitia via a mountain road, passing through the highly picturesque villages of Karidi, Palio Mitato, Krioneri and Roussa Ekklisia. The entire plateau is an ideal terrain for off-road riding and rough camping, full of dirt roads which form ring routes and pass through quaint villages or next to isolated farmhouses and country chapels. If you are up to it you can attempt a greater detour by turning south at Karidi toward Sitanos, in order to visit the medieval towers at Chandras and Etia and the ruins of ancient Praesos (see Route 16, page 372)

Carrying on south of Adravasti, the road (A3) goes through the large village of Ano Zakros and ends at the coast, where the Minoan palace of Kato Zakros is situated (see Route 15, page 363).

Practical information

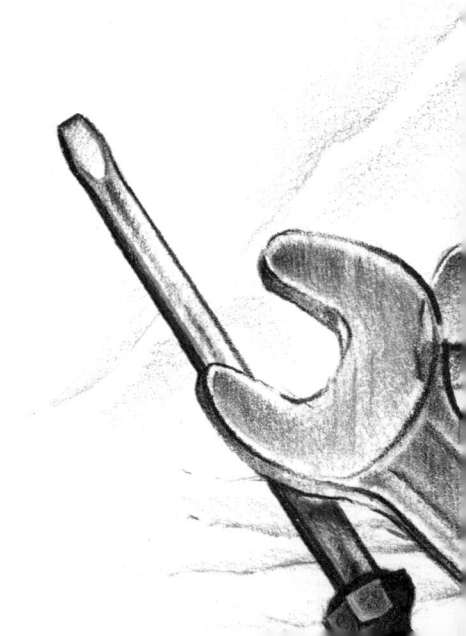

SERVICE

FIRST AID

Tel 551379

USEFUL INFORMATION ON THE LAW
Theodore Gazoulis, Ph.D., Attorney

As is well known, laws differ from country to country. But while the Greek Law is not so significantly different from that of other European countries, the distance between law and everyday practice **is,** as any first time visitor will soon notice. A great number of traffic violations go unpunished, sometimes regretfully so (when STOP signs are ignored, for instance), sometimes very rightly (when unreasonably low speed limits are not observed, or cyclists choose to ignore signs forbidding bikes). In what follows we will try to provide some basic information regarding the Greek Law and everyday reality, which should come in handy whether you are always violating traffic laws or are harmed by somebody else's behaviour.

1. The European Convention on Human Rights, which was signed in 1950, applies in Greece as well, and it is in fact above any contrary Greek law with the exception of the Constitution.

2. The Constitution of Greece deals with individual and social rights, and these concern not only Greek citizens but aliens as well (it is no accident that the Constitution speaks of "all persons" and "no person" where individual and social rights are stated). Especially important for the visitor of this country are the following articles: article 5 (regarding personality rights), 6 (on arrest and detention pending trial), 7 (specifying when there is a crime and forbidding any kind of maltreatment), 9 (providing that "each person's home is a sanctuary"), 13 (protecting freedom of religious conscience), 14 (allowing freedom of expression), 16 (providing that "art and science... shall be free"), 17 (protecting property), 19 (stating that "secrecy of letters... shall be absolutely inviolable"), and 20 (guaranteeing each person's right "to receive legal protection by the courts"). It is worth noting that the Constitution has been translated by the Translation Department of the Parliament in all major European languages and can be easily obtained.

3. Among the above, articles 6 and 7 are of special importance. Article 6 states that: *a.* "no person shall be arrested or imprisoned without a reasoned judicial warrant... served at the moment of arrest or detention pending trial, except when caught while committing a criminal act," and *b.* the person must be brought before the examining magistrate within twenty-four hours, and the examining magistrate "must release the detainee or issue a warrant of imprisonment" **within three days at most.**

    Article 7 provides that any person who has been illegally or unjustly detained and deprived of his or her personal freedom must be compensated.

4. Bodily search is allowed only when there is serious and reasonable suspicion that a crime has been committed. This must take place in private, as the Law explicitly forbids a group search or one that takes place in public. Needless to say, a person can only be searched by another person of the same sex. Also, keep in mind that bearing arms is prohibited and that the anti-aggression sprays which are allowed in other countries are considered to be illegal weapons. Should you happen to be found with one, though, do not tell the police officer "I didn't know it was punishable"; say that you "didn't know it was forbidden." You will certainly discover that it makes a world of difference!

5. Searching a person's vehicle or home requires the presence of a judicial representative and can only be done when there is reason to believe that it will lead to the confirmation of a crime.

6. In Greece the possession and use of drugs is punished by law. There is no distinction between "hard" and "soft" drugs, so if you are used to a different legal reality in your home country you must adjust to this one to avoid any unwelcome experiences!

7. If the Interpol is after you for terrorist action, you are bound to have a rough time... The Law is quite strict on this point, and Greek jails are not known for their comfort and luxury, especially in comparison to those in West Europe or North America...

8. Admittedly, everything said so far concerns pretty serious situations... If we now take a look at the most frequent type of encounter with the Law, which concerns traffic violations, we can note the following:

    Traffic violations fall under two categories: *a.* minor offences and *b.* misdemeanours.

PRACTICAL INFORMATION

   a. Most traffic violations are classified as minor offences. Foreign visitors definitely have an advantage here, because the punishments provided for by the Law are not directly applicable; fines are never collected on the spot, and vehicles are never immobilised with metal "claws." On the rare occasion your vehicle has been removed by a municipal or Traffic Police crane, you must pay a small amount to take it back from where it's kept.

   b. More serious offences are treated as misdemeanours. Attention must be paid here, because you can be arrested and led before a court hearing cases of flagrant crimes. Among other things, these offences include:

Driving without a driver's licence.
Driving without a permit or number plates.
Failing to obey the orders or signals of a police officer wearing his uniform.
Driving under the influence of alcohol or drugs.
Driving with the lights turned to the highest scale, so that other drivers are blinded.
Overloading a vehicle by more than 10% above the specified limit.
Exceeding the speed limit by 40 kilometres per hour or more, or, in case of highways and fast traffic roads, exceeding the speed of 140 or 130 kilometres respectively.

9. Should you be arrested, you have the right to contact a family member or friend, a lawyer, or the Embassy or Consulate of your country. In addition, you can ask for an interpreter.

10. If you are of Greek origin and have relatives in Greece, or if you are an alien but have a Greek address, you must make a statement to that effect, so that you are only detained by the police in those cases that Greek citizens are also detained.

11. Failure to insure a vehicle is regarded as a misdemeanour and is punished as such. Careful, then, because the green card must at all times be valid. In addition, considering the fact that many thieves show a decided preference for foreign vehicles, it would not be a bad idea to insure your bike against theft as well.

12. If you get involved in a traffic accident:

   a. In case there is only damage to property:

   If it is the Greek vehicle that is to blame, you must take down all necessary information and contact its insurance company. Use the form at the end of this book.

   If it is your fault, you must give the other driver a copy or slip of your green card - so that he can contact the international insurance office - and make a statement to your own insurance company as soon as you get back to your country (unless otherwise stated in your contract).

   b. In case a person gets injured or dies:

   You must immediately inform the police and see to it that the person is taken to the hospital. If you ignore this responsibility and take off, your action is considered a misdemeanour and is punished as such.

   Police will arrest and detain you (unless we are speaking of a minor injury). If you come from one of the European Community countries this will happen only if the injury is quite serious. In either case, what happens to you will be decided by the District Attorney in charge.

13. **Damage occurring in ships is not covered by insurance companies.** This is why it is always a good idea to visit the garage during the times passengers board the ship or get off. Should your vehicle be damaged in spite of your precautions, you must inform the port authorities and the captain of the ship.

14. If a policeman or other public official causes damage to your vehicle (while searching it, for instance), it is not enough to prove that the damage is attributable to him (as is true for other European countries); you must also prove that the act that caused it (the search conducted for instance) was illegal!

15. Certain acts are not considered penal offences in Greece and are, therefore, not punished by the Law. Sexual harassment is a good example.

16. If you have an accident as a result of a pothole in the road or a wrong sign, you have no chance of being compensated. According to the precedents, drivers must be aware of the condition of the roads and take their precautions!

17. Some driving habits may differ from the Highway Code, or even be opposite to what it states, and you can certainly not ignore them. Consequently, it is not enough to pay attention to the road signs, but you must also keep an eye out for what other drivers are doing; their behaviour may be illegal and unexpected!
18. If you want to allow a pedestrian to cross the street or if you want to hit the brakes as soon as the traffic light turns yellow, you better check what's happening behind you...
19. Be extra careful with pedestrians! They have never been educated on how to cross the street and will frequently make a run for the other side. Meanwhile, Greek courts will generally put the blame on the driver...
20. Keep in mind that in case there is an accident it is always more difficult for a foreigner to find witnesses! If you feel that the situation is fairly complicated, it might be to your best interest to contact the local motorcycle club, if there is one, and ask for their help.

A final note: Though the first encounter with the Greek roads may be a hard experience, or even painful at times, remember that, unlike other countries - such as Germany or the U.S. - where it is often useless trying to explain your point of view to the traffic police officer, a friendly conversation with the Greek officers may go a long way toward making your stay in this country as pleasant and trouble-free as possible.

IN CASE OF AN ACCIDENT

If you have a traffic accident in which there are only minor injuries and damage to property, the Highway Code states the following:
- All people and vehicles involved must stay at the site of the accident but without placing other vehicles at risk.
- Warning signs must be placed on the street in both directions to ward off further accidents.
- The police must be notified immediately.

If the collided vehicles are in the middle of the road and block the traffic, they must be moved to the side. **Before moving them, though,** take a few shots from as many angles as possible (close shots as well as distant ones), jot down the name of at least one witness who has seen their initial position, and record the accident on the handy table that follows. If the other driver refuses to give you his name - a totally outrageous thing, to be sure - take down his plate number and insurance company info - which you will find on a small card stuck on the windshield - as well as the names of a few witnesses, along with the place and phone where they can be reached. The latter precaution is especially important in any accident, let alone in cases that invite dispute. You should know that witnesses are often reluctant to volunteer their name and address, because they don't want to get involved and to be later forced to testify in court (if things get so far). Should they refuse to give you the information you need, do not insist too much because you'll only make them walk away. Take a good look at their faces instead, and when the police arrives point them out in the crowd. This will force them to provide the info requested.

Do not allow the other driver to leave before the police gets there. If you do, you run the risk of being fooled by an apologetic person, who will take full blame for the accident, only to go to his insurance company and deny the responsibility. This, of course, would make it very difficult for you to prove your case and to be paid for damages. If your motorcycle is badly damaged, you must be very careful to document the accident. Most insurance companies in Greece will do anything they can to avoid paying, and the only thing that will fully cover you is the Accident Report made by the police on the accident site.

If people die or get seriously injured, they should be taken to the hospital immediately. Everyone else, though, should stay there and wait for the police. The phone numbers of police precincts and first aid stations are given in this catalogue. You will also need to contact your insurance company in Athens, and for that you can start with the Directory Info: (01) 3236 733.

PRACTICAL INFORMATION

PLACE / TIME	DATE	TIME	PLACE	
VEHICLE	PLATE NUMBER	MAKE	TYPE	COLOUR

OWNER	NAME	
	ADDRESS	PHONE NUMBER

DRIVER	NAME	
	ADDRESS	PHONE NUMBER

INSURANCE COMPANY	NAME	
	INSURANCE CONTRACT NO	PHONE NUMBER

WITNESS A	NAME	
	ADDRESS	PHONE NUMBER

WITNESS B	NAME	
	ADDRESS	PHONE NUMBER

GAS STATIONS

Greece is full of gas stations! You won't face any trouble refuelling, but keep in mind that most gas stations are concentrated around the cities and along the national and main countryside roads. If you plan to go travelling in the mountains, make sure you leave with a full tank. On the maps of Greece that Road Editions has published almost all gas stations have been marked, so you can plan your route in advance keeping in mind how far your bike will allow you to go.

Official gas station opening times are 7:00 a.m. - 7:00 p.m. Monday through Friday and from 7:00 a.m. till 3:00 p.m. on Saturdays. Since 1992, though, opening hours have unofficially been left up to the owners, so most gas stations remain open till 9:00 p.m. and 10% of them never close. Also, keep in mind that the owner of an isolated or village gas station usually lives right next to it or above it, so if it isn't too late you can always honk or ring his doorbell and ask for service.

PRICE OF GAS

Super: 212 - 225 drachmas per litre.   Unleaded: 200 - 205 drachmas per litre

In 1991 price regulation came to an end and the tough competition brought the prices down to a relatively cheaper level. As a rule, gas is cheaper in the cities. The selling prices of each station must be mentioned on a special sign post.

TYRE REPAIR SHOPS

Tyre repair shops can be found in every town, large or small. They are usually located near the entrance or the exit of the town and they remain open till late in the evening. Most gas stations serve as tyre repair shops as well, or they at least have the necessary equipment to help in case of emergency. Both tyre shops and gas stations that provide adequate vulcanising services are marked on the Road Editions maps. But much too often tyre shops **not specialising in motorcycles** don't keep a stock of motorcycle tyres or inner tubes. They also lack a torque wrench, so after fixing the tyre it would be wise to make a stop at a good repair shop as soon as you can and to have the bolts tightened properly.

POSTAL SERVICES

Greece used to have some of Europe's worst post offices. Since the beginning of the 90's, however, an ambitious program to raise their level got off the ground, so today you can be sure that your postcards will not arrive after you return home!

Besides postcards, you can mail home anything you won't be needing during your trip and any large objects which you may have bought and then found too inconvenient to carry. You can also **receive** parcels - or letters - by using the poste-restante method. Just ask your friends to address them to you and to send them to a certain post office from where you'll pick them up. The address should look like the following:

John Davis
Central Post Office of Rethimno
POSTE-RESTANTE

PRACTICAL INFORMATION

Your letter or parcel will be kept for you at the post office for about two months and you can collect it by showing them your passport. Post office opening hours are 7:30 a.m. - 2:00 p.m. Monday through Friday. In Hania and Iraklio, however, the main post offices are open from 7:30 a.m. to 8:00 p.m., seven days a week.

MAKING PHONE CALLS

The telephone, as its very Greek name suggests, is a device meant to carry a speaker's voice (*phoni*) to a far distance (tele < ancient Greek *tile*, far). Unfortunately, a more appropriate name for it here in Greece would be tele - mix up, tele - confusion, or tele - party!

At least that's how things were until 1990! Because at that time an innovative spirit swept through the Greek telecommunications company known as **OTE,** and a large scale effort to upgrade services began. Part of this effort was the new, advanced-technology digital network that would change the picture in telecommunications. Another part, which was immediately visible in our neighbourhoods, was the gradual replacement of the old coin-operated public phones by the new **card phones** that have now spread all over Greece. By the summer of 1995 a total of 15,000 new card phones had been installed, making it a lot easier for tourists to call home. Cards are sold in all street kiosks and convenience stores and they cost 1300 drachmas a piece. Each card gives you one hundred units, so each unit costs 13 drachmas. A phone call to Germany means 15 units (or 195 drachmas) per minute if you call during the expensive zone (6:00 a.m. to 10:00 p.m., Monday through Sunday) and 12 units (or 156 drachmas) if you call during the cheaper zone (10:00 p.m. to 6:00 a.m.). A phone call to Italy means 12 units (or 156 drachmas) per minute during the expensive zone and 10 units (or 130 drachmas) during the cheaper zone. On the dial window of the phone you can see how many units you have left, and if you are running out of units you can replace the old card with a new one - before you reach zero - and keep talking. International calls can also be made from the OTE offices which you will find in every town and every large village. Opening hours: 7:30 a.m. - 3:00 p.m., Monday through Friday. In places with a lot of tourism offices stay open till 10:00 p.m.

BANKS

The banking network in Greece is quite extensive and well organised. There are 26 private or state-owned Greek banks with many branches, and 24 foreign banks with headquarters in Athens and possibly a few branches as well.

Most banks have installed automatic teller machines (ATM's) in their branches to offer 24 hour service. ALPHA CREDIT BANK has the densest ATM network and accepts Visa, American Express and Barclays cards, while the IONIAN BANK accepts only Visa, the NATIONAL BANK accepts Mastercard, Eurocard, and Cirrus, and the COMMERCIAL BANK Visa and Mastercard. Some of these banks have also installed Automatic Exchange machines (AEM's).

BANK OPENING HOURS
Monday - Thursday .....8:00 a.m. - 2:00 p.m. Friday........8:00 a.m. - 1:30 p.m.

DRUGSTORES

Drugstores are found in all towns and large villages in Crete, and they can be distinguished by the sign with the cross (green or red). As a rule, pharmacists are very well trained and they have a considerable knowledge of Medicine. They can easily diagnose most minor ailments and recommend the right treatment, so you don't always need to go to the doctor or have a medical prescription with you. Most of them speak English well and are very helpful with foreigners.

DRUGSTORE OPENING HOURS
Monday .... 8:00 a.m. - 2:30 p.m.
Tuesday .... 8:00 a.m. - 2:00 p.m. and 5:00 p.m. - 8:00 p.m.
Wednesday .... 8:00 a.m. - 2:30 p.m.
Thursday .... 8:00 a.m. - 2:00 p.m. and 5:00 p.m. - 8:00 p.m.
Friday .... 8:00 a.m. - 2:00 p.m. and 5:00 p.m. - 8:00 p.m.

Although most drugstores are closed on weekends, a few of them are open to help anyone who needs a medicine. To find out which drugstores are open you must go outside the door of one and read the list they've posted. This may not always be easy, though, because the list is written in Greek... If you can't read Greek and need a medicine, we recommend you go to the local hospital, medical centre or community clinic. There they should be able to help you, because there is always a drugstore (in hospitals) or at least a stock of medicines needed for emergencies.

TRAFFIC SIGNS

Traffic signs are more or less the same as those in other European countries. Warning signs are triangular and have a red frame around them set on a yellow background, signs of prohibition are round and have a red frame against a white background, and signs directing the traffic are blue.

Although on the whole road signs are adequate, if you want to drive safely you'd better not count on them one hundred percent. Consider the first 1000 kilometres a trial period in which you familiarise yourself with the Greek roads, and be very careful.

Keep in mind that, more often than not, speed limits are **unreasonably low.** This means that you will frequently see signs on the national roads or the main provincial roads that impose a speed limit of 40, 30, or even 5 kilometres per hour! These signs are the easiest way the authorities have found to prevent accidents at the most dangerous sites and should be looked upon as danger signals. However, do not take the speed limits too seriously, or you may be run over by a bus!

GETTING HELP ON THE ROAD

Your bike may or may not be a model of speed, comfort and economy, but one thing is for sure: its main job is to transport you. If, for any reason (serious damage or accident), it refuses to perform its duties, then it's **your** turn to transport it. But if the heat is unbearable, the distance too long and your motorcycle too heavy, pushing won't get you very far. You will need help.

The best help, of course, is the ...fast and free kind. If you are **very lucky** you will see help approaching after only a few minutes; it is the local shepherd in his pick-up truck making his appearance at the far end of the road. Wave him to stop and ask him from the depths of your heart to save you! Chances are that he will accept to carry your bike to a nearby repair shop or at least closer to civilisation. Climb on the back of the truck to hold your motorcycle (which should be fastened for safety reasons) and enjoy your trip to rescue. If the driver is very fast (as is often the case) it would be wise to keep your helmet on. At the end of the journey insist on giving him 5000 drachmas *ghia ti venzìni* (for the gas), although he will probably refuse to take it. If two or three hours pass by and nobody who can carry your bike appears, stop daydreaming and go get help.

If you are no more than 30 kilometres from a town, look at the town map where repair shops are listed. Next to the name of each one we have marked whether it has a pick-up truck. The transportation is usually free, but the repair will of course take place at the shop that provided it.

Does all this sound frightening? Well, the safest and wisest method of getting road assistance is, of course, taking care of things **before you are in need.** This is why you should be aware of your options: there are two Road Assistance companies helping Greek and foreign bikers, ELPA and INTER-AMERICAN, and both work with members.

ELPA

The oldest (and outmoded) Automobile and Travelling Club in Greece is ELPA. It has about 60 road assistance stations all over Greece and its advantage is that it co-operates with all major European automobile clubs. So you have two options: 1. You join an automobile club in your country that ELPA works with. When in need, you give ELPA a call and receive their help, which will be either completely free of charge or paid in accordance with the terms set forth in your contract. 2. You do nothing because you trust your bike completely. When the bike betrays your trust, you curse the moment you bought it and then call ELPA for a lift to the nearest repair shop. ELPA, of course, charges you according to the following rates: 18,000 drs. for transportation up to fifty kilometres, or 25,000 drs. for up to one hundred (the maximum distance). Whichever option you choose, here are their numbers:

ATHENS ....(01) 104   **PATRAS**....(061) 104   **IGOUMENITSA**....(0665) 25104

INTERAMERICAN

Your other (and better) choice is INTERAMERICAN, a large insurance company that has a road assistance department with 65 stations located all over Greece. As you are about to leave the harbour of Patras or Igoumenitsa, stop at the local INTERAMERICAN office and buy a six month insurance (the minimum possible). This will cost you 11,250 drs. and will cover you fully. If you need help just call them toll free, and they will carry your motorcycle free of charge to the garage of your choice, be it the closest one available or **at the other end of Europe!** The INTERAMERICAN telephone numbers are:

ATHENS....(01) 168 **PATRAS**....(061) 168 **IGOUMENITSA**....(0665) 25089

LEARN SOME GREEK

Whichever country you come from, you already know some Greek, although you may not be aware of it! The Latin alphabet on which modern European languages are based comes from the Chalkidic alphabet (one of the first Greek alphabets, that is), which was transplanted to Latium in Italy and was later adopted throughout Europe (in the course of many centuries). But apart from the alphabet, thousands of words in all European languages have Greek roots, not only in the sciences but in everyday communication as well. Even the name **Europe** comes from the Greek mythology. It was the name of a princess who captivated Zeus with her charms, and who was kidnapped and brought off to Crete, where she gave him three children among which Minos, the famous king of Crete.

The Greek language is quite beautiful and pleasant to the ear and has syntactic variety and an incredibly rich vocabulary. Admittedly, it's not the easiest language to learn, but learning it can become a fascinating adventure in itself, an exploration that will give you the greatest satisfaction once the object is accomplished. It is like having an invaluable treasure, because it is through the language that you can come in **direct contact** with Greek wisdom. And when we say "Greek wisdom" we mean not only what can be found in the Homeric epics, but also what is hidden in the simple stories of Greek peasants.

Following is a list of words and phrases that are not hard to learn and will facilitate your communication on specific occasions. They have been transliterated according to the table given above the list, so you would do well to look at it first if you want to pronounce them correctly. However, what is more important is **stressing the right syllable**, so pay attention to the little mark above the syllable that carries the accent.

ALPHABET
Notes

1. Certain sounds are rendered by a bewildering variety of letters and letter combinations in modern Greek, but do not be confused. Just note that the e sound in "be**ca**use" can be rendered by η, Η ι, Ι, υ, Υ, ει, ΕΙ, or οι, ΟΙ, (all transliterated as 'i' / 'i'); the e sound in l**e**ss is rendered by ε and αι (both transliterated as 'e'); the o sound in f**o**r is rendered by ο and ω (both transliterated as 'o'); and the ng sound in a**ng**le is rendered by γγ and γκ (both transliterated as 'ng').

2. Although in the following glossary we have transliterated words according to the table given here, you should expect to see variations in Greek road signs, restaurant menus etc. Note especially that **despite their pronunciation the Greek letters β, Β, γ, Γ, and δ, Δ are often transliterated as 'b / B','g / G' and 'd / D'**.

Letters

Greek	Transliterated as:	Pronounced:
Α, α	a	a as in sof**a**
Β, β,	v	v as in **v**eto
Γ, γ	y / gh	1. Normally as a breathy throaty version of the g in **g**un
		2. y as in **y**ou (especially before ι and ε)
Δ, δ	dh	th as in **th**at
Ε, ε	e	e as in l**e**ss
Ζ, ζ	z	z as in **z**odiac

PRACTICAL INFORMATION

Η, η	i / ì (when stressed)	e as in b**e**cause
Θ, θ	th	th as in **th**eory
Ι, ι	i / ì (when stressed)	e as in b**e**cause
Κ, κ	k	k as in **k**ite
Λ, λ	l	l as in **l**ife
Μ, μ	m	m as in **m**oney
Ν, ν	n	n as in **n**et
Ξ, ξ	x	x as in a**x**is
Ο, ο	o	o as in f**o**r
Π, π	p	p as in **p**et
Ρ, ρ	r	as a rolled r
Σ, σ, ς	s	s as in pe**s**t **(never z, not even between vowels)**
Τ, τ	t	t as in a**t**las
Υ, υ	i / ì (when stressed)	e as in b**e**cause
Φ, φ	f	f as in **f**un
Χ, χ	ch	ch as in Rei**ch**
Ψ, ψ	ps	ps as in ti**ps**
Ω, ω	o	o as in f**o**r

Combinations and diphthongs

ΑΙ, αι	e	e as in l**e**ss
ΑΥ, αυ	av /af	av before vowels, av or af depending on following consonant
ΕΥ, ευ	ev / ef	ev before vowels, ev or ef depending on following consonant
ΕΙ, ει	i / ì (when stressed)	e as in b**e**cause
ΟΙ, οι	i / ì (when stressed)	e as in b**e**cause
ΟΥ, ου	ou	ou as in t**ou**rist
ΓΓ, γγ	ng	ng as in a**ng**le
ΓΚ, γκ	ng	ng as in a**ng**le
ΜΠ, μπ	b / mb	always b (**b**oss) at the beginning of a word, occasionally mb (a**mb**ulance) in the middle
ΝΤ, ντ	d / nd	always d (**d**og) at the beginning of a word, usually nd (A**nd**rea) in the middle
ΤΣ, τσ	ts	ts as in pe**ts**
ΤΖ, τζ	dj	dj as in a**dj**unct

GLOSSARY

How to read the Greek in this glossary

To read the transliterated Greek in this glossary, take a look first at the two right columns of the above table (and at the notes preceding it). Also note that stressed syllables in multi-syllable words are marked with an accent, masculine and feminine endings are marked with a and b respectively, and singular and plural are marked with 1 and 2 respectively. (NOTE: Like French, Greek employs a polite plural form to address an older person or a person one isn't acquainted with; *"ti kànis"* and *"ti kànete"* both translate "how are you?" but the latter is more formal and polite).

Everyday basics

Ne	yes
Òchi	no
Endàxi	OK
Asfalòs	certainly
Kalimèra	good morning
Kalinìchta	good night
Kalispèra	good evening
A(n)dìo	good bye
Yàsou[1] / Yàsas[2]	hello /good bye
Kalòs ìrthes[1] / Kalòs ìrthate[2]	welcome
Efcharistò	thank you
Parakalò	please / you are welcome
Sighnòmi	excuse me / I am sorry
Dhen piràzi	It doesn't matter, it's OK
Perìmene	wait
Stamàta	stop
Èla	come!
Voìthia!	help!
Pàme!	let's go!
Kàtse kàto	sit down
Èna leptò	just a moment
Sighà	slow /quiet
Arghà	slow
Ghrìghora	quick
Tòra	now
Metà	later /after
Ìsos	maybe
Sichnà	often
Pànda	always
Potè	never
Pòte?	when?
Pou?	where?
Arketà	quite / enough
Polì	very / a lot
Lìgho	a little, somewhat /not much
Pos	how
Ti	what
Ke	and
Ghiatì	why
Tìpota	nothing / you are welcome
Ìsodhos	entrance
Èxodhos	exit
Anichtò	open
Klistò	closed
Màlista	yes (polite)
Kalì tìchi	good luck
Ti kànis?[1] / Ti kànete?[2]	how are you?
Kalà ìme	I am fine
Etsi kiètsi	so and so
Chàrika	pleased to meet you
Me lène...	my name is...
Borò na...	may I...
Tha ìthela na...	I would like to...
Dhen thèlo na...	I don't want to...
Katàlaves;	Did you understand?
Dhen katalavèno	I don't understand
Ti òra ìne?	what time is it?
Èskasa!	I am hot!
Kriòno	I am cold
Kàni krìo	it's cold
Kàni zèsti	it's warm / hot
Pràsino	green
Kòkino	red
Kitrino	yellow
Ble	blue
Màvro	black
Àspro	white
Plìo / karàvi / vapòri	boat, ship
Ti òra fèvghi?	what time does it leave?
Ti òra ftàni?	what time does it get there?
Isitìrio	ticket
Ghramatòsimo	stamp
Fàkelos	envelope
Kàrta	card / post card
Kìrie	Mr. / sir
Kirìa	Mrs. / Ms / mam
Dhespinìs	Miss
Ìme	I am
Ìse	you are
Ìne	he / she / it is
Ìmaste	we are

PRACTICAL INFORMATION

Ìs(a)ste	you are
Ìne	they are..
kalò	good
kakò	bad
krìo	cold
zestò	warm / hot
mikrò	small, little
meghàlo	big, large / great
orèo	beautiful, nice
àschimo	ugly
Ìme	I am
Yermanòs[a] / Yermanìdha[b]	German
Anglos[a] / Anglìdha[b]	English
Portoghàlos[a] / Portoghalìdha[b]	Portuguese
Italòs[a] / Italìdha[b]	Italian
Ghàlos[a] / Ghalìdha[b]	French
Ispanòs[a] / Ispanìdha[b]	Spanish
Olandhòs[a] / Olandhèza[b]	Dutch
Vèlghos[a] / Velghìdha[b]	Belgian
Elvetòs[a] / Elvetìdha[b]	Swiss
Afstriakòs[a] / Afstriakì[b]	Austrian
Norvighòs[a] / Norvighìdha[b]	Norwegian, Norse
Finlandhòs[a] / Finlandhèza[b]	Finn
Souidhòs[a] / Souidhèza[b]	Swede
Dhanòs[a] / Dhanèza[b]	Dane
xènos	a foreigner
Èlinas[a] / Elinìdha[b]	Greek
Elàdha	Greece
Ècho	I have
Èchis	you have
Èchi	he / she / it has
Èchoume	we have
Èchete	you have
Èchoun	they have...
àdhia odhìghisis	driver's licence
leftà / chrìmata	money
dhiavatìrio	passport
asfàlia	insurance
pinakìdha	number plate
ponokèfalo	headache
Milàs...	Do you speak...
yermanikà?	German?
italikà?	Italian?
ghalikà?	French?
anglikà?	English?
Ìme / Èrchome apò tin...	I am / I come from...
Yermanìa	Germany
Anglìa	England
Italìa	Italy
Ispanìa	Spain
Portoghalìa	Portugal
Vèlghio	Belgium
Olandhìa	Holland
Souidhìa	Sweden
Finlandhìa	Finland
Norvighìa	Norway
Dhanìa	Denmark
Elvetìa	Switzerland
Afstrìa	Austria
Pou ìne...	where is...
to tilèfono	the phone
o yatròs	the doctor
to nosokomìo	the hospital
i astinomìa	the police
to limàni	the port
to aerodhròmio	the airport
to estiatòrio	the restaurant
i tavèrna	the tavern
i tràpeza	the bank
o stathmòs tou trènou	the train station
o stathmòs tou leoforìou	the bus station
to tachidhromìo	the post office
to sinerghìo	the service station, the repair shop

Numbers

1	èna	60	exìnda
2	dhìo	70	evdhomìnda
3	trìa	80	oghdhònda
4	tèsera	90	enenìnda
5	pènde	100	ekatò
6	èxi	101	ekatonèna
7	eftà / eptà	200	dhiakòs(i)a
8	ochtò / oktò	300	triakòs(i)a
9	enèa / enià	400	tetrakòs(i)a
10	dhèka	500	pendakòs(i)a
11	èndeka	600	exakòs(i)a
12	dhòdheka	700	eftakòs(i)a
13	dhekatrìa	800	ochtakòs(i)a
14	dhekatèsera	900	eniakòs(i)a
15	dhekapènde	1000	chìlia
16	dhekaèxi	2000	dhìo chiliàdhes
17	dhekaeftà	3000	tris chiliàdhes
18	dhekaochtò	5000	pènde chiliàdhes
19	dhekaenèa	10,000	dhèka chiliàdhes
20	ìkosi	100,000	ekatò chiliàdhes
21	ikosièna	200,000	dhiakòs(i)es chiliàdhes
22	ikosidhìo	300,000	triakòs(i)es chiliàdhes
23	ikositrìa	400,000	tetrakòs(i)es chiliàdhes
30	triànda	500,000	pendakòs(i)es chiliàdhes
40	saranda	1,000,000	èna ekatomìrio
50	penìnda	2,000,000	dhìo ekatomìria

Shopping

Akrivò	expensive
Ftinò	cheap
Pòso kàni?	how much is it?
kànete èkptosi?	will you cut on the price?
Dhècheste pistotikì kàrta?	will you accept a credit card?
Maghazì	shop
Foùrnos	bakery
Bakàliko	grocery store
Èchete...	do you have...
Thèlo...	I want
Batarìes	batteries
Film	film
Ekìno	that
Aftò	this
Ti ìne aftò?	what's this?
Borìte na me voithìsete?	can you please help me?
Ti òra klìni?	what time does it close?
Ti òra anìghi?	what time does it open?

PRACTICAL INFORMATION

Time

mèra	day
nìchta	night
òra	time / hour
evdhomàdha	week
mìnas	month
chrònos	year
sìmera	today
chthes	yesterday
àvrio	tomorrow
tou chrònou	next year
pèrisi	last year
fètos	this year
Dheftèra	Monday
Trìti	Tuesday
Tetàrti	Wednesday
Pèmbti	Thursday
Paraskevì	Friday
Sàvato	Saturday
Kiriakì	Sunday

Accommodation

Xenodhochìo	hotel
Thèlo èna dhomàtio...	I want a room...
ya èna àtomo	for one person
ya dhìo àtoma	for two people
me dhiplò krevàti	with a double bed
me zestò nerò	with hot water
me toualèta	with a bathroom
ya mia vradhià	for one night
ya dhio vradhiès	for two nights
ìsicho	quiet
pio ìsicho	quieter
Borò na to dho?	can I see it?
Pòso èchi?	how much does it cost?
Èchi proinò?	is breakfast served?
I timì perilamvàni proinò?	is breakfast included in the price?
To klidhì	the key
Èchi pàrking?	is there a parking lot?
Pou tha parkàro ti motosiklèta?	where do I park the bike?
Pou tha parkàroume tis motosiklètes?	where do we park the bikes?
Skinì	tent
Borò na stìso edhò ti skinì mou?	can I set up the tent here?

At the service station

Sinerghìo	service station, repair shop
Màstoras	the mechanic
Motosiklèta	motorcycle
Chàlase	It broke down (bike) / it failed (e.g. engine)

Pròvlima	problem
(Ghnìsio) andalaktikò	(genuine) spare part
Dhen pèrni brostà	it won't start
Èchi pròvlima...	there is a problem with...
i batarìa	the battery
i mìza	the ignition
o kinitìras	the engine
i idhròpsixi	the water-cooler
to kivòtio tachitìton	the gearbox
Èchoun pròvlima...	there is a problem with...
ta ilektrikà	the electric system
i tsimoùches	the gaskets, the seals
ta karbiratèr	the carburettor
Anàvi to labàki tou ladhioù	the oil light is on
Vghàzi polì kapnò	there's too much smoke coming out
Zestènete polì	it overheats
Kàni èna paràxeno thòrivo	it makes a funny noise
Kòpike i dìza	the cable is cut
Èskase to làsticho	the tire was punctured / went flat
Thèloun rìthmisi i valvìdhes	the valves need adjusting
Thèli tèdoma i alisìdha	the chain must be tightened
Thèli ghenikò sèrvis	it needs a full service
Thèli alaghì ladhiòn	it needs an oil change
Thèli ighrà frènon	it needs brake fluid
Thèli takàkia	it needs brake pads

On the road

O dhròmos ya...	the way to...
Pào kalà ya...	I want to get to...
	Am I going the right way?
Pòsa chiliòmetra?	how many kilometres?
Pòsi òra?	how long?
Pou pas?	where are you headed?
Kalò taxìdhi	have a nice trip
Pào stin./sto(n)..	I am going to...
Kondà	close
Makrià	far
Dhexià	right
Aristerà	left
Ìsia / efthìa	straight / straight ahead
Pìso	back
Bros / Brostà	front / ahead
Pàno	up
Pàno sto	on
Kàto	down
Kàto apò	underneath
Ekì	there
Apò	from
Pros	to
Ethnikì odhòs	national road
Àsfaltos	asphalt

PRACTICAL INFORMATION

Chomatòdhromos	dirtroad
Pinakìdha	(road) sign
Chàthika!	I'm lost!
Pou ìme?	where am I?
Psàchno ya...	I'm looking for...
Parakalò pou ìne...	could you please tell me how to get to...
to kàstro	the fortress
o pìrghos	the tower / the mansion
to vounò	the mountain
i lìmni	the lake
i spilià	the cave
i thàlasa	the sea / the beach
to nisì	the island
o potamòs	the river
i eklisìa	the church
to monastìri	the monastery
ta archèa	the ancient ruins
to mnimìo	the monument
o dhròmos / i odhòs	the road / the street
i platìa x	x square / x circus
to kèndro	the downtown area
to mousìo	the museum
to perìptero	the kiosk
to venzinàdhiko	the gas station
to sinerghìo	the service station, the repair shop
to voulkanizatèr	the vulcanizer, the tyre shop
i ìsodhos	the entrance
i èxodhos	the exit

For the initiated...

Amàn! ... Expresses mild anger or surprise

Òpa! ... Basically means 'careful' but can be used in a variety of circumstances. A cry of warning when something is about to fall, or a cry of enthusiasm encouraging a tipsy dancer to 'give it all'

Rìchta! ... Offers even stronger encouragement, especially when someone is dancing on a table!

Pedhì mou! ... Expresses admiration for a person's gifts (especially the physical ones...) and openly suggests one's amorous intentions.

Ti ghìnete? ... Conventional greeting, almost a substitute for 'how are you'. The standard answer is 'fine' or ''feelin' shitty'' depending on the case.

Pos pài? ... As above.

Sòpa!	You don't say! (Expresses admiration, perhaps mixed with a little distrust, when our friend tells an incredible story).
Meghàle!	Boy! / You are somethin'! (Expresses admiration, perhaps with a touch of irony, when the story of our friend sounds probable).
Psònio!	Exclamation of utter satisfaction!
Ghoustàro!	As above, only somewhat milder.
Tòra màlista	Oh, great! (Expresses disappointment when things don't turn out exactly the way we planned them, for instance when a tyre goes flat).
Tin kàtsame ti vàrka	Expresses worry when things are bad (for instance when we fall off the bike).
Klàfta Charàlabe	Expresses utter despair when things are lousy (for instance when our bike is stolen...)
Malàka	Can be a swear word or the equivalent of 'hey, buddy'.
Re	Like bread, it goes with anything! When combined with the word 'malàka' it turns it into the worst swear word.

Food and drink

Miscellaneous

Tròo	I eat	**Fisikòs chimòs**	juice
Pìno	I drink	**Biskòto**	cookie / biscuit
Psomì	bread	**frighaniès**	toasts
Voùtiro	butter	**Sokolàta**	chocolate
Yaoùrti	yoghurt	**Alàti**	salt
Tirì	cheese	**Pipèri**	pepper
Avghò	egg	**Làdhi**	oil
Mèli	honey	**Xìdhi**	vinegar
marmelàdha	jam, marmalade	**Boukàli**	bottle
Nerò	water	**Machèri**	knife
Krasì	wine	**Koutàli**	spoon
Retsìna	retsina, resinated Greek wine	**Piroùni**	fork
Bìra	beer	**Potìri**	glass
Kafès	coffee	**Flidjàni**	cup
Zàchari	sugar	**Katàloghos**	menu
Tsài (me lemòni)	tea (with lemon)	**Loghariasmòs**	check, bill
Portokalàdha	orange juice / drink	**To loghariasmò parakalò**	the check please
Lemonàdha	lemon juice / lemon soda	**Trapèzi**	table
		Karèkla	chair
		Me	with
		Chorìs	without

Vegetables and vegetable dishes

Anginàres	artichokes
Arakàs	peas
Dolmàdhes	stuffed vine or cabbage leaves
Fasolàkia	green beans
Choriàtiki	peasant salad
Maroùli	lettuce
Pandjària	beets
Chòrta	greens
Patàtes	potatoes
Yemistà	stuffed tomatoes or peppers
Ghìghandes	giant beans
Domàta	tomato
Domatosalàta	tomato salad
Angoùri	cucumber
Angourosalàta	cucumber salad
Kolokithàkia tighanità	zucchini
Kolokithàkia vrastà	steamed zucchini
Melidjànes	egg-plant, aubergines

Meat

Brizòla moscharìsia	veal steak
Brizòla chirinì	pork chop
Kotòpoulo soùvlas	roasted chicken
Kotòpoulo schàras	grilled chicken
Krèas vrastò	stew
Kokinistò	meat cooked with tomato sauce
Lemonàto	meat cooked with lemon sauce
Frikasèe	fricassee
Kondosoùvli	roasted pork chunks
Kokorètsi	lamb liver wrapped in intestines and done on the spit
Paidhàkia	lamb chops
Souvlàki	skewered meat (pork or veal) / skewered meat with slices of tomatoes and onions wrapped in pita bread
Keftedhàkia	meat balls
Biftèki	burger
Soudjoukàkia	spicy meat balls
Sikotàkia	lamb liver or giblets
Loukànika	sausages
Patsàs	tripe soup

Greek specialties

Mousakàs	mousaka (egg-plant dish)
Pastìtsio	pasticcio (spaghetti dish)
Fasolàdha	bean soup
Tiròpita	cheese pie
Spanakòpita	spinach pie
Salingària	snails
Fàva	purèed peas
Fakès	lentil soup
Frikasè	fricassee
Youvètsi	roast lamb with pasta and tomatoes
Melidjanosalàta	purèed egg-plant salad
Taramosalàta	fish roe salad
Djadjìki	cucumber and yoghurt salad
Ròsiki	Russian salad

Fish

Frèska	fresh	Chtapòdhi xidhàto	octopus seasoned with vinegar
Katepsighmèna	frozen		
Astakòs	lobster		
Bakaliàros	cod	Barboùni	red mullet
Gharìdhes	shrimp	Sinaghrìdha	gurnet
Ghlòsa	sole	Fangrì	pagrus
Kalamaràkia	squid	Ghòpa	bogue, boce
Soupiès	cuttlefish	Marìdha	brown picarel
Xifìas	swordfish	Pèstrofa	trout
Chtapòdhi sta kàrvouna	charcoaled octopus		

Fruit

Karpoùzi	water melon	Fràoules	strawberries
Pepòni	cantaloupe / honeydew melon	Portokàli	orange
		Mìlo	apple
Stafìli	grapes	Achlàdhi	pear
Rodhàkino	peach	Sìka	figs
Verìkoko	apricot		
Keràsia	cherries		

Dessert

Baklavàs	baklava (thin-layered pastry with walnuts and syrup)
Kandaìfi	pastry with very thin vermicelli
Krèma	custard
Rizòghalo	rice pudding
Loukoùmi	a type of marshmallow
Chalvàs	halvah (usually made of cream of wheat, butter and sugar but comes in a great variety).
Pasta	pastry
Karidhòpita	walnut cake
Ghalaktoboùreko	custard pie
Ravanì	syrupy cake
Sàmali	pastry of Turkish origin
Pastèli	pastry made with sesame seed and honey
Paghotò	ice cream
Boughàtsa	cream-filled pastry

Snacks

Kalabòki	corn
Kàstana	chestnuts
Kouloùri	bread ring
Tost	toast
Loukoumàs	donut

PRACTICAL INFORMATION

As for coffee, the Greek name for it is **kafès**, but unless you expect the waiter to know how you drink it you must specify what you want. Here is how to order the most frequent types of coffee served in the Greek *kafenìa*:

Frappè ("shaken"): black / medium / sweet / with milk
Nes (instant coffee): black / medium / sweet / with milk
Ghalikò (filter coffee): black / medium / sweet / with milk
Elinikò (Greek coffee): black / medium / sweet

THE POLICE

Contrary to what happens in most places in Europe, the police on this island is so discreet that... it seems to do nothing. In the bigger towns policemen are generally occupied with administrative tasks, while in the villages they sit at the *kafenìa*, sipping their *rakì* and playing backgammon with the other villagers. Crime rates in Crete are very low and most of the time the presence of policemen around is a mere formality. In the summer, of course, with so many tourists visiting the island, there is bound to be some small episode, some drunkard making a fuss over something, or some absent-minded or inexperienced motorcyclist or jeep driver who rented a vehicle only to cause an accident. However, such episodes are merely an exception to the rule, an occasional disruption of the order that prevails.

The most likely encounter you'll ever have with the police is in a road block set up, where you will typically see a police car at the side of the road, one or two police motorcycles, and a cop signalling you to stop. Chances are that as soon at they see you are a tourist they will let you go with no further ado. If you are stopped for a minor violation (such as exceeding the speed limit), they have to be polite, but if they yell at you do not react immediately. After a minute or two they will... feel better, and they will let you go without a ticket, having accepted your sincere apology and the promise that you will now go slower than a bus. The magic phrase that gets through to them is *èleos, dhen tha to xanakàno* (have mercy, I won't do it again!)

Careful: never try to bribe a police officer. This method may be effective in Turkey and the ex-communist countries of Eastern Europe, but in Greece it simply won't work. The Greek policemen will feel deeply offended, and they will treat you twice as hard as they normally would. Should a cop ask you for money - a very unlikely thing but one that can't be ruled out - refuse politely and ask him for the ticket *(dhòste mou tin klìsi parakalò)*. Keep in mind that policemen are not entitled to collect money on the spot; they are there only to hand you the ticket.

1. IRAKLIO PREFECTURE

Iraklio
- First Police Precinct 282 243
- Second Police Precinct 284 589
- Tourist Police 283 190
- Traffic Police 282 031

Aghia Varvara .... (0894) 22 209
Aghios Mironas .... (081) 721 210
Arkalochori .... (0891) 22 100
Archanes .... (081) 751 811
Viannos .... (0895) 22 006
Zaros .... (0894) 31 210

Kamares .... (0892) 43 270
Kasteli .... (0891) 31 111
Kroussonas .... (081) 711 211
Matala .... (0892) 42 168
Moires .... (0892) 22 222
Mochos .... (0897) 61 222
Pirgos .... (0893) 22 222
Tilissos .... (081) 831 221
Timbaki .... (0892) 51 111
Chersonissos .... (0897) 22 222

2. RETHIMNO PREFECTURE

Rethimno
- Police Station .... (0831) 22 289
- Tourist Police .... (0831) 28 156
- Traffic Police .... (0831) 28 891

Aghia Galini .... (0832) 91 210
Amari .... (0833) 22 222

Anogia .... (0834) 31 206
Episkopi .... (0831) 61 207
Perama .... (0834) 22 349
Sellia .... (0832) 31 238
Spili .... (0832) 22 026

PRACTICAL INFORMATION

3. HANIA PREFECTURE

Hania
- Police Station ....(0821) 51 111
- Tourist Police ....(0821) 24 477
- Traffic Police ....(0821) 41 111

Alikianos ....(0821) 77 127
Aghia Roumeli ....(0825) 91 294
Anopoli ....(0825) 91 249
Vamos ....(0825) 22 218
Voukolies ....(0824) 31 209
Vrisses ....(0825) 51 205
Galatas ....(0821) 31 111
Georgioupoli ....(0825) 61 350
Elos ....(0822) 61 241
Kandanos ....(0823) 22 100
Kasteli Kissamou ....(0822) 23 333
Kolimvari ....(0824) 22 100
Maleme ....(0821) 62 209
Paleochora ....(0823) 41 111
Platanias ....(0821) 68 206
Sougia ....(0823) 51 241
Souda ....(0821) 89 316
Sternes ....(0821) 63 333
Topolia ....(0822) 51 210
Chora Sphakion ....(0825) 91 205

4. LASITHI PREFECTURE

Aghios Nikolaos
- Police Station ....(0841) 22 251
- Traffic Police ....(0841) 22 750

Ierapetra
- Police Station ....(0842) 22 560
- Traffic Police ....(0842) 24 200

Zakros ....(0843) 93 323
Kalo Chorio ....(0841) 61 262
Koutsouras ....(0843) 51 666
Kritsa ....(0841) 51 206
Mirtos ....(0842) 51 204
Neapoli ....(0841) 32 298
Palekastro ....(0843) 61 222
Pachia Ammos ....(0842) 93 250
Sitia ....(0843) 24 200
Tzermiado ....(0844) 22 208
Psichro ....(0844) 31 292

THE PORT AUTHORITIES

The Cretan coastline is very big, the port officers are very few, and illegal activities abound. If you see a ship emptying dirty waters near the coast, if you are annoyed at the dangerous show that some idiot is putting up with his motorboat just a breath away from the swimmers, if it pains you to watch someone destroy marine life with his blast fishing, pick up the phone and call the nearest port authority or police station. We can all do something to stop the senseless degradation of our natural environment.

1. IRAKLIO PREFECTURE

Iraklio ....(081) 244 956
Kali Limenes ....(0892) 42 188
Chersonissos ....(0897) 23 111

2. RETHIMNO PREFECTURE

Rethimno ....(0831) 28 971
Aghia Galini ....(0832) 91 206

3. HANIA PREFECTURE

Hania ....(0821) 98 888
Kasteli Kissamou ....(0822) 22 024
Paleochora ....(0823) 41 214
Souda ....(0821) 89 240
Chora Sphakion ....(0825) 91 292

4. LASITHI PREFECTURE

Sitia ....(0843) 22 310
Ierapetra ....(0842) 22 294
Aghios Nikolaos ....(0841) 22 312

FIRST AID

Public health care in Greece is provided by the National System of Health, otherwise known as ESY. ESY works through university clinics, hospitals (including their outpatient services), health centres (mini hospitals in small provincial towns), and community clinics (minimally equipped and staffed with young doctors who just got their degree).

All European Community citizens are entitled to free health care in the above institutions as long as they have with them the E111 form. This means that before leaving your home country you should make sure you get one from the Public Health Authorities. We should also note here that emergency cases are treated free of charge and that this applies regardless of nationality.

If, however, you have made a private contract with an insurance company, chances are that it will cover the cost of treatment in a private clinic. This is admittedly better than going to a public hospital, so before leaving on your trip it would be a good idea to look into this matter as well.

If you are near the town of Iraklio, and you have an accident or a sudden attack of illness, the best thing to do is to call the Ambulance Service (EKAB) at the number 166; they will send an ambulance right away and take you to the nearest hospital. EKAB ambulances are very well equipped to give first aid, and they always come with a doctor, so you should be in good hands.

The same phone number is good for any other area in Crete too, but in this case the procedure involves more steps. Dial 081 for Iraklio before calling the number and give them your exact location. EKAB will contact the nearest hospital, and the hospital will send its own ambulance to get you, or else they will give you the number of the nearest hospital or first aid station so you can call them yourself.

1. IRAKLIO PREFECTURE

Iraklio	Hospital	(081) 237 502	Kasteli	Health Centre	(0891) 31235
	Hospital	(081) 269 111	Kroussonas	Community Clinic	(081) 711 203
Aghia Varvara	Health Centre	(0894) 22 222	Malia	Community Clinic	(0897) 31 594
Aghii Deka	Community Clinic	(0892) 31 268	Marathos	Community Clinic	(081) 521 213
Aghios Miron	Community Clinic	(081) 721213	Moires	Health Centre	(0892) 23 312
Arkalochori	Health Centre	(0891) 23013	Mochos	Community Clinic	(0897) 61 333
Archanes	Community Clinic	(081) 751 882	Pefko	Community Clinic	(0895) 31 377
Viannos	Health Centre	(0895) 22 625	Siva	Community Clinic	(0892) 42 236
Gouves	Community Clinic	(0897) 41 202	Tilissos	Community Clinic	(081) 831 206
Zaros	Community Clinic	(0894) 31206	Chersonissos	Community Clinic	(0897) 22042

2. RETHIMNO PREFECTURE

Rethimno	Hospital	(0831) 27 491	Perama	Health Centre	(0834) 23 074
Aghia Galini	Community Clinic	(0832) 91 111	Pigi	Community Clinic	(0831) 71 001
Zoniana	Community Clinic	(0834) 61 298	Prassies	Community Clinic	(0831) 25 260
Melidoni	Community Clinic	(0834) 22 032	Sellia	Community Clinic	(0832) 31 237
Melonas	Community Clinic	(0833) 22 253	Spili	Health Centre	(0832) 22 533
Nithavris	Community Clinic	(0833) 31 224	Fourfouras	Community Clinic	(0833) 41 215
Panormos	Community Clinic	(0834) 51 214			

PRACTICAL INFORMATION

3. HANIA PREFECTURE

Hania	Hospital	(0821) 27 231	Kaloudiana	Community Clinic	(0822) 31 484
Alikianos	Community Clinic	(0821) 77 300	Kolimvari	Community Clinic	(0824) 22 204
Agh. Roumeli	Community Clinic	(0825) 91 151	Kontopoula	Community Clinic	(0821) 65 211
Aroni	Community Clinic	(0821) 63 336	Kournas	Community Clinic	(0825) 96 314
Vamos	Health Centre	(0825) 22 580	Maleme	Community Clinic	(0821) 62 360
Voukolies	Community Clinic	(0824) 31 204	Meskla	Community Clinic	(0821) 67 356
Vrisses	Community Clinic	(0825) 51 230	Platanos	Community Clinic	(0822) 41 227
Deliana	Community Clinic	(0824) 91 345	Rodovani	Community Clinic	(0823) 51 210
Elos	Community Clinic	(0822) 61 227	Tavronitis	Community Clinic	(0824) 22 395
Kalives	Community Clinic	(0825) 31 244	Souda	Hospital	(0821) 89 307
Kandanos	Health Centre	(0823) 22 550	Sphakia	Community Clinic	(0825) 91 214
Kasteli Kissamou	Health Centre	(0822) 22 222			

4. LASITHI PREFECTURE

Sitia	Hospital	(0843) 24 311	Kritsa	Community Clinic	(0841) 51 216
Ierapetra	Hospital	(0842) 22 488	Mirtos	Community Clinic	(0842) 51 222
Aghios Nikolaos	Hospital	(0841) 25 221	Neapoli	Hospital	(0841) 33 333
Aghios Georgios	Community Clinic	(0844) 31 205	Prina	Community Clinic	(0841) 61 595
Vrachassi	Community Clinic	(0841) 32 512	Stavrochori	Community Clinic	(0843) 51 134
Elounda	Community Clinic	(0841) 41 563	Tzermiado	Health Centre	(0844) 22 602
Zakros	Community Clinic	(0843) 93 265	Tourloti	Community Clinic	(0843) 94 300
Kato Chorio	Community Clinic	(0842) 31 203			

INFORMATION FOR THE MOTORCYCLIST
Agencies, Spare parts, Motorcycle repair shops

In Crete you will find agents representing all motorcycle companies. They are selected by the official representatives of each company that have their base in Athens, and they are in charge of the local network of sales both for motorcycles and spare parts. Therefore, the ultimate responsibility for the spare parts available - and for the authorised repair shops - lies in the hands of the official dealers in Athens. If you are unable to find a spare part or have to wait too long for it, or if the repair shop where you took your bike has done a bad job, do not take it up with the locals; it will get you nowhere. Instead, write a letter of complaint to the Athens agency and send us a copy as well.

Of course, in all professional communities you will find a number of capable and decent individuals working alongside crooks, and in most cases the latter, even though a minority, manage to spoil the whole picture. Motorcycle mechanics could be no exception.

Although we believe we have done our best to compile a reliable list, we are also counting on you to provide information on the repair shops that offered good service and, most important, on the ones that gave you a hard time, charged you too much, or worsened the damage instead of repairing it. With specific information or charges in our hands, we will be able to make a more accurate investigation and to publish in our next edition not only a list of recommended repair shops but also a Black List of the ones to avoid. It's really quite simple! Just take one of the shop's business cards, write your comments on the back or on a piece of paper, and mail it to Road Editions. We will take care of the rest.

The following agencies are responsible for the local network of sales as well as the quality of service at the authorised repair shops:

HONDA (H)
SARAKAKIS BROS. AEBE
71 Athinon Ave., Athens 101 73
Tel. 3472 204, Fax 3467 329

YAMAHA (Y)
YAMAHA HELLAS A.E.
14th kilometre of the Athens -
Lamia National Road
Tel. 6202 401, Fax 8077 309

SUZUKI (S)
SFAKIANAKIS AEBE
58 Spyrou Patsi, Athens 118 55
Tel. 3454 211, Fax 3476 191

KAWASAKI (K)
KAMMENOS E.E.
196 Syngrou Ave., Athens 176 71
Tel. 9567 721, Fax 9594 102

BMW (B)
INTERCAR A.E.
15th kilometre of the Athens -
Lamia National Road
Tel. 6203 991, Fax 6201.013

PIAGGIO (P)
PIAGGIO HELLAS E.P.E.
41 Kifissias Ave., Athens 115 23
Tel. 6496 803, Fax 6497 069

MOTO GUZZI (G)
MOTO GUZZI HELLAS
13 Ermou, Paleo Faliro 175 64
Tel. 9420 039, Fax 9423 901

GAGIVA GROUP (GG)
HELLINMOTO E.P.E.
77 Michalakopoulou St., Athens 115 28
Tel. 7486 009, Fax 7488 251

TRIUMPH (T)
TRIUMPH HELLAS A.E.
18 Ethnarchou Makariou St.,
Mesogion Ave., Athens
Aghios Dimitrios 173 43
Tel. 9255917, Fax 9255 918

HARLEY DAVIDSON (HD)
SMASH A.E.
96 Vouliagmenis Ave.,
Ano Glifada 166 74
Tel. 9648 337, Fax 9648 335

PRACTICAL INFORMATION

Tyres
Cretan asphalt roads are not very hard on your tyres, and if you started out with new ones you should not have to replace them. Still, if the need arises, you will find a stock in almost all motorcycle tyres. The local dealers have set up a very efficient business, and anything not already available can be brought from Athens in a matter of 24 hours. In Crete you will find the following brands (in all types):
DUNLOP **(D)**, METZELER **(MZ)**, AVON **(A)**, MICHELIN **(M)**, BRIDGESTONE **(B)**, PIRELLI **(P)**, BARUM **(BR)**

Lubricants
The narrow country roads with their steep inclinations, the low speeds imposed by the traffic conditions, and the very high temperatures of Crete can "knock out" even the best of engine oils, after only 2500 to 3000 kilometres. That is why you should take care to change the oil before your engine gets knocked out as well! You don't have to carry it from home, though; scattered all over the island are numerous sales points with all the brands available. Besides the products of the big oil companies that are sold at their gas stations, you will find the following brand names:
CASTROL **(C)**, ARAL **(A)**, VALVOLINE **(V)**, MOTUL **(M)**, BEL RAY **(BR)**
BARDAHL **(B)**, LABO **(L)**, ELF **(E)**, DENICOL **(D)**, KENDALL **(K)**,
WOLF **(W)**, PUTOLINE **(P)**, PRO HONDA **(H)**, TORCO **(T)**, ROCOIL **(R)**

Brakes
Even if you've replaced your old brake pads just before coming to the island, you will still need new ones after the first one thousand kilometres... Every 200 metres or so you'll be tempted or forced to squeeze the brakes, so you can admire a great view, sniff the air, take a surprisingly sharp turn, or avoid a car that suddenly gets in your way! The brand names available are the following:
DUNLOPAD **(D)**, FERODO **(F)**, VESRAH **(V)**, PREMIER **(P)**,
BRAKING **(B)**, AP RACING / LOCKHEED **(R)**, BREMBO **(BR)**, SBS **(S)**

The catalogue symbols
The letters in parentheses signify the kind of motorcycle, tyres, oil and brakes, as given in the previous lists. In the column entitled MOTO, the asterisk in parentheses **(*)** stands for all Japanese makes, the double asterisk **(**)** stands for all makes, Japanese as well as European, and the abbreviations next to the parentheses **(Sa., Se.,Sp.)** stand for Sales, Service or Spare Parts respectively.

SALES POINT	MOTO	TYRES	OIL	BRAKES
1. HANIA				
ANGELAKIS IOANNIS 8 Kolokotroni Square, Tel. (0821) 92 834		M),(MZ), (B)		
ATHINAIOS MOTO 125 Milonogianni St., Tel. (0821) 97 623	(*) Sp		(C),(M),(BR)	(P)
ATHITAKIS IOANNIS 18 Diktynnis St., Tel. (0821) 98 838		(D), (B)		

SALES POINT	MOTO	TYRES	OIL	BRAKES
FRANTZESKAKI O.E. 101 Kissamou St., Tel. (0821) 71 001	(Y) Sa., Se., Sp			
KALOGERAKIS MANOS 120 Milonogianni St., Tel. (0821) 87 575	(*) Se., Sp.			
KARAKIS NIKOLAOS 15 - 17 Kissamou St., Tel. (0821) 99 997		(D), (P), (MZ)		
KATSOURAKIS VARDIS 53 Kidonias St., Tel. (0821) 74 672	(HD) Sa.,Se.,Sp		(L)	(R)
KECHAGIAS STAVROS 12 - 14 M. Botsari St., Tel. (0821) 70 530	(P) Sa,Se.,Sp. (K) Sa.,Se.,Sp.		(M),(BR)	(P), (D), (S)
KOKOLINAKIS ANT. O.E. 155 Anagnostou Gogoni St., Tel. (0821) 87 878		M),(MZ),(B)		(S)
LAZAROU THANASSIS 74 Anapauseos St., Tel (0821) 91 229	(Y) Se		(B),(C)	(F),(V)
LEVENTAKIS EFTYHIOS (end of) Anagnostou Gogoni St., Tel (0821) 70 972	(*) Se., Sp.		(C), (BR)	(S)
MALMOS ANTONIOS 5 Kissamou St., Tel. (0821) 95 221	(**) Sa		(B)	(R)
MOTO ELECTRIC 62 Apokoronou St., Tel. (0821) 47 946	(**) Se.			
MOTO MANIA 2 Manoussogiannakidon St., Tel (0821) 75 193			(C)	(D)
MOTOEMPORIKI 89 Kissamou St., Tel. (0821) 87 790	(*) Se.			(BR)
NTENEKETZIS TH. 142 Milonogianni St., Tel. (0821) 74 538	(*) Se.		(BR)	(S)
PSAROUDAKIS G. 53 Markou Botsari St., Tel. (0821) 74 757	(*) Sp.		(C), (M)	(F)
STAVROULAKIS ST. 117 Anagnostou Gogoni St., Tel (0821) 75 844	(GG) Sa., Sp. (S)Sa.,Sp		(D), (V), (M), (C), (W), (BR)	(B), (BR), (S)
TOGOUSSIDI MARIA 15 Dimokratias St., Tel. (0821) 42 102	(P) Sa., Se., Sp.			
TSIMENIS - KIAPEKOS 104 Markou Botsari St., Tel. (0821) 76 160	(H) Sa., Se., Sp		(H)	
VLASTAKIS ATHANASSIOS Mikras Asias, Tel (0821) 76 729	(GG) Se., Sp		(M), (BR)	(S)

PRACTICAL INFORMATION

SALES POINT	MOTO	TYRES	OIL	BRAKES
2. RETHIMNO				
ARGYRIOU - KOTAKIS 112 Stamathioudaki St., Tel. (0831) 23 013	(*) Se	(MZ)	(M)	(P)
ATHINAIOS MOTO 7 Timotheou Venieri St., Tel. (0831) 50 882	(*) Sp.		(C), (M)	(P)
GAVRILAKIS MANOUSSOS 7 Timotheou Venieri St., Tel. (0831) 50 882	(*) Sp.		(C), (M)	(P)
ILIOPOULOS DIM. 1 Machiton Scholis Chorofilakis Tel. (0831) 51 808	(Y) Sa.,Sp.	(MZ)	(P)	
LAGOUDAKIS G. 62 Dimakopoulou St,. Tel. (0831) 29 408	(H) Sa.,Se,Sp.		(C)	
PAPADAKIS & CO. 9 Kriari St. Tel. (0831) 22 858	(P) Sa.,Se.,Sp. (K) Sa.,Se.,Sp (H) Sa.,Se.,Sp		(M), (C), (BR)	(P), (S).
PISSAS EMM. 4 Acheli St., Tel. (0831) 53 201	(**) Se.		(C), (BR)	(S)
PLEXOUSSAKIS 10 Iliakaki St., Tel. (0831) 20 911	(GG) Sa,Se.Sp			
PSOMAS IOANNIS 11 Kriari St., Tel. (0831) 55 262	(*) Se., Sp.		(BR)	(P),(V)
SPYRIDAKIS BROS. 13 Emm. Bachla St., Tel. (0831) 23 590	(S) Sa.,Se.,Sp.	(M), (P)., (B)	(W), (BR)	(F), (S)
STARENIOU BROS. 64 Kourmouli St., Tel. (0831) 27 150			(E)	
TZANAKAKIS G. 4 Sifi Vlastou St., Tel. (0831) 50 607			(C), (V)	
3. IRAKLIO				
ANDRIS EVANGELOS 39 Georgiou Papandreou St Tel. (081) 211 488	(P) Sa.,Se.,Sp. (K) Sa.,Se.,Sp.		(C), (V), (M), (BR)	
BIKE CENTRE 2 Ethnikis Antistasseos St., Tel. (081) 239 754	(**) Sa.,Se.,Sp		(C), (BR)	(R)
CHRONAKIS GIORGOS 13 Kantanoleon St., Tel. (081) 241 374	(HD) Sa.,Se.,Sp			
DANDALIS ALEXANDROS 36 Dimokratias Tel. (081) 230 148		(M)		

SALES POINT	MOTO	TYRES	OIL	BRAKES
DELIGIANNIS ARGYRIOS 5 Kapodistriou St., Tel. (081) 230 138	(H) Se		(H), (V)	(P), (D)
DELIGIANNIS ARGYRIOS 65 Knossou Ave. Tel. (081) 230 156	(H) Sa., Sp.			
DIAKAKIS E. A.E. 24 Dimokratias Ave. Tel. (081) 239 203	(GG) Sa,Se,Sp		(M)	
MARKAKIS IOANNIS 20 Archimidous St., Tel. (081) 223 170	(K) Se		(V)	
MORAITIS GIORGOS 68 - 70 Ikarou Ave. Tel. (081) 245 913	(S) Se.,Sp	(D)	(C), (V), (M)	(D)
MORAITIS GIORGOS 122 Irodotou St., Tel. (081) 242 414	(*) Sa.	(D), (MZ),(M) (B), (P)	(W), (M)	(F)
MORAITIS VASSILIS 147 Nikolaou Plastira St., Tel. (081) 284 714	(P) Sa,Se,Sp	(P),(M)	(C)	(P)
MOTOSTUDIO 142 Ethnikis Antistasseos St., Tel. (081) 225 621	(B) Sa,Se,Sp	(P),(M)	(V),(A)	(BR)
PAPADAKIS IOANNIS 53 Ieronimaki St., Tel. (081) 227 519	(*) Se		(C),(M)	(V)
PAPASTEPHANAKIS G. 93 Ethnikis Antistasseos St., Tel. (081) 228 524	(P) Sa,Se,Sp (H) Sa,Se,Sp			
PEIROUNAKIS ANT. 21 Ikarou Ave. Tel. (081) 220 058			(C), (V)	(P), (F), (V)
PLATAKIS SPYROS 155 Mausolou St., Tel. (081) 226 503			(K)	
PNEVMATIKAKIS IOANNIS Chrissostomou Ave. Tel. (081) 280 559		(D), (MZ)	(P), (V)	
MATIKAKIS MICH. iou Papandreou St., Tel. (081) 289 327	(S) Sa,Se,Sp		(C), (W), (V), (M)	(P)
PH 365 E.P.E. Ave. Tel. (081) 316 746			(M), (C), (V)	(F)
RIGAS E... ELOS 59 Christomi... ouri St., Tel. (081) 821 012		(A)		
SARANTINIDIS 65 Knossou Ave. (081) 230 156	(H) Sa., Sp.		(H), (BR)	
SPYRIDAKIS IOANNI... 60 Ikarou Ave. Tel. (081) ...0 764	(Y) Sa,Se,Sp.	(B)	(D), (R)	(F), (D), (S)

PRACTICAL INFORMATION

SALES POINT	MOTO	TYRES	OIL	BRAKES
TRIANTAFYLLIDIS G. 53 Papanastassiou Ave. Tel. (081) 210 681	(GG) Se., Sp.		(M),(BR)	(V)
VOGIATZIS EVANGELOS 54 Ikarou Ave. Tel. (081) 223 909	(S) Sa.,Se.,Sp.	(MZ)	(W)	(F)

4. AGHIOS NIKOLAOS

SALES POINT	MOTO	TYRES	OIL	BRAKES
ALTSIADIS D. Stavros Tel. (0841) 24 037	(Y) Sa.,Se.,Sp		(R)	
APOSTOLAKIS O.E. 2 Idomeneos St. Tel. (0841) 28 113	(P) Sa,Se,Sp (K)Sa.,Se.,Sp (H) Sa,Se,Sp		(M), (C)	
CHAROULIS GEORGIOS 124 Latous Tel. (0841) 24 325		(D), (MZ), (A) (M), (B), (P)		
ORPHANAKIS N. O.E. 22 Latous Tel. (0841) 24 413	(S) Sa,Se,Sp	(P), (M)	(W), (V)	(P), (BR)

5. IERAPETRA

SALES POINT	MOTO	TYRES	OIL	BRAKES
CHRISTAKIS PAN. 9 S. Kouta St., Tel. (0842) 27 058	(K) Sa,Se,Sp.			
DASENAKIS AP. 30 Nikiforou Foka St., Tel. (0842) 26 239	(Y) Se.		(C), (R)	(P)
FRANGOULI ZOI Kolokotroni Square Tel. (0842) 22 225	(Y) Sa., Sp.			
MARANGAKIS KON. 45 Kostoula Andrianou St., Tel. (0842) 28 065		(D), (M), (A), (MZ), (B), (P)		
TZOUVELEKAS KON. 1 Cooper St., Tel. (0842) 72 200			(B)	

6. SITIA

SALES POINT	MOTO	TYRES	OIL	BRAKES
CHAMILAKIS DIM. 27 September 4th St., Tel. (0843) 24 491	(**) Sa.			
MOTO HERMES 28 Itanou St., Tel. (0843) 24 491	(*) Se.		(M)	(F)
TSIMBIDAKIS - MISANTONIS O.E. 3 Papanastassiou St., Tel. (0843) 25 129	(*)Sa.,Se.,Sp.		(L),(C), (V), (R), (BR)	(P), (F), (D)
ZERVAKIS MICH. 26 Itanou St., Tel. (0843) 23 928 ,		(M), (B), (P), (MZ)	(C), (V), (R), (BR)	(P), (F)

AREA CODES IN GREECE

Achladokambos	.0751
Aghios Andreas (of Attica)	.0294
Aghios Kirikos (of Samos)	.0275
Aghios Nikolaos	**.0841**
Agiassos	.0252
Agrinio	.0641
Alexandria	.0333
Alexandroupoli	.0551
Aliveri	.0223
Amaliada	.0622
Amfiklia	.0234
Amfilochia	.0642
Amfissa	.0265
Amindeo	.0386
Amorgos	.0285
Anavissos	.0291
Ancient Olympia	.0624
Antiparos	.0284
Antirrio	.0634
Andravida	.0623
Andritsena	.0626
Andros	.0282
Arachova	.0267
Areopoli	.0733
Argos	.0751
Argos Orestiko	.0467
Argostoli	.0671
Aridea	.0384
Arkitsa	.0233
Arta	.0681
Astipalea	.0243
Atalandi	.0233
Athens - Piraeus	.01
Avlona	.0295
Axioupoli	.0343
Chalkida	.0221
Chios	.0271
Chrissoupoli	.0591
Delphi	.0265
Didimoticho	.0553
Dimitsana	.0795
Distomo	.0267
Domokos	.0232
Drama	.0521
Edessa	.0381
Egina	.0297
Egio	.0691
Elassona	.0493
Elefsina	.01
Eleftheroupoli	.0592
Epidaurus	.0753
Erithres	.0262
Ermioni	.0754
Ermoupoli	.0281
Etoliko	.0632
Farsala	.0491
Filiatra	.0761
Florina	.0385
Galaxidi	.0265
Gargaliani	.0763
Giannitsa	.0382
Githio	.0733
Grevena	.0462
Hania	**.0821**
Hydra	.0298
Ierapetra	**.0842**
Igoumenitsa	.0665
Ikaria	.0275
Inofita	.0262
Ioannina	.0651
Ios	.0286
Ipati	.0231
Iraklio	**.081**
Ithaki	.0674
Kalamata	.0721
Kalambaka	.0432
Kalamos Attikis (K. of Attica)	.0295
Kalavrita	.0692
Kalimnos	.0243
Kamena Vourla	.0235
Kapandriti	.0295
Karditsa	.0441
Karies Aghiou Orous (K. of Aghion Oros)	.0377
Karistos	.0224
Karpathos	.0245
Karpenissi	.0237
Kassos	.0245
Kastellorizo	.0241
Kastoria	.0467
Katerini	.0351
Kato Achaia	.0693
Kavala	.051
Keratea	.0299
Kerkira (Corfu)	.0661
Kiato	.0742
Kilkis	.0341
Killini	.0623
Kimi	.0222
Kineta	.0296
Kiparissia	.0761

PRACTICAL INFORMATION

Kithira	.0735
Kithnos	.0281
Komotini	.0531
Konitsa	.0655
Korinthos (Corinth)	.0741
Koropi	.01
Kos	.0242
Kozani	.0461
Kranidi	.0754
Lagonissi	.0291
Lamia	.0231
Langadas	.0394
Larimna	.0233
Larissa	.041
Lavrio	.0292
Lefkada	.0645
Leros	.0247
Livadia	.0261
Lixouri	.0671
Loutraki	.0744
Malakassa	.0295
Mandra	.01
Marathonas	.0294
Markopoulo	.0299
Megalopoli	.0791
Megara	.0296
Menidi	.0681
Messolongi	.0631
Methana	.0298
Metsovo	.0656
Mikonos	.0289
Milos	.0287
Mitilini	.0251
Nafpaktos	.0634
Nafplio	.0752
Naoussa Imathias (N. of Imathia)	.0332
Naxos	.0285
Nea Karvali	.051
Nea Makri	.0294
Orestiada	.0552
Oropos	.0295
Ouranopoli	.0377
Paleokastritsa	.0663
Pallini	.01
Parga	.0684
Paros	.0284
Patmos	.0247
Patras	.061
Paxi	.0662
Peania	.01
Pilos	.0723
Pirgos Ilias (P. of Ilia)	.0621
Platamonas	.0352
Poros Trizinias (P. of Trizinia)	.0298
Portaria	.0421
Portocheli	.0754
Preveza	.0682
Psara	.0274
Ptolemaida	.0463
Rafina	.0294
Rethimno	**.0831**
Rhodos (Rhodes)	.0241
Salamina	.01
Samos	.0273
Samothraki	.0551
Saronida	.0291
Schimatari	.0262
Serres	.0321
Siatista	.0465
Sifnos	.0284
Simi	.0241
Siros	.0281
Sitia	.0843
Skala (of Laconia)	.0735
Skiathos	.0427
Skiros	.0222
Skopelos	.0424
Sounio	.0292
Sparti (Sparta)	.0731
Spata	.01
Spetses	.0298
Stilida	.0238
Tembi	.0495
Thassos	.0593
Thessaloniki	.031
Thira (Santorini)	.0286
Thiva (Thebes)	.0262
Tilos	.0241
Tinos	.0283
Tirnavos	.0492
Tolo	.0752
Trikala (of Korinthia)	.0743
Trikala (of Thessalia)	.0431
Tripolis	.071
Tsangarada	.0426
Vergina	.0331
Veria	.0331
Vilia	.0263
Volos	.0421
Vonitsa	.0643
Xanthi	.0541
Xilokastro	.0743
Zagora	.0426
Zakinthos	.0695

AREA CODES ABROAD

The numbers in parentheses refer to the time difference between Greece and the country you are calling

ALBANIA (-1) 00355
Korytsa 00355824
Tirana 0035542
ALGERIA (-1) 00213
Algier 002132
ANDORA (-1) 0033
ARGENTINA (-5) 0054
Buenos Aires 00541
AUSTRALIA 0061
Cambera (+8) 00616
Melbourne (+8) 00613
Sydney (+8) 00612
AUSTRIA (-1) 0043
Salzburg 0043662
Vienna 00431
BAHREIN (+1) 00973
BELGIUM (-1) 0032
Antwerp 00323
Brussels 00322
BRAZIL 0055
Brasilia (-6) 005561
Rio de Janeiro (-5) 005521
Sao Paolo (-5) 005511
BULGARIA (0) 00359
Sofia 003592
CAMEROON (-1) 00237
Yaounde 0023722
CANADA 001
Montreal, Quebec (-7) 001514
Ottawa, Ont. (-7) 001613
Quebec, Quebec (-7) 001418
Toronto, Ont. (-7) 001416
CHILE (-6) 0056
Santiago 00562
CHINA (+6) 0086
Beijing 00861
Shanghai 008621
COLOMBIA (-7) 0057
Bogota 00571
CROATIA (-1) 00385
Dubrovnic 003850
Zagreb 003851
CYPRUS (0) 00357
Larnaca 003574
Limassol 003575
Nicosia 003572
Paphos 003576
CZECH (-1) 0042
Prague 00422
Brno 00425
DENMARK (-1) 0045
EGYPT (0) 0020

Alexandria 00203
Cairo 00202
ETHIOPIA (+1) 00251
Addis Abeba 002511
FINLAND (0) 00358
Helsinki 003580
Oulu 0035881
Turku 0035821
FRANCE (-1) 0033
Paris 00331
GERMANY (-1) 0049
Berlin 004930
Bonn 0049228
Cologne 0049221
Frankfurt 004969
Hamburg 004940
Munich 004989
GILBRALTAR (-1) 00350
HONG KONG (+6) 00852
HUNGARY (-1) 0036
Budapest 00361
ICELAND (-2) 00354
INDIA (+3) 0091
Bombay 009122
Calcutta 009133
New Delhi 009111
INDONESIA 0062
Jakarta (+5) 006221
IRAN (+2) 0098
Teheran 009821
IRAQ (+1) 00964
Baghdad 009641
IRELAND (-2) 00353
Dublin 003531
ISRAEL (0) 00972
Jerusalem 009722
Tel Aviv-Jaffa 009723
ITALIA (-1) 0039
Firenze 003955
Milano 00392
Napoli 003981
Roma - Vatican 00396
San Marino 0039549
Torino 003911
Venezia 003941
IVORY COAST (-2) 00225
JAPAN (+7) 0081
Tokyo 00813
JORDAN (0) 00962
Amman 009626
KENYA (+1) 00254

PRACTICAL INFORMATION

Nairobi	002542
KUWAIT (+1)	00965
LEBANON (0)	00961
Beirut	009611
LIBYA (-1)	00218
Tripoli	0021821
LIECHTENSTEIN (-1)	004175
LUXEMBOURG (-1)	00352
MALAYSIA (+6)	0060
Kuala Lumpur	00603
MALTA (-1)	00356
MEXICO (-8)	0052
Mexico City	00525
MOLDAVIA (+1)	00373
Kishinov	003732
MOROCCO (-2)	00212
Casablanca	00212
Rabat	002127
NETHERLANDS (-1)	0031
Amsterdam	003120
Hague	003170
Rotterdam	003110
NEW ZEALAND (+10)	0064
Wellington	00644
NIGERIA (-1)	00234
Lagos	002341
NORWAY (-1)	0047
OMAN (+2)	00968
PAKISTAN (+3)	0092
Karachi	009221
PANAMA (-7)	00507
PERU (-7)	0051
Lima	005114
PHILIPPINES (+6)	0063
Manila	00632
POLAND (-1)	0048
Warsaw	004822
PORTUGAL (-2)	00351
Lisbon	003511
QATAR (+2)	00974
ROMANIA (0)	0040
Bucharest	00401
RUSSIA	007
Moscow (+1)	007095
St. Petersbourg (+1)	007812
SAUDI ARABIA (+1)	00966
Jeddah - Mecca	009662
Riyadh	009661
SENEGAL (-2)	00221
SINGAPORE (+6)	0065
SLOVAK (-1)	0042
Bratislava	00427
SLOVENIA (-1)	00386
Ljubljana	0038661
SOUTH AFRICA (0)	0027
Cape Town	002721
Johannesburg	002711
Pretoria	002712
SOUTH COREA (+7)	0082
Seoul	00822
SPAIN (-1)	0034
Barcelona	00343
Madrid	00341
SUDAN (0)	00249
Khartoum	0024911
SWEDEN (-1)	0046
Stockholm	00468
SWITZERLAND (-1)	0041
Bern	004131
Geneva	004122
Lausanne - Montreux	004121
Zurich	00411
SYRIA (0)	00963
Damascus	0096311
TAIWAN (+6)	00886
Taipei	008862
TANZANIA (+1)	00255
THAILAND	0066
Bangkok	00662
TUNISIA (-1)	00216
Tunis	002161
TURKEY (0)	0090
Ankara	0090312
Instanbul	0090212
UN. ARAB EMIRATES	00971
Abu Dhabi (+2)	009712
Dubai	009714
UNITED KINGDOM (-2)	0044
Edinburgh	004431
Glasgow	004441
London	0044171 / 0044181
Manchester	004461
UNITED STATES	001
Atlanta, Ga. (-7)	001404
Boston, Mass. (-7)	001508 / 001617
Chicago, Il. (-8)	001312
Los Angeles, Ca. (-10)	001818 / 001213
Miami, Flo. (-7)	001407 / 001305
New York, N.Y. (-7)	001718 / 001212
Philadelphia, Pa. (-7)	001215
San Francisco, Ca (-10)	001510
Washington, D.C. (-7)	001202
VENEZUELA (-6)	0058
Carakas	00582
YUGOSLAVIA (-1)	00381
Belgrade	0038111
ZIMBABWE (0)	00263
Harare	002634

A FEW WORDS ABOUT ROAD EDITIONS

ROAD EDITIONS is a new publishing company that was founded in February, 1994, by two young people, Yannis Tegopoulos and Stephanos Psimenos. In this company we invested all of our time (including personal time), all of our energy (of the body as well as the mind), and all of our money (including our parents'!) We explored every corner of Greece, delved into an awful many books, talked with hundreds of people (from simple peasants to special scientists), took thousands of slides, and collected remarkably extensive travel material of great variety.

We then proceeded to work on this material with great care and published the travel guides of Unexplored Greece. At the same time, in co-operation with the Hellenic Army Geographical Service and the Forest Authorities, we made the most updated and reliable map of Greece, on a scale of 1:250,000 that allows great detail. (The map came out in six parts and is meant to accompany our travel guides). In addition we publish maps of all the Greek islands, on scales ranging from 1: 25,000 to 1: 100,000. The complete series will comprise 46 maps of unprecedented detail, featuring **all** the island roads as well as a wealth of practical information; hotels, rooms to let, restaurants, public transportation, sights, folklore items and historical monuments are just a few of the things you'll find on our maps.

In everything we did we kept in mind the people we are addressing: demanding travellers, who are not satisfied with what a massive tourist industry wants them to see, but wish to explore the most beautiful parts of

There is no limit to where we go but the road itself!

PRACTICAL INFORMATION

Greece and to have a genuine experience. An experience one can't have in overexploited tourist areas.

Though our publications are based on thorough field research and methodical work, we also owe a lot to the hundreds of people, Greek or non-Greek, who travel by bike and send us all that precious information. Thanks to you, we can keep improving our work and updating it on a regular basis. Once more, it becomes evident that travelling motorcyclists form a large international community with a very special mentality, a strong sense of solidarity and a special communication code. A code that is immediately felt when we hear the sweet "purr" of the engine, when we gracefully "dive" with our bikes, and when we travel on the road - sometimes "cool" and sometimes playful - with all our senses participating in the experience. All of us, who greet each other on the road, who have coffee together and form groups that share the same love for the loaded bike and what it stands for, have now got our own communication channel: the ROAD EDITIONS travel guides. Through this channel you can share the experience of your trip with other "colleagues" all over the world. We invite you to tell us about the beautiful places you saw, the hotels, the rooms, the camping sites you enjoyed, the restaurants and taverns that you liked, and the routes that pleased you most. Write not only about the good parts of your trip, but also about its bad moments.

On the next pages you'll find a simple questionnaire that could greatly help us with our work. We'd appreciate it if you took the time to fill in the form, tear it out, and mail it to us at your convenience.

You can write to the following address:
ROAD EDITIONS
41 Ilia Iliou St.,
Athens 11743
GREECE

Or you can reach us on weekdays (between 9:30 a.m. and 6:30 p.m.) at the following telephone numbers:
9296 535   9296 541   9296 542
Alternatively, you can send a fax (any time of the day or night) at: 9296 492

Even better, if you happen to be in the neighbourhood, we'd be very happy to have a chat with you at our offices. Welcome to Greece!

THE PEOPLE WHO WORKED FOR THIS BOOK

IRINI KARAFLI
Graphic Artist

Irini was born in Ano Kalendini of Arta in the year 1966. After finishing high school, she made the big jump from her village to Athens. She studied at the Gymnastic Academy, but with her next leap she landed at the printing house of G. TSIVERIOTIS, where she worked as a graphic artist, putting her artistic talents to use. In 1994 she made yet another leap, and from the first floor of the building that houses the TSIVERIOTIS printing-house she found herself on the fourth floor, where ROAD EDITIONS has its offices. Since then, Irini has been working on the company maps. She soon realised that she chose the hardest path to take, and she has often threatened us with a final jump off the window if we keep torturing her with the countless dirtroads, chapels, gas stations and all those tiny details that we keep feeding her computer each day! Yet we know that she loves us and that she'll stay with us till the end of the road.

VANGELIS JANNIS
Art Director

Vangelis was born in Ermoupolis of Siros in the year 1966. He had always wanted to become a cook, but Life cheated him! He ended up an Art Director, after three years of study at the Graphic Arts School of VAKALO and five years of hard work as a graphic artist. He has worked for several advertising companies and for MOTO, the most popular motorcycle magazine in Greece.

In any case, Vangelis does his work like a true chef. He demands the best ingredients (rejecting with abhorrence all bad pictures and long captions), mixes everything carefully in his electronic stew pot (an Apple computer), steams it (working under real pressure), and serves it with just pride. His delightful dishes include the cover of the ROAD EDITIONS travel guides as well as what you see on each page. Bon appétit!

PRACTICAL INFORMATION

MARINA ROUSSOU
Illustrator

They say that in any profession there is no such thing as "good, cheap and fast." The work will be good and fast but expensive, or it will be good and cheap but slow, or cheap and fast but of bad quality.

Marina is a rare exception to this rule. She has a great talent in painting and works with any kind of medium with remarkable ease; tempera, oils, powder, even advanced designing programs such as Photoshop, Abode Illustrator, Quark Xpress and Coreldraw are all tools that have yielded their secrets to her. She is actually at the beginning of her career, having just graduated from the Graphic Arts School of VAKALO, and cares more about art and its endless possibilities than she does about how much she makes. The energy she smilingly puts into her work is also rare, even for people of her own age. (She was born in Athens in 1973).

Marina handles all the illustrations in the ROAD EDITIONS travel guides (covers, drawings and diagrams of archaeological monuments etc). When she has a bit of time, she adds her own touch to the ROAD EDITIONS promotion materials, decorates our kiosk in the exhibitions we participate in, and makes interesting proposals that enhance our work. In short, with her work - as well as her lovely appearance - she makes the world a little more beautiful.

MARIA RAPTI
Secretary

Maria was born in Athens in 1961. She studied Political Sciences at the Athens Law School.

Though she is one of the very few people in ROAD EDITIONS that do not drive a motorcycle, she was hired as a true miracle worker. She has only to take charge of something and problems miraculously disappear. She types without the slightest mistake, but somehow manages to correct the original's mistakes as well. She reads **all** papers and magazines every day and files all items that could be of interest. She co-ordinates the flow of material between Stephanos Psimenos, the translators, the Art Director and the graphic artists. She keeps our accounts, takes care of supplies, keeps the client records, is the personal secretary of the Publisher and the General Manager, and still manages to finish her work by 5:00 p.m. If **that** isn't a miracle, I don't know what is!

STEPHANOS NIKOLAIDIS
Field Researcher

Stephanos was born in Constantinople in 1963. He studied mechanical engineering at the Kozani Technology Education Institute and Industrial Design in Eindhoven, Holland. Curious and resourceful by nature, he tried his hand at a number of unconventional things that charmed him: cross country skiing, bicycling, rope climbing, mountain climbing, hamster breeding, store-sign painting, lemon selling, animal nursing, and a lot more. He has always put his heart in everything he did.

Apart from a million other things, Stephanos is an experienced diver, who has worked for the Marine Antiquities Department in shipwreck excavations from Chalkidiki to Crete, and an active member of the most dynamic speleological association of Greece (the SPELEO), who has helped to explore and map over one hundred caves in Greece and has trained other cave explorers (and divers) as well.

For eighteen consecutive months, he travelled together with Stephanos Psimenos all over Greece, covering over 60,000 kilometres and taking the cold, the rain, the most frightful winds and the most exhausting heat with unflinching courage, almost as if he was on a pleasure trip. In fact, he proposed that our next trip be in the Unexplored Siberia!

LENA HADJIIOANNOU
Translator

Lena was born in Chicago in 1964, but grew up in Greece. She studied Greek Literature at the University of Athens and went on to explore the world of Comparative Literature at the University of California at Riverside where she did her graduate work. She has worked as a court interpreter and a translator (having completed a two-year program in Literary Translation at the French Institute of Athens), and since 1990 she has been teaching at DEREE COLLEGE.

Her interests include travelling (she is doing her best to explore every corner of the planet), foreign languages (of which she speaks three), folk dances, and good plays and books. She sees translation as a very interesting challenge and was very happy to take on this project, in spite of her other obligations.

Though Lena consulted a map while working on the translation, she believes that nothing compares to the real thing. This is why she has expressed a very strong desire: To be in total harmony with the spirit of ROAD EDITIONS, translators should accompany the field researchers on their trips!

MICHALIS MONTESANTOS
Translator

Michalis Montesantos was born in 1953 in Athens and has studied Geology in the USA. He has worked as a technical translator since 1982. Most of the 70's and 80's he was riding bicycles and hiking mountains in Europe, North America and a bit of South America too, while in the 90's he has limited himself to enduro motorcycling and the Cyclades isles.

His latest dream is to move to Paraguay in order to avoid premature stroke or mutilation in hectic Athens.

PRACTICAL INFORMATION

QUESTIONNAIRE

Please fill in the following pages and mail them to ROAD EDITIONS, 41 Ilia Iliou St., Athens 117 43, GREECE.

1. What is your nationality? ....

2. Put down the type of motorcycles and the number of people in your group.

TYPE OF MOTORCYCLE	ENGINE CAPACITY	NUMBER OF PEOPLE

3. How many times have you travelled to Greece?

☐ Never   ☐ Once before   ☐ Twice before

☐ More than three times

4. Apart from this travel guide, what other sources did you consult on Greece? Mention their strong and weak points.

5. Which maps of Greece did you use? List their strong and weak points.

....
....
....
....
....
....
....
....
....

6. What did you like best in Greece? (List in order of preference).

....
....
....
....
....
....
....
....
....
....

7. What bothered you most in Greece? (List in order of... annoyance)

....
....
....
....
....
....
....
....
....

PRACTICAL INFORMATION

8. Mark the type of accommodations you chose and how many days you spent in each of the following:

TYPE OF ACCOMMODATIONS   NUMBER OF DAYS

- [ ] Hotel   ....
- [ ] Rooms to Let   ....
- [ ] Organised camping ground ....
- [ ] Tent set up in the wilderness ....
- [ ] Someone's home   ....
- [ ] Chapel   ....

9. How many kilometres did you travel in Greece and how many days did your trip last?

KILOMETRES ....

NUMBER OF DAYS ....

10. Which month did you come to Greece?

....

11. Jot down some of the interesting places you discovered on your trip, the nice hotels, good restaurants and pubs etc.

....
....
....
....
....
....
....
....
....
....
....
....

12. Jot down anything you consider essential to improving the next edition of this guide: things you liked, things you didn't, mistakes, omissions etc.

....
....
....
....
....
....
....
....
....
....
....
....
....
....
....
....
....
....
....
....
....

13. If you like, provide your name and address. We'll send you a "thank-you" gift for your precious help and let you know about our new publications on Greece.

....
....
....
....
....

PRACTICAL INFORMATION

PEOPLE YOU MET ON THE TRIP

Name ....
Address ....
....Telephone number ....
Notes ....
....

Name ....
Address ....
....Telephone number ....
Notes ....
....

Name ....
Address ....
....Telephone number ....
Notes ....
....

Name ....
Address ....
....Telephone number ....
Notes ....
....

Name ....
Address ....
....Telephone number ....
Notes ....
....

Name ....
Address ....
....Telephone number ....
Notes ....
....

Name ....
Address ....
................................Telephone number ....
Notes ....
....

Name ....
Address ....
................................Telephone number ....
Notes ....
....

Name ....
Address ....
................................Telephone number ....
Notes ....
....

Name ....
Address ....
................................Telephone number ....
Notes ....
....

Name ....
Address ....
................................Telephone number ....
Notes ....
....

Name ....
Address ....
................................Telephone number ....
Notes ....
....

PRACTICAL INFORMATION

Name ....
Address ....
................................Telephone number ....
Notes ....
....

Name ....
Address ....
................................Telephone number ....
Notes ....
....

Name ....
Address ....
................................Telephone number ....
Notes ....
....

Name ....
Address ....
................................Telephone number ....
Notes ....
....

Name ....
Address ....
................................Telephone number ....
Notes ....
....

Name ....
Address ....
................................Telephone number ....
Notes ....
....

TRAVEL CALENDAR

Date ....

Departure from ....

　　　　　　　　Time ....Counter reading ....

Arrival at ....

　　　　　　　　Time ....Counter reading ....

　　　　　　　　　　　　Kilometres travelled in the day ....

Overnight stay at ....

Notes ....

....

....

Date ....

Departure from ....

　　　　　　　　Time ....Counter reading ....

Arrival at ....

　　　　　　　　Time ....Counter reading ....

　　　　　　　　　　　　Kilometres travelled in the day ....

Overnight stay at ....

Notes ....

....

....

Date ....

Departure from ....

　　　　　　　　Time ....Counter reading ....

Arrival at ....

　　　　　　　　Time ....Counter reading ....

　　　　　　　　　　　　Kilometres travelled in the day ....

Overnight stay at ....

Notes ....

....

....

PRACTICAL INFORMATION

Date ....

Departure from ....
　　　　　　　Time ....Counter reading ....
Arrival at ....
　　　　　　　Time ....Counter reading ....
　　　　　　　　　　　　Kilometres travelled in the day ....

Overnight stay at ....
Notes ....
....
....

Date ....

Departure from ....
　　　　　　　Time ....Counter reading ....
Arrival at ....
　　　　　　　Time ....Counter reading ....
　　　　　　　　　　　　Kilometres travelled in the day ....

Overnight stay at ....
Notes ....
....
....

Date ....

Departure from ....
　　　　　　　Time ....Counter reading ....
Arrival at ....
　　　　　　　Time ....Counter reading ....
　　　　　　　　　　　　Kilometres travelled in the day ....

Overnight stay at ....
Notes ....
....
....

Date ....

Departure from ....

                Time ....Counter reading ....

Arrival at ....

                Time ....Counter reading ....

                            Kilometres travelled in the day ....

Overnight stay at ....

Notes ....

....

....

Date ....

Departure from ....

                Time ....Counter reading ....

Arrival at ....

                Time ....Counter reading ....

                            Kilometres travelled in the day ....

Overnight stay at ....

Notes ....

....

....

Date ....

Departure from ....

                Time ....Counter reading ....

Arrival at ....

                Time ....Counter reading ....

                            Kilometres travelled in the day ....

Overnight stay at ....

Notes ....

....

....

PRACTICAL INFORMATION

Date ....

Departure from ....

              Time ....Counter reading ....

Arrival at ....

              Time ....Counter reading ....

                         Kilometres travelled in the day ....

Overnight stay at ....

Notes ....

....

....

Date ....

Departure from ....

              Time ....Counter reading ....

Arrival at ....

              Time ....Counter reading ....

                         Kilometres travelled in the day ....

Overnight stay at ....

Notes ....

....

....

Date ....

Departure from ....

              Time ....Counter reading ....

Arrival at ....

              Time ....Counter reading ....

                         Kilometres travelled in the day ....

Overnight stay at ....

Notes ....

....

....

Date ....

Departure from ....

                 Time .... Counter reading ....

Arrival at ....

                 Time .... Counter reading ....

                          Kilometres travelled in the day ....

Overnight stay at ....

Notes ....

....

....

Date ....

Departure from ....

                 Time .... Counter reading ....

Arrival at ....

                 Time .... Counter reading ....

                          Kilometres travelled in the day ....

Overnight stay at ....

Notes ....

....

....

Date ....

Departure from ....

                 Time .... Counter reading ....

Arrival at ....

                 Time .... Counter reading ....

                          Kilometres travelled in the day ....

Overnight stay at ....

Notes ....

....

....

PRACTICAL INFORMATION

Date ....

Departure from ....

              Time .... Counter reading ....

Arrival at ....

              Time .... Counter reading ....

                            Kilometres travelled in the day ....

Overnight stay at ....

Notes ....

....

....

Date ....

Departure from ....

              Time .... Counter reading ....

Arrival at ....

              Time .... Counter reading ....

                            Kilometres travelled in the day ....

Overnight stay at ....

Notes ....

....

....

Date ....

Departure from ....

              Time .... Counter reading ....

Arrival at ....

              Time .... Counter reading ....

                            Kilometres travelled in the day ....

Overnight stay at ....

Notes ....

....

....

Date ....

Departure from ....

                Time ....Counter reading ....

Arrival at ....

                Time ....Counter reading ....

                              Kilometres travelled in the day ....

Overnight stay at ....

Notes ....

....

....

Date ....

Departure from ....

                Time ....Counter reading ....

Arrival at ....

                Time ....Counter reading ....

                              Kilometres travelled in the day ....

Overnight stay at ....

Notes ....

....

....

Date ....

Departure from ....

                Time ....Counter reading ....

Arrival at ....

                Time ....Counter reading ....

                              Kilometres travelled in the day ....

Overnight stay at ....

Notes ....

....

....

PRACTICAL INFORMATION

Date ....

Departure from ....

                Time ....Counter reading ....

Arrival at ....

                Time ....Counter reading ....

                Kilometres travelled in the day ....

Overnight stay at ....

Notes ....

....

....

Date ....

Departure from ....

                Time ....Counter reading ....

Arrival at ....

                Time ....Counter reading ....

                Kilometres travelled in the day ....

Overnight stay at ....

Notes ....

....

....

Date ....

Departure from ....

                Time ....Counter reading ....

Arrival at ....

                Time ....Counter reading ....

                Kilometres travelled in the day ....

Overnight stay at ....

Notes ....

....

....

Date ....

Departure from ....

　　　　　　　　　Time ....Counter reading ....

Arrival at ....

　　　　　　　　　Time ....Counter reading ....

　　　　　　　　　　　　　　Kilometres travelled in the day ....

Overnight stay at ....

Notes ....

....

....

Date ....

Departure from ....

　　　　　　　　　Time ....Counter reading ....

Arrival at ....

　　　　　　　　　Time ....Counter reading ....

　　　　　　　　　　　　　　Kilometres travelled in the day ....

Overnight stay at ....

Notes ....

....

....

Date ....

Departure from ....

　　　　　　　　　Time ....Counter reading ....

Arrival at ....

　　　　　　　　　Time ....Counter reading ....

　　　　　　　　　　　　　　Kilometres travelled in the day ....

Overnight stay at ....

Notes ....

....

....

PRACTICAL INFORMATION

Date ....

Departure from ....

                Time .... Counter reading ....

Arrival at ....

                Time .... Counter reading ....

                          Kilometres travelled in the day ....

Overnight stay at ....

Notes ....

....

....

Date ....

Departure from ....

                Time .... Counter reading ....

Arrival at ....

                Time .... Counter reading ....

                          Kilometres travelled in the day ....

Overnight stay at ....

Notes ....

....

....

Date ....

Departure from ....

                Time .... Counter reading ....

Arrival at ....

                Time .... Counter reading ....

                          Kilometres travelled in the day ....

Overnight stay at ....

Notes ....

....

....

Date ....

Departure from ....

　　　　　　　Time .... Counter reading ....

Arrival at ....

　　　　　　　Time .... Counter reading ....

　　　　　　　　　　　Kilometres travelled in the day ....

Overnight stay at ....

Notes ....

....

....

Date ....

Departure from ....

　　　　　　　Time .... Counter reading ....

Arrival at ....

　　　　　　　Time .... Counter reading ....

　　　　　　　　　　　Kilometres travelled in the day ....

Overnight stay at ....

Notes ....

....

....

Date ....

Departure from ....

　　　　　　　Time .... Counter reading ....

Arrival at ....

　　　　　　　Time .... Counter reading ....

　　　　　　　　　　　Kilometres travelled in the day ....

Overnight stay at ....

Notes ....

....

....

PRACTICAL INFORMATION

Date ....

Departure from ....

               Time .... Counter reading ....

Arrival at ....

               Time .... Counter reading ....

                        Kilometres travelled in the day ....

Overnight stay at ....

Notes ....

....

....

Date ....

Departure from ....

               Time .... Counter reading ....

Arrival at ....

               Time .... Counter reading ....

                        Kilometres travelled in the day ....

Overnight stay at ....

Notes ....

....

....

Date ....

Departure from ....

               Time .... Counter reading ....

Arrival at ....

               Time .... Counter reading ....

                        Kilometres travelled in the day ....

Overnight stay at ....

Notes ....

....

....

Date ....

Departure from ....

　　　　　　　　Time ....Counter reading ....

Arrival at ....

　　　　　　　　Time ....Counter reading ....

　　　　　　　　　　　　Kilometres travelled in the day ....

Overnight stay at ....

Notes ....

....

....

Date ....

Departure from ....

　　　　　　　　Time ....Counter reading ....

Arrival at ....

　　　　　　　　Time ....Counter reading ....

　　　　　　　　　　　　Kilometres travelled in the day ....

Overnight stay at ....

Notes ....

....

....

Date ....

Departure from ....

　　　　　　　　Time ....Counter reading ....

Arrival at ....

　　　　　　　　Time ....Counter reading ....

　　　　　　　　　　　　Kilometres travelled in the day ....

Overnight stay at ....

Notes ....

....

....

PRACTICAL INFORMATION

Date ....

Departure from ....

              Time .... Counter reading ....

Arrival at ....

              Time .... Counter reading ....

                             Kilometres travelled in the day ....

Overnight stay at ....

Notes ....

....

....

Date ....

Departure from ....

              Time .... Counter reading ....

Arrival at ....

              Time .... Counter reading ....

                             Kilometres travelled in the day ....

Overnight stay at ....

Notes ....

....

....

Date ....

Departure from ....

              Time .... Counter reading ....

Arrival at ....

              Time .... Counter reading ....

                             Kilometres travelled in the day ....

Overnight stay at ....

Notes ....

....

....

INDEX

Listed below are all the major towns, villages, archaeological sites etc presented in this travel guide. Beaches are listed under the letter B, monasteries under M, gorges under G, plateaus under P, caves under C, archaelogists under A and roadbooks under R.

A

Achendrias 311
Achladia 371
Adravasti 374, **506**
Afentoulief 42
Afrata 196
Agalianos 279
Aghia Fotia 498
Aghia Fotini 319, 323
Aghia Galini 282
Aghia Paraskevi (Rethimno) 281
Aghia Pelagia 399
Aghia Triada (Lassithi) 360
Aghia Triada 285, **292**
Aghia Varvara (Iraklio) 326
Aghies Paraskies 462
Aghios Andreas 249
Aghios Eftychianos 301
Aghios Ioannis (Hania) 193
Aghios Nikolaos 48, 70, **476**
Aghios Titos 299
Agnion 207
Agriles 152
Ai Kyrkos 156
Ai Kyrgiannis 150
Akrotiri 141
Aktounda 279
Alikambos 185
Alikianos 149
Almirida 185
Alones 245
Amalthia 25, 330
Amari 278, 318, **322**, 325
Ambelaki 320
Amigdalokefali 216
Amnisos 427
Ammoudari 187
Amourgeles 337
Androgeos 25, 443
Anemospilia 460
Angathia 505
Anissaraki 157
Ano Assites 389
Ano Chorio 369
Ano Varsamonero 249
Anidri 159
Anopolis 191
Anogia 409, **413**
Apesokari 283
Apodoulou 326
Aptera 178
Aradena 193

Archaeologist
　Bosanquet, R.C., 373, 496, 504
　Davaras, Konst. 492, 493,
　Dawkins, R.M., 469
　Evans, Arthur, 45, 439, 446, 448, 455
　Halberr, Federico, 373
　Hatzidakis, Iossif, 410
　Hall, Edith, 487
　Hawes / Boyd, Harriet, 488
　Hogarth, D.G., 363, 469
　Marinatos, Spiros, 427, 462
　McKenzie, Duncan, 446
　Pendlebury, J.D.S., 446, 469
　Platon, Nikolaos, 365
　Sakellaraki, Efi,454, 456, 460
　Sakellarakis,Yiannis, 454, 456, 457, 459, 460
　Schliemann, Heinrich, 44
　Seager, R., 492,
　Soles, J., 492
　Tsipopoulou, Metaxia, 496
　Warren, Peter, 315
　Xanthoudidis, Stephanos, 493
Archanes 49, **454**
Ariadne 24, 25, 444
Arkalochori 337
Armeni (Hania) 184
Armeni (Rethimno) 277, 278
Argiroupoli 245, 247
Arvi 314
Asphendou 243
Aspra Nera 196
Assigonia 244
Asterion 24, 440
Asterousia Mountains 68, 302
Astratigos 196
Astrikas 228
Atherinolakos 360
Avdeliakos 344
Avdou 462, **466**
Axos 415
Azokeramos 506
Azogires 160

B

Barbarossa 40, 261, 497
Barotsis, Andreas, 381
Beach
　Aghia Irini 280
　Aghios Pavlos 281

PRACTICAL INFORMATION

Amoudi 256
Balos 207
Damnoni 255
Hiona 506
Hohlakia 502
Karoumes 507
Korakas 254
Loutra 306
Menies 197
Palm beach 258
Souda 254
Tholos 490
Triopetra 280
Tripiti 308
Tris Ekklissies 313
Vai 100, **501**
Bebonas 489
Belli, Onorio 464
Bouzomarkos 209

C

Caves
　Diktaio Andro 26, 469, 471
　Ideon Andron 26, 67, 329, **330**
　Aghia Sophia 221
　Harakas 160
　Kamares 68, **329**
　Melidoni 403, 408
　Sendoni 416
　Trapeza 469
Chalis, Vassilis, 42, 165
Chamezi 492
Chandakas 36, 378
Chandras 372
Charkia 424
Chochlakies 506
Choudetsi 462
Chromomonastiri 319
Christos 343
Chora Sphakion 175, 189
Chametoulo 361
Chersonisos 428
Chortatsides 39
Chrisopigi 371, 489
Coopers, Paul, 353

D

Daedalus 26, 442
Damaskinos, Michael 379
Da Molin, Francesco 149
Daphnes 49
Daskaloyiannis 41
Dikti, mountains, 61, 314, 337, 339
Diktynnaion 197
Dragmos 504
Drakona 181, 227
Drapanos 185
Drossoulites 253

E

Elafonissi 218
Eleftherna 417, 418
Eliros 152
Elounda **435**, 487
Embaros 332, 337
Epano Episkopi 371
Epimenides 291
Episkopi (Hania) 228
Episkopi (Rethimno) 245
Erimoupoli 502
Eteokrites 33, **372**
Ethia 311
Europe 24, 26, **296**, 439
Exandis 403

F

Falassarna **213**, 237
Faistos 285
Floria 235
Focas, Nikiforos 37, 334, 378
Fodele 399
Fourfouras 325, 329
Fournes 165
Fournou Korfi 313
Fourni 456
Frangokastelo 42, 251, **252**
Fres 183

G

Galouvas 240
Gerakari 279, 323
Gerondogiannis 358
Gianniou 256
Glossa 229
Gonies 466
Gorge
　Aradena 191, 193
　Arvi 312
　Asphendiano 187
　Aghia Irini 66, 151
　Aghios Nektarios 251
　Klados 66, **170**
　Eligia 66, 171
　Chochlakies 506
　Imbriotiko 187, **251**
　Kallikratiano 251
　Kamares 327
　Katre 187
　Kourtaliotiko 259
　Patsos 319, 321
　Perivolakia 358
　Prassiano 318
　Rokka 228
　Samaria 66, 170, **172**

Therissiano 165
Topoliano 221
Tripiti 66, 171, 307
Zakros 363
Gortina 291, **296**
Goudouras 358
Gournia 488
Gramvoussa, Imeri 207, 208
Gramvoussa, Peninsula, 207
Gramvoussa, Agria 207

H

Hania 40, 41, 43, 45, 50, 70, **118**, 149
Hatzimichalis Dalianis 252

I

Ierapetra 351
Ierapitna 34, **351**, 352, 373, 501, 503,
Imbros 251
Ippokoronion 185
Iraklio 70, **377**
Irtakina 157
Itanos 351, **502**
Itzedin, castle, 178

K

Kafouro 230
Kakodikiano, stream, 225
Kakopetro 229
Kalamaki 301
Kalami 184
Kalamios 223
Kalamos 417
Kalandare 417
Kalathenes 240
Kali Limenes 302, 303, 305
Kali Sikia 246
Kalives 184
Kalivos 417
Kandanos 234
Kallergis, Alexios, 39, 40
Kallikratis 243
Kalogeros 325
Kalokerinos, Minos, 44
Kalo Horio 360
Kalo Nero 357
Kaloros 181
Kamares 329
Kambi 182
Kambos 241
Kambos Kissou 279, 281
Kandanoleos 40, **149**
Kapetaniana 309
Karidi 374

Karines 259, 321
Karphi 470, 472
Kasteli Kissamou 203
Kastelos 249
Katelionas 374
Katofigi 337, 474
Kato Simi 340
Kavoussi 424, 488
Kazantzakis, Nicos, 388
Kedros, mountain, 278
Kefalas 185
Kefali 215, 217
Kelaria 506
Kera 467
Kidonia 120, 123
Kioporuli Pasha 381
Kiparissi 333
Kiriakoselia 182
Klisidi 506
Knossos 32, 51, **439**
Kornaros, Vincentzos, 40, 497
Kourites 27, 331
Kofinas 309, 310
Kokkino Chorio 185
Komitades 251
Kostogiannides 240
Koumassia 308
Koundouras 223
Kouroutes 329
Koustogerako 153
Koutsomatados 223
Koxare 259
Krioneri 507
Kritsa 345
Krotos 283, 306
Kroussonas 421

L

Labyrinth 442, 446
Lakki 167
Langada 506
Lappa 245, **246**
Lastros 490
Lato 346
Lendas 283, 304
Lefka Ori (mountains) 66
Levin 297, **304**
Ligaria 399
Likastos 334
Likotinara 185
Linosseli 154
Liopetra 495
Lissos 156
Listaros 301
Livadia 417
Lochria 327, 329
Loutro 191
Lyttos 463

PRACTICAL INFORMATION

M

Madaro 182
Makrigialos 357
Maleme 195
Males 343
Malia 429
Maneriana 235
Maniatiana 219, 223
Marathos 408
Margarites 408
Martha 284
Matala 301
Mathokotsana 343
Maza 157
Megala Chorafia 177
Melambes 263, 282
Melidoni (Hania) 183
Melidoni (Rethimno) 403
Meskla 166
Messara, valley, 283
Metaxochori 343
Mili 319
Miliarades 338
Mino 343
Minos 27, 440
Minotaur 27, 442
Miriokefala 244
Mirsini 490
Mirtos 313, 340
Mochlos 491
Monastery
  Arkadi 44, 325, **420**
  Atalis Bali 402
  Kardiotissa (Kera) 467
  Chrissoskalitissa 217
  Epanossifis 335
  Faneromeni 487
  Giagarolo 141
  Gouverneto 143
  Kapsa 358
  Katholikou 145
  Koudouma 309
  Martsalo 303
  Odigitrias (Hania) 199
  Odigitrias (Iraklio) 301
  Paliani 332
  Preveli 256
  Toplou 500
  Xera Xyla 434
Monastiraki 324, 325
Morosini, Francesco, 381
Mouliana 490
Mourne 259
Mournia 311
Mournies 43
Mouri 192
Myson 496

N

Nea Kria Vrissi 281
Nea Pressos 371
Neo Chorio 184
Nithavris 326
Nochia 227

O

Omalos 168
Orino 371
Orno, mountains, 369

P

Pagomenos, Ioannis, 157, 159
Palaiokapas, Konst., 199
Palekastro 504
Paleochora 160
Palia Roumata 233
Palialoni 185
Palio Mitato 507
Pantanassa 323
Papoura 469, 470
Paraspori 495
Partira 337
Pasifae 28, 442
Pashley, Robert, 43, 142, 156, 184, 263, 336, 501
Passalites 417
Patsianos 251, **254**
Patsides 454
Patsos 259, 321, 323
Pemonia 183
Perama 408
Perivolia 318
Petsofas 505
Peza 49
Phaidra 24, **29**
Pirgos (Hania) 235
Piskokefalo 371, 489
Plaka 185
Plakalona 201
Plakias 70, **255**
Platanos 213
Plateau of
  Askyfou 67
  Katharos 69, 343
  Lasithi 69, **469**
  Nida 68, 331, 409, 423
  Nissimo 69, 472
  Omalos (Hania) 66, **167**
  Omalos (Iraklio) 332, 338, 339
  Stroumboulas 408
  Vothonas 183
  Ziros 373
Plati 469

Polirrinia 237
Potamies 462
Praisos 351, **372**, 503
Prassies 318
Prince George 46
Prodromi 159
Profitis Ilias 333, 334
Provatas, Pavlos, 150
Provatopoulos, Georgios, 153
Psari Forada 313
Psilafi 154
Psiloritis, mountain, 68, 324, **328**, 331

R

Radamanthys 28, 291, 440
Ramni 183
Ravdoucha 196
Refuge Kallergi 169, 191
Rethimno 70, **261**
Retzepis, brothers, 263
Riza 342
Rizinia 167
Road books (R/b)
    R/b 1 (Voukolies - Sembronas - Palia Roumata): 230
    R/b 2 (Polirrinia - Sirikari - Kambos): 238
    R/b 3 (Mt. Vrissinas): 320
    R/b 4 (Patsos - Spili): 323
    R/b 5 (The beaches behind Mt. Siderotas): 280
    R/b 6a (Mt. Asteroussia/ Kali Limenes): 304
    R/b 6b (Mt. Asteroussia / Lendas): 306
    R/b 6c (Mt. Asteroussia / Moni Koudouma): 308
    R/b 6d (Mt. Asteroussia / Tris Eklissies): 312
    R/b 7 (Katofigi - Omalos Plateau - Kato Simi): 338
    R/b 8a (Riza - Males): 341
    R/b 8b (Males - Katharos Plateau - Kritsa): 344
    R/b 9 (Lassithi Plataeu - Kaminaki - Katofigi): 474
    R/b 10 (Anogia - Kroussonas - Psiloritis): 422
    R/b 11 (Kavousi - Ano Chorio): 370
    R/b 12 (Hamezi / Liopetra): 494
Rodakino 254
Rodopos 196
Rodopos, peninsula, 195
Rotonda 228
Roussa Ekklissia 500, 507
Roussa Limni 424
Roussolakos 504
Rouvas 413

S

Sanmicheli, Michele, 122, 380
Sarpidonas 28, 440
Sassalos 223, 235
Scordilo 371
Selakano 343
Selia 235, 254
Seliniotikos Giros 154, 169
Sembronas 232
Sgouros, Dimitrios, 199
Siderotas, mountain, 278
Sineniana 240
Sirikari 240
Sisses 401
Sitia 40, 45, 49, **496**
Sivritos 325
Sklavopoula 223
Sougia 154
Sphakia 188
Sphinari 215
Spili 259, 277
Spratt, T.A.B., 44, 287, 478
Stavrochori 371
Stavros 141
Strovles 222
Syia 155

T

Talos 29
Tavrokathapsia 289
Telephassa 24
Temenos 334
Theseus 27, 444
Theotokopoulos, Dominicos 40, 379, **400**
Therisso 46, 165
Thripti 369
Thripti, mountains, 69, 371
Thronos 324
Thimia 181
Timbaki 283, **285**
Topolia 222
Tourloti 490
Tris Ekklissies 310
Tsakistra 182
Tylissos 410
Tzermiado 472
Tzitzifes 183

V

Vafes 183
Vamos 184
Vamvakados 157
Vassiliana 229
Vathypetro 461
Velonado 249

Veneri, brothers, 166
Venizelos, Eleftherios 46, 47, **146**
Vistagi 325
Vizari 325
Vlithias 225
Voleones 323
Vorizia 329
Votomos 327
Voukolies 230
Voutas 222
Vrisses 177, **180**, 183
Vritomartis 197, 325
Vrissinas 249, **322**
Vrocastro 487

X

Xeniakos 337
Xerokambos 361
Xiloskalo 168
Xopateras 303
Xylouris, Nikos, 413

Z

Zachariana 240
Zakros, Ano 362
Zakros, Kato 363
Zaros 326, 327
Zeus 26, 296, 330
Zimbragos 229
Ziros 360
Zoniana 416
Zourva 166

The photographs appearing in this travel guide
were taken with a **SIGMA SA 300** camera,
SIGMA lenses **SAF 28-70** and **DL 70-300** and
a **SIGMA EF-430 SA** flashlight.
KODAC ELITE 100 films were used throughout.